*f*P

Other works by Kiron K. Skinner, Annelise Anderson, and Martin Anderson

REAGAN: A LIFE IN LETTERS

REAGAN, IN HIS OWN HAND

STORIES IN HIS OWN HAND

REAGAN IN HIS OWN VOICE

Reagan's Path to Victory

THE SHAPING OF RONALD REAGAN'S VISION: SELECTED WRITINGS

EDITED WITH AN INTRODUCTION AND COMMENTARY BY

Kiron K. Skinner
Annelise Anderson
Martin Anderson

with a Foreword by George P. Shultz

FREE PRESS
NEW YORK LONDON TORONTO SYDNEY

*f*P
FREE PRESS
A Division of Simon & Schuster, Inc.
1230 Avenue of the Americas
New York, NY 10020

For information regarding special discounts for bulk purchases,
please contact Simon & Schuster Special Sales at
1-800-456-6798 or business@simonandschuster.com

Manufactured in the United States of America

10 9 8 7 6 5 4 3 2 1

Library of Congress Cataloging-in-Publication Control Number 2004053333

ISBN 0-7432-2706-9

For Nancy Reagan,

who made it possible

Contents

Foreword

George P. Shultz

In 1974, I took up residence in California after serving as secretary of the treasury and, before that, as director of the Office of Management and Budget and as secretary of labor in President Nixon's cabinet. That fall, I got a phone call from Governor Ronald Reagan. He invited me to Sacramento for lunch, and I was glad to accept.

We sat around the lunch table for about three hours as I received the most intensive grilling about how the federal government worked that I had ever undergone. Governor Reagan wanted to know how the budget was put together, how the budget director worked on the process, what role cabinet members played, when and how the president weighed in, and what kind of alternative arrangements might work.

I mentioned one procedure I had used with President Nixon, presenting ten or so issues for him to decide, with the notion that these decisions and his thinking on them would give me the basis for handling other issues of comparable size in a way that he wanted. I told Governor Reagan that our approach with difficult cabinet members was always to give them an audience with the president. They could complain about what they regarded as my take on an issue, though in reality it was the president's. I suggested that after the cabinet member's presentation, he might admonish me for being overly generous and cut the terms back. That word would get around, I said, and would save him a lot of trouble. I don't know if President Reagan ever employed such a technique, but I was fascinated by his reaction. He saw the budget process as a process of negotiation as well as presidential decision.

I came away from this grilling on all manner of operational aspects of how the federal government worked with a clear impression: this man doesn't want just to *be* president; he wants to do the job, and he's thinking actively about how you go about making the presidency operate effectively. A year later, he launched his first full-scale presidential campaign.

As I worked later with candidate Reagan in 1980, particularly as chairman of his economic policy group, I saw first-hand his approach to a wide variety of issues. He clearly went about them more in terms of presidential policy than of campaign fodder. This realization that he had an agenda and a desire to put it into operation was one of the reasons that inspired me to put in so much effort on his behalf.

I also reflected on the negotiating aspects of our budget discussion. I could see from that discussion that Ronald Reagan liked negotiations, thought about the negotiating process, had practiced the art as president of the Screen Actors Guild, and enjoyed it. Later on, as I worked with him as secretary of state, this insight helped me to understand his objectives and how he wanted to go about achieving his goals. There were many people in the administration who wanted strength but did not want Ronald Reagan to use that strength as a basis for negotiation. I knew he was confident in his ability as a negotiator and was more than ready to stand in with the Soviet leaders. As it turned out, he did a masterful job of negotiating, and I was honored to help him do it.

This book of Ronald Reagan's radio addresses from the late 1970s is fascinating in many ways, but one theme emerges from placing the essays in chronological order. The essays, like my budget discussions with him, show how consciously Ronald Reagan was preparing himself for the presidency. He developed his ideas, he honed his way of expressing those ideas, and he worked on the mechanics of how you go about being an effective president—a president who turns ideas into reality.

Reagan's long-standing way of working is also apparent in this book. As is shown in *Reagan: A Life in Letters,* President Reagan often wrote letters and enclosed checks to those in need. He behaved similarly in his pre-presidential years; in some of his radio essays, Reagan informed his listeners about needy individuals and organizations. He used his radio program as a national platform to promote issues and causes that he felt deserved special assistance. In the radio essays, you see as much of Reagan's heart as his mind.

Historians who review the Reagan administration with all its dramatic changes in domestic, economic, national security, and foreign policy will be well advised to look carefully at this book and its earlier sister publications. They will see a fine mind at work, a gift of expression, the evolution of Reagan's thinking, and the conceptual underpinning of his presidency. Historians will be joined by a broad readership, and all will benefit from reading these informative and revealing essays. So dig in!

Introduction

Ronald Reagan's rise to national political prominence began on October 27, 1964, when he gave a televised campaign speech on behalf of Senator Barry Goldwater (R–Arizona), the Republican nominee for president. Speculation about Reagan running for president began following what became known as "the speech." During the next decade, Reagan's national political profile grew—and so did speculation about a presidential bid. On November 8, 1966, Reagan defeated Edmund "Pat" Brown, the two-term incumbent, for the governorship of California by a million-vote margin. In 1968, he became a "favorite son" candidate for the Republican nomination for president, briefly challenging Richard Nixon at the convention in Miami Beach, Florida. On November 3, 1970, he was reelected California's governor by defeating Assemblyman Jesse Unruh by a half-million votes. In 1972, he actively campaigned on behalf of President Richard Nixon's reelection effort. When he stepped down as governor of California in January 1975, Reagan was a seasoned political figure who was widely considered to be a future Republican presidential nominee.

It soon became clear from Reagan's actions that he was determined to run for president of the United States. As the popular ex-governor of California, he could have moved on to the private sector, giving speeches, serving on corporate boards, perhaps even making a movie or two—and making lots of money. He didn't. President Gerald Ford offered him the prestigious post of ambassador to Great Britain; he turned it down. He could have gone to Washington and served in President Ford's cabinet as secretary of commerce or transportation. He said no to the president.[1]

Instead Reagan followed a different path—a path that eventually led to victory, to becoming the 40th president of the United States.

Reagan faced a daunting gauntlet as he took his first steps along that path in 1975. The country had just gone through the trials of the Watergate political scandal. In January a bleak national poll was announced to Republican state chairs meeting in Chicago. It showed that "only 18 percent of the American people identified themselves as Republicans."[2] President Nixon was forced to resign on August 9, 1974. Democrats made substantial gains in the November 5, 1974, elections in both houses of Congress and in state legislatures.

On February 6, 1975, Reagan had his 64th birthday, one year short of when many people retire. While he had a growing band of supporters, many thought he was too old and had misgivings about his health and endurance. They doubted he could survive the long run for the presidency, to say nothing of governing for four—and perhaps eight—years.

Many thought he was far too conservative, a Neanderthal throwback, even more so than Barry Goldwater, whom Lyndon Johnson had defeated by a landslide just ten years earlier. He had no major financial support and his full-time staff was only half a dozen or so. Moreover, few politicians were in his corner—only one U.S. senator, Paul Laxalt of Nevada, and a couple of members of Congress.

Finally, and most important, Reagan faced the prospect of running against an incumbent president—a Republican one. It is tough enough to run against an incumbent president of another party, but it is nigh impossible to take out one of your own in a primary fight. In Republican circles, running against a president of your own party was "just not done."

But Reagan ran.

It was not supposed to happen this way. With Richard Nixon's election to a second term in 1972, Reagan's staff expected him to be running, if he chose to do so, for an open seat, not against an incumbent, let alone an incumbent of his own party. The field of candidates for the Republican nomination of 1976, they thought, might include Charles Percy, Republican senator from Illinois; John Connally from Texas, who had been Nixon's secretary of the treasury; and Nelson Rockefeller, who resigned as governor of New York in December 1973 during his fourth term.[3]

But that was before Watergate. When Richard Nixon resigned in 1974 and Gerald Ford became president, he also became the leading contender for the 1976 nomination. Ford was vulnerable, however. He had been selected to replace vice president Spiro T. Agnew when Agnew resigned in 1973 over another scandal. Nixon's first choice as a replacement for Agnew was John Connally, but the Congress objected. Thus, an unelected, second-choice vice president became the incumbent president.

Ford nominated Nelson Rockefeller to take the vacant vice presidency on August 20, 1974. It was a job Reagan probably thought should have gone to him. Reagan had told reporters that the executive experience of governors was often overlooked in selecting national leaders, and also stated that the new vice president should hold views consistent with the mandate of 1972, which he believed reflected the Republican Party's conservative and even libertarian philosophical basis, "a belief in individual freedom and the reduction of government."[4] Rockefeller's reputation as a member of the Eastern liberal establishment and left wing of the Republican party did not fit this description; his selection was viewed as an outrage by many conservatives.

Ford had never taken Reagan seriously, and Reagan had not even been on his final list of five candidates for the vice presidency.[5] Ford eventually asked Rockefeller to withdraw from the ticket for the 1976 election given Rockefeller's unpopularity within the party, but it was November 3, 1975, before Rockefeller made the announcement—well after the July 15, 1975, formation of Citizens for Reagan, which would become Reagan's campaign committee, and barely before the formal announcement of Reagan's candidacy on November 20. Ford's support with the general public had fallen, furthermore, after he pardoned Nixon on September 8, 1974.

In 1974, as Reagan was preparing to leave the governorship, Walter Cronkite, the famous newscaster, offered him the opportunity to do two commentaries a week on the CBS Evening News. Reagan would be balanced by Eric Sevareid, who would also do two commentaries on other nights.[6] Reagan's staff was ecstatic. That would give Reagan roughly 40 percent of the nightly news viewing audience, to say nothing of how much money he might make.

True, Cronkite did offer him a large audience, but it was under Cronkite's control. CBS television could have fired Reagan at will. They could have followed his commentary with a rebuttal or presented him as representing a far-out minority, the "other side." He could only speak twice a week, and he had no control over the news that night which would set the stage for his talk.

Reagan said no to Cronkite's offer. The answer he gave to Mike Deaver, a senior aide, was that "people will tire of me on television—they won't tire of me on the radio."[7]

That may not have been the real reason. Reagan was quietly intent on running for president. He needed a way to speak to the voters—millions of them. As he prepared for the 1980 campaign, he commented on how he had communicated with the public since he left the governorship in this February 5, 1979, letter:

> I am trying to avoid declaring until as late as I can in the year for a number of reasons. 1.) I think it is too early and 2.) I lose some valuable forums the day I declare, among them 300 radio stations (5 days a week), 100 newspapers (twice a week), to say nothing of all the speaking engagements. But, I am going to be in this race—don't quote me on that to the press, but you tell anyone who's interested that you are sure I am going to do it.[8]

What Reagan wanted was control of a large megaphone, one with which he could speak daily to potential voters on what he wanted to talk about.

On behalf of radio producer Harry O'Connor, actor Efrem Zimbalist, Jr. asked his old friend Reagan if he would be interested in doing a radio commentary that O'Connor would produce and syndicate nationally.[9] In October

1974, Peter Hannaford, assistant to the governor and director of public affairs, and Michael Deaver, an aide to the governor, presented Reagan with a comprehensive proposal that included O'Connor's offer, a nationally syndicated newspaper program, and speaking engagements around the country. Reagan liked the proposal and agreed to do it under the management of their new firm, Deaver & Hannaford, Inc.

Two strategy documents dated November 4, 1974, provided an outline and guide for Reagan's post-governorship activities, now two months away. "Testing the potential strength of a Presidential bid, without RR [Ronald Reagan] overtly stepping out of the 'mashed potato circuit' role he has described for himself" was discussed in "Ronald Reagan: Building a National Organization." In "Ronald Reagan: A Program for the Future," the upcoming nationally syndicated radio program and newspaper column as well as speaking engagements around the country were described as necessary components for Reagan to "maintain influence in the Republican Party; strengthen and consolidate leadership as *the* national conservative spokesman; and enhance [his] foreign affairs credibility."[10]

By January 8, 1975, three days after he had turned over the governor's mantle to Democrat Edmund G. "Jerry" Brown, Reagan had crafted his first set of radio commentaries. On that day, shortly before his first newpaper column would be published, he sat down in the recording studio and taped 13 commentaries.[11] The first one for which a handwritten draft has been found was on inflation. Radio stations flocked to his commentary and soon he was broadcasting *daily* on more than 200 radio stations.[12]

Reagan's broadcasts reached potential voters in virtually every nook and cranny of the United States. Occasionally the program was rejected regardless of its potential to attract advertisers. The KFI (Los Angeles) radio station manager wrote on December 4, 1974, "Thank you for sending the Ronald Reagan audition. We are not interested at this time." And then he added by hand: "—even sponsored!"[13] During his radio broadcasting career from 1975 to 1979, it is estimated that he spoke to between 20 and 30 million Americans a week.[14]

The personal campaign machine that Reagan built and ran from 1975 to 1979 was his pathway to the presidency. His speeches and columns were important and necessary, but his radio commentaries were the driving force. The radio program gave Reagan a national platform that no other politician had at the time.

Advertisers would occasionally withdraw sponsorship of Reagan's radio program because listeners complained about Reagan's views,[15] and a handful of newspaper editors who contended that Reagan appeared too much like a presidential candidate canceled his column.[16] As stipulated by the provision for equal opportunity by the Federal Communications Act, media outlets are to provide equal air time to qualified political candidates. On November 20, 1975, Reagan announced his intention to seek the Republican Party's nomination for the presidency. He devoted the next nine months to his campaign, and guest commentators and then Senator Barry Goldwater temporarily took over the radio program.[17]

On August 19, 1976, Reagan accepted defeat by President Gerald Ford at the Republican convention in Kansas City in a close race for delegates. Less than two weeks after the convention, Reagan was again writing radio commentaries. One of them, "Shaping the World for 100 Years to Come," was not only a statement of Reagan's political philosophy and abhorrence of nuclear weapons, but also a window into how he wrote his commentaries; much of the commentary was a restatement of his extemporaneous speech at the Republican Convention. Although his commentaries would sometimes be a restatement of one of his newspaper columns, speeches, or congressional testimony,[18] Reagan cast a wide net in looking for sources and subjects of his radio commentaries.

Reagan consistently read conservative magazines such as *Alternative: An American Spectator, Commentary, Human Events,* and *National Review*, and he often mentioned these sources in his commentaries. He quoted from many newspapers, including the *Los Angeles Herald Examiner, The New York Times,* and *The Wall Street Journal,* and government documents such as the *Congressional Record*. Reagan also relied upon books he was reading.

Reagan was a powerful speaker. He wrote legibly and had a soothing, captivating radio voice. But it wasn't his penmanship or his voice that drove him up this path—it was the ideas about which he wrote and spoke.

The manuscripts from which this book is drawn were discovered by accident. Kiron Skinner was the first scholar since Edmund Morris to be granted access to the private papers of President Ronald Reagan. Skinner discovered the handwritten drafts of Reagan's radio commentaries, letters, speeches, and other writings in 1996 and 1997 while doing extensive archival research in the private papers for her research on the end of the cold war.

Skinner along with Annelise Anderson and Martin Anderson undertook an analysis of the radio manuscripts, which yielded 1,027 commentaries. Six hundred and seventy three of the radio commentaries were written in Reagan's hand. He wrote another nine that were not, as far as we know, broadcast.[19]

Some of the remaining 354 commentaries were written by Reagan, but his handwritten draft has not been found in the archives, is lost, or was discarded—and thus they are not attributed to Reagan. The rest were written by his staff, primarily Peter Hannaford, and edited by Reagan. A database of the radio commentaries developed by Annelise Anderson is produced here as an Appendix.

Of the commentaries we know he wrote, almost one-third were on foreign policy or national defense, although those that compared socialist and capitalist economies also had domestic implications. Reagan's foreign policy essays dealt with issues ranging from apartheid in Southern Africa to the nuclear arms race and to the political efficacy of international organizations like the United Nations. He also reported on his trips abroad in radio segments.

More than two-thirds of the commentaries were explicitly on domestic issues, most often the economy—inflation, taxing and spending, unemployment, monetary policy, and excessive regulation. Energy and the environment were also frequent topics. Reagan also wrote about social security, Medicare and national health insurance, welfare, and education. He addressed issues such as illegal drugs and crime—and wrote a number of essays with religious or inspirational themes, about topics as diverse as John Wayne and the Bible. Reagan sometimes used his airtime to advocate causes he thought exemplified American values.

The five years leading up to 1980 were difficult years. The country was still dealing with the aftermath of the Vietnam war and Watergate. In foreign affairs the standard view was that the Soviet Union was an effective economic and military power, one with which the West would have to learn to live for a long time. In fact there was some doubt about whether the Western free-market democracies could compete effectively with centrally controlled systems that were less subject to the will of their constituents and could repress dissent. Many people thought the two systems would converge, becoming more like each other over time. The Soviet Union seemed to be intent on increasing its military might and expanding its sphere of influence in Africa, Asia, and Latin America. In the United States the activities of U.S. intelligence agencies were investigated, challenged, and restrained. The share of the U.S. economy devoted to national defense declined steadily from its Vietnam peak of 9.4 percent in 1968 to less than 5 percent in 1979, when Congress called a halt and declared that more resources needed to be devoted to defense.

The lack of confidence in the vitality of market economies was exacerbated by the difficulties of Great Britain and, later, the United States. The United States feared the "British disease"—high inflation and low economic growth, or stagflation. In the 1960s it had seemed possible to fine-tune the economy—to increase growth and employment at the cost of somewhat higher inflation. But this prescription seemed no longer to work in the 1970s. In addition, by the mid-1970s the Organization of Petroleum Exporting Countries (OPEC) dominated world oil markets and was able to curtail oil output and raise prices of crude oil; the increased cost of energy created additional problems for importing countries, especially in 1973 and again in 1979.

Taken as a whole, the essays Reagan wrote over this difficult five-year period were a powerful campaign weapon, allowing him to explain his views to tens of millions of potential voters. It is doubtful whether he could have become president without them. And when he did become president, the essays acted as his personal, handwritten policy platform for governing.

In early 1980, Reagan wrote:

> I am surprised at times that there is so much lack of knowledge about my positions. For several years except when I was running in '76 and now in the present campaign, I have had a five-day-a-week radio commentary

> on more than 300 stations nationwide. I took up virtually every subject mentionable and stated my views on those subjects, but I guess there were a lot of people who were not listening. Maybe, as the campaign goes on, there will be more awareness of where I stand on these various issues.[20]

The radio commentaries made it possible for Reagan to smoothly shift gears from running America's largest state to demonstrating that he was capable of becoming its commander-in-chief.

On March 7, 1979, the Reagan for President Committee was announced. On October 25, Reagan taped his last set of commentaries. On November 13, he announced his intention to seek the Republican Party's 1980 nomination for the presidency.

Two months before his victory on November 4, 1980, a television and radio trade magazine declared: "If Ronald Reagan reaches 1600 Pennsylvania Ave., he can figuratively give a low bow in the direction of Harry O'Connor who may be as much responsible for Reagan's nomination—and if he is elected—his election as anyone."[21] Reagan had reached America long before he accepted the Republican Party's nomination for the presidency on July 17, 1980, and before his November landslide.

A Note on Editorial Methods

In producing a printed version of what Reagan wrote in his own hand, we have followed the same methods we did in *Reagan, In His Own Hand.*[1] We show his own inserts in small italic capital letters when he used caps, in italics when he added in script rather than capitals. His deletions are shown with a single strike-over except where we could not read what he struck out. Unreadable strike-overs are shown with only a single "≠" symbol.

We have not corrected spelling or punctuation, nor have we expanded the abbreviations he often used. His placement of apostrophes in contractions, however, was as casual as the dotting of an i, and so we have located apostrophes (when he used them at all) in their conventional place.

Reagan's marginal comments and instructions are indicated by the dagger (†) symbol and are printed at the end of the document on which they appear. Asterisks are used to indicate editors' footnotes, and are at the bottom of the page. In the rare cases where editorial changes were made by someone other than Reagan or where we have inserted a word he left out, we present those edits in brackets.

The titles of the documents are the titles that Harry O'Connor of O'Connor Creative Services used in distributing them, rather than the even briefer identifiers Reagan used when he wrote them. The dates given are taping dates, each of which is the closest known date to the time of writing. The taping dates of course preceded the distribution date and can be estimated in those cases where it is unknown. Radio broadcasts were usually taped in batches of 15, although at first fewer were taped at a time. Sometimes Reagan would tape as many as 20 broadcasts, the additional ones held for distribution when he was traveling abroad or on vacation. The air dates can therefore be two to five weeks, sometimes more, after the taping date.

Reagan wrote his radio commentaries in two parts. First, he used a brief introduction or "teaser" to entice the radio audience to stay tuned to the station. He finished this part by saying "I'll be right back." Then, after radio commercials, he would read his essay for the day. Each of the commentaries ended with: "This is Ronald Reagan. Thanks for listening."

Three different versions of most of the radio commentaries can be found in the archives. One is Reagan's handwritten draft. The typed version of his draft prepared by his staff is also in the archives, sometimes including his own further editing for clarification or to shorten the length of the broadcast. The third version is the printed transcript of Reagan's taping session prepared by O'Connor Creative Services for distribution to radio stations so that they could see what was on the tapes or vinyl records being sent to them. Stations also used these transcripts to respond to listeners' requests for printed copies of the program. The O'Connor version does not include Reagan's teaser or his sign-off.

Part One

1975

Ronald Reagan concluded his two terms as governor of California successfully, with significant accomplishments on many fronts—welfare reform, the environment, health, education, and the budget. He had long since decided not to run for a third term. His arrangements for a daily radio address and weekly column were in place. His last day at the governor's office was Friday, January 3, 1975; on January 6 his successor, Jerry Brown, was inaugurated. Reagan taped his first batch of 13 radio addresses on January 8, and they began airing on the 20th.

At the time, Americans were concerned about many issues. Richard Nixon had resigned the previous August, and on September 8 he was pardoned by President Gerald Ford. In the wake of Watergate and the pardon, Democrats made substantial gains in the November 5 elections in both houses of Congress and in governorships. An economic recession that had begun in late 1973 following the Arab oil embargo and the significant increase in crude oil prices had continued throughout 1974, and would not end until the second quarter of 1975. Unemployment averaged 8.5 percent during 1975. Inflation, coming from a longtime high of 12.2 percent in 1974, slowed to 6.9 percent in 1975 but remained a great concern. Taxes were not indexed for inflation, and thus people found themselves paying higher taxes on wage and salary increases that primarily compensated for inflation. Gerald Ford persuaded Alan Greenspan to stay on as chairman of the Council of Economic Advisers. The 1975 deficit was over $50 billion, a record at the time.

Among other events of 1975, Margaret Thatcher became the leader of the Conservative Party in Great Britain on February 11; Ford signed tax-cutting legislation on March 29; the Cambodian government surrendered to the communist Khmer Rouge on April 17; South Vietnam surrendered to communist North Vietnam with the fall of Saigon on April 30; the report of the commission on CIA activities within the United States, of which Reagan was a member, was made public on June 10; the Helsinki Accords on détente, cooperation, and security in Europe were signed by more than 30 nations on August 1; attempts were made to assassinate President Ford, on September 5 and September 22; OPEC raised oil prices by 10 percent on October 1; President Ford asked the U.S. Congress to approve aid to New York City on November 26; the military government in Chile that overthrew Marxist Salvador Allende in 1973 continued to try to rebuild Chile's economy; and political transition in Southern Africa was under way.

In April, Reagan traveled to Western Europe. While in London, he gave a speech warning of the dangers of Soviet encroachment in Europe, and arguing that through Communist political victories in Portugal, the Soviet Union could undermine the southern flank of the North Atlantic Treaty Organization. He met with Margaret Thatcher, beginning a warm relationship that would grow in the years to come. He wrote a radio address about the trip on his return titled "Peace" in which he argues that strength is the basis for peace: "Power is not only sufficient military strength but a sound economy, a reliable energy supply and credibility—the belief by any potential enemy that you will not choose surrender as the way to maintain peace."[1]

On July 15, 1975, Citizens for Reagan was created, chaired by Senator Paul Laxalt, Reagan's only supporter for the 1976 Republican presidential nomination in the Senate. Reagan informed the Federal Election Commission that if he chose to run for president, this organization would be his campaign committee.[2] On November 20, 1975, Reagan announced formally that he would challenge President Gerald R. Ford for the nomination, and at that time suspended his radio broadcasts and newspaper columns.

Reagan's radio talks in 1975 set the foundations of his first full-fledged presidential campaign, which began late in the year. As he would in the following years, he addresed many topics, including economic issues (regulation, inflation, taxes, spending, and unemployment); domestic policy (energy, the environment, and social welfare programs); foreign policy (chiefly but not solely anti-communism); and inspiring stories of individuals and groups.

During the year, Reagan wrote his most cogent statements about the cold war. In commentaries titled "Communism the Disease," "Peace," and the "Russian Wheat Deal,"[3] he argued that the only way for the United States to guarantee peace and stability and prevent a global war was to maintain military strength and political and economic freedom. These things, he argued, would eventually erode the Soviet system because it was not durable enough to compete over the long run. The role of morality in foreign policy was at the core about how Reagan thought about the United States' involvement with the world. He argued that although power and political necessity were key components of grand strategy, so too was principle; for a moral foreign policy was the United States' distinguishing characteristic.[4]

Another dimension of Reagan's thinking about defense and foreign policy in 1975 had to do with defining and protecting U.S. defense perimeters in the Western Hemisphere. By the end of year, he was being closely associated with his famous phrase: "We bought it, we paid for it, it is sovereign U.S. territory and we should keep it."[5] He was talking about the Panama Canal, an issue he would address far more in the coming years.

Of the 209 radio addresses taped in 1975, we have found Reagan's drafts for 60. An internal staff listing suggests that he wrote others. In later years he wrote a much higher percentage of the commentaries.

A Cuba Documentary
February 14, 1975

Documentarys are supposed to be fact not fiction. I'll be right back.

The very word documentary ~~brings to mind the~~ *invokes an image of* ~~*the*~~ *research & a* painstaking ~~collection~~ *collecting* of factual material ~~and it's~~ *for* presentation. ~~as a printed or (in this electronic age) a pictorial essay. The reader or viewer theoretically comes away with understanding & knowledge of the *documented* subject *which he or she can rely upon as true.*~~ *Those who read or see a documentary are entitled to believe they've been given an objective, thoroughly documented treatise on whatever the subject might be.*

Not too long ago on this program I discussed Cuba and gave some requirements I thought should be met before Uncle Sam welcomed that unhappy island back into the family of American ~~nation~~ nations. ~~Since then one~~ *Now that was an editorial—an expression of opinion with which you could agree or disagree. Since then one* of our *TV* networks has presented (with a certain amount of fanfare) a quote, documentary, unquote & question mark. *It was* called "Cuba—The People." Was it really a documentary ~~The question raised I raise~~ *or was it an editorial effort—an expression of opinion* or was it *JUST PLAIN* propaganda? ~~*And if the latter—why?*~~

Basically the message was that soon Cuba will no longer be an "underdeveloped" country ~~because~~ thanks to the success of socialism. The question is—~~how~~ *how & when* did Cuba become an underdeveloped country? Prior to Castro ~~*it is my understanding*~~ Cuba led all ~~+~~ *her* latin neighbors in standard of living, literacy and any number of other desirable indices. For example *Cuba had more* Drs. in proportion to pop.; *more* automobiles, *higher* per capita income, *more* TV broadcasting & ownership of TV sets, *more* newspaper circulation and even greater attendance at movies. In ~~this latter~~ *movie going* they were 2nd only to us ~~in all the world.~~, *which means they were 2nd in the world.*

~~#~~ The so called documentary ~~contained~~ *was of Cuba now & showed* scenes of Cuban farmers plowing with oxen. I dont know how widespread that is but mechanized farming had reached a pretty high level *back in Cuba* B.C.—before Castro.

Let me read some lines from what has to be considered a real documentary—a report issued in May of 1962 by the Ec. Research Svc. *Service* of the U.S. Dept. of Agri. The report was entitled, "Agri. & Food Situation in Cuba."~~—Remember this was in 1962.~~ "In 1958 Cuba was self supporting in many foodstuffs such as meat, poultry, fish, eggs, milk, butter, & cheese, tubers, vegetables, coffee & fruits of which there was a great variety & abundance. In the season, oranges were sold in pushcarts, in Havana, peeled, iced & ready to eat—at 3, 4 or 5 for a nickel." *

"Under communism, food ration cards were introduced before the 3rd year of the revolution expired. Oranges have become so scarce that they can only be purchased in pharmacies with a Dr's. prescription."

I dont know whether the makers of the documentary intended selling *us* socialism, ~~as a~~ or whether they were *just* set up by their Cuban hosts but ~~there is no evidence today that Cuba is in any way as economically sound as it was before~~ *a truly objective documentary would have made it plain that the Cuba of today is not anywhere near as well off or economically sound as it was before* Castro imposed communism on the people. Indeed there is every reason to believe Cuba would be in ~~dire straits~~ *real trouble* without ~~a~~ *the* sizeable subsidy *it gets* from the Soviet Union.

In this day when we are flooded with so many words on every subject—it behooves us to check some of those words out before we accept them as gospel. And that goes for ~~me too~~ my words too—make sure you've heard all the facts before you make up your mind. ❖

Farm Facts

February 14, 1975

~~Virtually e~~*E*very hour of every day you are in contact with Agriculture. Almost everything starts on ~~the~~ a farm.—I'll be right back.

* The report confirms the substance of the quotation but does not include the specific quotation. *Agriculture and Food Situation in Cuba* (Washington, DC: Economic Research Service, U.S. Department of Agriculture, May 1962).

Not too long ago I was a guest speaker *in Las Vegas* for one of our Nat. ~~farm~~ agriculture groups. ~~I couldn't help but think that~~ some of the regular patrons of Las Vegas must have thought the farm visitors were *a little* out of place. *Well* I have news for them. A farmer of any kind is in a business that makes a crap table or roulette wheel look like *a* guaranteed annual inc.

Year in & year out the farmer bets the whole roll against weather, insects ~~plagues~~, plant or animal diseases and a supply & demand system in which he'*s* ~~has to fly~~ *flying* blind. He has no way of knowing whether everyone else is raising the same crop he decided to put in or if he'll have the mkt. to himself.

It can rain too early or too late or too much or too little & any one of those can make him a loser. ~~Now~~ Some years back one of our Sec's. of Agri. was getting around the country ~~soliciting~~ hearing at 1st hand the farmers views. One ~~fellow~~ *of them* was giving him a rough time with his complaints. The Sec. took a hasty look at his breifing papers and said, "Well now *wait a minute* you didn't have it too bad last year, you got 29 inches of rain." The farmer said, "Yes—I remember the night it happened."

A couple of years back when beef prices shot up the cattle growers took a lot of abuse they didn't deserve. For one thing there had been virtually no increase in ~~cattle~~ beef prices at the grower level for more than a decade—there had been a sizeable hike in the price of feed; the ~~stuff~~ grain that puts on that ~~final~~ finishing growth in the feed lot. And it takes about 4½ lbs. ~~for~~ of grain to make 1 lb. of meat. Arithmatic is a very exact science and when the grain price per lb. is higher than beef per lb. how do you ~~work~~ *come* out on that 4½ to 1 ratio of feed to meat? Then just to ~~make sure~~ top things off in that year of high priced meat we had winter storms on the western plains that killed thousands of animals. *In* One storm alone the toll was $100 mil. worth. That was also the year the workers in the packing houses struck for higher pay. The housewife was angry about the high price of meat—but was she mad at the right people.

March 24 has been named Agriculture Day. It is hoped that farmers will understand their own position as consumers but that others will take the time to find out what agriculture means to all of us.

~~Almost~~ It is true that Almost everything starts on a farm; the things we eat & wear but also chemicals, pharmaceuticals, cosmetics, soap & even ink. Less than 5% of ~~us~~ our people provide for 95% & have enough left over to export to other countries.

You've probably read about the disappearing family farm—replaced by the huge corp. farm. Well less than one tenth of 1% ~~our~~ *of* our 2.9 mil. farms are corporate. In these last few decades the Am. farmer has led America & the world in a technological revolution; ~~that and~~ his increase in productivity is the miracle of the 20th century. In just the last 10 years *his* production has gone up 20% while acreage farmed has gone down 6%. *On* One out of 4 acres the harvest is exported and without that our bal. of trade would be in a sorry state.

One farmer grows food & fibre for 51 of his fellow citizens and 4 out of 10 <u>non</u> farm jobs are dependent on Agriculture.

Maybe on March 24th we should all decide—at least for the day—not to complain about the high price of food. ❖

In the next three commentaries Reagan explores a controversial plan for employee stock ownership in corporations.

First proposed by Louis Kelso in his 1958 book, The Capitalist Manifesto, *the idea had attracted a small body of intense supporters, including Senators Russell Long and Hubert Humphrey. The theory was seductive; workers would gradually get to own much of the corporation stock and become wealthy. The implementation was more difficult. Critics raised questions about what would happen when employees had a choice between benefits and capital investment, and whether they would prefer higher salaries in the present to the possibility of larger salaries from long-term investment.*

Reagan, after consultation with his growing group of economic advisers, quietly and quickly dropped any further mention of the scheme. While the Kelso plan never received the endorsement of most economists, elements of the idea survive. Today, close to 10 percent of employees work for companies that have an employee-ownership plan.

Tax Plan #1
February 14, 1975

Has capitalism used all the tools available to it in the worldwide struggle with socialism.

I'll be right back.

The answer to the question I asked a moment ago is—no. ~~capitalism hasn't used all the *its* tools. *and*~~ In fact ~~it~~ *capitalism* hasn't used the best tool of all—*which is* capitalism itself.

~~A little~~ Roughly 94% of the people in *capitalist* Am. ~~derive their inc. from the capital ≠~~ make their living from wage or salary. Only 6% are *true* capitalists in the sense of deriving their ~~living~~ *income* from ownership of the means of production.

~~Now there is no question but that overall~~ *Of course* both groups enjoy the highest standard of living the world has ever known~~. However~~ ~~And~~ certainly far better than ~~any socialist state has ever been able to deliver to it's people.~~ *anything socialism has produced for its people.* ~~But why dont~~ ~~We~~ *We can* win the argument once & for all by simply making more of our people capitalists.

More than 100 yrs. ago Abe Lincoln signed the homestead act making it possible for *our* people to own land.* ~~That act set the pattern for~~ *of* ~~American capitalism.~~ *This was a revolutionary developement.* Ownership of land ~~by the ordinary citizen was~~ *in most of the world* ~~*had*~~ *had* not *been* ~~a universal thing-and most of the world~~ *possible for the ordinary citizen. Generally* land ~~was the property of the King and he doled it out to the aristocracy. The nobleman in the castle owned the land & the citizenry worked the~~ ~~the land it as tenants. O Thanks to our great expanse of virgin territory our homestead act offered ≠ many land reforms where property had been taken from one owner & redistributed to others. Here~~ *belonged to King or Emperor and thru him to the* ~~*aristocracy*~~ *favored aristocracy.*

The homestead act set the pattern for American Capitalism. Today 53 mil. Americans ≠ own their own homes. Now we need an industrial homestead act, and ~~it~~ *that* isn't impossible. ~~to get.~~ As a matter of fact any number of companies & corps. in Am. have tried *in* a variety of ways to spread ownership to their employees.

In S.F. a man named Kelso has evolved a plan ~~that~~ *which* a number of corps. have ~~also~~ already implemented. When a corp. needs to expand it usually ~~does~~ finances the expansion ~~in one of two~~ either by borrowing or by floating a new stock issue. Under the Kelso plan an employees trust is formed. ~~When the company expands the trust borrows the money from a bank or lending inst. The trust then ≠~~ ~~*with which it buys.*~~ *A company desiring to expand* ~~It~~ sells a new stock issue to this employees trust. ~~which~~ *The trust* in turn borrows the money from a bank or lending inst. using the stock as collateral. Each individual emp ~~owns~~ *winds up owning* stock in the co. directly proportionate to his ~~earnings~~ salary or wage level~~. in the And of course~~ ~~*Thus every emp*~~ *and* has a vested interest in the companys ability to prosper and increase earnings.

~~In~~*Over* the next 10 yrs. there will probably be $500 bil. worth of new investment. ~~This~~ ~~*It can be \$500 bil. of*~~ *for business & industrial expansion. It can be $500 bil. worth of corporate* ownership ~~in corporate Am.~~ by ~~corporate~~ employees. ~~This would lead to a~~An ever increasing number of citizens ~~who~~ *thus* would have 2 sources of inc. T~~heir~~ *a* paycheck & ~~their~~ *a* share of the profits. Could there be a better ans. to the stupidity of Karl Marx than mils. of workers individually sharing in the ownership of the means of production?

Some years ago an exec. of the Ford motor co. was showing the late Walter Reuther (head of the auto workers U.) through the Ford assembly plant in Cleve. Ohio.** Pointing to the latest in automated machinery He said, "Walter you'll have a hard time ~~selling~~ collecting ~~union~~ dues from those machines."

* On May 20, 1862, President Abraham Lincoln signed the Homestead Act. The legislation essentially provided public land free of charge for adults prepared to settle the land.

** Walter P. Reuther toured the Ford plant in Brook Park, Ohio, on June 10, 1953. See "Reuther Tours New Ford Setup," *Cleveland Plain Dealer,* June 11, 1953, p. 24.

Walter said—"You'll have a harder time selling *them* automobiles. ~~to those machines.~~"

The obvious answer neither of them thought of was ~~that~~ owners of machines can buy automobiles.

Tomorrow I'll tell you of another plan *one* ~~we can have~~ that would ~~make~~ *give* every ~~voting~~ registered voter in Am. ~~a~~ *an actual* share ~~in the o~~ *of ownership* in the industry of Am. ~~& we can start right now if Cong. will simply pass a bill.—This is Ronald Reagan. Thanks for listening.~~

~~And we~~

And it's possible to have that <u>&</u> the plan I've just described. All it takes is a bill by Cong.

This is R.R.~~—I'll be back~~ Thanks for listening. ❖

Tax Plan #2
February 14, 1975

† ~~We are still a new country capable of doing new & innovative things. Cong. should remember that. I'll be right back.~~ *Socialism makes promises only capitalism can keep. I'll be right back.*

Yesterday I told you ~~about a~~ of a plan used by some industrial corps. to make their emp's. stockholders—part owners of the firm.

Today ~~let me~~ I want to tell you about another idea for ~~making~~ *giving* every registered voter ~~in Am.~~ ownership in the entire corporate bus. & industrial structure of Am. This is not a scatterbrained, utopian dream of never, never land. It is a well thought out, fully documented program called "The Nat. Dividend Plan" which has the endorsement of "*many* well known economists & pol. scientists.

Lionel D. Edie & Co. a research subsidiary of one of the great financial inst's. Merrill~~,~~Lynch, ~~Pierce~~ PIERCE, Fenner & Smith did a feasability study and endorsed it. ~~without qualifi~~ Other endorsers include the Am. Enterprise Inst. the U.S. Chamber of Commerce and the U.S. Jr. Ch. ~~of~~, General Fed. of Womens Clubs, U.S. League of Savings & Loan Assns. & the Nat. Assn. of mgfrs."

~~Curiously enough this very simple, easy to implement plan does not have to be an alternate to the plan I discussed yesterday. We can have both. of them.~~

~~Right now the corp. tax on profits is 48%, which means every stockholder-regardless of the size of inc. is in a 48% tax bracket. An elderly couple with their savings invested in stocks has 48% of their~~

~~The N.D.P proposes setting a limit of 50% on the corporation tax and eliminating the individ. inc. tax on dividends. which at present is a form of *rather unfair* double taxation. You'll see the reason for this in a minute.~~ The corp. tax would be collected by the govt. as at present but instead of govt. spending it on our behalf we'd get to spend it ourselves.

Incidentally this plan is not offered as a substitute or alternate for the plan I discussed yesterday whereby employees could acquire ownership in the companys they worked for. We can actually have both and let me repeat what I said yesterday; we wont be taking anything away from anybody nor will those who benefit have to dig into their present savings.

Right now the Inc. tax on corporation profits is 48%. The Nat. dividend plan* calls for setting a ceiling of 50%. Investors would be assured that the corp. tax would never go above 50%. This should encourage more investment particularly since the plan would also end the present unfair double tax. ~~whereby~~ *Presently* ~~w~~*We* assess a pers. inc. tax ~~against the individuals~~ on the remainder of the profit when it's divided up between the shareholders. This would be cancelled, you'll see why in a minute.

The corp. tax would continue to be collected by govt. ~~Instead~~ However instead of govt. spending it in our behalf we'd get to spend it ourselves.

Very simply every citizen who ~~until~~ *was registered to vote* in the previous Fed. elec. would receive a pro rata share of the total corporation tax collected by govt. This means the registered voters of Am. would be ~~receiving~~ *sharing in* roughly half the profits of American industry.

Checks would be sent on a quarterly basis and it is estimated that when the prog. is fully implemented the payments to each individual would be ~~from at leas~~ $500 ~~a yr. or upward from tha~~t fig. *or more each yr.—TAX FREE.* An elderly couple ~~with~~ on a pension or soc. security would be getting an additional $1000 a year as their share of our industrial prosperity. Registered 18 yr. olds would have $500 a yr. ~~as a~~ to help them with their ed. And all of us would have a personal stake in helping our ec. to expand and produce more. One little known statistic ~~that~~ shows how we could all help to increase ~~this~~ our annual dividend: a 1/10 of 1% incrs. in ~~productivity~~ output per man hour adds a Bil. $ to the G.N.P. *A 2 or 3% incrs. would make us the worlds greatest producer.*

This basically is the plan. Tomorrow I'll give you more details including what we can do to ~~make this~~ make the Nat. Div. Plan a reality.

†*2nd tax plan script.* ❖

Tax Plan #3

February 14, 1975

† We can all own a piece of the action. It only takes an act of Cong.—I'll be right back.

This is the third day I've been talking about capitalism and a couple of ideas that could make all of us capitalists.

* See John H. Perry, *The National Dividend* (New York: I. Obolensky, 1964), and Martin R. Gainsbrugh, ed., *The National Dividend Plan: Pro & Con* (New York: The Conference Board, 1971).

When my old friend Cong. H.R. (Charlie Gross) of Iowa* retired last year he gave his colleagues a farewell valedictory address that ≠ challenged ≠ every one of them to start thinking about the next generation instead of the next election. For a quarter of a century he has been the conscience of the Cong. pleading constantly for statesmanship and responsibility ~~from that parliamentary body. They~~ *Very* seldom ~~voted as he urged them to vote but in~~ *did they support him in overwhelming numbers but in* their hearts every one of them ~~had to know~~ *knew* he was dead right and they were dead wrong.

In that final address he presented ~~to his colleagues the~~ *a* simple ~~plan~~ idea that could resolve ~~in many~~ *most* of our problems and make this Nat. once again the "Golden Hope of All Mankind." The idea *he presented* was not his. It ~~is~~*was* the work of a great many distinguished scholars & men successful in industrial America. It is known as *N.D.P.*.—"The Nat. Dividend Plan"—

As I told you Yesterday ~~I told you~~ it *is* simply ~~was~~ a plan whereby Govt. ≠ which is collecting *in tax* about ½ the profits of *all our* corps. would give that money ~~directly back~~ BACK DIRECTLY to the people~~. Each~~ *with each* registered voter ~~would get an equal share. getting~~ *sharing in the* ~~*share of the*~~ *benefits of free enterprise*. ~~I also told~~ ~~Now~~ I'm sure yesterdays broadcast ~~*however*~~ MUST HAVE left ~~wh~~ you with a few questions. ~~≠ *which* I'll try to answer them for you today.~~ *Let me see if I can give some additional facts & hopefully answer some of those questions.*

First of all N.D.P. ~~would~~ *will* not cause great disruption or damage to the necessary functions of the Fed. govt. It would be phased into operation over a 5 yr. period—20% a year.

The PRESENT corporation tax accounts for about 15% of ~~the govt's.~~ total ~~tax~~ *Fed.* revenue so ~~the ≠ yr.~~ *each yr. for 5 yrs.* the reduction ~~in revenues would only be 3%. & for each year thereafter~~ ~~*The same for each of the next* 4 yrs.~~ . *would be ⅕ of that or about 3%.* ~~But the Fed. govt's. ≠ revenues increase~~ NOW NORMALLY ≠ FED. REVENUES, GROW BY about 9% a year just from ~~normal~~ growth of the E.C. ~~≠ so each year govt. *revenues* would still be getting more money than it had~~ *be greater than they were* ~~the year before. In other words~~ *So* even though the govt. would be giving ~~up~~ back to the people ~~that~~ the corp. tax govt. would still ~~be increasing~~ *have an increase* in revenue ~~every~~ *each* year.

~~This dosen't take into account the~~ fact al~~so that N.D.P. would stimulate the ec There would be more~~ *In addition to this normal growth rate in revenues there would be an additional stimulant because of the money freed for* investment & ~~more~~ spending. ~~and that always~~ *This not only stimulates more ec. activity in the pvt. sector, it also* generates more tax revenues for govt. At the same time many govt. progs. could be reduced if not completely eliminated. Every family would be receiving tax free funds based on the number of regis-

* Congressman Harold R. Gross (R–Iowa, 1949–1975).

tered voters in the family. This would eliminate the need for many supplemental aid ~~grants~~ *programs* and the burocracys that supervise them.

~~Most~~ *In the main* Fed. spending does not create industry or generate production of goods which is the only true wealth of a Nat. *On the other hand increased activity in the pvt. sector does. It has a multiplier effect.* NDP. will involve distribution of earned $—$ the govt. is taking in taxes from pvt. indus. and theoretically spending in our behalf. The plan simply calls for letting each ~~# spend share~~ *one of us instead spend* his share of those $ the way each one of us chooses. I submit that we have ~~to as individuals~~ a better knowledge of our individual needs than govt. can possibly have.

Govt. still belongs to the people. Our congressmen know of this plan thanks to ~~Cha~~ former Cong. Gross. Now it is up to us to see that Cong. knows that we know of the plan. Our job is not so much to make Cong. see the light ~~as it is~~ but to feel the heat.

†*3rd on tax plan* ❖

Unemployment #1
February 27, 1975

Is a worker with a particular skill really unemployed if somewhere in the land an employer has a job for such a worker?—~~This is~~ I'll be right back.

A while back ~~I did some~~ *on these broadcasts* I talked about unemployment* and the way the govt. counts or perhaps I should say <u>mis</u> counts the unemployed. My intention was not to underplay the desperate situation of a person willing to work, needing work and unable to find it. The point I was making was that the percentage fig. given to us (often in scare headlines) *by the U.S. Bur. of labor statistics* was inaccurate, misleading and of no help whatsoever to those looking for work or those looking for workers.

~~Job skills are not evenly~~

Demand for *certain* job skills ~~are~~ *is* not evenly distributed across our land. Unemployed workers in one area are matched by unfilled jobs in other areas. There is little or no communication between employers and vocational schools as to ~~what~~ which skills are in demand and which are in surplus.

An item appeared recently in a Nat. magazine telling of the shortage in Am. industry of skilled tradesmen in the metal working fields. The prediction was made that in 5 yrs. or less metal working companies will be forced to cut back operations because they'll be unable to hire machinists, tool makers or die makers. One company operating in 6 states has a chronic problem right now. Most of their skilled emps. are age 60. ~~or over.~~ The youngest is 40. A*t* ~~al~~ a half

* In February 1975, the unemployment rate was 8.0 percent. *Economic Report of the President.* (Washington, DC: U.S. Government Printing Office, 1976), Table B24.

dozen locations they are in a constant search for personnelle. In one plant an opening for a toolmaker has gone unfilled for 2 yrs.

You and I as consumers are paying part of the price for this shortage in poor quality worksmanship because managers have to fill the gap with inadequately trained workers.

Now these aren't menial jobs with no future. Tool making is creative with new challenges daily and is well paid. Good tool & die makers are earning up to $18,000 a yr. and many go into business for themselves where their earning power is unlimited.

And yet a survey in the field of vocational training in one state found recent graduates numbered 105 trained in cosmetology, 181 clerical—~~not~~ tool & diemakers 0.

Thats only one field in this time of great unemployment. The Nat. Fed. of Independent Bus. which includes most of ~~the nations of employers of~~ those employing 500 or less workers of all types reports *that more than ⅕ of* its member firms have unfilled jobs and ~~a~~ ⅓ of those have been unfilled for more than 6 mo's. Half of ~~the employer~~ *the businesses* with job openings have been advertising in the papers and or using employment agencies. The pattern of labor shortage varies indicating as I said before that labor surplus & labor shortage is not evenly distributed. For example *in* the West & So. Central states including Texas ~~have~~ 32% of the businesses have job openings and 40% of these have been unfilled for 6 mos. or longer.

The article mentioned Calif. specifically as having fewer job openings and ~~suggested~~ suggested this reflects the tightening of welfare standards & closer supervision of unemp. benefits in Calif. Maybe that tells us something. One thing sure, it indicates that we need more information than just a misleading overall percentage fig. of how many people the labor dept. says are ~~loo~~ out of or between jobs. Why not a periodic census of job skills, ~~and where they are~~ *which are in surplus,* which are in short supply & where? ❖

Unemployment #2
February 27, 1975

Yesterday I was talking about unemployment and ~~asked~~ whether we should ~~legit~~ consider some one legitimately unemployed if there was a waiting market for his particular job skill in some other ~~state.~~ *TOWN OR EVEN ~~STATE:~~ IN SOME OTHER STATE.* ~~In other words have we decided that workers no longer need to seek jobs if this means moving?~~ *If we are going to give the unemployment figure as the overall national total shouldn't we also give the overall total of unfilled jobs?* Well intentioned but ridiculous govt. regulations and some court decisions have ~~just about established the rule that the~~ *had the effect of saying no one must leave home to find a job the* job must be brought to the worker. If this had been true ~~for the life of our country~~ *200 yrs. ago* we'd all still be living East of the Alleghenys.

During my last term as Gov. two skilled workers employed *in another state* by the same co. ~~in another state~~ decided they wanted to live in Calif. *So* They packed up their families and moved out here. ~~to the same town. In fact to the same neighborhood.~~ *to live continuing as neighbors in the same town.*

When They were unable to find jobs in their particular line of work ~~so~~ *they* applied for welfare. We had already instituted our very successful welfare reforms and, in keeping with the new procedures, got in touch with their former employer. He said that not only were their jobs still open if they'd come back but he had openings for 40 more ~~with~~ *of* their particular job skill. Forty two jobs waiting in one state and two who could handle ~~those~~ such work asking to be supported by their fellow citizens in another state. We refused them welfare.

But that didn't end the story. They sued the state and a judge ruled that we had to give them welfare; that not to do so was a denial of their right to travel and to live where they wanted to. Now it's true that one of our great freedoms is to be able to cross state lines and live wherever in Am. we choose. But ~~can we force our neighbors to support us~~ *do we have a moral right to be supported by our fellow citizens* simply because we want to live in a certain place. ~~Even~~ *even though there is no work for us in that place?*

I went to one of the lawyers on our staff and posed a hypothetical ~~case~~ question. ~~based on the judge's decision. Pointing~~ *I pointed* out that I would soon be leaving office ~~&~~ *but* that my line of work for most of my life had been motion picture acting. ~~I asked if I could return to my home town in Ill. where there is no *movie* work for and w~~

My question was, *in light of the judges decision* could I choose to live in my home town in Ill. and *would I* be eligible for welfare as an unemployed motion picture actor ~~although~~ *even though* there is no such work available ~~in that town?~~ *there?* It was his opinion that this was exactly what the judges decision meant.

Now dont send me a care package, ~~I'm not going to a former actor and I'll continue to live in Calif. and~~ motion picture acting is a closed chapter in my life. *And I'm not leaving Calif.* ~~I just wanted to point out how much room there is for *sense* common sense~~

I just used this as an example of how far we've strayed from ordinary common sense in our social reforms. ❖

Price of Beef
February 27, 1975

A steer is not all steak. Ill be right back.

Now I'm sure we all know that a beef animal isn't all steak. It consists of a variety of cuts some more tasty and desirable than others. But when I said a steer is not all steak—I had something else in mind. Actually that line is the title of an educational display by some fine young people in the 4H club over in Ariz.

Perhaps you aren't aware ~~th~~ of the growing ~~movement to~~ *attempt* to shame us into not eating beef on the grounds that we are feeding several lbs. of grain to cattle for ~~every~~ *each* lb. of beef we get back ~~& t~~*T*hat grain, *the argument goes,* could be used to feed the world-wide famine victems.

Well ~~as~~ the exhibit sponsored by these farm youngsters can be summed up in the words of a man who deals in meat. He says, "there are 4 meat quarters in a beef animal. The 5th quarter is the by products." In a lot of ways that 5th quarter has done more than the other 4 to enrich & even to lengthen our lives.

Before we take too seriously these sincere but ill informed people who see ~~meat~~ *cattle* as taking food from the hungry lets take a look at that 5th quarter we dont see in the meat market. Without it your tires might blow up in a mile and a half. One tire co. alone uses about 20 mil. lbs. of "stearic acid" a year. Stearic acid a by product of the beef animal is what keeps your tires cool. During last summers beef shortage this company had to cut back on production.

~~Here are some of the things that leave the packing house headed for~~ company. Here are some other things you wont see on a steak house menu, products from the bones, horns & hoofs, glue, gelatin (including the edible kind used in ice cream) case hardening steel, refining sugar, processed bone meal used as animal feed & fertilizer to grow ~~fo~~ more grain for the hungry.

That's only the beginning. There is neats-foot oil, plaster retarder, foaming fire extinguisher, paper boxes, sizing, wallpaper, sand paper~~,~~ and emery cloth. Would you believe cosmetics, camera film, band aids, spray on adhesives, vitamins, violin strings, ~~crotchet~~ crochet-hooks, combs & tooth brush handles?

In the field of pharmaceuticals we truly get into the life saving field—Heparin which keeps the blood from coagulating during an operation. It's also used in preventing blood clots. There are ~~drugs~~ *enzymes* used to aid babies digestion, epinephrine for asthma & allergies, Adrenal Cortex used in treating Addisons disease & to overcome shock. The list of really exotic medecines is too long ~~to~~ *for* this time slot but just as an example; we've known about diabetes since the 15th century. It took 400 years to find insulin and we found it in the pancreas of cattle. Today chemists feel they've only scratched the surface in developing useful things other than food from meat animals.

As for that grain were wasting—it is feed grain not eaten by humans and cattle only get that for about 100 days. Beef & Dairy cattle provide ⅔ of our protein and most of that comes from converting grass & brush on 40% of our land that would otherwise be waste because it couldn't be converted to raising crops. In the meantime our farmers are exporting 75% of our wheat & 57% of our rice to that hungry world. Lets pat bossy on the back with gratitude. ❖

In this commentary, Reagan offers his views on relying upon Arab oil and the ongoing energy crisis and offers some solutions.

Oil Talk
March 12, 1975

Do we have to wait for Cong. to do something about the energy crisis? I'll be right back.

If words could be burned as fuel Cong. would have the energy crisis solved & we'd be in the export business. They talk of rationing, gas tax to make it so expensive we'll buy less and a variety of regulations & controls. None of which has produced a single drop of oil.

We know we must develop new sources of oil as well as other energy sources so as to become independent of the Arab oil cartel. So far no program to do this has emerged from the puzzle palaces along the Potomac. *But* Even if we started tomorrow it would be several years before these new fuels would be available.

In the meantime we are consuming ~~about~~ 17 mil. barrels of oil a day ~~and importing about 2 mil. of that from the Arabs~~ *2 mil. of which we import from the Arabs* at a price that accounts for half the increase in the wholesale price index. Not only is part of our inflat due to ~~this~~ *the Arab* oil cartel ~~but the deficit~~ *so is the multi bil.* $ deficit in our balance of trade.

We know from experience that all the panaceas proposed by Cong.—rationing, controls and punitive taxes ~~dont~~ *wont* work in an economy as complex as ours. Any estimate of how much we'll reduce our oil consumption by adding a tax to make it more expensive isn't even a well educated guess. On top of that we'd better remember that govt. dosen't tax to get the money it needs—govt. always needs the money it gets. That punitive gas tax would wind up being spent on increased govt. and ~~when~~ *long after* the energy crisis was over the tax would linger on.

Now if you are going to write a letter to your congressman tell him to get on with the long range problem; finding tax incentives to encourage the production of new fuel; review of regulations and restrictions which presently interfere with the search for oil & other fuels. But dont for heavens sake encourage him to do anything about the short range problem—at least not while Cong. is thinking the way it is now.

Why dont we do something about the problems ourselves? One of the dignitarys of the Oil cartel told an American businessman recently, "I dont understand you Americans. You talk of destroying your economy when it is obvious you <u>waste</u> enormous amounts of this God-given resource." He was speaking of oil of course.

And he's right. The Fed. energy office estimates we waste as much oil as all of Japan uses. Our per capita consumption is 6X that of the Japanese & double that of the Germans. We use $\frac{1}{3}$ of the worlds total energy.

We can do something about that without any help from Cong. Let us cut the waste as we did ~~last year~~ when the Arabs were boycotting us. We can trim the fat without scratching a single muscle fibre in our industrial machine or without reducing our standard of living. If we just observe the 55 mile speed limit, cut out some unnecessary trips, double up with friends on an outing, a trip to the game or to a party combine errands into a single trip we can actually save 1 mil. barrels of oil a day. That is only $\frac{1}{17}$th. of our total consumption—surely 1 mile out of 17 is*n't im*possible. But that $\frac{1}{17}$th. will improve our balance of trade by 4 bil. $.

Then at home we can add to the savings by being a little more careful of the lights, the thermostat and so forth. We can bring down the price of oil, ~~and~~ help our country & do it all by ourselves if we make up our minds to it & if we start talking it to our friends & neighbors about how easy it is. Who knows once we've succeeded—Cong. may even take the credit for it. ❖

Tiffany & Company

March 12, 1975

Jewelry isn't made of *pulp* paper & printers ink—or is it? I'll be right back.

Some titles & names have ~~become~~ come to be literally part of our language ~~used~~ *able* to describe ~~some~~ *a* current event, a happening, a place or thing. The name of a jeweler in America is one such. You'd have to be way back in the hinterlands to find someone who wouldn't recognize the name Tiffany~~.~~ ~~The~~ and immediately connect it with precious stones & fine jewelry.

It is often used in conversation to denote class or prestige—For example someone wanting to describe ~~a~~ *the high quality of a* thing or place ~~as being of often~~ refers to it as ~~the~~ the Tiffany of it's kind.

Perhaps that's why Tiffany & Co. *of N.Y.* caused *something of* a ~~stir~~ *nationwide ripple* the other day. They didn't suddenly offer free diamonds or announce they were going into the hardware business. They just ~~published an~~ *PUBLISHED AN* advertisement* in Newspapers across the country. It didn't ~~even~~ mention jewelry but in the days since it has appeared in editorials; been reprinted by other businesses; ~~and *who* mailed *it* out to customers~~ quoted in pamphlets & for all I know printed in the Congressional record. I *sincerely* hope so because that above all is where it should be read & heeded.

Just on the chance that some of you might have missed it in spite of all the stir it caused I thought I'd read it to you as sort of a public service. So here it is—an ad by Tiffany & Co. "Is inflation the real problem? No it is not. Infla-

* The advertisement appeared in *The New York Times* on October 17, 1974, p. 3.

tion is simply the inevitable, final result of our follies. What then are the *real* causes of this national calamity? Here they are:

1. Spending exorbitant sums of taxpayers money unwisely by our govt.
2. Inhibiting the initiatives of the people with frustrating burocratic regulations.
3. Taxing savings & capital formation to death.
4. Govt. programs which have created critical shortages of essential materials & energy.
5. Giving away billions of $ to foreign govts.
6. Wasting untold money on foreign wars.
7. Tinkering with the ec. machinery with unsound panaceas.
8. Forsaking our religious heretage, not only in our schools, but everywhere; thus accentuating~~, not only~~ crime, immorality, greed & selfishness."

—End of ad. Printers ink on pulp paper but priceless pearls if we'll take them to heart. ~~7~~ ~~Tiffany From Tiffany~~ 8 Tiffany jewels for free ~~&~~ *in* a Tiffany of an ad.

Maybe not as flashy as that ~~met~~ *Govt. issue* costume jewelry we've been getting but ~~it~~ they'll wear better. ❖

Easy Voting
March 12, 1975

† How easy should it be to become a registered voter? I'll be right back.

Over recent years & without our paying much attention we've been making it easier & easier to become a registered voter. And whether we know it or not we've been making it easier & easier for voting blocks to swing elections even though the block dosen't represent a majority.

~~There is no question but that we should deplore the sizeable percentage of citizens who dont bother to register. b*But* is it~~ ~~true~~ ~~a proven fact that their reason~~ ~~they~~ ~~for not registering is~~ ~~that~~ ~~the complicated process of registration? If so how do we explain the percentage (this last elec. the large percentage)~~ ~~of registered voters~~ ~~who dont vote even after they've taken the trouble to register.~~

The proponents of easier registration would have us believe the non-voters are panting to vote only they find registering to do so impossibly ~~complicated~~ *complex* & difficult. ~~In Wash. & in many of our states (including my own) the drive goes on to permit registration by postcard, & *to* eliminate or *greatly* reduce residency requirements even to the point of allowing a citizen to register at the polling place on elec. day.~~

~~Shouldn't we be even more concerned about making it easier to cheat and~~

Is it true that our low voter turnout is due to the bother of registering? If it is how come *in* some elections where the issues or the candidates have excited the citizenry the voters dont seem to have much trouble registering & voting in overwhelming numbers? ~~Only 38% of the~~ *On the other hand only 38%* turned out in the '74 elec. & the majority of the 62% who stayed home gave every reason but registration difficulty as the reason for their defection.

If you dont mind a Calif. example let me ~~tell~~ give you an idea of what happens when you make it too easy. Out here we've had some court decisions plus the wording of the State Elections Code which have created something called "transient voting." Technically it's legal—morally it's on a par with ballot box stuffing. ~~The *CALIF* Legis. instead of correcting the language in the code is considering postcard registration & instant voters.~~

Very simply a voter is eligible simply by declaring his <u>intention</u> to live in a certain place. Wouldn't you know that Berkeley has been the scene of what has to be ~~the~~ *an* experiment in mobile voting blocks~~.~~ and some of the election results have been pretty upsetting to the ~~legit~~ more solid citizenry of that community.

In one election 2000 or more votes were cast in Berkeley than the total number of adult citizens in the city. *In 1972* 30 people voted from 1 address *a SINGLE FAMILY DWELLING* & 59 were registered to do so. ~~at that address—a single family residence. That was in 1972.~~ In 1973 6 people voted from that address even though the house had burned down 4 months before *the elec.* ~~& the lot had been cleared of the debris.~~ People with fixed abodes in 6 *other* Calif. cities & 2 in Pa. voted in Berkeleys elec. All it took was a statement 30 days in advance that they intended to ~~vote~~ live in Berkeley.

One man a former Mayor of Berkeley has led the drive that exposed ~~the irregulatory~~ *hundreds of* irregularities ~~I've mentioned plus hundreds more~~ *of the kind I've mentioned.* ~~and is for~~ *He's* working to get changes in the state code to correct the situation. ~~Meanwhile the~~ Meanwhile the Calif. legis. leans toward making things worse not better~~.~~ *and Cong. is talking of postcard registration* ~~*at the*~~ *for Nat. elections.*

Look at the potential for cheating, a John Doe can be registered in 3 or more counties ~~&t~~*T*here is no cross checking between counties. He can be John Doe in Berkley & J. F. Doe in the next county all by saying he intends to live in both places.

How is it in your state? And does your Congressman want postcard registration?

This is R.R. Thanks for listening.

†Pete H. This is the result of a letter from your friend Mike Culbert ❖

Indochina #1
April 1975

Should baseball players be the only ones judged on their batting average? I'll be right back.

We are being treated to a barrage of column & commentary ridiculing those who urge aid to S.V.N.* ~~on the grounds because~~ *on the grounds that* failure to support an ally will have a domino effect on other allies in other parts of the world. James Reston of the N.Y. Times a week before Easter discounted the domino theory as having no validity; ~~that~~ *He says* two small Asian nations ~~could~~ *can* have no bearing on the real international problems confronting us. He ~~ended up by saying,~~ *describes ~~the~~* "the domino theory" [as] almost as obsolete as the game of dominoes itself." **

It's strange that so many members of the press who insist that every statement ever made by an officeholder be brought forth ~~at the~~ whenever they think he is guilty of inconsistency have never thought of making the record public where their own pontifications are concerned. These men & women write with *GREAT* authority on any & all subjects ~~but seldom if ever do and their opinions influence~~ *and unfortunately they influence* public thinking to a great degree. *BUT* Would their influence be so great if like ballplayers their updated batting average was published with their columns & editorials?

~~In recent years some of the best known, of, the ones who solemnly tell us after a President speaks to us~~ *Those familiar voices we hear telling us with assurance after a Presidential address* what it was ~~he~~ *we* really ~~said,~~ *heard;* ~~have~~ *those who* told us ~~how~~ Castro was no communist, Ho Chi Minh was another George Washington and Mau Tse Tung & the Red Chinese were just agrarian reformers *never remind us of how often their pronouncements were wrong.*

~~Let me give you a collection *of statements* on one specific happening. I wont identify the individuals but assure you they are the well recognized voices of all 3 TV networks.~~ *FOR EXAMPLE* A few years ago Pres. Nixon made the hard decision to mine Haiphong harbor & stop the flow of ammuntion from Russia to the No. Vietnamese.*** He made the decision on the very eve of the summit meeting in Moscow. All arrangements had been made ~~and I'm sure great names of the communications media~~ *for the trip & most of the better known news analysts* who had ~~already~~ accompanied him to Peking were all packed *for the trip to Russia.*

His announcement of the action he planned against an enemy who had been killing American fighting men for several years stunned these ~~media~~ *well known men* & brought ~~forth~~ *FROM THEM* a flood of scornful criticism.

* S.V.N. stands for South Vietnam.
** James Reston, "The Domino Theory," *The New York Times,* March 19, 1975, p. 47.
*** On May 8, 1972.

~~Here are some of the lines~~ *ERIC SEVAREID:* "I would suspect that the summit will not come off"—that was the mildest although it was delivered with an arched eyebrow. ~~Another said~~ *CHARLES COLLINGWOOD* "Certainly the Moscow summit meeting from which so much had been expected is now in jeopardy." ~~Commentator no. 3 said~~ *MARVIN KALB:* "One casualty of the Presidents mining & blockade may well be his upcoming summit to Moscow. Those who began packing & dreaming of caviar are beginning to unpack & are returning to dry cereal." That was cuter than the bare announcement ~~by a 4th~~ *OF JOHN CHANCELLOR*—: "The summit is in jeopardy today." Then there was ~~the horrified~~ *RICHARD VALERIANI*['*s*] *SHOCKED* question "How can they receive him now." ~~The line~~ *TED KOPPEL REPLIED:* "I dont see how he can go." *& EDWARD STEVENS SAID,* "The Presidents announcment will be pretty hard for them to swallow. It practically killed the prospects of a summit."

So spoke the great modern day informers & interpreters, most of whom *then* dutifully accompanied the Pres. to Moscow a few days later to report on the very successful summit which all agreed did much to lessen world tensions. To my knowledge none have ever acknowledged ~~that he was~~ *THE PRES. HAD BEEN* right & they were wrong nor have they given ~~him~~ credit to the mining & the bombing of Hanoi for finally bringing an end to our participation in the war & the freeing of our prisoners.

~~And just as a postscript~~ *Ironically enough at the very time they were calling the Moscow trip off*—the Russians were so afraid ~~he~~ *the Pres.* wouldn't come ~~to Moscow~~ *that* Henry Kissinger ~~had to rush over & assure them he'd be there~~ *at their invitation was already in Moscow to calm their fears and assure them he would really be there.*

Tomorrow I'll get back to the domino theory & whether it's real or imaginary. This is RR Thanks for listening. ❖

*In 1975, there were over 11 million people on welfare.**

Welfare Program #1
April 1975

It's time to write your congressman again—I'll be right back.

Eight Demo. congressmen & fifty four Repub's. have joined together ~~to~~ in introducing a welfare reform program** that could save the taxpayers almost $2 Bil.—1.87 Bil. according to conservative estimates. It will—if passed—

* See the Department of Health and Human Services statistics at http://www.acf.dhhs.gov/news/stats/6097rf.htm.

** The National Welfare Reform Act (H.R. 5006) was introduced in Congress on March 17, 1975, by Congressman Samuel Devine (R–Ohio). It was never passed.

probably save more. We learned in our own w.f. reforms in Calif. that our real savings were far greater than our estimates. What is even more important these reforms will also benefit the truly, deserving needy who must have our help. In Calif. in addition to saving the taxpayers a Bil. $ we were able to incrs. the grants to the needy by 43%.

When we reformed W.F. in Calif. and halted an increase in caseload that was adding 40,000 people a month to the WF rolls, we did so by changes in our state regulations and local administrative rules. ~~This was enough to bring about a reduction in the WF~~ ~~*change the 40,000 a month increase in the*~~ ~~case-load~~ ~~that averaging 8000 a month.~~ ~~*to an 8000 a month reduction.*~~ *That reversed the trend & brought about an 8000 per month reduction in the rolls.* ~~But~~ We could not however change the multitudinous Fed. regulations imposed on us by the dept. of H. E. W. in Wash. Those reg's. offer (if reformed) an *even* greater potential for savings.

The plan being offered to Cong. is in effect an extension of the Calif. plan but one in which th~~ese~~*ose* Fed. regulations will also be reformed. One major change will require able bodied mothers on the "Aid to dependent children program" to work ~~at~~ *IN RETURN FOR W. F. GRANTS AT* public or community work projects halftime—80 hrs. a month. As one congressman put it "They get something—they give something."

Now there will be terrific oposition to this—charges of slave labor and that welfare mothers should be in the home with their children. Let me answer that latter charge 1st. ~~Among the present working women in Am. are~~ 40% of all the *Am.* mothers of children under 18 yrs. of age ~~&~~ *are working* & ⅓ of these have children under age 6. *As for pub. work projects being slave labor we were allowed to conduct an experiment in 35 Calif counties wherein able bodied welfare recipients had to report for such work. In one year we funneled 57,000 people from WF thru these work projects into prvt. enterprise jobs* In 1969 the House Ways & Means committee did a study in 11 cities and came to the conclusion that an increasing number of WF recipients were people who had been induced by social workers to quit jobs and opt for WF instead. In 8 yrs. the percentage of WF mothers who had <u>never</u> worked had been cut almost in half.

It is ~~hight~~ high time for WF reform at the Nat. level & reform is not a new idea. In 1935 F.D.R. signed the Soc. Sec. Act and announced: "We can now see the end of pub. assistance in Am." In 1962 J.F.K. signed a W.F. Reform bill* which he said would cost more to start with but which would eventually reduce the rolls by training people for useful work by stressing "self support & simplyfying W.F. Admin." In 1964 L.B.J. signed the Ec. Opp. Act (the Pov. Prog.) & said, "The days of the dole in our country are numbered."

In the meantime an exec. in H.E.W.** ~~instructed~~ *was telling* the professionals in the dept. "To think *BIG &* plan big." And they did. While 3 Presidents

* The Public Welfare Amendments (P.L. 87-543) were enacted on July 25, 1962.

** Department of Health, Education, and Welfare.

were making statements they sincerely believed were true and our Nat. pop. was increasing 11%, Aid to dependent children ~~was increasing~~ *increased* 216% & the overall WF caseload more than doubled while it's cost quadrupled.

The time has come to write your Congressman in support of WF reform. I'll tell you some more about W.F. tomorrow.

This is R.R. Thanks for listening. ❖

Welfare Program #3

April 1975

Should our judgement of welfare be based only on whether it raises the standard of living for recipients or should we also consider what it does to the character of the people who participate? I'll be right back.

For the last 2 days I've been talking about welfare and the need to correct some of the *COSTLY CUMBERSOME* burocratic nonsense that has ~~made~~ *taken* it ~~costly, cumbersome and~~ far afield from it's original purpose. Today I'd like to touch on ~~another troublesome facet,~~ what it may be doing to the spirit & character of our people.

~~Before I get into this and k~~*K*nowing how easy it is to be attacked as heartless & unfeeling let me state a few facts about my own position. First of all I believe in our responsibility to *help* those who for whatever reason are unable to provide for themselves & their families. Right now ~~I frankly~~ *I* believe we could do more for the truly needy ~~but we're~~ *if we weren't* spread too thin ~~because we're also~~ providing for the truly greedy.

Milton Friedman the noted economist once said "when you start paying people to be poor you wind up with an awful lot of poor people." From my own experience I am convinced that most welfare recipients are unhappy being on WF and would much rather be self sustaining & self respecting. I'm also sure however that encouraged by some ~~in~~ professional welfarists ~~they can~~ *many* lose ~~that~~ *their* desire to leave welfare and begin accepting it as a way of life—indeed a career in itself. When this can happen~~—then~~ we are destroying human beings not salvaging them.

There is ~~now~~ a Nat. Welfare Rights Org. ~~It is a kind of *an organization*~~ dedicated to ~~increasing~~ demanding ~~what it claims are the rights of its members, namely to have~~ a voice in ~~saying~~ how much of a workers earnings ~~should~~ *must* be shared with them. A few years ago a Mrs. Beulah Sanders representing this org. before the House Ways & Means Comm. ~~In her testimony she~~ said, "Everyone in this country has a right to share the wealth. The money has gone into the pockets of the middle class & if we dont get our share we're going to disrupt this state, this country & this Capitol."

Fed. officials have habitually said fraud ~~was~~ in WF was less than 1%. But

Dr. Richard Nathan while deputy under Sec. of H.E.W. said "Our prob. is we cant even detect fraud." Former Congressman Bill Scherle of Iowa * once told his colleagues; "Take the cap of the strongest, wealthiest, most freedom loving country in Hist. Give it an unemp. rate of only 2% but 1 out of 5 ~~citz. of that cap.~~ *are* on W.F. ~~*yet though*~~ ~~t~~*T*he median inc. is $10,500. ~~Still~~ *Yet* Fed. aid per cap. is 6X as much as it is for the citz. of Iowa. Then set up a fed. funded consumer complaint dept. in a model city project & what is the number one complaint of these deprived people? Jobs, housing—crime?—Their color TV sets dont work properly."

In 1968 C.O.RE (Com. on Racial Equality) told us why ~~ref~~ we should be supporting the *present* move in Cong. to reform W.F. They said: "Hand outs are demeaning. They do violence to a man, strip him of his dignity & breed in him a hatred of the total syst. Poor men want the same as the rest of us. They want to be independent, they want jobs & control over their own destiny." "W.F." they said, "is no answer. We ~~want the~~ *seek to* harness the creative energy of ~~the~~ pvt. enterprise to achieve a solution to Am's. crisis. We look to American independence of spirit to recog. opportunity, & to take advantage of it. It has happened in the past—it can happen again. This is R.R. Thanks for listening. ❖

On January 27, 1973, the United States, North Vietnam, South Vietnam, and the Viet Cong signed the Paris Peace Accords. A cease-fire and peaceful negotiations toward reunification were included in the terms of the agreement. Yet two years later, as Reagan records the commentary below, the Paris agreements are falling apart and the United States is completing its withdrawal as the country falls to the North.

Vietnam
April 1975

The lights are going out in S.E. Asia & soon a great silence will settle over the land. It wont just be the silence that follows when the fighting stops.

~~The other day the "Wall street Journal" carried an editorial bluntly pointing out that certain anti war voices are being heard warning against "recriminations" if & when Saigon falls. Then very bluntly the editorial suggested the warnings were self serving. They were aimed at "closing down debate. . . . before history makes it painfully clear that whatever the mistakes in V.N. our prescnce there was rooted in serious purposes."~~

A debate has already begun about whether the communist forces in V.N. will or will not eliminate great numbers of people if & when ~~th~~ Saigon falls.

* R–Iowa, 1967–1975.

Those who have been most vocal against ~~the~~ helping the S. Vietnamese in their fight to remain free pooh, pooh the idea and call it scare talk. Some of them I'm sure are aware *they wont have to eat their words* ~~that w~~With a surrender will come a lowering of a curtain around the entire ~~Nat.~~ *area*. We'll hear only what the conquerors want us to hear. There will of course be escapees, or correspondents who'll wait until they are safely out before telling us of atrocities they've witnessed. But like with the great slaughter in Red China there will be a reluctance on the part of many to believe these stories. Its easier not to believe them. And so the debate will never be resolved. The only losers will be the human beings who <u>will</u> be executed behind the curtain of silence.

Sometimes it seems the Europeans are more realistic about these things. They are already getting the word. A diplomatic report ~~in~~ *to* France ~~puts~~ puts the figure at 3600 already put to death in one town *alone* in the central highlands ~~when it was~~ taken by the communists a few weeks ago. Who were executed & why?—Well the usual types the conquerors will *already* have earmarked when they arrive—S.V.N. civil servants, former employees of Am. companies or *of* our military.

Why should this surprise anyone? In the library of the Hoover Inst. at Stanford U. you can see the Gestapo book listing *by name* the 10,000 Englishmen who were to be executed when the Nazis invaded England in W.W.II. ~~Di Th~~ Dictators have a very practical idea—eliminate anyone who has the potential to be a leader & who therefore could make trouble. *And above all strike terror to the hearts of the rest.*

Other reports received in Europe—In Rome the Jesuit society has been notified the Vietnamese Catholic bishop of Fa Lat has been executed. Why? He was a bishop wasn't he? The refugees add to the mounting horror with stories of wholesale slaughter of local police & govt. officials. They report that captured soldiers are tied together in ~~bunde bundlls~~ bundles & killed with a single grenade.

The London Daily Telegraph carries similar dispatches and adds "a minimum fig. of a million executions in the whole of S.V.N. if the communists take over does not seem far fetched and it could be much higher." Lets see, a million in a country of 19 mil. To give you an idea of what that means—if it were our own country that would be the same as executing between 11 & 12 mil. Americans.

The horror mounts ~~according to~~ *in* the dispatches to European capitols. To discourage the people from fleeing the communist advance one report tells of Viet Cong driving ~~Molotov~~ *Russian built* trucks at high speed over & through crowds of refugees. Others were shelled by artillery.

One of Britains leading experts on V.N. P.J. Honey has written: "No matter how the U.S. Congress may rationalize, no matter how Communist apologists in the free world may argue, no matter what conciliatory promises Hanoi or Liberation radio stations may broadcast, a Communist victory in S.V.N. will result in killings on a Vast scale."

We still have 1300 men ~~+~~ listed as missing in action over there. That was one of the cease fire terms violated by Hanoi. ~~They had promised we coul~~ *to* ~~*help help us*~~

This is R R. ~~I'll be right back~~

Thanks for listening. ❖

Government Computers
May 1975

† To err is human—it takes a govt. computer to really louse things up.—I'll be right back.

A New Jersey newspaper recently reported a story that bears repeating. It begins with a familiar scene. A ~~mother in law—wife~~ *woman* and her daughter in law having a *mid* morning cup of coffee at the kitchen table. The womans husband leaving to go down to the store for a few groceries. He's retired on a $642 a month inc. as the result of serious injuries *he has* suffered, in addition to which he has the curse of the coal miner, black lung disease.

Just after his departure the mail arrives. Mother opens a letter from the Soc. Security Admin. ~~and as the news~~ According to the news story it was a good thing she was sitting down. Her daughter in law saw ~~the~~ her alarm and asked "Whats the matter ~~m~~Ma?" Her mother said, "Its Soc. Sec.—they want Pops death certificate. They got him dead." "Dont tell him" ~~his daughter in law~~ he'll die of a heart attack," the daughter said.

Up to here the story gets a laugh—but not for long. That $642 monthly check has ~~dropped~~ *been reduced* to $281. *YOU SEE* The declaration by Soc. Security that the head of the household had passed away wipes out the disability benefits to which he is legally entitled. *After all a dead man can hardly be eligible for disability payments.*

The very much alive deceased and his wife—(widow according to Soc. Sec.) have patiently been making periodic trips ~~to~~ & phone calls to the S.S. Admin. offices in Perth Amboy N.J. trying to refute as Mark Twain once did the report of his death which he described as "somewhat premature." *

The officials according to the news story are sympathetic, courteous and a little bit embarrassed. They appear also to be unable to solve the problem. Heaven forbid they should tell a computer it's goofed. The head of the Perth Amboy office refused to discuss the matter with the press. He said, "regulation number one forbade such a discussion." He did say however that admin. officials in Baltimore had been notified of the mistake and that every effort ~~had~~

* What Mark Twain actually wrote, in May 1897, was: "The report of my death was an exaggeration."

was being made to restore the victem to the ranks of the living. So far they haven't suggested a trip to the Shrine of Lourdes.

One ~~hap~~ bright note—the familys financial plight has been eased a little. Soc. Security sent them a check for $710 to cover the cost of the funeral.

This is R.R. Thanks for listening.

†(From The News Tribune of Woodbridge N.J.~~)~~ Story of Stewart Busch.) ❖

Adoption

May 1975

One of the arguments for abortion is that it prevents the birth of unwanted children. Who says they are unwanted? Ill be right back.

During my last 2 yrs. as Gov. I did a weekly one hour T.V. question & answer program. ~~with~~ The questions*ing* ~~were from a no.~~ was done by highschool students—a different group each week ~~picked~~ chosen by the dept. of ed. The program was entirely unrehearsed. I had no hint of what the questions would be and only met each class a few min's. before the taping began. The program was aired on the ed. network & made available to our 1100 Calif. school districts for closed circuit class room use.

For me I have to say it was exciting & most enjoyable to meet these young people and *to* discover what concerned them about govt. & current issues. Several times ~~we~~ the subject got around to abortion and why the Gov. of Calif. opposed abortion on demand.

One day a pretty, fresh faced young lady, intelligent & sincerely concerned asked me if abortion wasn't preferable to making a young ~~girl~~ unmarried girl have a baby she didn't want & which would therefore grow up unloved & probably turn out to be a criminal. I gave an answer which apparently she hadn't considered. I told her there were literally mils. of people in this country who wanted but could not have children and who ~~had~~ waited eagerly sometimes for years to adopt the baby she had described; that such a child would not be unloved—very much the opposite was true.

There were always some raised hands & unanswered questions ~~when~~ *after* the cameras were turned off and I always tried to stay around to answer them even though we were no longer on the air. This day another equally attractive, wholesome girl had her hand half raised. I called on her but she didn't have a question. Instead she said "I am adopted. I think a great deal of my ~~par~~ folks & I think they feel the same about me." And then she added this unforgettable line—"I'm glad no one killed me."

I've just finished reading about the young mother in Columbus Ohio who is dying of cancer. ~~H~~ She has three handsome, lovely children Sheri age 12 Joey who is 10 & another daughter Amber 6. There is no question about the love in this family. The mother made her situation known through the press. She wants someone who will ~~love~~ *take* her children—keep them together & most of all love them.

The story I've just been reading quotes a spokeswoman for the hospital where the 32 yr. old mother is ~~a patient~~ *dying*. She says: "This is the 1st time anything like this has ever happened. We were totally unprepared." They have had to call in volunteers to handle the flood of mail from couples who want to take in her children. They are not unwanted nor will they be unloved.

God Bless America—This is R.R. Thanks for listening. ❖

In early 1975 the federal debt reached $500 billion, almost 19 percent of GDP.

George Meany and Economics
May 1975

George Meany* talking economics reminds me of the fellow who drowned trying to wade across a river whose *<u>average</u>* depth he'd been told ~~averaged~~ *was* 3 ft. I'll be right back.

I knew Geo. Meany some years back when I was an officer of a Union myself. And I like him. He's been in my home on one or two occasions. But I found myself resenting very much his tirade to a Congressional committee ~~which was presented on the television news just before the middle of May.~~

Briefly the point he made loudly & angrily was that one problem & one alone "unemployment" must be ~~dealtt~~ dealt with as if it had no connection with the entire ec. situation. He demanded a greater deficit—~~+~~$100 Bil, if need be, to create jobs.~~, and added that if the Pres. & Cong. had acted during W.W.II. the way they're acting now we'd have lost the war. Several times he repeated this country can afford such a deficit~~. *He went on to say a big rich country like ours can afford to go in debt.*

~~Well now *He said* a~~A big rich country like ours <u>can</u> afford to go in hock,—~~n~~<u>Now</u> & <u>then</u>—just as a solid citizen with ~~a few assets like~~ a pd. up home, some insurance & a ~~good guaranteed position with a good inc.~~ *reasonably good, safe inc.* can borrow to ~~tide himself over a bad time *say for* hospital bills or a temporary~~ lay~~off. finance his~~ ~~*the*~~ ~~kids college ed.~~ *meet the unusual or unexpected* *SUCH AS HOSPITAL EXPENSE OR MAYBE ~~OR~~ JUST TO SEE THE KIDS THRU COLLEGE*. But ~~what if~~ *we're talking* about a ~~not so solid citizen~~ *character* who already has a double mortgage on ~~his home~~ *the house,* owes install-

* George Meany (1894–1980) was a famous American labor leader, president of the American Federation of Labor and Congress of Industrial Organizations (AFL-CIO) from1955 to 1979.

ments on the furniture & ~~his~~ the car, has borrowed up to the limit on his insurance and is only working part time? ~~How much can he borrow?~~

Even the economist *so* beloved of the liberals, Lord Maynard Keynes * said Govt. should run deficits in bad times to stimulate the ec. but—& it's a much ignored but by those who claim to be Keynsian economists—he said in good times Govt. should accumulate surpluses & reduce the debt.

~~We have too many people in high place—like Geo. Meany who only read half of Keynes.~~

Franklin ~~Delano~~ Roosevelt said: "A govt. like a family can in time of emergency go into debt but if it continues to ~~do this~~ *SPEND MORE THAN ITS INC* in good times & bad~~—like a family it will as a~~ *a govt. like a* family will go bankrupt." (UNQUOTE) ~~Well We have been going into debt in good times & bad~~ Certainly a Nat. must borrow to see itself through an emergency like W.W.II. But we've kept on borrowing *until* ~~Now~~ our Nat. debt is greater than the *combined* debt of all the *other* Nat's. of the world. ~~put together & *yet* we're still lending these others *countries* money.~~ We're not ~~a country~~ *suddenly* faced with an ~~ec. recession~~ *emergency* debating whether or not ~~we should temporarily go into debt until times get better.~~ *to raise a short term loan.* The interest on ~~our~~ debt we *already* have is 10X bigger than our whole Nat. budget ~~was~~ when we *1st started* ~~down this path.~~ *running deficits on an annual basis.* ~~We've just heard~~

~~The N.Y. st. confess it must default on $800 mil worth of bonds & N.Y. city whose bud is 2nd only to that of the Fed. govt. is asking Uncle Sam to bail it out for $1½ Bil. a j just to meet it's payroll.~~

Yes we have unemployment and I've told you before how I feel about a person who wants to work & cant find a job. Few if any situations seem as tragic & desperate to me. But Geo. Meany ~~if~~ should know that govt. policies, ~~yes & cands. for office that he has supported for several decades now~~ *he himself* has supported & still supports are responsible for this countries insolvency, ~~and therefore The~~ inflation and the unemployment that inflation brings.

He wants a bigger deficit?

Here's what ~~inflati~~ *the* present deficit means to the working people ~~Mr.~~ Meany represents; ~~first of course is the confiscation by govt. of capital which should be available~~ *the Fed. govt. is* ~~*confiscating*~~ *taking most of the available money which should be used* to finance plant expansion, ~~replacement of machinery etc. to~~ increase production (which reduces inflation) and provides jobs. But it becomes more personal—those things we want to buy on the instalment plan ~~for instance,~~ the treasury dept. has already told the banks & lending institutions how much of their cap. must be earmarked for funding the government's deficit. This means ~~*one* your good credit rating wont matter much,~~ it will become harder & harder to buy things ~~with lower down~~ *with the usual down* payment & easy instalments. And those instalments ~~will come~~

* John Maynard Keynes (1883–1946) was one of the world's best-known economists.

(when they do) at ~~*if you can get them will include* higher & higher interest~~ rates. A bigger deficit means higher inflation, ~~means~~ a deeper recession, ~~means~~ more unemp. and there'll be George asking next time for a $200 Bil deficit.

~~This is R.R.~~

Sometimes I think the AFL-CIO economic advisors are the kind of economists who have a Phi Beta Kappa key on one end of their watch chains & no watch on the other.—This is RR— ❖

In 1975 federal, state, and local government expenditures were 31.1 percent of GDP. State and local governments spent 9.1 percent of GDP from their own sources. Spending in 1976 was virtually identical. Inflation in consumer prices for 1975 was 8.5 percent.

Congress vs. Local Government
May 1975

Sometimes maybe you think I'm too critical of govt.—I worry about that too. But then govt. comes over the hill with another zany.—I'll be right back.

Every time I soften up a bit and think maybe I should spend these few minutes giving helpful hints on gardening or how to keep your dog from ~~jumping~~ putting his paws on your new white suit, govt. comes up with a new one that stiffens my back. (Incidentally you can cure your dog of ~~leaning on you~~ *putting his paws on your white suit* by stepping on his hind feet when he ~~rears~~ stands up—not hard mind you. Just a little)

Here is a news item that should make all of us perk up. The Joint Ec. Committee of Cong. says a study of 48 states and 140 local govt's. reveals that loc. & st. governments are retrenching and cutting back spending by something in the neighborhood of $8 Bil. a year—and that's a nice neighborhood.

With govt's., Fed. St. & local, taking virtually half of every $ earned in the U.S. this news of reduced govt. spending should be cause for dancing in the streets. But that's not the way the Congressional comm. see's it. They are downright unhappy, and that should scare all of us for what it reveals about governments thinking.

The Comm. says ~~for local~~ this action by loc. govt. will remove $8 Bil. in overall purchasing power from the economy at a time when the Fed. govt. is attempting to pump up the sagging economy by increased Fed. spending.

Increased Fed. spending is the cause of inflation, inflation is the cause of the sagging economy and what makes them think that $8 bil. left in the hands of those who earned it wont be more wisely spent than if it is spent by burocracy? The truth is money spent by govt. does not have the multiplier effect of money spent in the private sector. Indeed govt. spending is a drag on the economy and slows ec. recovery.

The Congressman who chairs the comm. says: "We must find some method for stabilizing state & local govt. budget~~s~~ actions so that we can have all levels of govt. working together"—and he went on to ~~say~~ explain that he meant working together to solve the ec. problems.

It's time we all realize that govt. is not the ans. to our EC. prob. govt. is the problem—and this kind of ridiculous thinking makes that very clear.

St. & loc. govt's. do almost as much spending as the Fed. govt. and between them are responsible for about ⅓ of the G.N.P. I submit that is a percentage which a free enterprise system cannot long tolerate and remain free.

If you dont mind a personal recollection—every time we produced a surplus in Calif's. state govt. during these past 8 yrs. we gave it back to the taxpayers in the form of a one-time rebate or bonus. Usually we did this by way of the st. inc. tax. for example a $250 mil. surplus allowed us to tell the taxpayers to fig. their inc. tax and then only pay 80% of it, putting the other 20% back in their pockets.

The last such surplus rebate was by way of both the ~~sal~~ inc. & the sales tax and it amounted to $850 mil. ~~The~~ We had great resistance from the majority in the legis. who shared evidently the same phil. as this joint Cong. comm. One st. Sen. said he considered giving this money back to the taxpayers an "unnecessary expenditure of pub." funds." That one ~~takes a~~ makes you shake your head a little.

~~All told~~ *During the 8 yrs.* we returned to the people more than $5 Bil. The reason I tell this is because until 8 yrs. ago Califs. rate of ~~increase~~ inflation was consistently higher than the nat. average. For ~~the~~ six of the last seven years it was lower. ~~This is R.R.~~

Do you really need govt. telling you how your money should be spent—let alone spending it for you? This is R.R.— ❖

*Consumer prices increased 12.1 percent in 1974 and another 7.0 percent in 1975.**

Inflation as Tax
June 1975

Riddle—When is a tax not a tax?—Ans. When it's inflation.
I'll be right back

I know it's a cliché and we've all heard it & said it ourselves, that inflation is the cruelest kind of tax—hitting those ~~the~~ hardest who can least afford it. I wonder though if we really understand that inflation is in fact a tax

* *Economic Report of the President* (Washington, D.C.: U.S. Government Printing Office, 1980), Table B52.

INCREASE—, a way govt. can raise more revenue without ~~increasing~~ *raising* the ~~tax~~ rates. ~~What could be dearer to the heart of a spendthrift pol. than to be able to get money for his pet schemes without being accused of raising taxes?~~

Lets take capital gains. ~~to begin with.~~ This is the profit you make if something you bought a while back has become more valuable and you sell it for more than you paid for it. This can be a farm, a home, a lot you were going to build on and didn't, that old car that suddenly became valuable to a collector, ~~etc. and of course~~ stock you bought. ~~etc.~~

But what if ~~the~~ increased sale price ~~is only because the dollar has declined in~~ value? ~~*you receive*~~ *is* ~~*only*~~ *an increase in* ~~*the number of*~~ *dollars but they dont buy as much as they did?* If you sell your home for twice what it cost, but all homes are worth twice what they ~~originally~~ cost ~~only~~ because the *present* dollar today only buys what 50¢ bought a few years ago, then you haven't made any profit. ~~on the deal.~~ But the tax collector says you have. If you paid $20,000 and sell for $40,000 he says you've made $20,000 ~~profit~~ upon which you must pay a tax even though $40,000 today will only buy what $20,000 bought at the time of purchase. ~~Govt. takes it's share & you actually lose money on the deal.~~

The answer is very simple, but not too many politicians are going to suggest it. The ~~profit of~~ sales price should be computed in constant dollars—meaning the dollars should be valued at the ~~same~~ purchasing power now compared to their purchasing power when you first acquired the asset.

Let's turn to your paycheck because here ~~the~~ is where the govt. really profits from inflation. We have a "progressive" inc. tax. As your inc. increases you find the govt. takes a higher percentage, say, of the second several thousand dollars you earn than of the first. But now you get a raise ~~to~~ simply to keep even with ~~inflation~~—the increased cost of living. You are not better off ~~than you were~~. You can ~~only~~ *STILL* afford to buy ~~the same things in the same amount that~~ *only what* you could before the raise. ~~because the price of those things has gone up.~~ But that ~~raise~~ *increase in the number of $* put you into a ~~new~~ higher tax bracket. The govt. ~~increases the actual percent it takes from each of those $ dollars~~ *TAKES A GREATER SHARE OF THOSE NEW $* and suddenly ~~in spite of the raise you cant buy as much as you were able to buy befo the year before.~~ *YOU FIND YOU HAVN'T KEPT UP WITH INFLATION. AFTER TAXES YOU ARE WORSE OFF THAN YOU WERE BEFORE THE RAISE. NINE TIMES OUT OF TEN THOUGH YOU BLAME HIGH PRICES, NOT YOUR TAXES.*

~~Fiscal liberals hail this as a way to finance the expanded social programs so dear to their hearts.~~

~~Here is an example—the~~ *THE average* ~~$10,000 a year man of a few years ago today earns $15,000. a year—only to keep even with. He has actually kept ahead of inflation by something in the~~ ~~*That's an increase greater than the increase in the cost of living. He should be better off*~~ ~~Not by much but some—until he figures~~ ~~*and he is until he figures*~~ ~~his inc. tax. Then he learns he is a~~

SEVERAL ~~*HUNDRED* $ a year poorer than he was when he earned the 10.~~ *before ~~he earned the added $5000.~~*

~~There is a There is an answer—a very simple one. It has been proposed to the Sen. by Sen. James Buckley of N.Y. to a thunderous silence on the part of most of his colleagues. It is called indexing of the progressive inc. tax brackets. Adjust the brackets in time of inflation to reflect the depreciated value of the $ so that you dont pay a penalty for merely keeping up with the cost of living. You dont move up in the surtax brackets until you actually have increased your purchasing power.~~

~~Cong. is very busy talking tax reform. Start those cards & letters. Tell your representative & your Senators this should be part of that reform. If govt. had to feel the same pain we do from inflation; If govt. couldn't make an extra profit in inflation they'd do something to stop inflation. This is R.R.—~~

Lets take an example:—the man who earned $10,000 a yr. in 1966 ~~has~~ *earns* (if he is the average) $15,000 today. That $5000 increase is a little more than the increased cost of living. Actually $3800 of his raise is eaten up by inflation. Still he is $1200 better off than he was in 1966—but not after taxes. At $15,000 ~~you are~~ *he is* in a higher surtax bracket. The govt. takes the $1200 plus $159 more making him $159 worse off than he was in 1966.

There is an answer—a very simple one, a proposal by Sen. James Buckley of N.Y.* which has been greeted with thunderous silence by his liberal colleagues. He proposes what is called indexing the progressive tax brackets so as to reflect the lowered ~~value~~ *purchasing power* of the $. In other words you ~~dont~~ move up into ~~an increased~~ *a higher* tax bracket ~~unless *only if* your increased inc.~~ only to the extent that your increased inc. exceeds the increase in the cost of living.

In the example I just gave that $10,000 a year man would ~~stay~~ stay in the same tax bracket for ~~$13,800 of his~~ for $3800 of his $5000 raise and would only pay an increased rate on the $1200 if that moved him into a new bracket.

Cong. is very busy talking tax reform. This is a time to start those cards & letters. If govt. suffered the same pain from inflat. we do instead of making a profit on it they'd do something about it.

This is RR.—— ❖

Cost Overruns
June 1975

In the eyes of some, money wasted by the military ~~costs more~~ *is more expensive* than waste by other govt. agencies.—I'll be right back.

* Senator James Buckley (Conservative–New York).

In Wash. there is a govt. agency which truly is a friend of the ~~peo~~ taxpayer; The G.A.O.—short for General Accounting Office. G.A.O.'s function is to look for needless waste and to shed light in dark corners ~~of new~~ *where live* cost overruns and other extravagances. A cost overrun is ~~some~~ very simply the name given to ~~the cost of~~ any undertaking that ~~was~~ *is* supposed to cost X number of $ and winds up costing 2 or 3 times X number of $.

The theory is that once needless ~~or~~ extravagance has been exposed Cong. will in righteous indignation ride forth to smite ~~those~~ the guilty & defend the taxpayer. And sometimes some congressmen do but only when the extravagance is laid at the door of Nat. defense. Oh there are conscientious members of Cong. who ~~have striven~~ *strive* valiantly to curb the excesses of govt. spending but their words somehow are ignored by their colleagues & considered un-newsworthy by much of the press.

G.A.O. has no trouble getting attention when it reports on cost overruns in the acquisition of tanks ~~and~~ planes & other weaponry produced by quote—the industrial military complex—unquote. But a recent report by G.A.O. has been greeted with nationwide silence on the part of those who usually are most vocal about other reports.

It's possible this is due to the fact that this latest report astonishingly reveals that 269 recent govt. construction projects have ripped off the taxpayers by about $57 bil. and most of the extravagance was in non-mil. projects. ~~What is even more surprising~~ *in spite of the fact that*—¾ of the *audited* projects were mil. ~~but~~ 80% of the cost overruns ~~46 of the $57 Bil.~~ were in the ¼ ~~of non mil. projects.~~ *that was not military.*

The projects ~~were~~ originally approved as costing $76 Bil. ~~but they~~ finished up costing $133 bil. and according to the audit this was not due to inflat. The cost was hiked by changes and add ons. ~~The average incrs. was 75% but s~~Some ended up costing 10X the original estimate.

I know figs. *& STATISTICS* are hard to absorb in a single hearing—particularly ~~a~~ for those of you who are listening & driving at the same time. So let me try to sum it up. The Audit covered 269 projects—210 were mil. 59 non mil. The extravagant overruns for the 59 non mil. averaged 15X as much per project ~~for a total~~ accounting for 46 of the $57 Bil. in extra cost. That's more than enough to bal. the bud. It's also enough to make you wonder why Cong. is so quiet.—This is R.R. Thanks for listening. ❖

Business Profits, Myths & Realities

June 1975

~~If we knew as much about~~

According to the latest poll higher ed. should ~~have~~ *invite* ~~some resident~~ representatives of the business world ~~as~~ *to the* ~~visiting professors~~ campus for a spell.—I'll be right back.

Another poll has revealed that among college & U. students *the approval rate for* business & industry ~~rate~~ is about as high as it is for pickpockets & childmolesters. In fact the only group with a lower opinion of business than students is the faculty. And that makes it pretty difficult to be tactful about what I'm going to say next; namely, that the poll also reveals this low opinion is based on a considerable lack of knowledge about business & industry.

Just as one example, the great majority of students (and a greater majority of faculty) estimate business profits generally at 45%. Now it isn't hard to find the truth about that *one* and the truth is business profits in America average ~~4~~ 5%—just ⅑ of ~~what~~ higher education's estimate. Some may go 10 or 11%, but others go to zero—in fact *each year* 4 out of 10 businesses ~~each year~~ show no profit or even a loss. ~~each year.~~ At any rate the average, as I said, is 5%.

Frankly we cant afford this ~~kind~~ *lack* of understanding~~—(~~particularly in the halls of academia~~) because w~~We're talking about ~~the busin~~ *a* system which determines the way of life for all of us, and that very much includes those in higher education.

But let me "have at you" with some facts & figures and, just so you wont think I'm hand picking a set up, I'll use the industry that is presently ~~p~~*Public* ~~e~~*E*nemy ~~n~~*N*umber ~~o~~*O*ne in the anti-business world—oil. The halls of cong. ring with cries of "windfall" profits~~, conniving to~~ and proposals to curb them—with taxes of course.*

Here are some figures from a study of about 30 representative oil companies including some of the biggest names on the public enemies list. Last year this gross revenue was up 77% ~~from~~ *over* the previous year. So was their operating cost. Their net rate of profit was just 7%. ~~Even so net profits were *up 89% which gave them a 7% profit rate to a figure of 7%* but taxes were up 89%.~~ Ninety three ~~% of total revenues~~ *cents out of each revenue dollar* went for cost of operation & taxes—oh yes—taxes were *up* 89%, almost double what they were the year before. ~~Incidentally, that doesn't include another $32 Bil they collect for govt. in sales taxes, excise taxes & lease bonuses, making govt. a $72 Bil winner in the oil business, *by of* ½X as much as the total is in *company* profits.~~ It's interesting to note that in all the ~~long~~ inflation ~~level that's take~~ that took place between 1952 & 1972 crude oil only went up 21%. In just the last half of those 20 yrs. the cost *of* oil field machinery, casing & pipe lines went up 33%.

Last year our 30 companies invested $6 Bil. more than they earned in trying to find new oil, expanding & modernizing refineries etc. and 60% of that was spent here in America. ~~You see~~ When Cong. gets around to really ~~dealing with~~ *looking at* the energy problem which right now they are pretending will go away if they dont look ~~at it~~ they'll have to recognize how much ~~drilling~~ exploring it takes to find oil. ~~Only about 1 out of 40 wells drilled contains~~

* The windfall profits tax was signed into law in April 1980 and amended during the first Reagan administration.

~~Out of all the exploratory wells drilled in the U.S. only about 1 out of *of* 40 contains enough oil to justify commercial development. But that's another subject.~~

~~Well so much for oil—back to the original subject which is the lack of understanding.~~

We're using *the* oil industry as an example of the lack of understanding that prevails about business and how that can lead to govt. policies aimed at business which will have a shotgun effect on all of us. The truth is business profits in the U.S., while showing an overall increase for the year, were beginning to go down as ~~t~~ the year went on & ~~may~~ *will* very likely show a ~~lo~~ drop for 1975. ~~and t~~*T*hat means a lack of ~~tot~~ capital for expansion to provide jobs and to keep us competitive in the world mkt. The whole subject might be an interesting research project for higher education. This is RR— ❖

Law and Order
June 1975

I once appeared in a movie called "Law & Order."* If it were being made today the title would probably be changed. I'll be right back.

Not too long ago any discussion of crime & it's rapid rate of increase would find the term "law & order" used as a matter of course. Those who feel the courts have been too lenient and that permissiveness has played a part in crimes increase would use the term to describe what should be restored.

I played in a movie some years ago called "Law & Order." It wasn't a very good movie as some of you who stay up for the late show have probably discovered. But it was a story of a town marshall who was totally dedicated to preserving law & order hence the title.

The phrase is perfectly respectable (at least it always has been). We are a nation of laws—proud that we place our faith in ~~the~~ law rather than in men. And of course ~~our~~ civilization is built upon the ability of humans to live together in an orderly society.

In the last few years however the phrase has become unfashionable. Those who have made it so began looking askance at any who used the words. Their arched eyebrows were a reaction to what they had determined was an expression of bigotry. ~~& racial prejudice.~~ If pressed for an explanation they would inform you that "law & order" ~~was a~~ *were* code ~~la~~ words ~~for~~ that ~~really~~ *really* meant ~~you really were advocating~~ a call for racial discrimination.

By coincidence those who made the decision to outlaw this simple phrase are usually ~~the~~ against our penal system, against capital punishment and believe that society not the criminal is to blame for crime.

* Reagan starred in this 1953 conventional western movie.

Well in the 1st place I think this inference of bigotry is in itself bigoted. Not only does it impugn (without proof) the character of people for using an appropriate phrase to describe what is all too lacking today; but it casts a slur on an entire racial group. Are they not implying that our fellow citizens who happen to be black are so given to crime that ~~calling~~ *a call* for law & order is ~~aut~~ automatically a call for a curb on the Negro community?

The truth is Negros in America are victems of crime far out of proportion to their numbers. They are roughly ten or twelve percent of our pop. but more than half of all the murder victems are black.

If "law & order" is a code word for racism then explain away the survey done by American U. in the Nations capitol. It seems that the Negro residents of the Dist. of Columbia are calling for law & order far more than their white neighbors. 74% of them want sterner action against criminals. With whites it was only 61%. 82% of blacks compared to only 62% of whites ~~want~~ *think* tougher parole policies would cut down crime. On the death penalty there was a closer ratio. It was believed to be an effective deterrent by 56% of blacks & 54% of whites.

Our Negro friends are well aware that criminals are color blind. They practise no discrimination in ~~th~~ plying their despiciable trade.

Law & Order isn't a code word to ~~them~~ ~~n~~Negros—it's a cry for help and we'd better join in. This is RR—— ❖

UNICEF
July 1975

The Am. people are the most charitable and generous people in the world—maybe that's why once in awhile we get taken for a ride.—I'll be right back.

Col. Robt. D. Heine Jr.* has just ~~had~~ had a story published (a story I might add that appears to be fully documented) ~~that~~ indicating that advantage has been taken of American generosity.

The Col. asks if you were aware last ~~fall~~ *Halloween* when you gave trick or treat money ~~on Halloween~~ for UNICEF—(the United Nations Childrens emergency fund) that you were helping the communist takeover of S.VN? I'm sure the answer from all of us would have to be—"no we didn't know that."

We're not only a generous people—we're darned ingenious at thinking up new & different ways to raise money for good causes. Usually the idea is to make giving easier and a mite less painful. In that framework it seemed logical and pretty cute to have our children sally forth on Halloween with cannisters to collect money for other less fortunate children in other parts of the world.

The kids were successful. They collected $13,649,433 for Indochina

* Robert D. Heine Jr., was a reporter for the *Detroit News*.

alone—that is for the children of Indochina. It broke down to 61% for the communist enemy & 39% for S.VN. $6,313,130 went to Hanoi and almost $2 mil. more through Hanoi to the Viet Cong. I didn't really know the *V.C.* guerrila fighters had their children with them.

Now before you say it let me say it first; children dont start wars and cant be responsible for what their national leaders do; and yes the enemys children innocent of any wrongdoing should be helped not penalized if they are among the hungry & deprived of the world. So my remarks are not aimed at the fact that *the lions share of* our money wound up in enemy hands.

No—the Col. had more info. about ~~what our~~ the results of our generosity. In S.VN. we were in a position to check and make sure our benefactions ~~&~~ by way of the United Nations did go to the children. There our money bought food & medicine largely. Not so in N.VN. *No monitoring* ~~Not~~ was permitted to see that the supplies shipped in thru Haiphong & dropped off at Hanoi actually reached the children. A UNICEF spokesman is quoted as saying, "Unicef has no way to make sure the supplies to the communists got to children. They were dropped off at the airports & docks and we assume they were used as we intended." That would have been something to see—the children of Hanoi happily running trucks, bulldozers, heavy engineer construction equipment & construction tools & materials. Word of honor that was what Hanoi said it needed for the children of N.VN. Believe it or not they justified their choice by claiming it would be used to rebuild schools which naturally were the main targets of American bombers.

The Viet Cong being in the field got mainly food, clothing & hard to get drugs & medicines. Incidentally the VietCong even by their own estimates are only 15% or less of the pop. of S.VN. they received 2½ x as much ~~proportionately~~ in proportion to their numbers as did the rest of the S. Vietnamese.

Well I guess we should remember the name of the game was trick or treat. We got tricked & they got the treat.

I think next Halloween—we shouldn't be home. ❖

Socialized Medicine II
July 1975

Yesterday I promised to talk some more about the campaign to give us socialized medicine.—I'll be right back.

It's funny ~~what~~ (or would be if it weren't so serious) how far a little propoganda can go. A nat. poll was taken a little while back on the subject of health care. More than ¾ of those polled stated flat out that "yes there was a health care crisis in America. But then the pollsters got down to specifics. ~~with their questions.~~ They asked for personal examples such as "Do you have ready access to medical care?" "Are you satisfied with your Dr?" "Do you have any ~~trouble~~ *delay in* getting medical attention when you need it?" etc. etc. To these specific questions about 90% or better answered no—they themselves had no problems.

In other words they'd read & heard so much about a crisis in the health field they took it for granted that one existed. ~~b~~*B*ut when their own situation was questioned there was no crisis. It only existed for some one else but they didn't really know who. ~~It *it* was.~~ Again it's that mysterious "they" we're always hearing about.

One of the arguments used to support the claim that we need ~~is~~ govt. medicine is comparison of infant mortality figures. A favorite comparison ~~to~~ is the U.S. rate & the rate in Sweden.* Unfortunately they never tell us that no two countries are the same in their determining infant mortality. In America we register every birth and ~~count~~ base the rate on stillborn children ~~up to~~ as well as all who die in their first year. Sweden by contrast doesn't require a report of birth until after 5 years.

Nevertheless the Sen. from Mass.** I referred to yesterday who ~~is off~~ has been preaching govt. medicine for years charges us with having a progressive rate of deterioration. That isn't quite the case. In 20 years infant mortality in the U.S. has declined by 33%. Obviously we are improving not deteriorating. That is also evident from the figs. at the other end of the line. Our life span at the beginning of the century was 49 yrs. ~~toda~~ today it is 70.

If we want to continue comparing our system with Sweden there are long waiting lists there for all kinds of hospitalization. In Stockholm alone 4000—1800 of them for surgery. Minor operations have a waiting time of more than 6 months. As for costs when Sweden converted from vol. health insurance to govt. provided coverage it only took 12 yrs. for the total cost to increase to 9X what it had been.

The same story can be told with regard to Eng. More than 40% of the hospitals are over 100 yrs. old. Only 3 new hospitals have been built in Eng. since 1948. A woman having a baby will not have it in a hospital nor will a Dr. be in attendance. She will have it at home helped by a mid-wife unless it is her first or her Dr. claims she has a problem posing considerable risk.

The question we should ask is, who besides some politicians & some believers in more govt. is really asking for socialized medicine?

~~This~~ Just as a side issue—call it another example of burocracy the dept. of Health, Ed. & Welfare is now ~~screening~~ inspecting our hospitals. In one relatively new hospital they demanded that plastic bag liners in waste paper baskets be removed. If they caught fire they might develope dangerous toxic fumes.

* The Centers for Disease Control and Prevention (www.cdc.gov) base the infant mortality rate on the number of deaths per 1,000 live births. Data are based on reports by the countries. The U.S. infant mortality rate was 20.0 in 1970 and 12.6 in 1980. Sweden reported rates for the same years of 11.0 and 6.9 respectively.

** Senator Edward M. Kennedy, D–Massachusetts (1962–present).

O.S.H.A.—the occ.* safety & health agency had just been there & they ordered the hosp. to put in the bags to save the emps. from the risk of contamination in emptying the waste baskets.—This is RR.—— ❖

Community Work Experience Program
July 1975

Can welfare reform be permanent ~~until~~ unless & until it takes place at the top level in Wash.—I'll be right back.

Four years *& a few months* ago as most of you know Calif. launched a program** of welfare reform that was spectacularly successful. Actually reform was a must because we ~~had~~ were the welfare capital of the world. Of all the people in Am. receiving W.F. 16% were getting it in Calif. and the case load was increasing by 40,000 people a month.

Almost from the moment the reforms were instituted ~~we~~ this was reversed. The 40,000 a month increase became an average decrease of 8000 a month until by last Jan. we had almost 400,000 fewer recipients than we'd had when the reforms started. This saved the taxpayers about $2 Bil. but equally important it enabled us to increase grants to those with real need by 43%.

Now the Calif. welfare rolls are increasing and of course the recession is given as the reason. I dont deny that ec. conditions and increased unemp. have resulted in some change [and] we knew also that eventually we'd bottom out as we elimi[nated] the cheaters from the rolls. But I firmly believe that what we are seeing in Calif. is ~~bur~~ the welfare burocracy just simply returning to its old evil ways now that those who created the reforms are no longer riding herd on them.

Case in point. Part of our reform was a community work project requiring able bodied welfare recipients to work 80 hrs. a month at useful community tasks in return for their welfare grants. Those who opposed our reforms to begin with called this slave labor. H.E.W. in Wash. only allowed us to do this in 35 counties—mostly the rural ones as an experiment.

Now the legislature & admin. in Sac.*** have cancelled the program. They infer it was unsuccessful & quote some of the welfare burocracy to substantiate the inference. For example they speak of the few thousand work assignments that were filled ~~and~~ while indicating an unknown (but smaller) number left the welfare rolls rather than work. Frankly I challenge their claims and suspect it is only the first step in a return to the same old way of doing business which ~~treat~~ threatened to bankrupt the state.

In my last year in office we funneled 57,000 ~~people~~ *WF recipients* thru this

* Occupational.
** The California Welfare Reform Act of 1971.
*** Sacramento.

program into regular jobs. Many of them never served an hour in a work project but when they reported our job agents as we called them were able to get them jobs in the private sector. In addition thousands refused to report and were automatically dropped from welfare & never heard from again which is some kind of indication they had been on the rolls fraudulently & thus couldn't report without getting caught.

But lets look at the human side. Here are some reports we received. (I'll leave the names blank)—Blank was unable to get reg. employment due to his appearance & general work attitude. He reported & worked satisfactorily at a community job—was placed with a pvt. furniture repair shop & is now off WF.

Blank no. 2—53 yrs. old—2nd grade ed. 2 yrs. on welfare was put to work as helper to a school custodian—in 8 weeks he was hired permanently as a grounds man beginning at $495 a mo.

Blank no. 3—She had some accounting skills but was unable to find a job. Her assignment was to help the county auditor. After working 60 hrs. she was hired on a permanent basis as an account clerk. ~~That~~

Thats just a sample. Here is a letter from a local govt. official; "Except for a very few, all of the WF recipients have been good workers eager to earn their wf. grants. We now have 3 as permanent employees. I strongly feel the prog. is worthwhile not only to us but to the WF recipient & hope it will be continued." We have a stack of these letters containing such lines as—"To do away with this prog. would be an injustice to these people." "People aren't naturally lazy they just have to be properly motivated." & "Retain this program."

Well it hasn't been retained* because the welfare burocracy ~~did~~ dosen't want it—after all what would they do if all their clients went to work & became self supporting? This is RR—Thanks—— ❖

The North Vietnamese Army's final offensive in the spring of 1975 included taking over cities such as Da Nang and Hue. When this radio essay was written, a refugee crisis was under way in Vietnam as thousands of people fled the fallen towns.

Phu Quoc
July 1975

Did we tie up all the loose ends of our rescue operation in Indo China? There is a tragic chance we didn't.—I'll be right back.

* California Governor Jerry Brown (1975–1983) discontinued the Community Work Experience Program on July 1, 1975. According to Lou Cannon in *Governor Reagan: His Rise to Power* (New York: Public Affairs, 2003), p. 360, although it only served 9,600 people over a four-year period, it was nevertheless the inspiration for a number of other state and federal welfare programs.

~~Way back *During the Eisenhower years* when the French left Indochina and the the Geneva Accords set up the 2 nations of N. & S. VN. There was during one the Eisenhower years a migration~~

Let me set the stage by reviewing a little history. The war in VN. went on for so long it's possible some of us have forgotten the prelude to that war.

Indochina was French Indochina until ~~during~~ the 1950's when the colonial period ended and a ~~settlement~~ meeting of Nations including our own created N. & S. VN. as 2 separate & independent Nations. N.V.N. was already ~~in~~ under communist rule~~s~~ with Ho Chi Minh the unelected dictator. *S. VN. had to start from scratch.*

Part of the settlement called for the people of both countries to have *for a certain period of time* the right to move & live in whichever of the 2 countries they chose. ~~This A specified time period was set~~ It turned out to be a one *way* move. Few if any chose to go North but an estimated 1½ mil. went South. This resulted in the 1st of the many communist violations of the *terms of the* agreement. Long before the set period was up Ho Chi Minhs soldiers set up barricades at the dividing line & refused to allow ~~any~~ the north to south migration to continue. He probably suspected that if he didn't he'd have a lot of empty real estate on his hands.

Many of those who moved south did so for religious reasons. ~~an~~ They knew there would be no freedom of religion under Ho Chi Minh. A number of Catholic Priests led their ~~whole~~ entire congregations across the border. Now the border is gone and apparently the flight to freedom has begun again.

~~About 50 miles off the coast of S.VN. lies the island of Phu Quoc.~~ When Hue & Da Nang fell many of those same congregations moved to the island of Phu Quoc some 40 or 50 miles off the mainland. In fact some were carried there by American ships. It is believed there are about 42,000 refugees ~~[on] the island including hundreds of nuns and *a* thousands of orphans.~~

~~The refugees have weapons but only a limited supply of food & ammunition. They propose to resist—or perhaps I should be talking in the past tense. By this time it's possible the communists have taken the island. *There is no way to know their fate as of now. We do know the communist conquerors have seized the airstrips making rescue by air impossible but some are escaping in sampans under cover of night. A Swedish freighter reported picking up 52 survivors at sea a few weeks ago. You see their only chance is to head out to sea in their small boats and hope.* It's also possible they might just wait for them to starve. At any rate we know they were alright as of the latter part of May. We know that because the *our ships & naval vessels received* radio messages were received calling *pleading* desperately for ships to pick them up *help to come to their* rescue them. We know also that So. Korea, Taiwan, Chile & Canada have agreed to accept them as immigrants.~~

[on] the island including hundreds of nuns & 1000 orphans.

The refugees have weapons but only a limited supply of food & ammunition. It is reasonable to assume they will try to hide out if possible in the islands hills & mountains ~~for as long~~ until they are overtaken by the enemey or by starvation.

The communist conquerors have ~~landed &~~ seized & control the airstrips making rescue by air impossible but some are escaping in small boats & sampans under cover of night. Of course this means heading out to sea with only the hope of intercepting a passing ship or dying at sea instead of on the island. One ~~recent~~ *pickup of 52 people was recently* report*ed* ~~from~~ *by* a Swedish Freighter.

We know that So. Korea, Taiwan, Chile & Canada have agreed to accept them as immigrants. We also know that our own ships & naval vessels at least for a time have been receiving radio messages pleading desperately for someone to come to th~~ie~~*ei*r rescue.

The press has reported that ~~a briefing~~ Ron Nessen * in a White house press briefing on May 21st said with regard to Phu Quoc that "the evacuation of refugees *from V.N.* and their territorial waters is over." One wonders

I ~~wonder how many *if any*~~ if the ~~rad~~ anguished ~~radio~~ cries for help are still being heard by our radio operators or is there only silence now; the kind of silence we heard in Oct. 1956 when the Hungarian Freedom Fighters went off the air in Budapest.

Russian soldiers were battering down the doors as we heard the ~~mass~~ cry "People of the world—Help us! People of Europe whom we once defended against the attacks of Asiatic barbarians listen now to the alarm bells ring—People of the civilized world, in the name of liberty and solidarity we are asking you to help. The shadows grow darker. -Listen to our cry. God be with you & with us." Then came the silence.

I wonder if we're hearing only silence from Phu Quoc. Or is that the faint sound of alarm bells.

This is R R—Thanks for listening. ❖

Pollution #1
August 1975

Memory is far from infallible and when it comes to the "good old days" it leaves out a lot of the not so good. I'll be right back.

Not so long ago I found myself in ~~an~~ a discussion ~~of~~ concerning the state of the world with some young people including my own children. Strangely enough it wasn't old Dad who was nostalgic about the good old days & ~~pessimistic~~ *sour* about todays world. No, it was the "now" generation who were pessimistic about where we are & where we're going. They almost seemed resentful toward me because I'd known that other world of yesterday when life was simple & good with joy on every hand.

* Ron Nessen was President Gerald Ford's press secretary from 1974–1976.

Before I knew it my memory machine was functioning the way it's supposed to on a psychiatrists couch, dredging up particulars not just the rosy nostalgia that comes to mind when you hear an old song. Now dont get me wrong my memories are pretty happy and I enjoy closing my eyes now & then for a re-run or two. But I *also* find life exciting & good today, in truth better in most respects.

I looked at these young people and wanted them to feel good about the world they've inherited. They'd already covered such things as present day pollution, our grasping materialism & the commercial rip off in modern day merchandising. *So* For a little while they heard ~~of~~ about the *old* nightly chore of banking the coal furnace—~~put~~ (shoveling ashes on the ~~furnace~~ fire to keep the coals alive through the nite). ~~t~~*The* ~~earling~~ *cold* early morning ~~cold~~ journey to the basement to shake the grate ~~&~~, uncover the ~~coals~~ *embers* & shovel in coal & ~~the~~ dressing in the shivering cold while you waited for the house to warm. As for their *worry about air* pollution—*they were reminded that in that earlier time* every chimney in town ~~was~~ belch~~ing~~*ed* black ~~coal~~ smoke & soot ~~from~~ every day from Fall til summer.

Having been born in a small country town I could also tell them of that *nite time* walk thru the snow to that little wooden building out back of the house—a journey repeated in the morning. Summer brought the flies incubated in those outhouses *of which there was* one for every home & store & public bldg.

I went on about the apple barrel in the cellar, the ice box, the lack of fresh vegetables in ~~win~~ winter etc. But let me go back a century or more so this wont just be a personalized trip down memory lane.

Dr. John J. McKetta chairman of the Nat. Air Quality Commission has ~~published~~ written an essay * which does much to set the record straight on pollution & related subjects. In passing he gives ~~some~~ a capsule description of the really good old days about 150 yrs. ago.

"For one thing," he says, "life was short. Life expectancy for males was 38 yrs." It was a hard 38 yrs. too for the work week was 72 hours. For women it was even worse, their household chores ran to about a 98 hr. week. They scrubbed floors by hand, made clothes the same way, brought in firewood, cooked in heavy iron pots & fought off insects without pesticides.

There were no fresh vegetables except in their season of ripening so vitamen deficiency diseases were common. Epidemics were an annual occurrence & usually claimed the life of someone in the family. If we think water pollution is ~~ba~~ a problem now—it was deadly then. One typhoid epidemic in Phil. caused by polluted water carried off ⅕ of the population.

It was a time when most people never traveled more than 20 miles from

* "The 8 Surprises or Has the World Gone to Hell?" (January 21, 2004, communication from McKetta). McKetta joined the Department of Chemical Engineering at the University of Texas at Austin as an associate professor in 1946. He was appointed the E. P. Schoch Professor in 1972, and also served as the chairman of the National Air Quality Commission.

their birthplace, never heard an orchestra, *or* saw a play. As Dr. McKetta says "Perhaps the simple life was not so simple."

Because we've all been treated to so much mis-information about pollution I'm going to give you some more of the facts the Dr. has collected in the next couple of days. I think you'll be surprised & relieved because he says & proves that we are not on the brink of ecological disaster. This is R. R. Thanks—— ❖

Pollution #2
August 1975

Is murderous man responsible for *all* the endangered species—those birds & animals ~~who are~~ *seemingly* slated for extinction? Ill be right back.

I dont think any of us can hear of an endangered species of ~~bird~~ wildlife without feeling regret and a ~~certain~~ sense of guilt that mankind has brought this about. ~~We may~~ Most of us will never actually see a tiger in ~~the~~ his jungle home or an elephant in the wilds of Africa but ~~we've the knowledge that~~ *we enjoy just knowing* they are there.

Right now there are plenty of people working very hard to preserve the remaining few of whatever species is on the endangered list *and I'm all for them.* There are also many who are *not* going to rest until they have saddled all of mankind with a great guilt complex ~~*as the*~~ *for being the murderer of all sorts of innocent creatures of field & stream.*

Yesterday I gave you some info. collected by the chairman of the Nat. Air Quality Commission. ~~in the course of his work on that commission.~~ Well it seems ~~their~~ his ~~studies~~ *work with the commission* took him into the area of disappearing animal species. His conclusion was that while ~~man~~ it is possible that man may hasten (in some instances) the disappearance of some species he really has very little to do with it & cannot be held responsible.

About 50 species are expected to disappear during this century—just as 50 species disappeared in the last century & the one before that *& the one before that* and so on back for 3 bil. years during which *time* 100 mil. species of plant & animal life have become extinct ~~with~~ & man ~~having~~ *had* nothing to do with it.

We're really relative newcomers on earth and obviously ~~had~~ couldn't have played a part in the disappearance of mils. of creatures that existed before we ~~did~~ even arrived here. In fact the commission chairman points out ~~that we've failed to eliminate a single species of insect~~ *that* in spite of ~~the fact~~ our all out war against certain undesirable ~~ones~~ *insects* over countless years~~.~~ *we've failed to eliminate a single species.* And that brought him to another bit of surprising knowledge.

We may have jumped the gun ~~on~~ in eliminating DDT and other chlorinated compounds which supposedly ~~were endangering~~ *endanger* mankind ~~& elimi-~~

nating ~~*as well as* some bird species by thinning their eggshells. It seems the ex~~periments which led to this action were conducted in a manner that led to *no* positive conclusions.

I recall when I was Gov. ~~we had a~~ *a* Prof. in our great agricultural U. at Davis Calif. ~~who~~ used to lecture against doing away with DDT and ~~would~~ dramatized his lecture by swallowing a spoon full of pure DDT. Last I knew he was still hale & hearty.

Now we learn that on balance the desirable attributes of DDT may vastly outweigh its harmful effects. For starters there is Dr. Borlaug* ~~the~~ who won a Nobel prize for developing a new strain of wheat that can double food production per acre. That's quite something in a world threatened by famine.

He says if DDT is banned by the U.S. his *life* work is wasted. He has dedicated his life to finding better methods of feeding the worlds starving people. Without DDT & other important chemicals he says "that goal is unattainable."

According to the World Health Org. DDT has had a miraculous ~~effect~~ *impact* on arresting insect borne diseases & increasing yield from grain fields once ravaged by insects. Malaria deaths dropped ~~to 4~~ *FROM 4 MIL. A YEAR TO 1 MIL.* because of DDT. ~~and~~ sSimilar declines were shown in encephalitis & yellow fever. It is estimated that 100 mil. people ~~are~~ who ~~whou~~ would have died of these diseases are alive today. Incidentally recent tests have indicated the thinning eggshells could have been caused by mercury compounds rather than DDT. ~~To~~ *TOMORROW WE'LL GET DOWN TO THE DRs. FINDINGS ON AIR POLLUTION. IT MIGHT SURPRISE SOME OF OUR DOOM & GLOOM CRIERS.* ~~T Im going to give you some more of the Drs. surprises where air polution is concerned.~~ This is RR—Thanks—— ❖

Pollution #3
August 1975

Apparently we dont have to look for another world to move to just yet. We aren't going to smother in smog or run out of clean water. I'll be right back.

All of ~~f~~ us are concerned about the environment and I'm sure ~~all~~ *none* of us ~~*dont*~~ want to be remembered by our children & our childrens children as having left them a ravaged, polluted ~~world—a sort of~~ planetary garbage dump.

For a couple of days now I've been talking about the findings of the chairman of the Nat. Air Quality Commission, Dr. John McKetta. He has presented facts that put the matter of air pollution in a new perspective. If you've been reading that we are seriously depleting our oxygen & replacing it with toxic

* Dr. Norman Borlaug won the Nobel Peace Prize in 1970.

substances such as carbon monoxide you may be as pleasantly surprised as he says he was.

In the 1st place the theory ~~that~~ we've long accepted that our oxygen is created by growing green things is not true. The evidence according to the Dr. is overwhelming that the sun, ~~&~~ cosmic rays & water vapor in the upper atmosphere is the source. ~~& t~~*T*he supply of oxygen in the atmosphere is virtually unlimited & *is* not threatened by man in any significant way.

We know that automobile exhaust throws 270 mil. tons of carbon monoxide into the air every year & it has a life in dry air of about 3 yrs. Yet measurements show there is no ~~difference~~ increase at all in the ~~concen~~ concentration of C.O. (carbon monoxide) in our air. In Los Angeles where we have a real smog problem the C.O. concentration reaches as much as 35 parts per mil. Without our air inversion layer & ~~geop~~ geographic ~~problem~~ *situation* that fig. would probably be *only* 1½ PPM. ~~so you can see we~~ *Obviously a place like Los Angeles does* have a problem. But hear this—the carbon monoxide content of cigarette smoke is 42,000 p.p.m. In a stuffy room where a number of people are smoking the concentration is from 3 to 5 times as great as it is in Los Angeles on the worst day.

To sum up on carbon monoxide the Dr. reports that in the "broad expanse of our natural air carbon monoxide levels are totally safe for human beings.

Now before some one sets up a howl that I'm advocating an end to our fight for less air pollution—that isn't true at all. I want the bluest sky we can get and the purest air and I know that our cities can be made much more pleasant & less smelly. But it seems to me we can carry on the campaign to do this without a sense of panic that clouds our judgement & leads to costly mistakes.

Right now our main effort is directed toward oxides of nitrogen which comes out of the automobile tail pipe and cause the photochemical reactions which color the air a muddy brown. There is no question they are a problem in areas like L.A. where we have a more or less constant temperature inversion trapping the air.

But Dr. McKetta lists the findings in this field as his no. 3 shock & surprise. Nature *it seems* also produces oxides of nitrogen. As a matter of fact nature produces 97% of them. If we could successfully eliminate 100% of all the man produced polluting oxides of nitrogen we'd still have 97% of what we presently have. ~~and if we As the~~ He adds that sometimes he thinks nature must be laughing at us.

He proves ~~that~~ the possibility of that last observation with this astounding fact. The late Dr. Wm. Pecora * has calculated that all ~~of~~ *the* man made *air* pollution since the 1st man appeared on earth ~~is less *totals*~~ *and up to the present totals less* than the amount of particulates & noxious gases thrown into the air

* William Pecora was the director of the U.S. Geological Survey from 1965 to 1971 and served as the undersecretary in the Department of Interior from 1971 to his death on July 19, 1972.

by just 3 volcanic eruptions—Krakatoa (Java) 1883, Mt. Katmai Alaska 1912 & Hekla Iceland in 1974.

This is RR Thanks for listening. ❖

Hudson Institute on Education
September 1975

From local school boards to the Fed. office of Ed. in Wash. we are being told we must come up with more money for schools if we want little Willy to learn how to read. Ill be right back.

The professional educationists lobbies are at it again—(that is if they ever really stopped) demanding more money, more teachers and more control ~~of~~ over how our schools are run. The alternative they say is decline in the quality of ed.

Comes now a 300 page study by the Hudson Inst. on Primary & Secondary ed. and just for the record so you wont think Hudson is some tight fisted, anti ed. outfit, the study was funded by the Office of Ec. Opp. That's O.E.O. the completely liberal, govt. spending oriented Poverty Prog.

Frank E. Armbruster* directed the study and in his own words found, "ed. has become increasingly and alarmingly expensive." In the last 25 years, which certainly covers the period in which concern ~~of~~ over what Willy was learning has been greatest, student enrollment didn't even double. Actually we went from just under 29 mil. students to not quite 50 mil. But local, state & Fed. expenditures for pub. & private primary & secondary ed. went up to almost 10x what they were—from \$6.7 Bil. to \$61.6 Bil. In the last 15 years an enrollment increase of 18.3% was matched by a spending increase of 245%. I know I'm throwing a lot of figs. at you but they are important if we are to understand & be able to resist the incessant lobbying for more school spending. As a percentage of Gross Nat. Product school spending in these 20 odd years has more than doubled.

Now I'm sure none of us would hesitate for a second in approving even more spending if the record indicated that dollar for dollar we were getting our moneys worth; that ~~Will~~ the little Willys & Johnnies & Marys and Susans were getting a better ed. ~~o~~Or ~~if~~ even if it could be proven that more spending was necessary just to maintain the ~~present~~ past quality level.

Unfortunately we cant say that. Indeed the score board shows the very reverse is true. Achievement in both verbal & mathematical skills is steadily de-

* Frank Armbruster's study, "The U.S. Primary and Secondary Education Process," issued July 14, 1975, was the basis for his later book, *Our Children's Crippled Future: How American Education Has Failed* (New York: New York Times Book Company, 1977).

clining and the decline is most pronounced among the brightest of our children.

The College Board Scholastic Aptitude Test commonly called SAT is ~~the~~ taken by ~~more~~ *most* of our high school students who feel they may enter college. Thus you could say here is the final judgement among the most intelligent products of 12 years of schooling.

There has been a sharp and ~~consistent~~ *steady* decline in the average SAT scores for the last dozen or so years. ~~There has also been a cut~~ Even more significant & yes frightening is the fact that the number of students scoring in the highest bracket (750–800) has been cut almost in half.

To sum it up the greatest increase in cost per student in our history almost 150% in constant dollars has been matched by the greatest decline in results. ~~Maybe the next time there is a teachers strike~~ But dont worry—the educationists have an answer. ~~You~~ We are being taxed to provide special courses in our state U's. & colleges to teach the kids what they were supposed to learn in high school.—This is RR—Thanks for listening. ❖

Gun Laws, Drug Laws
October 1975

Sometimes I wish I could do more than *just* give a viewpoint. This is one of those times.

I received a letter I'd like to share with you. The writer was commenting on my stand against so the many proposals for gun laws. As you know & have heard me say I dont believe anything will be accomplished by making it harder for honest citizens to own guns. I do believe we could do much more with stiffer penalties for those who are convicted of using guns in the commission of a crime.

But that isn't why I want to share this letter with you. ~~Following~~

Following the comment about gun laws the letter reads; "I am a 19 yr. old female. I know a lot of—as you call them—thugs, drug pushers etc. I have participated in a lot of their activities since the age of 11—when I was strung out on Heroin.

Right now I, like so many others can buy any gun illegally for a small price. The gun laws will not change this. These guns are obtained through B.&E's," That means breaking & entering, "robberies & other illegal means. The honest folks are the only ones *who* wont be able to obtain them. I feel I am an expert on criminals having been exposed to them for so long and believe me if they are high & have a loaded gun—they'll use it without any rationality.

The decent folks need to protect themselves at all times. I guess I wouldn't be writing this except one of my best friends just murdered her husband in a fight—she loved him"—here the letter was a little difficult to make out but she seemed to indicate drugs were involved so that her friend was ~~a complete~~ irrational at the time.

She closed saying, "Drugs have made my generation lose their perspective. At 13 they are just as dangerous as the worst." She again commented on my view on guns (and then talk about a generation gap)—revealed she ~~hadn't~~ hadn't respected adults since "the ripe old age of 6."

And went on with these final haunting words, Stricter drug laws are needed—maybe one day if they were changed I'd be able to change too."

~~Of course I wish she had signed her name. Of course if she had I couldn't have shared this letter with you—a letter that will haunts me *must haunt all of us*—as a cry for help.~~

She signed it "Anonymous & yes I am ashamed to sign my name."

I wish she had signed it for it haunts me like a *childs* cry in the night. ~~from a child.~~ *And I'm afraid it will go on haunting me for a long, long time.*

~~I thought I'd share it with you. Maybe all of us need to be *more* aware and ready *attuned* to hear cries for help.~~

This is RR—Thanks for listening. ❖

Secret Service
October 1975

How far do we go in guarding civil liberties before we endanger the *very* lives of some in our midst—particularly the life of the Pres. of the U.S.? I'll be right back

Twice in 19 days attempts have been made on the life of the Pres.* ~~Other officials in govt. at virtually every level of govt. have come to accept as normal the threatening letter or phone call.~~ Everyone is asking why those entrusted with guarding the Pres. had no advance warning concerning the individuals who ~~thre~~ attempted ~~to assassinate the P him~~ *his assassination.*

Criticism has been leveled at the Secret Service. Congress investigates and demands to know why they ~~didnt~~ *dont* have ~~these~~ potential assassins identified, ~~tagged~~ & watched. And fearing the traumatic shock of another tragedy scores of proposals are made to maximize the safety of the Pres. by minimizing his freedom to walk the streets of the Nat. he serves. As Paul Harvey** said,

* On September 5, 1975, Lynette "Squeaky" Fromme, a follower of Charles Manson, tried to shoot President Gerald Ford in Sacramento, California. Seventeen days later, on September 22, 1975, former FBI informant Sara Jane Moore made a similar assassination attempt in San Francisco. Both women were given life sentences in federal prison.

** Paul Harvey's radio career began in 1933. He became Chicago's most widely heard radio newscaster in 1944; in 1951 ABC Radio Networks began carrying his broadcasts nationally. He is still on the air.

"someone trys to kill the Pres. and the only thing we can suggest is locking up the Pres."

~~Let's start with this,~~ Yes we should have better intelligence about possible assassins, & yes there was every reason to have the accused in both of the recent attempts under ~~closer~~ surveillance. Why didn't we? And who is responsible for the fact that we didn't?

The ~~truth is~~ *answer to that is,* some of ~~those~~ *the very people who are* asking these questions ~~are responsible~~ *the loudest,* including members of the media, the civil liberties union and the Congress of the U.S. It's time to jog our memories a bit as to whats been going on these past 2 yrs,

~~First let me say~~ I've had ~~the experience of~~ Secret Svc. protection several times ~~in~~ during my terms in office. I have the highest regard for that agency, for the calibre of men, their thoroughness, devotion to duty and ~~outright~~ overall professional know how & courage. There are fewer than 2000 of them overall. Think of that for a moment; Fewer than 2000 ~~for~~ assigned to security details for a number of individuals & for a variety of instalations. It dosen't take a genius to realize the Secret Svc. is a security force and has neither the manpower ~~or for~~ *nor the* resources for intelligence gathering.

When threats are made against those for whom the service is responsible ~~they keep~~ *the names* & what info. is available are kept on file. In addition the F.B.I., several other Fed. agencies, local & state police are provided with guidelines as to the kind of info. the Secret Svc. requires in doing its job. These groups forward info. & names of anyone known to pose a threat such as individuals who make unusual & persistent efforts to personally contact high govt. officials for redress of imagined grievances or those who have uttered threats against the Pres.

What we must remember however what has happened to that system over the past 2 years. Bella Abzug*—congresswoman from NY. chairs a subcommittee which leaned very hard on the secret service for gathering such info. Now the Secret Svc. list is less than 50,000 names when once it was 500,000.

The House & Sen. committees presently investigating intelligence activities have been extremely hostile to the keeping of files on American citizens regardless of evidence indicating a possible danger from those particular citizens. The Dept. of Justice has done away with its Internal Security Division. Congress had disbanded the Subversive Activities Committee** as no longer needed & the Sen. is moving to do the same to it's own Security subcommittee even though that committee is investigating the ~~lessen~~ *decline* of police intelligence activity.

Lets not forget the outraged editorials with which much of the press greeted the discovery that police intelligence units in cities such as Wash., N.Y. & L.A.

* D–New York, 1971–1976.

** The House of Representatives voted to abolish the Internal Security Committee (originally called the House Un-American Activities Committee until 1969) on January 13, 1975.

had accumulated files on people believed to have a potential for arson, murder and starting riots. Under the pressure city councils caved in & such files were ordered burned and police were forbidden to continue such activity.

The Attorney General of the U.S. has called for limiting the ability of the F.B.I. to proceed with domestic intelligence. ~~There are~~ *But in the meantime it is admitted that foreign terrorist groups are moving closer to America* ~~and~~ *in addition to* an estimated 15,000 terrorists *already* organized into 21 groups in the U.S.

~~We are all threatened by the same forces that threatened the Pres. and w~~We need more intelligence gathering ~~not less. The self righteous,~~ *and less* anti-intelligence hysteria in the media & the Congress. ~~endangers all of us and i~~If we dont get some common sense ~~soo~~ soon, someone is going to get hurt. This is RR—Thanks for listening.

Part Two

1976

Ronald Reagan devoted most of 1976 to his first full-scale presidential campaign. He lost the 1976 Republican nomination for president to Gerald R. Ford in the early hours of August 19, 1976, by a slim margin winning 47.4 percent of the delegate votes.

It had been a close campaign. Although Reagan lost the first five primaries, he won in North Carolina on March 23 and continued to roll up victories. When the primary season ended neither candidate was assured a first-ballot victory when they arrived in Kansas City in August. To attract uncommitted delegates from the Northeast, Reagan announced in advance his proposed choice of a running mate—Senator Richard Schweiker of Pennsylvania—perceived as a liberal Republican.

Reagan did score on one issue: U.S. Soviet relations.[1] In an interview on NBC-TV on January 3, President Gerald Ford had said: "Politically, I think any candidate who says abandon détente will be the loser in the long run."[2] Yet for Reagan, speaking against détente was a central part of his campaign. He demanded that détente be clearly reciprocal or the United States should quit that particular type of bilateral relationship. Reagan clearly stated his position in Exeter, New Hampshire, on February 10 in his first major foreign policy speech of the campaign.[3]

On March 1, President Ford declared: "I don't use the word détente any more. I think what we ought to say is that the United States will meet with the superpowers, the Soviet Union and with China and others, and seek to relax tensions so that we can continue a policy of peace through strength."[4] Soviet international behavior, principally its military buildup in Angola, was seen as a reason for jettisoning the term. But so was pressure from conservatives, including candidate Reagan, who opposed the way in which the United States was practicing détente.[5]

Reagan argued that the United States slipped into the military position of second best during the late 1960s and 1970s. He called for funding weapons programs such as the cruise missile, the B-1 bomber, and the Trident submarine. At the convention, to avoid a roll-call vote that Reagan would have won, a platform plank that criticized the way détente was being pursued passed by voice vote—a direct expression of disagreement with the Ford-Kissinger foreign policy.

After Ford accepted the nomination at the convention hall, he motioned for

Reagan to come from his skybox down to the podium. Reagan spoke spontaneously and eloquently about preserving freedom and avoiding nuclear war between the superpowers: "We live in a world in which the great powers have poised and aimed at each other horrible missiles of destruction that can in minutes arrive at each other's country and destroy virtually the civilized world we live in."[6] There was thunderous applause (and lots of tears) when Reagan finished speaking. He had lost the nomination but some thought he had won the future of the Republican Party.

Perhaps because of the response of the delegates in the convention hall or perhaps because of his own optimism and resolve, Reagan was not discouraged. He returned to radio broadcasting within days, doing the first taping on September 1, 1976. His newspaper columns resumed on September 17, now twice instead of once a week, and his radio broadcasts began airing September 20.[7]

Reagan's post-convention radio addresses are upbeat and strong, expressing confidence in the American people and in his own policies, which were strongly reflected in the party's 1976 platform. He continued to comment on both domestic and foreign issues. He compared the platforms of the two parties, specifically mentioning the cautionary language about détente in the Republican platform. He used another radio address to defend his selection of Richard Schweiker as his proposed running mate.

In addition to doing radio commentaries and newspaper columns, Reagan spoke widely on behalf of Republican candidates, including Ford, during the 1976 general election campaign. He campaigned in more than 20 states and taped a variety of television speeches and ads for the Republican National Committee. When Ford lost to Democratic candidate Jimmy Carter on November 2 by only 2 percentage points, Reagan became the leading contender for Republican Party's 1980 presidential nomination.

Reagan made one decision in September of 1976 that indicated his intent to remain in the political arena. He designated his campaign committee's surplus $1.5 million—unspent because of its late arrival as matching funds from the federal government—as seed money for a political action committee that would support Congressional candidates who shared his political philosophy. This he did even though he was legally entitled to keep the money for his personal use. The committee, called Citizens for the Republic (CFTR), came into being February 10, 1977. Lyn Nofziger was its executive director, and Reagan chaired it. Reagan worked hard to support other members of the Republican Party who would later do the same for him.

Shortly after the 1976 election, Ford asked Reagan to come to Washington to talk about the future of the Republican Party and especially the chairmanship of the Republican National Committee (RNC). Reagan met with Ford and a few other people in the Oval Office on December 9, 1976, and again on January 5, 1977. He expressed no interest in the chairmanship of the RNC; he had earlier declined Ford's offer of cabinet positions and the ambassadorship to Great Britain. He later expressed the view in correspondence that he could be more effective through his radio and newspaper commentaries than he would be chairing the RNC: "Remaining independent, I'm in a position to speak out in both those channels for the things we believe in as well as against those things our opponents may try to do."[8]

Reagan scored an important victory against President Gerald Ford at the 1976 Republican Convention when the delegates approved the inclusion of his explicit indictment of the Nixon and Ford administrations' Soviet policy in the platform. He refers to his statement in "Platforms C."

Platforms B
September 1, 1976

As I said yesterday the voters in Nov. will have a rare experience. Both parties have stated their philosophys in their platforms. The dif. is there for all to see.

I'll be right back.

Yesterday I summarized the Demo. & Repub. primaries on the economy, labor, taxes & energy.

Today we'll start with welfare. The Demo. platform calls for federalizing welfare with a guarant~~y~~eed annual inc. for ~~boh~~ both the non-working & working poor.

The Repub. platform in direct opposition says "no" to federalization of WF and to a guaranteed annual inc. It calls instead for a strengthening of local & state admin. of WF and the involvement of able bodied recipients in useful community work projects.

On abortion; the Demo. platform opposes a const. ban on abortion. The Repub. platform supports the efforts of those who would amend the const. to prohibit abortion on demand.

On compulsory School bussing the Demo's. concede this is a judicial tool of last resort. Repub's. declare segregated schools are morally wrong & unconst. but oppose forced bussing to achieve racial balance & favor consideration of an amendment to the const. forbidding the assignment of children to school on the basis of race.

On the whole subject of ed. the two platforms are ~~in~~ on opposite sides. The Demo. platform wants increased Fed. funding and control. The Repub. platform stresses state & local school district control with the Fed. govt. returning tax sources instead of grants to help in funding local ed.

On gun control the Demo. platform advocates laws to control the manufacture, ~~&~~ distribution *and posession* of handguns especially the low priced so called "Sat. night specials." It does uphold the right of sportsmen to own guns for hunting & target practise.

The Repub. platform supports the right of citizens to keep & bear arms and opposes Fed. registration.

The Demo platform proposes a comprehensive nat. health insurance program in which everyone will be compelled to participate. It would be funded by payroll & general tax revenues.

The Repub. party is directly opposed to such a program and maintains it would if enacted increase Fed. spending by more than $70 Bil. a year & require a personal inc. tax increase of approximately 20%.

In the all important field of agriculture the Demo. platform is less specific & generalizes with pledges ~~the~~ *for the* adoption of an agri. policy which, "recognizes that our capacity to produce food & fiber is one of our greatest assets."

Again in generalities it speaks ~~f~~ of doing more in the way of govt. loans, health care, transportation and rural developement.

The Repub. platform speaks in general terms of these same points—(services comparable to Urban areas) electricity, telephone service, transportation, available & adequate financial credit & employment opportunities to ~~help to~~ supplement small ~~farmer~~ *farmers* incs. Then it spefically opposes govt. controlled grain reserves & unrealistic regulations imposed by OSHA & EPA. Demands a stronger grain inspection prog; A govt. guaranty of access to the world market; protection against govt. subsidized foreign produce; labor laws that prevent work stoppages during the critical harvest season; better insurance protection from natural disasters, drought flood etc. and legis. to increase inheritance tax exemption to $200,000 for farms & small businesses.

Tomorrow we'll have one last go at the platforms and how they differ on foreign policy. This is RR Thanks for listening. ❖

Platforms C
September 1, 1976

This is the 3rd & last broadcast in which I've tried to summarize and compare the Demo. & Repub. platforms as adopted by the conventions. I'll be right back.

~~The D~~ I've spent these three days discussing the Demo. & Repub. platforms because it seems to me this is the first time in many years that the platforms have clearly enunciated the ~~id~~ dif. in philosophy between the two parties. Frankly I believe the voters should insist on their candidates making plain their stand on the respective platforms.

Harry Truman in 1948 said, "To me, party platforms are contracts with the people, and I always looked upon them as agreements that had to be carried out."

On the subject of foreign policy ~~the Demo.~~ *both* platforms ~~t~~ urge the continued reduction of tensions with the Soviet U. However the Repub. platform takes a strong stand for basing our policy on moral standards and commends "that great beacon of human courage & morality Aleksandr Solzhenitsyn." * Further the Repub. platform in a rare rejection of ~~past~~ policy previously pursued by a Repub. Admin. says, "in pursuing detente must not grant unilateral favors with only the hope" of future reward.

The Demo. platform calls for cutting the defense bud. by from 5 to 7 Bil. $ at the same time it demands that we maintain an adequate defense. The Repub. platform calls for a "superiority in arms" and advocates the developement of the B-1 Bomber, the Cruise Missile & the Trident submarine.

Where the Demos. call for "redeployment & gradual phaseout of the U.S. ground forces & withdrawl of nuclear weapons now stationed in Korea;" the Repubs. reaffirm committment of those troops "so long as there ~~is~~ exists the possibility of renewed aggression from No. Korea."

The Demo. platform advocates establishing peaceful peaceful relations with the Peoples Repub. of China—"including early movement toward normalizing diplomatic relations in the context of a peaceful resolution of the future of Taiwan."

The Repub. platform also supports contacts, trade & ~~normalization~~ *normalized* relations with China but bluntly & explicity maintains our treaty obligation & friendship with Taiwan.

The Demo. platform supports a new treaty with Panama and indicates that could include the terms already negotiated which of course means giving up sovereignty & eventual ownership of the canal itself. The Repub. platform has to be accepted as repudiating the previous negotiations & quotes the language of the 1903 treaty that our rights are, "as if we were sovereign in the canal zone." It goes on to say "the U.S. should in no way cede, dilute, forfeit, negotiate or transfer any rights, power, authority, territory or property vital to the U.S. & the defense of the Western Hemisphere."

Both platforms pledge continued support of Israel. The Repub. platform pledges "support for the people of Central & Eastern Europe to achieve self

* Following charges of treason in the Soviet Union in 1974, Aleksandr Solzhenitsyn, a famous writer and dissident, lived in exile. Solzhenitsyn was living in the United States when Reagan taped this commentary.

determination." And it supports continuation of the Voice of Am., Radio Free Europe, & Radio Liberty with adequate appropriations. It also is specific in demanding that the microwave transmissions aimed at the U.S. Embassy in Moscow be terminated immediately.

There is more—much more than I can comment on here. I recommend that everyone get copies of the 2 platforms & read them.—For once they mean something. This is RR. Thanks for listening,

Getting Back at the Bureaucrats A

September 1, 1976

Anyone who has been plagued by burocratic nonsense, forms to fill out, regulations to comply with even though they make little sense, has to be a fan of a Mayor in Texas. I'll be right back.

The Mayor of Midland Texas, ~~is~~ Ernest Angelo* will see that Midland never suffers the problems of N.Y. City**. As a matter of fact N.Y. would never have suffered the problems of N.Y. City if it had, had a few Ernie Angelos in City Hall these past 20 years.

As a former Gov. I can testify as to the ridiculous demands inflicted on state & local govt. by the paper pushers of the Potomac. And I know any of you listening who are in business or *who* farm can reel off personal horror stories of the hours ~~of~~ spent filling out govt. required paperwork and bowing to the demands of senseless regulations. Well give a listen you'll enjoy ~~what~~ the Mayor of Midlands revenge.

Mayor Angelo struggled ~~for 8 mo's. to hack~~ through a burocratic jungle of red tape in the U.S. Dept. of Housing & Urban developement to obtain for his city some Fed. funds that were due. It took him 8 long, frustrating months of paperwork, questionaires in duplicate, triplicate & quaddruplicate before he broke through into daylight.

Then one day the regional office of H.U.D. (that's burocratese for *the* Housing & Urban Developement~~)~~ *Agency*) requested a reserved parking space at the *MIDLAND* municipal airport. Mayor Angelo was delighted to comply with the request—if HUD would do a little complying.

He sent a letter to the Dallas regional office of Hud with copies to the Pres., Sec. Carla Hills and a few others in Wash. His letter requested 3 executed & 14 confirmed copies of their application. It further said, "Submit the make & model of the proposed vehicle to be parked in the space together with certified

* Ernest Angelo, Jr., a longtime Republican party loyalist, was the mayor of Midland, Texas, from 1972–1980. He was a personal friend of Reagan's and served as a delegate to the Republican National Convention in 1988 and as a presidential elector in 2000.

** New York City's banks refused to lend the city additional money. The city faced bankruptcy.

assurance that everyone connected with the manufacture, servicing and operations of same was paid according to a wage scale in compliance with the requirements of the Davis-Bacon Act*.

"Submit a genealogical table for everyone who will operate said vehicle so that we can ascertain that there will be a precisely exact equal percentage of whites, blacks & other minorities as well as women & the elderly.

Submit certified assurances that all operators of said vehicle and any filling station personnel that service same will be equipped with steel-toed boots, safety goggles, & crash helmets, & that the vehicle will be equipped with at least safety belts & an airbag in compliance with the Occupational Safety & Health Act.

"Submit environmental impact statements"—well you get the idea.—His letter went on for quite a few additional paragraphs citing all the red tape requirements (so dear to the hearts of those who toil & spin on the banks of the Potomac). ~~Then~~ *that would have to* be complied with before favorable consideration could be given to their request for a parking space.

Then Mayor Angelo added a postscript. He told them they could have their parking space without complying with all the aforementioned red tape.

I hope he made his point because the General Accounting Office in Wash. estimates the *yearly* cost of regulations at $60 Bil. The Fed. Trade Commission puts it at $80 Bil.—all waste due to regulatory overkill. Probably the correct figure is nearer the $130 Bil. the ~~Ec.~~ Council of E~~d~~conomic Advisors ~~*says*~~ estimate is prorated out at $2000 per family.

Maybe we'll talk some more about this tomorrow. ❖

Bureaucrats B

September 1, 1976

We are governed more & more by people we never elected, ~~and~~ *who* cant be turned out of office by our votes and who want more power than they already have. I'll be right back.

Yesterday I talked of how ~~much~~ govt. regulation & paperwork is adding to the cost of govt. & to the cost of living. There are some congressmen who need our help. They too are concerned about the effect of *Fed.* regulations on ec. activity, jobs, prices & the tax burden. They have formed a task force called "Gear"—for "Govt. Executive Agency Review."

So far their findings support the complaints of both business & consumers. For example they price govt. regulation of the airlines as adding $1 Bil. a year

* The Davis-Bacon Act requires that workers on federal and state construction contracts worth $2,000 or more be paid the "prevailing wage," which includes a specified hourly fringe benefit amount.

to our travel costs. The Rock Island R.R. went bankrupt after waiting 13 yrs. for the I.C.C.* to answer their request for a merger which could have prevented the bankruptcy. Two yrs. ago the Am. taxpayer put up $2 Bil. to ~~keep~~ foot the payroll for the regulators. Today the tab is $3 Bil. That's a 50% increase in just 24 months.

The Environmental Protection Agency & The Occupational Safety & Health Admin's. conflicting rules & requirements have ~~close~~ forced the closing of 350 foundries and thousands of small businesses according to Cong. John Myers** of Ind. He also adds that Fed. paperwork cost has gone up 150% in 8 yrs.

Cong. Ron Paul*** of Texas reports that under the Food for Peace program which was to feed the worlds hungry ~~and~~ at the same *time* reducing our own food surpluses, we have bought and shipped ~~to Syria~~ *abroad* in the last 20 yrs. $677 mil. worth of tobacco. Maybe we figure a smoke will make them forget how hungry they are.

There are *however* greater dangers to all of us than just this waste of money. ~~however.~~ For a number of years now the Fed. govt. has tried to get control ~~of~~ if not ownership of privately owned land in America. A decade ago they pushed the panic button on the supposed lack of recreational land and began gobbling up mining claims and other property. At that time a Fed. official announced that in the beginning the govt. had to encourage private ownership to get the land developed but now the goal was to regain govt. control of land.

More recently the device has been "land planning." Never does ~~govt.~~ *Wash.* state the true purpose. Land planning would leave you with deed to the property plus the right to pay taxes on it but govt. would dictate it's use. *When proposed openly as land planning it was defeated thanks to pub. pressure.*

Now there is another ~~one~~ plan. The E.P.A. has come up with something called "significant deterioration" standards for purity in ambient air. Very simply this means that any part of the U.S. where the air is cleaner than the air quality required by national standards can be prevented from doing anything to lower ~~it~~ air quality even though it equals or excels the standards set for air anywhere else in the *U.S.* ~~country.~~ There has been no public debate. This is not law passed by Cong. It is regulation pure & simple imposed on us by permanent civil servants.

What it means is that up to ⅔ of the U.S. will be permanently barred from any kind of growth or developement. Suppose you live in a rural area ~~and~~ of high unemployment and an industry wants to build a branch plant on the edge of town? E.P.A. can arbitrarily say "no." In fact even a school building with it's heating plant & adjacent parking lot could be ruled out by those omnipotent elitists along the Potomac.

This is nothing more than back door land planning; getting under the

* Interstate Commerce Commission.
** R–Indiana, 1967–1996.
*** R–Texas, 1976–1977, 1979–1985, and 1997–present.

guise of environmental ~~plannin~~ *protection* what they couldn't get openly. And the public works committees of both the house & Sen. have proposed enshrining these burocratic proposals in Fed. law. It is time to write your congressman. ❖

Women's March
September 1, 1976

I'm going to talk about a womens movement that isn't concerned with the sometimes controversy over womens place in the world. I'll be right back.

There is a savagery loose in the world. ~~and w~~While we can claim peace on the technical grounds that no nations are in a state of declared war, people are being kidnaped, highjacked, blown up and mowed down by rifle & machine gun fire~~, i~~Innocent people going about their daily work killed simply because they ~~were~~ *are* targets of opportunity.

Those doing the killing claim to serve a cause; redress of ancient wrongs, political differences, ec. imbalance and even religious differences. The innocents die on Cypress, in *Latin America*, Lebanon, Africa & in the North of Ireland.

We are naïve indeed if we accept the bloodshed ~~has~~ as resulting solely from the local ~~problems~~ *causes* proclaimed by the terrorist bands & guerillas. Behind the scenes an evil power, ~~the~~ helps provide the weapons, feeds the fires of hatred & intolerance because continued strife brings closer the dream of a communist dominated world. *Of course* The only killing in the communist world is the official execution of those who dream too much of freedom.

One of the most tragic trouble spots is Northern Ireland where for 7 years neighbor has taken the life of neighbor and done so in the name of God—the same God prayed to by both sides. There is ~~a~~ *a* non-~~sectarian~~ sectarian issue to be sure; the argument as to whether Northern Ireland ~~sho~~ should remain under British rule or become a part of the ~~Irish~~ Irish Republic. But the religious difference is very real ~~and~~ and lends an extra special bitterness to the dispute.

Just when you would think the killing had become so commonplace ~~is~~ as to be endured something happened a few weeks ago that resulted in a kind of miracle. ~~Bombs~~ During these 7 yrs. bombs have been exploded in crowded taverns & dept. stores, cold blooded executions have taken place and continual sniping has added to the toll. Then a few weeks ago 3 children of one family were killed by the I.R.A.* Ironically killer or killers & victems were on the

* The three children were killed while bicycle riding when a car, piloted by an IRA (Irish Republican Army) gunman, crashed into them after the 19-year-old driver was shot by British soldiers. Their deaths prompted their aunt, Mairead Corrigan, to found the Northern Ireland Peace Movement (later renamed Community of Peace People) with colleague Betty Williams. Both were awarded the Nobel Peace Prize in 1976 for their efforts.

same side. The children weren't the targets as far as is known. They just happened to be in the way when the guns talked.

One woman—Aunt to the 3 children spoke to another woman. Then the 2 set out to speak to others. Only days after the funeral a meeting of 2 or 3,000 women took place. They demanded an end to the killing and called on women everywhere to join them.

It has always been my belief that women brought civilization to the world. Without their influence we males would still be carrying clubs and in recent years we've come pretty close to ~~getting back to those clubs.~~ *doing that again.*

Just days ago 30,000 women from both sides Catholic & Protestant marched through Belfast ~~with~~ voicing one demand; "stop killing our children." In Dublin 20,000 marched in sympathy, smaller groups did so in other Irish towns. ~~They ask their sisters world wide to join them. There is a womens~~ In Belfast stones were hurled at them—by men of course, young men. They kept on marching. Women ~~joined~~ stepped off the side walks to join them. They ask their sisters all over the world to join them, to rally for an end to the killing.

What if it happens? Imagine the men in the Kremlin if they looked down on Russias women marching in the streets demanding ~~an end~~ peace. Why not? Does anyone have a better idea? ❖

The Tax Reform Act of 1976, signed October 4, 1976, attempted to increase taxes by closing so-called loopholes and changing capital gains rules. It greatly increased the complexity of the tax code.

Tax Reform
September 1, 1976

More than 100 yrs. ago a French economist named Bastiat * said, "When a nation is burdened with taxes nothing is more difficult or impossible than to levy them equally." I'll be right back.

It has been said that nothing in life is certain except death & taxes. Well we can add the certainty of Congress talking about reforming taxes every election year.

They are at it again with months & months of arguing in committee, then a ~~house~~ bill on the floor of each house & now a conference committee trying to reconcile the differences between the Sen. version & the House effort. All you

* The work of Claude Frédéric Bastiat (1801–1850) has been widely published and translated. See e.g., *Selected Essays on Political Economy,* translated from the French by Seymour Cain and edited by George B. de Huszar (Princeton, NJ: Van Nostrand, 1964).

& I can be certain of is that the inc. tax will still be too complicated to figure ~~out~~ without legal help and the govt. will get more money not less.

Why cant Congress get the message the people are sending; that the inc. tax needs to be simplified, that the progressive surtax brackets need to be adjusted so that a cost of living pay raise dosent put you into a higher tax bracket and that we are paying too much in taxes.

That last point of course dosen't ~~ha~~ really have to do with tax reform. It has to do with making govt. cost less & for Congress that is like going over Niagara Falls in barrell—the hard way—up stream.

The Congressional approach to tax reform is to talk loudly of loopholes, creating the idea that everyones burden can be lightened if only a mysterious "they" can be ~~made~~ prevented from escaping their fair share of taxes. The result is that when Congress finishes its loophole closing some taxpayers pay more, none pay less & govt. gets more money. ~~than it was getting before the reform.~~

I know it is difficult to follow figures reeled off by a voice on radio but let me try to shed some light on the whole matter of loopholes.

Taking 1972 figures the total earnings & inc. of the Am. people was $945 Bil. Of that amount $500 Bil was exempt from inc. tax. Aha! you say $500 Bil. worth of loopholes—who got the break? The answer is, you did.

$155 Bil. was that $750 personal exemption we all get for each member of the family. Another 70 Bil. was what those of ~~you~~ *us* take who use the Standard Deduction. Then $93 Bil. was inc. from Soc. Security benefits, welfare grants and unemployment insurance. None of these I'm sure you'll agree can be termed loopholes and they amount to 318 of that $500 Bil. of untaxed inc.

Alright—but what about the remaining $182 Bil.—that's a lot of loophole. Not quite. Surely none of us believe we should pay a tax on a tax so 36.2 Bil. is the deduction we take because of other taxes we pay such as property tax on our homes. Then there is interest $27.3 Bil. ~~worth~~ & 20 of that is int. on our mortgages. ~~We give~~ If we had to pay tax on that a lot of us couldn't afford to own a home.

Charitable contributions—money we give to church & worthy causes plus deduction for medical expense bring the total to more than $400 Bil. The balance covers all the other deductibles—casualty loss from accident, fire, flood, tornado, earthquake, ~~etc.~~ Investment loss, robbery, depreciation etc. Sure there is room in there for someone to take advantage of a legal technicality and get an undeserved break but those who do so are far fewer in number than pol. demagogs would have us believe. The truth is, to change the regulations ~~so has~~ *JUST* to catch ~~that the~~ *the occasional* few would deny a legitimate deduction to the many.

~~A few years ago a Sen. *a disgruntled govt. emp. on his way out* made headlines by charging roughly 100 people with 6 fig. inc's. had ma paid little or no inc. tax. The treasury dept. was able to show that*ere were* more than 16,000 in that earning bracket who averaged paying about 70% of there earnings in~~

~~tax and gave specific information as to why the 100 owed no tax. This didn't make the headlines.~~ ❖

Education (A)
September 21, 1976

For some time now a lot of us have been asking why cant little Willie read or do arithmatic and the answer is, he isn't being taught to do that. I'll be right back.

The story is told of the new young school master telling the old timer about progressive ed. He was ~~enthus~~ ~~ie~~enthusiastic about how the children were allowed to express themselves, play games, draw pictures, visit with each other etc. The old boy heard him out and then said, "we had that when I was in school." The young teacher said—"you did?" & he said, "Yep we called it recess."

A few weeks ago a nat. magasine carried a one page story by a lovely young lady 24 yrs. of age. She titled her story "Confessions of a Misspent Youth," * but dont let that title fool you. She was in no way a juvenile delinquent. She ~~was~~ *is* instead a victem of some of the ~~new~~ modern ideas ~~of~~ in ed. that have been around for a couple of decades or so.

Her parents were of that era when permissive ed. seemed to be the wave of the future. At age 4 (in 1956) she was enrolled in a small private school which she describes as a school without pain. It specialized in freedom—the freedom not to learn. The idea was to cultivate the innate creativity each child was believed to have.

According to this graduate of the educational sand box they had ~~h~~ different hours for each subject but they were free to dismiss anything that bored them. School policy forbade them from being bored, miserable, or made to compete with each other. In studying history by re-creating its least important elements. In early Am. history they made tepees, pounded corn and ate Buffalo meat. Another year they were maids & knights in armor and drank orange juice from tin foil goblets. As she says that was "the middle ages" but they never found out what the Middle Ages were.

There were other examples—copying hieroglyphics on brown wrapping paper without even knowing what the hieroglyphics stood for. They spent a lot of time being creative because they were told that was the way to be happy. At age 10 they were ~~p~~ functionally illiterate. ~~Readi~~ Reading didn't begin until 3rd grade. I have a set of the old McGuffey Readers—back when ed. was old hat. The 1st vol. is for kindergarten. ~~and~~

Sadly this young lady says that upon graduation ~~from~~ all the happy young

* Mara Wolynski, "Confessions of a Misspent Youth," *Newsweek,* August 30, 1976, p. 11.

children "fell down the hill." No matter what high school they went to they were the underachievers—more handicapped than any underprivileged ~~slum~~ SLUM children. One ~~young man~~ *of her fellow students* killed himself after flunking out of the worst high school in N.Y. at age 20. Others have put in time at various mental hospitals. Her own mother was advised to give her psychological tests to find why she was blocking out information. She wasn't blocking it out she didnt have any information to begin with. Rejected by all 4 yr. colleges she finally got a degree by way of a start in junior college.

She rejoices that her 8 yr. old younger brother was yanked out of the same progressive school when her mother finally saw the light and didn't want him to be like her.

Her *POIGNANT* closing line should be over the door of every teachers college in America. "And now I've come to see that the real job of school is to ~~see that the real~~ *entice the student* into the web of knowledge and then, if he's not enticed, to drag him in. I wish I had been."

~~Tomorrow~~ This is RR—~~Ill be right back.~~ Thanks for listening. ❖

Humphrey-Hawkins Bill (Jobs A)
September 21, 1976

Sometimes it seems that in halls of Congress "old bills" unlike old soldiers neither die nor fade ~~away~~ away. They just live on under different titles. I'll be Right back.

Congress has before it Sen. Bill 50 House Res. 50 ~~authored by & known as Humphrey Hawkins~~ entitled, "The Full Emp. & Balanced Growth Act." We first knew of this as the Humphrey, Javits bill. Fortunately it didn't get far *under that title* but now *unfortunately it is back* renamed the Humphrey, Hawkins bill.

It~~'s label~~ is as persuasive and grandiloquent in it's promise as the ~~cure all~~ pri~~nted~~ *label* on a bottle of patent medicine. It declares that every adult American has the right to, "opportunities for useful paid employment at fair rates of compensation." Surely no one wants to quarrel with that. *But* It sets a goal of 3% adult unemp. to be reached by 1980~~. Actually that~~ *which* is better than full employment.

~~It is generally conceded that d~~*D*uring times of peak emp. ~~such as in war time~~ the percentage of workers temporarily & voluntarily between jobs~~, first timers~~ *and those* looking for a *first* job ~~and those unemployed who were fired for whatever reason~~ total more than 3%. ~~of employables.~~

~~The bill~~ Hump-Hawk as it's called requires the Pres. to submit a complete plan every year for achieving "full emp. & balanced growth." That too sounds alright. He's supposed to use fiscal & monetary policy (which I'm sure can only mean deficit spending & printing press money) ~~and other tools. to~~ *tax re-*

vision & other tools. Here there seems to be some fuzziness because Wash. estimates the cost of the bill at anywhere from $16 Bil. a year to $44 Bil.

But that phrase "other tools" is the one we should watch out for. To begin with Cong. has to approve the Presidents plan or presumably come up with one of their own. Then if joblessness isn't reduced to the magic figure all sorts of employment & grant programs go into effect including pub. service employment & job training. We already have about 50 govt. agencies charged with training & assisting the unemployed. ~~That would become~~ *Make that* 51 because the bill calls for a new "Full emp. office" in the labor dept. to administer a reservoir of "last resort" Fed. jobs. (Right now there are only 4½ workers ~~in~~ for every pub job holder.)

The bill makes sure that these make work jobs pay equivalent to wage scales in the private sector which means a built in inducement for some to quit their present jobs for the guarantyd pub. job because it would mean a raise in pay.

In our experience so far with these emergency ~~job.~~ *pub.* job programs we've learned that they actually decrease employment because in many instances govt. entities only use the program to hire those they already intended to hire.

But there is much, much more to fear in Humphrey-Hawkins. Actually it follows a pattern once used in Italy by a fellow named Mussolini & ~~we~~ *then it was* called Fascism.

The annual plan would involve govt. allocating resources including labor. It creates govt. machinery for planning virtually every aspect of Am. life, projecting nat. goals for production, purchasing power etc.

These words may not sound frightening but think of their meaning & application. Govt. not the customers would decide how much of what should be produced. You may think you want a new car but if govt. decided refrigerators were more important, steel and other materials would be denied the auto maker. That of course would mean layoffs which also means govt. would begin telling free Americans where they would work & what kind of work ~~they'll~~ *they'd* do. Maybe it is a full employment program—but so was slavery. This is R.R. Thanks for listening. ❖

President Coolidge
September 21, 1976

Right now we are all cencerned with who will be our ~~next~~ *future* Pres. For whatever it's worth I'm going to talk about a Pres. from the past. I'll be right back.

The names of some Presidents are invoked by spokesmen of both pol. parties as "men for all seasons," ~~typical~~ epitomizing the greatness of America, Washington, Lincoln, Jefferson etc. Then there are Presidents whose names are brought up in party circles, hailed as great but if ~~recog~~ acknowledged by the other party ~~not~~ *at all with* NOT quite the same enthusiasm.

There are *also* two lists of Presidential names—one for each party ~~which are proclaimed~~ *usually held up to view* for strictly partisan purposes. Each party lists past Presidents of the opposing party as examples of that parties terrible record. ~~In the~~

The Demos. for example get laughs by mentioning Silent Cal Coolidge. And truth is many Repubs. chuckle a little and go along with the idea that he was a do nothing Pres. Sometimes I wonder if he really was a "do nothing" or was he a little like a Life Guard on the beach who also seems to be doing very little when there is no emergency. If you take a closer look he is quietly being watchful.*

Cal Coolidge ~~was~~ is good for laughs but not all of them are at his expense. There ~~is~~ *was* the ~~story of the~~ press conference where a persistent reporter asked the Pres. if he had anything to say about prohibition? Cal said "No."—"Any comments on the world court?"—"No." "What about the farm situation? Again the ans. was "no." The reporter said, "You dont seem to have any comment about anything." Coolidge said, "No comment & dont quote me."

Probably no Pres. has ever lived in the White House and maintained so unchanged his previous life style. Which in Coolidges case was the simple even frugal life he had lived on a New England farm.

Shortly after he became Pres. he sent his teenage son into the tobacco fields to work in the summer as he always had. One of the other workers surprised at this said to the young Coolidge, "if my father were Pres. I wouldn't be out here working in the field." Young Coolidge said, "If my father were your father you would."

But while "Silent Cal" seemed to be doing nothing as Pres. the Fed. budget actually went down & so did the Nat. debt. Consumer prices fell but unemp. stayed at the figure we only dream of—3½% which means everyone who wanted a job had one. Fed. taxes were cut 4 times.

The number of automobiles on our streets & highways tripled during his years in the White House and radio sales went up 1400%.

In just the 5 years from 1922 to 27 the purchasing power of wages rose 10%. It was a kind of "Golden era, *in other ways.* ~~in the entertainment world & in the sports arena.~~ Hollywood would never again be more glamorous and there were giants in the sports arenas whose names are still ~~have a~~ legend—the Manassa Mauler, Jack Dempsey, Knute Rockne, The 4 Horsemen, Red Grange, Babe Ruth & Big Bill Tilden. Now I'm not saying Pres. Coolidge was responsible for them but they were larger than life figures that went with Americas place in the world

* Reagan describes his respect for Calvin Coolidge in a letter to James Huntley in *Reagan: A Life in Letters,* edited by Kiron Skinner, Annelise Anderson, and Martin Anderson (New York: Free Press, 2003), p. 287.

~~So Silent Cal Coolidge was a do nothing Pres.~~

So what if he was a "do nothing" Pres. Do you suppose doing nothing had ~~anything~~ *SOMETHING* to do with ~~a balanced~~ ~~*balancing the*~~ ~~budget,~~ *reducing the bud,* reducing the debt & cutting taxes 4 times? This is R.R. Thanks for listening. ❖

Vietnam

October 18, 1976

A soft but ugly sound is beginning to filter through the bamboo curtain surrounding what once was free S. Vietnam. I'll be right back.

More than a year ago on one of these broadcasts I said a curtain of silence was ~~fall~~ falling over V.N., Cambodia & Laos as the conquering, communists established their rule. At the same time I predicted that one day sound would filter through the curtain of silence. We would learn piece by piece the story of what had happened to people whose only sin was a yearning for freedom & human dignity.

The time has come. When the wind blows in from the west across the Pacific one has the feeling that it carries the sound of soft moaning *such as* we once heard ~~as the~~ *when an* East wind blew across Dachau, Belsen & Auschwitz. Perhaps one day soon we'll add other names to those symbols of horror, names easier to pronounce—NV16, L1T.6—the communists are very practical. ~~The~~

No. V.Namese call their ~~camps~~ *camps* "Trai Cai Tao" which means "re-education camps." The S. Vietnamese call them "Trai Tap Trung" which means concentration camp.

Just as in that earlier time the horror story is beginning to come to us piece by piece from escapees, refugees whose loved ones have disappeared into the camps & now & then a European journalist. ~~perceptive journalist brings the story—to~~ It's still far from complete but somewhere between 200 & 300,000 South Vietnamese are being purified in the "re-education camps." The picture is one of inhumanly hard labor, starvation rations, disease & little or no medical care. And of course there is stern discipline we can call torture for short.

Our own returned P.O.W's. are familiar with what that torture might be. There is ~~being~~ kneeling on a hard surface until it becomes agony. Also being beaten while you are kneeling. Some are placed in metal boxes which we probably left behind. ~~We called these conexes. They were cargo containers.~~ *They are cargo containers we called conexes.*

The idea is that with the prisoner in the sealed metal box his captors beat on the metal sides with clubs until the din ~~becomes~~ *for the man* inside becomes excruciating. Former army capt. Ngo Dinh Ly escaped ~~from~~ this summer after undergoing this torture. ~~He made his way to Thailand.~~ *He says it can drive a man insane.*

In the line of work there is clearing minefields in which many die~~.~~, *but then what's a life if a mine is eliminated.* A job reserved for soft city dwellers or people of some education is ~~mixing~~ *making* fertilizer by mixing soil & human excrement with ~~their~~ *your* bare hands. This can be fatal too because no soap is provided for washing and ~~they~~ *you* must eat with ~~their~~ *your* bare hands. Dysentery is widespread and often fatal.

N.V.N. wants admission to the U.N. ~~w~~We vetoed their request.* Now a N. Vietnamese official says confidently the veto was due to our election. They'll try again after Nov. 2nd. He's confident they'll be admitted then. I hope he's wrong. This is R.R. Thanks for listening. ❖

Reagan's tale of the "welfare queen" is part of American political folklore, with many people doubting such egregious fraud ever took place. However, numerous articles in the Chicago Tribune *and* The New York Times *from 1974 to 1976 show that not only did the "welfare queen" exist, the fraud she committed was even worse than Reagan described.***

Welfare
October 18, 1976

A news item about welfare foolishness has brought back some campaign memories I'd like to share with you. I'll be right back.

The other day a news item told of a woman on Aid To Dependent Children who came into $14,544 cash through an accident claim. On the advice of welfare workers she went on a six week spending spree to get rid of the money so she could remain eligible for welfare.

That brought to ~~my~~ mind an example I cited during the primary campaigns of a Chi. woman ~~who was found to~~ *who was reported* to be receiving welfare

* The Carter administration stopped the policy of vetoing Vietnam's admission to the United Nations, and the country became a member of the international body in 1977.

** The "welfare queen"—so dubbed by the Chicago press in 1974—was an attractive 47 year old black woman whom Joel Edelman, the former director of the Illinois Department of Public Aid, described as being "without a doubt, the biggest welfare cheat of all time." Her name was Linda Taylor. She had three new 1974 cars—a Cadillac, a Lincoln, and a Chevrolet station wagon. She had dozens of false names, used over 30 different addresses, and had 25 phone numbers and three social security cards. She owned three houses that she rented. It was estimated that she received Social Security and welfare checks under as many as 80 names in different states around the country. In one year alone they estimated she received $154,000 in welfare. The authorities were reluctant to prosecute, perhaps because of embarrassment, but she was finally convicted in Chicago on March 17, 1977 of "welfare fraud and perjury" on a few of the charges against her. *Chicago Tribune,* September 29 (p. 3), 30 (p. 1), October 5 (p. 12), 12 (p. 3), 13 (p. 3), November 14 (p. 4), December 1 (p. 25), 10 (Sec. 2 p. 5); 1974; January 10 (p. 3), March 2 (p. 38), June 26 (pp. 1, 19), September 22 (pp. 1, 19), 1975; *The New York Times,* December 15, 1974, p. 58; February 15 (p. 51), 29 (p. 42), 1976; January 9 (p. 39), March 19 (p. 8), 1977.

under 80 different names at 30 different addresses. Even though the story had been widely carried in the press campaigns being what they are I would run into cynics who thought I'd padded the story for pol purposes.

Well thanks to the chief investigative reporter of the Chi. Tribune* I can verify & update my story. ~~and~~ *And* It ~~dosen't~~ *wont* do anything for the image of welfare workers who tried to hush the story up. They had been touting controls which they said made welfare fraud a minor problem when the "welfare queen" as she's now called ~~came on the scene~~ *suddenly burst* on the scene.

It all started with a reported theft of $18,000 in jewels & furs. Two Chi. detectives ended up arresting the robbery victem for filing a false police report. Apparently there had been no robbery. ~~and~~ *But* their investigation had turned up in the victems plush apartment ~~were~~ bundles of public aid checks and records. When they reported their findings to the pub. aid office, officials there passed the buck to the States Attorneys Office, he shoved it off on the Attorney General who promptly told the detectives to take it up with the Feds. ~~who~~ *The Feds* didn't want it at all so the detective told his story to the Chi. Tribune. Be grateful for a free press.—*it made the front page.*

A St. Senator chairman** of the advisory committee on pub. aid ~~said called~~ *termed* the case unbelievable and put two fraud investigators on it. They stated "We could spend the rest of our lives checking out all the cases on ~~Linda~~ *her* but it would be worth doing because she's taught us every possible loophole in the welfare regulations.

I said I would update my story of 80 names & 30 addresses. Here goes! The trail extends through 14 states. She has used 127 names, posed as a mother of 14 children ~~& an open heart surgeon.~~ *at one time, 7 at another, signed up* twice with the same case worker in 4 days and once while on welfare posed as an open heart surgeon complete with office. She has 50 social security numbers and 50 addresses in Chi. alone plus an untold number of telephones. She claims also to be the ~~wid~~ widow—let's ~~th~~ make that plural—of 2 naval officers who were killed in action. Now the *dept. of* agriculture is looking into the massive number of food stamps she's been collecting. *She has 3 new cars, a full length mink coat and her take is estimated at a mil. $.*

I wish this had a happy ending but the pub. aid office according to the news ~~accounts~~ *story* refuses to cooperate. ~~#~~ She's still collecting welfare checks she can use to build up her defense fund. This is RR. Thanks for listening. ❖

* George Bliss.

** State Senator Don A. Moore (R). George Bliss, "Walker Hid Aid Fraud: Legislator," *Chicago Tribune,* January 10, 1975, p. 3.

Government Forms
October 18, 1976

Congress has just passed a new tax reform bill. I dont think it will be greeted by dancing in the streets. I'll be right back.

More than 200 yrs. ago we said of George III, "he has sent hither swarms of officers to harass our people & eat out their substance." * I wonder what the Founding Fathers would say about the modern day swarm who harass & eat of our substance?

I know I've talked to you before in broad, general terms about the "blizzard of paper" we are asked (demanded is a better word) to send to Wash. The other day I was reading a roundup ~~of what that~~ of stories about individual victems of the *paper* blizzard. And then I read of the final passage & signing into law of the tax reform bill. It is 5 inches thick, (1500 pages) and economists who have studied it say they dont understand it. Happy next April to us all! The one thing we ~~do~~ *should* understand is the ~~govt. will be getting more money.~~ *Congress which talked for so long about helping the taxpayers by reforming the system has helped itself in this reform to an additional 1.6 Bil. $.*

The Nat. chamber of commerce has done some research on the ~~storm~~ *paper blizzard* and finds that of the 20 reports most frequently demanded by Wash. 13 are by the Internal Rev. Svc. Next in line is O.S.H.A.—the Occupational *Safety* & Health Admin. The Chamber was trying to help the Commission on Paper work ** which is suppose to be eliminating red tape.

Not only does the I.R.S. have the most forms they also take the most time & effort to fill out. By coincidence I.R.S. is the only agency exempt from any effort to reduce or simplify its paper work.

The Chamber found the citizenry in almost the same revolutionary mood our ancestors were in 200 yrs. ago. One businessman in the N.W. told of providing a 74 page report in 1973 for the Equal ~~Opp~~ Emp. Opp. inspector who personally visited his plant. In 1974 a second inspector refused to accept the report approved by ~~the 1st~~ his predecessor but finally settled for 145 pages. You are probably already ahead of me ~~but~~ on this one—yes in 1975 a new inspector refused to accept the program until the report reached 395 pages.

~~According to the~~ ~~my news source~~ *The same news source told of* a banker ~~did~~ *who* filled in a form writing "none" where that was the appropriate answer. The form with it's six required copies was returned to be re-done using a "O" where ~~the~~ the word "none" appeared.

* This is from the American Declaration of Independence, the tenth charge against King George III of England in a long list of grievances.

** The Federal Commission on Paperwork looked at the proliferation of government requests for information and the management of resulting data. Its recommendations led to the Paperwork Reduction Act of 1980. Information policy was centralized in the Office of Information and Regulatory Affairs, part of the Office of Management and Budget.

A midwest manufacturer can only spend half his time running his business. The rest of the time he's doing govt. paperwork.

A small engineering firm completed 1,342 St. & Fed. forms in one year. ~~Th~~ On a 5 day a week basis that's more than 5 forms ~~a day~~ to be filled out each working day.

I am not advocating an overthrow of the govt. by force & violence but isn't it time to buttonhole our congressmen when they come week ending home? ~~and~~ *Let's* ask them for proof that these reports do anything more than provide jobs for a bunch of burocratic paper ~~push p~~ shufflers. This is RR. Thanks for listening ❖

On September 19, 1976, Prime Minister Olof Palme was voted out of office, thereby ending 44 years of Socialist rule in Sweden. A non-Socialist coalition took power, and non-Socialists ruled the country until 1982.

Sweden I

October 18, 1976

Why dont we take warning from what has happened in other countries before we get as deep in the swamp as they are. I'll be right back.

When the English pound went into decline every fraction of a penny loss in value was & is reported each day in all the media. Not so widely heralded are the words of the socialist Prime Minister of Eng.* who has been betraying socialist gospel and doing penance. Having taken the "Right little, tight little Isle" down the road to a socialist Utopia which turned out to be a cracked plaster, quonset hut with a double mortgage, unemployed tenants and a roof blown off by inflation the present leader of the Labor, socialist party is calling ~~for~~ *on* private enterprise & the free marketplace for help.

Then there is Sweden the socialist, showplace. They have lived *for some 40 years* according to the gospel of Karl Marx. In any argument ~~with liberal leaning Americans~~ about the *shortcomings or* merits of socialism ~~they could always~~ *our own liberals would* fall back on Sweden citing its high standard of living, lack of unemployment and general ec. health. About ~~all~~ *any* of us who dont trust socialism could come back with was the element of free enterprise Sweden still allowed to exist. We'd say that was really what kept Sweden afloat but it wasn't a satisfactory argument because they'd say that was the kind of socialism they wanted for America. Come to think of it we're pretty well on our way to that kind of mix right now.

Maybe we'll be saved in spite of ourselves if the British P.M. will keep talk-

* James Callaghan.

ing & if we'll pay a little heed to the recent election in Sweden. ~~and~~ *If we'll* ask why—why after 40 years did the Swedes vote the socialist govt. out and the conservatives in.

Maybe a motion picture director can help us understand. Ingmar Bergman virtually a national hero in Sweden and pretty popular with moviegoers in our own country wants to leave Sweden & live in America. He has good reason. His govt. charged him with tax avoidance. The govt. wants him to pay taxes of $1.39 ~~for~~ *on* every $ he earns. That's kind of a losing proposition. Ingmar just handed them his fortune & walked away with only his talent.

~~This wasn't all that made the Swedish people unhappy. Swedens average man earns $8,800 a yr. His boss pays 25% *on top* of that for soc. security dues & payroll taxes. and the Ma average man~~ *he* ~~pays 40% of that~~ *his* ~~$8800 in taxes. Inflation is running at 10%. To try and keep it in check the govt. passed a new tax law that said the tax rate for shopkeepers, lawyers, authors & artists~~ *~~those~~* ~~earning $33,000 a year would be 102%. A distinguished author wrote a fairy tale~~

Swedens average man earns $8800 a yr. & pays ~~40%~~ *$3520* of that in tax. His ~~boys~~ boss ~~pays~~ $2200 ~~on top of that 8800~~ for soc. security dues & payroll tax.

To try & curb the 10% inflation rate the govt. passed a new tax law last year that made the rate for those earning $33,000—102%. A distinguished author wrote a fairy tale which ended with her supposedly stealing ~~7000 Kroner to pay the 2,000,000 Kroner~~ tax on ~~her 2,000,000 KRoyalties with 5000 left over for living for~~ *money from the national treasury to pay* the 102% tax on her royalty for the book plus something to live on.

The Sec. of finance told parliament "taxation was none of her business." Now they've had an election, ~~she's still writing~~ & there's a new Sec. of finance.* ~~This is RR. Thanks for listening.~~

Tomorrow I'll tell you some other things in Swedens socialism that made them vote as they did.

This is R.R. thanks for listening. ❖

Sweden II

October 18, 1976

Yesterday I talked about Swedens tax policies as something that might have ~~made~~ had something to do with the recent election. Ill be right back.

* Gunnar Strang served as the Swedish Minister of Finance from 1955 to 1976. Following the change in government in the fall of 1976, the Finance Ministry was dissolved and replaced with two separate ministries, the Budget Ministry and the Ministry for Economic Affairs. Ingemar Mundebo headed the Budget Ministry, and Gosta Bohman headed the Ministry of Economic Affairs.

Whenever govt. tries to do things that aren't properly govts. province ~~we~~ *the people* pay in the loss of freedom & individual rights. Yesterday I told you about Swedens tax policies which ranged from 40% of the average workers income to more than 100% of earnings above $33,000. I suggested this might have had something to do with the recent election when Swedens 40 yrs. of socialism ~~was~~ *were* repudiated by the voters.

But it wasn't just money in my opinion. Socialism, ~~collectivism, statism~~ exacts a ~~higher~~ price far dearer than money. In an effort to ease the tax burden the people of Sweden have resorted to barter. A dentist or doctor needing a few house repairs will exchange treatment for carpenter or plumbing work with a patient skilled in those crafts. *The shoe merchant & the grocer trade in each others stock.*

Govt. of course responded. The Sec. of Justice* took the position that crimes against society are more dastardly than crimes against individuals. In other words it's worse to be a tax dodger than a thief or a burglar. So under this philosophy and with govt's. natural tendency to invoke emergency as an excuse Swedens civil liberties began to erode.

A law was passed to "secure evidence in taxation cases." Tax authorities suddenly had the right to search any office or factory at any time without offering the usual evidence necessary to get a warrant. They did get a court order to search private dwellings but the citizen is not notified he's under suspicion nor is he warned of the coming of the tax authorities.

Professional privacy—the traditional relationship between Dr. & patient no longer exists where the tax police are concerned. In one case which fortunately got wide publicity the tax police not only checked a Dr's. files they then went through the files of thousands of patients back through the years,

Maybe it's time for us to ask if we are *still* safe in our books & records—one of the basic rights we fought for in the American Revolution. Internal Revenue dosen't think so and certainly their is violation of the private ~~nature~~ relationship between banker & depositor where questions of inc. tax are concerned.

It was probably the indignity of govt. invading ~~indi~~ their privacy more than the actual tax burden that prompted the people of Sweden to vote against 40 yrs. of socialist rule.

This is RR Thanks for listening. ❖

Tax Reform I

November 2, 1976

When is tax reform not tax reform? When it's a tax increase. And we've just had one. I'll be right back.

* Reagan is most likely referring to Lennar Geijer, who served as Sweden's Minister of Justice from 1969 to 1976.

In this election season we've been told the inc. tax structure is a disgrace; that it falls heavily on some & provides loopholes for others. Well the inc. tax is a disgrace but not *necessarily* for the reason I've just given. It costs all of us too much because govt. costs too much. It is so complicated even the person of modest earnings must get legal or professional help to find out how much he or she owes each April 15th. Eve~~n~~ *And* ~~t~~*T*he Internal Rev. Svc. employees ~~who are supposed to~~ *cant* help us ~~through the burocratic language of the tax forms cannot agree on what that language really says.~~ *because they dont understand the rules & regulations either.*

A man in Atlanta Georgia took all of his records to the I.R.S. office~~. Helpful hands~~ *where the staff on duty* at the time worked out a final fig. on what he owed the govt. He then took the same records to the I.R.S. office in Rome Geo. where he got a different answer. More than a little curious *by this time* he crossed statelines with those same records visiting all in all 5 different I.R.S. offices. ~~and~~ *H*e wound up with 5 dif. answers as to how much he should send the govt.—I hope he paid the lowest amount. *Maybe to play safe he added them up & divided by 5.*

~~We need a tax reduction but to have that the cost of govt. must be reduced.~~ We need tax reform that will simplify the process of finding out how much tax to pay. Ah! But haven't we just had a tax reform? Well in a way—yes. ~~You cant help~~ but ~~think of~~ *What else can you call* 1500 pages of new inc. tax law~~? as a The answer to that is, call it~~ *a book 5 inches thick? If we are honest we'll call what's just been cooked up by congress* a tax increase. ~~No matter how they juggled the rules and regulations around the bill passed by Congress and signed into law will net the govt.~~ *because the govt. is going to get* $1.6 Bil. more than it was getting under the old rules. ~~*And that in any language is a tax increase.*~~

It is true most of ~~this~~ *the increase* will come from ~~those~~ income on investments which means there will be less investment and therefore slower ec. growth, fewer jobs and less income to tax down the road aways. ~~Our capital stock per worker is increasing at half the rate it was in the 1950's.~~ ~~Could it be~~ ~~*It could be*~~ ~~that's why we have a higher percentage of workers unemployed~~ ~~*now*~~ ~~than we had 20 yrs. ago?~~ ~~*Yes it is*~~ *We dont have the plant & equipment to provide employment for a growing labor force.* But beware the Ides of March (if I can paraphrase Shakespeare). ~~That's about the time we'll be wading through the new tax forms.~~ The new tax reform is 1500 pages—as ~~5 inch. thick book and~~ *I said has been studied by* some pretty sound economists *who* claim ~~they~~ ~~*they've studied it but*~~ *they* cant understand it. So tax reform turne~~ds~~ out to be no tax cut for any, a tax raise for some and more headaches for all.

Oh yes—about those loopholes. It's time we recognized this as the big, perennial fairy tale it really is. About 60% of total deductions are non taxed ~~inc.~~ social security~~, &~~ *payments*, pension inc. and unemployment insurance plus the $750 exemption we all take for ourselves & our familys. ~~Then~~ O~~f~~*n* top of that ~~then~~ comes the standard non itemized deduction the average earner takes, int. on mortgage payments, medical costs, *local & state taxes* & contributions to church & charity. Actually 95% of all inc. tax deductions *the so called loopholes* are taken by people of average inc. or less.

We still need tax reform. This is R.R. Thanks for listening. ❖

Tax Reform II
November 2, 1976

Yesterday I talked about tax reform that wasn't tax reform. Now hear where some of your tax *money* is going. Ill be right back.

The other day a news story caught my eye and in case you missed it here are the highlights.

We all are familiar with that curved glass building on the Hudson in N.Y. City, the modern tower of Babel where the U.N. delegates toil so much & produce so little. But I was surprised & maybe you will be too, to learn there are some 10,000 U.N. employes in what is called the United Nations European Headquarters in Geneva Switzerland.

~~Those 10,000 employees are not exactly underprivileged.~~

I know it's customary to give some bonus or extra pay to overseas personell but I always thought that was to compensate for *the* hardship of living in primitive or unattractive areas climatewise etc. Geneva Switzerland ~~does~~ *hardly* qualifies as such. Let me assure you the 10,000 U.N. employees there are not exactly underprivileged.

Messengers who push a cart through the corridors doling out inter-office mail receive $413 a week. According to the ~~press a~~ *news story* a press officer who serves as liaison with the "German speaking press" gets $1000 a week. Secretaries struggle along on $350 and junior executives draw $555.

All 10,000 get at least 6 weeks pd. vacation a year. And among the other fringe benefits are allowances for their childrens schooling, extra pay for speaking foreign languages and extremely good pensions. Just one other thing I shouldn't overlook; because they work for an international org. they dont have to pay any income tax at all.

The director of the U.N. Press Division in N.Y. explains that under General Assembly Regulations they must pay the best prevailing rate in any community where they are stationed. Yes I can understand that a delegate or employee from an underdeveloped nation *where living costs & salaries are very low* must be paid commensurate with the pay scale of the land where he'll be ~~living~~ stationed but this still dosen't explain what's going on in Geneva.

~~The~~ An official at the Swiss embassy in Wash. says the average messenger working for the Swiss govt. in Geneva earns between $135 & $212 a week which is considerably less than *the* $413 *the U.N. pays*. He adds that by any standard U.N. pay scales are tops.

Perhaps you already know but in case you dont Uncle Sam still picks up ¼ of the total tab for *the cost of* the United Nations. Not too long ago Congress didn't feel that was enough and proposed increasing our contribution by $44 mil. We <u>are</u> a generous people.

This is R R. Thanks for listening ❖

When Reagan taped this broadcast, Rhodesia and Angola were deeply involved in civil strife as they moved from minority rule and colonialism to black rule and full independence. In Angola, despite the swearing-in of a transitional government on January 31, 1975, the three principal factions in the country descended into conflict. By summer, the transitional authority collapsed with the Popular Movement for the Liberation of Angola (MPLA) seizing most of the official offices in Luanda. In 1976, African nationalists Robert Mugabe and Joshua Nkomo came together in the Patriotic Front, which brought political pressure on the white-ruled government of Rhodesia. In 1980, Mugabe became prime minister of Zimbabwe, the name adopted for Rhodesia the previous year.*

Africa
November 2, 1976

I dont know about you but I'm concerned—scared is the proper word—about what is going on in Africa. I'll be right back.

Many Americans have interpreted our interest in Africa as an extension of our own desire to achieve racial equality and elimination of injustice based on race. I'm afraid that is ~~an~~ *a naive* oversimplification of what is really at issue.

First of all much of the conflict is between people of the same race. Blacks are killing Blacks in the guerilla war in Rhodesia and Angola where ~~the~~ peace has not really come as yet. Africas history is one of tribal divisions and warfare going back over the centuries. Ancient hatreds still exist.

I have a letter from a Rhodesian Senator who opposes majority rule. He says the countries black ~~majority~~ *population* is divided between 2 major tribes ~~the~~ who would be at each others throats if it weren't for the buffer offered by

* The National Front for the Liberation of Angola and the National Union for the Total Independence of Angola were the other two principal political factions in the country. During the final decades of the cold war, the Marxist MPLA received support from the Soviet Union and the other parties received support from the United States and South Africa. Despite a peace accord in 1994 and an attempt at a national unity government in 1997 and 1998, civil war continued. In early 2002, however, a cease-fire was declared and the warring parties began implementing the peace accord.

the Ian Smith regime.* Well of course you say that's a white Sen. trying to preserve the status quo. The Sen. is black & a cheif of one of those 2 tribes.—50% of Rhodesias Sen. is black.

Then the Sen. says, ~~"Rhodesia is a land of beauty. It's peoples over the past decade~~ "We are facing the brunt of a communist backed insurgency, the sole purpose of which is to overthrow our const. our way of life & above all our freedom."

Democracy, majority rule, is a desirable thing for people everywhere. But on the basis of freedom to vote and choose between rival political parties as we do democracy is not ~~the~~ a common thing in the ~~more than~~ almost half a hundred new & emerging nations of Africa. Only 5 (and that includes Rhodesia & S. Africa) have more than one pol. party. The rest are mil. or civilian dictatorships allowing no civil liberties. In most of Africa they believe in 1 man, 1 vote,—once. Whoever gets in power cancels out the opposition.

Mozambique is the staging area for the terrorist attacks on Rhodesia. It is completely totalitarian, *&* communist. Religion is outlawed & thousands of it's people (including an Am. missionary) are in concentration camps.

~~There I've said that word—communist. Well what~~ *What* does the Soviet U. have to say about the African problem? *Well* Moscow defines the goal as the use of black power to "strangle the imperialists (that's us) economically."

Pravda reveals very clearly what the African problem is all about and we'd better pay attention. ~~because it bears a hammer & sickle trademark.~~ Here it is translated from the Russian—outlining the, "losses they hope to inflict on the U.S."~~—Quote "In US im,~~ *Pravda says* "In U.S. imports the share of strategic raw materials imported from Africa amounts to 100% of the industrial diamonds, 58% of the uranium, 44% of the manganese, which is used in the steel smelting industry, 36% of the cobalt, essential for aircraft engines & high strength alloys, 33% of its oil and 23% of its chromium used in the mgfr. of armor, aircraft engines & gun barrels."

The African problem is a Russian ~~missile—complete with hammer & sickle trademark—aimed at us.~~ *weapon aimed at us.*

This is R.R. Thanks for listening. ❖

The Communes
November 2, 1976

The "counter culture" of the 60's is far enough behind us to allow, with the perspective of history some evaluation & judgement. I'll be right back.

* Ian Smith became the prime minister of Southern Rhodesia in April 1964 and continued to serve in that post when the country declared its independence from Great Britain on November 11, 1965, and became a republic on March 2, 1970. As black rule was being installed, Smith held the post of minister without portfolio from May to December 1979. He served in the Zimbabwean Parliament until 1987.

We remember the decade of the 60's as a time of riot in our streets and schools. It's easy to lay it all to the war in V.N. & the struggle for civil rights but this cant explain the social revolution entirely; the generation gap, "dont trust anyone ~~under~~ *over* 30" or the rejection of virtually every custom, tradition and rule of the adult world. There was rebellion against something called the establishment.

One of the symbols of the revolution was the rejection of the life style in which they had been raised and in which their parents still lived. Professing idealism, love for everyone (which still didn't keep them from stoning anyone in authority) they rejected privacy in their living arrangements and took up communal living. There were no more couples, just groups called communes, a rejection of the workaday, selfish, money grubbing world of their elders.

The communes aren't entirely a thing of the past. Some of the alienated still live that way even though they approach or have passed that dividing line of age 30.

~~A few years~~ Two members of the counter culture set out on an 8 mo. tour to find out how their contemporaries were doing. They visited communes around the country and wrote *of* their findings ~~up~~ in a book published by Doubleday entitled "The Children of the Counterculture." * The children they write about are not the children who took up communal living in the 60's. They are now parents and the book is about their offspring. Remember now the authors started their project while still as anti-establishment as the people they were writing about. One of them allowed her own pre-school children to puff on marijuana joints when they were being passed around. In their own words they believed "regular schools were prisons and Americans strangle their children with rules, routines & expectations." They seem to have changed a little and if you worry sometimes about being old fashioned in the way you raise your children, read their book even though it isn't very pretty.

There is a 10 yr. old commune lad whose mother seduced [him] when he was 6 so he wouldn't have any Oedipus complex or hang up. A 12 yr. old scrounges for pennies to pay for a mind control course. On the whole they found commune children illiterate, suffering emotional disturbances and unaware of even such things as flush toilets. Mainly their parents wanted them out of sight and mind.

By contrast some communes demanded a harsh conformity. Individualism—even crying was put down as childish self indulgence. This from parents who had chosen their drug, drenched life style as a rebellion against conformity. In one such commune they had their own school, a bare ugly place with straw mats on ~~the~~ *a* floor littered with orange peels and ~~gab~~ garbage. The authors saw a child with chicken pox pulled up off his straw mat & forced to at-

* John Rothchild and Susan Berns Wolf, *The Children of the Counterculture* (Doubleday: Garden City, NY, 1976).

tend a class. ~~As she~~ They wrote "the children of the flower children emerge less as human beings than experiments in radical philosophy."

The story of 10 yr. old Nina is the most poignant. She lives in the slovenly litter of the adults and her [self] "freaky" mother is baffled by her. Somewhere Nina must have seen a picture of how little girls live in that square, outside world her parents have rejected. In all the squalor her room is an immaculate island complete with neat bed spread, mirrors, curtains and teddy bears. Or could it be that in an odd moment mama revealed how she had lived when she was little? This is R.R. Thanks for listening. ❖

Bureaucrats Revisited
November 2, 1976

No matter how big our government grows it is still (if you wont think me sacriligious) capable of seeing the sparrows fall. I'll be right back

We should all be indebted to columnist James J. Kilpatrick for exposing how far and at what administrative cost the swollen forces of Fed. govt. will go to become involved with totally unimportant trivia.

Mr. Kilpatrick tells of a minor auto accident—a rear end collision in Toledo Ohio one afternoon last May. One of the cars involved sprung a seam in the gas tank resulting in a spill of about 2 gals. of gasoline. The patrolman at the scene properly called the fire dept. and the 2 gals of gasoline (obviously a fire hazard) were flushed into a storm sewer. The sewer runs into a ditch which in turn runs into the Ottawa river, which runs into Maumee Bay which opens into Lake Erie. All of these waters are under the purview of the Fed. Water Pollution Control Act.

While the firemen were efficiently ridding the accident scene of the threat of fire a Coast Guard ~~offi~~ inspector driving by on his way home witnessed this flushing of 2 gals of gas into Petersons ditch. And thereby begins a story attesting to the ridiculousness of ~~much~~ which govt. is capable.

Roughly one month later a report was filed with the Marine Safety office in Toledo citing the ~~owner~~ *driver* of the car with the leaking gas tank as the discharger of pollutants into the waters of the U.S. Another representive of the Coast Guard investigated & confirmed the report. A photographer was sent to photograph the scene of the crime. A Capt. reviewed the evidence & sent his report on to the chief of the Marine Safety Div. And 2 weeks later Gogolin & Sons Inc. received a letter threatening them with a civil penalty of up to $5000.

Oh yes—I should have mentioned the driver originally ~~sen~~ cited was driving a Van owned by Gogolin & Sons Inc. ~~Now~~ So the company was charged with discharging oil in harmful ~~amounts~~ quantities into Peterson ditch.

To any of you who may carry a cigarette lighter, take care when you fill it. Dont spill any of the fluid near a gutter or Big Brother will have you up for endangering the worlds water supply.

The final officer in this whole chain of events—the one bringing the charge against Gogolin & Sons Inc. followed up his ~~cha letter which~~ threat of a $5000 liability by asking how *THEY'D FEEL ABOUT a* $50 penalty? ~~would sit with Gogolin.~~ He said; "I have preliminarily determined that amount to be an appropriate penalty after a careful review of the investigatory report, based upon my assessment of the gravity of the violation."

To their everlasting credit Gogolin & Sons Inc. dug in their heels and said, "no." Elton E. Gogolin Jr. said: "Why a small businessman should be subject to this classic example of federal harassment is beyond rational comprehension." Amen!

Columnist Kilpatrick spoke to the Officer and expressed the thought that the matter seemed too trivial for a $50 fine. The Capt. replied, "Nothing is trivial." ~~Well~~ *And* that must be true of the total administrative effort & cost to the taxpayers that went into this 2 gal. gas leak caper.

Jack Kilpatrick thank you. This is R.R. Thanks for listening. ❖

Education II
November 16, 1976

~~As long as I talked about ed. yesterday I might as well have at it again today.~~

I wonder how many of you could write the letter I received recently. ~~from~~ I'm sure most of you will agree with it. I'll be right back.

Not too long ago I rec'vd. a letter from a lady in one of our mid-western cities—not a megalopolis like Chi.—just a typical middle size city. I wont embarrass her by using her name or even identifying the city which is pretty well known to me. But I will share her letter because in a way it is a cry from the heart of America.

She wrote, "Last week my husband & I attended meetings on the proposed integration of our schools." Now let me state this is not going to be a protest ~~because of~~ *against* integration. The writer of the letter is not a bigot, is not prejudiced and the school system in her city is integrated already. ~~and~~ *It* was long before any court decision simply because the towns & cities of middle America drew no line at accepting all the children in town.

Now however she says a committee has been set up by the school board because the proportions are not the same in each school. She explains, "As it looks now, Our children will be shifted around to suit the numbers game set down by the Fed. Courts. When people seem satisfied with their lives, schools etc. why do the courts and governments, Fed. St. County & City jump in & tell us we aren't happy and that how we feel is discrimination?

Again remember the schools in her city are all integrated and funding per student is absolutely equal throughout the system so quality of ed. is as equal as money can make it.

Her letter reveals that ~~the~~ no court order is hanging over them. The school board just thinks it should do something before orders might come. She says the parents are told, "there are no neighborhood schools yet that school 7 blocks from our house is still there." *

Here is her plea, "None of our schools are closed to minority children. We have had open enrollment for several years and very few children ever change schools. That seems to indicate that everyone is pleased with their school so why must a city go through this turmoil because a few men say it must be done? Dont the masses of people have any say about their lives anymore?" Well ~~She says~~ more & more Americans are asking that question.

The school board tells her it's a voluntary program. It turns out it's only voluntary on the part of the school board. The parents have their orders & it's do it or else. She writes, "If we were rich we could send our children to pvt. schools. If we were poor ~~we~~ *the* govt. would take care of us. We are middle class so they tax us, strip us of our rights, hassle us and then tell us work because some one has to pay all those needed taxs to pay for all those unneeded programs." Then she asks, "how do we keep from being strangled *& swallowed up* by govt? One day we may find we can do nothing without asking, 'May I.' " I love my country, believe in God, family & freedom. Govt. cannot be all things to all people. We must save our pride & our ability to do things for ourselves."

This is R.R. Thanks for listening. ❖

Campaign Reminiscence
November 16, 1976

I keep getting questions ~~once~~ on some of the things that took place in the campaign. One of the most frequent has to do with my Vice Presidential suggestion. I'll be right back.

Back during the primary campaigns I departed from tradition and named in advance of the Nat. convention ~~who~~ my choice as a Vice Presidential Cand. ~~would be if I were the party's nominee.~~ Just doing this caused a little stir but the real controversy ~~that arose~~ had to do with who I had proposed *and why*. ~~I still get questions as to why.~~

During the campaign when questioned as to who my choice would be my honest answer was that I didn't know. That answer was amplified however by a statement that he would be philosophically compatible with me. I still hold with that. It dosen't make sense to choose ~~for purely pol. reasons~~ someone of an opposite pol. persuasion ~~in the service~~ ~~*interest*~~ ~~of~~ *to* balance~~ing~~ the ticket philosophically.

* Reagan is quoting her letter; although the school board claims there are no neighborhood schools, there is a school seven blocks from her house.

~~But w~~When I named Sen. Richard Schweiker* of Pa. the shock wave was pretty considerable and the reaction was that I had gone contrary to ~~my reported campaign statements—I dont think I had and maybe you'd like to hear the story from me as to the why of his selection.~~ *what I'd expressed during the campaign*. Well here is the story.

The primarys & the state conventions were over and the business of trying to sway uncommitted delegates was going on. As a challenger I didn't have some of the natural advantages in that game that go with incumbency. ~~I had another worry.~~

Hunting delegates in the large North Eastern industrial states it became evident ~~that to be~~ *there was* ~~alienation of Repub's. there and~~ a kind of separation within our party. The N.E. seemed alienated from Repub's. in the rest of the country. I wasn't interested in ~~the nomination unless it was based on a chance of victory in Nov.~~ *winning a nomination so much as winning an election*. This led to ~~thinking~~ *the idea* of using the Vice Presidency to bridge the ~~difference~~ *gap* between the rest of the country & the N.E. ~~Hence Sen. Schweiker.~~

In asking ~~him~~ *Sen. Schweiker* to be part of the ticket I did not have to compromise principle nor did he. My chairman S and long time friend Sen. Laxalt of Nev. has *for 2 yrs* been Dick Scheweikers seat mate. He told me he thought ~~both~~ Dick & I would *both* be surprised at how much we had in common. ~~and h~~*He* was right.

~~I'll frankly admit w~~ When his name came up my first reaction was that we were not compatible philosophically; that he was indeed ~~a~~ liberal in all those areas where I am conservative. But we agreed to talk & did so for 5 hours.

~~Very simply~~ I found him frank to admit that many of the programs he'd voted for *in the Sen* had turned out to be failures. He is convinced we must discontinue our costly social tinkering & look to the private sector *as we bring deficit spending to an end & balance the bud.*

We agreed on the necessity for capital punishment, opposed gun control & favored mandatory prison sentences. We both believe Detente is a failure; ~~&~~ *that* we must be more firm in dealing with the Soviet U. We both are opposed to general amnesty or pardon for draft dodgers & deserters and ~~we~~ believe we should achieve a superiority in mil. strength. He ~~had already~~ *has* introduced legis. to restore bible reading & prayer in the pub. schools. And we both believe that the act of abortion destroys a human life.

Dick Schewiker has just successfully led the fight to ~~stop using~~ *halt the use of* pub. funds to pay for abortions.** I rest my case. This is R.R. thanks for listening. ❖

* R–Pennsylvania, 1969–1981.

** The 1976 Hyde Amendment to the House Labor–H.E.W. appropriations bill excluded federal funding for abortions through Medicare. Schweiker encouraged acceptance of the amendment in the Senate, and it passed on September 17. Future Congresses reenacted variants of the Hyde Amendment in annual appropriations bills.

New Directions was a group founded in 1976 to address international issues in the same way Common Cause addresses U.S. issues. Planners of the organization included Robert S. McNamara, Dr. Theodore Hesburgh, Margaret Mead, Cyrus Vance, and Russell W. Peterson, who would be its chief executive officer.*

Liberals
November 16, 1976

As a former New Deal Demo. and I suppose at the time ~~quite~~ *something* of a liberal I have come to the conclusion that liberals aren't liberal.

I realize I may be opening a pandoras box, (to coin a cliché) but like many others I've wondered at times if the terms liberal & conservative haven't been hung on the wrong doors.

Why should a belief in individual freedom, less centralized authority in govt. and more local autonomy be called conservatism? By the same token what is liberal about wanting more govt., govt. interference in the raising of our children, compulsory govt. medicine and the confiscation & forced redistribution of a sizeable percentage of each citizens earnings?

~~I challenge that I have~~

Can anyone say that I have not honestly described the fundamental difference between what we term liberal & conservative? Several days back I ~~described~~ *told you of* a new special interest organization, a kind of international "Common Cause" named "New Directions."** As a matter of fact figures prominent in "Common Cause," John Gardner for instance turn up in this new group. One of its brochures says "It will attempt to influence the non-governmental shapers of ~~foreign~~ *national* policy—corps. banks, universities and trade assns. It will organize people in local communities to respond to local manifestations of <u>global</u> injustice or irresponsibility. And when necessary it will take its case to court."

Now I grant you none of this seems sinister, indeed it has a high sounding note but one cant deny ~~a~~ *it is* rather generalized and non-specific. ~~note.~~ Who will decide what is a ~~glo~~ "local manifestation of global injustice or irresponsibility," and whether to take the case to court?

The founders of "New Directions" actually provide the answer but I doubt if they'll appreciate what *I* see as the only interpretation of that answer. I'll quote from the By Laws of New Directions, and let me interject ~~how~~ this too is typical of liberal movements, the Bylaws are determined *in advance* by the founders not by those who will subsequently make up the rank & file mem-

* See Gladwin Hill, "Citizen Action Unit Formed in Capital," *The New York Times,* Sept. 8, 1976, p. 13.

** Reagan taped a radio address called "New Directions" about this group on November 2, 1976.

bership. They read, "The governing body of New Directions shall be it's board of directors hereinafter referred to as the Governing Board. The Governing board shall have supervision, control & direction of the affairs of New Directions, it's committees and publications; shall determine it's policies or changes therein; and shall supervise the disbursement of it's funds."

~~The board by the way has already~~

Those who make up the rank & file membership will accept bylaws already adopted & in addition a governing board already in existence. ~~The Again~~ By a kind of intelectual inbreeding process the board is made up of names long associated with causes which shall we say see danger only if it approaches from the right—never the left. One journeyed to Hanoi in 1969 to lend moral support to Ho Chi Minh. Another saw nothing in Russias invasion of Czechoslovakia that could be called aggression. Statements & deeds like these are typical of other board members.

But my point is all associated with New Directions have impeccable "liberal" credentials but ~~their is~~ an elitism & lack of democracy characterise this newest expression of liberalism. This is R.R. Thanks for listening. ❖

Reagan's Proposition 1 to limit taxes and spending in California was defeated November 6, 1973. Michigan's 1976 effort also failed. Both state and federal taxes increased from 1972 to 1976 because of inflation of both taxable income and property valuations. California's Proposition 13, which limited property taxes, passed on June 6, 1978, setting off a spate of successful tax initiatives in other states.

Government Cost I
November 16, 1976

We all want the size, power & most of all the cost of govt. reduced dont we?—Or do we? I'll be right back.

Ask the man on the street, the housewife, the fellows at the club, everyone who pays taxes if we shouldn't have a reduction in the cost of govt. and ~~hence~~ *therefore* taxes and the answer will of course be a resounding yes. ~~I dont think anyone will disagree with this finding.~~ But that makes for a puzzlement.

A few years ago in Calif. we put an initiative on the ballot that would have limited the percentage of ~~the~~ gross earnings the state could take from the people in taxes. Every provision for flexibility in the event of emergency had been included and we could show with sound projections that growth of the economy would result in the state getting increased revenues in spite of the limitation. In fact ~~we could demonstrate that~~ under the limitation the state could STILL triple it's budget in 15 yrs. *but the taxpayers would save $45 Bil. during those years.*

Now I'm sure if you asked the people to vote on whether they wanted a bud. 3X the size we have now in just ~~13~~ *15* yrs. they'd say no. But ~~they also~~ *STILL THEY* voted no on the initiative known as prop. 1.

The state was taking about 8¾ cents of each dollar earned. With the help & support of some of the greatest economists in the country including recent Nobel prize winner Milton Friedman we had worked out a plan to gradually lower that percentage to 7¢ at the end of 15 yrs. The state however would continue to get more actual money each year because the lowered percentage was far less than the increase *in revenues* due to ec. growth.

I have since blamed that ~~lowered~~ lowering of the percentage for the defeat. Everyone who has a vested interest in the public trough rose up against prop. 1. The ed. lobby ~~sham~~ led by the Calif. Tchrs. assn. shamelessly used public funds—ed. funds if you will in their attack. Day after day children were sent home with leaflets & brochures to give to their parents.

Most of this literature & the entire campaign against Prop. I was based on an outright falsehood. ~~Ignoring the fact that t~~*T*he measure specifically forbade the state from *keeping the limit by* dumping ~~any~~ burdens on local govt. ~~they claimed over & over against that~~ *But ignoring this our opponents claimed* this would be done & local property taxes would ~~rise~~ *go up*. And because we ~~were~~ *would be* gradually lowering the ~~percentage taken in state taxes they were able to use the lie that~~ *limit to an eventual 7% they coined a campaign slogan that* if we were reducing the states share we'd have to get the money someplace.

I have believed that if we had settled for holding the percentage at the existing 8¾ cents they couldn't have used the lie. Now I discover I'm wrong. In the election just past Mich. put a measure on the ballot* to freeze the percentage of earnings *roughly 8½%* the state takes in tax ~~at the percent roughly 8½%.~~ *Except for that they had followed our plan.*

The same forces ~~snowballed to defeat do battle against it~~ *rose up to do battle;* the leadership of organized labor, pub. emp. associations & the teachers. The press reported children bringing literature ~~against it~~ home from school and they all used the same falsehood—it would increase local taxes. The measure lost.

How many more chances will we have? There are *some* 81.~~3~~ mil. people now dependent on tax dollars for there year round, year in year out living. There are only 70.~~4~~ mil. Americans working in the pvt. sector to support themselves & *their* 62.~~4~~ mil. dependents. ~~plus which they~~ *Those 70 mil.* pay all the taxes that support ~~those other~~ *the* 81 mil. This is R.R. Thanks for listening. ❖

Seven months before Reagan taped this radio essay, Foreign Secretary James Callaghan of the Labour Party became prime minister of Great Britain. He

* Proposal C was designed to amend the Michigan constitution to impose an 8.3 percent personal income limit on state taxes and spending. It was defeated on November 2, 1976. See also the radio address "Tax Limit," p. 98.

governed at a time of severe economic crisis, which included high oil prices, high inflation, unemployment, and a drop in GNP.

Britain
November 16, 1976

"There'll always be an England & England shall be free"—we sang those words a long time ago in W.W.II. I hope they are still true. I'll be right back.

Many commentators and pundits have called attention to the fact that the U.S. seems to follow a course set by the British. Many put us about 15 yrs. behind our English cousins in adopting social reforms pioneered by them.

Of late that has been a cause for alarm. Under the leadership of the ~~l~~Labor, Socialist party Britain has slid into seemingly unsolvable ec. problems. Inflation & unemployment are staggering and the value of the pound is ~~shrink~~ sinking like a modern day Titanic. Per man hour productivity in her industrial structure has gone down until the once vaunted Eng. craftsman is way behind his counterparts in all of the common mkt. countries. Still egged on by irresponsible labor leaders he asks for ~~still~~ shorter hours, higher pay and more "perks"—fringe benefits. Strikes for little or no cause are commonplace.

At last a voice has been raised and we as well as the British should ~~take~~ take heed. Surprisingly the voice comes *not* from the opposition party—the Conservatives but from a leader, indeed <u>the</u> leader of the Labor party Prime Minister Callaghan. He says, "The cosy world which we were told would go on forever, where full employment would be guaranteed by a stroke of the chancellor's pen, cutting taxes & deficit spending is gone." The P.M. it is said now sees socialism as an oversold superstition among the British working class.

If it is true that somehow we ~~p~~ take a parallel course to Britain then we'd better listen to what the labor P.M. ~~said~~ *told* the British Labor party at it's ~~Blackpool~~ recent convention. He obviously was not out to win a popularity contest and didn't but even those who jeered the loudest must have wondered if they could equal his courage.

"We must ask ourselves~~," he said, "~~unflinchingly," he said, "what is the cause of high unemployment?" And he answered his own question, "Quite simply & unequivocally it is caused by paying ourselves <u>more</u> than the value of what we produce. This is an absolute fact of life which no govt. be it left or right can alter. We have lived too long on borrowed money & even borrowed ideas and live in too troubled a world to be able in a matter of months or even a couple of years to enter the promised land."

He went on to say to his surly audience, "We used to think you could just spend your way out of a recession and increase employment by cutting taxes & boosting govt. spending, I tell you that option no longer exists and insofar as it did exist it worked by injecting inflat. into the ec." He added, "Higher inflat. followed by higher unemp. That is the hist. of the last 20 yrs."

Then he hit them with this, "We can only become competitive by having the right kind of investment at the right kind of level and by significantly improving the productivity of both labor & capital. Nor will we succeed if we use confetti money to pay ourselves more than we produce."

I wonder if Geo. Meany would like to ask him to address the AFL-CIO convention?* *And* While ~~he was~~ *he's* here ~~he could~~ maybe *he could* speak to Congress. ~~also.~~

This is R.R. Thanks for listening. ❖

On September 21, 1976, a car bomb in Washington killed Orlando Letelier, a former ambassador from Chile to the United States and cabinet member in the government of Salvador Allende.

Terrorism
November 16, 1976

It's possible that some who led the charge against the C.I.A., the FBI and police intelligence work in general ≠ *are* having & should have 2nd thoughts. I'll be right back.

In late Sept. *on the floor of Cong.* a liberal member ~~of Congress rose to~~ ~~*took the floor*~~ denounce*d* the "terrorist bombing *in Wash.* that took the life of a Chilean foe of that countries present govt. ~~The bombing took place in Wash.~~ Obviously the victem was to the left in his politics and the ~~obvious~~ *natural* assumption is that his murderer or murderers were of the ~~obv~~ opposite persuasion.

≠ Other liberal congressmen joined in demanding that the F.B.I. bring the murderers to justice.

On that same Sept. day *however* FBI director Clarence Kelly** was testifying before a committee of Cong. that his agency had reduced the number of domestic security investigations from a routine 21,000 or more a couple of years ago to a grand total at present of 626. Ŧ

This was the direct result of pressure by liberal policy makers who have been doing their best to dismantle and render ineffective all the agencies ~~that~~ whose function & responsibility is our safety. The Attorney General of the U.S. laid down the *anti*-security guidelines that now restrict the F.B.I. in its work.

Now let me interject right here I dont hold with unwarranted prying by govt. in the lives of any of us. But note that qualifying word "unwarranted." I ~~complain because~~ *object when* the census bureau which is supposed to count

* George Meany was president of the American Federation of Labor–Congress of Industrial Organizations, an umbrella union organization, from its founding in 1955 to 1979.
** Clarence M. Kelley.

us, busies itself with asking how many bathtubs we own. Governments *principal* responsibility is to protect us from each other. But at what point do we insist so much on privacy that our law enforcing agencies are unable to guard us against ~~modern~~ todays terrorism?

In ~~the~~ recent years we have been subjected to an alarming increase in bombings, arson, hi-jackings and asssassination. Last year there were more than 2000 bombings causing 69 deaths. In the last 5 yrs. 43 policemen have been killed in terrorist violence. ~~It is estimated that some 15,000 people are involved in about 2 dozen organizations.~~ Anti-Castro Cubans in Miami have been blown to eternity in a number of bombings. A bomb in N.Y. was directed against the Gov. of Puerto Rico, the New World Liberation Front claims credit for bombing the So. African consulate in S.F.

In the face of all this we have forced police in our cities to destroy mil's. of intelligence files on revolutionary groups. The House Internal Security Comm. has been abolished and I've told you about the restraints on the F.B.I. ~~Mainly~~ The principle attack ~~against~~ has been against ~~a~~ F.B.I. agents joining terrorist groups to learn their plans. But a few yrs. ago there was no objection when ~~a heroic~~ an F.B.I. agent joined the K.K.K. and identified the murderers of young civil rights activists. Had he been exposed his life would have been forfeit.

Well the F.B.I. estimates there are some 15,000 ~~individuals~~ *terrorists* in roughly two dozen groups or organizations in this country and they ~~are~~ threaten us from the left. ~~Now I~~ The only effective way of dealing with this kind of guerilla viciousness is to infiltrate as heroic agents once infiltrated the Klan.

Do you know if the F.B.I.—the C.I.A. and our local police do this I wont feel for one minute that my constitutional right of privacy has been endangered. This is RR Thanks for listening. ❖

During the 1976 presidential campaign, Governor Jimmy Carter declared: "I do not favor a blanket amnesty, but for those who violated Selective Service laws, I intend to grant a blanket pardon." On January 21, 1977, the day after he was inaugurated, President Jimmy Carter honored his controversial campaign pledge.

Pardons
November 30, 1976

†It goes without saying that a criminal is someone who breaks ~~the~~ the law. Is he any less a ~~lawbreaker~~ *criminal* simply because time has gone by since he broke the law? I'll be right back.

We the people traditionaly hold as one of the most admirable traits of those who take pub. office that they try to keep their campaign promises. But what if a candidate in campaigning expresses an intention to do something ~~*wh*~~ *if elected* ~~and there is good reason to believe the majority of people do not feel that what he has proposed doing should be done?~~ which the majority of people dont think should be done? *NEVERTHELESS* They elect him because the particular issue is outweighed by other considerations.

I believe we have such a situation with Pres. Elect Carter. He stated that while he would not favor amnesty for those who avoided service in the V.N. war either by draft evasion or desertion he would grant them a pardon & expressed the belief there was a difference. The dictionary goes to some length to explain no such difference exists. Amnesty means to pardon & vice versa.

Whatever our feelings about the *VN.* war those who fled our land broke the law. To grant a blanket forgiveness regardless of whether there is repentance or not; to ignore that while some may have been motivated by principle others simply were running for cover is to set a precedent that will haunt us for years to come.

There has never been a blanket amnesty after an American war. Lincoln pardoned deserters if they returned & served out their enlistments without pay. Coolidge granted amnesty to 100 deserters who had deserted after the armistice in WWI. In 1933 Roosevelt pardoned 1500 draft evaders—after they had served their sentences. After WWII Truman granted amnesty to 1523 out of 15,803 violaters after a review of each individual case. In 1952 he granted amnesty to peacetime deserters who left their units between WWII & the Korean war. There was no amnesty following the Korean war & indeed ~~there~~ going back to Geo. Wash. there has never been an unconditional amnesty for deserters or draft evaders.

Some 55,000 young men gave their lives in VN. Others will bear grievous wounds for the rest of their lives. I'm sure none of them wanted to go to war but they accepted the responsibility we all have to meet certain demands of the society in which we live.

Another group endured the longest most brutal captivity ever imposed on American fighting men~~.~~, ~~They endu~~ accepting unbelievable torture because they knew there are some things men must be willing to die for if civilization is to be preserved.

Now a few thousand wives, children & parents go through torture waiting for the final word on husbands, fathers & sons who are still unaccounted for—listed as missing in action. Some of these who wait and some of those returned Prisoners are asking their fellow Americans to help in a program to circulate petitions asking the Pres. elect to reconsider his position with regard to ~~pardoning those~~ *a blanket pardon.* They have written to all the former P.O.Ws. ~~they can reach but they need some help from all of us to mail out the petitions etc. Contributions would help~~ *asking for contributions to help with getting out the petitions.* They wouldn't mind if some of the rest of us pitched in. The address is Americans Against Amnesty—Box 1397 Albuquerque N. Mex.—This is R.R. Thanks for listening

† Pete lets put this in the 1st 5 on Dec. 2nd RR ❖

Twelve days before Reagan recorded this broadcast, Milton Friedman received the Nobel Prize for economics in Stockholm, Sweden. A protester shouted, "Friedman go home," and "Long live the Chilean people." *

Milton Friedman and Chile
December 22, 1976

When ~~I~~ *Dr.* Milton Friedman ~~head~~ *leader* of the school of economics at Chi. U.** received the Nobel Prize demonstrators were on hand to protest. ~~They were—if nothing else economically illiterate.~~ I'll be right back.

~~The~~ A great many people in America & the world have been sold a bill of goods with regard to one of our latin American neighbors—the country of Chile. This was evident recently when protestors demonstrated against the awarding of the Nobel prize for ec's. to Dr. Milton Friedman.

Dr. Friedman's qualifications for being named a Nobel laureate are beyond question and certainly ~~merit an~~ more outstanding than many who have received ~~a Nobel prize.~~ *that honor in the past.* ~~But~~ But the demonstrators weren't challenging his award on the grounds that he lacked ~~qualification~~ *stature* in his field. No the good & eminent leader of the *Chi. U.* school of economics was a target because he accepted an invitation to go to Chile about 2 yrs. ago.

Chile was *is* on the liberal list of places *not* to go because a military junta overthrew the govt. of Pres. Allendé.*** Allende it is true was elected to office~~.~~ *&* ~~T~~*t*he present govt. of Chile seized power by force. ~~and a~~*A*pparently that is only acceptable in ~~liberal~~ *some* ~~*circles.*~~ circles if the overthrowing is done by communists—Castro in Cuba, N.VN's. conquering of S.V.N., Russian tanks rolling into Czechoslovakia. The military rulers of Chilé dont meet that qualification.

Just for the record the late, supposedly, democratic (with a small d) Allende was a Marxist and proved it by seizing businesses, industries, banks & agriculture making them state owned. Then he ordered great wage increases while refusing to allow price increases. There was of course a breif period of seeming prosperity ~~but then came~~ *followed of course by* the inevitable inflation. ~~The~~ ~~m~~*M*oney was virtually worthless but *then* there wasn't anything to buy with it ~~anyway.~~ *because production had fallen off.*

~~When the~~ *At the time the* Allende regime was *over*thrown the inflation rate ~~was~~ *had reached* 1000%. That means a $ by the end of the year was worth a dime and in the 2nd year the dime ~~was~~ ~~*would be*~~ *was* worth a penny. Sales &

* "Americans Who Swept 5 Nobels Get $160,000 Prizes," *The New York Times*, December 11, 1976, p. 3.
** University of Chicago.
*** Salvador Allende Gossens.

production were at an all time low. *More than 400 industries were govt. owned as were all the banks.*

Upon assuming power the military junta invited Prof. Friedman & some associates sneeringly called by some "the Chicago boys," to come to Chile and talk *to them* about economics. ~~Around~~ *In true Friedman tradition* 20 months ago the Generals took the drastic ~~course~~ *action* politicians find so impractical. They set out to balance the budget, slashing spending ruthlessly. Austerity was the order of the day. They began selling to private citizens the banks & industries Allende had seized.—~~t~~*The 400* ~~*are down to*~~ *govt. owned industries were reduced to 50 and all the banks are back in private ownership.*

~~There was deep recession. But that recession~~ *The deep recession* bottomed out a year ago and slowly but surely the economy is improving. The rate of inflation is no longer 1000%. Last year it was down to 340% & this year it's ~~aroun~~ only half ~~of that~~ as much. Unemployment is down by one fourth and real wages—(purchasing power of workers) ha~~s~~*ve* gone up 10% over last year. The new Chilean govt. is inviting foreign capital to invest and in a kind of man bites dog twist is pressuring ~~govt.~~ business to be more free & less dependent on govt.

It seems when Milton Friedman talked someone in Chile listened. Wouldn't it be nice if *just once* someone in Wash. would ask—"What did he say"?—

This is RR Thanks for listening. ❖

Tax Limit
December 22, 1976

When is a conflict of Interest not a conflict of interest? When those who live on tax dollars have the muscle to prevent ~~cuts in~~ *limits on* govt. spending and taxing. I'll be Rite Back.

A few weeks ago I spoke about the Michigan tax limitation plan that was defeated by the voters on Nov. 2nd.* It had been based on the Calif. plan ~~known as proposition 1~~ which was defeated in 1972. Very simply both plans called for recognition that all efforts up to now to control govt. spending have failed and that the answer ~~lay~~ *lies* in establishing what percentage of the ~~peoples~~ *total* earnings *of the people* the govt. should be allowed to take in taxes. The Mich. proposal would have set that percentage at the present level 8.3%.

~~I called attention to the fact that t~~*T*he same groups opposed the plan in Mich. as in Calif. and used the same methods—namely falsehoods & distortions. ~~to achieve their purpose. Well now the facts are available and my charges have been proven correct. For one thing i~~*I*n both states the opponents were mainly those who have a personal stake in not limiting taxes because

* See radio address, "Government Cost I," p. 91.

they live on tax dollars. And the false*hoods* ~~charges~~ were that state costs would be transferred to local govt. causing an increase in property taxes. ~~Both~~ ~~i~~*I*n Mich. & Calif. the ~~ballot~~ measures specifically prohibited such a transfer. In Calif. we've just had an horrendous increase in property taxes without the limitation.

The Michigan Education Assn. is ecstatically claiming credit for the defeat of the tax limitation plan. But in their Nov. 8 bulletin they generously give credit to the other organizations who helped. They list 44 groups of which 31 are organizations dependent on tax $ for their existence ~~or the purpose for which they are organized. Then there~~ Among the others are ~~the AFL CIO, the United Auto Workers, League of Women Voters and other~~ groups who generally lobby for ~~govt.~~ social reform programs.

But the Mich. Ed. Assn. has the right to take credit even though the Gov. sent state employees ~~into~~ *on state time into* the hustings to campaign against the limitation. The Assn. spent $20,000 on Polls in Sept. which revealed the people were in *overwhelming* support of ~~limiting~~ a *limit on* state spending & taxing. This triggered the FRIGHTEND 93,000 teacher organization into putting $228,000 into the campaign.

The Exec. Dir. of the Assn. Herman Coleman says, "there was no question ~~but~~ that proposal c was seen as a threat by our union members everywhere in the state." He also says "the vote means the M.E.A. has come of age as a significant pol. force in this state. We have the ability to deliver." Incidentally the 2nd largest contributor was the Am. Fed. of St. County & Municipal Employees. Coleman further explains that a fair, flexible tax syst. is essential to upgrade the teaching profession including salaries.

A Dem. St. Sen. who chairs the Sen. Taxation Comm. sums up the teachers interest by saying, "If the issue passed they wouldn't have their cookie jar anymore." The educators have a pending demand for a 2% increase in the state inc. tax plus the right of teachers to strike.

In the Nov. 8 bulletin of Colemans organization there is a claim that they elected 75% of their endorsed candidates to the legislature. Their parent organization the N.E.A. boasts that on Nov. 2nd they elected 83% of their candidates to the U.S. Cong. Mr. Coleman says "We think we know how the game is played and how to succeed at it."

~~So much for the tax spenders.~~ It is time for the taxpayers to learn ~~ab a little about~~ how the game is played. ~~and~~ *With our employees lobbying for tax increases we'd better realize* that a percentage limit on taxes is our only hope. This is RR Thanks for listening. ❖

The following radio address was handwritten by Reagan and typed, but apparently never taped. Its typed version was found with other typescripts for the December 22, 1976, taping.

Planned Economy
December 22, 1976

In the interest of morale boosting and day brightening I'm going to see if I can make you feel better about this land of ours. Ill be right back.

A young executive of the Adolph Coors Co. in Colorado has found himself on the mashed potato circuit now and then speaking out for free enterprise. He's earned the right and it isn't the only way he's defened the American way.

Steve Ritchie is a graduate of the air force academy and a Vietnam Veteran. One of the most highly decorated Americans in our national history he has the Air Force cross, 4 silver stars, 10 distinguished flying crosses & 24 air medals. He's a little irritated by those people who would trade what we have for a govt. planned & controlled economy.

He points out that our poverty line—the income level that we declare is poverty in our society is 800% higher than the worlds average inc. ~~And~~ He emphasizes that is ~~the~~ *800% above the* worlds <u>average</u> inc. not it's poverty level.

His warning to us is summed up in his statement that, "Govt. controls, govt. regulations, and govt. planning are old, tired, rejected ideas that have never worked, and are not working anywhere in the world today."

Steve has inspired me to do a little comparing ~~with~~ of our situation with that of the most planned society in the world. ≠ One of our economists once said that if a Martian spaceship should circle the world looking for the best planned economy they would pick the one that wasn't planned—our own.

We all know we have inflation, high prices hang over us like a cloud. They are probably more on our minds than anything else. But let's do a little looking on the bright side. That most planned country I mentioned is of course the Soviet Union.

~~Now f~~For the comparison we have to deal in average earnings. We find the worker in Russia has to work anywhere from 2x to 10x as long as his American counterpart for the simple necessities of life and the occasional luxuries if they are available in Russia at all are fantastically higher than in America.

A Soviet worker puts in 3½ hours for hamburger an American can earn with 34 min's. of ~~work~~ work. For eggs it's 10 mins. in Am. & 97 in Russia. Apples that take 16 mins. of work here take 5½ hours there. Butter ~~is~~ *takes* almost 9x as much work in the Soviet Utopia, shoes 6x as long, soap more than 8 times. Your wife can bring home a new dress ~~for~~ and you'll only have to work ⅐ th. ~~of the time~~ *as long as* a Russian ~~would put in~~ husband. Thats something to remember when ~~that the~~ *she comes home with a* new Easter outfit.

There is one thing where they beat us—according to the shoppers who did the comparative buying. Potatoess would take 8 min. work in America & only 7 in Russia—except that there weren't any potatos ~~available~~ *for sale* in ~~the~~ *the* Russian ~~markets~~ *stores*. This is RR Thanks for listening. ❖

Part Three

1977

Jimmy Carter took the oath of office as president of the United States on January 20, 1977.

The terrain had changed. When Reagan wrote his 1975 essays, he was considering a challenge to a sitting Republican president, Gerald R. Ford. When he resumed his radio commentaries and newspaper columns in 1976, after he lost the nomination to Ford, he was supporting Ford against the Democratic candidate, Jimmy Carter. But once Carter took office, Reagan had a potential Democratic opponent. He did not attack Carter directly; he wrote about issues. But his essays express a lot of specific disagreement with administration policy on taxes, energy, foreign affairs, and defense.

Peter Hannaford and Michael Deaver, who together ran the public relations firm that managed Reagan's schedule, found him in greater demand than ever. Reagan was an invited guest on the Sunday morning public affairs television programs like *Meet the Press* and *Issues and Answers*. He appeared on television programs hosted by Merv Griffin and Phil Donahue. Tickets sold out when he was the featured speaker at Republican fundraisers.[1] In an August 1977 Gallup Poll, Reagan was the first choice of Republicans for the 1980 nomination by 26 percent to 16 percent over the nearest contender, Gerald Ford.[2]

One of Carter's first actions, on January 21, 1977, was to pardon the 10,000 or so men who evaded the military draft between August 4, 1964, and March 28, 1973. The pardon did not cover the 100,000 deserters or 500,000 servicemen who received dishonorable discharges, yet it was highly unpopular, especially among conservatives. Other Carter initiatives met with a more mixed reaction on the right; on January 27 Carter proposed a bill to cut some taxes, raise others, and create public service jobs, legislation that would eventually be signed in May.[3] In April he proposed an energy program of higher prices for fuel and various tax credits and rebates, but the proposals went nowhere and in October Carter blamed the oil industry. Carter approved plans for creating the Department of Energy on August 4.

One issue above all, however, energized many on the right, though they could not stop it. Turning the Panama Canal over to Panama had been an issue in the 1976 primaries; Reagan had first spoken strongly about it in the fall of 1975.[4] The Carter administration continued what the Nixon-Ford administrations had undertaken—bilateral negotiations that would result in two agreements—and Reagan continued to be concerned about the security implications. He did numerous radio commentaries on Panama and the canal in 1977 and addressed it in speeches.

A few days after one such speech, in early February, President Carter appointed Sol Linowitz and Ellsworth Bunker co-negotiators for the Panama Canal Treaties.[5] Reagan continued to oppose the treaties, especially in his newspaper columns and radio commentaries. On April 30, Ambassador Linowitz briefed Reagan on the negotiations during a lunch meeting at the Madison Hotel in Washington. Nancy Reagan and Peter Hannaford were also in attendance, and Hannaford later recalled: "We talked it over afterward, agreeing that it was something of a compliment for the Carter administration to assume that Ronald Reagan might have it in his power to mount so strong a campaign against a new treaty as a private citizen that he could derail its course."[6] The day after meeting with Linowitz, Reagan appeared on *Meet the Press* and said: "I do not believe that we should be . . . negotiating to give away the Canal or to give up our sovereign rights, and our rights of defense of the Canal, and I shall oppose that."[7] Reagan was now the leading conservative critic of the new Carter administration.

On June 9, Reagan gave a major foreign policy address in New York. One of his themes, often included in his 1977 radio commentaries, was that the Carter administration's foreign policy was marked by a double standard:

> If human rights around the world are going to be our principal concern, then we must adhere to a single, not a double standard in our policy. For example, if we deplore alleged violations of human rights in Chile, Argentina and Brazil, can we ignore them in Panama?
>
> Can we, on humanitarian grounds, carry on a constant drumbeat of criticism toward South Africa and Rhodesia at the same time we talk of recognizing a regime in Cambodia that has butchered as much as a third of its population? . . . [T]he new Administration's foreign policy has aimed most of its human rights criticisms at governments which are no threat to others and which, despite not always behaving precisely as we might like, have nevertheless been our friends. . . . [O]ur asserting a strong belief in human rights is an important part of our moral ethic. But, we need our friends.[8]

Reagan continued the critique of détente that he had made when he challenged Ford to be the Republican Party's presidential nominee the previous year: "We [the United States] saw détente as a relaxation of tensions and an opportunity, through trade and cultural exchanges, to gradually modify the Soviet system. They [the Soviets] saw it otherwise." This speech also attracted wide interest.[9]

President Carter and General Omar Torrijos Herrera signed the Panama Canal treaties on September 7, 1977. The next day the national spotlight was again focused on Reagan, when he testified before a subcommittee of the U.S. Senate Judiciary Committee on the Panama Canal treaties. The core of his testimony, for which a handwritten draft exists,[10] was that the canal was part of the U.S. defense perimeter; giving it to Panama would hurt U.S. strategic interests. In an interview for the September 19 issue of *Newsweek*, Reagan said: "No one can guarantee that we can keep this waterway [the Panama Canal] open to the world without the right of sovereignty, which we are giving away."[11]

Most of the country agreed with Reagan on the canal. In a September 27, 1977, Gallup Poll, 45.5 percent of the adults surveyed opposed turning the canal over to Panama; only 35.7 percent approved.

The Panama Canal treaties, foreign policy double standards with a long list of countries, and a flawed U.S.-Soviet détente relationship were among Reagan's main foreign policy themes in 1977. He addressed defense policy issues as well. For instance, in his radio commentaries Reagan questioned President Carter's announcement on June 30 that he would halt production of the B-1 bomber.

But the country's concerns were primarily the domestic economic situation and energy problems. In 1977—as throughout the late 1970s—respondents told the Gallup Poll that the most important problem facing the country was the economic situation—inflation, taxes, and unemployment—by a wide margin. Energy—shortages, fuel prices, and energy policy in general—held second place. Together they almost always accounted for well over 50 percent, outweighing foreign policy and national defense by a 5-to-1 margin.[12]

In his radio commentaries Reagan continued to hammer away at the economic problems of inflation, taxing, spending, and regulation. He criticized Carter's economic policy proposals, instead recommending across-the-board income tax cuts and the indexing of tax brackets for inflation, so that inflation would not continually increase the tax burden and provide government with additional funds to spend. Even more fundamental was Reagan's support for limiting the percentage of income the government could take in taxes. He reflected on the need to reform federal programs including social security and food stamps. He criticized overregulation and wasteful government spending and supported privatization of some government services.

By the end of the year, Reagan had solidified his position as President Carter's most forceful challenger from the right.

Korea
January 19, 1977

There are 2 Koreas as there once were 2 Vietnams. Are we being conditioned to sell out S.K. as we did S. Vietnam? Ill be right back.

News leaks from the inner sanctum of the Justice Dept. have led to a journalistic carnival over the doings of a S. Korean businessman Tongsun Park* who domiciled in Wash. D.C. According to the headlines Mr. Park & unnamed officials of the S. Korean govt. eased the rigors of life in the U.S. Congress by showering on an unspecified number of Congressmen gifts, ~~of~~ cash and trips to Korea.

The objective was to firm up opposition to those who would have us withdraw our forces from S. Korea. Now no one can condone bribery or influence buying but certainly we can understand the fear ~~engendered by those shrill voices urging our abandonment of another ally.~~ *which might have prompted* such an attempt. S. Korea has known freedom from Colonial rule for such a short time. And in that breif period of freedom the communist forces of N.K. swept across a border only 20 miles from the S. Korean capitol and almost im-

* Park Tong Sun, also known as Tongsun Park in the United States, reportedly offered money to some American legislators in an attempt to have them encourage their colleagues to support U.S. policies toward South Korea that the government in Seoul deemed favorable. See Richard Halloran, "South Korean C.I.A. Extends U.S. Activities, Seeking to Influence Government Policies," *The New York Times,* October 2, 1976, p. 6, and Richard Halloran, "Korean Chief Linked in Illegal Lobbying," *The New York Times,* November 9, 1976, p. 1.

posed a new slavery on the emerging free ~~Korea.~~ *nation.* We freed them from Colonialism & stood beside them against communist aggression.

Get to the bottom of possible wrongdoing in our Capital but lets not fall for the idea that our Congressmen were ~~forced to~~ *innocents seduced into* accepting gifts against their will.

In getting to the bottom of this sordid affair we shouldn't ~~focus~~ try to fix a one sided blame in such a way as to weaken the seams of an alliance which is every bit as valuable to ~~us~~ *the U.S.,* to the Repub. of China on Taiwan, *to* Japan, Australia & the other free nations of the Pacific as it is to S. Korea.

If trips by Congressmen to S. Korea are unquestioned evidence of illicit gifts & bribes then shouldn't we look at the justification for *fairly* recent junkets to Moscow, Peking, Havana *to* several new African nations and a score of other capitols? Will Congress investigate itself with the same killer instinct it displayed when it went after the CIA & the F.B.I?

What should bother us most is the one sided attention some elements of the press have been giving to the suspected S. Koreans who alledgedly gave the gifts and so little to the recipients of those gifts. As the saying goes—it takes 2 to Tango.

~~If I sound a little incensed *concerned* it is because one major paper in the Nations capitol has had shown no reluctance to go after Tongsun Park & S. Korea in general. Yet when it's own correspondent sent it the *in a* story about N. Korean *of having* diplomats, (scores of them in the N. Korean embassies of Scandinavian countries) had been caught red handed (forgive the expression) dealing in truckloads of smuggled contraband, the story didn't hardly *exactly* mad*k*e waves. The head *lead* line read "The Gang that Couldn't Smuggle Straight" and the tone was *smuggling* of liquor & dope was treated as a kind of light hearted escapade.~~

~~The same paper took paid ads from the N.~~

What makes the bias more evident is the way one paper *contrast in the way* one major paper has treated a scandal ~~story~~ involving scores of <u>North</u> Korean diplomats in several Scandinavian capitols who were trafficking in smuggled liquor & drugs. It titled the story "The Gang that Couldn't Smuggle Straight" and treated their criminal acts as a kind of lighthearted escapade. The same paper ~~took~~ printed Ads pd. for by the N. Korean govt. which railed against "U.S. Imperialists & their henchmen." ~~It~~ The ads called us criminals who occupied S. Korea by force. *But no S. Koreans are chanting Yankee go home.*

~~As I said a few weeks ago~~ *It would seem*—the campaign is on to persuade us to abandon another ally—this time it's S. Korea.—This is RR Thanks for listening. ❖

OSHA

January 19, 1977

Forgive the expression but "there is a light at the end of the tunnel~~l~~. We can fight city hall & even the puzzle palaces on the Potomac. I'll be right back.

Not too long ago I told you of the lady in New Mexico, (Pres. of a small co.) who turned away inspectors for the Occupational, Safety & Health Admin.—OSHA as it is called on the grounds that her const. rights under the 4th amendment were being violated. Her case was that govt. inspectors ~~backed by regula~~tions had no ~~write~~ *right* to come into a privately owned business on a hunting expedition for possible violations of safety regulations adopted by the govt. agency. ~~without u~~*U*nless those inspectors had a warrant showing probable cause. Her case was upheld by a panel of 3 Fed. judges.

Now a member of Cong. Rep. George Hanson* of Idaho has become the founding chairman of an org. called "Stop Osha," a happy brainchild of the Am. Cons. Union.** This dosen't mean that Rep. Hanson or the A.C.U. want to see workers maimed & killed by accidents in the places where they work. It does mean they recognize that OSHA hasn't succeded in reducing hazards for the numbers of workers suffering injury. But it has added bils. of $ to the cost of doing business to say nothing of the cost of OSHA itself. Nearly 600,000 people have been killed at their jobs since OSHA started and there has continued to be a steady increase in job related injuries. Nothing however can match the increase in regulations spawned by the busy bees at OSHA.

~~By~~ Ironically the General Accounting Office which is set up to ride herd on it's fellow members of burocracy report there are more than 300 hazardous conditions in—guess where—the working quarters of OSHA ~~itself~~ in Wash. D.C. In fact G.A.O. in it's own sleuthing found violations in several other govt. agencies in the capital. A goodly number of which would have resulted in costly fines had they been found in private businesses.

Congressman Hanson has done more than put his name on the new organizations letterhead. He encouraged and backed a S. Dakota businessman who like the lady in New Mexico is fighting OSHA as a matter of principle.

Let me repeat—no one least of all the average employer wants his employees to risk life & limb in the pursuit of their job. There are hazards to safety in many occupations and no one can guaranty that accidents wont happen. But OSHA spawning regulations by the 1000's; *REGULATIONS* that no can possibly ~~read~~ be familiar with; OSHA refusing to help employers by looking at their operations and pointing out where safety can be improved has, as the figures

* R–Idaho, 1965–1969 and 1975–1985.

** American Conservative Union, a conservative lobbying organization. The ACU also rates members of Congress on their voting records.

indicate done nothing to ~~make working men & women~~ *reduce ~~industrial~~ worker* related ~~inju~~ accidents.

What if OSHA instead of snooping busied itself with studying ~~the~~ the causes of industrial accidents & offered it's services to employers ~~to survey & recommend~~ *to help reduce those causes?* What if OSHA started out by ~~giving govt.~~ ~~*believing in their fellow citizens,*~~ believing that employers do want to protect the health & safety of their employees~~? and~~ ~~provided~~ ~~believing that provided a consulting service to make life safer for those who toil~~ ~~*Wouldn't it be more in keeping*~~ *and believing that provided a consulting service to help them?* What if OSHA remembered that this is ~~with~~ a nation created to be run by it's citizens ~~if the employees of those citizens and OSHA~~ *and those citizens are the employers of* every one who works for OSHA—not the other way around? This is RR. Thanks for listening. ❖

More About OSHA
January 19, 1977

The Occupational Safety & Health Agency commonly known as OSHA is having more trouble than a Liberian Tanker.* I'll be right back.

The other day I said it was possible to fight city hall and even the marble halls in Wash. ~~and I.~~ Here is ~~more~~ confirmation of that fact.

I ~~spoke of~~ *mentioned* a businessman in Idaho who had been encouraged by his Congressman George Hansen to stand up to OSHA. ~~as~~ This isn't a case of "lets you & him fight"—Congressman Hansen has accepted the chairmanship of an org. called "Stop OSHA."

Bill Barlow and his 4 sons have a plumbing, heating & electrical subcontracting business in Pocatello Idaho. They have 35 employees in ~~their this~~ *their* family owned business.

Bill said he knew that OSHA ~~snoops~~ would get around to him sooner or later. ~~*And* he did a lot of thinking & studying in the meantime.~~ *So in the meantime he did a lot of studying and thinking.* He came to the conclusion that such inspections BY GOVT. of private property ~~by govt.~~ were a violation of our const. rights under the 4th amendment. Incidentally OSHA ~~claims the right~~ *bases it's right* to ~~inspect~~ *search* without a warrant ~~bas~~ on Sec. 8(a) of the Occupational, Safety & Health Act.

Well when the inspectors finally reached the Barlow firm Bill said "not without a warrant." You'll remember *earlier* ~~I spoke some~~ *a lady* ~~*did* this in New~~

* The Liberian tanker *Argo Merchant* ran aground off the coast of Nantucket on December 15, 1976, spilling 7.5 million gallons of oil into the Atlantic Ocean. The primarily Greek-crewed ship had been involved in 18 other accidents since 1964, and there were charges at the time that Liberian ships were not subject to rigorous enough safety standards. Most "Liberian" vessels were actually owned by companies from America, China, and Greece, and were registered under the Liberian flag for convenience.

Mexico and a Fed. Court~~ upheld her.~~ ~~*in New Mexico had done this & been up-*~~*held by a Fed. Court.* In ~~his~~ *Bills* case however OSHA ~~de refused~~ *declined* to get a warrant ~~but~~ *and* obtained a court order instead. ~~His~~ *Bill* refused to ~~get~~ obey the ~~court~~ order and was cited for contempt of court. He petitioned for the empanelling of a 3 judge court ~~to~~ challenging the constitutionality of sec. 8(a) of the Osha act. On Dec. 30th in the U.S. district court ruled in his favor, ruled that sec. 8(a) is indeed unconstitutional that it "directly offends against the prohibitions of the 4th amendment of the Const. of the U.S. of Am." *

Bill Barlow still faces the "contempt citation but is hopeful it will be dismissed. So am I. Here is a citizen who like the farmers at Concord bridge took a stand for what he believes is right and thanks to him freedom is a little more secure for all of us.

This may well be a landmark decision. OSHA has announced it will appeal to the U.S. Sup. Ct. but in the meantime suspend further inspections in Idaho. Congressman Hansen has said this isn't good enough; that pending ~~the~~ *a* Sup. Ct. decision inspections everywhere should be suspended. He is introducing a resolution to that effect in Congress.

Powerful forces are ~~marshalling~~ *rallying to* support OSHA ~~to~~ and 1st in line is the AFL-CIO. Burocracy itself feels threatened because OSHA isn't the only agency that has been guilty of "search & find guilty" missions. The AFL-CIO claims that all govt. inspections are threatened but this is a scare tactic exaggeration.

The Court in it's decision specifically stated that heavily regulated industries, those for example having to do with food & drugs etc. could be ~~required~~ *subject* to warrantless inspections as a condition for obtaining licenses and that this would *not* be ~~in~~ a violation of const. rights.

The people should be on the side of Bill Barlow. All that he is asking & all that the District Court upheld is that shopkeepers, *FARMERS* and manufactures should have the same constitutional protection we give to suspected criminals; they cant be searched without a warrant showing probable cause.

This is RR Thanks for listening. ❖

The Real China?
January 19, 1977

We've been told that whatever else we may think about Communist China—at least it's people are no longer hungry. True or False? I'll be right back.

* The Supreme Court affirmed the ruling of the lower court that the warrant clause of the Fourth Amendment applied to commercial buildings as well as private homes in a 5–3 decision on May 23, 1978. It did establish, however, that OSHA had a right to inspect businesses by means of a warrant, and that OSHA did not need to establish "probable cause" of possible criminal wrongdoing when seeking a warrant for inspection. It could simply seek an inspection warrant of a business as part of normal administrative supervisory activities.

There is a weekly publication called "Human Events" headquartered in Wash. D.C. It contains a great deal of news about govt., International affairs & politics not always available in the regular press or TV news. A ~~month~~ *month* or so ago it carried an article by a well known scholar, a professor at Dartmouth Jeffrey Hart. Prof. Hart wrote of a study by two of his contemporarys Miriam & Ivan London,* having to do with what he called the obscurity that is ~~contempor~~ Red China.

All of us have been subjected to the reports of Americans & Europeans who have journeyed to Peking and returned with glowing accounts of the orderly society that has been created there. The publisher of the N.Y. Times has proclaimed; "I have immense admiration for the accomplishments of the Maoist revolution. . . . which for the first time in recorded history can feed & clothe its vast population adequately & by its own efforts."

Miriam & Ivan London, writes Prof. Hart, have managed to penetrate the before mentioned obscurity by modern techniques. They have taken the testimony of the thousands of refugees who continue to pour into Hong Kong and pumped it into computers. Admittedly refugee information tends to be unreliable. But the computers reject the accounts which disagree ~~and~~ *with* each other and put together the stories from *separate* individuals ~~who dont know each other but~~ *which* are in agreement until they have a "province by province" account of what is actually going on in China. They have also cranked into the computer veiled accounts from official directives, broadcasts etc. Their findings will soon appear in a book.

But in the meantime an ugly picture of the China behind the showplaces for foreign visitors emerges. It is a China of corruption, of pickpockets & thieves and prostitution. Ration coupons are sold and an underground commerce is carried on. Peasants labor endlessly for meals of rice gruel & sweet potatoes. In this China there has been massive famine and say the computers "beggars still [s]warm from disaster areas in the North into the more fortunate south."

Even while our own journalists were writing of Maos triumph over hunger in the years 1958 to '62 one of the most disastrous famines in modern history took place. The Londons go on to say this was not the result of a natural disaster. It was caused by mis-management & misguided communist party zeal. Crop failures took place in virtually every province. They quote a Peoples Liberation Army officer who went home to find his grandmother & uncle had starved to death. He told of trees stripped of bark by the ~~star~~ hungry people.

Prof. Hart says the Londons overall conclusions ~~of~~ are grim; food ~~prop~~ production lagging behind population growth; a bare subsistence economy with no surplus to cover disasters <u>but</u> plenty of food in those cities where foreigners are allowed to visit—the showcase cities.

* Jeffrey Hart, "Red Chinese Hide Widespread Hunger," *Human Events*, January 8, 1977, p. 19, and Miriam London and Ivan D. London, "The Other China: Hunger: Part I: The Three Red Flags of Death," *Worldview* (May 1976): 4–11.

I hope when the Londons book is ready Human Events will announce it. This is RR Thanks for listening. ❖

Capital Gains
January 19, 1977

Capital gain and inflation are about as untasty a combination as mustard on ice cream—I'll be right back.

B It's hard to get a great many people excited about the Capital Gains tax. ~~and b~~*B*ecause of that fact politicians aren't inclined to do anything about it except possibly increase it *WHICH THEY'VE JUST DONE.* A Capital gain is what happens when someone sells something of value for more than that someone paid for it. Govt. says a profit has been made and such profit must be taxed.

That sounds fair enough and since *such* capital transactions most often involve people with enough means to make investments in real estate, stocks, bonds etc. It's easy to see why there isn't widespread concern among the general public. ~~Of course there are cases~~ where govt. ~~shares claims a *share in a* one time windfall.~~ *But what about that* once in a lifetime windfall? Take the small struggling farmer who finds himself ~~in~~ and his farm in the path of progress. His scrubby acres become real estate quote unquote and after years of scraping along he sells for a price that puts him on easy street—~~at least before~~ *or did until* govt. ~~takes~~ *claimed* it's share.

Now a*n* ~~case~~ *argument* can be made as to whether there should be such a tax at all. Indeed in many countries far less free than ours there is no such tax. In 1942 the exec. committee of the Am. Fed. of Labor (believe it or not) angrily demanded of Pres. Roosevelt that the Cap. Gains tax be ~~th~~ cancelled. And they spoke truly when they said in support of their demand that such a tax reduced the investment in industry needed to provide workers with jobs. Those really were the good old days.

Today the A.F.L.—C.I.O. is the most powerful force urging ~~more~~ *a higher* Capital-Gains tax. Walter Reuther* has left this vale of tears but it would seem his influence lingers on.

I remember a night when Geo. Meany** sat in our living room talking of the struggle for power in the newly merged labor organization. He said Reuther openly advocated socialist measures in the exec. committee meetings. One of his goals was to re-shape one of our two major pol. parties in the image

* From 1946 to 1970, Walter Reuther presided over the United Automobile Workers, a union of auto workers.

** George Meany was the first president of the American Federation of Labor–Congress of Industrial Organizations. The organization was founded in 1955.

of the Labor-Soc. party of Eng. Meany at the time led the opposition to such a course.

But I'm not going to argue whether we should or should not have a Cap. gains tax. I'll save that for another time. Right now we have the tax and I'd like to point out an unfairness in it that literally puts ~~the~~ *our* govt. in the position of stealing from it's own citizens.

We have & have had for many years a continuing inflation which reduces the value of our dollar by several cents each year. ~~What you~~ This is not allowed for in govt. taxing policys. Suppose you are that struggling farmer I mentioned or you invested in some real estate, or ~~tax~~ stock or whatever say 10 yrs. ago. Now you decide to sell and you actually get double what you ~~paid~~ *invested* 10 yrs. ago. The govt. says half of what you get is profit and it takes ~~anywhere from a third to more~~ *upward of a third* of that supposed profit. But todays $ is only worth 40¢ compared to the $ you invested 10 yrs. ago. *So* You didn't double your money. You got twice the number of $ but you actually lost 20% on the sale—before govt. took it's bite. *You got back $2 for every $1 invested* ~~*by*~~ *but the $2 today* ~~*is only worth 80¢.*~~ *is only equal to 80¢ in the money you spent 10 yrs ago.*

Simple honesty dictates the*at* govt. should compute capital transactions in constant $ to see if there ~~was any~~ *actually was* a profit & if so how much~~.~~ *& tax accordingly.* ~~Try that on your~~ This is RR Thanks for listening. ❖

On January 21, 1977, one day after his inauguration, President Carter granted full pardons to all men who avoided the military draft during the Vietnam War by not registering or leaving the country. The pardon meant that the government gave up the right to prosecute thousands of draft-dodgers. Deserters were not pardoned.

Amnesty
February 2, 1977

I have a hunch we'll be allowed to forget the pardon given to ~~Vietnam~~ draft evaders very quickly as befits something in which we take so little pride. I'll be right back.

~~Back when we were still involved in the Vietnam war one of those incidents occurred~~

With the pardon of those who not only didn't heed the call of duty, but, went so far away they couldn't hear it, memories *of the Vietnam war* pleasant & unpleasant ~~were~~ *are* re-awakened. One that came back to me was of an incident so unique it's hard to believe it wasn't considered newsworthy. I can assure you it wasn't, certainly not by ~~so much of~~ the media which found so much immorality in our participation in the war & so little to criticize about Hanoi.

~~Over a period of about 5 years~~

The story has to do with 10 separate individuals who fought in Vietnam and returned to this country over a period of about 5 years. Some were officers, other enlisted men. ~~who~~ *They* had served in the army, navy, marine corps & airforce.

Their paths had never crossed in Vietnam. They didn't know each other and upon their return ~~to this country~~ they were scattered all over the U.S. They had only one thing in common besides being ~~Viet~~ Vets of the Vietnam war. Each of them were convinced of the rightness of our being there to help the Vietnamese people. Each of them wanted to do more to help.

Ten men in a nation of more than 200 mil. What would the odds be against even 2 of them ever coming together? But they evidently talked about what they felt and what they wished they could do. A listener would ~~hear~~ hear & say "you ought to know so & so he feels the same way." An address would be given. Two men would correspond. To brief it down eventually these 10 men, ~~were~~ strangers all, were in touch with each other.

There came a day when they journeyed to Wash. Their request sounded simple—"We are ~~v~~Vietnam veterans who want to do something to help the ~~v~~Vietnamese people before the American withdrawal. Will you send us back"? It sounded simple yes—but it took quite a bit of doing. They were now civilians asking to be ~~returned~~ sent to a war zone and they finally made it.

Their destination was the village of "Cat Lai" and they had decided on their mission. They wanted to build houses for disabled Vietnamese veterans. They called themselves the Cat Lai commune.*

Day in, day out they worked. The villagers accepted them and quietly understood. One of the happiest notes in this story is the lack of surprise on the part of the people in Cat Lai. What these 10 young men were doing was in keeping with what ~~they~~ the Vietnamese had come to believe was typical of Americans.

* According to Douglas Brinkley in a *Boston Globe* story of December 14, 2003, bestselling author Armistead Maupin originated the idea for the "Cat Lai Commune." The White House was searching for ways in 1971 to counter the anti-Vietnam attacks of former naval officer John Kerry, then a member of the organization "Vietnam Veterans Against the War." Maupin had served in Saigon as a naval protocol officer in 1969, and suggested to Admiral Elmo R. Zumwalt in a letter of June 3, 1971, that Washington send some Vietnam veterans back to the country to "do some good." He believed it would send a message to America that not all veterans agreed with Kerry's anti-war stance. The White House agreed, and on July 3, Maupin and nine other American veterans returned to Vietnam to build a 20-unit housing project for disabled South Vietnamese veterans. The Cat Lai goodwill ambassadors met with the White House in October when they returned, and Maupin himself was a guest at the 1973 inaugural celebration. However, Maupin later recanted his earlier support for Nixon and agreed with John Kerry that the war in Vietnam was wrong.

In the evenings they would sit around in the warm twilight having a beer with the villagers and the disabled men they were trying to help. On one of those evenings they told a young Vietnamese officer that back in America there were many Americans who thought the people of Vietnam would be better off under Hanoi.

He replied, "I think my country is the h—l of the world & you have come to this h—l to help us. We have been at war for thousands of years. We want peace more than anyone but we want peace without communism."

~~As the planes come in from Canada and Sweden~~

I dont know what finally happened to those 10 men or when they came home. But as the planes from Canada & Sweden bring others home I'm going to try and remember the Cat-Lai commune. This is RR Thanks for listening. ❖

Foundations
February 2, 1977

Normally a trustee of one of our prestigious foundations resigning would not be a particularly newsworthy event. Normally that is. I'll be right back.

We are a charitable people. So ingrained in our American culture is the voluntary support of good works, that we exempt from the inc. tax gifts to charitable & educational institutions. ~~Only in the last few years have some of the more extreme believers in, Government doing everything, complained about this tax exemption and *They have* tried to suggest that somehow a person voluntarily giving money to support medical research, education or charity to the needy is guilty of tax evasion.~~

This native generosity has led to the creation of great multi-million dollar foundations staffed by eminent scholars & researchers. Their endowment is invested in stocks, real estate & bonds, *IN SHORT AMERICAN INDUSTRY,* the income from which is tax free and finances the foundations contributions to educational research, public services & good works in general.

~~Whether it is~~ *Whatever* the reason many, if not most of the great foundations, have more & more ~~been guided by a liberal philosophy~~ *tended* to believe in big govt. Their scholarly works explore more ways for govt. to busy itself in the peoples affairs. Often they present studies to show how much more govt. we can afford, urging the people to recognize that govt. is a good buy.

Of late their pro-govt. & anti-marketplace bias has caused some to question their continued right to tax exempt status. The case made is pretty legitimate. We have never recognized the ~~right to influencing~~ *influencing of* legislation as deserving of favored tax treatment. Naturally those who bring this up are denounced as quote, "right wing" unquote. ~~o~~Or ~~other~~ something similar, "reactionary, unprogressive, neanderthal etc.

One of the greatest of the foundations was set up by the heirs of Henry Ford ~~the~~ Senior who launched the great motor company which bears his name. The Ford foundation, ~~is multi bil. dollar in size and~~ *WITH virtually unlimited resources,* subsidizes battalions of intellectuals who devote their energies to ~~flogging~~ whittling away at the ec. system which created & supports their source of affluence—the ~~Ford~~ foundation itself.

Recently after 33 yrs. of service Henry Ford II resigned as a trustee of the foundation.* Mr. Ford has tended to be quite liberal. ~~m~~*M*ore often than not he supports Dem. candidates for public office *all of* which makes his farewell address ~~more~~ *to the foundation which bears his family name more* than a little surprising.

"The ~~F~~*f*oundation exists and thrives on the fruits of our ec. system" he said. "The dividends of competitive enterprise make it all possible. A significant portion of the substance created by U.S. business enables the foundation & like institutions to carry on their work. In effect the foundation is a creature of capitalism—a statement that I'm sure, would be shocking to many professional staff people in the field of philanthropy. It is hard to ~~recognize~~ *discern* recognition of this fact in anything the foundation does. It is even more difficult to find an understanding of this in many of the institutions, particularly the universities that are the beneficiaries of the foundations grant programs." ~~End quote~~ *So said Henry Ford the II.*

Very plainly Mr. Ford ~~accused~~ *was accusing* the largest tax free foundation in the nation of using tax free money to undermine the ec. system without which it couldn't exist. An official of the Carnegie Foundation was outraged, "Is that what the Ford foundation is set up for, to promote free enterprise?" he asked. Funny—he never questioned its right to destroy free enterprise. This is R.R. Thanks for listening. ❖

In the wake of Watergate, Congress and state legislatures passed legislation on campaign financing and ethics in government. Legislation in 1974 amended the Federal Election Campaign Act of 1971 to limit federal campaign contributions and expenditures, but independent expenditure limitations were invalidated by the Supreme Court as a restriction on political speech in 1976. The Ethics in Government Act, requiring greater financial disclosure and further attempting to reduce conflicts of interest, was passed in 1978.

* Henry Ford II resigned as a trustee of the Ford Foundation on January 11, 1977, saying that the foundation had spread itself too thin and that the staff should be more appreciative of the free enterprise system that provided the money in the first place. He also criticized the "fortress mentality" of the organization that failed to encourage innovative thinking in favor of maintaining old programs.

IBM

February 2, 1977

Who was it that said something to the effect that "the more things change the more they remain the same"? I'll be right back.

Out of all the trauma of the last few years, ~~the charges, counter charges, & accusations which often were taken as proof of guilt,~~ came legislation nationally & statewide to eliminate conflicts of interest. ~~and~~ *The* new (and in my opinion) ridiculous election laws ~~were~~ are examples of govt. by hysteria.

There was the offer of I.T.T. to guaranty a sizeable portion of the sum offered by merchants, hotels & restaurants to lure the Repub. Nat. Convention to San Diego *in 1972*. Never mind that cities customarily do this ~~to~~ in the competition to host the nat. pol. conventions. Never mind that the Repub. Nat. committee turned down the offer by I.T.T. and then took the convention to Miami. I.T.T. was involved in ~~a suit~~ *legal* difficulties with the Justice dept. and the oder of chicanery was in the air.

Now we have the new laws and assurances ~~that~~ *against* conflict of interest but is anything really different? William Safire has written a column proving it isn't.* He points out that never in our history has one corporation so completely dominated the top levels of an admin. And he isn't talking about I.T.T. or 1972.

Our new Sec. of St.** is a director of I.B.M. and a member of the exec. committee. The Sec. of Defense*** is an I.B.M. director and chairs the audit committee. The Sec. of Housing & Urban Development (H.U.D.)**** is a director of I.B.M. & advises management on executive compensation. The new attorney Gen.***** and the top advisor to the Pres. are both members of the law firm that represents I.B.M. in Atlanta. The under Sec. of St. is a partner in the law firm that represents I.B.M. in the far west.

The Presidents science & technology advisor****** is a V.P. and chief of technology for I.B.M. Two of the Presidents first choices ~~of~~ for other cabinet positions (they are not in the cabinet however) were an I.B M director & a former Vice Pres.

Now Mr. Safire does not hint at collusion or suggest that any of the individuals he has mentioned are in any way questionable as to character. But one cant help but be aware of a greater tolerance in this instance than was afforded in some earlier ~~cases incidents.~~ *incidents.*

* William Safire, "Think," *The New York Times,* January 17, 1977, p. 36.
** Cyrus R. Vance served as Secretary of State from 1977 to 1980.
*** Harold Brown, served 1977–1981.
**** Patricia R. Harris, served 1977–1979.
***** Griffin B. Bell, served 1977–1979.
****** Frank Press, served 1977–1980.

You see for a year & a half the U.S. govt. & I.B.M have been engaged in the most extensive anti-trust case in our history. The govt. wont be finished presenting it's case until the end of next summer and then I.B.M will begin presenting its hundreds of witnesses.

The new Attorney General will have to remove himself from the biggest case in the justice dept. But as Mr. Safire points out the justice dept. lawyers can not forget why. It's like inadvertently seeing an opponents hand in a card game. No matter how honest you are you cant force your mind to forget the cards you saw. Will IB.M. competitors trying to do business with govt. ~~not~~ be able to believe there is no prejudice when they run into this IB.M. alumni group?

Again Mr. Safire does not suggest conspiracy but he does suggest no one thought to look at the way the puzzle when put together would spell out the potential for conflict. This is RR Thanks for listening. ❖

Congress
February 2, 1977

Isn't this the era of "sunshine laws" no more secrecy or closed doors in ~~Congress~~ govt. Or was that just something to get us through the election. I'll be right back.

~~I think all of us from time to~~

Congress is back in session ~~and with~~ *and with* great fanfare & self congratulations ~~told~~ *informed* all of us ~~were informed of~~ *that* a new code of ethics would bring ~~a~~ *the look of* Camelot ~~back~~ to the House of Representatives. The bearer of this good news was the new speaker of the House Congressman Tip O'Neill.

Either he lost his voice after that announcement or ~~he~~ decided one such gift from on high was enough. There was no fanfare or even a whisper when he changed the House rules by way of a "privileged resolution."

A "privileged resolution" is one that slides smoothly & silently through the legis. process without debate or explanation. This one had to do with the customary procedure when a court or grand jury decides it has to look into the doings of a member of Congress.

For example *UP TIL NOW* if ~~the~~ *a* court or grand jury issued a subpoena for the payroll records or expense accounts of a member or members *OF THE HOUSE* the subpoena was printed in the Cong. record & voted upon by the House. Publicity followed ~~usually as the press became aware of course &~~ *as a matter of course and the capitol press corps were made aware.* ~~and so~~ You & I ~~read~~ *would then read* about it ~~with~~ *over* our morning coffee.

The ~~#~~ new speaker just pulled the curtain on that. From now on when a House members ~~is~~ *RECORDS ARE* subpoenaed ~~to present evidence~~ only he (or she) and Speaker O'Neill will know about it. There will be no voting on it nor will it be announced in the Congressional record.

~~Now~~ Now here is an interesting aspect—if the subpoena should be directed to the Speaker himself only he would have ~~that~~ knowledge of it. What was all that furor about an imperial Presidency?

The Senate was busy doing a little changing on it's own and in my opinion democracy was the loser. Once again it was the new leadership. Sen Robt. Byrd called it modernizing the Senate. Actually it makes it easier for the majority to ram through legislation without some of the debate that now & then ~~took~~ *takes* place.

I'm sure all of us from time to time have wondered about the filibuster and whether it was a legitimate tool in the legislative workshop. Then we'd find ourselves thankful when ~~we our~~ *a controversial* matter came along and we were on the side of those who filibustered. In the movie "Mr. Smith Goes To Wash." it was the only weapon "Jimmy Stewart" had to block ~~the~~ a nefarious special interest bill and thanks to him evil was thwarted & right triumphed.

Two years ago the Sen. weakened the filibuster by reducing the ⅔ vote required to limit debate to only 60%. Now Sen. Byrd's resolution * provides that after the 60% have voted, individual Senators speaking time will be cut in half, a time limit will be imposed on total debate and by a ⅔ vote debate can be virtually ended.

One Sen. of the majority leaders own party has described what's going on as "cutting off a dogs tale one inch at a time." What makes or has made our Senate a unique deliberative body is ~~the~~ protection ~~of~~ *for* the minority viewpoint. It is not unusual for a filibuster to focus the peoples attention on an issue to such an extent that the majority view in the Sen. is discovered to be at odds with the will of the people and ~~we are spared a mistake~~ *a mistake is avoided.*

Isn't it strange that some who have argued the loudest about the right of dissent would deny that right to their fellow Senators? This is RR Thanks for listening. ❖

On November 1, 1977, President Jimmy Carter signed legislation increasing the minimum wage from $2.30 to $2.65 on January 1, 1978, and then to $2.90, $3.10, and $3.35 on January 1 of the following three years.

* Byrd's resolution failed, but the Senate did adopt time limits in 1979 and made the limits more stringent in 1985. (Richard S. Beth and Stanley Bach, "Filibusters and Cloture in the Senate," Updated March 28, 2003, Congressional Research Service Report RL 30360, Library of Congress.)

Minimum Wage
February 2, 1977

The minimum wage stands at $2.30 an hour and a push is on to increase it. Can we do that without paying the price ~~in~~ *of* an increase*d* unemployment.* I'll be right back.

The other day, in answer to a question from an audience, I expressed my view that the minimum wage is a factor in unemployment. Criticizing the minimum wage can lead to arguments high on emotionalism but low on reason & rationality.

It is pure demagogery to charge that questioning the minimum wage means one wants to see workers reduced to a starvation level income. I think all of us would ~~th~~ like to see everyone who works for a living rewarded with enough to have some of the luxurys that make life worth living. But the minimum wage is not going to bring that about or even help bring it about.

We have an overall unemployment rate of nearly 8%. The smallest group of unemployed fortunately ~~are~~ *is made up of* heads of households. The largest—teenagers. Teenage unemployment is about 2½ times the rate for all workers or about 20%. For black teenagers ~~the rate is double that. or~~ *double it. The rate is 40%.*

Now lets look at a little history. In 1954 the minimum wage was 75¢ and black teenage unemployment was 16.5%. By 1968 the minimum wage had risen to $1.60 an hour and unemployment of black teenagers had gone up to 25%. Remember too that in '68 we had full employment because of the Vietnam war. Now the minimum is $2.30 and as I said unemployment ~~is 40%.~~ among black teenagers is *NOW* 40%.

Actually that $2.30 should be considered as closer to $3.00 because of about 70 cents in additional fringe benefits. But the push is on to make the actual cash level $3.00 with of course a proportionate hike in the*ose* compulsory fringe benefits. Based on past performance that would further hike unemployment in general, teenage unemployment in particular and especially among young black Americans.

I'm aware that there is ~~no~~ *little* chance of persuading the present Congress to cancel the minimum wage *nor am I suggesting such a move* even though fact & figure indicate that it ~~simply has made~~ *has eliminated* a great many ~~jobs~~ marginal jobs. ~~cease to exist. And I am not suggesting such a move.~~

But with all the evidence available why should even an irresponsible Congress be unwilling to try a two tier system designed to meet the problem of the greatest group of unemployed? By two tier I mean continuation ~~f~~ of the present minimum for the general working population ~~(but for heavens sake let it~~

* The average unemployment rate for 1976 was 7.7 percent. *Economic Report of the President* (Washington, D.C.: U.S. Government Printing Office, 1977), Table B-29.

be a ~~figure which does not wipe out more jobs.) and a substantially lower min-~~imum for teen-age & part time workers.

I know that labor leaders have complained employers would ~~substitute~~ substitute teenagers for adult workers but I dont think we're even talking about the same kind of jobs. Western European countries have tried the 2 tier system & find it works well and does not in any way threaten the jobs of older & more experienced workers.

We might find we ~~we~~ *had* not only reduced our overall unemployment but ~~have~~ *had* achieved some ~~sizable~~ *beneficial* side effects. We could concentrate *on* the most important unemployment problem—the family wage earner. ~~j~~Juvenile deliquency might be reduced if idle ~~youths~~ *young people* had ~~a chance to~~ *something* to do & honest earnings to spend. And a lot of resources now being wasted on ineffectual social tinkering could be put to better use. This is R.R. Thanks for listening. ❖

With Jimmy Carter settling in as president for the next four years, Reagan returned to one of his main policy concerns—taxes and the economy—and wrote three commentaries focused on the paperwork and legal thicket of the Internal Revenue Service.

Taxes I
February 2, 1977

This is going to be more about taxes & more about fighting city hall—only in this case *it's* the Internal Revenue Service. I'll be right back.

With the 1500 pages of inc. tax reform Cong. passed last year* we're all going to find it's harder than ever to tell the tax collector how much we owe him. Two men in Texas one an employee of a radio station the other a certified public accountant have written an article outlining the procedure in appealing an inc. tax case. But they've done more. Maxwell Green & Roy Carden have at the same time revealed the virtually unlimited power the Commissioner of Internal Revenue has over all of us. They've also suggested a constitutional remedy available to us. And they have generously told me I can ~~use~~ *pass* their findings on to you.

Most everyone has to employ ~~extra~~ outside help these days in figuring out his or her inc. tax. Yes, there is the simplified form but lately even that is getting complicated. If you <u>are</u> one of those who seeks out a tax advisor you know that when the job is done you both are confident that the deductions you've taken are allowable. ~~and y~~You send your tax forms & money off to Wash. poorer but square with the law

Of course you dont expect to be one of those whose ~~"return~~ "tax return"

* Tax Reform Act of 1976.

will be audited. But a certain percentage are each year. When *& IF* it happens ~~you'll~~ *you may* be shocked, angry & frustrated. The I.R.S. agent ~~will~~ *may* tell you that you owe the govt. more money—additional tax, plus interest, plus penalties because the Commissioner has ruled that some of the deductions you took are not allowable. And they are not allowable because he says so.

You go to your tax advisor to find out what you can do. This will usually ~~make~~ *add to* your anger. He'll ask how much they want & usually it will be an amount that will cause him to say "pay it." His explanation ~~bein~~ will be that it's so much less than the cost of fighting that you are better off. Of course it's a chunk of money you dont think you owe & that you hadn't counted on having to give up *which adds to it's value in your mind.*

What are your choices? The tax advisor will ~~remin~~ tell you that under the tax law the Commissioner has authority to interpret the code and write the regulations. So if he has interpreted your deductions as non-allowable he has the unlimited resources of govt. to fight any legal action you may take. In effect you will be paying your own costs and ~~a share of his~~ as a taxpayer contributing to his. But if you want to go ahead you can appeal. If that dosen't work you can go to the Appellate division. In the first appeal you and your accountant or lawyer will face an Audit Supervisor but he works for the Commissioner. If you choose the appellate division you face a panel of hearing officers—who are also on the payroll of I.R.S.

If they rule against you—you still have 3 choices; small claims court (if the amount is less than $1500.), Tax court or Fed. District Court. I trust you are remembering a little something called court costs.

Tomorrow I'll let our 2 authors take you down that road aways. This is R.R. Thanks for listening. ❖

Taxes II
February 2, 1977

Today let's see what happens if you take on the Internal Revenue Service in some of the ways open to you. I'll be right back.

Yesterday I listed some of the things you can do if those fellows at I.R.S. come around & tell you ~~that sometime in the last 3 yrs.~~ they've decided you owe more than you paid in any one of the previous 3 yrs.

You are mad at the agent delivering the bad news that on top of disallowing some of your deductions you owe interest and a penalty—they dont call it a fine.

You file a written appeal. You are then invited to what I.R.S. calls an informal conference with—guess who?—The agents boss. He checks the agents findings—makes sure you & the agent aren't having a personality clash and, barring a miracle decides against you.

Now you carry on and head for the Appellate division. This is a panel of hearing officers also employees of I.R.S. So are the people who will present the Agents findings. You & your tax advisor are the only ~~f~~ people in the room who arent members of the club. About your only chance is if your tax man can come up with some provision of the tax code the agent slipped up on. ~~and~~ *Then* you hang him out to dry. That isn't likely.

Alright so now you are 2 down and headed for the Small Claims Court. The amount at issue remember has to be less than $1500 for you to take this route. Everything is real informal—you wont need a lawyer (they say). No rules of evidence. Just a bunch of good old boys who want to get to the bottom of this. Of course this judge—a lawyer himself cant really forget all the law he's learned. The I.R.S. agents are legally trained & very experienced in taking cases to Small Claims Court. You are outgunned & outnumbered. Three down.

You are still mad & determined so here you are in Tax Court. The judge is one of 16 appointed for 15 yr. terms by the Pres. He will attempt to ~~rule~~ make a ruling based on the tax code. That is if the code is specific enough to make such a ruling possible. If not he'll probably rule in favor of I.R.S. You're not likely to win unless there has been a flagrant violation of the code by the Revenue agents. Rarely the chief judge might review the decision and call for a hearing by the entire court. Remember through all these steps you & your advisor are the only ~~people~~ *members* of the cast whose wages aren't paid out of the funds collected by Internal Revenue. Four down.

Of course there is the Fed. District Court & here there will be a jury of your ~~peers~~ *peers* who are not on the Fed. payroll. First however you must pay the I.R.S. the disputed tax, the interest & the penalty. Then you ~~can~~ sue to get it back. ~~Of course~~ If the jury decides in your favor that's what will happen—~~you'll get your money back—or will you?~~—*or will it?*

The Commissioner of Internal Rev. can appeal the case to the Circuit Court of Appeals. That's really no hardship for him—he has the unlimited resources of the Fed. govt. to call on. You of course are paying for *a* lawyer, your tax advisor & possibly clerical help ~~& yo~~ *as well* as other expenses.

~~Your case~~ *The decision* will be reviewed by a panel of 3 Fed. judges ~~and~~ strictly on the basis of the law & how it applies to your case. Again it becomes a question of whether I.R.S. is in gross violation of the code and remember I.R.S. wrote the regulations that implement that code.

It ~~y~~ the lower court decision is reversed you are down to big casino or perhaps I should say up. Your last recourse is the U.S. Supreme Court. Is it really worth it in cash or are we doing this for principle?

Tomorrow the last chapter*—tune in & find out what happens to John Q. Taxpayer. This is RR. Thanks for listening. ❖

* "Taxes III," published in *Reagan, In His Own Hand,* edited by Kiron K. Skinner, Annelise Anderson, and Martin Anderson (New York: Free Press, 2001), p. 281. Reagan finds citizens' rights on tax matters are limited; he recommends a tax limitation amendment to the Constitution.

*Taped two months into the Carter presidency, this radio broadcast is further evidence that Andrew Young was incurring the wrath of many critics, including prominent conservatives, for his views on foreign policy. Two years later, as the criticism mounted, Young resigned as the U.S. ambassador to the United Nations.**

Cuba II
March 2, 1977

I'm sure we are all conscious of mans inhumanity to man but every once in awhile a single instance or the mis-treatment of an individual reminds us all over again. I'll be right back.

A few weeks ago our new ambassador to the United Nations publicly expressed the view that we should normalize relations with Cuba. By coincidence I assume Dictator Castro appeared on TV *2 DAYS LATER* and expressed his desire for normal relations with the U.S. beginning with resumption of trade.

That would be a good beginning—for Mr. Castro. ~~His~~ He has much more to gain from trade with us than we do. His countrys ec. is creaking along with consumer goods of every kind in short supply and productivity far less than it was in the bad old days of freedom.

The question is, should trade be the first approach to normal relations, diplomatic recognition etc? ~~with~~ We are signatories to the U.N. declaration of Human Rights.** We ~~justified si~~ *rationalized* signing the Helsinki pact on the grounds that it might make life easier for some of those enslaved behind the iron curtain & elsewhere.*** Why shouldn't we tell Castro that normal relations might follow the ≠ adoption by him of some of the simple humanitarian customs we consider normal?

Chilé a country ≠ often accused by some ~~of us~~ *among* us of denying civil liberties to it's people, nevertheless has ~~ofl~~ offered to exchange pol. prisoners

* The political furor that prompted Young's resignation arose from his private meeting with Zehdi Terzi, the representative of the Palestine Liberation Organization at the United Nations. Some American Jewish leaders felt that Young was seeking to negotiate with the PLO, while black leaders declared that Young was the target of an opposition campaign. President Jimmy Carter wrote in his memoirs that "Andy had *not* violated the United States agreement with Israel concerning the PLO, but he should have informed the Secretary of State more fully about the controversial meeting. A mountain was made of a molehill—another indication of the politically charged character of the Middle East dispute." *Keeping Faith* (New York: Bantam Books, 1982), p. 491.

** On December 10, 1948, the Universal Declaration of Human Rights was adopted by the United Nations General Assembly.

*** Reagan is referring to his criticism of President Gerald Ford for signing the Helsinki document at the Conference on Security and Cooperation in Europe in Helsinki, Finland, on August 1, 1975, and leveled this charge repeatedly during the Republican primaries the following year.

~~with~~ for some of the people being held by the Soviet U. and other communist countries. On Dec. 18 they had their first success. The Soviet U. freed *& exchanged* Vladimir Bukovsky for ~~the~~ a veteran *Chilean* communist Luis Corvalán.*

But so far they have had no success in trying to exchange another jailed Chilean communist for a Cuban prisoner Major Huberto Matos imprisoned by Castro in Oct. of 1959 almost 18 yrs. ago.**

It seems that his crime was in saying that the Castro govt. was being infiltrated by communists and that he didn't want to be associated with it. This was only a few months after Castro had seized power and Matos was one of the mil. leaders who had helped him do this. He was removed from his mil. command, placed under arrest & jailed for quote—"betraying—unquote the revolution. ~~For the last 5 years~~ For the last 5 years he has been allowed no visitors.

Our govt. is aware of his situation. His wife Maria has been seeking help to obtain his release. She has written Pres. Carter asking him to intercede; to appeal to Castro to accept the Chilean offer of an exchange. ~~She~~

She has also met with staff aides of Sens. Case & Kennedy & Rep. Edward Koch*** all of whom have been quite vocal in their protesting of the ~~lack of~~ *violation* of human rights—in Chilé. So far she has had no success.

In her letter to the Pres. she wrote, "Can you provide the needed hand to obtain the release of my husband? You have called for a new morality in foreign policy and I believe that you are genuinely interested in human rights. That is why I'm asking you to appeal directly to Pres. Castro urging him to accept the Chilean offer."

Mrs. Matos last word from her husband was a letter smuggled out of the prison 2 *YRS. AGO*. He said, "if my spiritual state is holding up, I cannot say the same for my physical state." He told her his left arm was paralyzed and he was nearly blind, then added, "I am old & ailing. I am a shadow of the man who entered prison in Oct. 1959."

Major Matos is just one of thousands imprisoned in Castros Cuba. Let normalization of relations with us begin with justice for all of them. This is RR. Thanks for listening. ❖

* The United States mediated the exchange of Vladimir K. Bukovsky and Luis Corvalán Lepe at the Kloten Airport in Zurich, Switzerland.

** After Fidel Castro's rise to power in January 1959, Huberto Matos was imprisoned on the grounds that he criticized and sought to undermine the new regime in Cuba. He spent the next 20 years in prison.

*** Senator Clifford Philip Case (R–New Jersey, 1955–1979); Senator Edward M. Kennedy (D–Massachusetts, 1962 to present); and Congressman Edward Irving Koch (D–New York, 1969–1977).

Seabrook
March 2, 1977

The severe ~~cold of this~~ winter in our Eastern states ~~should have~~ *could be of* some benefit if it would focus attention on the price we are paying to humor certain special Int. groups.

I'll be right back.

We all want clean air, clean water, the beauty of nature preserved and on the side a place to live, to work and a ~~cet~~ certain amount of comfort. A great many people in the East were denied the latter this winter when fuel ran low, businesses closed and their homes became frigid, unheated iceboxes.

There can be no denying that excessive regulation of the energy industry set us up for the horrors of this, coldest in a century, winter.

Recently the Wall St. Journal recounted the problems of one utility co. in trying to add to our available supply of energy. They named their story "The Seabrook Scandal." * Seabrook is the location picked by Pub. Svc. Co. of New Hampshire to build two nuclear power plants to provide power for all of New England.

The Co. was given a go ahead *by the Nuclear Regulatory Commission* to start construction last summer. The approved design was for ~~a~~ plants that would pump sea water into the cooling system and then back into the Ocean through an elaborate tunnel. The environmental admin. in the area declared the plant met E.P.A. standards. Everything looked fine at that point even though construction had been delayed 2 full years by the regulatory burocracy.

Then the regional administrator reversed himself last Nov.** This threw the problem to his superiors in Wash. So far they have made no decision. The hang up happens to be over whether harm will be done to some clam larvae.

Since E.P.A. (the Environmental Protection Agency) wont give an answer the Nuc. Regulatory Commission ~~a~~ has now become doubtful about letting construction ~~get~~ continue. The answer may be to scrap the tunnels & use cooling towers. This could mean having to find an entirely new & different location. In the meantime while the burocrats do what burocrats do best, "hem & haw & stall" each month of delay costs the Utility Co. $15 mil. Not only does no one know <u>what</u> the answer will be—they dont know <u>when</u> it will be. At $15 mil. a month that is heavy. With the right or common sense answer New Eng. could be getting elec. power by 1981. That is more delay than is neces-

* "The Seabrook Scandal," *The Wall Street Journal,* February 1, 1977, p. 20.

** On November 9, 1976, John A. S. McGlennon, the regional administrator for the Environmental Protection Agency, announced that he was reversing his initial approval of a plant-cooling system for a nuclear power project in Seabrook, New Hampshire. See John Kifner, "Nuclear Plant in New Hampshire Loses Approval of Cooling Plan," *The New York Times,* November 10, 1976, p. 16.

sary but if the decision is cooling towers there is no way of knowing when if ever there will be power because it is possible the plants cant be built at all.

Already years have been spent getting the original permission. Then in good faith P.S.C. started construction—$140 mil. worth so far. Total investment is estimated at around $600 mil. How much of that can be salvaged if any is anyones guess—that is if the project must be called off.

Once again we run into the ec. mythology so prevalent that lets us think somehow a corp. absorbs and writes off a loss of this kind. First of all what business can absorb $600 mil. in dead loss. The truth is all of this will have to be recovered from future sales of electric power. Which means the people of New England will pay hundreds of mils. of $ more in utility bills just because some burocrats fumbled and stumbled.

~~The only~~ But we can spread the blame a little. It is doubtful there would have been the costly delays and reversed decisions if there had not been a radical fringe of the environmental movement determined to halt the developement of nuclear power at any cost. Now as the Wall st. Journal says they've learned they can kill off the generation of elec. power simply by causing delays that make the costs prohibitive.

This is RR Thanks for listening. ❖

Added Inflation

March 2, 1977

We know that govt. causes inflation by spending more than it takes in—but then it adds to inflation indirectly by regulation & Statute. I'll be right back.

~~I've talked about govt. regulations on these and the~~

Many times on these programs I've talked about govt. regulations & how they impose on our freedom. I've also talked about taxes and given examples of how so called business taxes must wind up in the price of the product meaning we pay ~~for~~ all of them when we line up at the counter to make a purchase.

To inflation & taxes lets add another cost to all of us which is the indirect inflation brought about by excessive regulation and govt. statutes.

In spite of all the talk and congressional debate regulations are ~~increasing~~ multiplying like spores ~~from~~ *on* a fungus. In 1974 it ~~was~~ *all* the talk seemed to be heading toward some kind of action. But also in 1974 the Fed. Register needed 45,422 pages to list all the new U.S. govt. decrees & regulations that year. That was a 25% increase in pages over the preceding year. Funk & & Wagnalls new encyclopedia—25 volumes a stack of books 3 ft. high only had 12,000 pages.

Those regulations add to the cost of doing business in a variety of fields and many ways which means they add to the cost of the ~~th~~ things we buy. For example Congressman Bill Armstrong of Col.* estimates, "Restrictive ~~practices~~ rate policies of the Interstate Commerce Commission add $5 Bil. per year in excess freight rates passed on to the consumer."

Sen. James McClure of Idaho** confirms this by calling attention to a Brookings Inst. study which put the ec. loss caused by I.C.C. regulations in 1968 alone as ranging from a low of ~~3.78~~ about $3.8 Bil. to a high of almost $8.8 Bil.

Congressman Armstrong also gave an example of what we pay for some of the reform programs over & above the tax cost for implementing ~~the~~ *those* programs. Obviously we all support anti-pollution efforts but we'd also like to know whether we are getting cleaner air & water at the best possible price. In 1972 Congress jumped on the pollution bandwagon. It was the newest & best pol. cause since Motherhood. In just 4 yrs.—by 1976 ~~it had added~~ $127 Bil. *HAD BEEN ADDED* to industrial costs which of course added to the inflationary spiral as prices went up *in* each of those 4 yrs. for ~~the products of industry~~ *the industrial products* we buy.

Last year the Congress adopted rule reforms including a requirement that new spending schemes ~~include~~ *carry* an ~~environmental~~ "*inflationary* impact statement;" ~~as to~~ an estimate of what effect the spending program would have on the rate of inflation. You cant fault that as an idea for slowing down the increase in the cost of living.

But apparently Congressmen reserve the right to disobey their own rules or at least to make exceptions. One of their colleagues Rep. Bauman*** from Maryland has just blown the whistle on the growing practice of committees which pass spending programs out to the floor with a simple ~~claim~~ *assurance,* quote—"no inflationary impact" unquote. He gives as one example the suspension of food stamp regulations which wound up ~~cos~~ adding up to a Bil. $ in cost.

All told he says the grand total for 11 different bills is about $22 bil. in added govt. cost. Yet all eleven were reported out of their respective committees with the flat declaration that they would not ~~add~~ *contribute* to inflation.

When we are already spending some $50 Bil. over & above our revenues there is no way you can increase that ~~spending~~ deficit by almost 50% without adding to inflation.**** This is R.R. Thanks for listening. ❖

* R–Colorado, 1973–1979; also served as U.S. senator (R–Colorado, 1979–1991).

** R–Idaho, 1973–1991.

*** Robert E. Bauman (R–Maryland, 1973–1981).

**** Reagan's experience as president would be that deficits need not add to inflation if not accommodated by an inflationary monetary policy.

Sports and Religion
March 2, 1977

I'm going to tell you a little story out of the sports pages & hope it will make you feel as good as it made me feel. I'll be right back.

A few weeks ago having covered the news section, then the comics and the editorial page of the morning paper (and I do it in that order) I turned to the sports section. This dosen't mean that sports come last on my list of priorities—far from it. I'm just a creature of habit, set in my ways.

My eye was caught by a *4 COLUMN* photo of a basketball team & coach on the bench, heads bowed, ~~some with their heads in as if in~~ *or RESTING on their crossed arms. I read the* caption thinking this must be a team ~~gr~~ that had just suffered a terrible defeat. I was wrong. Their heads were bowed not in grief but in prayer. They ~~are~~ *play* under the title "Athletes In Action"—(A.I.A.)* and as the caption writer couldn't resist pointing out they are a team that prays together & plays together.

A.I.A. ~~is~~ the sports arm of Campus Crusade for Christ is headquartered in Tustin Calif. and hopes to represent the United States at the world championships in Manila in 1978. They may very well make it. Recently they overwhelmed ~~No. 1 ranked~~ *the countrys top ranked team,* U. of S. F. 104 to 85 then rode over Nevada Las Vegas (also highranked) 104 to 77. Nev. went into the game ~~with A.I.A.~~ averaging 53 rebounds a game—they got only 33 and A.I.A. had 64.

This is an amateur team and plays colleges & U's. who can take the defeats handed them because they dont ~~share~~ appear in their win, lose record. A.I.A.'s record at the time of the photo was 78 wins 14 losses *TOTAL RECORD—they are 25–6 for the season*—all on the road. They have no home base. ~~O~~

One of their players turned down a no cut 2 year contract with a pro team that would have brought him $230,000. There are other former U. stars who were high draft choices for pro ball. Their inc. is $700 if single, $900 if married and it is not for playing basketball.

They are ministers. When half time comes they dont go to the locker room for the coaches input on what to do in the 2nd half. They towel themselves off, pick up microphones and ~~preach~~ tell the crowd of their belief in God.

The news article said the reaction is mixed. Sometimes they get attentive audiences but sometimes on college campuses they are booed, ~~&~~ jeered ~~at by~~ *and cursed* by small but noisy groups. As one of them said though "We just try to rise above it." And they must succeed because between 2 & 3000 people have responded to their half time messages by accepting God. In addition another 10,000 have responded by mail asking for more information.

* Athletes in Action is a Christian sports ministry group that operates at both the university and professional level. It also fields its own teams in some sports and has offices in Xenia, Ohio.

Whereever they are, at home or on the road they address civic groups or speak in churches and hold clinics in ~~se~~ high schools and with coaches. And all the time they have a basketball team that some say could go up against the Pro's and give a good account of ~~themselves.~~ *itself*. After all they have beaten the No. 1 college team and in the midwest broke a 48 game home winning streak of another top ranked U. team.

They have a faith that has enabled them to gamble that they can buy TV time for thousands of $ and put their games on television as ~~dell~~ delayed telecasts. I'm going to start looking for them, they just may be the best amateur team in the country and can get even better. ~~Because of religio~~ Some of the nations top stars are interested in joining them when their college days are over and the bait isn't basketball it's faith in God.

This is RR Thanks for listening. ❖

President Jimmy Carter's first economic plan was proposed January 27, 1977. Reagan takes the opportunity to support across-the-board tax rate cuts. In May 1977 Carter signed a tax cut bill and a jobs bill, both larger than Carter had proposed.

Economic Plan
March 23, 1977

† This time it isn't *pol.* party partisanship that will hurt us; It's Congress versus the exec. branch. But whoever wins we the people lose. I'll be right back.

The Pres. has submitted an ec. plan to Congress calling for a rebate of $50 to part of the people* and a govt. plan for putting some of the unemployed on the public payroll. There is also a tiny break for business, tax wise which it is claimed will stimulate bus. & industry to expand thus providing more jobs. *UNFORTUNATELY IT IS TOO TINY TO DO ANY GOOD.* It is not a good plan but ~~certainly~~ *still* it is *a little* ~~*better than*~~ better than the amended version turned out by the House Ways & Means Committee. Their version is a concession to the anti-business bias which characterizes them philosophically.

~~The leader The White House version~~ ~~*plan*~~ ~~ran into~~ Congressman Al Ullman** ~~of the~~ *chairman* of the Ways & Means Committee ~~who~~ was so determined to do things his way that we now have an ec. monstrosity which will solve nothing and mess up much. Mr. Ullman titles his plan the "jobs tax credit program." It has a supposed stimulant to encourage companies to hire new workers. But the AFL-CIO director of Research calls it "an admin. nightmare." The chief economist for the U.S. Chamber of Commerce is equally ve-

* Not all taxpayers would get a rebate.
** Congressman Albert Ullman (D–Oregon, 1957–1981).

hement in his denunciations *and those two arent usually on the same side.* ~~and a~~*A*n economist for the liberal Brookings Inst. says it "encourages employers to substitute parttime workers for fulltime workers & low inc. workers for moderate income workers." Actually the plan only reaches ~~a limited segment of the labor force,~~ the unskilled & low paid, least productive sector. The Asst. Sec. of the Treasury says it ignores 66% of the work force.

Maybe by the time you hear this it will be all over, ~~but we've seen already a confrontation head on between those who still believe in~~ *and we'll be trying, once again,* the social tinkering, ~~the patent medicine~~ & snake oil cures that have failed so many times ~~and a~~ *in the past.*

A bi-partisan group in Cong. who believe the free market can handle inflation & unemp. if govt. will just get out of the way, *has come up with something better but no one seems to be listening.*

For 4 yrs. a young N.Y. Congressman Jack Kemp* has been urging on his colleagues a tax plan ~~which is~~ based on common sense & backed by a record of proven success. ~~In fact t~~*T*he pattern ~~from~~ *for* his plan comes from the early '60's. and ~~the then~~ Pres. John. F. Kennedy. It calls for an across the board tax cut ~~that will~~ *to* provide needed incentives for long term ec. growth.

The Carter plan & the Ullman distortion of that plan will both add to the deficit & therefore to inflation. Kemps plan calls for each inc. tax bracket ~~being~~ *to be* lowered about 15%. ~~This would really only put the brackets~~ *Ullman & his cohorts scream that* ~~reducing across the board gives~~ *this would give* a break to those with higher earnings. ~~& so it does~~ *Yes*—the same break given to those ~~in~~ *with* lower ~~incomes~~ *earnings.* The top tax brackets will ~~be percentage wise~~ be just as much higher than the lower ~~rates~~ as they are right now.

In 1962–63 John F. Kennedy chose this way to get "the country moving again." He cut the 91% bracket down to 70 and the 20% bottom rate to 14%. His Keynesian advisors swore the govt. would suffer great losses of needed tax revenues. Indeed they ~~published their projections~~ *predicted* that between 1963 & 1968 ~~a total of 6 yrs.~~ tax revenues would decline from ~~2.3~~ *2.4%* in '63 to a drop of 24.4% in '68 *for*—a six year loss of 89%.

Instead the stimulus to the ec. was so immediate that actual tax revenues ~~went up 7% the 1st yr. and~~ totaled a 54% increase over the 6 yrs. The doom criers were off in their projections ~~a total of~~ *by* 143%.

If we look back in hist. to the Eisenhower years & earlier we find this is always the result of reducing taxes across the board. ~~Of course both~~ *Congressman Ullman has chosen failure over a* record of certain success. This is RR Thanks for listening.

† —(This probably should be the 1st recorded on the 23rd) ❖

* R–New York, 1971–1989.

Taxes
March 23, 1977

This is the season for paying taxes—also for hearing a lot of demagogery about those who supposedly have found some devious way to escape paying. I'll be right back.

A short while ago the morning paper gave a few paragraphs to a news release from the treasury dept. The headline on the story read "182 Pay No Inc. Tax Despite Making $200,000 or More." The story itself has become an annual report it seems, since an outgoing under Sec. of Treasury--3 days before the inaugural in 1969--told a Congressional Committee we faced a possible tax revolt by the middle class because there were, "many high inc. Americans who paid little or no Fed. Inc. Tax." * This of course was a serious distortion of fact.

Congress acted like Cong. and in no time at all we had the tax reform of 1969—probably the worst tax legis.*lation* in the memory of any of us. Ever since, those inclined to sensationalism & demagogery come riding forth at tax harvest time to inflame people's passions, charging there is skullduggery abroad in the land.

In spite of inflation the earning level chosen for the stories remains that $200,000 figure. ~~a~~*A*nd, as in this most recent news item, the indicted individuals are always referred to as rich. Now I'll agree $200,000 is a healthy income, but it ~~dosen't~~ *isn't* automatically ~~mean~~ *accompanied* by great wealth. Those could be one time earnings for a golf pro having a hot season on the tournament circuit. Earnings at that level are not uncommon to athletic stars in a variety of sports who ~~may~~ will only have a few years of such earnings--and no allowance is made by the Internal Rev. Svc. for the shortness of the earning period.

One has to wonder if the purpose of the annual story is to make taxpayers angry by intimating that a few greedy conspirators get a free ride while average citizens strain to pay their yearly tribute. *IF SO* You'd think the Treasury Dept. would realize it was admitting failure on it's part to treat everyone fairly.

~~T~~ If the dept. feels it must ~~realize~~ release this info. each yr. why dosen't it also offer an explanation about the 182 non taxpayers & why they paid no tax. The year before there were 244.

In 1969 Congress was provided with an explanation for each one of the cases *in* the departing under secretarys bombshell. Some had lost law suits that took more than their entire years income, some had business losses that wiped

* For a review of the statement of Secretary of the Treasury Joseph W. Barr see "Treasury Secretary Warns of Taxpayers' Revolt," *The New York Times,* January 18, 1969, p. 15, and Eileen Shanahan, "Mills Will Examine Tax Returns of 155 Who Paid Nothing," *The New York Times,* March 22, 1969, p. 1.

out earnings, catastrophic losses such as fire or flood and a few had earned & paid their taxes in a foreign land. One stuck in my mind—he had reported gambling winnings of $200,000 but he could also prove he lost $440,000 doing the same thing. The head of I.R.S. *SAID* the only way they could get *at* him was to charge an amusement tax.

Lets look at this latest news story again. There were 41,361 persons who had incomes of $200,000 or more. Less than ½ of 1%—182 individuals paid no tax. Are we to believe that the other 41,179 were smart enough to earn $200,000 or better but not smart enough to find those illicit loopholes found by the 182? That is if ~~such~~ *we assume* such loopholes *do* exist.

Why not a story about the fact that a few years ago only 3% of all inc. tax payers were up in the surtax brackets & now, due to inflation, more than 30% are; not because they are better off financially, but mainly because cost of living pay raises put them up in higher tax brackets even though their purchasing power hadn't increased by one $.? That story ~~would~~ might make us mad but we'd be mad at the right people—the members of Cong.

This is R. R. Thanks for listening. ❖

In the next three commentaries on the regimes of Salvador Allende Gossens and Augusto Pinochet Ugarte, Reagan reiterates the views he expressed in his December 1976 commentary, "Milton Friedman and Chile," and he further indicts Socialist leadership in Chile.

Chile I
March 23, 1977

One of our delegates to the United Nations ~~found it necessary to~~ *decided he had to* apologize ~~for~~ on behalf of the rest of us for actions he says we took against Chilé. I'll be right back.

~~On~~ *A few weeks ago, on* March 8th, ~~in a meeting of the U.N. Human Rights Commission Brady Tyson U.S. delegate said~~ *our delegate to the U.N. Brady Tyson said,* "We would be less than candid & untrue to ourselves & our people if we did not express our profound regrets for the role some govt. officials, agencies & private groups played in the subversion of the previous democratically elected Chilean govt." * He was speaking, of course, of the election of the late Pres. Salvador Allende. Thank Heaven our govt., by way of State dept. & White House, immediately disavowed ~~his~~ *Tyson's* apology & made it plain he was speaking only for himself. ~~But Nevertheless the Tyson apology got worldwide press. And~~ *Yet,* in spite of that disavowal our govt. does maintain a

* Brady Tyson's statement is found in "U.S. Official Expresses 'Regrets' for Role in Chile but is Disavowed," *The New York Times*, March 9, 1977, p. 1.

discriminatory policy against the present Chilean regime. ~~despite the fact that Chilé is probably the most pro American of all the Latin Am. nations.~~

In Congress particularly the attitude is, first that Allende ~~*In Sept. of 1970*~~ was truly elected by the people in democratic style~~;~~, *&* 2nd that he was deposed in Sept. of 1973 by a military coup covertly aided & or directed by the C.I.A. & U.S. military. It is time to put these assumptions into proper perspective & to focus a little illumination on the whole Chilean situation.

In Sept. of 1970 Allende won 36.2% of the vote in a 3 way race. Thus he was not the choice of 63.8% of the voters. Normally one would expect a run off election. Under the Chilean const. however the Congress is empowered to ratify a winner. ~~in~~ The Congress did ratify Allende as ~~but~~ Pres. *but* only after he signed a Const. amendment reaffirming freedom of the press, ed., electoral process and the non-involvement of the military in pol. matters. ~~The amendment was titled a "Statute of Guarantees."~~ Following his election by the Congress, Allende told a ~~f~~French journalist Regis DeBray,* "I signed the amendment as a simple tactical necessity to gain power."

There is little or no evidence to support Mr. Tyson's statement that the U.S., through either the military or the C.I.A. rigged, ran or even participated in the subsequent overthrow of Allende. ~~There have been admissions indicating~~ *We apparently did give* some small campaign assistance to one or the other of ~~Allendes~~ *his* opponents in the election but ~~then~~ the Soviet U. ~~gave Allende 20 mil. in campaign aid.~~ *was giving the Allende ~~≠~~ campaign $20 mil.*

After he assumed office, no foreign govt's., including our own, played any significant part in the failure of Allende's Marxist experiment. ~~The U.S.~~ *We* withheld relatively minor amounts of aid or credit, but this had to be expected in the face of ~~Allendes~~ *his* seizure of private assets owned by Americans.

All the facts, few of which have been made available to Americans, make it plain that Allende's 1000 days as Pres. were a disaster for the people of Chilé~~.~~ ~~indeed a daily disaster. He excited & polarized extremists of both sides and actively encouraged violence.~~ One witness on the scene for all those 1000 days has said, "If Allende was the creator of the Chilean Marxist Experiment he also was without doubt it's executioner. The record speaks for itself for those who are willing to listen."

I hope you are willing to listen because on the next broadcast I'm going to ~~give some talk about that actual record. First of all~~ *give that record.* ~~w~~ With the Soviet U. spreading it~~'~~s influence in Latin America as energetically as it is I think we~~,~~--the Am. people~~,~~--should have the facts about a Latin Am. neighbor who apparently is ready to be an ally of the U.S. Especially a neighbor with a long record of enlightened democratic traditions similar to our own. This is R.R. Thanks for listening. ❖

* Following a stay in Cuba, Regis Debray was captured in Bolivia while traveling with Ernesto "Che" Guevara, a revolutionary, and sentenced to 30 years in prison. Many world leaders and eminent scholars championed Debray's case, and in 1970 he was pardoned. He went to Chile and wrote a book based on interviews with President Salvador Allende. In the 1980s and 1990s, Debray was a foreign policy adviser to President François Mitterrand.

Chile II

March 23, 1977

~~Yesterday~~ Last broadcast I said I would give the record of the late Pres. Allende of Chilé and his 1000 days in office ~~The~~ leading to his overthrow & death. Ill be rite back.

On Sept. 11th 1973, Pres. Salvador Allende of Chilé was overthrown ~~by~~ *in* a mil. coup that probably received more world-wide media coverage than any similar event in history. At 1:45 on the afternoon of the 11th--fifteen minutes after his supporters had surrendered--he committed suicide with a gun which bore a gold plate in its stock inscribed with the words: "To my good friend Salvador Allende. Fidel Castro."

≠ A barrage of propaganda, aided & abetted by the world communist press, tried to portray this as a democratically ~~initiated~~ conceived govt. reflecting the will of the people ~~of Chilé,~~ overthrown by ~~amb~~ politically ambitious mil. leaders.

Allende's downfall was the direct result of shameful ec. mismanagement, deliberate violation of his nation's const. & laws and terrorist tactics imposed on his people. The chief foreign correspondent of the London Times, Dave Holden, said; "Unfortunately nobody with even a nodding acquaintance with economics could have classified the management of the Allende govt. as anything but disastrous."

When Allende took office the govt. had $343 mil. in reserves. Three yrs. later Chilés <u>deficit</u> was more than $300 mil. The admitted inflat. rate was 508%, but economists charged the figs. were rigged to hide a real inflat. rate of $700%. Either fig. was a world record for inflat~~.ion rates~~.

The govt. ~~inst~~ had increased the amount of paper money ~~842%~~ *670%* in 2 yrs. The consumer price index had gone up 842% ~~by 1983~~. ~~Wheat prod. was down 45%, corn 75% &~~ *Agricultural production was down* 22% *and* copper, ~~production~~ *which makes up* ~~(~~80% of Chilés foreign export,~~)~~ *was* down 25%.

Allende had assumed control of all the banks & therefore of all loans, savings & fluid financial assets essential to business. ~~With printed~~ *Using* printing press money, massive spending programs were instituted mainly to benefit the roughly ⅓ of the people who were Allende's constituency. By June of 1973 the govt. had confiscated 282 large industries which produced more than ½ of the countries output. Almost 6000 farms ~~were seized~~ ≠--*40% of the agricultural land*--was seized (much of it at gunpoint) and redistributed, ≠ again to Allendes followers. In the summer of '73 there were great food shortages & those who couldn't afford to deal in the black market lined up for hours to buy rationed necessities.

In May of '73 Chilés Sup. Ct. unanimously denounced the Allende regime for "disruption of the legality of the nation." ~~because it refused to uphold a criminal courts decision to evict persons from illegally seized private property.~~ One month later a 2nd Sup. Ct. resolution charged the Pres. with illegal & unconst. interference in legal affairs that fell within the exclusive competence of the Judicial power. A few weeks later the *MEMBERS OF THE* 2 houses of Congress appealed to Allendé to reestablish legality "before it is too late." They cited the danger inherent in his, "creation of a parallel army in which numerous foreigners are collaborating." These foreigners were primarily Cuban and they were featherbedded on the payrolls of the ~~seized~~ confiscated businesses & ~~indust~~ *industries.*

By Aug. the Congress charged the Pres. with widespread violation of Human Rights and the Bar Assn. issued a report concluding that only Cong. was competent to legislate & determine the extent of Presidential Power.

Tomorrow I'll try to cover the final days & the specific events leading up to the overthrow. This is RR. Thanks for listening. ❖

Chile III

March 23, 1977

In the summer of 1973 Chilé was a revolution looking for someplace to happen. There was no question as to whether the govt. would fall--only when. I'll be right back.

Allende, the late Pres. of Chilé, has been described as a gentle man of the people. Maybe so but he declared *in 1970* that if *the* Congress didn't make him Pres., "Santiago would be painted red with blood." When he was questioned as to how he could keep a campaign promise to provide a quart of milk *every day* for every Chilean child he replied, "when we run ~~of~~ out of 4 legged beasts, we'll milk the 2 legged kind."

By 1973 his presidential retreat in the Andean foothills was the training center for a 15,000 man private army equipped with Russian weapons. ~~His~~ *The commander of his* personal bodyguard ~~commander~~ was a Cuban assassin nicknamed "Easy Trigger." The mil. instructors were Cuban & so were most of the 15,000 man force.

~~His~~ *In that final summer,* On June 27th, ~~in that final summer~~ his hand picked cheif of the regular army, Gen. Gonzalez, was involved in a street incident ~~in the Capitol~~ that reveals the pol. climate. A woman driver passing the General's car stuck out her tongue at him. Despite the heavy midday traffic he gave chase firing 2 shots at her car. Overtaking her he put his pistol to her head, called her an ~~unrepeat~~ unrepeatable name & demanded an apology. This was too much for ~~the crowd of~~ several hundred ~~people on the street. They rescued the woman &~~ *bystanders who went to the womans rescue.* ~~t~~The Gen. ~~was lucky to~~ *barely* escaped with his life.*

On June 29th a single armored regiment--in ~~a comic~~ *an almost* comic opera

* For this story about General Carlos Prats Gonzalez, see Jonathan Kandell, "Chile Declares Emergency in Capital Region After Disorders," *The New York Times,* June 28, 1973, p. 18.

move--launched an attack on the Presidential Palace. The tanks went through Santiago stopping at all the traffic signals and running out of gas in front of the Palace. Let it be noted, the regular army ~~not the Presidents personal *gang* army~~ put down the abortive attack.

But Allende ~~went~~ *seized the opportunity to go* on the air and ~~urged~~ *urge* his followers to take over all industries and enterprises. ~~It is significant~~ The workers, who responded & took over 244 factories, were surprisingly prompt & well armed.

~~Civilian morale was at zero.~~ In July the transportation workers walked off the job, joined by most other unions & professional assns. Food virtually disappeared. Medical care was available only for emergencies. Municipal services ceased, electric & tel. service was a sometime thing & there was no gas at the gas stations.

On Aug 7th A radical, communist org. known as M.I.R.* *SUPPORTED BY ALLENDES LDRS IN COM* ~~+~~ was revealed ~~*on Aug 7*~~ as having infiltrated the navy with a plot for *mutiny &* murder. ~~600 top mil. Allendes top Congressional leaders were involved.~~

On the 22nd of Aug. 300 army wives appeared before Gen. Gonzalez' home ~~& demanded~~ *demanding* his resignation. The Gen. had fire hoses turned on them.

The Admiral commanding the navy resigned; and, still hopeful of avoiding civil strife, top naval officers begged Allende to appoint as his successor Admiral Jose Merino.** The Pres. agreed & ~~Mer~~ on Sept. 7th Merino went to the Palace to be sworn in. *But,* Allende reneged on his promise and the embarrassed Admiral returned to his ship.

All day & night on Sept 8th shocked senior naval officers met & conferred. By now ~~they *the naval officers*~~ *they* had learned of "Plan Zeta"--~~*the*~~ *an* MIR plot to murder *on SEPT.* 18th. 600 key mil. figures & civilian leaders.*** ~~on Sept. 18th. On~~ Sunday Sept 9th ~~they~~ *the naval officers* sent a simple msg. to the Army & Air force commanders, "D-day is Tues. The hour is 0600." The two generals gave a one word ~~response~~ *answer* "conformé"--meaning concur.

On Sept. 11th. ~~whatever~~--*regardless of what* the propagandists ~~might~~ *say about it*--the Chilean military freed the people of Chilé.

This is RR. Thanks for listening. ❖

Swine flu was the 1976–77 version of influenza. The government's vaccination program ran into problems.

* The Movement of the Revolutionary Left.

** Vice Admiral Jose Toribio Merino was head of Chile's First Naval Zone.

*** The existence of Plan Zeta (also known as Plan Z) is still under dispute and is seen by many as the military's public excuse for overthrowing Allende. The military held that Plan Zeta was a Marxist plot by MIR to destroy the Chilean military and take control of the country.

Murphy's Law
March 23, 1977

~~Back in the mid~~

I must confess to being one of the estimated 40 mil. Americans who had a Swine-Flu shot. You do remember Swine-Flu don't you? I'll be right back.

Back in the middle '30s on a New Years Eve a song swept the country and for the few hours preceding midnight seemed to be the only song anyone wanted to hear. It was ~~a~~ silly but easy to sing—catchy is the word. It literally played itself out on that New Years Eve. Oh you heard it occasionally after that but it's peak was reached ~~in the~~ between sunset & midnight on that one holiday.

Now I don't know what this has to do with Swine-Flu but for some reason it popped into my mind when I read some articles about the epidemic we didn't have and the flurry over whether to vacinate or not.

There is a thing called Murphy's Law.* It is—"Whatever can go wrong will go wrong." And the Swine-flu vaccination ~~law~~ certainly proved the truth of Murphys law.

On March 24 [1976] the Pres. announced the govt. would provide "every man, woman and child" with Swine Flu immunization. Trouble started within 24 hours. Dissent with the idea came from such diverse circles as the N.Y. Times, Health Research Groups, Dr. Wolfe & even the inventor of Oral Polio vaccine, Dr. Albert Sabin. He however by June had changed his mind.

Congress passed a $135 mil bill including $110 mil. to buy the vaccine & $26 mil. to subsidize state health depts. State officials screamed because that only pro-rated out to 13 cents a shot & cost would be $1.10.

On June 2nd HEW officials announced a slight technical problem. One of the 4 vaccine mgfrs. had produced 2 mil. doses of the wrong vaccine. The Fed. Drug Admin.'s Bureau of Biologics had given them the wrong culture strain. Later in June officials of the Nat. Inst. for Allergy & Infectious diseases reported problems in determining the proper dosages for children. It seems that enough to stop the flu would cause too many side effects.

In July 2 firms said they wouldn't participate unless they were given liability protection. Finally Congress after great debate offered such protection not only to the mgfrs. but to Dr's. involved in the free public immunization clinics.

By Aug 1 all signals were go and the drug firms announced 101 mil. doses on hand. They would be ready by the Sept. 15 starting date. But some one must have learned to count in the "new math." On Aug. 27 the firms said they

* According to one account, Murphy's Law originated in 1949 with a comment by Captain Edward A. Murphy, an engineer at Edwards Air Force Base in California, criticizing a technician for an incorrectly wired test device: "If there is any way to do it wrong, he'll find it."

couldn't make shipment before Oct. 1 and only ¼ of the 101 mil. doses were on hand. Then they told the shell shocked planners of mass immunization that only 65 mil. doses would be ready for shipment by <u>Nov</u> 30th.

Finally the program got off the ground. Then the press began reporting deaths of ~~elde~~ elderly people connected with the vaccinations. Local health depts. began closing down the program. Then the 1st case of swine flu was reported in Missouri. But the "confirmed" on that case was withdrawn & he didn't have ~~it~~ swine flu after all. Then came the charge that a certain paralysis resulted ~~fr~~ from some vaccinations. The debate still rages on that one. There were 12 deaths ~~who~~ in cases where there had been vaccination but there were 9 where there had been no shots given. And it seems no one knows what does cause that particular paralysis.

The argument will go on I'm sure for years about whether the program was right or wrong. But one thing is certain—Murphys Law was upheld.

This is RR Thanks for listening. ❖

Redwoods

April 13, 1977

~~The present excuse being used by the Congressman~~

This may come as a shock to those who think the nation is becoming an environmental wasteland but we dont need a Nat. Park to save the Redwoods. I'll be right back.

Congressman Phil Burton of Calif.* has introduced a bill to add 50 or 75,000 ~~additional~~ acres of Redwood forest land to California's Nat. Redwood park. He plays on a misconception that somehow the great Redwood trees are in danger of being lost forever and only the enlarging of the present Nat. park can save them. That isn't true.

~~Lacking the truth about the Redwoods~~ *Still* I'm sure that *lacking the truth* many Americans are ready to march ~~further~~ forth under ~~Mr.~~ *the* Burton~~s~~ banner. ~~After all t~~*T*he giant Redwood trees *of Calif.* are unique in all the world and must be considered a Nat. treasure. Standing in one of the Cathedral like groves of giant trees *IS A MOVING EXPERIENCE &* one can feel very close to God and very humble. ~~It is a truly moving experience.~~

Why then am I critical of ~~the~~ *the* Congressman? ~~Burton? Because~~ The answer ~~to that one~~ is ~~because~~—we dont ~~*t*~~ need his bill or a Nat park to preserve the Redwoods. Thanks to an org. called "Save The Red Woods league" virtually all the superlative trees, ~~what I called~~ the Cathedral like groves, have been incorporated into state parks already. The league for decades has been raising

* D–California, 1964–1983.

money to buy these groves & give them to the park service. And for the most part the lumber companies have been most cooperative in not cutting the superlative trees until the league could make the purchase. Somewhere near 200,000 acres have been preserved with only about 4000 scattered ~~a~~ *acres of* superlative trees still in private hands.

The Redwood forests are a major part of the economy in Northern Calif. providing ~~j~~ thousands of jobs ~~for~~ in the lumber industry and an extremely fine wood for home building & ~~furnt~~ furniture. ~~The industry is~~ Closely regulated by the state, *the industry* ~~and~~ has achieved or is close to a sustained yield basis—cutting no faster than replacement growth. Still it has been subjected to constant harassment by some who apparently want ~~no harvesting of Redwoods at all.~~ *every Redwood tree left standing.*

This is unrealistic. ~~and unnecessary. The Redwood is a fast growing tree,~~ ~~t~~*The* VAST *Redwood* forests ~~cover a vast area & the trees being lumbered are not the great spectaculars.~~ *are not made up of the giant 1000 yr. old trees one sees on the picture postcards.* ~~Redwoods~~ *Redwoods* are fast growing ~~and grow to~~ *reaching* lumbering size in ~~no more than~~ *about* 40 yrs. ~~We are not going to run out of Redwood forests.~~ *Our great grandchildren will see as many Redwoods as we see today.*

For years th*ere* ~~opponents of the industry~~ *have* ~~demanded a nat. park.~~ *has been a demand for a Nat. Redwood park.* Finally Congress gave in with no real enthusiasm & ~~perhaps even less understanding of the true situation.~~ *no understanding of the extent of the magnificent Calif. state parks.* As Gov. at the time I had to tell the chrmn. of the Congressional committee a park was unneccesary from the standpoint of saving the trees.~~—that had been done~~ *They had already been saved* but possibly a nat. park would ~~halt the harassment & give~~ *calm the waters & bring* stability to the ~~northern part of our state.~~ *industry.*

~~The present~~ *So we have a* nat. park *which* would have little attraction if it were not between 2 of Calif's. most beautiful state parks ~~and indeed r~~Roughly half of the 55,000 acre nat. park consists of what ~~is~~ was already state park land. To illustrate what I said about the lack of need for a nat. park ~~to save the Redwoods~~ the Fed. govt. bought roughly 27,000 acres of which ~~only 3 Almos~~ *almost 16,000* were cut over ~~of non timber land.~~ *or open land without trees.* By contrast the state park portion *is* 28,000 acres of which about 20,000 ~~were~~ *are* superlative & old growth big trees with only about 4000 acres in cut over & non timber land.

The excuse for enlarging the Nat. park is that a buffer zone of Redwoods must ~~surround~~ *be provided to protect* the present park boundaries. But if a buffer zone is added to the park wont that call for another buffer zone to protect the buffer zone and that can go on until you run out of trees.

This is R R. Thanks for listening. ❖

Capital Punishment
April 13, 1977

A few years ago 70% of the people of Calif. voted for the re-instituting of Capital punishment.* Now a visitor to ~~the state~~ *Calif* has told state legislators ~~why we shouldn't have it.~~ *the people are wrong.* I'll be right back.

A short while ago a former Attorney Gen. of the U.S. one time anti-war activist and defeated candidate for the U.S. Sen. Ramsey Clark visited Sacramento Calif. Appearing before a ~~group of~~ *State Sen.* Committee he called for limiting all prison sentences to 5 yrs. maximum even for 1st degree murder. He said punishment in itself was a crime. He then expounded on the standard bleeding heart line that prisons weren't the answer; that we must do away with poverty, ~~misery,~~ *lack of ed. &* broken homes. ~~etc.~~ *Do all that* and crime ~~would~~ *will* cease to be.**

A few months ago on one of these broadcasts I reported on a scientific study by two eminent scholars debunking this whole, ~~prison & poverty~~ "*society* ~~a~~is the cause of crime" approach. The study had shown by fact & figure that crime was reduced proportionate to the increased severity *& certainty* of punishment & vice versa.

But Mr. Clark touched a nerve with me when he ~~told~~ *reminded* the Senators *that* Calif. had carried out an execution in 1968*** and then ~~he~~ asked, "did that reduce the murder rate." Having been Gov. at the time *of that execution* I feel called upon to reply. No I dont think one execution ~~could~~ reduce*d* the ~~crime~~ *murder* rate by any measurable degree. But ~~I know one man who thinks it deterred at least one possible murderer.~~ *one Californian has reason to believe that execution* ~~*prevented one murder—his own.*~~ *PREVENTED AT LEAST 1 MURDER—HIS OWN.*

During the week of that ~~last~~ execution ~~in Calif.~~ an elderly storekeeper in San Francisco was victem of a robbery. The husky young robber ~~had held *holding* the storekeeper on~~ *threw him to* the floor ~~and~~ *and* tried to stab him. ~~As the *The* storekeeper s~~Struggle~~d~~*ing* to avoid the ~~descending~~ *descending* blade ~~he~~ *the storekeeper* desperately cried out "You'll get the gas chamber if you do." ~~The robber paused for a second *moment* and then got up &~~ *The knife*

* On February 18, 1972, the California State Supreme Court decided that the death penalty was illegal. Nine months later, on November 7, 1972, Californians voted for Proposition 17, a ballot initiative that reinstated capital punishment. On December 7, 1976, however, the California State Supreme Court struck down the capital punishment law.

** Appointed attorney general by President Lyndon Baines Johnson in 1967, Ramsey Clark served until 1969. Reagan is referring to Ramsey's news conference in Sacramento on April 11, 1977. See Jerry Gillam, "Prison Term Limit of 5 Years Suggested," *Los Angeles Times,* April 12, 1977, part 1, p. 3, and Larry Liebert, "Clark Comes to Lobby Against Executions," *San Francisco Chronicle,* April 12, 1977, p. 6.

*** The only execution during Reagan's governorship actually occurred on April 12, 1967. Reagan refused clemency to Aaron C. Mitchell, who had killed a policeman.

~~*stopped*~~ PAUSED *for a moment in it's descent—then the robber* ran out of the store. The intended victem wrote me that he was convinced the great ~~press~~ attention given the execution *at the time* by the Press ~~at the time~~ had saved his life. Not statistical evidence—just one mans opinion.

But there are statistics which tend to refute the foolishness of a Ramsey Clark. In the years from 1930 until the mid 50's. murder ~~was~~ *was* actually decreasing in ~~Calif~~ the U.S. It fell from more than 10,500 in 1935 to less than 7500 in 1955. During those years ~~as many as 1600 1600~~ *capital* punishment was consistently enforced in most of our states with ~~several hun~~ *executions numbering* in the hundreds each yr. Then in the early 60's. the crusade against capital punishment began to roll. By 1964 there were only 15 executions ~~*in the U.S.*~~ and ~~in 1968 it~~ *4 yrs. later* they stopped all together. ~~during the moratorium while the Sup. Ct. pondered the constitutionality of cap. punishment.~~

Murderers weren't being put to death but murderers were putting others to death; 12,500 in *19'68*, 18,500 in ~~19~~72 and more than 20,500 in 1975. ~~In the 20 yrs. of decline & abolition of the death sentence *the number of* murders increased *tripled*.~~ *A 200% increase in 20 yrs.*

Prof. Isaac ~~Erlich~~ *Ehrlich* of the U. of Chi. offers an explanation of the relationship between crime & punishment.* He says most human acts, including crime are based on costs & benefits. If the cost for doing murder is death and a criminal is aware of ~~ti~~ this he may decide as the young man in the store did that the price is too high.

Prof. Erlich also said that ~~in~~ *during* the years we began saving the lives of murderers we traded the lives of 8 victems for every murderer we didn't execute. That~~'s an~~ *kind of* inflation ~~rate~~ we cant afford.

This is RR Thanks for listening. ❖

Reagan was a leading conservative opponent of the Panama Canal treaties. He argued against them in speeches around the country, and in 1977, at the height of the political debate, he devoted numerous broadcasts, like the one below, to Panama and the negotiations. Handwritten copies exist for these commentaries.

Panama
April 13, 1977

A few weeks ago I read an ad in a Fla. publication that said, "There is no Panama Canal. There is an American Canal in Panama." Someone wants us to forget that. I'll be right back.

* Isaac Ehrlich, assistant and associate professor of economics at the University of Chicago, 1969–1978.

In the next few months we're going to be treated to a sophisticated public relations campaign designed to convince us we really want to give away the Panama Canal. The govt. of Panama has hired an American P.R. firm, headquartered in Wash., to do a nationwide sales job on the American people. The fee is somewhere between $150,000 & $200,000 for a 6 month's campaign, which should buy a fair sized snow job.

It is interesting to note that the firm selected by the Panamanian govt. is one ~~which deals in~~ *experienced in* matters political. The owner is reported to be former Dem. Nat. Chmn. Strauss but the pol. spectrum ~~≠~~ *is pretty* well covered. ~~by those running the operation.~~ Former Goldwater campaigner and participant on the Repub. side in the last campaign, F. Clifton White, will be among those running the operation.*

No one, of course, can know in advance what the advertising theme will be. ~~They could portray~~ *Could be* the canal ~~*a*~~*is* obsolete and ~~really of no great importance to us. Or it could be presented as a~~ *unimportant; or it is a* last vestige of ~~capitalism~~ colonialism ~~which we should give up to win friends in Latin America~~. Then, of course, there is the ever-present threat that enraged Panamanians ~~affronted by our presence in their country~~ will rise up and do violence to us & the canal.

Any, or all, of these could be the basis for the ~~Publicity~~ *sales* campaign. ~~But they would be~~ *And all of them are* as phony as some of the old-time Hollywood publicity used to glorify, ~~some~~ not so epic, screen epics.

~~While one can only guess at what will be said w~~ *We* can be a little more sure of what they wont tell us. There will be no mention of the fact that Gen. Torrijos, Panamas dictator, was not chosen by the people. He seized power at the point of a gun 9 years ago. No reference will be made to the amt. of shipping going through the canal each day, and how much prices would go *UP* if those ships had to go 'round the "Horn." Or, how much prices would go up if someone like the Gen, instead of non-profit Uncle Sam, were setting the toll fees.

We've already been conditioned to accept that Panamanians are at a boiling point over this issue, so I'm sure the P.R. campaign will make no mention of the stories Ronald Yates of the Chi. Tribune, has been filing from Panama City. Yates has found that Torrijos is not an ~~ob~~ object of affection in Panama, and the poor & unemployed want desperately for us to stay in control of the canal.** A number of our Congressmen & Senators have heard the same thing from businessmen & Panamanian leaders, but they only ~~whisper~~ it *express* themselves in whispers.

* Robert S. Strauss was chairman of the Democratic National Committee from 1973 to 1976. Senator Barry Goldwater (R–Arizona, 1953–1965 and 1969–1987) was the Republican nominee for president in 1964. F. Clifton White is a political strategist who worked on behalf of Goldwater's presidential candidacy in 1964.

** Ronald Yates, "Panama's Dictator Tells U.S. to Get Out, Poor Beg Us to Stay," *Chicago Tribune*, March 27, 1977, p. 1.

Mr. Yates found that those with little to lose (except their lives) were bolder. Singly, & in groups and freely giving their names they ~~said things like~~ *are quoted as* saying, "All of us would fight for America to keep the canal." We would never fight against the U.S." The ~~same spokesman openly and backed by a group of his fellow citizens~~ *one who said that also* said "~~We have nothing against America or the Canal zone because we know as long as America has control of the canal there will be jobs for Panamanians~~. *The only people in Panama who have ever given the U.S. trouble are Communists, rich university students, and parasitic intelectuals who live off the blood & sweat of people like us.*" Another ~~citizen~~ said, "Running the canal is a complex thing. As soon as the Panamanian govt. gets it's hands on the controls, forget about the canal as a means of getting ships between the Atlantic & Pacific Oceans." His friends tried to persuade him not to talk because he would be taken away by the police. He shrugged them off and said, "The Americans are the only friends we've got. Poor people dont have nobody else." An old woman summed it up when she told the Tribune reporter, "You ask the General how he got so rich in 8 yrs."

This is RR. Thanks for listening. ❖

Michael Manley, a Socialist, was the prime minister of Jamaica from 1972 to 1980 and from 1989 to 1992.

Jamaica

April 13, 1977

Lenin said, "We will take Eastern Europe, organize the hoardes of Asia & then move into Latin America. We wont have to take the U.S. It will fall into our outstretched hand like overripe fruit. I'll be right back.

In a series of broadcasts a few weeks ago I told of how Pres. Allende of Chilé had taken his country to the very brink of a communist takeover before he was stopped by the Chilean military.

History does repeat itself. It's almost like a re-run on T.V. If you missed Allendes destruction of Chilés economy, his buildup of a private army aided & abetted by Cuba and his elimination of civil liberties tune in on Jamaica.

That island Nation sitting astride the sea lanes leading to the Panama Canal is well on it's way to becoming a communist, indeed a Soviet sattelite. This should worry us ~~not only~~ because of it's geographical position ~~but~~ *and* because it is a source of bauxite & aluminum.

Somehow with so much media attention fixed on Africa very few of our Nation's guardians in Wash. seem aware that Prime Minister Manley is following the blueprint drawn by Allendé. He openly expresses his intention to model Jamaica after ~~his the~~ *HIS* communist neighbor to the North, Cuba. And like Chilé ~~before~~ under Allende there are thousands of Cubans, many of them part of Cubas secret police training communist Cadres in Jamaica.

Several hundred Soviet agents are also enjoying the climate and handing out advice. A student exchange program is a 3 way deal between Cuba, the Soviet U. & Jamaica. Manley has made all the proper statements; he admires the Soviet U., supports the national liberation efforts of the African people *AND WANTS TO SELL THINGS TO E. EUROPE* ~~etc~~. He has also adopted *all* the standard communist procedure's.

Jamaicans who complain about the spreading Marxism receive a certain official attention. Under an emergency act they are "detained." Several hundred are already in jail including the leaders of the opposition political party. There is increasing violence and the usual ~~pressure on~~ *efforts to curb* the press.

Like Allende, Manley is organizing a "peoples militia" that already outnumbers the army & police force put together. But he hasn't stopped there. Cuban experts are selling Communism to the police & military.

Expropriation of American owned ~~of~~ aluminum companies hasn't exactly taken place yet. They've just had to give 51% control to the Jamaican govt. which more & more is becoming Prime Minister Manley. Banks are being nationalized as well as private businesses. Getting away from Jamaica isn't easy for Jamaicans. They can leave but they can only take $50 ~~with them~~ *when they* go. Taxes on a $12,500 inc. are 60%, private land is being confiscated, there are price controls and a growing number of ~~controls~~ *regulations &* restrictions ~~of~~ *on* industry.

And as with Chilé under Allende economic problems are growing. Foreign investors are not coming to Jamaica and Jamaican Drs., lawyers and businessmen are leaving regardless of the $50 limit. Tourists once a major source of income for the island have been scared off by the violence & vandalism. Tourist trade is down to about ¼ of normal.

But guess who is to blame for all these troubles according to Prime Minister Manley—the C.I.A.

This is RR. Thanks for listening. ❖

The United States Supreme Court upheld its landmark Miranda decision on the admissibility of confessions in court by ruling for the defendant in a 1968 Iowa murder case a few weeks before this commentary was taped.

Miranda

April 13, 1977

We thought we were through with the Warren Courts Miranda decision, but it's alive and well by a 5 to 4 Supreme Ct. ruling. I'll be right back.

Some years ago the U.S. Sup. Ct. ruled that a man *named* Miranda could not be convicted on his voluntary confession ~~to a crime of violence~~ *of rape &*

murder because his lawyer wasn't with him at the time & he hadn't been advised by the police that he didn't have to say anything. He went free for a very brief time and then was back for committing the same kind of crime. Of course, no one could bring *back* the victems. ~~back.~~

Since that time, as we've seen in countless crime shows on TV, the police must read an arrested individual his "rights." "You have the right to remain silent etc. etc." That's one line a lot of actors dont have to learn anymore, they've said it so often.

In real life the "Miranda Decision" has resulted in some great mis-carriages of justice as suspects, due to technical error, have gone free even though there was overwhelming evidence of their guilt. Then the Sup. Ct., under Chief Justice Burger,* modified the ruling and a measure of common sense returned to the courtrooms of the land.

Let me make it plain, we must preserve the rights of the accused. Indeed, that was one of the principles we fought a revolution to secure. But we must not forget govt's. obligation to protect the law abiding.

The Miranda decision came back into the Sup. Ct. by way of Iowa a few weeks ago, and ~~f~~Five justices used it to grant a new trial to an escaped mental patient who had been convicted ~~of for for~~ *for the rape &* murder of a 10 yr. old girl on Christmas Eve in 1968.

Chief Justice Burger and three of the Assoc. justices vehemently dissented with their 5 colleagues but to no avail. So once again a confessed killer has, on a legal technicality ~~has~~ a chance to go free.

Briefly here is the story. Little Pamela Powers, 10 yrs. old, disappeared on Christmas Eve 1968. ~~Accordin~~ Robert Williams was arrested in Davenport Iowa and driven to Des Moines by *the* police. He was informed of his rights at least 4 different times and had a lawyer present in Davenport when he said he would tell the whole story in Des Moines.

On the auto trip, a detective who knew that Williams, in ~~sp≠~~ spite of his record of sex offenses also had a kind of religious quirk, mentioned the importance of giving the little girl a "Christian Burial." Actually no one knew whether the missing girl was dead or alive. But the detective who was guessing mentioned the weather forecast of ~~an~~ impending snow and how that would make finding her body difficult. Williams led the police to her body.

It is true the police had promised he wouldn't be questioned during the ride. ~~Actually he wasn't~~ *But was he,* questioned? A very intelligent detective made a couple of observations, one having to do with the weather. He <u>should</u> get a medal. But the court's ruling was that Williams lawyer should have been present.

Now it remains to be seen if 9 years later ~~W.~~ he can be convicted again. ~~o~~Or is there another victem fated to suffer as *little* Pamela did?

~~Yes w~~We want "one nation indivisible—with justice for all"—including little girls who have a right to grow up and live happily—if not forever *at least*

* Chief Justice Warren E. Burger.

until they have ~~lived ≠ and their lives as~~ *become whatever* God intended ~~they should.~~ *them to be.* This is RR Thanks for listening. ❖

Student Letter
April 13, 1977

Are you worried that perhaps our sons & daughters are being led to believe that socialism offers advantages capitalism cant match? I'll be right back.

Economists (at least the *good* old fashioned kind) have written countless books and essays trying to explain that a free mkt. economy is superior to the collectivism of Karl Marx. There really shouldn't be much of an argument with ~~th~~ all the examples we have for comparison. Everywhere there is a socialist nation there is *a* failure to meet the needs of the people *of that nation* ~~without~~ except by calling on *CAPITALIST NEIGHBORS FOR* outside help. ~~from capitalist neighbors.~~ Still it is the socialist world that is expanding while the free world grows smaller.

Well how would you like to feel a little better about the whole thing? I received a letter a couple of weeks ago that brightened my whole day. Paul A. Leonard a Sophomore at Mayo High school in Rochester Minn. wrote to tell me ~~of an experiment~~ he had listened to some of these radio broadcasts. Then he wrote, "In view of your support of free enterprise, I thought that you might be interested in an experiment that I recently conducted in my history class. Fifteen volunteers were selected with an eye to an approximate balance of athletes and non-athletes, boys & girls. The volunteers were not informed of the purpose of the experiment.

The 1st day a socialist-like system was set up. The subjects were informed that they had "volunteered" to do pushups, in return for which they would be given candy."

Now pushups & candy! What do they have to do with socialism? Well Paul Leonard explained ~~that~~ *to* the 15 volunteers that they would do pushups with a limit ~~on~~ of 30 on how many anyone would have to or be allowed to do. For every 5 pushups they would each get a piece of candy. And here is where the pol. science comes in. The total number of push ups ~~done by~~ *accomplished* by the volunteers would be divided by 15—(the number of volunteers) and each would receive a piece of candy for every 5 pushups. Those who could do 30 and those who couldn't get off the floor once would share equally in the candy.

Four managed to do the maximum & the over all average was 16.2 pushups so everyone received 3 pieces of candy. That was half the experiment—the socialist half. The next day was capitalisms turn. The volunteers found they were going to do push ups again—same limit, no more than 30 and same reward, one piece of candy for each 5 push up's. Just one difference—they were capitalists this time—no averaging. They would *each* get one piece of candy for every 5 pushups that each one was able to do. In other words there was an incentive for each one to do his or her very best.

The average of 16.2 on the socialist day went up to 21.2 ~~almost a~~ *more than* a 30% increase in productivity and this time almost half of the volunteers, 7 not 4 did the maximum of 30. ~~Every one of them improved~~ ~~*them except the top 4*~~

I gathered from Paul Leonards letter that he really wasn't too surprised about that. If I could deliver a personal message to Paul, *SOPHOMORE AT MAYO HIGH* it would be, "congratulations ~~for proving simply & suddenly you've~~ *Paul you've demonstrated you understand* the difference between the magic of the free mkt. system & the idiocy of Karl Marx. There are some pretty eminent PH.'Ds in Ec's. who cant figure that out." This is R.R. Thanks for listening. ❖

In 1978 arson was added to Class I (also known as Part I) crimes—common, serious crimes likely to be reported to the police—by Congressional mandate, increasing the number from seven to eight.

Arson
April 13, 1977

It is possible that one of the most costly crimes in the nation is being ignored, in spite of the fact that it is increasing at an unprecedented rate. I'll be right back.

We know that our ancesters way back in dim antiquity discovered ~~th~~ fire could be a useful tool. We dont know when they discovered it could also be used maliciously for spite or revenge; to murder, maim and, more lately, provide illicit profit.

About twenty five years ago the handful of men in Calif. who were engaged in fire/arson investigation formed an org. now known as "The Calif. Conference of Arson Investigators." They recognized the need for training & ed. in their field. They were also convinced that many fires of so called "undetermined cause" were, in fact, fires deliberately started for one reason or another.

In these 25 years, their investigative work has become a science, not only in the determination of arson, but in identifying other fire problems. We are now ~~ack~~ *aware* of structural design ~~problems~~ *faults* whereby stairwells, elevator shafts & air ducts become natural chimneys resulting in the rapid spread of fire. Their work has led to improved building materials with fire retardant qualities and better appliance design to eliminate fire causing malfunctions.

One would think this knowledge indicated the situation was well in hand and we were on our way to happier & less dangerous times. *We might think that but we'd be wrong.* Back in 1970, while I was Gov. we had a task force ~~a~~

study gr~~oup *called the "Arson* Information Study Group." They brought me a~~ report that in the years 1967 to 1970 the total number of fires in Calif. increased by 19%. The cases of detected arson increased 87%. This report led to the forming of the 1st arson detail within the State Fire Marshal's office.

The report, taking data from other states, indicated that arson was a crime costing the Nat. 800 mil. $ a year—more than 4 times the cost of the next most costly crime: ~~autobi~~ auto theft.

Just recently, I recv'd. a letter from one of the men who served in that study group and the Arson investigating team in Calif., James Timmons, now doing the same work for one of our Calif. cities. Reminding me of what had been learned in our state he said ~~the~~ "Nat. Fire Protection ~~Agency~~ *Assn.* data indicates arson fires have been increasing at a steady rate of 10% a year since 1968. Those are just the cases where arson is proven. They estimate half the fires of undetermined cause are in fact arson.

Then Mr. Timmons asked some pertinent questions maybe we all should be asking. Why are less than ½ of 1% of fire & police personnel assigned to arson investigation? Why do so many cities & towns have <u>no</u> trained personnel in this field? They report they have no arson—just an awful lot of fires of undetermined cause. Why does the F.B.I. not classify the nations most costly crime as a Class 1 crime? Indeed, the F.B.I. crime reporting system does not recognize the existence of arson. And, finally, why did the International Assn. of Police Chiefs recently recommend against having the F.B.I. classify Arson as a Class 1 crime?

I have the greatest respect for law enforcement agencies and for those who fight our fires. If there are answers to these questions, I'd like to hear them and I think you would too. This is RR Thanks for Listening. ❖

A Renewable Source

May 4, 1977

With energy now the number one issue and Americans being asked to sacrifice on an, ~~"War~~ "as if we're at war" basis, dont you think we are entitled to all the facts?—Ill be right back.

Nuclear energy continues to be shunted aside in the proposals being made by govt. ~~to~~ as to how we're going to meet our energy needs in the years to come.

We are told that industry & power generating plants must switch from natural gas & oil to coal. We're also told the clean air regulations will not be compromised to allow for the additional pollution ~~which~~ burning coal will bring. And, there will be stricter regulations imposed on the mining of coal. We are <u>not</u> told that it will cost about $50 Bil. to convert Am. industry back from oil & gas to coal.

A C.I.A. report is quoted to prove we only have a few years supply of oil & gas left in all the world. A U.N. report saying we have enough oil for 100 yrs. (in which time we surely can come up with alternate sources) is not quoted. Nor is a report that with more freedom to make *the* price of natural gas compat~~i~~*a*ble with costs, we have a 1000 yrs. supply by conservative estimate.

The cleanest, most economical and efficient energy source—nuclear power is dismissed out of hand. The issue of possible proliferation of nuclear bombs is raised if we increase the number of nuclear power plants in the world. But, we cant stop other countries from having them, so, if there is such a danger we cant prevent it by ourselves. The Naderites raise environmental objections citing radioactive polution, risk of nuclear disaster and, finally, that Uranium to fuel the plants is in as short supply as oil.

~~One~~ That last point brings us to the underlying fact in all of the energy debate; we are talking about finite fuels. Coal, oil, gas, uranium are all energy sources which conceivably will be used up.

Right at hand, however, still in an experimental stage, but far enough along ~~to~~ *for* us to know it is practical in the immediate future if we continue our developmental effort, is a renewable fuel that is literally perpetual motion realized. It is the breeder reactor which generates nuclear power and produces plutonium at the same time which, in turn, produces more nuclear power.

The Pres. has ordered a halt to further development citing *environmental & other* dangers as the reason. But Wash. is sitting on an environmental report prepared for the Energy Research and Development Admin. that says just the opposite. This E.R.D.A. document, 500 pages, known as 1554-D was prepared by the Savannah River Laboratory and has been in the administration's hands since Feb. In short, the report says, "there is no safeguards related reason to delay the development of fuel cycle facilities to demonstrate reprocessing, including plutonium conversion—and storage."

~~The~~ Capitol Hill researchers were led a merry chase in trying to track down this document. Finally, invoking the freedom of Information act, a copy was obtained. It is an extensive, obviously costly & thorough report. Not only does it make plain there are no insuperable ~~difficulties~~ safety problems with plutonium, it states that recycling plutonium ~~in some respects so~~ *is safer than not recycling it.*

Why are we not supposed to know that a practical source of energy is at hand which regenerates it's own fuel, meaning the supply is inexhaustible?

This is R.R. Thanks for listening. ❖

Rhodesia
May 4, 1977

Every red blooded American likes to think Uncle Sam cant be pushed around. We also like to think he's too big & honest to push someone else around. I'll be right back.

Other govt's. friendly & *not so* ~~un~~friendly maintain information offices in Wash., ~~some I believe in N.Y.~~ to see that news advantageous to them will be disemminated through our news outlets. One of these is the Rhodesian Information Office. It is duly registered under the Foreign Agents Registration Act of 1935 * ~~which is~~ administered by the Dept. of Justice.

Such an office allows us a viewing window on this faraway country which otherwise would remain pretty much unknown to us. It's size dosen't warrant the maintaining of American news bureaus there.

Under that 1935 act these foreign info. offices are subject to a periodic audit—a checkup to see that the info. it hands out meets certain requirements as to reliability etc. Usually these audits are pretty routine and carried out in a friendly courteous manner. After all aren't we the worlds leading exponent of free speech?

But several weeks ago three U.S. agents walked into the Rhodesian info. center unannounced and began a minute inspection which was headlined by one paper as a full fledged investigation of "the Rhodesian Lobby." **

By coincidence this surprise visit followed ~~on top of~~ *right on the heels of* a discussion in the U.N. Security Council (chaired by our Ambassador Andrew Young) of a British resolution to close down the Rhodesian office. It seems that under an informal arrangement we have for some years now made American dollars available in return for Rhodesian money which Am. missionarys & businessmen need for doing business in Rhodesia.

The U.N. resolution is aimed at halting that exchange which would leave the Rhodesian office out on a limb indeed out of business. The only objection has come from *of all people* the Russians but only because they want a tougher resolution which would include cutting telephone & cable communication with Rhodesia. Come to think of it that figures with what they probably have in mind.—A curtain of silence ~~for their~~ *to screen* a *BLOODY* takeover by Russian armed Guerillas.

But forget the Rhodesians for a moment and think of what this resolution *when passed* would mean ~~when passed~~ to all of us. The United Nations—that tower of Babel ~~b~~ stained with hypocracy would be making law for the U.S.

* Reagan is most likely referring to the Foreign Agents Registration Act of 1938.
** John Goshko, "Rhodesia Lobby Under Scrutiny By Justice Dept., *The Washington Post,* March 29, 1977, p. A5.

without any action by our own Congress. That is a surrender of sovereignty we should never permit.

Then of course we should ask ourselves if we are ready to also abandon our principle of freedom of info.; ~~or~~ *Our* right to have access to news from Rhodesia or any & all other countries of the world. One wonders why we haven't heard from the Am. Civil Liberties Union about that.

But to get back to the Rhodesians themselves—we've already imposed trade restrictions on them and the question is why? It's true they do not grant majority rule but it's also true they are proceding to do so in exact conformity with the plan proposed by our former Sec. of State.* That plan called for a 2 yr. transition period leading to a peaceful transfer of authority as voted by the people themselves. The Rhodesian govt. agreed to do this.

The U.S., ~~the~~ Eng. & the Black Nationalist leaders of several factions also agreed. ~~to the proposal.~~ Then the pro-marxist nationalist leaders re-neged and demanded an immediate takeover without regard to the wishes of the majority. The position of Gt. Britain & our own govt. in ~~all of this~~ is *the face of this has been* somewhat less than noble ~~and so~~ *as* is the U.N. resolution.

This is RR Thanks for listening. ❖

Lawnmowers
May 4, 1977

Do you remember when lawn mowing was a simple thing your father told you to do~~,~~? ~~o~~Or if already grown up you did as a weekend chore? Those days may be gone forever. I'll be right back.

My friend, *columnist* James J. Kilpatrick, ~~has~~ has thrown a journalistic spotlight on another longtime American institution that is about to be improved out of existence by the multitudinous humanitarians who dwell on the banks of the Potom~~i~~ac.

Some of us still have memories of an earlier day when our fathers would rise from the breakfast table and say "the lawn needs mowing." Or, if there were more than one male offspring in the family he might be more subtle, like asking, "whose turn is it to mow the lawn today?" Of course, in later life if you were lucky, a loving wife stood between you & your golf clubs & said "the ~~lawn~~ neighbors are going to complain if we dont do something about the lawn pretty soon."

In this latter-day adult experience modern technology had lessened the labor and even put a little fun in the job. We have power mowers and there is

* For a recent first-hand account of U.S. diplomacy toward southern Africa as the transition to black rule was under way during the 1970s, see Secretary of State Henry A. Kissinger, *Years of Renewal* (New York: Simon & Schuster, 1999), pp. 903–1016.

no way to describe the pleasureable adventure of gassing up the machine & then engineering it around flower beds & sidewalks. ~~Now however~~ Innocently we ~~assu~~ *took* for granted that only the tulip bed or possibly the garden hose, left carelessly on the lawn, were in any danger. That however was B.C.—P.S.C.—before the Consumer Product Safety Commission.

Now we find that it is we who are in danger. How could we have gone so long enjoying our weekend toy, pulling the starter cord, scaring the dog with the satisfying roar of the 1½ horsepower motor without realizing that we were in deadly peril?

But over the hill to *the* rescue has ridden the Consumer Product Safety Commission. We may have to wait a bit for their proposed standard to be implemented, but at least we've been made aware.

Their principal recommendation is for a "dead mans" control—that should give you an idea of the risk you've been running. This is for the walk behind mower *& the kind you ride*. If you should fall in a faint, or carelessly take your hand off the handle bar to mop your forehead, the deadly blades of the mower will stop in 3 seconds.

Jack Kilpatrick has suggested the possibility that the Commission staff responsible for this proposal has had little, or no, experience in mowing a lawn. He points out that "real world" lawn mowing is a series of interruptions; moving a ~~trycycle~~ *tricycle*, garden furniture, a toy or whatever. In real life, under their proposal, every interruption will find you pulling that rope to re-start the motor.

But this kill-the-engine gadget is only one of the quote improvements unquote contained in the 200 page proposal.* An easier starter is demanded to ease the pain of all that rope pulling. The bottom line is a sizeable increase in the cost of ~~m~~*p*ower motors and a major re-tooling by manufacturers in an almost $2 Bil industry. There are 40 mil in use and about 33 mil. a year sold. Ec. analysis by the Commission itself indicates that smaller manufacturers will be put out of business with a loss of between 1 & 2000 jobs. They estimate a 20% drop in retail sales and they acknowledge that customers who do pay the added price will undoubtedly go to the nearest mechanic & have the control disconnected.

Mr. Kilpatrick quotes a staff member of the commission who summed it all up in these words, "We will be mandating a product that most customers do not want at a price they cannot afford to pay." This is R.R. Thanks for listening. ❖

Warner Bros. Pictures bought the rights to the Kidco story for a reported $500,000, and in April 1984 released the movie Kidco. *In 1980, Kidco Presi-*

* Reagan lost this debate. Today a "dead man's switch" is a standard safety feature on power lawn mowers. See the Code of Federal Regulations 29 CFR 1910.243.

*dent Dickie Cessna and his sisters used that money, along with their $3,000 monthly income from Kidco, Inc., to purchase the California coastal city of Gorda as a tax shelter. Floods later washed out the town, forcing Kidco to declare bankruptcy. As an adult, Cessna went on to serve in the Air Force and later became the general manager of an upscale golf course in Southern California.**

Kidco
May 4, 1977

Out here in Calif. the State Board of Equalization has moved in on some corporate shenanigans and made sure that Kidco ~~Corp~~ *Inc.* will meet the State requirements for doing business. I'll be right back.

Kidco Inc., of Ramona Calif. has had, among other commercial pursuits, a contract with an equestrian center to clean the sawdust, woodshavings & manure out of the stalls. Kidco does this in return for getting the use of the material they remove from the stable. The corporate profit comes from composting this material and then selling it as fertilizer to ~~several~~ nurseries & a country club.

Recently the Calif. Board of Equalization declared this constituted sale of a tangible product, therefore a sellers permit was required and sales tax due retroactively to the date the arrangement began. The Pres. of Kidco Inc. was ordered to appear before the board with the books & records of the Corp.

Richard Cessna Jr., the Pres., stated that ~~not~~ Kidco, having been incorporated outside of Calif., he was not aware of the need for a sellers permit. As for the sales tax, he had a pretty good argument and one that sounded ~~prett~~ reasonable. Sales tax had been paid *already* on the wood shavings & ~~on the horse feed when it was~~ *other material when it was in the form of feed* purchased by the equestrian center and he didn't think it was due again. ~~just by virtue of~~

At any rate, Pres. Cessna appeared before the Board of equalization. The meeting was amiable with no such burocratic procedures as fines or punishment. Kidco will get a sellers permit and begin to pay sales tax.

~~Now if you are wondering why all of this should be told as posessing some newsworthiness~~

Now if this seems to be a rather routine and minor bit of corporate, govt. disagreement hardly worth becoming a radio event, let me add a few details. Pres. Richard Cessna Jr., Pres. of Kidco Inc., is 12 yrs. old. Vice Pres. of Kidco is his 9 yr. old sister, Ne-Ne. Sister Bette, age, 11 is sec. of the corp. and their half sister June, 14 is treasurer. The owner of the equestrian center from whence comes Kidco's stock in trade is their father. I'm sure the Calif. St.

* "Life Is Mellow in a Town Owned by Four Youths," *The New York Times,* November 6, 1980, p. A-16. Also "Fairfield Golf Course GM Values Service," *Daily Republic,* December 26, 2003.

Board of Equalization found the situation a little unusual. *Make no mistake about it, Kidco is a very real, legally registered corp.*

The kids do all the work themselves, plus some other money-making activities such as street & driveway cleanup in the community. I dont know what the overall annual inc. of the corp. is but the hearing did bring out that *in* one recent month the gross receipts were $3000.

Maybe this incident is an indication of our changing world. Once upon a time we taught our children the fundamentals of free enterprise and thrift with jobs like paper routes, mowing lawns and, of course, the traditional summer lemonade stand at the front curb.

But it's a different world, one in which the alphabet is more than A,B,C,. If you are going to be in business it's F.T.C., B.L.S., I.R.S., N.L.R.B. and all the multitude of alphabetical agencies, Fed., St., & Loc., that are now involved whenever & wherever buying & selling takes place.

I take my hat off to Mr. Cessna Sr. and hope with all my heart, the officers of Kidco corp. have not been discouraged or made cynical by their first experience with the intrusive ~~but~~ *and* benevolent hand of officialdom. ~~This is R R. Thanks for listening.~~ Just the same I'm a little nostalgic for the good old days.—This is RR Thanks for listening. ❖

Lord Chalfont

May 4, 1977

Everyone knows the Berlin wall was built to keep East Germans from going West. But was it designed to let some East Germans go West in a hurry if the occasion called for it? I'll be right back.

On these broadcasts I have, on occasion, called ~~to~~ attention to the massive buildup of the Soviet military forces and the fact that those forces ~~were~~ *are* by every criterion designed for offensive action.

Also on these broadcasts I have on at least 1 or 2 occasions passed on the observations of a member of the British Parliament, Lord Chalfont.* ~~He~~ *His Lordship* seems to have an ability to observe and point out with amazing clarity, obvious ~~points~~ *things* that make us wonder why we have failed to notice them ourselves.

The latest such has to do with the Berlin wall. Certainly this ugly affront to all that is humane & decent has been talked about, written about and photographed ad infinitum. It is hard to think that anyone, anywhere in the world where news is available is not aware that this structure is a barrier to freedom, designed to keep the beneficiaries of enlightened socialism from straying across the border into the affluence & comfort of miserable, imperialistic capitalism.

* Lord Alun Gwynne Jones Chalfont.

The East German police who man the wall are not guards on watch to keep someone in the West from scaling the wall to gain entry to their workers paradise. They are there for one reason & one only—we are told—to keep people within the communist world. Barb[*ed*] wire, trained dogs, land mines, electric current through the wire of course automatic ~~rifls~~ rifles are the guards tools. So far they have killed ~~a num~~ *quite* a number of men, women & young people who yearned to breathe free.

Now Lord Chalfont points out an interesting fact, he says, "If one examines a little more closely the East German frontier guards who patrol the wall, it becomes clear that they ~~combine~~ *constitute* something substantially more than a prison service. They are equipped with tanks, artillery, heavy machine guns, and other modern mobile weapons."~~—rather~~ His Lordship adds—"rather more, one would think, than they need to deal with the occasional dissident citizen making a terrified dash for the West.

"It may be, of course that they are also *there* for purposes of military defense. Someone in the Kremlin may really believe that one day the Allied soldiers in West Berlin are going to burst irresistably out of their barracks and annihilate the 100,000 Russian & E. German troops who surround the city.

Then Lord Chalfont calls to our attention something which as far as I know has never been openly discussed or even mentioned. He asks "If that is really the case, there is something else which needs to be explained. —What is the reason for that strange concentration of E. German troops at Glienicke, a point on the Berlin Wall opposite one of the principal Allied airfields? If they are defensive in purpose, why do they need the latest bridging equipment? The only water obstacle is in front of them in West Berlin. Why do they need chemical warfare vehicles? And perhaps most significant of all, why is the sector of the East-West border immediately in front of them the only sector along which no concrete wall has been built?"

Thank you Lord Chalfont. I'm sure if we try we can think of a possible answer to those questions.

This is RR Thanks for listening. ❖

Bill Niehouse
May 4, 1977

†The name Bill Niehouse is hardly a household word but it's a name we should be familiar with if we believe in our right to be protected by our govt. I'll be right back.

On Feb. 27, 1976 Wm. Niehouse* was abducted from his home in Caracas Venezuela by "leftist guerillas." He was an employee of an American firm

* William F. Niehous was freed on June 30, 1979, in a gun battle between Venezuelan police and guerrillas.

doing business ~~there~~ in Venezuela, Owens-Illinois Co. He was not engaged in any kind of James Bond adventurers, he worked for Owens-Illinois [and] lived in Caracas with his family. He is the victem of a crime.

The ransom demands came—first there must be ~~a~~ *the* publication of a leftist manifesto in the N.Y. Times, London Times, Paris Le Monde and Venezuelan "El Nation." Owens-Ill. complied with the demand and the manifesto appeared in all but the Venezuelan paper. The govt. of Venezuela refused to allow it to be printed in that country.

The next demand called for $114.00 to be paid to each employee of Owens Ill. in Venezuela. Owens-Ill. complied, at which point the Venezuelan govt. announced the co. had broken the laws of the country and for so doing must sell their possessions to the govt. While not totally expropriation of the American company it was about as close as you could get. ~~to it~~ As of two months ago the business negotiations were at a standstill.

Demand number 3 arrived. It called for an outright payment of ransom. The Venezuelan govt. refused to ~~allow~~ permit any such payment but also refused to allow anyone to say it wasn't permitted.

Mrs. Niehouse had naturally become of interest to the news media in Caracas. But with this third demand her interviews were cut if any reference to ransom was made or asked about. One television station was closed by the govt. and a newspaper taken over.

Donna Niehous stayed in Venezuela for six months. She was under constant surveillance. Her house was bugged and her phone tapped. Two policeman lived in the house as part of the surveillance not ~~to~~ as a measure of protection for her.

During the period when the messages were coming from the kidnapers letters came from her husband assuring her he was alive & well. Then in July an attempt to make a token payment to the kidnapers was aborted by the Venezuelan police. Nothing has been heard from the kidnapers or the police since that time.

The police continue to make arrests and the govt. *has* announced that everyone involved has been arrested and the case is solved. But where is Bill Niehous?

There is only this post-script.—Donna Niehous was recently called to Venezuela to see if she could identify any of the persons under arrest. She positively identified one suspect and apparently his fingerprints ~~verif~~ prove he was present at the kidnaping. But they have been unable to get any information from him. Possibly because he is held as a pol. prisoner and in Venezuela pol prisoners ~~have a way of~~ usually walk away free.

Mrs. Niehous and literally hundreds of friends have written to the State Dept. & the White House. Each has received a form letter reply, "We are doing everything we can. We must allow the Venezuelan govt. to handle it."

I still say a govt. has no reason to exist unless it is willing to pledge it's total resources to help even one citizen where ever he may be in the world if that citizens *Const.* right to life, liberty & the pursuit of happiness ~~are~~ *is* being unjustly denied.

This is RR Thanks for listening.

† We should send copies of this script to our friends in the House & Sen.)

Send 2 copies also to Mr. Francis J. Reilly 1100 East Landis Vineland N.J. 08360 & mark one for Mrs. Niehous. ❖

John Kearney was indicted on April 7, 1977, on several counts of conspiracy and unlawful wiretapping. Former FBI Acting Director L. Patrick Gray and former FBI officials Mark Felt and Edward Miller were indicted on similar charges four days later. Attorney General Griffin B. Bell dropped the charges against Kearney because of evidence that the orders came from superiors within the FBI. The charges against Gray were dropped on December 11, 1981, on the basis of "unconvincing evidence." Felt and Miller underwent a lengthy three-year trial, were convicted in November of 1980, and were pardoned on April 15, 1981, by President Reagan for their service to the nation.

F.B.I.
May 25, 1977

More than a century ago a French Philosopher said of us ~~Americans that they differed from Europeans in~~ that when an American saw a problem, he crossed the street, talked to a neighbor and soon a committee was formed to deal with the problem. Well we're at it again. I'll be right back.

Some weeks ago on this program I told of the ~~former retir~~ed retired FBI agent who is being prosecuted by the Justice dept. for having used wiretaps, mail openings etc. to get a line on the revolutionary Weatherman organization.

All of this took place several years ago before the agent John Kearney had retired. It seems that Mr. Kearney had done nothing that wasn't standard operating procedure at the time. And certainly the best interests of our people and the nation called for knowing in advance what activities were being planned by the Weatherman activists.

It is hard to understand how the Justice depart thinks the interest of the nation will be served by proceeding with this, after the fact, prosecution of a man who served his country & his fellow citizens ~~well &~~ honorably & well. The Attorney Gen. himself has expressed sorrow about the ~~whole affair~~ *case*—which makes one wonder why he doesn't drop the whole thing. He has even declared that John Kearney will face ruin even if he's found innocent because his entire life savings will be used up in defending against the charges.

This charging of an FBI agent with a crime for carrying out orders has reduced *TO ZERO* the morale of ~~a~~ every agent. ~~to zero.~~ The Bureau, a proud service with a unique record is being treated as if it were some kind of "secret police" guilty of harassing and persecuting the law abiding. Personally I dont know of any governmental agency more entitled to the respect and gratitude of the Am. people.

~~I'm sure that over the years this FBI agents have looked into the background and activities of people who turned out to be completely above suspicion. I'm also sure the Bureau never hounded or persecuted *embarrassed* these people and anyone who might have~~

It has guarded against sabotage in times of war, carried on a tireless crusade against organized crime and aided local law enforcement in every way possible. Now in a climate of fear, mistrust and hysteria not only the Bureau but police intelligence of every kind has been attacked as somehow threatening us with a police state. ~~Meanwhile~~ It is in this climate that former agent John Kearney is being prosecuted.

When I spoke of this before, I closed the broadcast expressing the hope that a committee to come to the aid of John Kearney would be formed so I could contribute to his defense fund. Well that hope has been realized and there is such a committee.

Former *U.S.* Senator James Buckley,* former U.S. Ambassador Clare Booth Luce and former Sec. of the U.S. Treasury dept. William Simon are writing letters around the country to friends ~~&~~, associates & others asking for help to finance the "Citizens Legal Defense Fund for the FBI." Contributions should be sent to the committee, Suite 608, 95 Madison Ave. N.Y. City 10016. I'll repeat that address in a few seconds so be ready. The monies received will be turned over to the Special Agents legal fund of the Soc. of Former Agents of the Fed. Bureau of Investigation which will assist Kearney ~~t~~ *in* the forthcoming trial.

Now I said I'd repeat that address—it is, "Citizens Defense Fund for the FBI," Suite 608—95 Madison Ave. N.Y. City 10016.

I know this is something I haven't done before but in a time when *dozens of* govt. agencies are snooping into every facet of our lives without restraint of any kind it seems to me there is a great injustice in hounding an agency whose snooping is aimed at our protection.

This is RR Thanks for listening. ❖

Why Government Costs Money

May 25, 1977

The cost of govt. has gone up 340% in the last 20 yrs. That is 3½ times the increase in profits & more than 1½ times the increase in wages. I'll be right back.

* Conservative–New York, 1971–1977.

On these broadcasts I have frequently pointed out how much govt. has ~~& is increasing~~ *been, & continues to be, increasing* in cost. And, I've called attention to the fact that govt. costs are not included in the factors used to compute the cost of living index. When govt. tells us the inflation rate, it is the rate before taxes. That's why we could be told that between 1974 & 75, for instance, real wages—meaning purchasing power—went up 9%. We were not told that <u>after taxes</u> real purchasing power had gone down 3%, in spite of the 9% raise in pay.

I've not hesitated to blame the Fed. burocracy for this increase in govt. costs. But, without retreating from that position, let's recognize that we, ourselves, and our local ~~elel~~ elected officials can also have a a hand in the ever-rising tide of govt. spending.

Let me give you an example, which I'm sure, is just one of hundreds & hundreds of *similar* cases that have taken the cost of govt. up to almost $7500 per year for every household in America.

A French statesman* & economist more than a century ago said, "public funds seemingly belong to no one and the temptation to bestow them on some one is irresistable." At the Fed. level in bureaus & agencies, with the power to dole out grants to individuals & local or state govts., custom has it that success is measured by how efficiently that money is handed out. Emptying the bucket becomes the very reason for the existence of the govt. entity.

Cap Weinberger, when he was Secretary of H.E.W., told me of coming to the end of ~~the a~~ *one* fiscal year with $17 mil. left over in a student aid program. He was ordered by the Cong. to use up that money, so had to send agents out to campuses to find students who would accept the grants~~—It *That*~~ WHICH was hardly an insurmountable ~~problem~~ *task,* as you can imagine.

Now comes a news item about a Fla. city with a $475,000 Fed. grant to build a firehouse. The city had no need for another firehouse. It could return the money to Wash.~~—(you know those <u>free</u> Fed. funds~~) or it could go ahead and accept ~~them~~ *it* ~~but then~~ *and begin* construction within 90 days.—those are the rules.

At least 2 commissioners, bless them, wanted to return the money, but in a 3 to 2 vote it was decided to accept $300,000 and build the un-needed firehouse. It *just is* hard to let that seemingly free money get away.

To justify building the firehouse and keep it from standing idle for the period of as much as 8 yrs. before ~~a~~ another fire company is needed—that is if city growth should call for it even then,—it was decided to put an emergency medical service vehicle & crew in the building.

One of the "no-vote" commissioners called attention to the fact that the city already has 3 medical stations and dosen't need another. He also pointed something else out. The $300,000 ~~of~~ *in* Fed. money, of course, came out of the same pockets the city has to get into for it's revenues. And, the city will have to dig deeper into those pockets because it will cost $185,000 a year to keep that

* Claude Frédéric Bastiat (1801–1850).

~~medi~~ un-needed medical team in that un-needed firehouse. If they do need the firehouse in 8 yrs. they will have spent 8 x 185,000 or $1,480,000 to have that free $300,000 bldg. available. And that's why govt. costs are going up.

This is R.R. Thanks for listening. ❖

Marijuana
May 25, 1977

Peter Bourne newly appointed head of the "Office of Fed. Drug Abuse Policy" has told ~~a~~ *members of a* Congressional Comm. he favors removal of Fed. penalties for possession of small amounts of Marijuana. I hope they ~~dont agree~~ *turn him down*. I'll be right back.

A few days ago I was approached by ~~a small group of~~ *several* young men who wanted to know my stand on Marijuana. They frankly told me they were users ranging from pretty ~~regularly~~ regular by one to now & then by the others. Just as frankly I gave my opinion that it was definitely harmful to health and probably represented a dangerous threat to an entire generation.

It is estimated conservatively that more than half of all ~~our~~ Americans between the ages of 18 & 25 have tried Pot, Grass, the Weed or whatever other names are given to Marijuana. Another finding puts use by high school freshmen (now we're down to age 14 or 15) at almost half. Whatever the figure, use by youngsters is referred to by the "Nat. Inst. on Drug Abuse" as *of* epidemic proportion.

In my discussion with the young men their defense ~~of marijuana~~ was chapter & verse from the clichés being uttered and repeated in what can only be called a public relations campaign in behalf of ~~the weed.~~ *marijuana.* ~~I was told i~~*It* ~~was~~ *is* less harmful than alcohol or even tobacco; it ~~was~~ *is* a mild intoxicant at worst but ~~mainly~~ *really just* a pleasant relaxant.

~~I've I'm familiar with the sources of some of this pleasant but also~~ *They were not familiar* with the facts refuting these easily sold clichés. For example a sketchy experiment in Jamaica ~~in which it is claimed~~ *was quoted to the effect that* 30 ~~workers~~ *laborers* were tested ~~is quoted as proof that~~ *and it was found that* their ~~output of labor~~ *labor output* was increased by smoking Pot. The experiment of course didn't show that at all. What it did prove was that ~~work~~ productivity declined. The workers ~~j~~ just thought they were doing better because being stoned they ~~didn~~ weren't aware of the boredom of their jobs.

Peter Bourne * used the relaxing of the Marijuana laws in Calif. ~~who~~ (a re-

* Special Assistant to the President for Health Issues. Bourne resigned in 1978 after he was caught writing a sedative prescription for a staff member for whom he used an assumed name. Rumors were also spreading that he had used cocaine at a Christmas party for the National Organization for the Repeal of Marijuana Laws. (www.pbs.org)

laxing I hasten to add which took place after I left Sacramento) to persuade the Congressmen that such a course had proven beneficial. He did not however quote the present chief of the Bureau of Investigation & Narcotics Enforcement of Calif. who has testified that since the change in the law there has been a sharp increase in the use of Marijuana an increase he puts at some 55%. ~~The increase in a~~Arrests of juveniles for driving under the influence of drugs has increased ~~in Calif.~~ more than 70%.

But Mr. Bourne and others who press for decriminalization & even legalization are signaling to young people that marijuana is harmless or in the parlance of the day "real cool." They and our young people should read "Keep Off The Grass" a report published by "Readers Digest Press" and authored by Dr. Gabriel Nahas of Columbia U. He confirms other research findings by reputable scientists that marijuana is far from harmless. It interferes with mental function, the grasp of reality and the reproduction of cells by the human body. ~~T~~*H*abitual smoking of "pot" weakens the body's ability to fight disease and can affect ~~the~~ children yet to be born to those who indulge.

I asked my young questioners something we all ought to be asking ourselves. Obviously these scientists have no ulterior motive,—no axe to grind in ~~suggesting~~ *declaring* that marijuana is harmful. But what is the motive ~~of~~ behind the propaganda campaign to sell the idea that it isn't? ~~There must be some reason for this constant continuing effort.~~ In my own opinion it's rather obvious; decriminalization leads to legalization and legalization leads to commercialization. Already a number of marijuana trade names have been registered in Wash. looking toward the day. Can you see the billboards ~~now~~ that will spring up in the land—"Smoke x brand & fly higher"? There's a whole new *MONEY MAKING* industry ~~MONEY MAKING~~ waiting to be born.

This is R.R. Thanks for listening. ❖

Consumer prices increased 5.8 percent in 1976 and 6.5 percent in 1977, but the rate would go up to 7.6 percent in 1978, 11.3 percent in 1979, and 13.5 percent in 1980. Although deficits were viewed as inevitably inflationary at a time when the Federal Reserve Board (FRB) increased the money supply to accommodate them, FRB chairman Paul Volcker and Alan Greenspan demonstrated that this did not have to be the case. Their stable monetary policy depended on the support of the President. Reagan concludes in this essay that spending limits and indexing the tax code for inflation would end inflation.

Inflation
May 25, 1977

If I seem to devote a number of these broadcasts to inflation, it's because you & I spend more on inflation than we do on just about anything. I'll be right back.

At the recent Ec. summit in London one of our top ranking staffers, in replying to press questions, said, "inflation has so many causes it has to have many different answers—there is no single cure." If one of the advisors to our govt. on ec. & fiscal matters actually believes that, you & I are in deep trouble.

We are undergoing the longest, sustained period of inflation in our Nation's history. Just since WWII it has cost Americans, in the loss of purchasing power ~~in~~ *of* their savings accounts and the value of their insurance policies, more than one trillion dollars.

But let's come down to more understandable figures and see how this loss occurs. ~~If you put a dollar in the bank *10 YRS. AGO* or~~ ~~some other~~ ~~*invested it* in any way that would return a 6% interest~~ ~~just 10 yrs. ago~~ ~~and let the interest accumulate & be compounded annually your dollar would be $1.79 today.~~ If you placed a dollar ~~*10 YRS. AGO*~~ in a savings account, ~~or annuity or any investment where it would draw 6% int.~~ *10 yrs. ago, and if it drew 6% interest* compounded annually; today, 10 yrs. later, your dollar would have grown to $1.79. But it takes $1.78 today to buy what $1 would have bought in 1967. Now if you are a cheerful soul, *LOOKING ON THE BRIGHT SIDE,* who always says the glass is half-full instead of half-empty, you'll say, "well at least we didn't lose anything—in fact we made a penny."

No you didn't. That $1.79 is before taxes and the 79 cents in interest is taxable income. To make it very simple, you are not a penny ahead. After taxes, you are loser by a considerable amount.

What does this have to do with the cause—or as our representative at the London Ec. Conf. would have it—the many causes of inflation? It has everything to do with it. The cause of inflation is govt. Nikolai Lenin, father of the Russian revolution, knew whereof he spoke when he said, "The way to take over a country is to debauch the currency. Thru a continued policy of inflation a govt. can quietly & unobservedly confiscate the wealth of its citizens." And, dont let that word wealth fool you. It refers to the earnings & the savings of the workers in our land.

When politicians want to continue govt. spending on social programs they think will win votes, but know they cant raise taxes any higher than they are, they turn to inflation. Oh, they dont call it that. It's called deficit spending, borrowing against the future—when they'll no longer need our votes. Inflation is caused by govt. spending more than govt. takes in ~~and i~~*I*nflation can be eliminated by reducing govt. spending to match govt. revenues.

Our progressive tax system is geared to the number of $ we earn, not their value. We earn a greater number to even-up the lower value of each $ and end up paying a higher inc. tax. As purchasing power is reduced, we become more dependent on govt. which has more & more of our money.

I do not charge that inflation is a conspiracy in the sense that politicians knowingly set out to rob the people. To tell the truth, ec. illiteracy is their greatest problem.

Sen. Paul Laxalt* has made a practical proposal to ~~th~~ his colleagues in Wash.; prohibit the Fed. govt. from increasing the percentage of the Gross Nat. Product it spends. Let govt. spending increase each year only as much percentage-wise as the G.N.P. increases.

A colleague in the House,—representative Lawrence Coughlin,** proposes indexing of the tax system so it reflects changes in the cost of living. These 2 measures would end inflation by removing govt's. profit from inflat. This is R.R. Thanks for listening.

It was international news when on April 30, 1977, Nguyen Kong Hoan, Tran Van Son, and Tran Van Thung, Vietnamese defectors, held a press conference in a Japanese fishing town and appealed to the United States to give military aid to Vietnamese who wanted to overthrow the Communist government that had taken over the country two years earlier.

Vietnam
June 15, 1977

People do change their minds—sometimes tragically too late. The least we can do is hear their apology & perhaps learn from it. I'll be right back.

A former member of the S. Vietnamese Nat. Assembly, ~~and later~~ leader of the "peace bloc"*** which opposed Pres. Thieu**** and *which* rejected strongly ~~+~~ our intervention in Vietnam has escaped TO JAPAN with two of his former colleagues. Interestingly enough his anti-war activity had made him an honored figure among the No. Vietnamese conquerors. He was ~~made~~ a member of the Nat. Legislature in Hanoi until he escaped.

He and his 2 companions ~~f~~ have asked, from the safety of Japan, for ~~mil~~ Am. mil. assistance to those who want to overthrow the North Vietnamese Communist's~~—who now rule all of Vietnam.~~ The 3 ex legislators frankly & sadly admit their complete turnaround. They say they wanted relief from the war and all it's destruction but now they realize how precious was the freedom they once had and which has now been lost.

When an American journalist skeptically asked if the So. Vietnamese people after more than 30 yrs. of war would actually take up weapons and fight again the answer was an emphatic "yes."

Meanwhile in Paris where representatives of the Admin. are proceding with talks leading to normalization of relations with the Vietnamese conquerors an

* R–Nevada, 1974–1987.
** Congressman Robert Lawrence Coughlin (R–Pennsylvania, 1969–1993).
*** Ngyuen Kong Hoan.
**** Nguyen Van Thieu, president of South Vietnam (1965–1975).

open letter to the U.S. was distributed by Vietnamese exiles. Calling themselves the Vietnamese Comm. for Human Rights they begged the U.S. not to establish relations with Hanoi until it ended it's brutal repression of freedoms.* ~~and freed the hundreds of thousands now in concentration camps.~~

One sentence in their letter cannot be denied. It read; "Whether you accept it or not, the U.S. bears a great part of the responsibility before World History for the annexation of S. Vietnam by the Communists and for the imprisonment of hundreds of thousands of their own allies." Unfortunately "human rights" weren't being discussed by our team in Paris.

Other things concerning Vietnam are being discussed in a variety of places all having to do with tax dollars taken ~~by~~ from the American people.

The admin. has granted licenses for $5 mil. in private aid for Vietnam through charitable groups. Those of course aren't tax dollars but they're coming up. The U.N. Development Program has agreed to send Hanoi $44 mil. We put up 20% of ~~that~~ the budget for that program.

The World Bank to which we give a full ¼ of it's funds is expected to approve major loans to Hanoi. It's affiliate I.D.A.—the Internat. Development Assn. makes 50 yr. loans at no interest to 3rd world nations and has about $6 Bil. a year for development loans.

The Bank has sent a mission to Vietnam which has been described as "a useful and constructive start to the Banks relationship with a unified Vietnam." I suppose calling it a "unified Vietnam" is alright if ~~that's the way~~ you'd describe a lion that just had a lamb for lunch—*as* unified.

Hanoi didn't just listen at that meeting. They presented a shopping list as long as your arm. It ranged from vast irrigation systems, expansion of elec. power to factories for building railroad equipment. Maybe we could send them "Amtrak."

In Paris direct aid to Hanoi wasn't denied—we just said it would have to wait until we'd established normal relations. Then magnaminously the Vietnamese handed us 20 more names of men missing in action. That only leaves about 1150 or so to be accounted for.

We're writing a chapter for the history books we wont be happy to read. This is RR. Thanks for listening. ❖

Oil II

June 15, 1977

On my last broadcast I gave you a lot of statistics on oil—how ~~much~~ *little* we were told we'd have back 60 odd years ago and how much we've found since.

I'll be right back.

* Diplomatic relations between the United States and Vietnam were established on July 11, 1995.

On the last broadcast I cited the ominous and repeated warnings we heard in 1914, 1920, 1939 and yes, in 1977 about how soon we were going to run out of oil. I was also pretty critical of the present energy proposals with their emphasis on conservation and their lack of emphasis, or apparently no interest at all, in developing new energy sources.

But it's occurred to me that maybe I came off sounding as if I disapproved of conservation and that is hardly accurate. As a matter of fact not only do I believe ~~it~~ in it in general but particularly with regard to petroleum. *But* I'm not talking about conservation as a temporary energy crisis expedient. Oil is so important to something called the petrochemical industry we shouldn't be burning it in furnaces at all.

It is true that petroleum originally was seen only as a fuel & lubricant but today we have an even greater use for it as the basis for plastics, drugs, medicines & a host of other extremely useful products. Burning it to heat a boiler ~~is as useless~~ is as ~~foli~~ foolish as coming upon a cabin in the frozen wilderness and setting it on fire for *TEMPORARY* warmth instead of using it for lasting shelter.

Granted we cant discontinue present uses of oil overnight but we can do more *than we are doing* to develop alternative sources of energy. Nuclear power & the breeder reactor are the most likely substitutes and govt. is the greatest obstacle to their immediate use. A combine of regulations makes ~~building of a nuclear power plant take almost 3 times as long in America~~ ~~*TO BUILD A NUC. POWER*~~ ~~as it~~ *it take almost 3 times as long to build a nuclear power plant in America than it* ~~*does in*~~ does elsewhere in the world. At the same time govt. controls have reduced our production of petroleum and interfered with exploration ~~and~~ *leading to* development of new producing oil fields.

On the ~~last~~ previous broadcast I called attention to how many times our govt. in ~~p~~ the past ⅔ of a century has told us we were running out of oil. And how many times new fields were ~~developed~~ *discovered* so that the predicted doomsday never ~~arrived~~ happened.

During those years ~~though~~ *of discovery* govt. had ~~an~~ a policy of encouraging exploration including the much maligned oil depletion *TAX* allowance. ~~in the inc. tax law.~~ In these latter days however a punitive attitude toward the oil industry has prevailed. The incentives are gone & a network of regulations ~~has~~ makes ~~ex~~ wildcatting so high risk few are tempted. About 80% *of* the finding of new oil has been done—not by the giant oil companies but by independents and they have been *the* hardest hit by govt's. punitive policies.

The new energy proposals do little or nothing to reverse the recent course. Certainly they dont take into consideration the lag time in finding new oil. We are all aware that todays biggest source of oil is the OPEC combine of Arab states but do we remember ~~one of the oil companies drilled & drilled~~ *the search in the sands of Araby went on* for 8 years before ~~produ~~ ~~finding~~ a producing well~~.~~ *was found.* It took almost as long on Alaskas North Slope. Only recently ~~did~~ *was* the North Sea discovered to be the source of new oil. Most of the world ~~is~~ remains to be explored and will be if govt. will only remember how we did it a few years ago.

This is RR. Thanks for listening. ❖

Economic Fairy Tales
June 15, 1977

Has gradualism put a fear in our hearts that keeps us from taking forceful action to right things we know are wrong. I'll be right back.

Many decades ago the Fabian ~~socialist~~ movement was born. It~~'~~s purpose was to impose socialism on the world through gradual and silent encroachment. The Fabians believed that by ~~securing~~ achieving certain programs not perceived by the citizenry as socialistic the world would one day awake to find it had accumulated so many of socialisms goals that it might just as well go the rest of the way.

So far the Fabians have been pretty successful. ~~Much of what we see as just excessive regulation & unwarranted govt. interference is based on Marxian precepts.~~ *And* Their success could be used as ~~an~~ evidence that gradualism is the way to get things done.

I'm sure the Fabians, *HOWEVER*, didn't have anything to do with ~~a~~ the gradualism which keeps those *of us* who want less govt. & more freedom from doing something about it. The gradualism I'm talking about is our tendency to ~~say~~ believe ~~that we must gradually reverse the trend of the last 40 yrs.,~~ that to suddenly wipe out unnecessary and unwanted govt. programs would result in chaos.

Two years ago Leonard Read, head of the Foundation for Ec. Ed. exposed the fallacy of this fear inspired gradualism with 3 classic examples.

Going back to ~~1946 when,~~ *the early '30's*--the depression & New Deal days--he reminded us of the Nat. Industrial Recovery Act—known then as NRA. It~~'~~s symbol was a blue eagle, which was a pretty shabby way to treat an eagle. NRA was fascism pure & simple~~,~~ --govt. control of bus. & industry. Their courage ~~sh~~ destroyed by the traumatic experience of the 1929 crash & subsequent depression business & industrial leaders embraced NRA. But after a year or two of govt. interference the honeymoon was over. Bus. wanted to rid itself of the pol. monster. ~~b~~*B*ut—gradually. They were convinced *that* to end it suddenly would wreck the economy.

Then in May of 1935 the Sup. Ct. declared the Blue Chicken (no one called it an eagle anymore) unconstitutional. As of that moment every provision of NRA was abolished. There was no ~~chaos~~ *chaos*. The ec. indicators started upward and while the depression would continue until W.W.II--business was better not worse.

Reads 2nd example came with V.J. day ~~ending~~ *& the end of* WWII. Pres. Truman greeted the news of victory by ordering cancellation of all War contracts. They amounted to $45 Bil. He was told this would ruin the ec. He replied, "Cancel them." Telegrams were sent ordering all contractors to halt all production. There was no pandemonium, ~~and~~ production of long denied consumer items took over and again the ec. indicators moved up--no one went bankrupt & ~~no jobs were lost.~~ *there was full employment.*

The 3rd example was also post war. The allied command in Germany had imposed Keynesian ec's. & all manner of controls on the German industrial complex. ~~Then t~~*T*hey chose Dr. Ludwig Erhard as their *GERMAN* Ec. advisor. *Then* One Sunday evening Dr. Erhard went on nationwide radio and announced, "Beginning tomorrow morning all wage, price & other controls are off." The allied planning commission told him he could be imprisoned for such *an* unauthorized action. They said, "you have modified our controls." He denied this. He said "I haven't modified your controls; I have abolished them."

He was ordered to appear before the Allied Commander our Gen. Clay* who (bless him) ~~said~~ told Erhard he was the economist and he would have the General's backing. ~~Well w~~We all know that chaos & disaster did not result from the Dr's. precipitate action. An ec. miracle did; the recovery of W. Germany that astounded the world. ~~Well s~~So much for gradualism. This is RR—Thanks for listening. ❖

Health Costs

June 15, 1977

Everyone it seems is aware that health care in America has been increasing in cost faster than the ~~other price~~ *general cost of living*. But how many know who's to blame? I'll be rite back.

The other day my friend M. Stanton Evans** wrote a column in which he said; "From start to finish, the current mess in medical pricing is a creation of the govt. There will be no hope of ~~a~~ remedy until that simple fact is recognized & acted upon." He was commenting on the Presidents proposal for fixing hospital rates by govt. order to curtail quote—"the devastating inflationary trend," ~~of~~ unquote of hospital costs.

Stan Evans has properly fixed the blame where it belongs, on the impact of bil's. & bil's. of *taxpayer* dollars pumped into the health care system through Medicare & Medicaid. Now a fair question is why & how does Fed. spending

* General Lucius D. Clay, head of the U.S. Occupation Zone in Germany following World War II.

** M. Stanton Evans wrote a syndicated column from 1973 to 1985 and has written several books.

on health care raise the price? And the answer is the increased utilization that takes place when normal restraints are eliminated.

If you & I feel a touch miserable on a bleak winter day, ~~low~~ *chances* are we take a couple of aspirin, go to bed early & ~~figure we'll~~ call the Dr. if we dont feel *any* better the next ~~day.~~ *morning.* Likewise if something does hospitalize us our first question is, "Dr. how soon can I go home?" And that question is prompted at least in part by our knowledge of how much the *hospital* room is costing per day.

~~To be fair we have to admit t~~*T*he increase in health insurance has had some effect on increased costs. ~~Now that this~~ *With a* 3rd party ~~is~~ paying the tab,—even though it's out of our insurance premiums, we all relax a little and dont hurry to leave the hospital quite as soon as we did when we ~~pa~~ wrote out the check ourselves. But by far the big impact is govt.

Total figures can be confusing. For example the fact that Govt. expenditures for Medicare & Medicaid went from $7 Bil. to more than 40 in 10 yrs. can be laid to more people, inflation and a number of things ~~that tend to make the numbers meaningless. There is h~~*H*owever one figure ~~that~~ cant be talked away~~—the cost *spending*~~ *how much is the cost* per person. ~~We dont have figures later than 1975 but t~~*T*he startling fact is that from 1965 to 1975 per capita health care spending by govt. went up ~~$~~813.6%.

The Council on Wage & Price Stability ~~said~~ *says;* "The rapid growth in private third payments is dwarfed by the growth in public expenditures resulting from Medicare & Medicaid." Right now roughly 40% of all health care spending is by govt. ~~In 1975 g~~Govt. ~~was~~ *is* picking up the tab for 55% of all hospital bills. Thus a lot of those normal restraints I mentioned have been replaced by a "skys the limit" attitude.

You see the govt's. method of spending is based on cost. ~~In other words, t~~*T*o get more a hospital administrator only has to spend more. So why fight a demand for higher pay by hospital employees? Order that new equipment that looked so good in the medical journal, relax that daily close watch on extravagance in ordering supplies. Since three fourths or more of hospital costs are for staff it ~~was~~ *is* easy for hospital overhead to increase and of course it is prorated out on a per room basis.

A Frenchman named Bastiat more than a century ago said; "public funds seemingly belong to no one & the temptation to bestow them on some one is irresistable."

This dosen't mean we should blame the hospital administrator. Would ~~he~~ we do any different in his place? His task of trying to make each dollar go farther, saying no to a pay raise for hardworking nurses, ~~knowing the hardship for many patients, and then along comes Uncle Sugar just saying "whatever the cost send me the bill." This is RR Thanks for listening.~~ trying to hold the price down for the patient can be frustrating. Then down the chimney comes Uncle Sugar saying "just send me the bill." Well more Uncle Sugar is not the answer. This is RR Thanks for listening. ❖

Names
June 15, 1977

What's in a name? That's a well-known cliché question which could become something of a study if a new idea in marriage catches on. Ill be rite back.

In a recent edition of the journal "Alternative" ~~a~~ published by "The Saturday Evening Club, a gentleman named Joseph McGrath wrote tellingly of something that could change our society more than switching to the metric system.*

Mr. McGrath had seen an item in his local paper about an upcoming marriage. The thing that had caught his eye was the announcement that the young couple in keeping with some of the ideas floating around these days intended to keep both their surnames. They would as a married couple be known as the Schwamm-Bukowskis not Mr. & Mrs. Bukowski.

Now if I'd seen that item I must confess I probably would have shrugged it off as a little silly but certainly their right if that's what they wanted to put on their mailbox. But Mr. McGrath while conceding that latter point has a more inquiring mind. He looked into the future not only of the Schwamm-Bukowskis but the future of society if such an idea catches on.

Envisioning parenthood for the happy couple Mr. McGrath does some supposing. Suppose a daughter Janet is born—Janet Schwamm-Bukowski who grows up and marries a young man who also has a dual name (the idea having caught on). Janet Schwamm-Bukowski and ~~John~~ *Jack* Krenwinkel *(KRENWINKEL)*-Roget become the Schwamm-Bukowski-Krenwinkel-Rogets.

Time passes and they are blessed with a son they promptly name Frank. Reaching the age of 21 Mr. McGrath envisions Frank Schwamm-Bukowski-Roget falling in love with and marrying a lovely young lady Juanita Halloran-Schwamm (no relation) Morningside-Lucarelli. This nice young couple being sentimental & nostalgic over an earlier time, name their first born after a favorite great-grand-Uncle named John Smith. And there it is on the birth certificate—John Smith Halloran-Schwamm-Morningside-Lucarelli-Schwamm-Bukowski-Krenwinkle-Roget.

Without getting into additional generations Mr. McGrath then took up some of the associated problems started by the young couple—the Schwamm-Bukowskis who set us off on this course. Roll calls at the start of the school day could conceivably take until lunch time.

Of course, he points out, there would be rejoicing on the burocratic front. The computers would be humming like crazy and the Form 1040 would have to have a lot of additional lines. Telephone directories would be a new industry in themselves. And how about all those monogramned items—towels bed

* Joseph McGrath, "The Game of the Name," *Alternative: An American Spectator* (June–July 1977): 10, pp. 26–27.

linen, handkerchiefs & even shirts. Monogrammed jewelry, tie clips, cuff links, earrings etc.—well we'd probably just have to give up on those. But how about those conventions and business meetings where a sticker bearing your name is stuck to your lapel? It would become an 11 by 14 placard hung around your neck like a bib.

Mr. McGrath carried his vision of the future to other problem areas—the engravers of tombstones for example. He may have created a *new* parlor game. Try it at your next social gathering. I've thought of one already probably because of an earlier occupation of mine. Cant you hear a sports announcer now saying, "John-Smith--Halloran-Schwamm-Morningside-Lucarelli-Schwamm (no relation) Bukowski-Krenwinkel-Roget is fading back to pass." I wonder if we could get Miss Schwamm & Mr. Bukowski to reconsider? This is RR Thanks for listening. ❖

Private Property
July 6, 1977

† "You cant fight City ~~h~~*H*all" that's a statement as American as Moms apple pie. But do you know it, just may not be true. I'll be right back.

A young couple in Fullerton Calif. with a collection of antique furniture and a yen (now fulfilled) to restore an oldfashioned home are fighting City Hall and may be winning. A lot of their neighbors hope they are and the rest of us should hope so too. Govt's. at every level have shown an increasing arrogance ~~about~~ in recent years with regard to private property rights. It's time they were reminded that an individuals right to possess and control his own property is fundamental to freedom itself.

Carole & Matthew Slobin (like so many of us) had a dream. It wasn't an impossible dream ~~even though~~ *but it* did take 8 yrs. to fulfill. Now for almost a year & a half the Fullerton Park Commission & the City Council have been making the dream a nightmare.

The dream was to find an old fashioned home, restore it, furnish it with their collection of antiques and raise their children in it. Both the Slobins work, Carole teaches 1st grade and has always felt a responsibility to make her 1st graders ~~know~~ aware of how wonderful their country is.

Well a year ago March the Slobins found their old house. It had been built in 1916 on something more than a full acre. They put their life savings into restoring it and planned to landscape the entire acre plus.

But in that same month of March a year ago the Fullerton Park Commission had looked at the property with the idea of making it a mini-park. There are two regular parks within half a mile. When the city received a letter from the Slobins stating they had purchased the property and were in Escrow the park idea was dropped.

As work on the house was completed the Slobins made a slight alteration in their dream; they wouldn't landscape & garden the entire property. There was an energy crisis and Californias worst drought in 100 yrs. They decided to build two rental houses on the back half of the lot, each having about a 90 by 100 ft. lot.

The planning commission approved and so did the neighbors. But when the Park Commission & the City Council learned of the new plan back they came with the mini-park idea. The Slobins were threatened with condemnation procedings in spite of all their restoring & the fact the old house had become their family home complete with mortgage.

Perhaps I've gone too fast. I failed to mention that last year when the Slobins first bought the place & then heard about the citys plan for a park they got the signatures of 100 neighbors who evidently preferred to have the Slobin dream than the mini-park. They were told then to go ahead that the city would drop it's plan.

This last June with the park idea reborn a city council meeting was called for a public hearing on the matter. The surprised council found 150 opponents of the park bearing signs that said "Save the Slobin Home," "Listen To The People" & "No Mini Park." There was in addition a petition bearing 2400 signatures of people in the area who dont want the park. The local paper has also editorialized against the park.

The meeting was adjourned with no action taken but another public hearing was scheduled (under pressure) for Aug. 23rd. Possibly the council thinks the people will cool down over the summer. ~~Lets hope not. It's nice to know~~ *I dont think so.* The Slobins held an open house for their new friends, 700 came, many bearing gifts. It's nice isn't it to learn that you can fight city hall?

This is RR Thanks for listening.

† (Let's make this the 1st Broadcast in next taping because of dates involved) ❖

The Hatch Act
July 6, 1977

Was the Hatch Act of 1939 passed to ~~pr~~ restrict the rights of govt. employees or to protect them? This is a question we all should be asking. I'll be right back.

The ~~Congr~~ House of Representatives has voted to eliminate the law known as the Hatch Act. ~~Becau~~ And because this program is being pre-recorded prior to my going out on the mashed potato circuit it's possible by the time you hear this the U.S. Sen. has done likewise.* With all my heart I pray it has not.

* The U.S. Senate considered the bill to repeal the Hatch Act in the summer of 1977 but did not vote on it.

Eliminating the Hatch act is one of the major features of the administrations so called election reform proposals which might better be termed the ~~election~~ *voter* fraud act. During the House debate the Hatch act has been portrayed as some kind of monstrous restriction on the rights of Fed. employees. They have been pitied as 2nd class citizens *who are being* denied the inalienable rights available to the rest of us. And if you didn't look very carefully to see who was spouting this drivel you probably never noticed that it wasn't coming from those put upon, quote—2nd class citizens—unquote, at all. Probably because pub. employees remember better than the rest of us why the Hatch act was passed in 1939.

Well it's time for a reminder; time to recall the massive scandals, the coercion of govt. workers that was standard operating procedure at election time. It was commonplace THEN for Fed. employees to be ordered to attend partisan pol. rallies, to switch their party registration and to be shaken down for pol. contributions.

Congressman Joe Fisher of Va.* tried to tell his ~~collea~~ fellow House members what it was like to be a govt. employee ~~in~~ pre-1939. They should have listened because he spoke from experience. ~~Congres~~ Rep. Fisher was a civil servant in Wash. in 1939. He said govt. workers hailed the Hatch act as ~~a~~ landmark legislation to protect ~~and~~ them and better their working conditions. It banned pol. coercion and restricted employees own activities in campaigns yet it did not prohibit them from supporting candidates of their choice or wearing campaign buttons or contributing if they so desired.

A poll taken while Congress was debating the repeal causes one to wonder who the members of the house thought they were pleasing. Common Cause usually on the liberal side of any issue opposed eliminating the Hatch act and provided the poll results. Of the total respondents to the D.M.I. (Decision Making Info.) poll, 74% opposed changing the act as did 71% of Union members. That is significant because ~~labor~~ the Union hierarchy was promoting the repeal. Among pub. employees 81% of the non unionized govt. workers & 61% of those in unions did not want the Hatch act tampered with. But politicians and labor bosses did.

Govt. workers know better than anyone the subtle pressures that can be applied so they aren't very impressed with promises they've heard that they will be protected. Those making the promises are the ones who voted to ~~remove~~ *take away* the protection they already have.

Forms of compulsion are many if someone wants to ~~use~~ invoke the multitudinous rules & regulations ~~as~~ to make their lives miserable or to ~~make~~ *put a* "dead end" sign in the path of their career. *It's very easy to let a govt. employee know that if he or she wants to get along—he or she better go along.*

I saw enough examples of this when I was Gov. and conscientous state employees cooperated in efficiencies & economies displeasing to the entrenched

* Congressman Joseph Lyman Fisher (D–Virginia, 1975–1981).

burocracy. It can be done so subtley that you are powerless to help the victim or even prove it's going on.

If when you hear this the Sen. has not yet acted—write your Senator.

This is RR Thanks for listening. ❖

In April 1975, Communists took control of Vietnam and Cambodia. Reports of human atrocities perpetrated by the Communist regimes appeared regularly in the Western press.

Cambodia
July 6, 1977

A few weeks ago I told of a book co-authored by John Barron & Anthony Paul of "Readers Digest" titled "Murder of a Gentle Land." I'll be right back.

"Murder of a Gentle Land" is the well documented story of what has happened to Cambodia since the communist takeover. The authors, both experienced journalists toured refugee camps in Thailand, monitored Cambodian radio & press reports, interviewed hundreds & hundreds of Cambodian refugees and then cross checked the stories they heard to establish their veracity.

The crime is unquestionably pre-meditated, cold blooded murder of possibly ⅓ of the entire population of Cambodia. And the method of killing covered the entire spectrum of mans inhumanity to man back through the ages; starvation, thirst, beating, butchery by blade and of course shooting. The victems ranged from the tiniest of babes to the aged & infirm. The murderers ~~were~~ are the communist rule[r]s of ~~that~~ what remains of Cambodia.

Since that broadcast the authors have submitted testimony to the ~~House~~ *human* rights sub-committee of the House Internat. Relations Comm. ~~Anthony Paul sub~~ John Barron appended a letter from Anthony Paul to his testimony. Paul had just returned from another several hundred mile trip through the refugee camps. He wrote "I had expected some evidence of slackening of terror in Cambodia. It is true that fewer refugees are escaping from that country into Thailand—the present rate about 100 a month—but the stories they bring suggest the killings have not yet stopped."

The authors testimony didn't get much press attention, but one Wash. journal, "Human Events" ~~covered~~ *reported* the continuing story of barbarity & bloodshed—including the account of a British correspondent who has toured the refugee camps. Ian Ward of the London Daily Telegraph says "Daily acts of unspeakable barbarism continue to be perpetrated in the name of this once gentle country's Communist revolution." He confirms *the victems number* more than 2 mil. ~~victems~~ so far.

Mr. Paul told of a 27 yr. old philosophy student named Mam Hom who told him the slightest form of irregular behavior was punished with *often* brutal ~~execution~~ *and immediate execution.* He related the case of a 20 yr. old girl seized and carried off, her arms tied behind her back.~~—h~~Her crime?—Reading an Eng. language textbook. Two days later he came upon her about 15 ft. off a jungle path. She had been buried up to her neck. ~~Mam said s~~She was still alive, her head & mouth moving but no words or sound came from her. He could only hurry by. Later he learned she had died.

Barron's testimony ~~said~~ was that a tragedy of terrible proportions has befallen the people of Cambodia & will continue so long as the legislatures of the world remain silent.

Human Events reports that one Congressman on the committee a former anti-war liberal was appalled by what he heard. Calling it one of the most monstrous crimes of the century he said, "The question is, what can we do about it? We have to bring this criminal regime to it's senses."

Am I wrong or wasn't this the type of thing the United Nations was established to eliminate? But whether the U.N. protests or not—and the odds are against it wouldn't we feel better if our own Govt. expressed it's repugnance and in a voice heard round the world proclaimed that Cambodias present rulers are unfit to ~~join~~ associate with the *world* family of nations?

This is RR Thanks for listening. ❖

Spending
July 6, 1977

Budget Chief Bert Lance* was overheard saying, "not to worry govt. ~~can~~ *dosen't* have the time & energy to spend enough to bankrupt us." Somehow that doesn't make me feel better. Ill be right back.

To suggest that the tax collector is limited ~~by~~ ≠ *as to* how much he can lift from our pockets because govt. just cant spend money fast enough to really hurt us is like saying we dont need a limit on ducks because there are more ducks than hunters.

Some time ago I told of the town that couldn't resist taking $300,000 *in Fed. funds* to build a fire station it didn't need. The excuse ~~was~~ the town fathers used to justify this was the possibility the fire house might be needed in 8 yrs. In the meantime an *unneeded* emergency medical team will be put in the bldg. just ~~to~~ for appearances. Over the 8 yrs. that will cost the taxpayers $1,480,000 for their free $300,000 bldg.

Well that is not a rare & isolated case. Winter Park Fla. asked the Ec. Development Admin. for $883,500 to build a new library. There is no evidence to

* Director of the Office of Management and Budget. On September 21, 1977, he resigned his position because of allegations of unethical behavior within the National Bank of Georgia.

suggest that was not a legitimate request ~~for~~ to fill a legitimate need. But apparently business hadn't been too brisk at E.D.A. And you know what can happen to a Fed. agency if it comes to the end of the fiscal year with money left over.

E.D.A. was heart & soul for the Winter Park library. It would not only spring for the 883,000 ~~it but~~ it urged the city to accept ~~2.65 mil~~ *$2,650,000* which is more ~~that~~ than half the citys entire annual budget. For a while a few of the city fathers wanted to turn down the money on principle but principle lost.

Of course the town had to come up with some projects to keep E.D.A. legitimate but that was easily handled. There were tennis courts, bike paths, a baseball grandstand, all told about 20 projects were thought of to justify the enlarged Fed. grant.

I really think Bud. Director Lance has underestimated the energy & the inventiveness of the Santa Claus helpers who dwell in the Potomac puzzle palaces. It's a plain case of survival with them. If they stop giving away goodies they disappear.

Maybe it will brighten your day a little however to learn that the recently convicted "Welfare Queen of Chicago" * served a useful purpose. Even govt. was shaken to find that an enterprising individual could collect welfare under 127 different names, hold 50 social security cards and get widows benefits from a couple of non-existent husbands.

Her achievement triggered an investigation into a number of coincidental incidents where names listed on the public payrolls were also showing up on the welfare rolls. So far there have been 3,183 such duplications including some who were on the payroll for salaries up to $17,500 a yr. All in all 62% of the cases ~~are~~ show, quote—irregularities—unquote. Indictments have been brought against some, several hundred have been removed from the welfare rolls and the investigators have moved on to a list of another 4500 names. Losses to city, state & Fed. govts. (which means to the taxpayers) stand so far at about $10 mil.

Last word is that Detroit ~~has~~ is undergoing a similar experience and a U.S. Attorney is proposing similar investigations should be launched in every major metropolitan area.

Rather than depending on Mr. Lances optimistic hope that lack of time & energy will limit pub. spending why dont we set a limit ~~of~~ on what percentage of total earnings govt. can take in tax?

This is RR Thanks for listening. ❖

* See the radio commentary "Welfare," p. 75.

Government Cost
July 6, 1977

Every once in awhile another example pops up to illustrate why govt. costs so much. Since it's your money I figure you should know about it. I'll be right back.

Over in Tulsa Okla. the Corps of Army Engineers is moving about a fifth of its operation ~~into~~ out of it's present quarters and into a ~~newly built~~ *new* ~~*buil*~~ *office* building at roughly 4 times the ~~present~~ rent *NOW* being paid. The figures are ~~realling~~ *really* interesting. The engineers are leaving almost 21,000 sq. ft. of office space for which they pay $2.89 a sq. ft. to move into *only* 16,000 sq. ft. for which they'll pay (make that we'll pay) $11.88 a sq. ft.

The operation that is moving represents only about 22% of the Corps' Tulsa headquarters. The other almost 4/5's of their offices are located in the old Fed. bldg. which has 75,000 sq. ft. of vacant space and which was remodeled 10 yrs. ago at a cost of $700,000 for use by the engineers.

~~Now let me clear the air on one point.~~ Apparently none of this is the doing of the engineers. The Business Service Center of the General Services ~~of~~ Admin. is in charge of this move. According to the ~~new~~ *cheif* of ~~the admin~~ *G.S.A.* the new more costly office building is the only building in Tulsa which meets "Standard 101 of the Nat. Fire Protection Code" called "Code for Life Safety from Fire in Buildings & Structures." He says the govt. is really getting tough about the fire regulations. Standard 101 is a book with 16 chapters. ~~and each chapter has 4 or 5 sections.~~

The City Fire Marshal of Tulsa says he doubts any building in Tulsa ~~including the fancy new tower selected by the G.S.A.~~ can meet all the requirements of Standard 101 ~~I'm sure you've already guessed t~~*T*he Fire Marshall isn't saying downtown Tulsa is a fire trap—he's indicating Standard 101 like so many govt. documents goes beyond the bounds of common sense & reason. To their credit the Corps of engineers had asked for other locations but were turned down by G.S.A. ~~The Fire Marshall says the city operates under the "Building Office and Coide Admin." code and the new tower builders said to the city when construction was underway "tell us what you want for fire safety & we'll include it." To me this indicates that all of Tulsa's downtown office buildings must meet the same fire safety requirements.~~

A lot of questions come to mind in this whole thing beginning with why the 1/5 of the Engineers Operations, ~~weren't~~ ~~*aren't*~~ *aren't* over in the Federal Bldg. with the other 4/5 where there is vacant space amounting to more than 4½ times as much space as they are moving into. If the Fed. bldg. dosen't meet the rigorous ~~re~~ requirements for fire safety laid down in Standard 101 why haven't the rest of the engineers been moved out? A spokesman for the Corps can only say, it will be up to G.S.A. to say when the bldg. is no longer suitable for use by Fed. employees. That answers another question; Standard 101 isn't a code that can be enforced on buildings in general. It's just a code for the protection of Fed. govt. employees. Taxpayers can work and earn in less protected quarters. And just between us I'm sure with every bit as much safety as govt. employees are provided.

According to the Tulsa Tribune the shortcomings of the building the engineers are leaving consists of the following; one stairway is 4 ~~inches~~ *inches* too narrow and there was some concern expressed about the distance to the rest rooms.

Don't feel guilty if you cant ~~under~~ *make* sense ~~of~~ out of what they're doing. Let me read a paragraph from a memo on another subject—zero budgeting by the "Office of Management & Budget." When you can understand this paragraph everything will become clear to you. "Agencies may use whatever review and ranking techniques appropriate to their needs. However the minimum level for a decision unit is always ranked higher than any increment for the same unit, since it represents the level below which activities can no longer be conducted effectively. <u>However</u>, the minimum level package for a given decision unit may be ranked so low in comparison to incremental levels of the decision units that the funding level for the agency may exclude that minimum funding level package." See.

This is RR Thanks for listening. ❖

Reagan airs his concern about the national debt, a problem that would continue to grow during his presidency.

Quiz
July 6, 1977

I dont know how well this is going to work on Radio but I'm going to give a quiz, so brace yourself. If you're driving though, dont raise your hand if you know the answer. I'll be right back.

"Readers Digest" recently printed a quiz by Ralph Kinney Bennett * and, of course, provided the answers. Good thing, too, because there would have otherwise been a great many frustrated readers. ≠ I'm sure Mr. Bennett wont mind if I paraphrase his questions for brevitys sake and try them on you.

To start with, which of the following items is the ~~fast~~ *fastest* growing cost item in the family budget; food, fuel, housing~~,~~ *or* something else? The answer is "something else" and the "something else" is govt. In 10 yrs., cost of living has gone up 40%, taxes have risen 65%. No. 2, Total govt. spending (Fed. St. & Loc.) per household is close to $3000, $5000, $7500. ~~To get it over with quick~~ It's that 3rd fig.—$7383 for each household in the land.

* Ralph Kinney Bennett, "Quiz on Taxes and Spending," *Reader's Digest* (April 1976): 108, pp. 95–98.

The money govt. takes from one citizen to give to another—redistribution of earnings~~;~~. ~~i~~*I*s it ⅕ of the bud., ⅓, ½ or impossible to determine? You are right if you settled for half. It's increased 56% in the last 3 yrs. and now is $218 Bil.—a little more than half.

There is so much talk about this next one I'm sure most of you will get it. The Nat. debt—the amount govt. spends over & above what it takes in—is it $50 Bil., going down from the $200 Bil. it reached in the V.N. war, no debt at all or more than $500 Bil? The answer—it's on it's way to $600 Bil. at a rate of $1 Bil. a week. ~~About $575 Bil. right now.~~

Listen carefully to this one. Mr. Bennett asks if the interest on the *Nat.* debt ~~hs~~ has more than tripled in the last 10 yrs., is equal to the combined budgets of Calif., N.Y., Mich & Ohio, or is *it* more than double the total budget of the dept. of agriculture? ~~You are right if you said~~ *Ready? The correct answer is* yes to all three. It has gone from $12 Bil. in 1966 to $38 Bil. today. It is the 3rd largest item in the Nat. Bud. *right* after Domestic Assistance & Defense, and, at the present rate of increase, will reach $50 Bil. in 2 years,

The next one is a true or false. The Fed. govt. has no significant outstanding financial commitments beyond those listed as part of the Nat. debt? Quick say false! I haven't time to list them all, but from TVA to Soc. Security ~~but~~ almost a dozen other obligations ~~total~~ *of the Fed govt. amount to* more than $3 trillion, over & above the Nat. debt.

Another "true or false" was a statement that Govt. borrowing has no effect on borrowing by private citizens and, of course, the answer is govt. takes about half the capital we need for mortgages, buying cars etc. Mr. Bennett also asked if Fed. spending has grown faster, slower or at about the same rate as our G.N.P which has increased 275% in the last 20 yrs. *The Answer* Fed. spending has increased 400% & St. & Local *govts.* 520%.

I havent time for all the questions in the Quiz, but one more had to do with the number of pub. emps. not counting military. ~~Are they~~ *Is it* 1 out of 30 working Am's. 1 out of 17, 1 out of 9 or 1 out of 6? The last is correct. Actually the ratio is 4½ Pvt. emps. to 1 pub.

Not part of the quiz but a figure that belongs with these others is, that in a 20 yr. period while the number of pub. emps was increasing by 128% their combined salaries increased 786% going from ~~ab~~ around $17 Bil to ~~abou~~ more than $162 Bil.

Have a nice day. This is RR Thanks for listening. ❖

National health insurance has been advocated since the beginning of the twentieth century when it was on the Socialist Party platform in the 1904 election. After President Carter took the oath in 1977 the U.S. Department of Health and Human Services conducted a survey of the cost and extent of health insurance in the United States. Later in 1977 Congressman Ronald Dellums introduced the National Health Service Act, which was one of the most comprehensive health care proposals put before the Congress. It did not pass.

Medical Care
August 15, 1977

We're being pushed closer & closer to compulsory govt. health insurance with no question being raised as to whether it is wanted or needed. I'll be right back

For years now America has had a pluralistic health care system. There are govt. hospitals for veterans, govt. paid care for the needy, pub. institutions for psychiatric patients and various rehabilitation programs and for the most of us private medical care for a fee paid by the patient. Can anyone say this system of private medicine augmented by govt. programs has not worked?

Americans are living longer (72.5 yrs.) Infant mortality in the last 15 or 16 yrs. has dropped almost 40%, our general death rate is down 14% and *DEATHS FOR* women ~~dying~~ in childbirth have fallen more than 70%. Low income people go to Dr's. twice as often as the more affluent and 3 times as often as they did in the '30's. *We have 1 Dr. for every 581 people & 1 employed registered nurse for 230.*

Th~~at~~*ose* last items should quiet those who are now proclaiming high costs have put health care beyond the reach of the average ~~system.~~ *citizen.* They talk of catastrophic illnesses and $50,000 medical bills as if ~~they~~ those are routine. No one denys such things do take place but only 9/10 of 1% of Americans will have a medical bill of even $5000 in a single yr. and 80% of those are financed by already existing govt. programs.

Something called Pub. Health Ins. started in Am. almost 125 yrs. ago. At that time it was coverage against steamboat & railroad accidents. We've come a long way since then. More than 183 mil. of us are protected by hospital insurance, 170 mil. have surgical insurance and more than 160 mil. are covered for Drs. fees. As for catastrophic illness 150 mil. Ams. have policies with high benefits ranging from ceilings of $50,000 to no ceiling at all.

Most of the more than $100 Bil. Americans spend on health each yr. is paid by insurance companies, charities, businesses & govt. some 67% in all. The remainder is out of pocket and that includes over the counter drug store purchases of even such items as rubbing alcohol.

I realize figures are hard to follow when you are hearing them on radio but listen to these if you will and I think you'll have to agree there is no need for anyone to push the panic button. A 1970 survey of out of pocket medical expenses including health insurance premiums found 6% of the people had no expense at all, 11% spent less than $100. The biggest grouping—40% had expenses of $100 or more but less than $500, 26% had bills of 500 to $1000 & 16% spent $1000 & up. This hardly sounds like we need a compulsory catastrophic insurance program which will add $370 to everyones tax burden each year.

Admittedly health costs have gone up since 1970 but not as much as food or housing. ~~We have one doctor for every 581 people & one employed registered nurse for 230.~~ As I've said catastrophic insurance alone would raise taxes $370 a year for each one of us—can you imagine what comprehensive insurance would cost? Right now some savings are realized because we're allowed a tax deduction for medical costs above a certain amount. But if you are in a 2~~5~~0% bracket you are still paying 80% of the bill yourself. I~~s~~*f* there *is* an argument that most of us dont buy or cant afford as much health insurance as we should have~~?~~ govt. can remedy that without adding any new burocrats or administrative overhead. Let the govt. give us a tax credit for any health insurance premiums we pay. A tax credit means we subtract the amount of the premium from the inc. tax we ~~give~~ *owe* the govt. Thus at no added expense to ~~himself~~ *ones self* a citizen can afford health insurance of his own choosing. ~~Medicaid & Medicare take care *of most* of those with little or no tax to pay and~~

This is RR Thanks for listening. ❖

Dream World
August 15, 1977

A story has just come to me from a Wash. paper. ~~of~~ It is several weeks old but ~~timeless in it's ability to make~~ *it can still* set your head *to* spinning. I'll be right back.

A friend sent me a clipping from the Wash. Star—several weeks old now but ~~it is~~ so mind boggling I just have to pass it on. It was on page 10 not the front page which in itself makes one wonder if we've become so blasé we are beyond being astounded by anything.

The lead paragraph ~~says~~ tells of policemen in several jurisdictions across the nation who are familiar with an individual they call Al. They refer to him as affable, likeable, calm & intelligent but then with some surprise they add that Al has no remorse.

~~They~~ The affable Al they are speaking of is Allen Leroy Anderson who has pleaded guilty or no contest to 3 murders—has been charged with 3 more & is the number one suspect in yet another 2. Authoritys in 7 states think he may be responsible for more.

Seven of the victems were shot execution style in the back of the head the other *in Calif.* was bludgeoned to death with a hammer. ~~A h~~*H*omocide officers quotes "affable Al" as saying he got angry with the man over a business deal and just didn't have his gun handy. He was caught near Malibu Calif. when police stopped a van stolen from the man he'd killed, they also recovered his 22 calibre revolver.

But this isn't a Calif. story. It began on June 1 1976 when Anderson broke parole at a "halfway" house in *the state of* Wash. where he was being counseled. He stole credit cards & the Directors car and lit out reportedly because his homosexual lover had turned on him during a group therapy session. His first victem according to detectives was a 76 yr. old woman who ran an antique store. She objected to giving him her money even though he threatened her with a gun. Finally annoyed with her protests he said, "If you want *to* die, I'm the guy who can help you." He told detectives "I blew her brains out. The others were easy."

The "others" he spoke of included a young man in Va. whose body, bound hand & foot was found in an apartment. He had been shot in the head. Anderson has been indicted in that case but is less willing to talk [about] it than the others.

He left quite a trail starting with that first stolen car. His ~~recep~~ receipts for purchases made with the stolen credit cards were like a 2800 mile paper chase. But the mind boggling part of the story starts with ~~his~~ the neat arrangements he has made for his future.

Having confessed to the Calif. hammer murder he then plead guilty to a murder in Minn. (where the case wasn't very strong) on the condition that he serve his time in Minn. where he has friends & family. He has also arranged that his Calif. sentence be served concurrently. In other words by going to prison in Minn. he will also be credited with having served his time in Calif.

But complicating his plans was the problem of a murder he'd committed in Fla. Like any good citizen with a problem he wrote to Wash.—to Sen. Humphey & V.P. Mondale. He wanted their help in keeping him from being extradited to Fla. Under some thing called the interstate compact he was sent to Fla. for trial but with the understanding he'd be returned to Minn. to ~~serve~~ serve his prison term. No reflection on the Fla. climate. It just so happens Fla. has capital punishment and "affable Al" sure is opposed to that. ~~He is~~ *In fact he claims he didn't kill anyone in Texas for that very reason.* He just slipped up in Fla. and wasn't aware they had an electric chair on active standby. The Fla. jury voted 10 to 2 for the chair but he'll be in Minn. until 1994.*

Al wants to write a book, a publisher suggested the title, "Eight bullets: Eight bodies." He prefers, "Therefore I shall do it Myself." He says that describes his disappointment with our society.

If Calif. had Capital punishment the title could be, "One bullet: ~~One~~ *TWO* bod~~y~~*ies*" and one of those would have been his. This is RR Thanks for listening. ❖

Tom Hayden
August 15, 1977

Govt. by the people will only work if the people work at it and we haven't done that very well of late. I'll be right back.

* Allen Leroy Anderson came up for parole in January 2001; his appeal was denied.

~~The g~~Govt. directing us in Wash. and in many of our state capitals for that matter was chosen by little more than ¼ of the people. In the general election 27% voted Democratic, 26% voted Repub. and 47% sat on their hands. In other words 73% of the voters did <u>not</u> vote for those who now hold office.

In Calif. we've had a couple of special elections ~~to~~ *less than a year after the '76 general election to* fill vacant seats in the state legislature. ~~less than a year after the '76 general election~~ In one only 30% of the people voted & about 25% in the other. This means the winners were the choice of about 15 or ~~1~~ 16% of the electorate in their districts. Will Rogers once said, "Pub. officials are no better & no worse than the people who elect them but they are ~~all~~ better than people who dont vote at all."

Let me use Calif. as an example of what can happen to all of us if we dont change our ways and accept *our* responsibility to see that govt. truly represents the will of the majority. Suppose the rank & file, average, conscientious citizens are fairly divided among the 30% or so who ~~turned out for that one election.~~ *bother to vote?* But suppose there is a small, well organized group ~~who are~~ determined to exert more power than ~~their~~ *its* numbers justify? This group can become the deciding factor both in a primary contest to determine who the nominee will be and in the general elec. to put that nominee in office.

I said I'd use Calif. as an example but I assure you we have no monopoly on the kind of activity I'm about to describe. Early last spring in Santa Barbara Calif. a large, well attended conference was held. It was called the "Calif. Conference on Alternative Pub. Policy." Actually it was an outgrowth or follow on to the '76 U.S. Sen. campaign of Tom Hayden. ~~and he was the head honcho of the meeting.~~ It is fashionable to describe Hayden these days as a pol. activist. A few years ago he was one of the foremost revolutionaries when no one bragged about living only a stones throw from the campus. Now people cluck in astonishment that he got a surprising percentage of the Dem. vote when he challenged, then incumbent Sen. John Tunney. Remember what I said about a small unified voting bloc when the turnout at the polls is light.

The Santa Barbara meeting ~~had such luminaries as Congressman Ron Dellums of Berkeley who is called radical more than liberal~~ was like a re-union of all the anti-war demonstrators of the '60s, the hard corps shock troops of the campus violence ~~and the far out groups~~ who marched, rioted and ~~rock~~ threw *rocks* for causes. They gathered to endorse a new cause which they would support in a new & different way; a kind of uptown, wear a necktie to fool them, way.

Out of the meeting, led by Hayden has come the "Campaign for Ec. Democracy"—(C.E.D.)* Hayden describes it as an umbrella ~~group~~ *org.* of

* Hayden lost his 1976 campaign and subsequently helped to found the Campaign for Economic Democracy (CED), a statewide grass-roots political movement. The CED was involved in a number of causes, including rent control laws in Southern California. The organization remained active in California politics until the mid-1980s, when it was reconstituted as Campaign California.

coalition groups to break up the alleged power of corp's. He estimates they can round up a mil. to a mil. & a half followers starting with the ex-campus rioters. Their purpose?—To win elections local & statewide, to lobby, to support those who are allies & replace those who dont come through.

First priority is to win control of corporations. But in the process to build a network by electing their people to water districts, local air pollution control boards, planning commissions, boards of permits, equal rights commissions etc. All the offices so many of us dont pay any attention to and dont bother to vote for *BUT WHICH CAN CAUSE SO MUCH TROUBLE IF HELD BY TROUBLE MAKERS.* And they'll succeed famously as long as we dont bother to vote. ~~This is R R. Thanks for listening.~~ You say you dont think they can do it? We didn't think they could burn down the schools either, did we?

This is R R. Thanks for listening ❖

Business
August 15, 1977

It's supposed to be politically dangerous to defend business these days but when govt. blames bus. & industry for the problems govt. itself has caused—it's hard to keep quiet. I'll be rite back.

The ~~j~~*J*oint ~~e~~*E*c. ~~e~~Committee of Congress commissioned a study which ~~has~~ was made public early this summer. In the report two Wis. professors charged that in 1974 the top 17 supermarket chains, "overcharged the consumers $662 mil. because of lack of competition."

Now first of all with inflation hiking the prices on us every week it's like shooting fish in a rain barrel to make such a charge. We're all mad enough to believe it. ~~Second however~~ *But* dosen't the fact that they could use the term "the top 17 supermkt. chains" (indicating there are others who aren't *IN* the top *17*.) ~~indicate~~ suggest there must be ~~a certain amount~~ *some kind* of competition?

Why dosen't business itself answer a charge like this. Maybe it does but not in an effective way. The Chairman of the Board releases a reply to the press but who sees it or what guaranty is there that it will even be printed. And telling it to the Congressional committee is like ~~hollering down a well.~~ *spitting into the wind.*

~~Well anyway here is what~~ *But* they could say *possibly* in some of their ads where they'*d* ~~know~~ *be sure* it ~~would~~ *would* be ~~printed~~ *seen that* the top 17 supermarket chains couldn't have cheated us out of $662 mil. in 1974. ~~That's~~ *You see that's* more than 3 times as much as their total net profit ~~for the year~~, which ~~just~~ happened to be a little less than $200 mil.

In that particular recession year when unemp. was going up—(but not as fast as inflation) those 17 mkt. chains averaged a profit margin of less than ½ a cent on each dollar of sales. As a matter of fact the total profit~~s~~ of all the *super* mkt. chains *INCLUDING INDEPENDENTS* in 1974 was less than $800 mil. The Fed. govt. spends that much by about noon every day. But that's a mere detail that didn't prevent one congresswoman from charging—again because of lack of competition—that consumers are over charged about $300 for food every year.

Now in 1974 the average family food bill was about $2700 & of that amt. only $11 represented profit for the supermkt. That of course is the average for all supermkt's. If you did your shopping in the most successful of the chains that profit jumped to a whole $30. If on the other hand you spent your $2700 in the supermkt. chain at the bottom of the profit scale—it lost $16 on you. So if you are being ripped off (as the congresswoman says you are) for $300 a year, you'd better look under the bed because the mkt. isn't the burglar.

Of course we could ask the lady if she is concerned ~~that~~ *because* the per capita cost of govt. is increasing 3½ times as ~~mu~~ fast as the cost of food; Or ~~why we~~ *how* our govt. can, by it's own mistakes, lose, in medicaid & welfare 7x as much each year as the ~~total~~ profit made by the entire super mkt. industry?

One of the Wis. Professors in the congressional study was formerly a part of the burocracy, employed in the Fed. Trade Commission. At that time he claimed supermarkets profit was 1¼ bil. dollars too high. That was double what they actually made. Now he's charging it is $662 mil. more than it should be but that's only for the top 17 mkt. chains and as I said that's more than 3 times as much as ~~profits~~ *their actual* profit.

What reason can there be for this assault on an industry our best economists say is highly competitive? Can it be just a bias against our free mkt. system or is it the old Wash. game of looking for a scapegoat~~?~~; someone else to blame for the inflation Wash. itself is causing?

One footnote in closing; this years Fed. deficit alone would pay ½ the food bill for the entire Nation.

This is RR Thanks for listening. ❖

Inflation

Augnst 15, 1977

Inflation is still a confusing mystery to most of us. Is it possible the word itself contributes to our lack of understanding? I'll be right back.

Someone has said something to the effect that the more things change, the more they remain the same. Whoever said it must have had Washington in mind.

We are enduring the longest period of quote "inflation" unquote, in our nations history and something else we've never known before—worldwide inflation. Solemnly ~~our~~ high officials in every nation talk of the need to do something about it. But what they end up doing in the name of stimulating the economy is ~~a gigantic~~ *to make the* average citizen the patsy in an economic shell game he doesn't understand.

Very simply govt. votes to go on spending as much but usually more than it has been spending. At the same time using terms like stimulating the economy, increasing employment or providing more for the unemployed it creates an illusion of effective action. For example it proudly proclaims it has pumped more money into the economy. And it has—printing press money.

In the last 10 yrs. our govt. has, by simply running the printing presses at the Treasury Dept. increased the supply of money in circulation more than 4 times as much as the increase in goods & services available for purchase. We foolishly feel richer because we have more money. But then we discover prices have gone up, we call it inflation and get mad at the storekeeper, the manufacturer or even labor. Here we just got rich & those greedy so & so's are going to make us poor again.

It's that word inflation that does us in. In these 10 yrs. when the money supply has increased 112% and the goods & services for sale have only increased 24% ~~we~~ they have devalued our money by 44¢ on the dollar. Prices haven't gone up. The newly printed $ dollars should read 66¢. And that's only in comparison to the dollar of 10 yrs. ago, think what it's worth in comparison to those dollars we had in 1939 or even 1946 at the end of the war.

Rising prices dont cause inflation, inflation is the cause of rising prices. It would be far more honest and less confusing if they'd quit talking about the cost of living index and simply tell us by how many pennies & nickels & dimes they've reduced the value of our money every year. Of course if they did that we'd probably quit going along with the shell game.

Why does govt. ~~do this~~ play this game to begin with? Well it allows them to spend money they haven't had to raise taxes to get. They can get away with it because unlike raising a tax our money is whittled away a few cents at a time. ~~a~~*A*nd when we do catch on we blame (as I said before) the wrong people.

Oh yes! And the politicians help us blame the wrong people. Along about vote buying time they come over the hill like the cavalry with all kinds of plans for protecting us from venal & greedy profiteers; consumer protection agencies, more regulations & even price controls. All of which makes them look like heros saving us from the bad guys.

If we look back at even fairly recent history we'll see that whether the ~~politicians~~ politicians intended it or not, when inflation reaches a certain point nations go totalitarian. Socialism or Fascism takes over & ~~act~~ actually they are the same thing.

At the recent London Ec. conference ~~won~~ *one* of our officials declared inflation is caused by many things & therefore requires many cures. If he really believes that he had no business being there. Inflation is caused by one thing—govt. spending more than govt. takes in. It will go away when govt. stops doing that.

This is RR Thanks for listening. ❖

In 1977, Reagan delivered several commentaries on Rhodesia (Zimbabwe). He labeled the Patriotic Front, headed by Joshua Nkomo and Robert Mugabe, a terrorist organization and argued that it would not bring about stable black rule.

Rhodesia

August 15, 1977

Some weeks back I quoted from letters written by a Rhodesian cabinet minister to point out the hypocrasy of our position with regard to Rhodesia. I'll be right back.

The United States has joined with the 3rd world voting bloc in the U.N. ~~in~~ *by* imposing sanctions on Rhodesia. Our rationale is that Rhodesia is a nation predominantly black but governed exclusively by a greatly outnumbered white minority. In a sense this is true but it also ignores the effort being made in Rhodesia to achieve majority rule.

The U.S. & Great Britain in an effort to persuade Rhodesias Prime Minister Ian Smith to hasten the transfer of govt., secured his promise to achieve majority rule ~~in~~ within 2 yrs. ~~There is no doubt h~~*H*e is keeping that promise. In the meantime however 2 black nationalists, both died in the wool Marxists have repudiated the plan which they too had signed. Their terrorist guerrillas have brought bloodshed & death to hundreds of Rhodesians mostly blacks. Aligned in what they call "The Patriotic Front," they say they want no orderly, peaceful transfer they want an immediate takeover & the establishment of a communist govt.

And for no reason anyone can understand our govt. appears to support these self declared leaders who are nothing more than terrorists ambitious for power. One ~~+~~ journeys to Moscow for advice, the other to Peking.

The cabinet minister whose letters I quoted ~~from~~ is a black chief of one of the two principle tribes in Rhodesia. ~~J.S. Chirau~~ *J.S. CHIRAU.** ~~He~~ is Pres. of the council of chiefs, leader of some 230 chiefs & several hundred headmen. He has resigned from the cabinet to lead the black majority opposition to the guerrillas and it is estimated he has the support of almost ⅔ of Rhodesias blacks.

When I picked up a Newsweek magazine in late July & saw an interview with Chief Chirau** ~~and Ian Smith~~ I thought you might be interested in how much more sense he makes than does our Ambassador to the United Nations.***

The chief had just returned from a visit to London where he had submitted

* Jeremiah S. Chirau.

** "The Chief's Plan," *Newsweek*, July 18, 1977, p. 36.

*** Andrew Young.

a plan to the British govt. ~~It~~ Newsweek asked what his plan was. He answered, "A system of black govt. that would guarantee law & order, preserve our private enterprise economy & keep Zimbabwe ~~out~~ (the African name for Rhodesia) out of Marxists hands." Then he outlined a plan for a Pres. with executive powers, 2 houses of parliament & 2 provincial assemblies for the two principal tribes, the Mashonā and Motabeli. All this would be brought about through free elections with universal suffrage for everyone over 18.

Asked about restrictions on candidates he ruled out only those who refused to renounce terrorism. This of course would disqualify Nkomo and Mugabe the self annointed "Patriotic Front," who he said would get less votes than the communists got in Spain. He added, "If the Marxist terrorists succeed, we will become the victems of the greatest tyranny in Hist. It would mean the victory of a small handful of people whose only claim to support is that they possess the majority of rifles, machine guns, mines & mortars all made in Russia."

Significantly on a continent where the answer *offered* to white racism is usually an equally unjust black racism *Mr.* Chirau responded to a question about excluding whites; "Rhodesia could not survive without them (the whites). Their property & rights will be fully guaranteed. But we must act quickly to reverse the white exodus now under way."

In the same edition of Newsweek* *Rhodesian Prime Minister* Ian Smith was interviewed & declared, "The new govt. should be made up of the best people we have available, black & white." When he was asked if a black majority govt. with white participation were seen to be working did he think he would have our support against the ~~Com~~ Soviet-backed guerrillas he said; "I doubt it." ~~They will auto~~ He believes we will automatically be on the side of the "Org. of African Unity" which is manipulated by the Soviet U. Wouldn't it be nice if we could tell him we'd be on the side of decency & common sense for a change? This is RR Thanks for listening. ❖

Government Costs

September 6, 1977

We fought a revolution 200 yrs. ago over taxation without representation (among other things). Now what can we do about taxation with representation.

I'll be right back.

"The "Tax Foundation" has just released it's 19th Biennial, "Facts & Figures on Govt. Finance." ~~And~~ If we followed the ancient custom of be-heading the bearer of bad tidings the Tax Foundation would*n't* ~~be headless by now.~~ *have use for a hat anymore*. As it is, bless them for giving us the sad facts of govt's. cost.

* "Smith's 'Internal Solution,' " pp. 34–35.

For all levels of govt. Fed. State & Local in 1977 spending pro-rates out to $9,607 per family or almost half (47%) of average family inc. in America which is now $20,400. If we go back to 1950 we get the full jolt of how swiftly govt. costs are increasing. In that year govt's. at all levels took only $1,615 for each family.

Total spending for this year is more than $715 Bil. Almost $450 Bil. of that is Fed. and something under 270 bil. is for state & local govts.

Ralph Waldo Emerson, 100 yrs. ago said, "In a free & just commonwealth, property rushes from the idle and imbecile to the industrious, brave & persevering." Either that isn't true or we're no longer a "free and just commonwealth." A young man in N.Y. won the state lottery last spring which sets him up with $1000 a week for the rest of his life. Of course he has the same tax problems we all have so his net is something more than $600 a week ~~but~~ *still* he's no hardship case. Well according to the report I just read he recently lost his ~~job~~ *supermarket* managerial job ~~with a supermkt.~~ for refusing to carry out orders. With $600 plus $ a week outside inc. a fellow can be a little independent. The point is, he applied for his $90 a week unemp. insurance and went camping.

But Congressman John Ashbrook* has given us an example of ~~how~~ why Fed. spending has skyrocketed the way it has. With as many buildings as they build in Wash. you'd think they'd be pretty good at it but practise has not made perfect.

Congressman Ashbrook has made public a report by the General Acctng. Office on the Nat. Visitor Center.** Dont ask me what that is or why we need it. But like The Kennedy Center, Rayburn Office Bldg. and the R.F.K. Stadium to say nothing of Metro, Washingtons rapid transit system it's going to cost a lot more than the original estimate. Top figure for bringing it into operation was $87.5 mil. Now it is estimated at $180 mil.

Part of it opened ~~July~~ on our birthday July 4 1976, more than 8 yrs. after it was authorized. I say part of it because one wall is incomplete, major structural, mechanical & electrical problems will require repair & re-doing. Also the parking facilities are still non-existent.

The original plans called for a 4000 car lot costing $11 mil. They are now hoping to have a 2000 car ~~capacity~~ *lot* for $40 mil.

It's things like this which make you understand why no one cheers when the White House tells us by not deregulating the price of natural gas consumers ~~have been saved~~ *will save* $70 bil. by 1985. It is estimated consumers will have to come up with $100 bil. to pay for imported liquefied gas to make up for the natural gas we wont have because of the price limitation.

This is RR Thanks for listening. ❖

* R–Ohio, 1961–1982.

** A major renovation of Union Station in Washington, D.C. began in conjunction with the nation's bicentennial. The project, called the National Visitor's Center, never came to fruition, but Congress funded a $160 million renovation of the station completed in 1988. The National Visitors Center is now located in the Treasury building.

Cuba I
September 6, 1977

Before Fidel Castro opens a U.S. charge account and starts using our easy credit plan it might be well to check his character references again. I'll be right back.

Since the admin. announced (in the interest of human rights no doubt) that we were going to normalize relations with Castros Cuba wondrous things have happened. They've beaten us in a basketball game, American businessmen tour Havana dreaming of branch offices & new sales territories and the wife of one of them tweaks Fidel's beard & finds him cute.

Sen. George McGovern* and the Cuban dictator munch ice cream cones together & the Sen. discovers he is a personable, well informed fellow. Apparently better informed than the Sen. who shows no sign of knowing that the 15,000 Cuban mercenaries ~~of~~ in Africa are only the tip of an iceberg. "West Watch," quarterly journal of the "Council for Inter-American Security" says Cuban agents have been active ~~in~~ on the continent for more than 10 yrs. and lists 14 African states where they are operating. British journalist Robert Moss** estimates there are more than 20,000 (not 15) in Angola and gives specifics on their Russian arms which include everything from heavy tanks to multiple rocket launchers & Mig fighter planes.

If all of the testimony available on Cubas long time support of so called liberation movements is added up there are 25 to 30,000 Cubans in Africa & *many* hundreds more ~~in~~ have ~~& are operating~~ *operated ~~& still~~* in the past ~~&~~ *or* still are *operating* in Jamaica, Panama, Portugal, Vietnam & No. Korea. They have ~~traine~~ trained exiles who attempted to launch guerrilla warfare in the Dominican Republic as well as the terrorists who plague Argentina. Bayard Rustin writing in "New America" a socialist journal describes Cuba as doing the Soviets dirty work in Africa, the Caribbean & Latin Am.

But what should be the ~~hardest~~ *most difficult* thing for Americans to swallow is the testimony of our own former war prisoners in Vietnam. It is bad enough that we rewarded their years of suffering and their heroism by ducking out on our allies, surely they are entitled to be heard on the subject of Cuba. So far the national press has said nothing about their shocked disbelief that we could be negotiating with ~~Cuba.~~ *Castro.*

Col. George E. Day,*** former P.O.W. and ~~recipient~~ *holder* of the Congressional medal of honor has written that Cuban embassy officials in Hanoi inflicted some of the worst tortures on our men. They sold the No. Vietnamese the idea they were experts on brainwashing and could ~~convert Americans~~ *re-*

* D–South Dakota, 1963–1981.

** Editor of *Foreign Report* (1974–1980).

*** Colonel George E. "Bud" Day.

educate a dozen American Servicemen so they would come home preaching the communist line. When brainwashing failed they turned to plain brutality.

Col. Day tells of one of our Airmen who was raped, ~~and~~ bullied & tortured for 24 hrs. until his mind was gone. Then he was ~~suj~~ subjected to electric shock therapy (so called) with an antiquated machine that not only left *massive* burns on his arms & head but finished off what was left of his brain.

He was last seen by his fellow prisoners in Oct. of 1970. Whether murdered or just left to die, he never returned. Col. Day writes with regard to recognizing Cuba that he is, "appalled, amazed & frightened," ~~that our govt.~~ *that men like Sen. McGovern, Andrew Young & the Pres.* would have the uncommon, bad judgement & poor sense of responsibility to Americans to aid the cause of these international outlaws."

To forgive is divine but not while Castro is arrogantly declaring (as he did a few weeks ago) that he has no intention of halting his efforts to bring ~~about~~ terror & revolution to the world.

This is RR Thanks for listening. ❖

Cuba II
September 6, 1977

This is a difficult time for Americans to determine what is propaganda and what is proper ~~with regard to~~ *in choosing* our FUTURE course with Cuba. I'll be rite back.

The tourist traffic to Cuba is increasing. Most recent visitor to the island, travelling in an air force jet was U.S. Sen. Frank Church.* He spent 4 days with Fidel Castro and ~~left~~ departed for home saying, "I leave with the impression I have found a friend."

~~Castro returned the complement calling the Sen. very capable, very clever—a capable politician & a courageous one.~~

Lest we lose our perspective with all of these carefully staged tours let me read a letter ~~which was sent~~ ~~*written*~~ *written* to Pres. Carter ~~last May by Juanita Castro~~ *by* the exiled sister of the Cuban dictator.

~~She writes;~~ "My name is Juanita Castro. I am the sister of the communist dictator of Cuba Fidel Castro. However I am also a Cuban woman in exile who loves her country and has put its liberation above personal gain & family ties.

I have chosen liberty, Christianity & patriotism over slavery, atheism & treason. You Mr. Pres. must now choose how your name will go down in history. I speak to your conscience & through it to the Am. people.

I come to remind you of those killed by communist Cubas firing squads for

* Senator Frank Forrester Church (D–Idaho, 1957–1981). See Karen DeYoung, "Castro to Permit Americans' Kin to Leave Cuba," *The Washington Post,* August 12, 1977, p. A1.

trying to be free. I come to remind you of communist Cubas concentration camps & jails where torture & murder are everyday occurrences. I come to remind you of the enslaved people of Cuba muted by terror and waiting, hoping, struggling for liberation.

I come to tell you that those ≠ who state that the lifting of ec. sanctions against Cuba and or the establishment of relations with its communist govt. do not constitute condoning or accepting its actions are wrong. This argument ~~takes~~ would not have stood up to the realities of an Auschwitz or a Dachau under Hitlers Germany and ring hollow & bankrupt before the realities of their counterpart in communist Cuba.

I come to ask you, why after your pronouncements concerning Human Rights, you do not vigorously advocate that these be respected in Cuba before even trying to renew relations of any kind with the communist govt. of Havana.

I come to remind you of the Congressional resolution of Oct. 3, 1962 and of the innumerable conventions, doctrines & treaties that oppose such action. I come to remind you Mr. Pres. of that day in Fla. when you shouted: "Democracy yes, Castro no."

Last but not least I come to warn you Mr. Pres. that my brother Fidel Castro and the international communism he represents are not interested in this country's friendship but only in the ec. gain that would accrue to his regime from this move and in the increase ~~in~~ *of* his pol. prestige that such action would bring.

At the beginning of your War of Independence in 1775 Benjamin Franklin wrote to his old friend in Eng. Wm. Strahan: "Look upon your hands! They are stained with the blood of your relations!" Mr. Pres. I submit that your decision in this matter might well determine if you will ever again be able to look at yours."

Juanita Castros letter was addressed to the Pres. but in truth it was written to all of us and all of us must be part of the answer. Has Sen. Church or any of us for that matter "found a friend?"

This is RR Thanks for listening. ❖

Government Can Cost Less I

September 6, 1977

We all criticize govt. for things it dosen't do well but is govt. at every level doing things it shouldn't be trying to do at all? I'll be right back.

I've often said that when govt. tries to do things that are not proper functions of govt. it cannot do them as well or as economically as the private sector. Now I'm beginning to wonder if we've gone as far as we could in determining just what are the proper functions ~~in~~ *of* govt.

I'll yield to no man in my respect for & appreciation of the men who fight our fires. So I intend no criticism of them when I bring up the question of whether they should or should not be employees *of* govt.

The other day I discovered by way of Robert Poole Jr. Pres. of the "Local Govt. Center"—a nonprofit research ~~center based in Santa Barbara Calif.~~ *org.* that more than a dozen towns and cities in our land have no fire depts. and no more *fire* problems than cities that do.

One of the dozen is Scottsdale Ariz. It contracts with Rural/Metro Fire Dept. Inc. a private concern that has an employees profit sharing plan, employs both men & women and pays time & a half for overtime. One additional dif. also—it's trucks are painted yellow not the traditional fire engine red. ~~Sco~~ This is not some new experiment, Scottsdale has used Rural/Metro Inc. for 25 yrs. and just recently signed on for another 5.

How does Scottsdale compare to more traditional communities? Well the latest figures available for comparison show that the per citizen cost ~~of~~ *for* fire protection in Scottsdale is less than ¼ the nat, average of cities in its population range. And before you ask the next logical question—fire insurance rates in Scottsdale are ~~the same as~~ *in the class 5* rating which is good and compares with all other well run cities it's size (96,000 pop.)

There is another statistic used to determine fire protection quality—what are per-capita fire losses over a period of years? The nat. average is about $12. In Scottsdale it's only about $4.50. Bolstering these figures is the fact that Scottsdale has been recognized by the Nat. Commission on Productivity for 8 significant innovations in fire fighting. It has also received commendations from the "Institute for Local Self govt. & the N.Y. City Rand Inst.

One of the 8 innovations is something called the snail, a remote-control robot invented by the company *& built* at a cost of only $3000. Operated by 1 man it does the work of 4 and goes into action on treads with a 2½ inch hose in areas too hot or dangerous for fire fighters—(700°). Other improvements include "attack" trucks with an onboard water tank, ~~&~~ pump & hose. There are pickup trucks with 2 man crews for the 75% of cases which are minor, rubbish, grass fires etc.

There is much more that can be told about Rural/Metro, ~~but it would take too long. But Very~~ *but very* simply it comes down to this; because the company operates to make a profit it has the strongest incentive to be efficient & cost effective. And since 90% of fire fighting cost is personnell and much of the personnell cost is for people who are paid to wait for something to happen Rural/Metro has modernized the volunteer concept.

~~They~~ Scottsdale city employees form an auxiliary force of paid reservists. Those who serve must pass stringent selection procedures and undergo a rigorous training program, for which they receive a $50 monthly retainer & $6.38 an hour for training & duty. They are on call for 1 week out of four. During his on week each reservist carries a portable paging unit. Adding in these reservists & the regular company employees Scottsdale uses only ⅔ the man power of the average city it's size. This is RR Thanks for listening. ❖

Government Can Cost Less II
September 6, 1977

This is more about things govt. is doing that might better be done by the private sector & which would be done better at lower cost. I'll be right back.

On the last broadcast I told of how Scottsdale Ariz. & a dozen other cities in our land were ~~using~~ *hiring* a private, profit making company to provide fire protection with no loss of quality & great savings to the taxpayers. Since fire dept's. are so universally thought of as one of those things only govt. can do I got curious about other governmental functions & whether ~~other cities & counties~~ some of them might lend themselves to the Scottsdale pattern.

The answer is (and I'll admit I was surprised) yes. Rochester N.Y. began increasing it's contracting out of govt. chores in 1974 and has reduced the number of city employees by 12%. Private firms take care of some of the street ~~maintenance~~ and all the building maintenance and operate all but one of the city parking garages. Vehicle repair and grave digging are contracted out. The city manager considers all of this as still experimental but is going ahead with a plan to have private garbage collection in one part of the city. He's interested in the competitive feature and what it might do to perk up the city run depts.

Other cities have been even more extensive in their contracting & at it longer. Twice as many cities use private firms for garbage collection ~~as~~ rather than city refuse dept's. and a survey has found that on the average the cost for ~~govt. doing it~~ *govt. garbage collection* is 68% higher ~~than when it's done for profit.~~ *than when it's done by a private, profit making concern.* Among the better known cities who are moving to private contracting are New Orleans, Charleston S.C., Dallas, Portland Oregon & Omaha Neb.

Just about every public service is being provided somewhere by private contractors at considerable savings to the taxpayers.

In Houston Texas instead of using ~~crime fighting,~~ *highly* trained policemen for routine protective duties, private security guards are employed to ~~protect~~ *guard* municipal court bldgs. & even the City Hall *FREEING THE POLICE FOR CRIME FIGHTING DUTIES.* San Francisco has contracted a number of parks & recreational facilities out to private operators and is now making a profit *on these facilities* instead of showing a loss to the taxpayers. Another Calif. city is saving 20% through private management of a municipal golf course. More & more school cafeterias are being operated by private contractors—even one by a ~~chain~~ hamburger chain and they ~~are~~ have turned money losses into profitable operations.

At another level of govt. Orange Co. in Calif. is contracting out it's data processing for 7 yrs. at a price of $26 mil. The county is getting better service & expects to save $11 mil. ~~On~~

One of the best incidents has to do with Minnesotas Hennepin county. County staff had proposed construction of a major food service plant as part of it's new medical Center. Then someone asked a simple question: "What does a county govt. know about preparing 3½ mil. meals a year?" I doubt anyone even tried to answer the question. There must have been an instant realization that ~~such~~ food purchasing, storage, preparation and serving on such an institutional scale is a pretty complicated business for beginners. At the same time there was recognition that a number of private firms have been in that line of business for quite a while. Hennepin Co. contracted with a private concern, set standards of performance, quality & cost and estimates it saves about $1 mil. a year.

It's something worth looking at in everyones home town. And think what might happen if the idea ~~were~~ reached Wash.

This is RR Thanks for listening. ❖

Lightning strikes precipitated a blackout starting at 9:34 p.m. on a hot July 13, 1977, night. Nine million people in New York City lost power for up to 25 hours.

Blackout

September 6, 1977

I have been waiting for information on one facet of the big blackout story in N.Y. and finally have it. I'll be right back.

Utility Companies ~~like some~~ *more than* some other industries are vulnerable to charges of villainy and so it was no surprise that Con-Edison in N.Y. would be pilloried for the recent blackout in ~~the~~ "Fun City." *To hear some tell it you would think the Company planned the whole thing.*

The attacks were made more bitter than usual by the looting that broke out in several neighborhoods. Of course those with no charity whatsoever for Con Edison were understanding and played the sorrowing parent where the looters were concerned. Our Ambassador to the United Nations* *even* took the attitude that stealing is something everyone does when the lights go out.

The Brooklyn Dist. Attorney has released some figures which contradict those bleeding hearts who saw the looters as just hungry people who had a chance to eat for a change. It seems 48% were regularly employed (many by the city itself) 41% were in anti-poverty or educational programs funded by govt. and fewer that 10% were on welfare.

The hunger excuse dosen't hold up *either* when you see a breakdown of the looters targets. There was that automobile dealer who lost more than 50 cars, 39 furniture stores, 20 drugstores, 17 jewelry stores, 10 clothing stores & only 6 groceries. *The looters had an appetite but not for food.*

* Andrew Young served as UN ambassador under President Carter until 1979 when he resigned due to public outrage over his clandestine meeting with Palestine Liberation Organization members.

But to get back to Con Edison. I kept wondering when if ever someone would look back down the last few years to see whether consumer minded politicians might have put thumbs down on requests by the company to expand or upgrade their facilities. After all a utility company isn't exactly a free agent. Yes it is a privately owned, profit making business but it is also a govt. regulated monopoly controlled by politically appointed utility commissioners.

Victor Reisel the noted columnist and expert on labor affairs did look back over the years and found *that* a "yes" several years ago instead of a "no" could have made the blackout impossible.

Con-Ed (as it's called) made application to build a hydro-elec. generating plant on the banks of the Hudson near West Point. The company explained the need & the possibility of power shortages ~~withou~~ unless the plant were built.

But environmentalists would have none of it. First it would mar the scenery. Con-Ed replied to that with plans to put it it completely underground. Opponents said the concrete tube bringing the water from the river to the turbines would still be visible. Then fishermen got into the act & said the warm water returning to the river would interfere with & reduce the Striped Bass in the Hudson. Con-ed volunteered to build and maintain a fish hatchery to keep the river stocked. This too was turned down which adds to the suspicion that we have an element in this country who just dont want any additional power plants—period & all their environmental complaints are excuses to ~~leg~~ *hide* their real purpose.

Had that generating plant been built there would have been no ~~lootin~~ blackout, no looting, no small merchants wiped out in the Big Apple.

Con-Ed still has the plans for the underground plant & the fish hatchery—even though scientists now say the maximum loss of Striped Bass would be less than 5%. ~~Who w~~

Who really was the villain last July 13 & 14th?

This is RR Thanks for listening. ❖

Furbish Lousewart
September 6, 1977

~~Hold~~ Stop the press
Usually it takes a bursting dam with it's subsequent disaster to make the news. This time it's a dam going up not falling down.

I'll be right back.

Some time ago on one of these broadcasts* I told about ~~the~~ *a* giant electric power project; a multibillion dollar construction job that had been ~~halted~~ stopped before it could start. ~~in~~ It was the Dickey-Lincoln power program in

* "Endangered Species," July 6, 1977. Published in *Reagan, In His Own Hand,* p. 329.

northern Maine intended to supply energy to ~~the~~ a large section of the Northeast.

The project was halted when it was discovered the huge hydroelectric dam essential to the program could not be built. Federal law prohibits use of Fed. funds in any construction that could harm plant or animal species included on the rare & endangered list of the United States Fish & Wildlife service.

And there on the banks of the St. John river in the area ~~that would~~ *to* be flooded ~~when the dam was built~~ *by the building of the dam* someone found about 200 weeds. They were a particular kind of weed—a sort of wild snapdragon known as the Furbish Lousewort. The Furbish Lousewort is on the endangered species list. ~~and those~~ Furthermore some supposedly knowledgeable people said those were the only 200 *FURBISH LOUSEWORTS* left in the world. So scratch one power project.

I found it a little hard to believe that all the rocks & rills & templed hills in Maine & elsewhere had been scoured for Furbish Louseworts and so stated on this program. If no one knew the 200 were there until they were getting ready to build a dam and accidentally stumbled on them wasn't it possible they might stumble on some more?

I also remember suggesting that weeds aren't all that hard to grow; that possibly they could gather seeds from the 200 or even transplant ~~the 200.~~ *some of them.* After all a few more winters like the last one a without an adequate power supply and some New Englanders might get on that endangered *SPECIES* list.

Well I'm happy to tell you *I've learned*—thanks to the N.Y. Times that the ~~Corps of~~ Army Corps of Engineers were having some of the same thoughts. They like to build dams and didn't take kindly to being shut out by a weed called the Furbish Lousewort. They enlisted the aid of George Stirett a naturalist *FROM* New Brunswick & Dr. Charles Richard a botanist from the U. of Maine.

These gentlemen along with some other scientists who were interested in the situation discovered, apparently by doing a little hiking that Furbish Louseworts ~~grow~~ can be found ~~in at least 5 different locations~~ on both sides of the St. John river in at least 5 different locations that wont be affected by the building of the dam.

Furthermore Dr. Richards did a little research and found the Lousewort reproduces by seed and can be transplanted outside it's original habitat.

I wonder if they'll grow in Calif? It would be quite a conversation piece to have a weed that stopped a $700 mil. dam. I wonder too if one of these days I might be doing a broadcast about the emergency situation in Maine where a weed called the Furbish Lousewort ~~was threatening~~ *had become so prolific it threatened* the states agricultural Industry

What we really should wonder is—will environmentalists find another reason why the dam shouldn't be ~~fi~~ built?

This is RR Thanks for listening. ❖

Pot
September 27, 1977

Wash. has given voice to the idea that criminal sanctions for possession of small amounts of marijuana should be lifted. I'll be right back

A recent editorial in a metropolitan paper approved ~~the~~ *a* statement emanating from Wash. about removing Fed. criminal sanctions for possession of small amt's. of marijuana. The editorial writer said, "Experience so far shows no significant increase in marijuana use or abuse."

This was too much for Daryl F. Gates, Asst. Chief Dir. of Operations, Los Angeles Police Dept. ~~And may I interject the L.A. Police Dept.~~ is one of the ~~finest~~ *finest police forces* in all the cities of the world. Chief Gates took pen in hand & wrote a letter to the editor.* He asked, "What experience?"

~~Calif. reduced it's *marijuana possession* penalties to about traffic ticket status on Jan. 1, 1976. I had vetoed legislation of this kind. Prior to that time the state~~ *Not too long ago Calif.* had a pretty sound law that gave a judge flexibility to reduce a felony conviction to a misdemeanor in cases such as the youthful experimenter. There were also provisions to allow users to choose attending a treatment center with no filing of an arrest record. The people of California overwhelmingly ~~voted~~ ~~down a~~ *repudiated a* ballot measure to decriminalize marijuana. But on Jan. 1, 1976 a new law went into effect reducing penalties for marijuana possession to about the level of a traffic ticket.

Chief Gates in his letter to the editor said that prior to the new law ~~L.A. had steadily reduced the seizure of marijuana from to an all~~ *in 1975 seizure of marijuana* ~~was~~ *totaled 4900 lbs. which gives some measurement of probable use.* When the relaxed law went into effect confiscation of the drug jumped to almost 18,000 lbs. In addition he said the marijuana was also of the more exotic type containing a much higher percentage *of* THC the intoxicating agent. Alarmingly the depts. juvenile division, narcotic section experienced an almost 50% increase in juvenile arrests for possession or use of marijuana in 1976 and so far in '77 an additional 20% increase.

~~The~~ Chief Gates wrote, "This apparent trend of increased usage by children was also ~~apparent~~ *evident* in a recent study in San Mateo County" and he added that "the age of the user became progressively lower as the law became weaker."

Summing it up his letter read; "This evidence indicates that when the Legislature reduced the penalties for marijuana use & possession there was a marked increase in marijuana importation and in its use among our young people.

Marijuana trafficking is a lucrative business, and one can only conclude

* Editorial, "Of Pot and Punishment," *Los Angeles Times* Sec. 2, p. 4, August 4, 1977. Gates's letter was published on August 22, 1977 (Sec. 2, p. 6).

that it's possession and use are encouraged when the legislature continues to deemphasize the criminal consequences. The end result," he says, "of such legislative leniency is that the traffickers of this intoxicating drug are virtually free to drain the vitality from our youth and our society with the approval of our legislative representatives."

I hope the editorial writer also reads letters to the editor.

This is RR Thanks for listening. ❖

Hospital Costs
September 27, 1977

Why are hospital costs so high? And can they be made lower by simply issuing a White House order that they shouldn't be so high? I'll be right back.

The White House has proposed placing a 9% limit on the increase in revenue a hospital can get—*from private patients.* One reputable and respected hospital admin. has said the goal is laudable but the proposal itself is unsound, unfair, unrealistic, unworkable and will result in hospitals being less able to serve the people. ~~That is a rather all inclusive~~ *That's a rather positive* statement ~~that~~ *and* dosen't tiptoe around the subject. And he is right.

~~But there is justification for his forthright declaration.~~ First of all such a blanket price fixing makes no allowance for hospitals that are presently being run on an efficient, economical basis. It dosen't allow for the fact that about 70% of hospital costs are payroll directly affected by inflation. ~~And with considering inflation~~ *And* what of the hospitals faced with ~~bringing~~ *buying expensive new* equipment ~~up to date~~ to keep pace with new medical procedures? ~~This is of course also true of supplies & the effect inflation has had.~~ *Then there is the effect inflation has had on restocking supplies.* One hospital supply officer pointed out that in 1976 24 cases of sterile water *USED IN SURGERY* cost $63.48. By the spring of '77 10 cases cost $64.45.

Probably the best example of shortsightedness or perhaps just plain "lets not talk about it" was the failure of the White House to touch on how much govt. has to do with increased hospital costs. For example the increase in govt. decrees demanding changes in *LABORATORY* safety standards, ~~in laboratories,~~ *and* regulations covering electrical, fire & elevator rules which require expensive *re*novations. Govt. programs also boost the number of health care recipients and the amt. of service provided those recipients.

Lets take a look at some of the rules & reporting requirements mandated by not one but several govt. agencies. Hospitals must report monthly & annual days of inpatient care, by age group, by services & by type of financial coverage. Outpatient visits must be reported in the same manner. ~~a~~*A*lso emergency room visits.

Total annual minutes of anaesthesia administered ~~Count & report~~ *must be reported as well as the* number of xray exams and the number of films used in these exams. Report the number of births for the year; The number of children served. Report the number of physical therapy treatments, the number of blood transfusions (and here is one)—report the number of outpatients admitted as inpatients.

Each hospital must give a certain amt. of "charity care" each yr. & have multi-lingual signs posted telling the patients this charity is available. Operations must be reported by type & number. Are you beginning to understand why when you ring for the nurse she's ~~a~~ *SOMETIMES* a little while in getting there? It's all that paperwork.

And oh yes ~~about that limit on increase in charges~~; about half of reimbursement rates are set by govt. ~~usuall~~ at less than actual cost so the private patients have to pay more to make up the difference. In socialized medicine there wouldn't be any private patients to be tapped so guess who'd pay then?

~~Back to regulations~~—Hospitals must obtain a signed certificate as to need for hospitalization and estab. a "time limit" for hospital stay. Detailed records must be kept on services provided, by date and by individual performing the service. Periodically the "race" of each patient must be reported for a given day.

These are only a few ~~but~~ of many requirements and I'm sure as you heard them you wondered ~~what~~ of what use all that paper ~~work was~~ *could be* to govt. except to make work for burocrats. This is RR Thanks for listening. ❖

Olympics
September 27, 1977

As 1980 edges closer I'm sure many of us will find our thoughts turning to Moscow and the Olympic games. I'll be right back.

Some time ago on one of these broadcasts I told how the Soviet U. thru ~~some~~ *several* of it's ~~spiritual~~ unofficial allies—you might in the absence of formal ties call them ideological soul mates—was working to shut Israel out of the 1980 Olympics. At the time I indicated a little unhappiness with the International Olympic Committees tendency to waffle a bit when a stand on principle is called for.

The committee was established from the beginning to be above politics, absolutely independent of any & all govt's., supreme authority & sole owner of the ~~Olyp~~ Olympic games. Membership on the committee is pretty exclusive, new members can be appointed only by recommendation of established members of the committee.

Each new committee member takes a solemn oath to keep himself free "from all pol., sectarian or commercial influence." Now that pledge didn't ~~call~~ cause any problems in an earlier day but in the world as it is now obviously no citizen of a totalitarian country could take such an oath. And yet the roster shows the Soviet U., Bulgaria, Rumania, Poland, Czechoslovakia *CUBA* & E. Germany represented on the committee by full fledged members in good standing. Can it be we're wrong and totalitarians will permit a certain freedom in the name of sport?

No, it seems the Internat. Olympic Comm. solves this problem as it has so many others. The oath was waived for these members. The late Avery Brundage Pres. of the Olympics for 20 yrs.* said that "unfortunately there are large sections of the world today where the form of govt. precludes full independence of it's citizens." Alexander Solzhenitsyn puts it a little more bluntly.

But in 1969 it was also ruled that such non-independent members could never total more than 10% of the membership. And last June in observance of that quota the comm. turned down recommendations from ~~Eastern block~~ iron curtain countries—the "Peoples Dem. Repub. of Korea (that's No. Korea) included. Now that sounds better—or it did until the committee decided to boost it's membership by accepting citizens from such bastions of freedom as Mali, Mongolia & Libya.

It is not known whether they were asked to take the oath of independence. Possibly they weren't since the individuals chosen are ~~members~~ *Presidents* of their national Olympic committees & are therefore fully accountable to their govts. And those govts. are not exactly our idea of a Republic or a Democracy. ≠ In Mali the power ~~lies in~~ *all of it,* is vested in the Revolutionary Military Council. In Mongolia it is the Communist party & in Libya it is Col. Qaddafi** the absolute Dictator.

One thing is certain, they are all ~~soul br~~ solid allies of the Kremlin and will be helpful in seeing that the 1980 Olympics in Moscow are successful, ~~with~~ *as* success *is* defined by the Kremlin.

I've always suspected the Russian Athletes do as well as they do because they think there are real bullets in the starters gun. ~~This is~~ *If there were I wonder if the International Comm. would protest.*

This is RR Thanks for listening. ❖

Tax Limitation

September 27, 1977

"Nothing is certain but death & taxes." That's an old truism. But that ends the comparison between the two. The death rate is going down. Tax rates are going up. I'll be right back.

A few years ago in Calif. we tried to persuade the citizens to establish a limit on the percent of earnings *our state* govt. could take from the people in taxes.

* Avery Brundage was president of the International Olympic Committee from 1952 to 1972.
** Muammar Qaddafi.

Last year the same attempt was made in Mich. In both cases ~~we~~ *the proposal* ~~were~~ *was* defeated.* ~~Those~~.

Those who mounted opposition to the idea were, as you might expect, groups who gain their livlihood from tax dollars; ~~They defeated the proposal in both~~ ≠ Pub. employee groups, Teachers Federations and special interest groups enjoying subsidies of one kind or another. In both states they resorted to falsehood to win their case. I know that sounds blunt and a little harsh but it is absolutely true. They were successful in convincing the voters that somehow govt. would, in spite of the limit end up getting more *in* taxes not less and that was a lie.

Maybe ~~it was~~ *a percentage limit on taxes is* an idea that has to be around for a while before it is really understood enough to make the lies ineffective. ~~I hope so on.~~

Stop & think about it for a moment. Our family budgets are based on spending limitations. ≠ We know generally ~~how much~~ *what percentage of our income* we can afford for rent or mortgage payments; what has to be set aside for food & household expenses; what percentage can go for savings or insurance. Why shouldn't we collectively decide ~~t~~ what percentage we can afford to spend for govt?

It is presently the biggest single cost item in the family budget and it is increasing faster than anything else we buy. In 1930 total govt. costs were only 10% of our earnings. By 1950 the figure had gone to 25.8%. By 1975 (and I suppose it's about the same today) it had reached 44%—44 cents out of every dollar earned.

Govt's. only source of revenue is about 70 mil. Americans working, earning & paying taxes. These are the people employed in the private sector. Yes govt. emp's. *also* pay taxes but their *TAX* dollars first had to be taken from the 70 mil. Let me do a little dividing and give you a frightening answer. Next year govt's. in the U.S. Fed, St., & Local will cost $715 bil. (⅔ for Uncle Sam, ⅓ for the St's. Co's. & Cities) That pro-rates out to ~~about~~ $10,215 for each one of ~~the 70 mil. workers of Am.~~ *YOU WHO [ARE] EMPLOYED IN THE PRIVATE SECTOR*.

Out of the Calif. & Mich. efforts has come a National Tax Limitation Comm. located in Briarcliff Manor N.Y. One of the leaders is Wm. Rickenbacker the economist & another is Lewis Uhler who was part of our effort in Calif. They have authored a study called "A Taxpayers Guide to Survival." The address is *NAT. TAX LIMITATION COMM.* Box 1000—Briarcliff Manor N.Y. so dont write me or the station. *I'll repeat it at the end of this broadcast.*

There is no indication whatsoever that govt. costs are leveling off. In 1965 Eng. was taking the percentage in taxes we are taking now 44%. Their rate of increase was similar to ours but they started earlier. Today Eng. is taking almost 60%. We'll be getting there soon.

There really is only one way to stop ~~this~~ the ever increasing percentage of

* See also "Government Cost I," p. 91, and "Government Cost II," *Reagan, In His Own Hand,* p. 270.

our earnings taken by govt. ~~& d~~Determine what is the proper share, what we can afford to spend on govt. and then fix that percentage into law. No one knows better than the burocrat himself where the useless fat is in his dept. Faced with the possibility of his whole ~~dept. and~~ program being closed down he'll eliminate the fat in order to stay in business.

That booklet and that address again, "A Taxpayers Guide To Survival"—Nat. Tax Limitation Comm. Box 1000 Briarcliff N.Y.—This is RR Thanks for listening. ❖

All states except New Hampshire have passed mandatory seat belt laws; the first was passed by New York in 1984. Air bags were mandated by the Department of Transportation in the late 1990s.

Air Bags
September 27, 1977

Now and then we read something about air-bags in ~~aut~~ automobiles to, quote "protect our lives"—unquote, but do we know we're about to be stuck with them? I'll be rite back.

About 95% of our automobiles are equipped with seatbelts and we'd all be better off if we used them. Their ability to protect us and even to spare us painful bruises in minor, bumper denting accidents is a proven fact.

It could be we're going to wish we had used them even if we never have an accident. The Dept. of Transportation in Wash. which succeeded in having them installed in cars *IN THE 1ST PLC.* is pretty upset with us because we dont automatically hook them up every time we step on the starter.

They did a lot of fussing about making it compulsory for us to wear them but couldn't figure a way to put an inspector in every car to make sure we did. You'll remember one of their efforts was that inter-lock seatbelt device that rang buzzers and wouldn't let you start the car until the belt was hooked up. It only took Congress about 2 weekends back in the home district finding out how mad we all were to get that changed.

But now the Dept. of Transportation has figured a way to save us in spite of ourselves. It is the air bag. And they've passed a regulation that we have to have ~~them~~ *one* whether we want ~~them~~ *it* or not.

At first glance it looks like a pretty good way to save lives in head on collisions and incidentally that's the only time they work. If you are traveling 22 miles an hour or faster and you plough into something head on or nearly so the bag located beneath the dash instantly inflates & you find yourself plunging into a soft ~~ball~~ balloon instead of a hard windshield so far so good. ~~But~~ and maybe even worth the $2,000 or so it will cost you over the life of your car.

They ~~cost~~ *add* about 200 to $300 to the price of the car when you buy it and another 3 to $600 every time it inflates and has to be refilled. Now that's still a fair price if it saved your life. But it's pretty expensive if it just happened to pop open by mistake and about 7½ out of 100 do that. Then of course there might be additional costs if it did that accidental popping while you were ~~n~~ navigating a curve at about 55 miles an hour. I understand they are experimenting to see if they can make them so they dont extend above eye level. That of course would be a simpler problem if we were all the same height.

Of course you wouldn't have to bother with the seatbelt.—~~w~~ Which is too bad, because the seatbelt protects you f in a side collision or a roll over, ~~&~~ *even a rear ender &* the air bag doesn't. Incidentally almost half of all accidents are that kind. Very simply the Nat. Highway Traffic Safety Admin. has found seatbelts are 5½ times better than air bags at saving lives & 2½ times better at preventing injuries.

One thing I haven't checked out is information I've received that the air in the air bag isn't air. It's a highly toxic gas.* If true it's something *else* to be considered.

Isn't this whole idea another thing that should be left to us & the free mkt. If any of us would like to install such a devise in the family car shouldn't that be our decision to make? By what right does a govt. agency force us to buy something for our own protection at considerable cost? It really is none of their darn business.

This is RR Thanks for listening. ❖

Camps

September 27, 1977

Politicians campaign on a promise of getting govt. off our backs but govt. stays right there and gets heavier by the day. I'll be right back.

Our govt. or at least some people in it have found a new area where we are unprotected and govt. must ride to the rescue. You probably thought a hike in the country or summer camp for the kids was a part of growing up and contributed to health and happiness ~~of~~ *for* Mary & Tommy. Well thanks to our ever watchful & omnipotent guardians in Wash. the ~~tr~~ ugly truth has come out, mortal danger lurks in every bed roll & pup tent.

That's the bad news. The good news is that the Fed. govt. is going to eliminate the hazards of camping through burocratic rule & regulation.

Congress is debating a piece of legislation called the, "Youth Camp Safety

* Air bags' contents consist of two chemicals, which react at impact, creating nitrogen gas that then inflates the bag. One of these chemicals, sodium azide, is a highly toxic gas and is potentially fatal. See the Centers for Disease Control at www.cdc.gov and "A New Safety Look in Chemicals," *BusinessWeek,* June 5, 1978.

Act." It will (if passed) marshal an army of Fed. inspectors to ride herd on YMCA. ~~camps,~~ Boy ~~Scouts~~ *& GIRL SCOUT*, Church groups, and private camps. No longer will a Scout have to—"Be prepared"—Wash. will relieve him or her of ~~that~~ any need to continue that time honored motto.

Under the bill any group going on a hike would henceforth file a detailed itinerary in duplicate with the Fed. govt. A scout camping out alone to meet an Eagle Scout requirement would be subject to a fine under the act. Campers who cooked for their fellow campers would need a certificate from a Fed. inspector.

How do you suppose we've managed to live so long without knowing a steak fry or a weiner roast~~s~~ was a criminal act? Why if Jimmy Carter throws another one of those catfish frys for the neighbors it could be a bigger scandal then the "Tea Pot Dome."

But seriously it is no laughing matter. Another Fed. burocracy could be in the making. The legislation proposes something called the, "Office of Youth Camp Safety"—within the dept. of H.E.W. (where else?) Already existing laws and regulations pertaining to camps would be duplicated and inspectors would be hired to monitor these rules which have worked very well without such policing.

Right now camps are licensed and required to meet standards of sanitation, environment & water control, vehicle equipment and driver permits, even compliance with regulations of the Occupational Safety & Health Admin.

If what they are proposing sounds silly and incidentally very, very expensive it sounds sillier when you look at the record. By actual statistics summer camps are safer than our schools and believe it or not our own homes.

The death rate in camps based on child-weeks of camping is almost ⅓ less than the rate in the general population. As for injuries the rate in our schools is 5 times greater than it is in camping. In other words a child is safer in a summer camp than in school or at home.

I hope there are enough former Boy & Girl Scouts, Summer Camp alumnae and just plain veterans of cookouts and overnight hikes in Cong. to deep six this as yet unborn burocracy before yet another freedom is lost.

This is RR Thanks for listening. ❖

Energy
October 18, 1977

Cover up is the name of the game in Wash. and right now the game is energy & how to cover up how much of it we have. I'll be right back.

The House of Reps. rammed through the Presidents energy *plan* pretty much as ordered ~~reporting all~~ *after listening to* the frightening stories ~~of out of~~

~~the~~ *the* White House ~~of how~~ *told of* dark ~~the~~ nights ~~would *were to* suddenly become.~~ *to come.* ~~The shortage of natural gas & oil was so measurable~~ ~~t~~*T*hey almost gave us the day & hour at which the tanks would run dry. You wanted to ask if that was Eastern~~,~~ *or* ~~Central, Mountain or~~ Pacific time?~~—standard or daylight savings? And should we synchronize our watches.~~

By the time the Senate took the matter up a little more ~~reason~~ *common sense* was prevailing & with good reason. The doom criers in the Sen. filibustered, cots were brought in for the all night sessions and finally the weary Solons came up with a compromise. It isn't as good as it could be but at least ~~they passed~~ *it's* a program for gradual de-regulation of the price on natural gas.

Of course this now has to go to a joint conference committee ~~of~~ *to* reconcile the differences between the House & Sen. versions so more compromise is likely.

But one thing was demonstrated—the value of the cumbersome, slow moving pace of the legislative process. It gives time for even the best hidden facts to come out. Just think if we had acted on the White House declaration that we'd be running out of feul ~~by th~~ before the turn of the century—now only 22 years & a few months away.

~~First the news leaked out~~ *As the days went by we learned* of a report by the ~~Administrations~~ *Exec. branches* own Energy & Research Developement Admin. which was so optimistic about future supplies the Whitehouse sat on the report to protect it's own credibility. The ERDA staff responsible for the report was hastily reassigned to other ~~tasks~~ *duties* and their chief ~~was sent to~~ *wound up* walking a beat in flatbush. One of the optimistic utterances of the now muzzled group was that at $2.50 a 1000 cubic ft. instead of Mr. Carters $1.75 the nation would be awash in natural gas.

With that hole in the script covered the House went forward with the Presidents plan. But Whoops! Dr. Vincent McKelvey Dir. of the U.S. Geological Survey a carrer scientist with U.S.G.S. for 20 yrs. was making a speech in Boston. He mentioned a 4000 yr. supply of geo pressured gas in the gulf of Mexico, also a large amount of oil still to be found in the U.S. The Dr. is an expert on geology but a rank amateur on politcis.

The White House quickly covered with a C.I.A. report (you remember CIA) that the Russians would run ~~of~~ out of oil by 1985 and start buying it from the Arabs. Dr. McKelvey sincerely interested in helping out said "No the Russians" ~~are~~ *are* floating on a sea of oil."

Dr. McKelvey is no longer Dir. of *the* U.S. Geological Survey. He's in an obscure office down the hall someplace. ~~For~~ *In* 98 years the agency has only had 9 directors. They are ~~appointed by~~ *nominated by* the Nat. Academy of Sciences & Presidents have always accepted them & not fired them.*

* On September 6, 1977, Secretary of the Interior Cecil D. Andrus announced that Vincent K. McKelvey would be replaced by the end of the year.

Dr. Joseph Barneo of Israel who was the U.N. Dr. of Nat. resources says present estimates of recoverable oil are only 1% of what is there. The other 99% can be recovered by the law of supply & demand. In 1942 our estimate of crude oil reserves was 600 bil. barrells. By 1970 the estimate was 4 tril. Russian Scientists now place it at 12 Tril.

The law of suppy & demand still works. We dont need ~~an~~ a new energy dept. we only need deregulation.

This is RR Thanks for listening. ❖

Despite a range of charges about Brigadier General Omar Torrijos' regime, a month before this broadcast President Carter and the Panamanian leader signed the Panama Canal treaties.*

Panama III
October 18, 1977

We are told the new Panama Canal treaties will make it easier to guard the canal against sabotage. I'll be right back.

Of all the arguments given in support of the Canal treaty none are more ridiculous than to say that the canal will be in greater danger of sabotage if we dont give it to Panama. Obviously we must be thinking of Panamanian radicals as the saboteurs. But some of those radicals are outraged by the terms of the treaty. *One was so upset he burned himself to death in Sweden as a protest.***

We have gone through 4 wars without the canal being sabotaged. Actually it is next to impossible to do while we control the canal zone. If we ratify the treaty the zone will be policed by Panamanians. In fact there wont be a zone, it will all be Panama.

~~Then as a~~*A* reporter asked me the other day "how can we guard the canal against a missile attack?" We cant, but if it's going to be a nuclear missile war why would an enemy bother with *the* canal. His missiles will be dropping on our cities & factories. There would be no need to waste a missile on the canal.

No the real threat to us has to do with the Marxist leanings of the present govt. of Panama & the possibility of an arrangement similar to what Castro has with Russia. In May of 1957 the Wash. Evening Star carried a story that the Soviet U. had launched a propaganda offensive against the U.S. and Central Am. to incite Panama into demanding control of the Panama Canal.

* A few months after this broadcast, a U.S. Senate Intelligence Committee report stated Torrijos' brother, Moises Torrijos Herrera, was dealing drugs and the Panamanian leader ignored it. See Adam Clymer, "Senate Report Asserts Torrijos Ignored Drug Dealing by Brother," *The New York Times,* February 22, 1978, p. A1.

** In September 1977, Leopoldo Aragón died in an act of self-immolation.

Torrijos did not participate in the 1969 coup that overthrew the elected ~~P~~Govt. of Panama. His colleagues thought him too erratic. The leaders were Boris Martinez, Escobar Bethancourt & ~~Torrijos~~ *the husband* of Torrijos sister. Bethancourt leader of the communist party decided to dump Martinez ~~and~~ *after the coup*. Brother in law persuaded him to set Torrijos up as chief of the Nat. Guard & subsequently head of state.

~~I can only quote what is the history as reported in Panama.~~ Torrijos is reported as having been a youthful member of the marxist organization known as "Young Veraguas." His parents founded what is now the most powerful *communist* cell in Panama. On Nov. 19 1968 Drew Pearson identified Torrijos as a communist.*

This last July a Russian mission met with Torrijos, Bethancourt & the ever present brother in law. On July 19 Panama signed an ec. pact with the Soviet U. & it was reported they discussed a sea level canal to be financed ~~th~~ by the Soviets & the estab. of a naval base. "Brother in law," hailed the agreement as having deep historic ~~experience~~ *significance* for the Am. Continent.

In Aug. Intelligence International of Eng. quoted an article in "Red Star" the official Soviet mil. magasine. It was later carried in Cubas "Bohemia." Major Sergei Yunorov wrote, "Due to its privileged location as the juncture between S. Am. & the rest of the continent including the canal that permits U.S. warships to operate simultaneously in the Atlantic & Pacific the canal zone must be considered by the Soviet U. as a priority zone. A 2nd zone (from which to attack Panama) is the isthmus to the No. of Panama. The Canal itself can be attacked as well from Colombia." As a third choice he calls for converting Cuba & Puerto Rico into bases from which Moscows plan can be consummated.

This is RR Thanks for listening. ❖

Steel

October 18, 1977

Layoffs have hit the steel industry and one wonders what individual hopes & dreams have had to be canceled or at least put off. I'll be right back.

Across Pa. & Ohio the fires have been banked in steel mills and thousands of steelworkers have been laid off. The law of averages ~~says~~ *would indicate* X number of families have seen some plan or other shelved til better times.

Abe Abel Pres. of the U.S. Steelworkers of America has had to put ~~a~~ *on* hold ~~on~~ a life long dream. His dream was a lifetime *JOB* guaranty for every steelworker, portal to portal pay—on salary from his own door step back to that

* Drew Pearson and Jack Anderson, "Panama's Junta Has Red Background," *The Washington Post*, November 19, 1968, p. B13.

door step at the end of the day. And of course all the fringe benefits to solve whatever problems might arise for the worker or his family, health care, *life* insurance, the whole thing.

With all respect to Mr. Abels dream and his strenuous efforts to make it come true possibly that dream has something to do with the current layoffs. In the last 5 yrs. he has managed to increase the basic hourly earnings of steelworkers almost 66%. It costs the industry $96.32 per worker for each ≠ 8-hour day.

A few years ago he was negotiating for 450,000 steelworkers. Then it was 400,000 and now it is *only* 340,000. In 1976 American steel users imported more than 14 mil. tons of foreign steel. That was a 20% increase over the year before and going on 15% of our total steel supply. Much of this was coming from W. Germany & Japan where newer plants with more modern equipment increased per man hour productivity which we couldn't match.

Still I dont believe the layoffs can be laid completely to the wage differential between Am. workers & their foreign counterparts. I have an uneasy feeling that perhaps there has been overproduction of steel worldwide. If so that's a tougher problem to solve than differences in wage scales.

~~Then t~~*T*here is another factor affecting price. ~~brought on by govt.~~ The American steel industry is subject to 5000 regulations issued by 27 Fed. agencies ranging from the Environmental Protection Agency to the Occ. Safety & Health Admin. Many of these have called for massive investments in equipment ~~required by the Fed. regulations~~ none of which increased productivity by one ounce of steel but all of which increased production costs.

Mr. Abel and many of his cohorts in the heirarchy of organized labor would have to admit they themselves have supported the social reforms that led to *many of* these regulations. More & bigger govt. is part of their pol. phil.

I'd like to suggest a dream for not only the steel but for all American industry. Call it a seminar, a study, research or just a rap session. ~~but w~~Why cant labor, management and some objective economists sit down around a table, everything off the record and see what each could contribute to the health of the industry? What factors are keeping us from being competitive in the world mkt? And before we lay it to wages *alone* remember we've always had a higher standard of living & for decades we led the world in production & sales. The dream they could discuss *around that table* could be the American dream & how to restore it.

This is RR Thanks for listening. ❖

Land
October 18, 1977

Is there a concerted plan by govt. to quietly gain control of land in America either by outright ownership or through regulation of private property? I'll be right back.

~~Going back over the years one can see a consistent pattern of moves to increase govt.~~ ~~*Fed.*~~ ~~control over land in this country. About 30 yrs. ago Pres. Truman openly declared that land reform was long overdue in America.~~

A dozen years ago a truly concerted drive by the Fed. govt. to add to it's real estate holdings began with a program to provide *MORE outdoor* recreational facilities. Longtime mining claims were canceled and privately held land condemned. A Fed. official involved in this program stated that, "in the beginning the govt. encouraged private ownership to get the land developed but now it was necessary to get control back in govt. hands."

There was a limit of course to how much property the govt. could justify as required for outdoor recreation. But the environmental ~~boom~~ *movement* solved that problem, ~~and~~ land planning bills began to pop up in Wash. and they are still around. These of course permit private ownership but with govt. authorized to say what can & cant be done with the property.

~~Back when territorys became states~~ I believe ~~all land within the new states boundaries was to belong to the state for ultimate sale to individuals. It would be interesting to see if this was changed by law or just overlooked by Wash. The Fed. govt. is the biggest real estate owner in all the land~~ ~~*today*~~ ~~owning up to as much as 80% of some states total area. It owns about half of Calif.~~

Now however the assaults are many & varied. There are bills in Congress to declare millions of acres of Nat. forest land—wilderness area. This of course does not increase govt's. land holdings but it takes land presently available for multiple use, grazing, lumbering, mining & recreational and limits it strictly to preservation with roads, trails & vehicles banned. ~~*And of course sometimes it becomes necessary to take pvt. property.*~~

In many cases this would cancel grazing leases that have been in effect for generations. Under these leases ranchers have developed water and improved forage at their own expense with govt's. encouragement & assurance ~~that~~ *of* continued use of the land.

In Calif's. Curry & Del Norte counties 328,000 acres of commercial timber land & *the entire econ. of the 2 counties* is threatened by one bill in Cong. ~~The entire econ of the 2 counties is threatened.~~

A court decision has been interpreted as giving the Corps of Engineers jurisdiction over <u>all</u> <u>wetlands</u> including land that was under water 50 yrs. ago. In some cases ~~the~~ such land is *now* the site of factories, housing tracts, farms & schools—*all subject to the Corps of Engineers jurisdiction.*

In 1902 the govt. built many irrigation projects and to prevent profiteering limited farm size to 160 acres. Fair enough. But the condition was waived sometimes when the Fed. govt. was only a partner in local & state programs. Now the 1902 law is being invoked and private owners are being ordered to reduce their holdings to 160 acres even though such a limitation is uneconomic and cannot possibly work with todays farming methods.

The govt. is also involving itself in the disposition of the property. One regulation would prevent a citizen from buying the land & leasing it out if the owner lived more than 50 miles from the ~~farm~~ *land. If you want to own land 1000 miles away & rent it out what business is that of govt?*

The ~~worst~~ most unfair move is in Calif's. Imperial valley. More than ½ a century ago farmers built a canal to the Col. river and reclaimed *the* barren desert. Later the Fed. govt. over their protests that a new canal was unnecessary went ahead & built the American Canal. The Sec. of Interior in writing guaranteed the Imperial Valley farmers *they* were exempt from the 160 acre limit. Now the govt. has cancelled this guaranty ~~and ordered the~~ *& ordered the break up of the farms* saying the promise never should have been made. Maybe not—but once made it should be kept.

This is RR Thanks for listening. ❖

Prices for crude oil tripled in late 1973 with the Arab oil embargo and increased further in 1975, but levelled off in 1976 and 1977. Conservation and alternative energy sources became major issues. Prices would increase dramatically again in 1979 and 1980, reaching $34 per barrel.

Energy I

October 18, 1977

Dutiful citizens are driving 55 mi. per hour (or thereabouts) to save gas. Thermostats are set too ~~warm~~ *high* for comfort on a hot day & too low on a cold one. We have an energy crisis. I'll be right back.

Just supposing as the century draws to a close Our guardians in Wash. warn us of worse times to come. Mass unemployment ~~threatens~~ as industries close down for lack of fuel; our balance of trade ~~is~~ in dangerous imbalance and ~~our~~ *a further* deterioration of our once high standard of living. The govt. pleads for even greater sacrifice on our part *to hold off catastrophy.*

Then *one day* we open the morning paper ~~one day~~ and are confronted by 4 inch headlines announcing a sensational scientific breakthrough. There is available a new material which when dropped in water creates steam which *in turn* generates electricity.

An amount ~~which could~~ *of this new material small enough to* fit into an ordinary bathroom or large closet ~~could~~ *will* supply the ~~whole countries~~ *entire nations* electrical needs for a year. And we have enough *on hand* for more than

100,000 years. ~~the~~ The cost *is* equivalent to oil ~~at 2.5 gals. for at almost~~ *if oil cost about* a penny a barrel. and it is nonpolluting.

There is dancing in the streets—interrupted *suddenly* by an announcement from Wash. that we cant ~~have~~ *use* this magic answer to our energy shortage. Thats quite a script isn't it? ~~/~~

Well Except for the dancing in the street the story I've just outlined is true. The magic material is the waste from our present nuclear power plants. ~~You know—t~~That stuff the doom criers tell is us is too dangerous to store anyplace on or in the earth.

Plutonium 239 is produced in our nuclear power plants. When it is mixed with uranium 238 the ~~useless~~ *worthless* waste left over from making enriched uranium for power plants it regenerates itself and in breeder, reactor*s* ~~plants~~ can produce 100 yrs. electricity just from the present waste on hand. The breeder reactor actually produces more fuel than it uses as it generates electricity.

So why the stop order from Wash? For one thing the fear of creating Plutonium 239 which can be used in nuclear bombs. But other countries, the Sov. U. included are going forward with this new energy source. Our refusing to utilize it wont reduce the risk of ~~some~~ *other* countries developing nuclear weapons at all—too many others are doing it.

The other holdup is a campaign of slander & half truth about Plutonium 239 being ~~so toxic that is called~~ the most toxic substance known to man. That isn't quite true—Botulism is 1000 ~~more time~~ *times more* toxic *and it's been around quite a while.*

Two nuclear critics* are largely responsible for the mis-information being used to keep us from going into breeder reactors. It should be known that these 2 gentlemen earn their living by opposing nuclear power. An investigating committee of the U.S. Nat. Acad. of Science as well as dozens of our top radiation research scientists have declared the ~~statements~~ findings of these 2 messengers of doom totally invalid—so what are we waiting for?

This is RR Thanks for listening. ❖

Energy II

October 18, 1977

In my last broadcast I talked of the breeder reactor as a source of electrical power which can meet our needs for 100,000 yrs. I'll be right back.

* One of the critics to whom Reagan refers is probably Robert Pollard, who resigned from the Nuclear Regulatory Commission to become the senior nuclear safety engineer for the Union of Concerned Scientists. A major study of reactor safety, chaired by physicist Norman Rasmussen, was published as "Reactor Safety Study: An Assessment of Accident Risks in U.S. Commercial Nuclear Power Plants" (WASH-1400), U.S. Nuclear Regulatory Commission, 1975, and extensively reviewed in 1976 and 1977.

The breeder reactor using the atomic waste from our present nuclear power plants boggles the mind with it's potential. It not only can satisfy our nuclear needs for 250 years just from the otherwise useless rubble in our present wastepile but it creates more fuel than it uses. It sounds like mans age old dream of perpetual motion.

The Pres. is opposed to going ahead with the process because it would result in great availability of Plutonium 239—the stuff of which nuclear~~s~~ bombs ~~is~~ *are* made. But isn't it too late to worry about that since France, West Germany, Britain, Belgium, Japan, Brazil & the Sov. U. are already underway & ahead of us in the breeder reactor field. Plutonium 239 is generally available with or without our producing it.

There is another anti-plutonium element active however with an entirely different motive than that of the Pres. Actually this group is for the most part made up of those who oppose every other aspect of nuclear power.

The Nat. Council of Churches was led down the road of opposition to nuclear power by it's own investigating commission. Eleven of the 21 members of that commission had already taken a stand against nuclear power prior to their appointment to the commission. The other 10 were clergymen & lawyers with no knowledge or expertise in the field.

The most potent enemies of plutonium & nuclear power are for the most part environmentalists—some truly sincere and some outright professionals riding the cause for their own purposes. But whether well meaning & truly dedicated or just playing for pay they are politically influential in todays world where special interests get attention out of proportion to their members.

What you & I must realize is that just possibly their cause is much broader than whether electricity should be generated by nuclear power or some other source. Are the anti-nuclear forces the same who blocked the Maine power project because the dam to provide hydro-elec. generation would endanger a weed called the Furbish Lousewart? Are they also the ones who have blocked the TVA dam on the Little Tennesee River in the name of a 2 inch fish called the Snail Darter? Are they the ones who blocked a coal burning power plant in Utah in the name of environmental protection?

In other words is there a larger purpose behind their anti-nuclear stand or their ~~environ~~ environmentalism? Is their goal in reality to block any increase in energy supply & even to reduce it with the idea that by stopping progress the world will remain as it is. The deer "will loll in his rilly place" as the poet put's it and we'll give up many of the latest electric powered gadgets that have made life a little easier and yes more simple by any definition but theirs.

They do leave unanswered a number of important questions. What kind of jobs will the people get who now work at making those gadgets? Of course they could I suppose find work in the re-opened buggy whip factories and harness shops.

This is RR ~~I'll be right back~~ *Thanks for listening.* ❖

Breaking up the oil companies became an issue during the energy crisis of the 1973–79 period. The Federal Communication Commission's (FCC) equal time provision requires that legally qualified political candidates be treated equally when air time is sold or given away. See the Federal Communications Act of 1934, Section 315, as amended.

Equal Time
October 18, 1977

Sometimes it seems the fairness doctrine—the equal time provisions for radio & TV are like the recipe for mule & rabbit stew; one rabbit to one mule. I'll be right back.

As you know doubt are aware Birch Bayh of Ind.* & some other members of Cong. in both houses are of the opinion the major oil companies should ~~be~~ undergo divestiture. That is a polite word which means the companies should be broken up.

I wont go into whether divestiture is a good or bad idea or whether it would or would not benefit the economy. One thing is certain however, it wouldn't produce any more oil or make us less dependent on the Arabs. But that isn't the subject of this commentary.

~~Last~~ *In the* Spring *of* '76 it seems that Texaco Inc. ran a commercial on WTOP-TV in Wash. some 53 times in all. The word "divestiture" was never mentioned. Nevertheless a somewhat liberal (make that really anti-business) group called "Energy Action Committee," protested to the Fed. Communication Commission that the ads were against divestiture. ~~and t~~*T*he committee demanded equal time.

The F.C.C. ruled that WTOP had not carried enough pro-divestiture material in it's news programs to balance the ads and gave the station 10 days to respond. As a matter of fact WTOP had made Texaco tone down it's ad specifically to avoid the problem it now faced. But rather than do battle with the F.C.C. the station made available to the "Energy Action Comm." a total of 30 spot ads—16 60-second spots & 14 30-second spots.

At 1st glance you might say "fair enough" but a 2nd look reveals something of a catch. Texacos ads had been censored by the station so they were bland commercials with no mention that Congress was even considering anything called divestiture. And Texaco paid the regular price for such commercials. The Energy committee ~~will get~~ *was given* it's ads free and ~~now *then* we've learned they wont *wouldn't* be~~ *they weren't* censored even a little bit.

One of the free ads was a dramatic little epic called "Mugging." An ordinary citizen is held up in a dark alley by a fellow dressed as an Arab using a gas

* Senator Birch Evan Bayh (D–Indiana, 1963–1981).

nozzle as a weapon. The mugger takes the victems wallet and runs away. Act III he takes off his ~~≠~~ Arab costume and stands revealed as an American corporate exec. ~~1~~ who laughs as he counts the loot he's taken from John Q. Citizen. Close with a voice over warning "We'd better break up the oil monopol~~iesy~~ before it breaks us."

Of equal subtlety is the sponge ad. This one shows a sponge with the 48 mainland states superimposed. A pair of hands starts squeezing the sponge to background music of "America the Beautiful" while ~~a pile of~~ money piles up beneath the sponge. The voice over explains the hands belong to the oil industry.

All of this in the name of *the* fairness doctrine. It is of course totally unfair, ~~and~~ utterly ridiculous and the F.C.C. should be ashamed of itself. Come to think of it—dont we all feel a little ashamed?

This is RR Thanks for listening. ❖

Investigative Agencies
October 18, 1977

I've spoken several times about the price we could pay for what we've done to muzzle the FBI & the C.I.A. *NOW* The bills are ~~already~~ coming in. I'll be right back.

Some time ago on these broadcasts I deplored the extent to which our govt. yielding to pressure from a number of groups best described as "bleeding hearts," had reduced the crime fighting ability of ~~our~~ *the FBI* & the counter-espionage *ability* of the ~~≠~~ *CIA*. I also told of how Philip Agee ex-cia agent turned Marxist was going to be allowed to return to the U.S. *with a promise from the justice dept. of immunity from prosecution.* A late bulletin on him—he's evidently doing a new book or has done it already. The Soviet News agency Tass says Agee will name "all the organizations & persons that were connected with U.S. intelligence services in the past 30 yrs." That could be quite an extensive execution list.

But that isn't what I set out to tell you. ~~about.~~ An agency like the F.B.I. may spend years setting up an undercover agent in an inside position where he can gather evidence & information on a crime ring or ~~crim~~ specific criminal operation. The agent so set up is in a way really set up. If he is by any chance exposed he may pay with his life. At the very least all ~~his the~~ *his* work is wasted and the crime hunt must begin all over if it can begin at all.

Here is the story of ~~such an F.B.I. under~~ *ROBERT CASSIDY F.B.I. UNDER* cover agent.~~—his name Robert Cassidy.~~ Dont worry I'm not blowing his cover. ~~Sad to say t~~*T*hat has already been done by the U.S. Justice Dept. ~~which~~ under which the F.B.I. operates.

Cassidy had successfully infiltrated a shipping company in Miami. He was gathering a wealth of material having to do with waterfront corruption in Miami & N.Y. It was possibly the biggest & most successful ~~cover up~~ undercover investigation in shipping history.

But it seems that a previous Cassidy assignment ~~was~~—a kind of peripheral one ~~in~~ *was in* connection with the F.B.I.'s look into the Socialist Workers Party activities, ~~The S.W.P is a~~ *a* Trotskyite radical group. The grand jury is investigating the F.B.I.s conduct of this operation to see if any of the rights of the Trotskyites had been violated.

~~Th~~ Since Cassidys role *in that case* had been a very minor one the F.B.I. proposed that he give a deposition—a sworn written statement *concerning his part ~~in the~~ ~~t~~ ~~c~~ASE*. ~~The Justice~~ *The Justice* dept. said absolutely not. Agent Cassidy would appear in person in open court.

And thus the Justice Dept. guardians of our safety ended the investigation into waterfront corruption which had been proceding so ~~well~~ superbly by blowing the carefully arranged cover and revealing Robert Cassidy to the world of crime as an undercover agent of the F.B.I.

It is almost incomprehensible that anyone least of all the chief law enforcement agent of the entire Nat. could so confuse priorities but that's the way it is in the wondrous wasteland by the Potomac.

This is RR Thanks for listening. ❖

Pushers

November 8, 1977

Serious charges involving the highest figures in the govt. of Panama have been made recently in Wash. having to do with traffic in narcotics.

I'll be right back.

I would hope that the debate over ratification of the Panama Canal treaties could be held on the level of ~~the~~ whether the treaties ~~were~~ *are* good or bad for the U.S. I have thought long & hard about the charges of drug traffic*k*ing in Panama and whether I should make reference to them. And frankly I've been very reluctant to touch on the subject.

Now however I feel there are some questions every American has a right to ask. ~~I'm going to ask them here now. For example i~~*I*s it true that the charges of drug trafficking are so substantial that Att. Gen. Bell* briefed the Pres. on ~~them~~ Oct. 3rd & then passed the same info. on to leaders of the Sen. & House Intelligence panels and if so what was that information?

~~The rest of the questions are, i~~*I*s it true that the "Drug Enforcement Agency" ~~contains explosive information, that the March 1974~~ *files for March 1974 describe Panamas head of the secret* police as a liaison man between Tor-

* Griffin B. Bell.

rijos & Castro in charge of setting up bank accts. & ~~launder~~ *laundering* narcotics money ≠? Is it true that the 1975 files contain information that a Ramiro Rivas & Torrijos tried to buy a transportation co. as a cover for moving drugs? Do the same files for the month of Feb. ~~identify~~ *describe* the Generals brother as using Panamanian Air Force planes to transport drugs?

Is the story published last month in the Wash. Star true that a brother of ≠ Gen. Torrijos now serving as Panamas ambassador to Spain was indicted 5 yrs. ago in N.Y. City on Fed. *charges of* narcotics smuggling; ~~charges~~ & that such an indictment is still sealed in the Eastern Division of N.Y.?

The Panama Canal sub committee chaired by Rep. Murphy of N.Y.* reported to it's parent group the Merchant Marine & Fisheries panel in Jan. of 1973 that Panama had become the conduit through which passed massive quantities of dope. Quoting a study by the Dir. of our Bureau of Narcotics & Dangerous Drugs in 1971 the report said "Panama is one of the most significant countries for the trans-shipment of narcotic drugs to the U.S." The report added that nothing was being done to ~~halt~~ *interrupt* this traffic in Panama saying "This may be due to high level apathy, ignorance and/or Collusion."

Questions again, Is it true ~~that~~ that in 1972 our Bureau of Customs stated that heroin smuggling reached into the highest levels of Panamanian officialdom & included the brother of Gen. Torrijos & the foreign minister Juan Tack?

Is it true that a young man was arrested in N.Y. in 1971 carrying 150 lbs. of Heroin and escaped prosecution because he ~~carried a carried~~ *was travelling* on a diplomatic passport issued by the Gen's. brother & signed by Juan Tack?

Is it true that a prominent Panamanian official was arrested in the Canal Zone & sent to Dallas Texas charged with ≠ sending $1 mil. worth of Heroin to Dallas? And is it true that the ~~present~~ Panamanian govt. mobilized it's full resources in an angry protest ≠ attempting to have him returned to Panama?

When Congressman Murphy made his report it was interesting that the foreign minister of Panama expelled 3 Am. narcotics agents from Panama within 24 hours.

Aren't we justified in asking for these answers ~~if~~ before we ~~make a~~ *enter* into a treaty relationship as important as the one now being urged upon us?

This is RR Thanks for listening. ❖

Youth and Crime

November 8, 1977

Violence on TV was the defense theme ~~of~~ *in* a recent murder trial where the accused was a 15 yr. old youngster. I'm afraid our problem isn't that simple. I'll be right back.

* Congressman John Michael Murphy (D–New York, 1963–1981).

One wonders at times what the ancient Romans talked about in those twilight days of the great empire. Were there ~~prophets~~ *individuals* with greater foresight than the majority who actually predicted the downfall, who sensed the greatness was gone? If so what did they advance as examples to prove their contention?

They could have pointed to the "mob"—Romes name for those permanently on the dole who demanded more & more of a share from those who worked. Then too there was the lack of patriotism, the need to ~~f~~ fill Romes legions with foreign mercenaries. Or did they ever criticize the bloodthirsty circuses in the coleseumn & worry about the growing TASTE FOR sadism among the people?

Is violence in our entertainment, the increasing number of free for alls in our athletic contests a cause or a symptom? A few months ago one of our national magazines did a shocking piece about youthful ~~crime~~ *criminals* in America. The shock wasn't in the statistics although they were bad enough—(more than half of all serious crimes committed by youngsters age 10 to 17) but in the savage cruelty displayed by mere children.

The article told of a 16 yr. old luring a motorist into an alley and shooting him 6 times. He's back on the street, free because witnesses failed to appear for the trial. Then there was the 17 yr. old whose first of 22 arrests occurred when he was 11. Only 4 days after he was charged with attempted murder he raped & murdered a young nurse. Another who started his career at 11 (he's now 19) was nicknamed Touché because of his handiness with a switchblade.

A 15 yr. old tied up an 11 yr. old neighbor castrated him, stabbed him & cut off his head. He has admitted doing the same thing to the ~~b~~ victems 12 yr. old brother only his body has never been found. Because the killer was a juvenile he was released from prison when he became 18.

A teenager in N.Y. explained in a radio interview how he started to rob elderly women at age 12. He said, "What's to worry? If you're doing wrong do it while you are young because you dont do that much time." Another 15 yr. old raped a housewife at knife point even while the police were surrounding the house. When they caught him he taunted them, "what are you going to do send me to youth hall? I'll be out in a few hours."

Probably the record (at least so far) is the 6 yr. old boy who siphoned gas out of a car (that in itself is pretty advanced for a 6 yr. old) then he poured it over a sleeping neighbor, struck a match and watched him burn to death.

Apparently there is equality among the sexes where sadistic crimes are concerned. In Chi. the police finally rounded up a girl gang, ages 14 to 17 whose ~~h~~ hobby was beating up elderly victems. Their latest was a 68 yr. old man brutally beaten for no reason except that the girls seemed to be indignant toward their victems.

I could go on listing cases ~~but~~ by the hundreds but there is a sameness to them—cruelty, senselessness, utter lack of remorse and yes a lack of punishment.

This is RR Thanks for listening. ❖

Free Enterprise
November 8, 1977

We've all seen the Greyhound bus ads on TV, the cheerful fellow leaning out the bus window saying "and leave the driving to us." Greyhound wishes the govt. would.

I'll be right back.

I've done a number of these broadcasts on the subject of govt. regulation and unwarranted govt. interference in the running of business. Maybe we talk about this too often in general terms and dont get down to a specific case of a man trying to run a business and what his problems are.

Gerald H. Trautman chief exec. officer of the Greyhound corp. has been speaking to business groups around the country on "Free Enterprise in Our Third Century." He says when he 1st took the Greyhound job he could spend virtually 100% of his time managing the business. That was 10 yrs. ago. Now over a ~~third~~ *3rd* of his time is devoted to dealing with "intrusions, actual & proposed, of the Fed. govt." He describes the Fed. burocracy as some kind of weird science-fiction monster that has taken on a life of it's own & is out of control of Cong.

Here are some of Greyhounds actual experiences as described by Mr. Trautman. Greyhound happens to have the best safety record in the transportation business and not by accident. He gives credit to well considered safety rules and strict training.

But one day the company was hailed into Fed. court by the U.S. Labor dept. The govt. charged the company with discrimination because it had an age qualification for it's drivers. Greyhound should hire drivers without any restriction as to age. The company had to go through a full trial at great cost & loss of employee time to "repel this intrusion by the Fed. govt."

Next the Equal Emp. Opp. Commission attacked because Greyhound has a height requirement. After years of experience the companies safety people had set a minimum of 5'7" for drivers. E.E.O.C. charged this discriminated against people who weren't 5'7".

Weary from the 1st experience the company even though it felt it could win decided to let the govt. have it's way. That brought on a follow up. E.E.O.C. demanded that Greyhound pay some $19 mil. to unspecified, unnamed individuals who might have been employed in the past if they hadn't had that 5'7" height requirement. The govt. said the $19 mil. was it's estimate of back pay due these unknown people.

To add to the ridiculousness of this demand the letter was just signed "Betsy." Mr. Trautman points out that when someone in govt. tells you, you ought to hand out $19 mil. that someone at least should have a last name.

One last example. The I.C.C. has ordered the co. to provide a terminal in every town of 15,000 pop. & up ~~if the bus~~ through which the busses run and keep those terminals manned & open day & night. If the I.C.C. has it's way

Greyhounds operating costs would be increased by $187 mil. and bus fares would have to be increased by 50%.

Mr. Trautman tells his audiences this basic truth; "we have written the most remarkable chapter in the history of mankind with a pen called profit, and the rest of the world stands in awe of that accomplishment." Amen!

This is R.R. Thanks for listening. ❖

Vietnam was admitted to the United Nations in September 1977. Two months later, when this broadcast was taped, the international body was hard at work to revive the war-torn country and to integrate it into the international community of states.

Aid to Vietnam
November 8, 1977

This might be called one of those good news bad news items. The good news is that Russia wants to rebuild Vietnam. The Bad news—they want us to pay for it.

I'll be right back

A few weeks ago on one of these commentaries I told you how Congressman Bill Young of Fla.* had led the fight to prevent direct aid from going to the ~~promise~~ *treaty* breaking rulers of Vietnam. Now we are finding out there are other ways to remove the epidermis from a cat.

In the United Nations the Russians along with their fellow communists in 13 other countries—mainly iron curtain satelites have introduced a resolution authorizing the Sec. General to rehabilitate Vietnam socially & economically (they left out morally). This would be done through the United Nation's Developement Program.

It is hardly an act of overwhelming generosity on the part of the Russians. They contribute about $8 mil. to that fund—we contribute 200 mil. If the Russians ~~& their allies~~ want to help their blood (& blood stained) allies let them—*but* without our help. ~~But~~ *Of course* it wont be that way. Already our U.N. representatives are lobbying Congress, passing the word *that* they dont want to be forced to vote against this *UN* resolution.

The U.N. Developement Fund has already ticketed Vietnam for $44 mil. over the next 5 years along with $30 mil. to Idi Amin in Uganda & 13.5 mil. to Castros Cuba. When Congressman *Bill* Young protested this *action* our *own* U.N. delegates cried, "dont politicize the United Nations." That's like saying "Tammany Hall" was a social club.

Make no mistake about it forces in our govt. are determined that the conquerors of S. Vietnam, the treacherous aggressors of Hanoi are going to get the

* Congressman C. W. "Bill" Young (R–Florida, 1971-present).

bil's of dollars we had offered to all of Vietnam as part of the Paris Peace agreement which Hanoi brutally violated the min. our forces ~~in good faith~~ withdrew from Vietnam.

Their vehicle is the World Bank plus ~~these~~ other U.N. institutions such as the one I've mentioned. United Press Int. has reported an interview with Tran Duong, Dir. of Vietnams Central Bank in which Duong says the U.S. will pay the 4¾ Bil. dollars ~~we~~ promised as part of the Paris Peace Accords. He explained that we will put the money in the International Development Assn. ~~The I.D.A. is~~ the window in Mr. McNamaras* world bank where the soft loans (no interest & 50 yrs to pay—if ever) are handed out.

Our contributions to the banks current replenishment fund is almost 2½ bil. dollars. Right now the world bank is currently negotiating two loans to Vietnam. One is for a water project in the Mekong Delta. Those of ~~you~~ *us* who live in the West will ~~recall~~ *note, our* water projects aren't doing as well as ~~the Hanois murderous~~ *the bandits of Hanoi* seem to be doing with theirs.

Do we the American people whose elected representatives have said *in our behalf* "no" to helping Hanoi, have to stand by while non-elected burocrats calmly circumvent the will of the people? Not if we'll let our congressmen know how we feel about this kind of hypocrisy. There are good men in the Congress who need our help now to curb the ≠ arrogance of appointed govt. employees.

This is RR Thanks for listening. ❖

The Individual
November 8, 1977

Every once in a while we are made aware of the personal tragedy of an individual or family incidental to ~~but~~ *and* caused by the impersonal dealings of govts.

I'll be right back

Georgie Anne Geyer is a syndicated Wash. columnist who ~~ju~~ happens to support the proposed Panama Canal treaties. Nevertheless she authored a column recently ~~in~~ which ~~she~~ *did* not show the advocates of the treaties in a favorable light. She was fair, objective & true to the finest principles of her trade in bringing to our attention a great & tragic injustice.

On Sept. 1st a one time, highly respected Panamanian journalist Leopoldo Aragon exiled to Sweden took his own life. Standing in front of the American Embassy in Stockholm he set himself on fire ~~in~~ *to* protest the Canal treaties.

I remember reading the news item and whether it was the way in which it

* Robert S. McNamara served as secretary of defense from 1961 to 1968, and as president of the World Bank from 1968 to 1981.

was written or carelessness on my part, it was my impression he was an advocate of the treaties. Thanks to Miss Geyer I now know better.

The widow of Leopoldo Aragon is an American. Their two daughters are attending college in this country and apparently their mother lives in Wash. where she told the whole story of her husband & the events leading to his suicide.

As a journalist in Panama he had somehow seen an American document dated 1967 saying that the U.S. hoped for a strongman type rule ~~(of the type Panama now has)~~ *in Panama which they subsequently* got in the mil. takeover by Torrijos. Our govt. wanted this to facilitate getting a canal treaty. Aragon made his discovery public and for doing so was sent to Coiba—Panamas devils island. Here he underwent torture that almost cost him his life and from which according to his wife he never recovered mentally.

Through many international contacts he was finally released and exiled to Sweden. He told of one experience at the beginning of his time in the Coiba island prison. The prisoners had to run the gauntlet, chased like animals with the guards running among them beating them with clubs.

Rose Marie Aragon tells the tragic finale & the events leading up to it. She had worked at one time in the State Dept. and had top secret clearance. She tried to get a visa for her husband to leave Sweden & come here to join his family. He was refused a visa on the grounds that he might become a nuisance & cause *a* disturbance because he was opposed to the treaties. Well he very well might have done just that. You see he felt the treaties would further strengthen the hand of the Panamanian dictator.

When our congress held hearings in Oct. on human rights in Panama a State Dept. spokesman was asked if the dept. had made any effort to find out why Freedom House had rated Panama the worst violator in this Hemisphere. He replied the State dept. had made no such effort.

A widow & her two daughters must wonder a little about their own country, this land of the free which would deny admittance to a tortured, mentally disturbed man. ~~whose only reply was to die in a tower of flame~~ *Denied the right to join his family, to speak for a cause he believed, he chose to die in a tower of flame* before our embassy in a foreign land.

Perhaps those middle echelon functionaries in the State Dept. should be made to read the words inscribed at the base of the Statue of Liberty.

This is RR Thanks for listening. ❖

Taxation

November 8, 1977

For some time now tax reform has been simmering as usual on the Wash. back burner with constant hints that a move to the front burner is imminent.

I'll be right back

Here we go again proving that taxes *like the weather* are something everyone talks about but I'm not sure about the last part of the truism that no one does anything about them. In fact I'm very much afraid govt. is going to do something about them and ~~if the course of history remains unchanged~~ *when it does* we'll all be worse off.

~~There is no question that something should be done about taxes but not with politics as the 1st consideration.~~ We know govt. costs 44 cents out of every dollar earned. The U.S. is last among the industrial ~~states~~ nations in the proportion of gross domestic product being *re*invested in our means of production. ~~& o~~Our annual rate of ec. growth since 1960 has been lower than any other nat. except Grt. Brtn.

In 1950 govt. costs pro-rated out to $1,600 per family—today they are $9,600 and yet taxes are not a factor in computing the cost of living index.

Lets take a look at a city & state that once had the highest per cap. inc. in America & the highest standard of living—Boston Mass. Today Mass. has become such a welfare st. with so much redistribution of inc. that last year for the 1st time "transfer payments"—the money given thru welfare to increase incomes above what the people can earn for themselves—amounted to more than the ~~states~~ total return on investments, savings, rent & industrial cap. in Mass.

The average intermediate bud. for a family of 4 in Boston is $18,090 almost $3000 more than the cost for a similar family in the rest of the country—~~This is not~~ *not* because prices are higher in Boston—taxes are~~;~~. ~~t~~*T*wo in particular, the state inc. tax & property tax.~~es~~

Can we have real tax reform which very simply must mean lower taxes for everyone ~~& therefore lower govt. costs~~ as long as politicians think of taxes as a means of controlling the people? Govt. does not tax to get the money it needs—govt. will always find a need for the money it gets.

Back in New Deal days an under Sec. of the treasury spelled out our tax policy. He said, "taxs must be used for more than just raising revenue.~~s"~~ They can be used to control the ec. & to penalize particular ec. groups & individuals."

When you hear the phrase "tax expenditure" ~~does~~ *do you think* it means some govt. spending program? Wrong! That is Wash's. term for money it lets you keep. Since a change in the law a few years back the Treasury Dept. must report to Cong. on "tax expenditures~~.~~," ~~These are taxes not collected from you because of deductions allowed you~~ *which is the term govt. uses for income tax deductions you are allowed to take* such as the int. on your mortgage. The govt. calls it ~~a "~~govt. ~~expenditure"~~ *spending* when it allows you to keep your own money. Can we deny *that* the basis for such an assumption ~~is~~ *has to be* govt's. belief that all our earnings *rightfully* belong to govt. ~~and w~~What we are allowed to keep over & above taxes is ~~a decision to be made by govt. In effect a grant *a gift* to us by govt. of the money *of govt. money*~~ *a gift to us from them.* And all the time you thought it was the other way round.

~~This is RR Thanks for listening.~~

There can be no real tax reform ~~by officials who~~ *as long as govt.* subscribes to such a theory.

This is RR Thanks for listening. ❖

Energy

November 8, 1977

We've all heard (maybe until we are about fed up) of the proposals before cong. to solve the energy prob. There is another engery plan we haven't heard too much about. I'll be right back

Back around the turn of the century the Germans (possibly due to their lack of natural resources) became interested in organic chemistry. Their scientists explored the ~~using~~ *use* of organic wastes from farms, ~~leaves & stalks,~~ *and such things as* sugar & even coal ~~to~~ *as a way to* create other useful products. They experimented with breaking down the molecular structure with chemicals and it is said managed *even* to produce butter from coal.

It was inevitable that when Hitler began planning his world conquest he would seek an answer to the shortages of fuel that helped bring about ~~the allied victory in WWI.~~ *German defeat* in the 1st World War. He called upon German industry *Beginning in 1936* to create a synthetic fuel industry ~~beginning in 1936. And he got it somewhere around 1939.~~ ~~*They had it in production some*~~ *within 4 years*. We've had longer than that since the Arab oil boycott and Congress is still *JUST* talking. Maybe the difference is that ~~even in~~ *in spite of* Germanys national socialism Hitler turned the problem over to private business to solve.

Germany fought W.W.II. ~~on~~ *using* synthetic natural gas, liquid petroleum gas, motor fuels, fuel oil, lubricants & even high test aviation gasoline made from coal. Production increased ~~every month~~ *steadily* until the output was 100,000 tons a month. All of this was for the war machine, the civilian sector was left to fend for itself. Our own ~~demands~~ needs today are ~~man~~ *much* greater than that but so is our potential production capacity.

~~What I'm getting to is that~~ *Now a few decades later* at Texas A&M. ~~funded by Union Carbide, Dow Chemical & Diamond Shamrock~~ a University team *of 10 researchers* is sifting through 175 tons of ~~records~~ captured German ~~documents~~ *papers*—some 400,000 documents in all. In this mass of records are the secrets of Germanys synthetic fuel production. The documents are scattered throughout 6 nations. ~~Here i~~*I*n our own country ~~*the data is*~~ *they are* crammed in crates in the nat. archives & other govt. buildings. There are ~~306~~ *more than 300* reels of microfilm of 300,000 pages of original German data collected by a mission of scientists & engineers who followed our armies into Germany in WWII.

Interviews with German scientists about what may be found in the bales of records ~~indicates~~ *has revealed that* some key documents ~~may~~ have been lost. ~~but o~~On the other hand documents have been found dealing directly with the conversion of coal to oil~~. Such~~ *including* detailed information ~~has been found as~~ *such as* repair manuels, blueprints locating every pipe & valve of the refinerys. ~~the Germans built. In~~ *It's hard to believe but in* all these years ~~the crates, boxes & bundles of paper~~ *this mass of scientific material stored* in 23 depositories of ~~the~~ 6 countries hasn't been read by anyone. ~~There are no indexes~~ *Now without indexes or guides of any kind,* the Texas A&M team ~~has to~~ *is* reading, ~~&~~ sifting & cataloging. ~~The team has *They have*~~ *The team has* chosen one goal to begin with—to find all the records they can having to do with making oil from brown coal or lignite.* It is estimated Texas has about 110 bil. tons of lignite in that state alone. There is no way to calculate how much we have nationwide but it will last for ~~a long, long time~~ *several centuries.* This whole project is funded by Union Carbide, Dow Chemical & Diamond Shamrock. ~~congress thank heaven is not involved but~~ Uncle Sam is lending a hand in a practical way. The University prepared material is stored in the Energy, Research & Development Admin. computers where it is available to anyone. This may ~~be~~ *turn out to be* the most practical energy program we could possibly have ~~This is RR Thanks for listening.~~ *& it's been laying around for more than 30 yrs.*—This is RR Thanks for listening. ❖

Restitution
November 8, 1977

You know it's awfully easy on a commentary like this to report on the things that need correcting to such an extent that ~~you~~ *one* contributes to pessimism. Well not today.

I'll be right back.

I confess to trying to bring to your attention items of information that might have escaped your attention or which haven't received much coverage in the press. Very often these have to do with burocratic inroads on our freedom, injustices etc. This can lead to a onesided, discouraging perspective when in truth we live in the best of all possible places among the ~~finest~~ most generous, creative people on earth. Today I'd like to tell you what some of these people are doing about one of our more serious problems—crime in Am.

Robert Poole Jr. is Pres. of the Local govt. Center, a non-profit research org. in Santa Barbara Calif. He does a monthly newspaper column reporting on

* The Texas A&M University researchers began looking at the German documents in 1975, but abandoned the project five years later. The chemical process of turning coal into gasoline is well known, but is generally considered uneconomical (*Dallas Morning News,* September 4, 1990). However the search for an economical synthetic fuel continues.

~~things~~ problem solving at the local level, providing alternatives to the idea that all wisdom must start with Wash.

Mr. Poole recently pointed out that some place along the line we have forgotten or overlooked the idea that a criminal should have the responsibility to undo the harm he has done to the victem of his crime. Instead we have corralled some 200,000 prisoners and support them at a cost of about $3 Bil. a year while at the same time we ignore the victem.

But here & there alternatives are being tried. Very simply a restitution contract is negotiated between the prisoner & ~~the~~ his or her victem. The court of course must sanction this. The convicted is released from jail and allowed to go to work. His pay is divided to compensate the victem, support his own family and pay taxes which help support the program. Sometimes he lives in a residential facility to which he must return each nite & weekend, sometimes he may be allowed to live at home.

Let me tell you of one case described by Poole which illustrates how this old but new idea works. The offender broke into ~~the~~ *a* Tucson home ~~of an elderly, invalid woman~~ and stole ~~the~~ *a* color TV set. He was caught and soon found himself in the county prosecutors office face to face with his victem, an elderly, invalid woman whose life virtually centered around that color TV set.

With the proseccutors approval a deal was worked out. Not only would he return her TV set, he would also paint her house, mow her lawn and drive her to the Doctor for her weekly check up. By doing this he escaped going to jail & the people of Pima county were saved the several thousands of dollars it would have cost to keep him there.

In Georgia a pilot program was started 2 yrs. ago in 4 cities. In the first 18 mos. the offenders (85% had committed felonies) paid back to victems $127,000 paid $242,000 in taxes (St. & Fed.) returned $343,000 for their room & board, $139,000 for the support of their families, put away in savings accts. $84,000 and contributed 4212 hours of unpaid pub. service work. The bottom line is that ⅔ of them completed the program successfully & were released.

Minn. has had a pilot program for 5 yrs. and is now going statewide. The Fed. govt. has parceled out a grant to several cities ~~&~~ nationwide and will use these ~~to~~ as a test on how best to set up such programs. Already however there is no question that the program makes sense. The victems get restitution and an added plus is far more successful rehabilitation of the criminal than anything ever tried before. That's kind of good to hear.

This is RR Thanks for listening. ❖

Freedom

November 8, 1977

The other day I told a group of students that my wish for them was that they could know *in this land* the freedom I had known when I was their age.

I'll be right back.

Sometimes I wonder if we haven't talked freedom, free enterprise etc. so much & so long as abstract theory that people—particularly young people dont just tune us out. Speaking to some students the other day I referred to freedoms lost in this land during my lifetime. And I got a question—what freedoms? what was I talking about?

It reminded me of a TV play I'd once done *in* which I played a Soviet Major during the occupation of Budapest.* In the play I turned out to be something of a nice fellow and let two Hungarians go with this line, "I never knew what freedom was until I saw you lose yours."

But facing these students I had to search for an answer. This is what I came up with; when I was their age there was no such thing as a drivers license. Your father began teaching you to drive the family car when he thought you were old enough and after you'd driven him crazy asking why weren't you old enough.

You passed your drivers test when he said "yes you can take the car on your date tonite." Believe me he ~~wou~~ didn't say that until he was as sure as it's possible to be that you knew how to drive.

Now maybe you'll say that's not a good example; that drivers licenses are a necessity. Are there any fewer accidents today than there were then? Is there a better test of your ability than a parent turning you loose at the wheel of several thousand dollars *of* investment of ~~his~~ hard earned money? What about 12 yr. old farm kids driving tractors on their fathers farm & plowing a field yet?

Well this led to other examples. When I was 14 yrs. old I got a summer job with an outfit that was rebuilding & selling old homes. Before the summer was over I had laid hardwood floor, shingled ~~roff~~ roof, painted & worked on foundations. And at summers end I had my first years tuition for college in the bank. Can that be done today? No! ~~y~~You'd have to ~~be licensed~~ *get a govt. license* to do ~~almost any type~~ *just about every kind* of work *I did.* ~~and govt.~~ *And just* as it does with driving, ~~decides whether you are capable~~ *govt. not the fellow who hired you would decide* whether ~~I was~~ *you were* capable.

In a recent debate with Ralph Nader a distinguished scholar recently threw the obvious example of lack of freedom at Ralph & did so ~~delib~~ deliberately, sure of the answer he'd get. "What right" he challenged "does govt. have to say you cant ride a motor cycle without a ~~helm~~ helmet?~~"~~ You aren't endangering anyone but yourself?"

Right on cue came a typical Naderism. ~~"~~If a helmetless rider splashes himself on the pavement, a govt. subsidized ambulance will pick him up, take him to a govt. subsidized hospital. If he dies he'll be buried in a govt. subsidized cemetery and govt. welfare will begin paying for the support of his widow & orphaned children. Therefore ~~we~~ *govt.* cant let him fall down & go boom. In

* Reagan hosted the *General Electric Theater* television program from 1954 until 1962. He played Soviet Major Vasily Kirov with Carol Lawrence and Vic Morrow in an episode entitled "The Iron Silence." It aired September 24, 1961.

other words we are all now stamped—"Property of the U.S. Govt. Do Not Fold, bend or mutilate."

This is RR Thanks for listening. ❖

An Angry Man I

November 8, 1977

I'd like to tell you about & quote the findings of an Angry man who lives in Ohio. ~~and the~~ *What he has* to say should make all of us a little angry.

I'll be right back.

Mr. F. J. McIntyre, a prof. engineer founded the Columbus Water & Chemical ~~C~~ Testing Lab. in 1931. He is a life member of the Am. Waterworks Assn. & the Water Pollution Control Fed. And he believes the environmental crusade is one of the greatest hoaxes ever perpetrated on the people of this country.

That's a strong statement but Mr. McIntyre has done a study of pollution and the things we've done to supposedly reduce pollution. His conclusion is that the benefits have been few and some even ~~been~~ imaginery. But the ec. damage, loss of production & plant closings have been *very* real.

Then he points out that pollution is a tool of nature and if nature didn't have that tool there would be no coal, oil or natural gas. He says pollution is natures way of reprocessing; that without it the earth would be covered with dead vegetation & animals, & none of us would be here.

Coming to mans pollution—, to stop it, he says, we would have to eliminate the automobile & other machines, not fertilize our crops or use insecticides & we'd all be dead of starvation within a year. He gives examples obtained from his own & others research to illustrate such declarations.

Industry & the automobile spew about 400 mil. tons of carbon monoxide into the atmosphere ~~every day~~ *each year.* This fig. he says is from Dr. Robbins of Stanford Research who also says those 400 mil. tons are around 10% of the more than 3 bil. tons produced each yr. by nature. He says *one acre of* decaying vegetation in swamps, rice paddies & forests produces about 1½ tons of Methane gas each yr. The haze which gives the Great Smoky Mt's. their name is due to hydrocarbons given off by the vegetation.

Now lest you think Mr. McIntyre is against everything environmental he isn't. He realizes as we all should that there are congested areas where pollution can be & is dangerous to those crowded into such an area. I can offer Los Angeles as an example where our prevailing winds pile air pollution against a ring of mt's. which it cant surmount because of an air inversion layer. But Mr. McIntyre believes control of pollution should be in the hands of scientists who understand natures law and wouldn't try to override it with man made laws.

Comparing natures polluting ability to mans he points out that the Miss.

river dumps 500 mil. tons of solids into the Gulf of Mexico every day. For man to equal that he would have to empty 15,000 railroad cars a day into the Gulf.

McIntyre cites natures laws that too much of anything is poisenous, a moderate amt. inhibiting and a small amount stimulating. Therefore anything can be condemned if given in large enough quantities. As an example he points out that if any one of us would refrain from ingesting <u>any</u> salt for 60 days and then take that 60 days normal amt. all at once—it would kill us.

His research has come up with some astounding ~~answers~~ *facts* not only on pollution but sliding over into energy because of the relationship between the two. I'll tell you about them on the next broadcast.

This is RR Thanks for listening. ❖

An Angry Man II
November 8, 1977

Quoting from the man I'm going to quote today, "using the words of someone else is called plagiarism, but when you use the words of many it's called research."

I'll be right back.

On the last broadcast I told of the research ~~*done*~~ ~~by~~ *a Mr.* F. J. McIntyre ~~prof. of engineer of~~ *has done on* the environmental crusade and his belief that much of the crusade has been more costly than worthwhile. I ~~gave~~ *reported on* some of his findings which illustrate that nature itself is a far greater polluter than man and promised some more examples from his research.

He asks us to recognize that technology is a friend not a foe and points out that while Warfarin *for example* will kill rats it can be used as a control in human blood & heart problems.

Many cities banned the sale of phosphate detergents but of course did not ban the sale of eggs, milk & meats all of which have high phosphate levels. McIntyre used this example to point out that if we outlawed <u>all</u> phosphate detergents our domestic sewage disposal systems would only show a 25% reduction of phosphate content.

This led to an example of how we have fouled our rivers *lakes & oceans* by dumping unacceptable nutrients into our streams. He points out that by obeying natures laws those same nutrients ~~those same nutrients~~ *could be returned to* the land not as pollutants but with great beneficial results. One inch of sewage effluent per week will increase the yield of corn from 63 bushels per acre to 114. & just about double the alfalfa yield.

Colorado Springs has 2 water systems—one for drinkable water & one for treated effluent used for irrigation. There are no problems of public nuisance or health. San Francisco does the same with it's Golden Gate Park.

The study crossed over from pollution to energy but in the area where they overlap today—nuclear power. There is a widespread ~~belief about~~ *fear of* the radiation danger from nuclear power plants. The truth is there is more radiation from watching TV than there is from the nuclear plant producing the electricity ~~for that~~ *that runs the TV* set.

In 2 recent European tests animals were isolated from all radiation by being placed in lead lined cages then lowered into mines where they were even shielded from cosmic rays. The scientists found that after 4 generations of total protection from radioactivity there were malformed off spring & they were all extremely susceptible to diseases. In other words like so many things—radiation in the proper amt. is beneficial. In the improper quantity it is deadly.

Oil of Calamus is a flavor additive in food now banned as cancer causing. You'd have to drink 250 quarts of Vermouth a day to equal the amt. that caused cancer in rats. Safrole once *was* used to flavor root beer & hard candy. Again to equal the level fed to the experimental rats a human would have to drink 613, 12 ounce bottles of root beer a day or eat 220 lbs. of hard candy everyday.

Dr. Phillip Handler, pres. of the Nat. Acad. of Sciences says, "Exaggeration is the other pollution peril."

Well that winds up the story of the angry man in Ohio—~~Mr.~~ Engineer ~~J. C.~~ F. J. McIntyre.

This is RR Thanks for listening. ❖

On April 15, 1978, the Supreme Court ruled that the snail darter was protected as an endangered species under the 1973 act.

Snail Darters

November 29, 1977

Our little friends the "Snail Darters" are in the news again. Tragedy has befallen some of them. I'll be right back.

Some time ago on one of these broadcasts ~~th~~ I reported that a $116 mil. ~~dol~~ dam of the Tenn. Valley Authority had been kept out of operation for about ~~2~~ *4* years because of a tiny minnow type fish—the Snail Darter. Closing the dam & creating a lake to generate elec. power would interfere with the Snail Darters spawning habits and the Snail Darter is on the endangered species list.

To refresh your memory there are about 77 dif. kinds of Darters each differing in some characteristic of color or markings. You & I ~~wou~~ probably would think they all looked the same. They are about 2 inches in length & we probably couldn't tell them from a minnow or a guppy. The last time I mentioned them I reported that Congress had appropriated $9 mil. to try moving them to some other part of the Little Tenn. river or to some other river where other kinds of Darter lived. The estimate was that there were about 10,000 of them left so that pro-rated out to $900 per fish.

Well they are back in the news & the 1st thing we learn is that there aren't 10,000, there are only about 1400. Unless Cong. has done some refiguring about that appropriation that makes them price out at about $6400 per fish. Maybe more because now there aren't 1400—that's why they are in the news.

Wildlife scientists with the help of skin divers have been moving the ≠ fish to a new spawning area above the non-operating ~~dam~~ Tellico dam. In this operation ~~a fish foul up killed~~ 94 of *the* nearly extinct creatures were killed in a foul up. About 600 had already been moved without trouble to the Hiwassee *(HIWASSEE)* river. The remaining 800 were to be moved upstream in the Little Tennessee.

Now if I'm right about the cost of this operation we've just lost more than $600,000 worth of fish. But before our environmentalists get excited and declare ~~they~~ no one should have tried to move them; that it was the move that did them in, the scientists say "no." It is suspected that the net the skindivers were using had a residue of poisen left over from a previous operation. They were using the net to count & examine the catch when they began to belly up and leave this mortal coil. There is no word as to whether anyone tried mouth to mouth resuscitation.

Out of this news story came one additional fact about Snail darters. They are so named not because of any peculiar marking but because of what they eat. Now that leaves me with a ~~worrisome~~ *bothersome* question. Has anyone taken a look to see if those snails they feed on are endangered by the dam?

This is R R Thanks for listening. ❖

Visas

November 29, 1977

Visa, Visa who gets the visa—the visa to enter the U.S. as a visitor? Apparently very few of our friends. I'll be right back.

Recently I commented on some strange decisions by our state dept. with regard to who could & could *not* get a visa to enter the United States. A *Black* leader of the ≠ guerillas ~~causing~~ terrorizing Rhodesia gets a visa but two Black leaders of major tribes in Rhodesia who are opposed to a communist takeover are refused.

It's hard not to be paranoid when there seems to be a leniency toward those who are or *who at least* ≠ lean to*ward* ~~communism~~ *the Soviet block*. Now we add an even stranger case than the ones I mentioned in earlier broadcasts.

Wilfred Burchett is an Australian journalist and certainly that would be no reason to keep him out of our country. He has authored a book about the Vietnam war which I am sure he'll be promoting as he crisscrosses our country on

* Wilfred Burchett, *Grasshoppers and Elephants: Why Viet Nam Fell* (New York: Urizen Books, 1977).

a speaking tour.* And even though his book tells why we were wrong and the communists were right that shouldn't keep him out or prevent his speaking to student groups, which he'll be doing.

But there are other facets to Mr. Burchett which do call for at least a raised eyebrow. He was charged with trying to force Am. Prisoners of war in the Korean conflict to confess they had used germ warfare. In the Vietnamese war it was reported that he was a leading propagandist for No. Vietnam. Later he sued an Australian publisher for libel over such charges. Several American & British p.o.w's. went to Australia ~~to~~ and testified on behalf of the publisher. The court found in favor of the publisher and ordered Burchett to pay $100,000 in ~~court~~ costs.

There is more. A defector from the Soviet U., a former K.G.B. agent Yuri Krtkov told a U.S. Senate Internal Security Sub-committee that Burchett was employed by the K.G.B.; ~~He~~ *that he* served as a spy & a propagandist. An earlier trip to this country was hastily cancelled according to press reports when it became know[n] the Sen. subcommittee ~~intcded~~ intended to subpoena him for questioning. ~~by the~~

Now maybe the State dept. will claim the visa was granted to avoid the problems created by Senator McGoverns amendment to the dept's. appropriation bill. ~~If so the alibi hardly holds water.~~ The amendment declares that in order to refuse a visa the State dept. must get approval from the Speaker of the house & the chairman of the Sen. committee on Foreign Relations. This hasn't kept them from refusing visas to such applicants as the Panamanian ~~in~~ exiled to Sweden who wanted to join his American wife & children. You'll remember him as the man who burned himself to death in front of the American embassy in Stockholm.

Now ~~before~~ you *may* say, "communist or no communist he has a right to express his views & our students have a right to hear them."~~—let me say~~ *Well* I agree completely; ~~I agree~~ so long as our students get to hear all kinds of views and ~~so long as~~ those expressing the views ~~are willing to~~ identify themselves~~.~~ *and* ~~In other words let them hear from a communist who says *says* he is a communist.~~ *dont pretend to be something else.*

This is R R Thanks for listening.

(Facts on which based from L.A. Herald Examiner Nov. 2) ❖

On June 30, 1977, President Carter announced "one of the most difficult decisions" of his presidency; he halted production of the B-1 bomber.

National Security
November 29, 1977

Production of the B-1 bomber has been halted, there are rumors that our cruise missile (which we were told made the B-1 unncessary) is less effective than we thought—what exactly is our situation? I'll be right back.

On Sept. 24th the Wash. based paper Human Events published an exclusive interview with Maj. Gen. George Keegan recently retired chief of Air Force Intelligence.* The Gen. is now Exec. V.P. of the U.S. Strategic Inst. ~~His interview should be required reading especially in Wash.~~

In answer to a question as to why he was concerned about the Sov. mil. posture he replied; "There is virtually no area in which the traditional free world superiority or superior ability to defend itself has not been eroded seriously, has not been surpassed by Soviet weaponry & forces." He went on to say that in a nuclear exchange Soviet cities might be destroyed but their extraordinary civil defense shelters would hold loss of life down to 5 million. Our own losses would be a possible 160 mil. dead.

Expressing a concern that a series of misjudgements & miscalculations on both sides might lead to nuclear war Gen. Keegan expressed a belief that we could avoid this. He said; "Prudent & adequate investment in security & defense is basically what is required." *And added;* "In my opinion we are not doing that today."

Time wont permit the entire interview so let me just quote some of the answers this man who headed up our Air Force Intelligence gave to the editors of Human Events. "Six years ago the Pres. was privately briefed that if there were a nuclear exchange the Soviets would enjoy a 10 to 1 advantage over the U.S." He was referring to casualties. He believes now the ratio could be as much as 40 to 1. His words; "In a nuclear war today, we as a nation in the U.S. would die, the Soviet U. would survive."

Speaking of bombers he said; ~~What~~ "The Soviets have doubled the size of the factories producing the Backfire bomber." We of course have been told the *aging* B-52's will be polished up as a substitute for the cancelled B-1. The Gen. says; "The B-52 is a tired old airplane that was never designed as a low-level bomber. The idea that the B-52 or a 747 could deliver the cruise missile is pure nonsense."

He listed the Soviets defenses as 5000 radars to our 300, 12,000 SAM missiles (the kind that knocked down our B-52's in Vietnam) over the horizon radar that can track our missiles & planes from takeoff and a high energy beam which could possibly neutralize our missiles in flight.

He added another bit of information. All our Salt ~~Aggreements~~ *Agreements* deal with missile silos or launchers because when you launch a missile from a silo—that's it for that silo. Not any more where the enemy is concerned. The Soviets can re-~~fir~~ *load* & re-fire from their silos. The Gen. gives as his considered judgement that they have 3 to 5000 ICBM's we are not counting when we compare our relative strengths.

His last line in the interview—"We are infinitely less capable than we were 10 yrs. ago."

This is RR Thanks for listening. ❖

* "Could U.S. Survive First Strike by Soviets?" *Human Events,* September 24, 1977, pp. 1, 6, 10–11.

National Health Insurance I
November 29, 1977

With energy, Salt talks & the Canal so much in the news you might not have noticed that Nat. Health Ins. is moving up on the outside.

I'll be right back.

For purposes of clarity and outright honesty in discussing proposed Nat. Health Insurance plans, ~~on this broadcast~~ I shall refer to them as Socialized medicine for that's what is really being proposed.

A series of regional meetings sponsored by the dept. of H.E.W. has been scheduled and the first one ~~kicked things off~~ in *took place recently in* Wash. ~~recent~~ly. The hearings of course have to do with socialized medicine for America. If the Wash. meeting~~s~~ was an indication of things to come the only ~~subject~~ question to be decided is which proposal ~~of~~ *for* socializing health care do we get. There didn't seem to be anyone present putting in a plug for the system we've been using, which happens to ~~be~~ offer the best medical care in the world.

Let me ask you—do you think there is a health care crisis in the U.S.? If the polls are correct 9 out of 10 of you just said "yes." But now let me ask you about yourself. Do you have ready access to a Dr. if you need one? Are you relatively near to hospitals or medical centers if you should ~~need~~ be in need of the services they offer? Would it be impossible for you to get medical ~~health~~ *help* in a reasonable time in case of an emergency? Again if the polls are correct 9 out of 10 of you answered yes to those questions. In other words 9/10 of you have been conned into believing there is a health care crisis but 9/10 of you think it applies to someone else.

We have the highest ratio of Drs. *& Nurses* to patients ~~of~~ *in* all the world. Less than ½ of 1% of our people live in counties where there is no hospital or medical ~~clini~~ *treatment* center—but most of those aren't more than 25 miles from such ~~an inst.~~ *a facility.*

The L.A. Times recently ran a pro-con set of articles on socialized med. (they used that other name for it.) The advocate for it ranted about greed in the health care field. ~~&~~ *He* ended up with proposals for 10s. of 1000's of new Drs. & Nurses all trained at taxpayers expense; every Dr. ~~& Nurse on~~ *& Dentist* on govt. salary, pub. ownership of all drug & medical equipment co's. and *then* said all of this could be provided for only 80% of present health care costs.

That must have been his laugh line. ~~It was pretty ridiculous.~~ Total health care costs last year—govt. & private *together* were $140 Bil., a tidy sum. But Sen. Kennedy & Cong. Cormans* ~~p~~ *Sperm to worm* plan ~~(which has been dubbed Sperm to Worm in its completeness)~~ is ~~judged~~ *priced* by H.E.W. at $248 Bil. The 2nd most popular plan & one which I'm sorry to say some de-

* Congressman James Charles Corman (D–California, 1961–1981).

featists in the Med. Assn. have ~~t~~ caved in on would cost $243 Bil. Then there is one the insurance co's. think they could live with—and *perhaps* on, which would cost $234½ Bil. All of these are from studies by H.E.W. which of course is heart & soul in favor of socialized med. And ~~here we are told there is a crisis in a program (the one we already have) which only costs $140 Bil.~~ *yet our crisis ridden present health care system costs around $100 Bil. less than the best govt. can come up with.*

Maybe there is a cue to these contrasting prices in some statistics about patients in govt. run ~~hospitals~~ ~~*medicine*~~ ~~the Veterans Admin.~~ hospitals & in pvt. hospitals. ~~Med.~~ *Med.* patients ~~average lingering~~ *spend an average of* 8 days in ~~a~~ pvt. hospitals. ~~When govt. pays the bill at the V.A. it's~~ *The same kind of patients in our Veterans hospitals linger* 26.5 days. Nursing costs per *pvt.* paitent average $218. *In the V.A. Hospitals it's $580 of our tax money.*

Why dont we let well enough alone.

This is RR Thanks for Listening. ❖

National Health Insurance II

November 29, 1977

The last broadcast I compared some health care cost figures ~~between~~ *on* private hospitals & those run by govt. Today I'd like to talk about the comparison we should be making~~:~~. Ill be right back.

The believers in socialized med. (which for selling purposes they refer to as National Hlth. Ins.) occasionally try to arouse our guilt feelings by saying how far we are behind other more enlightened nations. ~~And yet they shy away from any real comparison.~~ They talk of *a total* govt. medical program~~s~~ replacing our present pluralistic ~~plan~~ system of govt. help for the needy ~~&~~ *plus* private fee for service ~~paid by the patient~~ but shy away from any actual comparison with nations which have total govt. *run* health care.

One of the most persistent advocates of govt. medicine Sen. Kennedy visited a nursing home in Denmark for 2 hours and was quite pleased with what he saw. Apparently however he never heard the Danish Administrator of their socialized health plan say, "Dont ask me how to control med. costs."

Virtually all of Europes socialized medicine is afflicted with rising costs, under funding, burocratic ineptness, decline in Quality of care, over usage, personelle & facility shortages & lack of capital for scientific modernization.

In Eng. they have resorted to cutbacks & sweeping reforms. Still a Sr. official says, "Yes we have gone too far. Waits for med. service are growing longer—fees have doubled." An Eng. Sociologist says, "Med., nursing & paramedic personnell most of whom enthusiastically accepted the challenge of British Nat. Health service & enthusiastically tried to treat patients as patients are now soured, disenchanted & militantly organized in their own special interest. Pub. Administrators override the independence of Prof. med. opinion. Progress raises expectations which cant be fulfilled. The best Prof's. are few in number therefore it's impossible for more than a few to receive the best care. The latest scientific techniques rest upon expensive equipment—therefore only a few enjoy it's benefits." Then came this telling line, "Neither socialized nor pvt. med. can change these basic facts.—But socialized med. induces the belief that it can."

A year or so ago the people of Sweden voted Karl Marx out after 40 years of Socialism. Maybe this statement by a Swedish official explains why. It sounds a little like England. "Waits for med. service are growing longer. Fees have doubled. The New Hosp. in Stockholm stands half completed for lack of funds. Dr's. leave the country in the summer to escape confiscatory taxes" (the inc. tax rate ~~on~~ *at* $33,000 of earnings is 102%) "Alcoholism, Drug Addiction, V.D., Mental Illness & Suicide rank among the highest anywhere."

A comment from France "We spend all our time filling out forms." Holland has suspended med. training for lack of funds. Israel has cut back on free prescriptions because people were taking medicines they didn't need *JUST* because they were free. Russia—the low quality of para-medic service is so out of hand abuse of the system is now a cap. offense.

~~Well~~ Is there anything in those comparisons to make us want to imitate any of them? As I've said before, "you cant socialize the Dr. without socializing the patient." Isn't it time we as patients gave the Dr's. a hand in their fight to keep medicine out of govt's hands?

This is RR Thanks for listening. ❖

Automobiles
November 29, 1977

Of late we've been told *that* Americas love affair with the automobile is over, that ~~we must turn to~~ *people want* some other method of transportation. True or False? I'll be right back.

When rush hour comes it's hard to believe the automobile is on the endangered species list. Still there are those who believe it ~~s~~ *should be. That it is* an anti-humanity tool of destruction, destroying our cities, polluting the atmosphere and threatening us with mayhem & instant death.

Personally I've always believed the automobile ~~was~~ *gave us* one of the truly *last* great freedoms. ~~—the freedom of mobility.~~ For the first time the ordinary man could go where he wanted to go, when he wanted to, choose his own ~~route~~ ~~*path*~~ departure ~~time~~ & arrival time free at last from timetables & fixed routes.

Now ~~at last~~ a book has been written defending the motor car. B. Bruce-Briggs a young urbanologist at the Hudson Inst. think tank has written a book called, "The War Against The Automobile." * Claiming that the N.Y. publishing industry has marketed dozens of books against the highway & the automobile Briggs claims his must be the first book to present an argument for the family jaloppy.

He ~~claims~~ says we have the best mass transportation system in the world,—our auto-highway complex, and that every country would like to imitate us. "It is the automobile that moves the great mass of Americans," ~~yet it is~~ he writes, "yet it is under attack from a number of sources, informed & uninformed, idealistic & selfish."

A member of what has to be called the intelligentsia he takes on his teammates in that league and accuses them of waging an "upper class struggle against the standard of living, individual freedom & pride of the great mass of Am. people."

He denies that the automobile has destroyed the cities or that cities should be for people not cars; that it has ruined mass transit~~,~~ *or* is unsafe. And he defends the motor industry against charges that it has suppressed other types of engines in favor of the present ~~type~~ *kind*. He even ~~defends~~ *denies* it is the greatest producer of smog.

Pointing out that Detroit made seatbelts available before ~~Na~~ Ralph Nader or the Nat. Highway Traffic Safety Admin. were ever heard of he argues that the Safety Admin. hasn't made cars any safer than the manufacturers were already making them. In ~~fact~~ *addition* he quotes ~~the~~ an admin. report that no study that has been conducted proves *that* annual safety inspections prevent accidents.

On Smog he doesn't claim it's good for us but he quotes a study by the Nat. Acad. of Sciences & the Nat. Acad. of Engineering that concluded there was no evidence that photochemical oxidants were responsible for any deaths.

Briggs identifies the Generals in the war against the automobile as a "New Class" of intellectuals, journalists, burocrats & academics who are anti-materialist and opposed to the basic values of Am. society. And he declares, "the automobile has been one of the greatest blessings to mankind, providing the masses with the mobility *& freedom* previously reserved for the rich." He says, "The new class considers most of the achievements of our society as childish & foolish."

Well—which side are you on in this "War Against The Automobile"? ~~I'm~~ *I'll tell you where I stand—I'm* going out to the parking lot ~~myself~~ and ~~pat my~~ *give my* gas buggy *an affectionate pat* on the trunk~~.~~ *& tell it how much I care.* This is RR Thanks for listening. ❖

* B. Bruce-Briggs, *The War Against the Automobile* (E. P. Dutton, 1977).

This commentary was written as a radio address but never recorded. It was distributed through King Features Syndicate as a newspaper column on January 28, 1977.

The Execution
January 1977

The other day in Utah a ten year moratorium ~~in~~ was broken and a convicted murderer was executed. According to some the world will never be the same. I'll be right back.

Just the day before the execution of Gary Gilmore,* columnist Morrie Ryskind quoted another famed columnist Franklin P. Adams who wrote some years ago, "At the time of a cold blooded murder, no punishment seems severe enough for the slayer; but at the time of cold blooded execution, no crime seems horrendous enough to warrant the penalty."

There is no question but that human sympathy is more or less easily aroused as the ~~formal, prescribed~~ date ~~of an execution~~ draws near and we know that a fellow human being is going to be put to death at a prescribed hour. Those who sincerely oppose capital punishment very often contribute to the emotional impact by adding to the drama, ~~the human tragedy~~ to emphasize their point that we should eliminate the death penalty.

I happen to believe (as I know I've said before) that the ~~capital~~ death sentence is a deterrent and society has a right in ~~our~~ it's own defense to take the life of those who with pre-meditation & planning commit murder. ~~But this isn't going to be a discussion of~~ I dont like to use the term capital <u>punishment</u> because in my opinion we should emphasize the self defense idea and not think of the penalty for murder as ~~only~~ punishment alone.

But this isn't going to be another discussion of the merit or demerit of the "supreme penalty" as it is so often called. We've been through a traumatic experience with the Gilmore execution, oddly enough it seems because in this case the condemned man wasn't fighting <u>for</u> his life but instead wanted the sentence carried out.

Thanks to the Am. Civil Liberties Union and others we now have been treated to every bit of information about Gary Gilmores life, his habits, his views until an almost carnival atmosphere was beginning to grow. His life

* Gary Gilmore was executed January 17, 1977. The Supreme Court declared the death penalty "arbitrary and capricious" and thus unconstitutional under existing state statues in 1972 (*Furman v. Georgia,* 408 U.S. 238) but ruled a more limited law constitutional in 1976 (*Gregg v. Georgia,* 428 U.S. 153). Gilmore refused the appeals to which he was entitled and was the first person executed after the 1976 Supreme Court decision. Norman Mailer wrote a book about Gilmore (*The Executioner's Song,* New York: Random House, 1979) as did Gilmore's brother, Mikal (*Shot in the Heart,* New York: Doubleday, 1994). A&E Entertainment produced a movie, *Gary Gilmore: A Fight to Die,* A&E Biography, 1996.

story will be a motion picture and who knows what other commercial tie ins will be attempted.

He is dead & I truly ~~p~~ ask God *to* have mercy on his soul. But shouldn't the issue of Capital punishment be determined on a less emotional basis than whether *or not* this one man who confessed ~~the~~ *his* crime & agreed ~~the~~ *his* trial was fair ~~and the sentence just~~ *should pay* the ~~sent~~ *penalty* he himself said was just?

The day after, one newspaper placed a picture of the execution chair on front-page center and captioned it, "the place where Gary Gilmore was shot, *where he* bled & died." Another had a cartoonists picture of ~~tab stone tablets riddled with bullet holes~~ *the stone tablets Moses brought down from the Mountain. They were shown riddled with bullet holes* and the commandment "Thou Shalt Not Kill" in bold black type. ~~and so it went.~~ *And of course the "thou shalt not kill" referred to the firing squad.*

If the eternal debate is carried on in this way then what about the murderers victems? ~~His~~ *Their* names ~~isn't~~ *aren't* ~~a~~ household words. ~~Why no pictures of the spots where he was *they were* shot, bled & died? There were no pictures *no interviews* of those who wept for him *them*. As I understand it he *one* was a fine young man working his way through law school. Clerking at a motel desk W hHe was held up & robbed—then he was forced to kneel and was *lie down. He was* executed with a shot through his *the* brain. *as was the other young man. Both were fathers of infant children.* Ah! but that happened quite a while *a long yesterday* ago. The wheels of justice are turning slower these days.~~

~~But shouldn't we wonder a little about his thoughts, the goodbyes he would like to have said & who still weeps for him?~~

~~This is R.R. Thanks for listening.~~

One was a young man working in a gas station to earn his way through law school. The other a hotel manager earning money to go back to school. Both were fathers of infant children. They were robbed then made to lie on the floor where they were executed with shots through the head. Why no pictures of where they were shot & bled & died? There were no pictures ~~of~~, no interviews of those who wept for them. Ah! but that was a long yesterday ago. The wheels of justice are turning very slowly these days.

But shouldn't we wonder a little about their thoughts, the goodbyes they would like to have said~~?~~ & who wept and still weep for them?

Does anyone even remember their names. ~~This is R.R. Thanks for listening.~~ ❖

Part Four

1978

In 1978 Reagan devoted considerable effort to campaigning for House and Senate candidates. Yet we found a higher percentage of original drafts of 1978 radio addresses than in any other year—83 percent. His commentaries and columns were almost all about national policy issues, but he did not directly criticize President Jimmy Carter. He was far more explicitly political on behalf of Republican candidates. Nevertheless his major topics—in this year as well as in 1977 and 1979—were issues on which he disagreed with the Carter administration.

Reagan was quite active on the foreign affairs front. "The accepted wisdom tells us," Reagan declared in his stump speech, "that no midterm election is ever won on the issue of foreign policy. Perhaps so. But remember: We could win an election and lose a country if we fail to discuss the issues of peace and freedom."[1] In 1978, peace, freedom, and the security of the United States were major foreign policy themes in about one-third of Reagan's radio commentaries. CBS-TV invited Reagan to reply to President Carter's televised "fireside chat" on the Panama Canal treaties. In his rebuttal, aired on February 8, Reagan emphasized the argument, made repeatedly in radio commentaries, that the Panama Canal was part of the United States' defense perimeter: "Being in the middle point—the vital center—of the free world is not an easy responsibility. . . . The Panama Canal is vital to the free world and that world depends on us. . . ."[2]

The following month, Reagan gave a speech in which he critiqued the Carter administration's foreign policy. In addition to discussing the administration's approach to human rights abroad and détente, Reagan described the Soviet Union's move into Ethiopia as an attempt to gain a strategic advantage in the Horn of Africa and increase its reach to the Arabian peninsula.[3]

On April 10, he pledged his commitment to Israel's safe place in the Middle East and presaged his presidential rhetoric when he spoke before the Bonds of Israel. Reagan described the Soviet Union as having an evil influence: "There is an evil influence throughout the world. In every one of the far-flung trouble spots, dig deep enough and you'll find the Soviet Union stirring a witches' brew, furthering its own imperialistic ambitions. If the Soviet Union would simply go home, much of the bloodshed in the world today would cease." Later, he said: "The barbarians of today's world are combat-lean and hard, hungry for all we've created. They talk of the brotherhood of man but they would destroy the God of Moses and extinguish with an evil darkness a light man has been tending for 6,000 years."[4]

Shortly after this speech, Reagan traveled to Japan, the Republic of China (ROC), Hong Kong, and Iran. In three radio taping sessions before his trip he recorded 20 commentaries instead of the customary 15, creating an extra batch that would be sent out while he was abroad. While in Japan, Reagan met with U.S. Ambassador Mike Mansfield and the two had a serious conversation about U.S.-Japanese relations. As president-elect, Reagan would ask Democrat Mansfield to continue serving as the U.S. ambassador to Japan.[5]

In a speech before businessmen in Taipei, Reagan criticized the Carter administration's move to normalize relations with the People's Republic of China (PRC): "In my opinion the realities of American politics are such that our government would not be persuaded to move any closer toward so-called 'normalization' this year. After all, we have national Congressional elections this November and elected representatives do not like to have to answer for unpopular policies."[6] Reagan was unsuccessful in persuading the Carter administration; on December 15, President Carter announced that U.S.-PRC diplomatic relations would be established and formal U.S. ties to the ROC would be broken. Back in the United States, Reagan's May 15 taping session included five essays about his travels and one more general essay on security in the Pacific region.[7]

By the time Reagan appeared on CBS-TV's *Face the Nation* on May 14, the U.S. Senate had ratified the two Panama Canal treaties. During the interview, Reagan was asked what was going to be his next major foreign policy issue. He replied that it would be the Senate ratification of SALT II. He did not call upon the Senate to reject the treaty, but his viewpoint was apparent: "[I]f the leaks [about the SALT II negotiations] are true . . . then, yes, I think you're going to see quite a fight in the Senate, and it will cross party lines."[8] It was an issue on which Reagan's position would eventually prevail. Reagan reported on numerous critiques of the arms control measure in radio commentaries in 1978.

Later in the year, on November 25, he went to London where he met with Margaret Thatcher, who would become prime minister of Great Britain in 1979. Reagan traveled from there to Paris, Bonn, Berlin, and Munich. Reagan wrote radio essays about his trip to Europe, and, as Peter Hannaford has observed, Reagan's "impressions foreshadowed the tone of *President* Reagan's policy views toward Europe."[9]

On the domestic front, consumer prices increased faster than in 1977 at the very high rate of 9.0 percent, up from 6.7 percent. Unemployment edged downward from 7.1 percent of the labor force to 6.1 percent. The economy—and the rising taxes that accompanied inflation—continued to concern Americans. Inflation was also reflected in rising property values and assessments, and homeowners were experiencing continual property tax increases.

Reagan supported California's Proposition 13 to limit property taxes, which was passed by a 64.8 percent vote on June 6, 1978. A dozen other states would join the tax revolt. Reagan also supported across-the-board federal tax cuts and was specific in his support for the tax-cutting measure introduced in the Congress by Representative Jack Kemp (R-New York) and Senator William Roth (R-Delaware). The Kemp-Roth proposal called for cuts in marginal personal income tax rates of 30 percent over three years—10 percent each year.

In June, Reagan met with a group of Democratic intellectuals—Norman Podhoretz, Midge Decter, Nathan Glazer, and Irving Kristol—at a dinner arranged by Bob Tyrrell of *American Spectator.*[10] They were to become the core of the "neoconservatives"—Democrats disillusioned with U.S. foreign and defense policy and the excesses of the 1960s who supported Reagan in 1980.

Martin Anderson arranged for Reagan to spend time with several people whose support would be important to a presidential candidacy, especially George Shultz, who had held several cabinet posts during the Nixon presidency and had supported Ford in the 1976 primaries, and Alan Greenspan, who had chaired Ford's Council of Economic Advisors. On June 19, 1978, Reagan was a dinner guest at the Shultz's home on the Stanford University campus, where he spent several hours in a round-table discussion with George Shultz; Alan Greenspan; Caspar Weinberger, who had served in Reagan's California cabinet; William Simon, who had been Nixon's treasury secretary; and Hoover fellows including Martin Anderson, Annelise Anderson, and Michael Boskin.[11] Reagan and Greenspan also had breakfast together the following morning.

The same month Reagan met with his own group of informal advisers and asked each of them to express their thoughts about a Reagan presidential candidacy.[12] He made no commitment, but he was clearly laying the groundwork.

The November elections brought the Republicans three additional seats in the Senate, 12 in the House, and six governorships. It was less than the typical gain of the opposition party in an off-year election, partly because people approved of Carter's efforts in achieving the September 17 Camp David accords between Israel and Egypt. Democrats continued to be the dominant party, holding 276 of 435 House seats, 59 of the 100 Senate seats, and all but 18 governorships.

On December 17, OPEC announced plans to raise oil prices again in 1979, and by the end of December the problems of Mohammad Reza Shah Pahlavi in Iran had reached crisis proportions. In addition to Iran, political crises earlier in the year in Nicaragua (the imposition of emergency power by President Anastasio Somoza Debayle to address a strike calling for his resignation) and in Afghanistan (the rise to power of Mohammad Taraki, a Communist, following the overthrow of President Mohammad Daud Khan) suggested that the tectonic plates of the international system were shifting. Jimmy Carter was heading into a difficult year, though it still seemed far from likely that a Republican could win the White House in 1980.

Christmas
January 9, 1978

†Well the holidays are behind us, the decorations put away, the tree long gone, even the after Christmas sales are ~~past~~ *over* & we're looking forward to Spring.

I'll be right back

All the traditions associated with Christmas were observed as usual in the past holiday ~~system~~ *season* including the chorus of complaints that ≠ over commercialization is robbing the day of its true meaning. I'll have to confess I cant join that chorus. Somehow the ads offering helpful gift suggestions when we are all filled with the spirit of giving, the decorations on the streets & in the stores, the familiar carols add to the Christmas spirit for me~~.~~ *and dont really strike me as crass or insensitive money grubbing.*

I~~'m far more~~ *am disturbed however* about something I read over the holidays which could really rob Christmas of it's meaning for millions of us who see it as more than just the birthday of a great & good teacher. I realize there are those who by religious belief consider Jesus a very human prophet whose teachings about love for one another, treating others as we would like to be treated ourselves are sound patterns for living; that he is to be respected but not worshipped.

But for many of us he is much more. He is the promised Messiah, the Son of God come to earth to offer salvation for all mankind. It was disturbing therefore to read that in many Christian seminarys there is an increasing tendency to minimize his divinity, ~~and~~ *to* reject the miracle of his birth and regard him as merely human.

Meaning no disrespect to ~~others~~ the religious convictions of others I *STILL* cant help wondering how we can explain away what to me is the greatest miracle of all ~~and one~~ *& which is* recorded in history. No one denies there was such a man, that he lived and that he was put to death by crucifixion.

Where then you may ask is the miracle I spoke of? Well consider this and let your imagination if you will translate the story into our own time—possibly to your own home town. A young man whose father ~~was~~ *is* a carpenter grows up working in his fathers shop. He has no formal education. He owns no property of any kind. One day he *PUTS DOWN HIS TOOLS* & walks out of his fathers shop. He starts preaching on street corners and in the *NEARBY* country side. Walking from place to place *preaching all the while even though he is in no way an ordained minister* he never gets farther than a*n* ~~mile~~ area perhaps 100 miles wide at the most.

He does this for 3 yrs. Then he is arrested, tried & convicted. There is no court of appeal so he is executed *at age 33* along with two common thieves. Those in charge of his execution roll dice to see who gets his clothing—the only posessions he has. His family cannot afford a burial place so he is interred in a borrowed tomb.

End of story? No this uneducated, propertyless young man who preached on street corners for only 3 yrs. *WHO LEFT NO WRITTEN WORD* has for 2000 yrs. had a greater effect on the entire world than all the Rulers, Kings & Emperors, all the conquerors, the generals & admirals, all the scholars, scientists and philosophers who ever lived—all put together.

How do we explain that?—Unless he really was what he said he was.

This is RR Thanks for listening.*

† May I have 3 or 4 copies of this when you get it typed? RR ❖

American Farm School I

January 9, 1978

Many Americans are critical of our foreign aid programs—not because they lack generosity but because of an uneasy feeling their sacrifice is being wasted.

I'll be right back.

"Give a hungry man a fish & he'll be hungry tomorrow. Teach him how to fish & he'll never be hungry again." Unfortunately that quotation has not al-

* Reagan received a letter disagreeing with this commentary from Rev. Thomas H. Griffith. Reagan's response, dated March 1, 1978, is printed in *Reagan: A Life in Letters,* edited by Kiron K. Skinner, Annelise Anderson, and Martin Anderson (New York: Free Press, 2003), pp. 276–77.

ways guided us in our efforts to help others through foreign aid. But today I'd like to tell you about a program that does meet that test.

A few months ago friends of mine in S.F. told me of their interest in helping something called the American Farm School. Thanks to them ~~I was~~ *Nancy & I were* visited by a young lady who works out of an office ~~in N.Y.~~ *at*—380 Madison Ave. N.Y. City. The sign on that big city office door must seem a little strange to native New Yorkers—"American Farm School."

If they'd drop in & ask a few questions they'd learn as ~~I~~ *we* did from ~~my~~ *our* charming visitor that the Am. Farm School is about 20 min's. from downtown ~~Thess~~ *THESSALONIKI* in Northern Greece. It is an agricultural & technical training center on 400 acres with a girls school featuring home economics & crafts & a boys school with specialties in Farm Machinery, Animal Husbandry & Horticulture. It was founded in 1904 and owes it's existence to one man who had a dream and made his dream come true.

John Henry House, a Congregational minister was a missionary in the Balkans for 30 yrs. During that time he became increasingly aware of a sociological trend. Village boys had learned to despise village life~~. He~~ and make their way to the cities. ~~He be~~ Rev. House believed a change in education ~~to~~ could result in a new or perhaps a revived ethic that it was not degrading for educated people to work with their hands.

The Rev. was that rare combination of practical & visionary. He dreamed of founding an educational inst. that would develop the "whole man, the head, the heart & the hand." He believed that ~~an~~ *a* school patterned after Hampton Inst. in Virginia, Tuskeegee in Alabama & the Penn School for girls in So. Carolina * could train young people to be leaders, modern farmers & make them content to stay down on the farm—down on the farm in Macedonia.

Rev. House was 60 yrs. old *in 1902* when he & two missionary friends bought 53 acres of parched, waterless land in a bandit-infested part of Northern Greece.** If they were to convince their students (to be) they had to start with land as poor as that of the poorest farmer. House had raised the money for the project himself. The American Board of Commissioners for Foreign Missions did not share his vision & considered it outside the scope of the missionary endeavour for which he'd been sent to the Balkans.

Rev. House was not a man to give up on a dream. He took his wife to see the

* Reagan is referring to three institutions established to educate blacks emerging from slavery in teaching, agriculture, and workmanship skills. Founded in 1868, Hampton Normal and Agricultural Institute (now Hampton University) educated blacks, but a program for Native Americans was added in 1878. The Normal School for Colored Teachers (now Tuskegee University) was opened in Tuskegee, Alabama, on July 4, 1881. The Penn School was started in South Carolina in 1862 to educate Sea Island slaves who were freed as the Civil War began. It was later known as the Penn Normal, Industrial, and Agricultural School, but in 1948 the private school was closed and was converted into a community center.

** The Thessaloniki Agricultural and Industrial Institute, which became known as the American Farm School, was founded in 1904.

~~first instalment of his dream~~ *land he had chosen for his venture.* Standing on the 53 windswept barren acres she asked: "Whoever will you get to live in this place?" He answered "You my dear." And live there she did. Thus was started the Thessaloniki Agricultural & Industrial Inst. which was to become the American Farm School. I'll bring you up to date on this, next broadcast ~~& think you'll~~ and I'm sure you'll be a little more proud of America the Beautiful.

This is RR Thanks for Listening. ❖

American Farm School II
January 9, 1978

On the last broadcast I told of how a 60 yr. old missionary with a dream started an inst. in Greece which is probably the best American Aid Program we have. I'll be right back

~~When~~ ~~&~~ Rev. House & his wife Susan started ~~to make~~ *scratching at* 53 barren acres in Northern Greece ~~&~~ *in 1902. Their harvest?*—A beautifully landscaped campus and 400 acres of productive farmland with several hundred Greek boys & girls learning & working. ~~was really only a dream~~

They dry farmed, dug wells, ~~&~~ prayed to God *and built a tiny schoolroom.* ~~The first students brought to the campus more than 70 yrs. ago were~~ ~~*had been*~~ ~~orphaned by~~ *Their first students were a hand full of orphans, refugees from* the masscre of Macedonian peasants ~~when northern Greece was ruled by the Ottoman empire.~~ *by the Turks.*

From that beginning ~~T~~the Thessaloniki Inst. became the American Farm School & is one of the oldest educational landmarks ~~on~~ *in* war torn Macedonia. It has survived wars, pestilence, drought & malaria. Today it is a middle level technical school open to those who've had nine years of schooling.

Rev. House never lived to see one part of his dream come true—the creation of a girls school ~~in connection~~ *on the campus.* It was his stated belief that, "when you educate a man you ed. an individ. When you ed. a woman you ed. a whole family."

In 1917 his son *Charles* a graduate engineer at Princeton returned to Greece where he had been brought up. His father was aging and he pitched in to help what had now become the American Farm School. When John House died in 1929 Charles took over. He understood & loved the Greek farmer. The school is not an American outpost on Greek soil. Of it's graduates 6 out of 10 are today farming in their native villages, others have gone on to get additional training and some have returned to teach and carry on the tradition of John & Susan House.

In 1945 when the program of electrification began in Greece the Farm School graduates were the 1st to harness electricity for farm use.

Charles died in 1961 but the school carries on led by Bruce Lansdale who is as dedicated to the Founders dream as was the founder himself. With the exception of years in college in Am. he has lived in Greece since 1925 and has known the Am. Farm School since childhood.

The students get a total ed. an academic program plus homemaking skills & crafts for the girls and modern farming for the boys. They pay $350 a year which is ½ the cost per student. All the work is done by the students, the housekeeping chores & the farming. They have a shop where ~~the their~~ *the girls* handiwork is sold.~~& the~~ *This & the* produce ~~from the farm no~~t ~~only meets their needs but is sold.~~ *raised by the boys provides* Almost ½ the *schools* budget. ~~is met by~~ ~~*in this way.*~~ A small percentage of help now comes from the Greek govt which pays to send ~~adults~~ *FARMERS* to the school for special courses. Our own Foreign aid program A.I.D.* helps with some construction needs which leaves 37% to be raised by private donation both in Greece & the U.S.

Talk of dropping a pebble in the water & watching the rings spread across the surface—the school now has a ~~foreign~~ *STUDENT* exchange program *WITH OTHER COUNTRIES* and there are special summer courses in the ancient arts & crafts of Greece *which makes for an interesting summer vacation for even a touring American.*

Time wont permit a listing of all the ~~facets but~~ *programs offered by the school but* you can get complete information or if you *JUST* want to help a truly successful bit of Am. neighborliness write The American Farm School—380 Madison Ave. N.Y. Up around Thessaloniki no one says, "Yankee go home."

This is RR Thanks for listening. ❖

Taxes
January 9, 1978

There is a stirring among the people of this great land which could signal increasing irritation with high taxes & centralized control over their lives.

In Calif. a court** decision ~~about~~ has ~~rule~~ *outlawed* the traditional financing of pub. schools by local property tax on the grounds that some school districts are poorer than others in real estate values. Naturally this has ~~had the effect of~~ *caused an automatic* turn to the state as the only source of funding some 1100 districts on an equal base.

Calif. dosen't face this problem alone. More than 20 states—perhaps your own—have switched from local property tax funding since 1971. That was the year a high powered movement began to centralize school funding at the

* President John F. Kennedy started the Agency for International Development (AID) in 1961 to oversee economic aid programs.

** *Serrano v. Priest,* 5 Cal.3d 584, 1971, a California Supreme Court case.

state level. Those pushing the move were very well aware that control of funding would also mean control of education and that was really their goal.

Up in Maine a statewide property tax was adopted in 1973 with the enthusiastic support of the Maine Tchrs. Assn. an affiliate of the Nat. Ed. Assn. Prior to 1973 the citizens of each Maine community met at annual town meetings and voted on the ~~items (inclu~~ *budget for* specific local programs including ed. Since their decisions had a direct effect on local property tax rates, economy dictated those decisions.

Under the new system the state set the uniform property tax rate and then returned to each community an amt. based on the number of children enrolled in school. This meant of course that some towns found themselves supporting their own schools as well as schools in other towns. At first those "other towns"—the ones benefiting from the new system were happy as clams.

Of course the towns that had to share their revenues had a legitimate beef and they weren't long in starting to complain. But they weren't alone in their misery for long. School budgets began to move skyward as the public school establishment lobbied for *and got FROM THE ST. LEGIS.* all the things it had always wanted. And of course the statewide property tax climbed right along with those skyrocketing school budgets.

The people of Maine did more than just complain. On Dec. 5th they went to the polls in a statewide referendum and voted 3 to 2 for repeal of the statewide tax. Their campaign went up against the school estab. and the Nat Conf. of St. Legislatures which has been plumping for a statewide system all over the country. The move to repeal was, for the most part a grass roots affair & the issue was local budget control.

It is interesting to note that this did not become a contest between the payout towns & the towns on the receiving end. In both kinds the people voted for local control.

If this action by the people of Maine is the forerunner of a national move toward more authority & autonomy at the local level and a return of such by the Fed. govt. to the states, govt. will cost less and we might look around some day & find inflation "went that-a-way."

This is RR Thanks for listening. ❖

Our Country

January 9, 1978

Abraham Lincoln said "a man can disagree with those in govt. without being against his country or it's govt." I'll be right back.

I have disagreed with those in govt. on many of these broadcasts. I'm sure I will continue ~~do~~ *to* do so. But just to keep the record straight let me make plain my criticism is not directed against this system of ours which is unique in all the world. ~~Rather do~~ I criticize those I believe are turning away from & repudiating the very principles which brought us greatness, eroding individual freedom, robbing us of independence and the right to control our own destiny.

I thought of this the other day when I read an account of a meeting to launch an Australian visitor *here* on a 3 month tour of campus appearances. The visitor is ~~not~~ hardly a typical representative of the land down under. He ~~has~~ has been identified as a collaborator *WITH OUR ENEMIES* in 2 wars, Korea & Vietnam~~,~~. ~~each time with our enemies.~~ A Russian defector ~~said~~ *claims* he has been a Soviet K.G.B. agent. He is telling our college students what is wrong with America and his message is not just a complaint about burocratic ineptness. According to him our enemies are the White knights and we are the dragons who must be slain before we devour all that is good & noble in the world.

Well I offer in rebuttal the words spoken a few years ago (when we were still involved in the Vietnam war) by a widely known & respected Canadian commentator who became angry at the rest of the world for, as he put it, kicking us when we were down.

God bless him. Gordon Sinclair went on the radio & said, "it is time to speak up for the Americans as the most generous and possibly the least appreciated people in all the earth." *

Then he went on to say; "As long as 60 yrs. ago, when I first started to read newspapers, I read of floods on the Yellow river & the Yangtze. Who rushed in with men & money to help? The Americans did. Germany, Japan & even to a lesser extent Britain & Italy were literally lifted out of the debris of war by the Americans who poured in bil's. of dollars in ~~aid~~ aid & forgave others bils. in debts. When the franc looked to be in danger of collapsing in 1956 it was the Americans again who propped it up.

"When distant cities are hit by earthquake it is the U.S. that hurries in to help—Managua Nicaragua is one of the most recent examples.

"The Marshall plan, the Truman policy, all pumped bil's. upon bils. of dollars into discouraged countries. Now newspapers in those countries are writing about the decadent war mongering Americans.

"I can name you 5,000 times when the Americans raced to the help of other people in trouble. Can you name me even one time when someone else raced to help when the Americans were in trouble." Mr. Sinclair said he wouldn't blame us if we thumbed our nose at the rest of the world. I'm grateful to him but I hope there'll be no nose thumbing. I hope we'll keep right on being the first to arrive when help is needed.

This is RR Thanks for listening ❖

* "The Americans" aired June 5, 1973, during Sinclair's radio show "Let's Be Personal" on CFRB radio in Toronto, Ontario.

Crime
January 9, 1978

The stories ~~of~~ *about* perpetrators of crime turned back on the streets are, it seems, becoming more frequent and the crimes more vicious. I'll be right back

We talk of human rights & civil rights but is there any greater right—human or civil than the right of an honest man to his life, the right of a child to ~~be~~ walk *on* the streets ~~of his or in~~ without fear or a ~~woman~~ *housewife* to feel secure in her own kitchen?

I have just received a letter from ~~a~~ *the* father of a young man who was brutally murdered on New Years Eve 5 yrs. ago. His letter was a cry of protest because one of his sons two murderers has been free on parole after only 2 yrs. in prison and now has ~~even~~ been discharged from parole & is totally free.

The Judge who sentenced the man to 2nd degree murder & the prosecuting attorney are both outraged. They had spent 16 days in court, *one* presenting & the other listening to the ~~brutal~~ *shocking* evidence of the brutal crime. The Judge says of the parole, "It is a miscarriage of Justice." Two years for a brutal murder like that?" The Prosecutor expressed disgust with what he called "another failure of the system." And he asks, "what is a human life *really* worth when compared to the degree of punishment?"

The victem of the crime was a young man 24 yrs. of age with a wife and young child. ~~He was murdered to cover the crimes already committed against him.~~ The murderers ~~both~~ one about 21 the other a year younger were both on parole for previous offenses. Having beaten the victem & abused him in other ways they decided he'd have to die so ~~they~~ their paroles wouldn't be revoked.

The testimony at the trial showed that in the hours before his death the victem had been beaten, sexually abused and then bound hand & foot and stuffed in the trunk of a car. He was taken to a remote country road where he was shot in the back of the head & twice in the back.

At the trial the two killers tried to blame each other. On May 9, 1974 they were found guilty; one of murder in the 1st degree for which he was sentenced to life imprisonment. Under Calif. law he'll be eligible ~~in~~ *for parole* 3½ yrs. from now. The other was given a 5 yr. to life sentence *FOR MURDER IN THE* 2ND *DEGREE.*. He is the one who was paroled after 2 yrs. in prison and now a yr. & a half later has been released from further parole.

A spokesman for the parole board which in our state ~~has~~ is now called the "Community Release Board" said there was nothing wrong in the decision to release him because the board didn't have the full details of his involvement in the crime. Is it asking too much to suggest that a board having the power to ~~turn someone~~ *send a* convicted murderer back into society should take the time to get the details?

As Cicero* said: "The safety of the people shall be the highest law."

* Marcus Tullius Cicero (106–43 B.C.)

But in Calif. a father writes "AFTER 2 YRS. the murderer of my son goes free but my son is dead."

This is RR Thanks for listening ❖

Pot

January 9, 1978

The Los Angeles Times Saturday editions feature some ~~interesting~~ human interest columns which in turn produce some interesting letters to the editor. I'll be right back.

On last Nov. 21st I read a*n* ~~column~~ *article* by a mother about her teenage son and his experience with marijuana.* She told of her first awareness of a change taking place—a change in *the* personality of her son and of his admission that he was smoking pot. One phrase she used in describing this change was that she watched his "eyes growing dimmer."

Her story had a happy ending. He stood before her one day, his eyes no longer dim and told her he had quit because he finally realized what the weed was doing to him. Her ~~article~~ *story* ended with ~~her~~ *the* statement that she looked at her son and, "knew he had become a man."

On Dec. 3rd the Times printed a page of letters ~~be~~ it had received in response to this story.** I couldn't believe the viciousness ~~of~~ *&* the ~~anger~~ outrage of the writers. One accused the mother of practising "parental fascism." Most of them carried on about one generation forcing it's standards on another and ~~all~~ made it plain that in their view she was some kind of monster for disapproving of marijuana.

Then on Dec. 17th ~~2 weeks later~~ in the same editorial section there appeared a response to the letters by a local teacher named Patrick Kennedy.*** He wrote; "I could not in good conscience sit back & not reply to those opinions about marijuana use & teenagers." He ~~spo wrote~~ TOLD of the experience sometimes exhilarating, sometimes heartbreaking in being close to 200 teenagers, seeing their struggle with the problems of growing up. ~~He~~ Speaking of them as a generation "needing & UNCONSCIOUSLY seeking moral guidance & structure," he asked, "if parents are not responsible to provide a moral atmosphere, stressing the values they find important, who is responsible?" Answering his own question he said, "this is not parental fascism—it is ~~a~~ parental commitment to the most sacred of all tasks: to see that the young get a good start with heathy roots & a straight growth in the proper directions." He called it a responsibility that is being ~~shi~~ avoided by too many of us & that our society is paying the price.

* Elizabeth Larson, "A Teen-Ager Goes to Pot, But Feels His Way Out," *Los Angeles Times,* Nov. 21, 1977.

** *Los Angeles Times,* Dec. 3, 1977, Part II, p. 5.

*** *Los Angeles Times,* Dec. 17, 1977, Part II, p. 6.

He asked the letter writers if they had ever been closely involved with bright young teenagers; "Have they seen those bright eyes slowly become dimmer, the once quick minds less attentive? Have they experienced the slow growth of paranoia in the eyes of these students; the inability to look you in the eye any longer with that innocent look of trust & friendship"?

Telling of the heartbreak in seeing that happen he ~~answered those who defended~~ *said of* "Pot." "It poisens the mind in the sense that when a problem arises in the life of a teenage pot smoker he or she dosen't solve the problem. It's too easy to avoid it by getting high. So they reach adulthood without ever facing or overcoming adversity."

~~Mr. Kennedy agreed with the mother for saying her son was now a man because her son was taking responsibility for his own life.~~

A lot of parents should be very happy if their sons & daughters are students in the classes of Patrick Kennedy.

This is RR Thanks for listening. ❖

Panama
January 27, 1978

I'd like you to hear what one of our Panama Canal employees—a Panimanian himself has to say about the doings of govt. ours & Panamas.

I'll be right back.

On a recent visit to Panama two U.S. Senators Paul Laxalt & Bob Dole* met with the Panama Canal Zone Civic Council. The Council is made up of representatives of the various towns in the Zone.

One of the council members who spoke to the Senators was a Zone fireman. He was born in the Zone to parents from the West Indes so he is legally a Panamanian. In his heart he is American and in his heart he is against the treaties which would give the canal to Panama.

He spoke with a heavy West Indian accent which I wont attempt to imitate but listen to his words. He's a man in his 40's, black and concerned as are most of the canal employees that they will face retribution if the treaties are ratified because of their loyalty to the U.S.

~~He said~~ He was quite emotional as he ~~said~~ *spoke:*

"The employees that you see here working, the ones that come from the United States and the ones that are employed locally, we are a breed of people—a breed of second, some third generation, whose fathers come here and built this place.

"They're probably turnin' over in their graves wanting to find out what's

* Senator Paul D. Laxalt (R–Nevada, 1974–1987) and Senator Robert J. Dole (R–Kansas, 1969–1996).

wrong with the United States government. What's this business about givin' away the Panama Canal? To who? Are we working for what? We sacrifice all the time. We give of ourselves . . . freely. Yes, we came here and worked for 10 cents an hour. We are going to defend it. Regardless of what anybody wants to say, we stood here in 1964 and we defended it." (He was speaking of the riots.) "And we dare anybody to come over and take it away from us. That's the kind of feelin's that I have. I am tell[ing] you that.

"You are never making me an American citizen which I know that I'm entitled to be because I was born and grow up in the Canal Zone under the American flag. And trained western style. I don't know anything about Communism or whatever. I read, write English. That's the language I know. The money in my pocket—"In God we trust"—that's what it writes on there. It's American money. And it's the only kind of money I care to spend.

"So what you think I'm going to do? Sit here and let some tinhorn terrorist come over here and tell us what we should do. Uh? This is our country. We built it. This Panama Canal was built by this people and it was paid in blood, sweat, and tears. Are you going to tell me the United States government just—just give it away like that?"

At this point he was interrupted by another member of the Council who said, "This man is very dramatic but he is 100 percent right."

The fireman continued; "I know that I'm right. That's the reason why my kids at home—three girls and a boy—they're going to be in the United States Navy and Army. They're not to go through this what I'm going through. Never happen. I'm going to see to it. And any day that this treaty comes into effect I'm going to tell you this: you'll have an exodus to the United States. Employees—black and white—will be going out of here."

I hope he knows how many Americans feel the same way. ❖

Oil

January 27, 1978

The oil industry has been blamed in some quarters for contributing to inflation because of the surge in gasoline prices which followed the Arab oil price hike.*

I'll be right back.

Not too long ago I told about the editor of an oil industry trade paper who had figured out that at 45¢ ~~for a cup of coffee~~ *a cup* (which he had paid) coffee was $600 a barrel compared to ~~$6 for domestic &~~ $14 for Arab oil.** Then he wondered why there were no congressmen demagoging about the

* OPEC increased oil prices from $12.70 a barrel to $13.66 in the summer of 1977.

** The radio address "Coffee," taped November 29, 1977.

high price of coffee with *all* the usual charges of monopoly, withheld reserves & obscene profits.

Well his editorial didn't stop the demagogery. ~~and~~ I'm afraid most of us look at the familiar signs & bill boards of the major oil companies & find it easy to believe at least some of the tirades against the oil merchants. With that in mind I decided to see what the truth might be and I was surprised and maybe you'll be too.

Try this on for starters—since 1958 the cost of mailing a letter has gone up 333%. The price of gasoline has only gone up 88%. Makes you wonder about that new $10½ Bil. energy dept. in Wash. dosen't it?

Sen. Jackson* *of Wash.* has found a few things ~~to~~ *in the oil industry to* criticize. ~~about the~~ But if the price of gasoline had gone up as much in his home state as those tasty apples they raise there Washingtonians would be paying $1.46 a gal. Sen. Muskie of Maine has had some unkind ~~questions~~ *things* to say about the petroleum peddlers but if gasoline had gone up in price to match Maine lobsters it would sell for $2.85 a gal. While we're at it let's take the dollar itself—we wont be taking much. Over the last 40 yrs. ~~it~~ *the dollar* has shrunk a little. It's worth a fraction under 26¢. But you can still buy a gal. of gas for less than one of those 26¢ dollars.

~~There are some surprises too when we look at the monopoly charge that has~~

High on the list of things the oil industry is accused of is that it enjoys ~~a~~ being a monopoly. Congress debates divestiture—a bill to break up the major oil companies. Now ~~if~~ monopoly means domination of the industry by a few companies, reduced competition and limited entry into the business by others.

Well that was my next surprise. There are more than 10,000 companies competing with each other in oil & gas exploration & production; 133 companies operate 264 refineries & more than 100 pipe line companies transport crude oil, natural gas liquids & refined products.

In the wholesale side of the industry there are 15,000 companies selling petrolium products to over 300,000 retailers—90% of whom are independents. Would it surprise you as it did me to learn there are more than 1500 different brands of gasoline for us to buy? That's not much of a monopoly.

There is a direct ratio between ~~the~~ increased production in America & energy. Four million jobs are created for every bil. barrels of oil found in this country. I hope the new energy agency** in Wash. knows that~~.~~ *because we'll need 19 mil. new jobs by 1985—thats 5 bil. barrels of oil.*

This is RR Thanks for listening. ❖

* Senator Henry M. Jackson (D–Washington, 1953–1983).

** President Jimmy Carter signed legislation creating the Department of Energy on August 4, 1977.

Regulation
January 27, 1978

A recent poll reveals that less *than* one ~~of~~ out of three people think there is overregulation by govt. of American business & industry. I'll be right back.

We have a long way to go in making govt. more responsive & less intrusive if as the poll says less than a third of our citizens believe there is no overregulation of ~~Ameri~~ business & industry in America. Perhaps our problem is that most people upon hearing the term "business & industry" automatically think of great corporations with legal depts. of their own, auditing staff & banks of computers.

This of course ignores reality. Our Take the letter a relatively small law firm ~~wrote~~ *sent* to the Congressman representing the district in which the firm is located. This firm has instituted a retirement plan involving profit *& ownership* sharing for ~~a~~ *its* few employees. One line in the letter informed the Congressman that the ERISA act of 1974* having to do with pensions had resulted in MAKING the cost of administering the law firms *retirement* plan greater than the plan's benefits.

Then came these lines, "There should be some provision for reducing the complexities & paperwork for small business. We only have 8 employees. A sole proprietor with only a couple of employees can hardly justify the administration costs if he complies with all of the ~~red tape.~~ present requirements." Now remember this is a law firm which ~~means it~~ *obviously* is better equipped than most to handle ~~the~~ *such* technical requirements. The letter gave an example of burocratic bungling when it stated that on Nov. 17 the firm had received from the Dept. of Labor a request for a 9 page summary of it's plan to be filed on Nov. 17. Incidentally the Internal Rev. Svc. already had the information the Dept. of Labor was demanding.

Now comes evidence that the concern expressed in the letter for smaller (non-lawyer) employers is well founded. In Annapolis Maryland a man who repairs sewing machines decided to hire one employee. It seems this ~~requires~~ *takes* more than just running an ad and offering someone a salary. He had to write for employer's state & Fed. tax forms.

From the state he received a stack of forms including two notices he was required to put on the wall of his shop telling employees how to complain about unsafe or unsanitary working conditions & how to apply for unemployment compensation. ~~From t~~The Fed. govt. ~~he got~~ *sent him* a packet containing 44 forms ranging from 1 to 30 pages each. He said, "I wouldn't have time to do my sewing machine work if I had to read all this."

But that isn't the real price we're paying for the blizzard of paper govt. demands. The proprietor explained that he had thought he could help the unem-

* Employee Retirement Income Security Act of 1974.

ployment situation a little by teaching some boy or girl a trade. He added, "But they dont make it easy for you at all."

The I.R.S. concedes his complaint is a familiar one among small businessmen but "ho-hummed" that most of them eventually get used to it. Maybe—but just maybe a lot of them like the sewing machine man change their minds about hiring someone.

This is RR Thanks for listening. ❖

Welfare Reform
January 27, 1978

Welfare & the ~~weather~~ need to reform it is getting to be like the weather—everyone talks about it but no one does anything about it. I'll be right back.

Back in 1971 when Calif. started it's highly successful welfare reforms the weeping & wailing was ~~enough~~ *enough* to make your blood run cold. But most of it came from those who had no need for welfare themselves. ~~but~~ *They* delight in bleeding for others. And a goodly share came from the professionals & organizers who saw a career threat in what we were trying to do.

One such was the head of an organization dedicated to protecting the rights of those on welfare. Testifying before a Congressional committee she said, "Everyone in this country has a right to share the wealth. The money has gone to the middle class & if we dont get our share we're going to disrupt this country & this Capitol."

We found in Calif. that tens of thousands of able bodied welfare recipients would like nothing better than to become self supporting. We found also that the welfare system dosen't encourage this. ~~and so m~~Many of these people fall into a lifestyle ~~that~~ *which* after a while renders them virtually incapable of entering the competitive job market. Treating only the material needs of man will not endow him with nobility of spirit, creativity & the unselfish desire to become productive.

~~until we can help people become self-supporting. Getting people off welfare should be the goal, not while we figure out a way to get them working~~ ~~*back to*~~ ~~work. increasing their number.~~

One day after our reforms had ~~gone into~~ *been in* effect *for a while,* I received a letter that began—"Dear Sir—I am one of those people who left Calif. & it's welfare rolls when you started your reform program." Right there I wanted to stop reading. I thought the letter would ~~be a tale of woe, blaming me for hunger & misery in the name of economy.~~ *accuse me of being heartless and cruel and that I had ~~t~~ brought hunger & unhappiness to the writer.* I was wrong. The letter went on to say; "I'd like to thank you. My life is much brighter now. I lived for years in public housing with my 2 sons, drawing a welfare check because it was so easy. And the longer I did it the easier it got and the lazier I became. I wouldn't even get married and lose the security of that check. When you started cleaning up the welfare mess the govt. was creating I figured it was only a matter of time before I was told to find a job. So I decided ~~it was time~~ to do something. I had $520 I'd saved out of that poverty I was supposed to be living in. I ~~wen~~ *came* to Alaska where my family lived. ~~and~~ *I* found working was fun & a ~~better~~ lot better than daytime TV. I've got a lot more self respect & pride now." And then she thanked me again.

~~Over a three year period in Calif. some 400,000 people left the welfare rolls and some~~ ~~*some* of them wrote letters like this one.~~ Welfare is really not the complex problem govt. pretends it is. All we have to do is think of it as a temporary helping hand until we can assist someone to become self supporting. And that means we recognize it for what it is—charity & charity is a noble word. We should judge our success by how much we decrease the need for welfare. The failure of the present programs is indicated by the vast increase in the number of recipients. Welfare is a dangerous drug destroying the spirit of people once proudly independent. Our mission should be to help people kick that particular drug habit. This is RR Thanks for listening. ❖

Jobs

January 27, 1978

In the last 2 yrs. private industry & business in America ~~has~~ *have* created 7 mil. new jobs at no cost to the taxpayer. Govt. hasn't done quite that well.

I'll be right back.

Back in 1971 Cong. ~~sup~~ spurred by the recession of 1970 passed a measure called the Comprehensive Employment & Training Act. It was to be a temporary program costing $1 Bil. The money was to be doled out to the state & local govts. which would in turn hire the hard corps unemployed in fields such as law enforcement, health & ed. etc.

The temp. program is still with us only now it costs $6 bil. a year. It has *also* been proposed ~~NOW~~ as a part of the much talked about welfare reform ~~starting at~~ ~~*and*~~ *going to* $9 Bil. ~~Number one~~ *Well* with one out of five workers in the U.S. already on the pub. payroll, more govt. jobs doesn't seem to be a practical answer to unemployment.

But more importantly the record of the Comprehensive Employment & Training Act—called CETA for short is a story of boondoggles & scandal. Here & there special interest groups have managed to get grants which helped pay for their own staff~~.~~ *and could hardly be called legitimate pub. service jobs.*

One county in my own state of Calif. came up with a program that won a Golden Fleece award from Sen. *Wm.* Proxmire* *of Wis.* The Sen. gives his

* Senator William Proxmire (D–Wisconsin, 1957–1989).

Golden Fleece trophy each month for the biggest and/or the most ridiculous example of wasteful govt. spending. In this Calif. case $400,000 of CETA money is being used to hire about 85 people who will do a door to door survey. They are counting all the dogs, cats, & horses living in or near the 160,000 homes & apartments in the county.

The awarding of the "Fleece" brought the project to the attention of the citizenry of that particular county & they felt just about the same as Sen. Proxmire did. But the counting goes on and will continue through the Spring.

Defending the program CETA's local director said the Dept. of labor doesn't, "weigh the projects merits." He then went on to say that an idea would have to be "illegal or extremely ridiculous," before the Dept. would cancel the funds. And while he admitted that counting animals might sound ridiculous it really isn't.

County officials defended the nose count on the grounds that they might pick up revenues by turning up unlicensed animals. ($400,000 ~~?~~ worth?) Then there was the matter of animals not vaccinated for rabies. Well no one can question the seriousness of a ~~rabid animal~~ *rabies epidemic* but there hasn't been a single case of rabies among dogs & cats in that particular county for more than 10 yrs. No—the program ~~was~~ is well deserving of the Senators monthly award.

It does bear out what the French economist Bastiat* said more than a century ago, "Public funds seemingly belong to no one & the temptation to bestow them on someone is irresistable. This is RR Thanks for listening. ❖

Father & Son
January 27, 1978

There is a quotation, "The saddest words of tongue or pen are these—it might have been." I'm sure all of us at one time or another have *sadly* used another phrase, "If only I had"—

I'll be right back.

Not too long ago on one of these broadcasts** I quoted an anonymous source to the effect that if all of us knew on a certain day the world was ending, the roads, ~~&~~ streets & telephone lines would be jammed with people trying to reach someone to say "I love you." Since then ~~I've heard from~~ some of you ~~relating~~ *have* written to express agreement with that unknown author. ~~of that statement a~~And some have begun a sentence with the words, "If only I had"—or "hadn't" as the case might be.

Back in W.W.II a ~~f~~ father wrote a letter to his soldier son in the form of a poem:

* Claude Frédéric Bastiat (1801–1850), a well-known French economist.
** "Looking Out a Window," *Reagan, In His Own Hand,* p. 18.

Dear Son:

I wish I had the power to write
The thoughts wedged in my heart tonight
As I sit watching that small star
And wondering where and how you are.
You know, Son, it's a funny thing
How close a war can really bring
A Father, who for years with pride,
Has kept emotions deep inside.
I'm sorry, Son, when you were small
I let reserve build up that wall;
I told you real men never cried,
And it was Mom who always dried
Your tears and smoothed your hurts away
So that you soon went back to play.
But, Son, deep down within my heart
I longed to have some little part
In drying that small tear-stained face,
But we were men—men don't embrace.
And suddenly I found my Son
A full grown man, with childhood done.
Tonight you're far across the sea,
Fighting a war for men like me.
Well, somehow pride and what is right
Have each changed places here tonight.
I find my eyes won't stay quite dry
And that men sometimes really cry.
And if we stood here, face to face
I'm sure, my Son, we would embrace.
Son, Dads are quite a funny lot,
And if I've failed you on some spot
It's not because I loved you less
But just this cussed manliness.
And if I had the power to write
The thoughts wedged in my heart tonight,
The words would ring out loud and true,
I'm proud, my Son, yes proud of you.*

He signed it "Dad" and walked down to the corner *& dropped it in the* mail box. As he returned home and reached his own door step he was handed

* An undated newspaper clipping found with Reagan's draft claims the poem was written by A. H. Riness after his son Kenneth was killed in WWII.

the war dept. telegram ~~that~~ *the one that* began with the *FATEFUL* words "We regret to inform you."

I'm glad *THAT* I can believe his son ~~knows he wrote~~ *KNEW he had written* that letter.

This is RR Thanks for listening. ❖

*This is the first of three radio addresses on the Panama Canal Reagan wrote in the weeks before the Senate ratification of the treaties on April 20,1978.**

Panama Canal Debate
February 20, 1978

† We are coming to the climax ~~with regards to the~~ *of the debate over the* Panama Canal treaties with many Americans unaware of ~~the growing body of~~ *the increasing* evidence that these treaties are a disaster.

I'll be right back.

It seems more & more as if the U.S. Senate is engaged in a race between treaty advocates & opponents & *is* not acting as a deliberative body willing to take whatever time is necessary to weigh every aspect of the issue; to sift every new bit of evidence & analyse every available viewpoint.

Item: An eminent scholar in Panama says, "the canal is not a solution right now. It is a problem." He is speaking of ~~the real p~~ *what he calls* Panama's real need which is for the "gradual creation of an honest, efficient, responsible govt. deriving it's power from the people under law." He then suggests that a new plebescite in Panama on amendments to the treaties would topple the regime of Gen. Torrijos.

Item: From an Eastern financial establishment comes word that Torrijos who has already run up a debt of some 2 to 3 bil. dollars in these nine years is arranging for 50 to 100 mil. dollars more in long ~~range~~ *term* bonds payable out of canal tolls—after the treaties are approved.

~~Then we recall that t~~*T*he payment figures in the treaties ~~are not final figures but~~ are couched in ambiguous language ~~about~~ to the effect that they can be adjusted to reflect inflation or "other relevant factors." ~~Then t~~*There* ~~is the line that~~ *For example,* Panama shall receive, "a just & equitable return on the nat. resources which it has dedicated to the efficient management, defense . . . etc. of the canal."

~~Then there is i~~ *In* the neutrality treaty ~~*is the line*~~ ~~another blank check sentence~~ *we read,* "Tolls & <u>other</u> <u>charges</u> for transit & ancillary services shall be

* The others are "Canal," March 13, 1978 (not published), and "Canal," April 3, 1978, *Reagan, In His Own Hand*, p. 208.

just, reasonable, equitable & consistent with the principles of international law." I defy anyone to tell us what that means.

Item: We know that Torrijos on his visit to Libya's ~~told the~~ fanatic *leader* Quaddafi, ~~whose help he sought~~ ~~*announced he had come to*~~ ~~seek Quaddafi's help in his "struggle"~~ with the ~~U.S. He~~ openly proclaimed his ties with the Soviet U. in describing his fight "for national liberation."

This becomes an important item in view of a ~~recent S~~ story ~~*dated Sept.*~~ in the highly respected English Intelligence Digest. It reads; "plans are being formulated at the Patrice Lumumba U. in Moscow for the establishment of a subversive network in the U.S. using the illegal immigrants from Mexico. This is linked to developments throughout the Central American area. The U.S. border with Mexico is left open effectively for pol. purposes & plans are being made in Moscow and Havana to train Mexican activists who will, at the right time stimulate nationalist claims to those parts of the U.S. 'stolen from Mexico.' But first the Pan. Canal has to be eased from U.S. control." In Jan. the Digest said: "The Pan. Canal is but one domino in a line & the U.S. Govt. finds itself in a heads & tails losing situation. If Cong. ratifies the treaty there will be tremendous pressure upon Panama because control of the Canal is a prize too rich for either Moscow or Peking to ignore."

This is a time for Congress to take it's time and let the legislative wheels grind slowly but exceedingly fine.

This is RR Thanks for listening.

† Because of a chance the Sen. might vote on the canal soon—maybe this should be taped 1st RR ❖

On January 24, 1978, a Soviet satellite equipped with a nuclear reactor fell apart over Canadian territory.

Spaceships
February 20, 1978

A Russian satellite crashed to earth in the ~~Candian~~ Canadian north woods and the recovered debris was radioactive. But is that all we have to worry about?

I'll be right back.

When an earth orbiting Soviet satellite re-entered the earths atmosphere, disintegrating and scattering wreckage across the frozen northland of our neighbor~~,~~ Canada there was grave concern when it developed the wreckage was giving off radioactive rays. The White House expressed concern and relief that the orbital path was over sparsely populated country. Others speculated about future accidents in which the debris would land in a crowded city and a few voices protested that we should ~~abandon~~ stop cluttering up space with our man made hardware.

Without writing off for one minute the legitimacy of worrying about radioactivity from whatever source, may I suggest we have a far greater worry. What was the function of the space vehicle that crashed to earth? In what way was it serving it's masters in the Kremlin?

The answers to those questions give us far more to worry about than radioactivity from a repeat failure. The N.Y. Times carried the answers in a story that hasn't been ~~widely~~ picked up by much of the media so far. Cosmos 954 was a naval reconnaissance satellite carrying a powerful radar able to scan the worlds oceans locating naval vessels of the U.S. & our allies. Information about location & number of ships could be radio'd to Soviet ground controllers.

We've been pretty smug about our apparently superior sophistication in space technology ~~so these were~~ *but* this piece of hardware shows a very high level of sophistication on the part of the Russians. In fact our own experts didn't believe such a space born radar was possible because of the tremendous power needed to beam radar signals. The Soviets developed a nuclear reactor small enough to be put on a spacecraft—hence the radioactivity *in the snows of Canada.*

I've said before—"while we are trying to avoid a war the Soviets are planning how to win one." It has only been a short time ago that we learned they have been developing "hunter-killer" satellites." Former head of air force intelligence ~~(~~until his retirement *Maj.* Gen. George Keegan * has ~~stated~~ described our strategists as "startled" 2 yrs. ago when the Soviets launched a new version of their killer which could home in and destroy a target in space during a single earth orbit. The Russians are also believed to be developing orbital bombardment vehicles & laser weapons.

Our military leaders fear that destruction of our communications satellites could leave the Pentagon unable to communicate with ships, planes, submarines, ~~&~~ missile silos & even ground forces. Over the past 10 yrs. the Soviets have launched at least 33 satellites as either "killers" or targets for the "killers." There have been ~~su~~ 15 successful operations and 8 of these were with the new manueverable interceptors.

We have embarked on a catch up program which will have us armed with very sophisticated space weaponry sometime in the early '80's. Let's keep our fingers crossed.

This is R.R Thanks for listening ❖

Redwoods

February 20, 1978

Perhaps by the time you ~~read~~ *hear* this the House & Senate will have come to agreement about adding 48,000 acres to the ~~Red Nat.~~ *REDWOOD NAT. PK.* & they should be ashamed of themselves. I'll be right back.

* Major General George J. Keegan Jr. retired from the U.S. Air Force in 1977.

No one can quarrel with the idea of preserving the great Cathedral like groves of Redwood trees which are found only in Calif. And likewise it's hard to be against a Nat. park when one thinks of the exceptional beauty spots preserved now in parks like Yellowstone & Yosemite. Why then do I call the idea of a Nat. Redwood park silly? I think I have an answer.

The L.A. Times in an editorial recently referred to the long struggle that, "led first to the creation of the original 58,000 acre park in 1968 and the subsequent effort to add 48,000 acres to the preserve." I believe the people of the U.S. who are being asked—make that told—to put up millions & millions of dollars for the added acreage plus $40 mil. or more ~~for~~ *on* a job training program for the lumberjacks & others who will be thrown out of work should know first of all there isn't a 58,000 acre Nat. Redwood park.

Back in 1968 when die hard preservationists were going all out for a Nat. park the Fed. govt. discovered that virtually all of the great Superlative Redwoods ~~were~~ *the Cathedral like groves are* already preserved in ~~282 sq. miles~~ *a number of state parks* totaling 282 sq. miles—that is more than 180,000 acres. The only way there could even be a pretense of a Nat. park ~~was to take~~ *would be to include* one of our *already existing* Calif. state parks. The Fed. govt. bought 28,000 *acres* not 58,000 ~~acres~~ and ~~also~~ 16,000 of those acres ~~were~~ *were* either non timber ~~land~~ or cut over land. Only 320 acres consisted of the Superlative trees *plus 10,000 acres of old growth Redwoods similar to the kind used for lumber.*

When I left office *5 yrs. later* nothing had been done to ~~complete the arrangement for incorporating a state~~ *incorporate the state* park into the Nat. holding. The promise of more than 1½ mil. visitors a year as a boost to the local community turned out to be about 35,000 ~~and the opening of 40,000 acres of~~ *nor had the Bureau of Land management opened the 40,000 acres of* commercial type forest ~~(owned by the Fed. govt.) to timber cutting had not been completed.~~ *to timber cutting which had been promised to avoid hardship in the lumber indus.* I dont think it has even now. The State park that was supposed to make ~~a Nat.~~ the Nat. purchase look like a park has almost 6 times as many acres of Superlative trees & ~~as~~ twice as much old growth forest. It only has ¼ the open or cut over land as the Feds bought. *I'm sure this is*

~~The~~ known to Sen. Cranston & Congressman Burton of Calif.* who honcho'd this measure through the 2 houses of Cong. I wonder if it is to all those others who voted "aye"?

The 48,000 acres approved for purchase are not the ancient, giant trees that we have ~~+~~ already preserved in those 282 sq. miles of state park. This purchase is for a so called buffer zone and is ~~run~~ *a* run of the mill ~~Redwood forest~~ mix of Redwoods & Pine trees. ~~W~~ I have no doubt the push will continue to acquire more thousands of acres of timberland to act as a buffer zone for the buffer zone.

* Senator Alan Cranston (D–California, 1969–1993) and Congressman John Lowell Burton (D–California, 1974–1983).

Again I say, "the Calif. save the Redwoods league"—(bless them)—with cooperation not opposition from the lumber companies has *already* saved basically all the Superlative Redwoods without a Nat. park.

This is RR Thanks for listening. ❖

Farm Day

February 20, 1978

† Farmers have been much in the news lately but how many of us know how legitimate their complaints really are? I'll be right back.

†† March 20th is Agriculture day or Farm day which ever you choose. It's an annual event staged by the entire Agri-business combine to make us more knowledgeable about the Am. Farmer & what he means to all of us.

In these decades of continued inflation we've heard the complaint, "Food prices are too high." We should ask, "compared to what?" ~~Fo~~ Food the thing we buy most often has become an easy target for gripes about inflation. And of course the villain is the producer of food—the farmer. But if he's really the villain why is he parading those tractors in protest?* Well maybe because he is caught worse than anyone else in the cost, price squeeze.

Let's take just one crop—in 1976 wheat was selling for $3.33 a bushel. In 1933 it was selling for only 72¢. But ~~in~~ today $3.33 will only buy what 55¢ would buy then and now ~~what is selling for~~ *the price of wheat has dropped to* $2.30 & that's less than it costs to grow it.

The wheat farmer gets ~~about~~ 2½¢ out of the loaf of bread you buy. The wrapper on the loaf costs almost 3¢. If the farmer contributed the wheat free of charge there wouldn't be much of a drop in the price of bread. But of greater significance (and consumer advocates please note) if the price of wheat doubled, the price of bread would only go up 2½¢.
~~3¢.~~

Wheat is just one example. In ~~Japan~~ *France* a ~~consumer~~ *worker* ~~at~~ has to put in almost 2 hours, in Russia 2¼ hours and in Japan 4½ hours to buy 1 lb. of sirloin steak. In America ~~it's~~ *he works* 24 min.

Twenty five years ago 1 out of 7 Americans farmed and ~~they~~ *each farmer* raised food for 16 people. Today ~~it's~~ only 1 out of 22 *are farmers* and each one produces enough *food* for himself & 55 others. In the last 25 yrs. the farmers per man hour rate of production has increased 5.3% a year,~~. That's~~ more than

* Farmers drove tractors in parades to 30 state capitols and Washington, D.C., on December 10, 1977, to protest low farm prices. Farmers also gathered in Washington in January 1978 to meet Congress as it convened. The March 15, 1978, march of farmers occurred after this commentary was written, and the "tractorcade"—tractors converging on Washington from around the country—occurred in February 1979. William Robbins, "Tractors Carry Farmer Protest to Washington and 30 Capitals," *The New York Times,* Dec. 11, 1977, p. 1.

Following are four facsimile drafts of Ronald Reagan's radio addresses, in chronological order. His broadcasts of the finished talks can be heard on the accompanying compact disk.

(Women) (1)

I'm going to talk about a womens movement that is'nt concerned with the sometime's controversy over womens place in the world. I'll be right back.

There is a savagery loose in the world. While we can claim peace on the technical grounds that no nations are in a state of declared war, people are being kidnapped, highjacked, blown up and mowed down by rifle & machine gun fire, innocent people going about their daily work killed simply because they targets of opportunity.

Those doing the killing claim to serve a cause; redress of ancient wrongs, political differences, etc. imbalance and even religious differences. The innocents die on Cyprus, Latin America, Lebanon, Africa & in the North of Ireland.

We are naive indeed if we accept the bloodshed as resulting solely from the local causes proclaimed by the terrorist bands & guerillas. Behind the scenes an evil power, helps provide the weapons, feeds the fires of hatred & intolerance because continued strife brings closer the dream of a communist dominated world. Of course the only killing in the communist world is the official execution of those who dream too much of freedom.

One of the most tragic trouble spots is Northern Ireland where for 7 years neighbor has taken the life of neighbor and done so in the name of God — the same God prayed to by both sides. There is a non sectarian issue to be sure; the argument as to whether Northern Ireland should remain under British rule or become a part of the Irish Republic. But the religious difference is very real and lends an extra special bitterness to the dispute.

Just when you would think the killing had become so commonplace as to be endured something happened a few weeks ago that

Women's March (September 1, 1976)

(2)

resulted in a kind of miracle. ~~Bombs~~ During these 7 yrs. bombs have been exploded in crowded taverns & dept. stores, cold blooded executions have taken place and continual sniping has added to the toll. Then a few weeks ago 3 children of one family were killed by the I.R.A. Ironically killer or killers & victims were on the same side. The children were'nt the targets as far as is known. They just happened to be in the way when the guns talked.

One woman — Aunt to the 3 children spoke to another woman. Then the 2 set out to speak to others. Only days after the funeral a meeting of 2 or 3,000 women took place. They demanded an end to the killing and called on women every where to join them.

It has always been my belief that women brought civilization to the world. Without their influence we males would still be carrying clubs and in recent years we've come pretty close to ~~getting back to those clubs~~ doing that again.

Just days ago 30,000 women from both sides Catholic & Protestant marched through Belfast ~~with~~ voicing one demand; "stop killing our children". In Dublin 20,000 marched in sympathy, smaller groups did so in other Irish towns. ~~They ask their sisters world wide to join them. Stones were~~ ~~women~~ In Belfast stones were hurled at them — by men of course, young men. They kept on marching. Women ~~joined~~ stepped off the side walks to join them. They ask their sisters all over the world to join them, to rally for an end to the killing.

What if it happens? Imagine the men in the Kremlin if they looked down on Russias women marching in the streets demanding ~~an end~~ peace. Why not? Does anyone have a better idea?

Terrorism (November 16, 1976)

Radio: Terrorism

(1)

It's possible that some who led the charge against the CIA, the FBI and police intelligence work in general are having & should have 2nd thoughts. I'll be right back.

In late Sept. on the floor of Cong. a liberal member took the floor denounced the "terrorist bombing in Wash. that took the life of a Chilean foe of that countries present govt. Obviously the victim was to the left in his politics and the natural assumption is that his murderer or murderers were of the opposite persuasion. Other liberal congressmen joined in demanding that the F.B.I. bring the murderers to justice.

On that same Sept. day however F.B.I. director Clarence Kelly was testifying before a committee of Cong. that his agency had reduced the number of domestic security investigations from a routine 21,000 or more a couple of years ago to a grand total at present of 626.

This was the direct result of pressure by liberal policy makers who have been doing their best to dismantle and render ineffective all the agencies whose function & responsibility is our safety. The Attorney General of the U.S. laid down the anti-security guide lines that now restrict the F.B.I. in its work.

Now let me interject right here I don't hold with unwarranted prying by govt. in the lives of any of us. But note that qualifying word "unwarranted". I object when the census bureau which is supposed to count us, busies itself with asking how many bath tubs we own. Government's principle responsibility is to protect us from each other. At what point do we insist so much on privacy that our law enforcing agencies are unable to guard us against todays terrorism?

In recent years we have been subjected to an alarming increase in bombings, arson, hi-jackings and assassination. Last year there were more than 2000 bombings causing 69 deaths. In the last 5 yrs. 43 policemen have been killed in terrorist violence. Anti-Castro Cubans in Miami have been blown to eternity in a number of bombings. A bomb in N.Y. was directed against the Gov. of Puerto Rico, the New World Liberation Front claims credit for bombing the So. African consulate in S.F.

In the face of all this we have forced police in our cities to destroy mil's. of intelligence files on revolutionary groups. The House Internal Security Comm. has been abolished and I've told you about the restraints on the F.B.I. The principle attack has been against FBI agents joining terrorist groups to learn their plans. But a few yrs. ago there was no objection when an F.B.I. agent joined the K.K.K. and identified the murderers of young civil rights activists. Had he been exposed his life would have been forfeit.

Well the F.B.I. estimates there are some 15,000 terrorists in roughly two dozen groups or organizations in this country and they threaten us from the left. The only effective way of dealing with this kind of guerilla viciousness is to infiltrate as heroic agents once infiltrated the Klan.

Do you know if the F.B.I. - the C.I.A. and our local police do this I won't feel for one minute that my constitutional right of privacy has been endangered. This is RR Thanks for listening.

Radio Freedom

The other day I told a group of students that (1)
my wish for them was that they could know
in this land the freedom I had known when I was their age.

I'll be right back.

Sometimes I wonder if we haven't talked freedom, free enterprise etc. so much & so long as abstract theory that people — particularly young people dont just tune us out. Speaking to some students the other day I referred to freedoms lost in this land during my life time. And I got a question — what freedoms? what was I talking about?

It reminded me of a TV play I'd once done in which I played a Soviet Major during the occupation of Budapest. ~~In the~~ the play I turned out to be some thing of a nice fellow and let two Hungarians go with this line, "I never knew what freedom was until I saw you lose yours."

But facing these students I had to search for an answer. This is what I came up with; when I was their age there was no such thing as a drivers license. Your father began teaching you to drive the family car when he thought you were old enough and after you'd driven him crazy asking why weren't you old enough.

You passed your drivers test when he said "yes you can take the car on your date tonite." Believe me he ~~was~~ didn't say that until he was as sure as it's possible to be that you knew how to drive.

Now maybe you'll say that's not a good example; that drivers licenses are a necessity. Are there any fewer accidents today than there were then? Is there a better test of your ability than a parent turning you loose at the wheel of several thousand dollars investment of hard earned money? What about 12 yrs. old farm kids driving tractors on their fathers farm & plowing a field yet?

Well this led to other examples. When I was 14 yrs. old I got a summer job with an outfit that was rebuilding & selling old homes. Before the summer was over I had laid hard wood floor, shingled roof, painted & worked on foundations. And at summers end I had my first years tuition for college in the bank. Can that be done today? No! You'd have to get a govt. license to do just about every kind of work I did. And just as it does with driving, govt. not the fellow who hired you would decide whether you were capable.

In a recent debate with Ralph Nader a distinguished scholar recently threw the obvious example of lack of freedom at Ralph & did so deliberately, sure of the answer he'd get. "What right" he challenged "does govt. have to say you cant ride a motor cycle without a helmet? You aren't endangering anyone but yourself?"

Right on cue came a typical Naderism. "If a helmet less rider splashes himself on the pavement, a govt. subsidized ambulance will pick him up, take him to a govt. subsidized hospital. If he dies he'll be buried in a govt. subsidized cemetery and govt. welfare will begin paying for the support of his widow & orphaned children. Therefore govt. cant let him fall down & go boom. In other words we are all now stamped—"Property of the U.S. Govt. Do Not Fold, bend or mutilate."

This is RR Thanks for listening.

Radio: (Salt Talk) II
Nat. Defense

(1)

Yesterday I talked about violations of the ~~Salt~~ SALT treaty by the Russians and our failure to utter a single protest. I'm going to talk a little more about our Nat. defense. I'll be right back.

A short time back the Los Angeles Herald Examiner Wash. bureau reported on a meeting of the Sen. Armed Services Committee. Sec. of Defense Brown & another Brown, Gen. George Brown chairman of the Joint Chiefs of Staff appeared together before that committee.

Gen. Brown is in his final year as our nation's top mil. commander. Sitting beside the Sec. he made a statement that can only be construed as contradictory to the policies of ~~his commander in chief~~ the present admin. He said: "I worry about the day coming when we are not going to be able to stand up to an aggressor."

In a week of such appearances before congressional committees the Gen. was careful to avoid any hint of disloyalty to his commander in chief but he explained that as his service comes to an end he did not want to be accused later on of acquiescing.

When a Sen. remarked that his warnings marked a great change from some of his past statements the Gen. did not hedge in his reply. He said that, "uppermost in his mind was the fact that this would be the last time he would submit a posture statement to Congress. "I feel it would be wrong," he said, "if somebody 5 years from now asked, 'Where was George Brown during all of this?' and looked up the record and I had said, 'Don't worry it's all right.'"

Telling the Senators the $126 bil. defense budget was too small he said it should have contained funds for the B-1 bomber, the M X mobile Land Based missile, new infantry combat vehicles and a number of 2 other programs.

Aware of the Defense Sec. beside him he said "I don't think he is complacent". He did not ask for approval of the present budget but said the time necessary to repair the current imbalance with the Sov. U. made a "quick fix" impossible. And he made it clear that the risk to our security—already high, would increase.

He made it clear that Congress had to share in the blame for our precarious position. "Each year", he said, "I have been a party to this action. We've come to Congress with a reduced program only to have an average of 5½ billion dollars taken out of it every year".

When a General who has been as loyal to his civilian superiors as Gen. Brown has been speaks so forthrightly of our danger we'd better listen. It doesn't cheer me up one bit to have a defense dept. spokesman say the differences between the Gen. & the Sec. were only "of degree", that they were on good terms. He added, "the Gen is representing the uniformed mil. & takes a slightly more worried position". If he's worried it's time for us to worry.

This is RR Thanks for listening.

double the rate of productivity for all other industr~~y~~*ies.* ~~which has averaged only 2.4% in this quarter of a century.~~ If ~~the rest of Am. industry~~ *non-farm production* had matched the farmers increase ~~in productivity~~ there would be no inflation. ~~today.~~

~~But d~~During these 25 yrs. the ~~farmers~~ *cost of food* as a percentage of our after tax income ~~fell~~ *has fallen* more than 30%. It now only takes 14.8% of ~~the average family inc~~ ~~*after tax*~~ *our* inc. after taxes to put food on the table. *And only about 5½ of that 14.8% goes to the farmer.* We eat better for less money than any other people on earth. And yet a congressman about a year or so ago asked ~~a man~~, "when are we going to see dollar a pound steak again?" The man *he had questioned* replied "Mr. Congressman 20 yrs. ago your salary was $12,500 a year now it's $42,500 & ~~going~~ *on it's way* to $50,000 or more. We'll see dollar a pound steak *again* when we see $12,500 a yr. Congressmen again."

The farmer is receiving fewer dollars than he did a year ago and the ~~$~~ *dollars* buy less but he's paying more for every thing he buys. On Ag-day—March 20th say a prayer for the American farmer & a thank you.

This is RR Thanks for listening.

† Make sure this one goes on air prior to March 20. RR

†† Send copy to Ernie Marshal in Kansas City—I think we have his address. RR ❖

Steel

February 20, 1978

Everyone who ever lived through the great depression must have felt a spinal chill when the announcements came of layoffs & shutdowns in the steel industry. I'll be right back.

There are charges of dumping of steel on the U.S. mkt. by Japan. Dumping is the term used to describe selling at below cost with the Japanese govt. making up the loss to the Japanese steel companies. Appeals were made to our govt. to take retaliatory action.

Possibly there was some dumping—I dont know, but the problem of the *U.S.* steel industry is a little more complicated than that. For example in 1976 our labor costs averaged $12.22 an hour compared to Japans $6.31. Since then Steel *in our country* has agreed to a wage contract that will raise the hourly pay 30% over the next 3 yrs. In 1977 steelworkers pay averaged $12.75 an hour compared to ~~all~~ the workers in all manufacturing getting $7.79.

But before we jump all over labor as the sole villain let's look at some other factors in steels dismal decline. In 1955 we produced 39% of the worlds steel. By 1976 that was down to 17%. That drop was almost directly proportionate to the decline in capital investment in American industry which means reduced need for steel. Profits in steel went from 4.6¢ on each dollar of sales in 1975 to 1.4¢ in the first half of '77.

The truth is Japan and some of our other competitors in the world mkt. have modernized plant & equipment and have thus increased their rate of production per man-hour. Not only have low profit rates kept us from ~~the~~ needed modernizing so has govt. emphasis on a lot of nonproductive regulations which ate up capital without increasing productivity. OSHA descended on the industry with 67 different rules ranging from ladder design to noise prevention. The Enviromental Protection Agency has added costs that over the next few years will be 3 times as much as the industrys normal profit margin. A host of other agencies up to & including the White House have ~~adde~~ *added* to the hamstringing.

In all these harassments the steel union has been silent but maybe that will change. Former Pres. of the Steelworkers has publicly stated, "Does stepping up the efficiency of each worker mean work speedups, job eliminations? Hardly. It does mean cutting down on excessive absenteeism, tardiness, turnover & overtime. Lets put our brainpower to work to create more efficient manufacturing processes, & better equipment. But then lets use them. Labor has always sought more wages & benefits. But Labor also knows that to obtain more, we must produce more."

If this could signal an alliance between labor & management in opposition to ~~gov~~ ~~unne~~ *unneccessary* govt. regulation & in favor of more realistic tax policies plus a real effort to increase per man hour productivity American steel could take care of itself in the world mkt.

This is RR Thanks for listening. ❖

Labor

February 20, 1978

† I'm a life time member of an AFL-CIO union and have always upheld the right of workers to organize but I cannot support the so called Labor reform bill ~~sent~~ *now* before the Congress. I'll be right back.

On Jan. 25th the Senate Human Resources Committee reported out & sent to the floor of the Senate the Labor Reform Bill which is a high priority item on Organized labors agenda. The Pres. has pledged to Mr. Meany * & company his support of this bill.

While called a labor reform bill it is in fact a measure wherein govt. will give labor special advantages in ~~their~~ *it's* effort to recruit members & to organize workers in non-union plants. Management will be given no comparable rights.

The AFL-CIO has been declining in membership in recent years and ~~is~~

* George Meany was president of the AFL-CIO from 1955 to 1979.

smaller b by ~~*has given* 500,000 FEWER members in *than it had* just the *it had*~~ last year. It's ironic that the Heirarchy of ~~*it had*~~ labor seeks this govt. recruiting help because just possibly their partnership with govt. may be ~~at~~ the ~~root of~~ cause of their shrinking membership.

Back at the time of the merger the late Walter Reuther, C.I.O. leader, influenced the ~~new *each* ≠~~ leadership of *the* newly formed alliance to get things from govt. which heretofore labor had tried to win *FROM MANAGEMENT* at the bargaining table. Maybe their success has made them less necessary to workers now. ~~and p~~*P*olls suggest rank & file members find the leadership too powerful & too involved in politics. Whatever the reason there is a growing desire on the part of many workers both in & out of unions to have freedom to choose.

Faced with losing their power the Union Chieftans have come up with Senate bill 1883 & House Resolution 8410 which they call mere technical amendments but which are in reality very significant changes in the Nat. Labor Relations Act. An enlarged Nat. Labor Relations Board will undoubtedly have more power and a definite pro-labor, anti-management bias.

Today ~~the~~ only 1 out of 5 workers is in a ~~u~~*U*nion & Unions have been losing more than half the elections conducted under ~~Union~~ *Govt.* supervision even though 80% of them aren't contested by management.

Perhaps todays Union bosses should go back & read again the words of the great labor statesman who created the Am. Fed. of Labor instead of trying to get govt. into a partnership to force compulsory union membership on workers who dont want it. Samuel Gompers in his last speech to a labor convention said; "There may be here & there a worker who does not join a union of labor. That is his right no matter how wrong we think he may be. It is his legal right & no one can dare question his legal exercise of that right." * Gompers said over & over again there could be no real strength in a union unless the members had freely chosen to join out of personal conviction.

It will be a sad day for the working men & women of America if the "Labor Reform Act" is passed by Cong. & signed into law. Only "we the people" can prevent that from happening.

This is RR Thanks for listening.

† This one should go fairly early in the taping schedule. And a copy should be sent to the writer of the attached letter. RR ❖

Reagan expresses the view here that the outcome of excessive government spending was inflation, reduced investment in the private sector, and, ultimately, recession. During the 1980 campaign he muted his prediction of "a gigantic economic bellyache," but this essay reveals that he did not think restoring the vitality of the U.S. economy would be easy.

* Quoted in Florence Calvert Thorne, *Samuel Gompers–American Statesman* (New York: Philosophical Library, 1957), p. 24, from a February 1919 report in the *American Federationist* on Gompers' speech before the Council of Foreign Relations, December 10, 1918.

Economy
February 20, 1978

We have been told the Fed budget will be $500 Bil. plus, with a built in bud. deficit of $60 Bil. plus. We have not been told the cost & possible deficit of non-budget programs. I'll be right back.

The Fed. budget for the fiscal year beginning next October first will top a half a trillion dollars which is some 60 bil. more than revenues will bring in. That isn't the entire story. There have come to be,—in recent years, a number of programs outside the budget and they too have deficits. To put it briefly govt. spending continues to accelerate, eating up scarce capital resources and fueling the fires of inflation plus recession. It is impossible not to believe that ahead lies a gigantic ec. bellyache.

Writing of this one economist Hans F. Sennholz* says, "our ec. situation is very precarious. World trade & commerce which are important pillars of the working & living conditions of all people, are held together by a thin dollar wrapper that may tear at any time. If it should burst because it is getting thinner with every turn of the U.S. printing presses, the world may fall into an abyss of a depression, deeper & longer than the Great Depression. And the U.S. dollar would suffer losses in purchasing power at unprecedented rates."

I know it's hard for many of us who knew the dollar when it could be turned in for gold or silver to think of that familiar green bill as so ailing & anemic. But since 1933 when the govt. took our gold from us and replaced it with paper unredeemable in gold we've had printing press money and history records no nation ~~that~~ as ever making imitation money work over a long period of time. The temptation to speed up the presses without considering the consequences is too much ~~of~~ for most politicians to resist.

Sennholz very simply states that the present admin. has in this it's first year planted the seeds for a serious recession. He cites the labor-law revisions & minimum wage; the new Soc. Security tax increase and the taxes & tight controls on the energy industry plus the acceleration of govt. spending. "Many economists" he says, "are convinced that the international paper-dollar standard is destined to lead to worldwide hyper-inflation and ec. disintegration." And he adds "The coming year may bring us one year closer to the catastrophe."

He also says this does not have to be. *HE MEANS WE* ~~We~~ are still the masters of our ~~f~~ own destiny. If you & I will insist that morality itself dictates we must as a nation live within our means. The integrity of the dollar can be restored if we'll cut through the Wash. doubletalk & demand that the budget be balanced. Stop & think for a minute—the proposed budget is more than 500 bil. & the ~~deficit~~ deficit about 60 bil. Can anyone honestly believe that we cant

* Hans F. Sennholz is a monetary economist who has written widely; he was president of the Foundation for Economic Education, Irvington-on-Hudson, New York, from 1992 to 1997.

find 12% of fat in that Fed. budget? The govt. spenders usually counterattack by saying, "which program would you eliminate?" What if we reply, "dont eliminate any (although there are plenty we can do without) just make every dept. every bureau, agency & program reduce it's expenditures by 12%.

~~Senhol Sennholz says~~ *Let me close with a few more words from Sennholz.*— "If Americans were to renew their faith in individual freedom & self reliance, in morality rather than politics, we could look forward with unbounded hope. Let us begin to be today what we hope to be tomorrow."

This is RR Thanks for listening. ❖

On October 5, 1977, President Jimmy Carter signed two United Nations covenants on human rights that the UN General Assembly had adopted in 1966 but that previous American presidents had decided not to sign.

Treaties
February 20, 1978

When & if the Sen. finally disposes of the Panama Canal treaties ~~the~~ it will be confronted by an equally thorny & unexplainable treaty ratification request.

I'll be right back.

"A mans home is his castle." That is a time worn truism, cliché, trite saying or whatever else you want to call it. But it was born of a right we all have & take for granted now with little thought of how it came to be.

When our Founding Fathers—(that little band of men whose like the world has seldom seen)—gathered to draw up the Const. the right of an individual to own property was very much on their minds. In most of the world prior to that time the rulers, be they King, Emperor or tribal Chieftan could award someone title to property & could also cancel the title. The framers of our Const. had seen the colonists homes seized on the whim of Geo. the III.* They had decided this must no longer happen. So the 5th amendment to our Const. reads, "No person shall be deprived of life, liberty or property without due process of law; <u>nor shall private property be taken</u> for pub. use without just compensation."

The American worker with his house & lot, the farmer plowing his own ground, the shopkeeper—we have all accepted this as the very basis of our freedom. And I'm afraid we've forgotten it was not always this way. Now of course we've become aware that under a different title rulers in large parts of the world have returned to the age old policy of land belonging only to the govt. It is called Marxism.

For a great many years the United Nations has had before it two covenants, the Covenant on Civil & Pol. rights & the U.N. Covenant on Ec. Social and Cultural Rights." And both specificaly omit the right to own property or to be

* George III, King of Great Britain and Ireland, 1760–1820.

protected from ~~a~~ arbitrary seizure without compensation. Ownership of property is not,—according to the covenants—a basic human right.

Presidents Truman, Eisenhower, Kennedy, Johnson, Nixon & Ford steadfastly refused to sign these covenants because of this omission which is so contrary to American tradition. In 1966 there was an effort made to amend the covenants to include property ownership as a human right. It was voted down. Obviously the socialist & communist countries could not accept such an affront to their totalitarianism. Right now the biggest block to normalizing relations with Castros Cuba is his seizure of Am. owned property without compensation.

What is apparently little known by the American people is that Pres. Carter has signed both of these U.N. covenants which nullify in effect the inalienable right of an individual to own property—if they are ratified by the U.S. Sen. U.N. treaties become the law of the land superceding all other laws.

We'd all better be ready to write our Senators when these treaties are submitted ~~to the Sen.~~ *for ratification.*

This is RR ~~I'll~~ Thanks for listening. ❖

Four months after this commentary was taped, the U.S. Supreme Court upheld the constitutionality of special admissions programs at colleges, but also declared that Allan P. Bakke, who had challenged one such program, must be admitted to the University of California at Davis School of Medicine.

Bakke

February 20, 1978

In our laudable effort to right ~~some of~~ the wrongs resulting from years of bigotry & discrimination we sometimes find ourselves committing ~~a~~ *another* wrong.

I'll be right back.

There is a case presently on appeal before the Supreme Court known nationwide as the "Bakke case." Most of you ~~are~~ have heard of it I'm sure and probably know something of what it's about. It has caused controversy and even resulted in demonstrations on some of our campuses. Not the violent hassles we had too much of back in the '60s but demonstrations nonetheless.

Because the issue is one of controversy arousing in some ~~a~~ anger at the name "Bakke" as if he is somehow a bigot working against the effort to redress ancient wrongs I thought I'd provide some information that isn't generally known.

~~We know t~~*T*here was a time when various professional schools were virtually out of ~~bonds~~ *bounds* for the economically disadvantaged & this of course included many of our minorities. It was not necessarily a reflection of prejudice, it was just that entrance standards were so high a great many ~~from~~ *young* people from poor backgrounds couldn't meet those ~~educational standards.~~ *requirements*. In view of this there have been efforts to see that each entering class includes a certain percentage of those who were heretofore ≠ excluded.

At the U. of Calif. medical school in Davis this effort resulted in what can only be called a quota system even though quota is a very unpopular term. At any rate 16 entrants were permitted each year in the school of medicine whose scores were below the normal requirement.

Allan Bakke is a Vietnam veteran who first applied at Davis in 1973. He is now suing the U. of Calif. on the grounds that his const. rights were violated. ~~The whole story~~ This is the case now on appeal before the U.S. Supreme Court.

The whole story however makes it pretty evident that Mr. Bakke is not an impulsive troublemaker or sorehead. Aspiring medical students take 4 preliminary tests estimating their verbal skills quantitative skills, scientific skills & general information.

In 1973 the average grades in those 4 tests for the regularly accepted applicants were 81, 76, 83 & 69. The special entrants scored 46, 24, 35 & 33. Bakke scored 96, 94, 97 & 72. He waited a year without complaint & tried again in 1974. The average this time was 69, 67, 82 & 72. For the quota students the average was 34, 30, 37 & 18. Bakke scored 96, 94, 97 & 72 the exact same high marks he had made in 1973. But again he was passed by.

The cumulative total for the regular entrants was 309 & the special group 138 in 1973. Bakkes total was 359. In 1974 the accepted groups scored respectively 290 & 119. Again Bakke scored 359. It was then—after two attempts that he filed the suit now pending before the court.

I believe it is right that we have a program to ensure equal opportunity for those aspiring to the professions. But surely we can come up with something that dosen't result in the kind of injustice done to Alan Bakke.

This is RR Thanks for listening. ❖

Salt Talks II
March 13, 1978

Yesterday I talked about violations of the ~~Salt~~ *SALT* treaty by the Russians and our failure to utter a single protest. I'm going to talk a little more about our Nat. defense. I'll be right back.

A short time back the Los Angeles Herald Examiner Wash. bureau reported on a meeting of the Sen. Armed Services Committee. Sec. of Defense Brown & another Brown, Gen. George Brown chairman of the Joint Chiefs of Staff appeared together before that committee.*

* Secretary Harold Brown and General George S. Brown appeared before the Senate Armed Services Committee on February 7, 1978.

Gen. Brown is in his final year as our nations top mil. commander. Sitting beside the Sec. he made a statement that can only be construed as contradictory to the policies of ~~his commander in chief &~~ the present admin. He said: "I worry about the day coming when we are not going to be able to stand up to an aggressor."

In a week of such appearances before congressional committees the Gen. was careful to avoid any hint of disloyalty to his commander in chief but he explained that as his service comes to an end he did not want to be accused later on of acquiescing.

When a Sen. remarked that his warnings marked a great change from some of his past statements the Gen. did not hedge in his reply. He said that, "uppermost in his mind was the fact that this would be the last time he would submit a posture statement to Congress. "I feel it would be wrong," he said, "if somebody 5 years from now asked, 'Where was George Brown during all of this?' and looked up the record and I had said, 'Dont worry it's all right.' "

Telling the Senators the $126 bil. defense budget was too small he said it should have contained funds for the B-1 bomber, the MX mobile Land Based missile, new infantry combat vehicles and a number of other programs.

Aware of the Defense Sec. beside him he said "I dont think he is complacent." He did not ask for approval of the present budget but said the time necessary to repair the current imbalance with the Sov. U. made a "quick fix" impossible. And he made it clear that the risk to our security—already high, would increase.

He made it clear that Congress had to share in the blame for our precarious position. "Each year," he said, "I have been a party to this action. We've come to Congress with a reduced program only to have an average of 5½ billion dollars taken out of it every year."

When a General who has been as loyal to his civilian superiors as Gen. Brown has been speaks so forthrightly of our danger we'd better listen. It dosen't cheer me up one bit to have a defense dept. spokesman say the differences between the Gen. & the Sec. were only "of degree," that they were on good terms. He added, "the Gen is representing the uniformed mil. & takes a slightly more worried position." If he's worried it's time for us to worry.

This is RR Thanks for listening. ❖

Budget
March 13, 1978

In presenting the new Fed. budget of more than $500 bil. the President described it as "lean & tight." That's a little hard to digest.

I'll be right back.

Is it possible that Fed. spending or for that matter all govt. spending has grown so great that we've become numbed and cant envision the huge figures—bils. trillions even? For example ~~do~~ can we ~~even~~ envision the enormity ~~if~~ of half a trillion dollars ~~if~~ Wash. will spend in 1 year even if we picture it this way—if 2000 yrs. ago we had started spending $700,000 a day every day, we'd just now be at the point of having spent ~~a half a trillion~~ what our govt. will spend in 1 yr.

Maybe it's impossible for us to picture spending $700,000 a day even once let alone 730,000 consecutive days. It should shock us I know to think of our govt. spending $57 mil. an hour round the clock every day including Sundays & holidays. That's $1.37 bil. a day. If it doesn't then try this on; 1929 (prior to the crash) wasn't a bad year as far as governmental services were concerned. I dont recall anyone complaining because the Fed. govt. wasn't telling us how to run our lives. The total Fed. budget was $2.6 bil. ~~i~~In ~~these~~ *the* 50 yrs. *from then* until next years budget we've increased our annual spending by 20,000% while population has only increased 80%. Spending has increased 250 times as fast as population.

And dont let anyone tell you the men in uniform are to blame. Nat. security is supposed to be the primary responsibility of the Nat. govt. Just 10 yrs. ago almost half the Fed. budget 43.6% was for defense now it's only ¼. Today a full half or more of the budget is for social welfare programs of all kinds.

Today we have more people dependent on govt. than we have working & earning in the pvt. sector to support themselves, their families & the govt. The Brookings Inst.* put's those dependent on tax dollars for their year round living at 81.3 mil. people. Govt's. only source of revenue ~~is the~~ *consists of* 70.2 mil *citizens* on pvt. payrolls.

I've thrown a lot of figures at you but I still dont think I've described or made understandable how much $500 bil. is so one last try—that is ~~1406~~ roughly $2~~5~~300 a year for every man, woman, child & baby in America. If you are part of the average family—2 adults, 2 children—a family of 4, your share of the Fed. bud. for the coming year is $9200 and we haven't even mentioned state & local govts. *You've got a right to feel sorry for yourself. Fed employees average $4000 a year more money than you make.*

It took the U.S. 173 yrs. until 1962 to hit the 1st $100 Bil. bud. We added the 2nd 100 bil. in just 9 yrs., 4 more yrs. to add the 3rd, 2 yrs. to add the 4th & 1 yr. to make it ~~4~~ that ~~"tight lean" 5th fifth~~ 5th ~~bil.~~ 100 bil. for the, "tight lean" half a trillion dollar bud. Some of you ~~*who*~~ have children *who* wont even have gotten rid of their braces by the time ~~it~~ it's a full trillion dollars.

Isn't it time we borrowed an expression from our good Americans of latin descent—"Ya Basta"—we've had it.

This is RR Thanks for listening.

* The Brookings Institution, a liberal Washington, D.C., think tank.

Mineral King
March 13, 1978

Are we justified in a suspicion that the Fed. govt. has quietly & without ~~public~~ notice to the people embarked on a policy of land ~~holding~~ hoarding & perhaps even land grabbing? I'll be right back.

Thirteen years ago—in 1965—the U.S. Forest Service under a mandate from Congress & at the direction of Pres. Johnson initiated an action to develop the recreational potential of a Calif. beauty spot known as Mineral King* ~~with~~ *WHICH ADJOINS SEQUOIA NAT. PARK*. This decision was not in response to any request or proposal by private interests. The govt's. position was that development of this ~~area~~ *PORTION OF THE NAT. FOREST* was badly needed & in the public interest.

In reply to the recreational *development* prospectus issued by the U.S. Forest service 7 potential developers submitted proposals. ~~Let me point out that Mineral King is a valley in *on* the Nat. Forest area *land* climbing up to the boundaries of the Sequoia Nat. park.~~ Walt Disney productions was chosen from among the 7 applicants and began developing a plan for ~~a~~ year round recreational use of the ~~valley~~ *area*.

There was nothing new in the govt's. decision to open public land in this manner. ~~Indeed~~ Working partnerships between govt. & private enterprise ~~for recreational facilities~~ have created many of the nations most popular recreational facilities. ~~on public land.~~

As I said, Pres. Johnson issued the directive for the Mineral King development. It was subsequently approved by the ~~next 2 Presidents. My predecessor as Gov. of Calif & I endorsed it.~~ *2 PRESIDENTS WHO FOLLOWED HIM. The Gov. of Calif. who preceded me endorsed it and so did I.* ~~t~~The Calif. legislature ~~did likewise~~ *approved it* & so did the Board of Supervisors of the county in which the area is located.

In good faith the planners at Disney went forward with a variety of plans for govt. approval involving much creative effort & great expense. But suddenly a hue & cry was raised by what can only be described as a very small group of ardent preservationists opposed to the development. Their abuse was directed at Disney Productions as if the whole thing had been originated by the company.

This special interest group has to be aware that there are 50 mil. acres ~~(virtually half of Calif.) is public lands~~ *of public land in Calif.* That is virtually half the entire state. Within a 100 mile radius of Mineral King there are over 2½ mil. acres of classified wilderness or roadless areas—Nat. parks~~,~~ & monuments ~~& wilderness areas~~ for nature lovers.

* Mineral King is a canyon of approximately 15,000 acres at the southern end of the Sequoia and Kings Canyon national parks.

Mineral King would be a ski & winter sports development. Only 15,000 acres *of Pub. land* in all of Calif. is designated for this purpose. Mineral King is the only area in ~~the~~ S. Calif. offering a ~~potential~~ suitable site and there are 1 mil. skiers in So. Calif. It would retain it's natural beauty and give 600 permanent jobs in an economically disadvantaged area.

In late Jan. the White House asked the Congress to support a bill including ~~the~~ Mineral King in the Sequoia Nat. park.* This would end the 13 yrs. planning and cancel the development of a high quality year round public winter & summer recreational facility. A bank, one of the foremost sources of finance for winter recreational developments has thrown up it's hands & announced it will no longer advance money for such projects. It says the probability that bureaucratic red tape will ~~even prevent them from~~ *prevent them* FROM *ever* becoming reality is too great. Is public land really for the public or for an elite few who want to keep it for their own use?

This is RR Thanks for listening. ❖

Local Control I
March 13, 1978

Can you think of anyone who would be more careful about spending your money than you are? That's why the closer the taxpayer is to the spending the more he'll get for his money. I'll be right back.

The whole principle behind our system of autonomous local govt's., sovereign states and finally a Fed. govt. with limited powers is the preservation of individual freedom by keeping as much govt. as possible ~~close~~ as close to the people as possible.

With few exceptions money spent by local govt. ~~is~~ has less waste & administrative overhead than we find at the state level and less ~~of~~ at the state level than we find in the Fed. behemoth. For one thing people are more aware of local spending, better able to see the result and more likely to hold their local officials responsible. After all they live in the same community. I'm willing to admit N.Y. City might be an exception.

The U.S. Statistical Abstract reveals some pretty convincing evidence to support the statements I've just made. For every elected official at the local level there are 19 full time govt. employees. At the state level there are 290 burocrats for each elected officer and in our National govt. the ratio jumps to 5,800 burocrats for every elected official. Dividing 19 into 5800 we can see that we have about 300 times more ~~account~~ *voter* control over bureaucrats spending at the local level than we do at the Fed. level. And make no mistake about it actual spending for the most part is done by those permanent em-

* Legislation passed in October 1978 took control away from the United States Forest Service and made Mineral King part of Sequoia National Park.

ployees of govt. Our only control over them is by way of holding our elected representatives accountable and registering our approval or disapproval at the polls—come election day.

Let's look at one example—education. ~~Som~~ About 1950 funding of grade schools & high schools began to shift to the state with healthy increases also in Fed. grants. Local school districts ~~28 years ago~~ *in 1950* were putting up 66% of the money with state & Fed. making up the other 34%. By 1976—the last year for which we have the figures local govt. was not ~~paying~~ *carrying* ⅔ of the load—it wasn't even paying half. State & Fed. govts. paid 52% of school costs & local govt. paid 48%.

At first glance you might say that's great for the local community—until you realize we ~~are still~~ *the same* old taxpayers are putting up the entire 100%—just funneling it through different tax collectors *and the higher you go in govt. the greater the overhead.* Now what has this change meant to us? Well for one thing our locally elected school boards dont have as much to say about content of textbooks, curriculum & methods of teaching as they *once* did. If we have any complaints we'll have to track down some faceless burocrats at the state or national level.

Then there is the practical matter of cost. Since 1950 the total cost ~~of primary *secondary* ed.~~ has gone from $6 bil to $70 bil. Ah! But you say there has been an increase in the number of students plus inflation. True. But in constant dollars adjusted for inflation the per-student cost is 3 times what it was before we started getting so much state & Fed. help.

I'll tell you more about this on the next broadcast.

This is RR Thanks for listening. ❖

Local Control II

March 13, 1978

On the last broadcast I pointed out that school spending had skyrocketed since 1950 when the real increase in Fed. & State funding of ed. began. I'll be right back.

Adjusting dollars for inflation the actual cost ~~of~~ of educating public school students *since 1950* went from $504 per pupil *then* to $1400 *IN 1976*. That is an increase in real dollars of 180%. If you dont adjust for inflation the increase is around 1000%.

Part of the reason for this has been a great growth in the educational burocracy. In 1950 there was one full time school employee for every 19 students. Today it is one for nine. The greatest increase has been in non-teaching, mainly administrative personne~~ll~~*l*. For teachers alone the ratio went from 1 to 28 in 1950 to 1 teacher for 21 pupils in '76. ~~In other w~~ To sum it up as we transferred much of educational funding to the State & Fed. level we tripled the cost per student & doubled the burocracy.

Now of course we would have no complaint if educational quality had risen to match the increase in cost & staff. Unfortunately the reverse is true. We were on a rise in educational performance from back in the '30's ~~until~~ (when we *really* began to keep statistics until ~~about 1960~~ *the early '60's.* <u>Fed</u> aid actually began about 1962, ~~and~~ so did Fed. control over ed. and so did the decline in educational quality, as measured by the Scholastic Aptitude Tests. ~~This~~

This was not the only indicator. There are state educational testing programs. In one state the score changed from a 10 yr. rise of about 13½% ~~to~~ in reading & 16 in math. to a *A 10 YR. DROP OF* 13% ~~drop~~ in reading & *an* 18% drop in ~~readin~~ *math.* ~~the following 10 yrs. A number~~ *Dozens* of other states have recorded similar declines—all coinciding with the creation of the U.S. office of ed. & the rise of state ed. burocracy.

The state with the lowest spending per student and the lowest percentage of personal income devoted to ed.—New Hampshire—has the highest average score in Scholastic Aptitude tests. ~~New~~

New Hampshire also has the lowest percentage of state aid to local schools (16%) which means the least interference with local control. ~~Mass. has the highest per pupil spending. The average for the nation.~~ The national average of state aid to schools is more than double that of New Hampshire—39%. By contrast Mass. has the highest per student cost and the highest percent of personal inc. devoted to ed. In scholastic Aptitude Tests it ranks below the Nat. average.

The only thing you can say for increased state & Fed. aid to ed. is that it will result in higher costs, ~~and~~ more educational employees & less supervision by the taxpayers.

The Nat. Ed. Assn. has long lobbied for a U.S. Dept. of Ed. & massive increases in Fed. aid. As a cand. the Pres. told the N.E.A. convention he would strive for a separate dept. of ed. and a $20 bil. increase in Fed. spending for ed. He said he believed the Fed. govt. should provide ⅓ of the cost of ed. This would ~~lower~~ *reduce* local ~~spending~~ funding to less than 20% which would virtually eliminate local control of ed.

This is RR Thanks for listening. ❖

Crime
April 3, 1978

Here is another one of those impossible ~~to~~ to believe *BUT TRUE* stories that explain why crime continues to be a major problem in our land. I'll be right back.

Several weeks ago the press routinely carried a story about a U.S. Supreme Court decision that goes a long way toward explaining why the "bad guys" just may be winning in the war on crime.

Out in Rolla Mo. [Montana] a state patrolman saw an unkempt, unshaven stranger with no luggage of any kind trying to hitchhike his way west on an interstate highway. Patrolman Herbert J. Hoffman went on his way ~~without~~ *without* pausing. But when he saw the same man an hour later this time 3 miles away trying to hitch a ride south on a local highway he became suspicious enough to stop and ask to see the man's identification.

While the hitchhiker Thomas Carl Jones sat in the patrol car Hoffman made a radio check and learned that Jones was wanted in Pennsylvania for the theft of a revolver. ~~There was more.~~ Pennsylvania authorities also wanted him for questioning in the bludgeon murder of his aunt. (He was later charged with that crime) Hoffman had already taken possession of a .38 caliber revolver so all in all it looked like a good bit of police work had resulted from his ~~suspi~~ alertness & suspicion of the hitchhiker.

A Pennsylvania court refused to allow the gun or statements Jones had made to patrolman Hoffman to be introduced as evidence. The judge said the patrolman didn't have "probable cause" to suspect Jones of criminal activity. He further ruled that even though ~~he~~ *Jones* had only been detained & had talked voluntarily to Hoffman, the patrolmans uniformed presence constituted authority & force.

The Dist. Attorney said that the gun & the voluntary statements ~~of~~ made by Jones to Hoffman had been the critical evidence he was counting on. The Judges decision was upheld by the Pennsylvania Supreme Court. ~~and~~ ~~t~~*T*he U.S. Sup. Ct. refused to review the case. According to the Dist. Attorney it is highly unlikely that Jones will be prosecuted for the murder of his aunt.

This is another one of those "exclusionary rule" cases. An arresting officer is held to be in technical violation of someones constitutional rights therefore no evidence found by him can be used ~~as evidence~~ *in court.* It is so contrary to common sense that officers have complained if they stopped a man for running a red light & found a bleeding baby in the rear seat they could *still* only charge the man with ~~runn~~ a traffic violation.

We tried to get a solution to this "exclusionary rule" which is not a ~~law or statute but simply case law based on a judicial ruling in Calif.~~ in Calif. while I was Gov. but the trial lawyers assn. and a permissive legis. refused to act. ~~The~~

~~≠ The "exclusionary rule" is not a law it is merely a what is called, "case law." It is based on a judicial ruling.~~ ~~We tried to solve this problem in Calif. while I was Gov. but couldent~~ We proposed that in cases of technical violations by a law enforcement officer the citizen be allowed to sue the ~~govt~~ governmental body employing the officer at the govt's. expense but that any evidence ~~be~~ found by the officer be admissable in court. Not perfect, but it would give ~~producti~~ *protection* to the citizen unjustly hassled by law enforcement at the same time it kept our courts from turning *the* sometimes obviously guilty back out on the streets.

Personally I think patrolman Hoffman of Mo. did exactly what he should have done.

This is RR Thanks for listening. ❖

Although the Carter Administration objected to the tax deductibility of business meals, they remained fully deductible until 1986.

Three Martini Lunch
April 3, 1978

A member of the 4th estate has commented in print about the Internal Revenues campaign against the 3 martini lunch. ~~It~~ *He* warrants quoting. I'll be right back.

~~In the last campaign~~ The Admin. in Wash. is pretty upset about the tax deductibility of the business lunch. I dont know how much additional revenue if any the govt. would get by making such luncheons non-deductible. I suspect there wouldn't be any; not after you figure the decline in restaurant business and the possible layoff of waiters & bartenders.

But in touting their case the tax collectors ~~bled~~ *bleed & weep* for the working man who cant deduct his bologna sandwich. This has led a newspaper man to do an article that appeared in the ~~With~~ Wichita Eagle & Beacon and which was mailed to me by a reader of that paper. I thought you'd be interested in what he had to say.

Identifying himself as a working man *HIMSELF* he said he really hadn't been too worked up about the unfairness of allowing a deduction for the 3 martini lunch & not the bologna sandwich. ~~He says~~ *It seems* he rarely eats a bologna sandwich. He's, "partial to pastrami & corned beef with an occasional ham & swiss cheese for a change of pace."

Still he says, "to get a tax deduction out of the govt. you have to start by getting the camel's nose—in this case the bologna sandwich—under the tent." Once the working mans bologna sandwich becomes deductible, it is a cinch that in a few years Cong. will amend the law to let working men deduct pastrami, corned beef & probably even grilled cheese."

But then our philosopher becomes realistic and recognizes the govt. isn't really interested in creating a tax deduction for the working man—it just wants to eliminate the deduction for business lunches whether they go to 3 martinis or not. He points out that since 3 martinis have about the same effect as a hit on the head with a hammer the 3 martini drinker probably couldn't care less whether they are deductible or not.

Then he gets down to the real nitty gritty; tax deductions are created to achieve a desired result~~;~~. ~~a~~*A* deduction for interest on mortgages encourages home building etc. He says tax reform always fails because the reformers always want to do away with deductions and ~~everyone who has a deduction~~ *the only deduction the taxpayer* wants eliminated is the one his neighbor has ~~& which he's denied.~~ *which he cant have.* Therefore he proposes that govt. increase *the number of* deductions. We all love them so much we probably wouldn't even notice that the tax rate had increased to make up for the lost revenue. We'd be having to much fun bragging about the ~~de~~ deductions we were taking. There could even be a social gain. Sec. of H.E.W. Califano * could quit jaw boning against smokers & give a tax deduction instead for quitting the habit.

Suggesting that maybe Congress isn't ready for such advanced thinking ~~he~~ *our writer* comes back to the bologna sandwich and says we should mobilize the pol. clout of the workers to make bologna sandwiches deductible.

Today Martinis—tomorrow bologna—*then* pastrami ~~next week~~ & maybe *even* a day when us hot soup ~~for lunch~~ fellas will take a deduction. And it all started with *3* martinis.

This is RR Thanks for listening. ❖

Spies
April 3, 1978

A student of Russian & Chinese affairs Lennart Frantzell brings us up to date *by way of Nat. Review magasine*** ~~&~~ on what some countries are doing about spies. I'll be right back.

In our country today there is almost a feeling that nothing is lower than a spy catcher. At least it seems that way with our continuing Vendetta against the F.B.I., the C.I.A. and even local police intelligence units. But espionage is regularly practised by most nations in this less than peaceful world and we're naive if we dont think there is a constant effort by the Soviet U. to infiltrate the most sensitive agencies in our govt.

~~It was 1974 when~~ *In 1974* the world learned that Chancellor Willy Brandt of W. Germany had an East German spy literally at his elbow.—*** ~~his own pol. aide was unmasked.~~ Unknown to the Chancellor of course this enemy agent had worked his way up to being the Chancellors top pol. aide.

The West Germans did not fool around. They set out to develop drastic new methods of tracking down spies. They estimated ~~at~~ *there were at least* 6000

* Joseph Califano, secretary of Health, Education, and Welfare from 1977 to 1979.

** Lennart Frantzell, "Tales of Nadis," *National Review*, March 3, 1978, p. 281.

*** Chancellor Willy Brandt resigned following Guenter Guillaume's confession that he worked for the Communist security forces and was in the East German Army. Guillaume was Brandt's assistant for party affairs.

East Germans plus another 1500 ~~Soviet, Czech, Polish, Hungarian—well just list all the iron curtain countries.~~ *from the Soviet U. and all the iron curtain countries.* Actually the espionage effort was based on flooding W. Germany with so many agents posing as refugees that the govt. couldn't possibly catch them all.

To counter this the West Germans developed a system of feeding all known info. about refugees into a computer. Previously this info. had been scattered among ~~a number of~~ *several different* agencies. Now gathered together it ~~was~~ *is* matched against a computer program made up from the behavior patterns & personal characteristics ~~of~~ typical of agents already exposed. Each pattern ~~gave~~ *gives* them a set of parameters which ~~could~~ *can* be made more specific as time ~~went~~ *goes* on.

The new plan went into operation early in 1976. By late May they had bagged a top agent who was serving as Sec. to several officials in the Foreign ministry ~~They also picked up~~ *plus* 15 spies in the Defense ministry. By Autumn of last year another 8 had been caught & the year end total was 35 arrested while another 35 had fled the country.

It's interesting that the West Germans made public what they [were] doing. This saved a lot of time & money because sizeable numbers of agents took off for the border without waiting to see if the computer would ~~snag~~ *expose* them. One couple sent a cable explaining that their sudden disappearance had been caused by a death in the family. A banker told of an accident in Denmark which would prevent his returning to Germany. There was a dying grandmother, a sick wife—any number of excuses for departure. Some city govt's. found themselves suddenly without pub. employees. Employees were lost to Nuclear *power* plants, a fuel research team~~,~~ *&* the rocket division of a firm with Nato contracts.

The personnel chief of the Hamburg Criminal investigating Division & Pres. of the Union of German Police Officials was picked up with 5 other spies. An Englishman ~~with a~~ *and his* German wife ~~were~~ *were* caught 48 hours before they were to cross the border into E. Germany. Documents were found in their home which led to a Sec. in the Chancellors office. She had previously passed a security check with flying colors.

Does anyone want to say, "it cant happen here?"

This is RR Thanks for listening. ❖

Regulators
April 3, 1978

Washington is still talking about relieving the citizenry of some of the ~~nitpicking~~ *burden of* petty regulation & nitpicking but in the 1st 10 mo's. of 1977 the Fed. workforce added 52,000 emp's.

I'll be right back.

† Almost a year ago the Wall St. Journal called attention to the fixation, the mindset of those who man the Fed. regulatory agencies. Encouraged by activist, ~~publi~~ special interest lobbies, the regulators apparently are incapable of trusting the American people to do the right thing.

~~There is great~~ The Journal gave some examples of this ingrained mis-trust. The administrator of the program set up to monitor and regulate pension funds ~~is~~ worrying because his investigators couldn't find more evidence of wrongdoing was typical. This is the program called "ERISA." Since it was passed thousands of smaller business pension funds have closed down because of the costly administrative overhead ~~covered~~ *required* by the act. But that isn't the point of this commentary.

The Director of "Erisa" complains that his investigators are not turning up enough cases of wrongdoing by pension plan administrators.* Some of us would be encouraged by that and conclude there was more honesty & ~~less w~~ *less cheating* than we had anticipated. That however is not govts. reaction. The Director wants more investigators, better trained in what will make a good court case & greater use of computers. In other words his program is necessary, there ~~is~~ *HAS TO BE* wrongdoing, he *JUST* needs a bigger dept. to find it.

The Comptroller of the Currency provided another example for the Journal. His office isn't getting enough complaints from consumers about Banks ~~not complying~~ *Failure to COMPLY* with Fed. ~~regulations~~ *rules* regarding disclosure & anti-discrimination. ~~regulations. He Now of course the failure to comply must be going on so the Comptroller decided Banks should~~ *NATURALLY THERE CAN BE NO DOUBT THE BANKS ARE NOT COMPLYING & THE CUSTOMERS DONT KNOW HOW TO MAKE A PROPER COMPLAINT SO THE SOLUTION IS, BANKS MUST* give their customers brochures ~~telling~~ *EXPLAINING TO* them what to complain ~~about and~~ *about & how to do it. The Banks will* provide forms for their complaints addressed to the Comptroller.

Mrs. Eleanor Holmes Norton** who heads up the Equal Employment Opportunity Commission has a different problem. She gets plenty of complaints from citizens who think they are being mis-treated by the boss but when the investigators look into ~~them~~ *these complaints* they find they dont have a case. The E.E.O.C. evidently yearns to go to court with class action suits but too many complaints have no basis in fact.

That does not give Mrs. Norton joy. The commission now will be more systematic in digging up it's own cases. ~~with agents~~ *Agents will be* better trained in how to make a complaint into a court case. She is sure there will be an increase in class action suits as soon as this can be done.

There is great danger in all of this burocratic witch hunting. When govt.

* "The Unrelenting Army," *The Wall Street Journal,* January 6, 1978, p. 6.

** Eleanor Holmes Norton chaired the United States Equal Employment Opportunity Commission from 1977 to 1981, and has been the Washington, D.C., delegate to the U.S. Congress since 1991.

loses respect for the people, the people lose respect for govt. It has been said that each form of govt. has a particular characteristic. ~~w~~When that characteristic is lost the govt. falls.

A Dictatorship exists because of fear. ~~When~~ *Let* the people lose their fear & the Dictator is ousted. A Kingdom can only last so long as the people have affection for the Royal ~~house.~~ *family.* A Dem. Republic can only last as long as the people have virtue. Americans do have virtue. Will ~~they~~ *we* continue to have it if govt. treats us like criminals?

This is RR Thanks for listening.

† Send Copy to name on attached paper—RR ❖

General James
April 3, 1978

We've had some ugly times in this melting pot we call America but every once in a while we're reminded of a capacity we have for greatness. I'll be right back.

Several weeks ago the salutes were fired, the bugles sounded taps and a 4 star General of the U.S. Air Force was laid to rest in ~~Arli~~ Arlington cemetery. He lies in that place we've set aside for heros and ~~people~~ *it is* fitting that he should *be there* for none ~~have~~ *has* deserved it more.

General Daniel "Chappie" James Jr. is younger than many of his rank who rest on those Virginia hills; 58 years old when his great heart gave out.* That fine columnist Pat Buchanan wrote in a tribute to General James; "There is the bravery of the soldier in battle, and the man against the mob. There is the moral courage of the individual swimming against the tide of contemporary dogma." Pat has eloquently summed up the ~~story~~ *heroism* of "Chappie" James.

I'm sorry to say I never had an opportunity to meet the Gen. face to face although we talked on the phone a number of times. He ~~had been put~~ *was* in charge of the homecoming arrangements 5 yrs. ago for those other heros—our returning P.O.W's. It was during that period that as Gov. we talked to each other by phone ~~since~~ *as* those men ~~came back~~ *returned* from Vietnam by way of Calif.

It was in one of those calls that for some reason he felt it was necessary to tell me he was black. I was surprised—not that he was black—I was well aware of that ~~& of his remarkable Mtary. career.~~ *and told him so trying hard*

* Daniel "Chappie" James Jr. was the first black four-star general in the United States Air Force. On being promoted to that grade on September 1, 1975, he was assigned as Commander in Chief, North American Air Defense and Aerospace Defense Command, and served in that position until his retirement on February 1, 1978. He died 24 days later.

not to add—"so what." My surprise was that he felt ~~it necessary~~ *he had* to interject that in the discussion we were having *which was* about the flood of requests we were both getting for appearances by the P.O.Ws. ~~I'm afraid I My reaction was that perhaps in this era of image making he felt it was necessary to tell me because it might make a difference in some way. I told him I was aware of~~

~~I must confess to thinking that perhaps he~~ *I wondered if he* felt he had to tell me because ~~in his mind~~ he thought it might make a difference to me. ~~And I chalked it up to some misconception he had about my attitude.~~

Now thanks to Pat Buchanan I know better. Chappie James the 17th child in his family grew up near Pensacola Fla. in an America that had *not* awakened to the fact it had a racial problem—a problem he would do some thing about ~~i~~ *in his* own way.

As a boy mil. pilots at a nearby base would give him airplane rides in return for chores he did for them. At Tuskegee Inst. in Ala. it was only natural that he signed up with the all black cadet unit that became the famed 99th pursuit squadron in WWII. He ~~was~~ *became an officer but stayed* a 1st Lt. for 7 yrs. ~~but he took it.~~ *It was unfair but he didnt complain.* He flew ~~100's of~~ *more than 100* missions in Korea earning almost ~~as~~ *that* many decorations. In Vietnam he was teamed with Col. Robin Olds. ~~and t~~*T*hey became famous as "Blackman & Robin"—a take off on the *then* current "Batman" TV show. ~~of those days.~~ He came home a General and took on campus ~~dissidents~~ radicals & protestors in defense of this nation.

He ~~added 3 more stars on his shoulders becoming a member of~~ *became a 4 star General joining* that exclusive club which includes U.S. Grant & ~~Gen.~~ *John J.* Pershing. ~~He knows The dark days of discrimination, bigotry & prejudice and never let it make him bitter.~~ *He had known times when he was not allowed to enter an officers club. That didn't make him bitter.* He was able to see past that to the real greatness of this land. His photo as a fighter pilot hangs in the Pentagon and on it he has written; "I fought in 3 wars & 3 more would not be too many to defend my country. I love Am. and as she has ~~her~~ weaknesses or ills I'll hold her hand."

Do Right
February 20, 1978

~~Each generation challenges the morés & customs of the past and that's as it should be—so long as youth doesn't discard proven values simply because they are old.~~

~~I'll be right back.~~

It's nice to think that maybe ~~todays~~ the younger generation dosen't have any faults that becoming a parent & a taxpayer wont cure. I'll be right back.

Every generation thinks the preceding generation left the world in a mess for them to straighten out. Each generation challenges the morés & customs of the past. We did it, our parents before us did it & our childrens, children will do it. There's nothing wrong with that as long as ~~we dont~~ *some generation* dosen't discard time tested, proven values simply because they are old.

Charles Edison, son of the great genius Thomas Edison has written something I thought you might like to hear. He tells that a reporter once asked his father if he had any "advice for youth." Thomas Edison replied: "Youth never takes advice" & went about his business. Then Charles writes:*

~~Charles Edison~~

"Like my father, I doubt that my advice will be taken. Youth seems to like to learn the hard way—on the battlefield of their own experience. However, here are some thoughts derived from my travels through seventy-three years of life.

My "advice" is double edged: it is presented to youth and, by the same token, to our country. For our country and its youth are synonymous. My generation—and the generation immediately preceding it—will soon be a memory—either pleasant or unpleasant, depending on the effect our lives had on our country. It is you—the young people of America—who will be taking over.

The basic ingredient of my advice is a resurrection of honor. Honor, an old-fashioned word, but one that encompasses everything—duty, responsibility, knowledge and adherence to one's heritage and traditions, respect for the eternal values. An honorable man can live a life free from fear. He knows his duties to his family, his community and his nation, and will exercise them to the best of his ability. He is aware of his responsibilities—first to himself and then to the world around him. He takes the trouble to learn his background—his family, his nation and his God—and uses this knowledge to enrich his own life and the life of all around him. The honorable man cherishes the heritage made available to him by his family, by the founding fathers of his nation and by the thousands of years of history in which men strove for freedom and decency. He knows and respects the eternal values which have come to him from all these years and from all these peoples. A man's honor is the greatest treasure he owns. It will make him rich beyond all dreams of avarice.

And so, the essence of my advice is to seek out the meaning of honor and, once this is realized, to exercise honor as the basic force of life."

Then Charles Edison sums it all up in this infallible guideline for individuals & for ~~govt~~ governments.

"When in doubt—do right."

This is RR Thanks for listening. ❖

* Originally published in Jesse Grover Bell, *Here's How By Who's Who* (Cleveland, Ohio: 1965); quoted with permission of the Charles Edison Fund. Edison was a businessman, secretary of the Navy, and governor of New Jersey. He died in 1969.

Life and Death
February 20, 1978

Every now & then something serves to remind us that how you live is of far greater importance than how long you live. I'll be right back.

No matter how ~~much~~ *many times* we say ~~it~~ that death is a normal part of living, a part of Gods plan for all of us, we still tend to be shocked and grieved when it comes to those near & dear to us. Now let me hasten to make plain that of course we feel grief and sorrow when a loved one leaves us. ~~That is one~~ *But that* sorrow ~~at being left without the companionship of~~ *is for ourselves because of the loss in our own* lives of a beloved companion.

But I'm speaking of the grief *the regret* we feel for the person who has had to depart this life. We speak of the waste if the deceased is young and has not lived out his or her more than 3 score & 10. And ~~certainly it takes all our faith~~ *all too often we fail* to remember *that* if our Judeo-Christian tradition means anything, ~~that~~ the departed has simply moved on to what we've been ~~told~~ *assured* is a better life.

A few weeks ago a little boy died in Santa Barbara Calif. His life span a mere 7 years before Leukemia took him. We have to feel sorrow for the Mother & Father ~~who had~~ *whose dreams* for him ended so quickly but surely his brief time here served a purpose every bit as much as if his life had been measured in decades not years.

At 7 years he is described as having an *unusual* understanding *of suffering &* of God. A volunteer with a group which works with the dying & their families recorded (at Edouardo's* request) his thoughts about dying & even his wishes as to his funeral. In answer to a question as to why he wanted to die—(you see he had asked the Dr's. to disconnect the life support systems) he said, "Because I am so sick. When you are dead and a spirit in Heaven you dont have all the aches & pains. And sometimes if you want to, you can visit this life but you cant come back into your own life. If you *dont* hang on to your body & let yourself ease away it is not so painful *Death is like a passage way, a walk into another galaxy.*" These are the words—the wise words of a 7 yr. old boy. He went on to say, "Sometimes Dr's. want to save people very badly. They try everything to cure them.~~"~~ I dont feel good and I am too sick to live on."

His mother tells *of* the final moment. He said "Mother turn off the oxygen. I dont need it anymore." She did as he asked and says "I turned it off then he held my hand and a big smile came to his face and he said 'It is time.' "Then he left."

His mother summed it all up when she said "It was a privilege & an honor to go through this with my son. I hope it helps parents talk things over with ~~t~~

* Edouardo de Moura Castro's story was reported in Bill Downey, "7-year-old Dies with Dignity," *Santa Barbara News-Press*, January 20, 1978, pp. A1 and A3.

their children & doctors. If he's done this in his short life, then it will have been worth it."

We can all learn from a very remarkable 7 yr. old boy and surely his life had meaning for all of us.

This is R.R. Thanks for listening. ❖

Government Security
March 13, 1978

It's surprising that more press attention hasn't been given to a recent meeting of the *Sen.* Subcommittee on Criminal Laws and Procedures. I'll be right back.

It was just before mid-Feb. that ~~that~~ *a* Sen. sub committee ~~which for years was chaired by the late Sen. John McClellan~~ heard testimony by two representatives of the Civil Service Commission. Alan Campbell, chairman of the commission & Robt. J. Drummond Jr. ~~the commissions~~ director of Personnel Investigations told the committee what some had suspected was *INDEED* true; ~~that~~ known members of terrorist organizations and even communist party members can ~~actually~~ *not only* become civil servants in govt. but can rise to the most sensitive of govt. positions. ~~On top of that t~~*T*heir subversive connections & associations are deliberately left out of the Commissions files.

Mr. Campbell said that membership in any kind of organization is protected by the Privacy act. The Civil Svc. Commission does about 25,000 full field investigations every year and he ~~said~~ *added,* it is ~~incr~~ *increasingly* difficult to obtain pertinent information about potential govt. employees. You see investigators are instructed to inform each source of information that the information and the identity of the informant will be given to the person being investigated upon request. This does not exactly inspire an informant to tell all.

It seems ridiculous but it is even difficult to get reports of criminal records ~~of~~ of prospective employees. Here again the reason is the Privacy Act and Fed. regulations. Local law enforcement agencies balk at revealing *conviction & arrest* records. This is true of large states like Calif., N.Y. & Ill. and at least 90 cities in other states. In other words there is a near collapse of the Fed. govt's. personnel security program.

It boggles the mind when you consider that this lack of ability to investigate involves prospective employees in the Pentagon, Foreign service officers and ~~thousands of and *and*~~ *many who* are being hired for other extremely sensitive positions.

The Sen. committee ~~is well aware of~~ *well remembers* the cold war days in the decade following WWII when communists in a great many critical agencies created a massive subversion problem in our govt.

Sen. Thurmond* asked Wm. Campbell; "You have to have some kind of criteria that enables you to make determinations as to what kind of activity constitutes proper course for believing that ~~individual~~ *applicant* in question may not be loyal to the U.S. Would you agree to that?" Campbell replied there should be such criteria but when he was asked, "Do you have such criteria today?" He answered "No sir we do not." Then he was asked if it weren't true that the commission itself had ruled that applicants for Fed. employment could not be asked whether they were committed to the violent overthrow of our govt. or whether the*yir* sympathies lie with another govt. The answer was that legal counsel had advised the commission such questions would violate the Privacy Act.

Senators pressed for answers on specific terrorist groups and whether membership in them would bar an individual from govt. service. The answer was always no, in addition to which the Director admitted the Commission intended to destroy it's files on 2200 questionable organizations.

It makes you wonder if the inmates aren't running the asylum.

This is RR Thanks for listening. ❖

Sports

March 13, 1978

A judge in Ohio made a decision having to do with the equality of the sexes and the sports world may never be the same. I'll be right back.

In a Federal Court in Ohio a judge ruled that state and federal guidelines providing for separate male & female sports are unconstitutional, and that girls must be permitted to take part in contact sports such as football. I would have missed this entirely if it hadn't come to my attention in a column by M. Stanton Evans.**

Stan says the judge even went so far as to say "there may be a girl lurking out there somewhere who will become the greatest Quarterback in history. The Judge ~~als~~ was pretty ~~f~~ verbose on the subject. He went on to say: "It has always been traditional that boys play football & girls are cheerleaders. Why so? Where is it written that girls may not if suitably qualified, play football?" Stan answered that one in his column. "The answer is written in the book of nature and the rules of common sense."

~~Stan~~ *He* went on to ~~discuss~~ *point out* very intelligently *and in medical terms* the physical differences between women & men. They are real and they are inescapable facts of nature. ~~but~~ Men are constructed differently with a higher

* Senator James Strom Thurmond (D–South Carolina, 1954–1964 and R–South Carolina, 1964–2003).

** M. Stanton Evans. "Unisex Sports Decision Latest 'Victory' for Female Athletes." *Human Events*, February 25, 1978, pp. 7–8.

ratio of muscle to body weight. He pointed out that girls compared to boys have narrower shoulders, less cardiovascular capacity, lower center of gravity and that running & throwing are not as natural to the typical feminine body.

But enough of that. The Judges decision opened up a 2 way street that brings all kinds of possibilities to mind. Suppose there is an Amazon type here & there who can throw a football 60 yards and even scramble to escape a blitz by some charging front 4. She makes the grade & is in line for the Heisman trophy. Seriously I dont deny this is possible.

But lets turn around & look in another direction. As I said the Judge opened the street both ways. We presently have Girls basketball, softball, soccer and a number of other sports. So here comes 'Joe Muscles,' 6 foot 4—225 lbs. who didn't quite make it on the varsity. He still wants to play basketball and so he plays—on what used to be the all girls team.

Since the, not quite good enough Joes, undoubtedly outnumber the occasional Amazons who ~~make~~ win a place on the varsity, a lot of girls happily playing on the girls teams could find themselves permanently on the bench. You buy a ticket to see the championship girls basketball team do it's stuff and five hairy chested male rejects from the varsity take the floor.

If you think this is far fetched—brace yourself. In Connecticut Little League they made the game gender free and in 1976 a team of mostly boys won the "Girls" softball championship. A player on the losing—all girls team disappointedly said, "They're so much bigger physically."

This is RR Thanks for listening ❖

Throughout the late 1960s and 1970s, the Japanese charged that there were too many "shokkus" (shocks), or unexpected changes, in U.S. policy toward their country. While visiting Japan in April 1978, Reagan discussed this issue in a speech to business leaders: "I firmly believe that there must be a strong element of predictability in our relations. Sudden, unannounced sharp departures from the existing pattern of relations would be harmful, even counterproductive. Neither side must perceive the other as attempting to gain a unilateral or selfish advantage, and we should be patient with each other." The broadcast below was taped shortly after he returned from Asia.*

Japan I
May 15, 1978

For the next few broadcasts you are going to be subjected to something of a travelogue that took me around the world.

I'll be right back.

* Quoted in Peter Hannaford, *The Reagans: A Political Portrait* (New York: Coward-McCann, 1983), p. 163.

For the last few weeks you've been hearing commentaries I pre-recorded before setting off on a round the world flight that was definitely not non-stop. In the next few broadcasts I'd like to talk about some faraway places that have a great bearing on our security & economy.

Nancy & I flew to Honolulu for an overnight stop where I participated *briefly* in an economic conference before flying on to Tokyo the next day. That flight took us across 5 time zones & the international date line which has always intrigued & sometimes confused me.

Out there in the vast and trackless Pacific on a Friday afternoon we came to that dividing point at which a day was taken out of our lives. Friday *instantly* became Saturday. Of course if you turn around and return by the same route ~~back to Calif.~~ you'll get the day back again. ~~and~~ We've done this a few times before but this time we would continue on West until we finally reached Calif. As far as I'm concerned we've permanently lost a day unless sometime we do the trip in reverse. I found myself wondering all sorts of things such as, wasn't there a split second when it was Saturday for those in the front of the plane and Fri. for those in the rear. Or what happened if a ship were becalmed astraddle the line and passengers could walk back & forth from Sat. to Fri. & back to Sat.

Well enough of that. I want to make one thing clear we were not on a vacation. The 4 day schedule in Tokyo ~~was~~ included 2 speeches, a question & answer session with the Foreign Correspondents Assn., ~~and~~ a full round of meetings with business & industrial leaders, ~~and~~ meetings with various cabinet ministers, and with Prime Minister Fukuda.* We had previously met in 1971 when he was ~~Foreign~~ *the* Minister of Foreign Affairs.**

An American in Japan has to be impressed with the vitality and energy of the people. You come away with an uncomfortable feeling that they have something we once had & took for granted but which if we haven't lost entirely we are in danger of losing. Their per man hour productivity far exceeds ours and the rate at which it is increasing is almost double ours.

A shopping trip or even a coffee break in a café leaves you with two impressions. One is of unfailing, cheerful courtesy *on the part* of everyone you do business with and the other the full reality of how anemic our American dollar has become. I'd like to meet an American who couldn't be shocked by a $40 price tag on a canteloupe. At that rate it's cheaper to eat money.

Incidentally the next time I'm caught in rush hour traffic I'm going to remember the all day long curb to curb traffic in Tokyo where we never saw a bent fender or an unwashed car.

* Prime Minister Fukuda Takeo.

** Reagan was governor of California in 1971 and traveled to several Asian countries, including Japan, as a representative of President Richard Nixon. Reagan was reassuring Asian allies of U.S. commitment to them even though Henry Kissinger, the national security adviser, was meeting with the leaders of the People's Republic of China to prepare the way for normalization of bilateral relations and for President Nixon's historic visit to the country in February 1972.

Next broadcast I'd like to talk about our balance of trade problem and Nat. Security.

This is RR Thanks for listening. ❖

Women
May 15, 1978

In all this time of womens lib and controversy over womens place in the world I happen to believe if it weren't for the ladies we men would still be carrying clubs.

I'll be right back.

In spite of all the jokes men like to tell about women drivers I think almost all men know in their hearts that women have been the single most civilizing influence in the world.

Years ago I read of an incident that took place in India during the days of British Colonial rule. It is not a make believe legend but an actual happening. I was reminded of it on our recent trip and thought you might like to hear it.

The scene is a dinner party in one of the palatial homes in India, a typical cosmopolitan gathering including a British Col. of the old school and a visiting American business man. The rest were Colonials, Indian notables etc.

Somehow the conversation had gotten around to heroics, courage and what makes individuals perform noble deeds. The British Col. was holding forth on the idea that men have that extra bit of control which in time of stress makes them able to resist panic and with courage do the dangerous thing that has to be done. Women on the other hand, according to the Col. are not gifted with that measure of control and therefore grow hysterical, faint or stand helpless to act in the face of danger.

As he was going on in that vein the American happened to notice the hostess signal *to* one of the servants who leaned over her chair while she whispered something to him. The American thought nothing of this until he saw the servant returning to the room carrying a saucer of milk. Passing the table he set the saucer on the floor just outside the glass doors which opened on to the patio. Suddenly ~~he~~ *the American* remembered,—*in India* a saucer of milk is snake bait—Cobra bait to be exact.

He saw the servants standing against the dining room wall and it was obvious they were frightened & tense. Quickly he looked around the room. There was no furniture that could conceal a snake. He looked overhead thinking possibly it could be on a beam but there were no beams, it was a tile vaulted ceiling.

Then he realized there was only one possible place a snake could be—under the table. His first instinct was to push his chair back and run but he knew this could cause the snake to strike one of the other guests. The Col. was still holding forth. The American interrupted him & said, "Col. lets have a test and see who has the most control. Let's see how many of us can remain absolutely silent & motionless for 5 min. I'll count to 300 as a measure of the time and no one must move or utter a sound.

Everyone went along with the idea and the countdown started. It had reached 280 when a King Cobra slithered from beneath the table and through the patio doors to the saucer of milk. The servants slammed the doors with the snake on the outside.

In the excitement that followed the Col. shouted, "that proves my point, this man could have saved himself but he thought of a plan to save the rest of us." The American said, "Just a minute Col." turning to the hostess he asked, "How did you know there was a Cobra under the table?" She said, "It was on my foot."

This is RR Thanks for listening. ❖

Education

May 15, 1978

In a rare show of bi-partisan statesmanship two Sen's. (Dem. & Repub.) have called for an income tax credit for parents paying tuition to educate their children. I'll be right back.

Tens of thousands of independent & parochial schools, elementary, secondary & college level have gone broke in recent years. Unable to charge a tuition high enough to keep pace with rising costs they've had to close their doors. This is a tragic loss to education. The very existence of the independent school helps preserve academic freedom and the diversity which is typical of our land.

To reverse this trend two Senators sponsored a bill providing for an income tax credit for half the tuition up to a ceiling of $500 per child. A credit of course means they subtract that amount from the inc. tax they owe. This would apply to both public and private schools. Now I realize public school tuition only ~~occurs~~ *occurs* at the college level so the benefit at elementary & secondary levels would only go to parents whose children were enrolled in independent or parochial schools.

The ed. lobby has risen in unholy wrath calling this a plot to destroy the pub. schools. That's a bit of hysteria when you consider that 90% of all students attend pub. schools. Only 10% are in private schools. Incidentally they have seized upon that word "private" to make this seem like a tax break for the rich. The word "private" does conjure up an image of exclusive prep schools & Ivy League colleges and while there are, of course some of those ~~they~~ *there* are far more local parochial schools & small independent liberal arts colleges existing in genteel poverty.

In the heated debate little has been said about the fact that the tax credit would probably help the schools more than the parents. Hard pressed to meet increased costs a school could raise tuition with the assurance that it wouldn't mean any actual increase in price to the parent. The result would be salvation for many otherwise doomed educational institutions.

Nevertheless the Wash. Post editorially predicts ~~doom~~ destruction of the educational system if the tax credit is adopted. In a particularly ridiculous bit of demagogery, Albert Shanker—(Pres. of the Am. Fed. of Tchrs.)—who numbers among his contributions to ed. a vast increase in the number of teachers strikes says the tax credit, "would amount to taxpayers subsidizing private schools." He is echoed by the Pres. of the Nat. P.T.A.* who declares, "the pub. would be taxed twice—once to support pub. schools through existing programs & a second time to subsidize the pvt. schools through tuition tax credits." They must be using the new math, to come up with that distortion of fact.

The parent paying tuition to an independent school is paying his full tax also to support the pub. school but his children are not adding to the cost of public ed. They pay for something they dont take.

What do Mr. Shanker & Madam P.T.A. Pres. think will happen if the ~~10% now privately enrolled~~ *INDEPENDENT SCHOOLS CLOSE DOWN & THE 10% attending them are* suddenly enrolled in the pub. school system? Mr. Shanker will probably call for a teachers pay raise because of the added burden. The school boards will demand a bigger budget to handle the increased enrollment and presto! everyones local taxes will be hiked. Is that really better than giving a tax break to people who are presently supporting 2 school systems?

This is R.R. Thanks for listening. ❖

Alger Hiss

May 15, 1978

I doubt if we've seen in this country a more determined effort to re-write history than we are seeing today with regard to communist subversion in the post world war II years. I'll be right back

From the Academy Awards performance (by way of one Oscar winner), to well written dramas & documentaries on TV, feature motion pictures, novels & articles there is an orchestrated campaign to revive the term McCarthyism and re-write history. We are supposed to believe there was no communist subversion, no use of communist fronts to lure innocent dupes into supporting communist causes and no effort *by communists* to infiltrate govt., industry & the media.

* Grace Baisinger served as the president of the National PTA from 1977 to 1979.

Being a veteran of the battle to keep the motion picture industry out of the hands of communists back in the late 40's when their power was such that ~~they~~ *by* use *of* a jurisdictional labor dispute they almost closed the industry down I find the ~~present~~ documentaries shamefully dishonest & the dramas based on falsehood.

A recent campus incident triggered this *indignant* outburst. At dear old Rutgers a visiting speaker on campus held hundreds of students spellbound with his account of the horrors of McCarthyism. Then a questioner in the audience broke the spell. He stood and asked the lecturer if it wasn't true that 3 different defectors from the Soviet secret police (now known as the KGB.) had ~~not~~ identified the speaker in sworn testimony as an agent of Stalins secret police? Had the speaker not been found guilty of perjury by a jury & his conviction upheld by our entire judicial review process? And hadn't a re-nowned scholar, sympathetic to the speaker studied the entire file on his case and concluded that he was indeed guilty? ~~The a~~Ashen faced *the* speaker *ALGER HISS* refused to comment.*

Now Alger Hiss has paid his debt to society (as the saying goes. He served his time in prison and therefore should be given his chance to go straight, by society.

The truth is society has done very well by ~~him,~~ *HISS*, no one has tried to persecute him or hound him. But he has become one of the focal points ~~for~~ *of* the present campaign to re-write the history of that era. He is being presented as an innocent victem of the thing called McCarthyism, martyred by intolerant witch hunters.

Well in the 1st place the late Sen. McCarthy** hadn't been heard from when Alger Hiss was charged with being a member of the Soviet underground. But the scholar mentioned by the questioner at Rutgers should end the myth of martyrdom.

Prof. Allen Weinstein of Smith College believed so much in the innocence of Alger Hiss that he invoked the freedom of information act to get all the trial records & secret govt. files on Hiss. Carefully, painstakingly he studied the more than 30,000 pages. Then in 1976 he informed Hiss that he had spent ~~the~~ 4 yrs. researching the case because he believed in his innocence but that he was now convinced of his guilt.

Prof. Weinsteins book entitled, "Perjury: The Hiss-Chambers Case," should be read by all who want the truth about that era. It is especially credible coming as it does from one who ~~t~~ wanted the answer to be different. It's also ~~as~~ exciting as a "who done it" & most informative. "Perjury: The Hiss Chambers Case" published by Knopf.

This is RR Thanks for listening. ❖

* *National Review*, March 31, 1978, p. 385.

** Senator Joseph R. McCarthy (R–Wisconsin, 1947–1957).

A month before this broadcast was taped Secretary of State Cyrus Vance and Andrew Young, the U.S. representative to the United Nations, traveled to Salisbury to support the British-American plan of racial power sharing in Rhodesia. Robert Mugabe and Joshua Nkomo of the Patriotic Front, who sought a dominant position in the transitional government, opposed the plan. Two years after this broadcast, Mugabe would become the prime minister of Zimbabwe, the name bestowed on the former Rodesia.

Rhodesia
May 15, 1978

If you are feeling a little queasy you might not want to hear the first couple of paragraphs in todays commentary. I'll be right back.

The other day in the mail I received a full page ad from the St. Louis Globe Democrat. It had been taken out by an individual who had just returned from his 24th trip to Rhodesia.

The ad consisted of photos taken in Rhodesia with identification & explanation printed beneath each photo. They were not pleasant to look at & the printed word was even less pleasant to read. There were pictures of Rhodesian citizens ~~(always Black)~~ always black & always dead, their hands tied behind their backs. They lay sprawled on the ground where they had fallen as bullets from Russian made automatic weapons mowed them down.

In one photo the innocent victems had been burned alive. There was a hard to look at picture of a ~~tribal~~ village chief. He was still alive. His lips, ears & hands had been cut off. The caption said his wife had been forced to cook & eat them.

There was only one picture of a white Rhodesian, a tiny baby girl, only child of a young farm couple. Her parents were at work in the fields when the guerrillas, perpetrators of all these horrors came to their farm home. The nursemaid, a young black girl tried desperately to save the baby. She was clubbed to the floor and the baby was then bayonetted a dozen times.

These guerillas are the forces of Joshua Nkomo & Robert Mugabe who call themselves & their murderous gangs, "The Patriotic Front." They claim they are fighting for majority rule in Rhodesia & one man, one vote. Since 1972 they have killed an estimated 9000 of their fellow Rhodesians—mainly blacks.

In the meantime three black leaders of more than 85% of the black population of Rhodesia have joined with Prime Minister Ian Smith to bring about majority ~~rule~~, one man, one vote rule. These 4 have such support from the people that our Sec. of State on his *recent* visit to Rhodesia was greeted by large crowds of black Rhodesians bearing signs proclaiming their support of the present plan.

But our govt. says it will not accept the agreed upon interim govt. of Rhodesia unless it includes ~~th~~ Nkomo & Mugabe. And so we continue the ridiculous economic sanctions prescribed by the U.N. bringing hardship & more guerilla killings ~~on~~ *to* the ~~black & white~~ citizens of Rhodesia, black & white.

What makes our attitude impossible to understand is that Nkomo & Mugabe still claim they are fighting for majority rule & one man, one vote. But the new interim regime has not only ~~proclaimed~~ proclaimed majority rule & one man, one vote, it has invited ~~the 2 Nkomo~~ *Nkomo & Mugabe* & their guerillas to return to Rhodesia & take part in the election. There will be total amnesty, no reprisals, release of all pol. retainees & govt. help in reuniting the marauders with their familys. Nkomo & Mugabe have ~~even~~ been asked to participate in forming the new govt. ~~& have~~ *They* refused.

It boggles the mind to hear our govt. in the face of all this refusing to accept the interim govt. because it does not include Nkomo & Mugabe.

This is RR Thanks for listening ❖

Dulles Airport
May 15, 1978

How concerned are you about the beauty or lack of it in an airport bldg. when the plane you're in is on final approach on a dark rainy night? I'll be right back.

American commercial aviation has ~~an~~ *a* safety record unequaled in *all* the world but even so we still occasionally hear that dread news flash of a plane that didn't make it. As one who occasionally flies into Washingtons Dulles airport a recent story in Electronic Engineering Times ~~so~~ worried me more than a little bit.

The air traffic controllers, those gentlemen who sit there eyes glued to a radar screen, talking planes into a safe landing at Dulles have a complaint—a very legitimate complaint. It has to do with the performance *in wet weather* of the F.A.A. (Fed. Aviation Admin.) surface detection system. ~~in wet weather.~~

What we're talking about is the radar called the A.S.D.E.-2 which is used in bad weather to track aircraft after they drop to altitudes of 40 ft. or less. The ~~rotating~~ *radiating* antenna is housed in ~~a~~ what is called a spherically shaped radome. I think that means it's in a *round* ball shaped shelter. That ball is made of a rubberized canvas. When it rains or snows (*which is* when it's needed most) the moisture settles on the ball and is soaked up by that rubberized fabric. This reduces th~~is~~*e* power of the signal returns and the air controller sees a white spot on his screen instead of the moving blip ~~that is~~ *made by* the airplane he's tracking. Incidentally this system is in use at about a dozen other airports and the same complaint is made at all of them.

F.A.A. engineers have been experimenting with different designs & shapes for the radome to find an answer to the problem. They have come up with one that looks like an upside down tea cup. John Curran chief of Dulles airwavefacilities field office says this shape they've found *is* the answer. "The moisture drops roll off the dome like rain falling off an overhanging roof," says Curran.

Well you'd say that solves the problem; We trade in the oversize tennis balls for oversize inverted tea cups and we're all safer on a rainy day. Unfortunately Dulles is in ~~the natio~~ or adjacent to the nations capitol. The change of shape is being blocked for aesthetic reasons by the Dept. of Interiors Advisory Council of Historic Preservation. Washingtons Fine Arts Commission also objects to the proposed new dome shape.

~~It seems~~ How did they get into the act? Well it seems that the Dulles airport terminal bldg. was recently nominated for the Nat. Register of Historic Places by the Sec. of Transportation upon the advice of the Advisory Council of Historic Preservation. This is a group that oversees the care of such designated bldgs. So anything that ~~tries~~ *threatens* to change the appearance of the airport bldg. is carefully looked at.*

I hope by the time you hear this sanity has come to someone in Wash. but at the moment the new & safer dome has been rejected & the F.A.A. controllers who help get the big birds safely down has lost to the Fine Arts Commission.

For me I dont care whether it looks like an upside down tea cup or an upside down garbage can I'm for giving those controllers ~~want~~ *what* they want.—*especially when the weathers bad.*

This is RR Thanks for listening. ❖

Castro's Prisons

May 15, 1978

I've just read of another businessman's junket to Cuba in pursuit of trade. I'd like to tell you about a businessman who's just returned from there.

I'll be right back

While American businessmen continue to visit Cuba dreaming of trade deals to come, one businessman has recently returned from a 14 yr. Cuba visit. His dream was a nitemare as he described it to a group of reporters last March.

Frank Emmick had a successful business in pre-Castro Cuba. Then when the U.S. severed relations with the new govt. he closed down his operation. Five militiamen beat him & threw him in the Ocean for dead. He was alive however and made his way to the Swiss embassy. A Swiss official took him to the airport but he was refused permission to ~~return to the U.S.~~ *leave Cuba.*

He was subsequently charged with being a C.I.A. agent. This allegation incidentally has never been substantiated by the slightest bit of evidence. Never-

* The Dulles terminal building was designed by Eero Saarinen. It has been extensively modified for security purposes since the March 10, 1978, determination that it is eligible for the National Register of Historic Places.

theless he was thrown into a dark refrigerated room where stripped to his underwear he stayed for 5 months, sleeping on the bare floor.

Removed from there he was told his sentence was death and transferred to a dungeon where he spent 9 months during which time 159 of his fellow inmates were taken out & executed.
~~taken out & executed.~~

~~Again he was tried—this time~~ *Then he was given* a full dress ~~trial~~ *formal trial* with Geneva observers & western correspondents present. ~~Nevertheless he was again sentenced to 30 yrs. on the same C.I.A. charge.~~ *Still charged with being an agent he was sentenced to 30 yrs. in Prison.*

~~He spent~~ *For* 6 yrs. ~~in~~ *he was in* Las Cabanas Fortress where roughly 5000 men were crammed into a bldg. built for 500. There were no sanitary facilities & little medical attention. In 1970 he was assigned to another prison where conditions were better but in spite of ~~a~~ *a* known history of heart trouble he was given a cell that required climbing 40 stairs 3 times a day. And as could be expected he had a heart attack that almost caused his death. Two years later he was back in Las Cabanas where conditions had not improved. It was here that he had his 2nd heart attack. He waited a week for hospitalization.

In Dec. of 1977 he was transferred to a new prison which looked modern & beautiful on the outside but on the inside was a boiler in summer & a freezer in winter. The sewage from the 4th floor leaked through to the 1st floor. ~~& there was no escaping it.~~ By now however ~~he was being treated kindly~~ *treatment was better* because the Cubans thought they could make a deal with the new admin. in Wash.

Last Jan. 2 of our visiting Congressmen interviewed him & obtained his release.* ~~There are, still, according to Emmick 4 more American businessmen still in those Cuban prisons.~~ He had spent 14 yrs. & 3 months in Castros Gulag. He says there are 4 American businessmen still there.

The morning after his lunch with the reporters one of the Congressmen who had arranged his release phoned him and tore him apart for talking about his experiences. Then he asked "Are you going to keep your mouth shut." Emmick quietly answered: "No. I no longer will be intimidated. I am now free & in America."—God Bless America. ❖

Health Care
May 15, 1978

Our govt. continues to distort & outright falsify figures in order to justify it's insistence that we *MUST* have nationalized health service.

I'll be right back.

* Congressman Richard Nolan (D–Minnesota, 1975–1981) and Congressman Frederick W. Richmond (D–New York, 1975–1982). See Frank Emmick, "An American's 14 Years in Cuban Prisons," *The New York Times,* August 12, 1978.

By saying it over & over again, proponents of govt. medicine have tried to make us believe that health care costs are spiraling out of sight. And I'm afraid they have been fairly successful. The average citizen would probably respond if a pollster asked about medical costs ~~"~~that "yes they were rising faster than prices of other commodities." But the average citizen would be wrong because like all the rest of us he's been subjected to a snow job put together by the busy planners in the Dept. of H.E.W.*

It is true that a dollars worth of medical care 10 yrs. ago costs $1.85 today. But a dollars worth of plumbing repairs 10 yrs. ago costs $2.10 today. I'm not picking on plumbers—for auto repairs it's $1.90 and the same figure for Blue Jeans. A dollars worth of *POSTAGE* stamps 10 yrs. ago cost $2.22 today, shingling your roof $2.33 and to top it off Soc. Security costs ~~are~~ have gone up twice as much as *THE INCREASE IN* health care costs.

Now how does H.E.W. justify it's contrary opinion about medical care? Well it does it by proving that Disraeli** was right when he said, "there are lies, blankety blank lies & statistics."

H.E.W. dosen't take 10 yrs. figures. H.E.W. just tells us how much medical costs jumped in 1975 & 76—and forgets to tell us that the recession inspired price controls weren't lifted on medicine until 1975—a year after they were lifted on every thing else.

When price controls are removed there is a thing called a bulge. The consumer price index jumped as much for other commodities in 1974 as it did for medical care a year later. It continued *to* rise for 2 more years and in the *3rd year* leveled off. The bulge in the consumer price index for health care levelled off in the 2nd year.

If we wanted to play H.E.W.'s game we could take just *the* period beween 1965 & 1973 and find that, yes medical costs rose faster than other prices and govt. was to blame. That was the period when govt. went into medicine by way of medicaid and added tremendously to the total expenditures for health care.

Sec. of H.E.W. Califano*** has said Englands national health care program should be our model. He should take another look. Over an 8 yr. period hospital staff in Eng. increased by 28% while the number of hospital beds occupied dropped by 11%. Typical of any govt. program is this next figure—the number of administrative & clerical staff jumped 51%. There was talk of a shortage of nurses but the ratio of beds per nurse fell from 2 to 1½. And amazingly in view of all this the greatest growth was in the line up of patients waiting to be admitted to the hospitals. The input of resources went up & the output of services went down.

* The Department of Health, Education, and Welfare, which later became the Department of Health and Human Services.

** Benjamin Disraeli, British prime minister in 1868 and again in 1874–1878.

*** Joseph Califano was secretary from 1977 to 1979.

The Sec. should find a better model—perhaps the system we already have. This is RR Thanks for listening. ❖

On April 10, 1978, Arkady N. Shevchenko, a high-ranking Soviet official at the United Nations, defected to the United States.

National Security
June 5, 1978

It's getting harder & harder to understand what our State Dept. and others involved in foreign policy are trying to do in the spirit of détente. I'll be right back.

For some time now we have made it increasingly difficult for the F.B.I. & the C.I.A. to gather information about the Soviet U. and it's possible intentions. Now a security windfall drops in our lap and ~~we try to~~ *it seems as if we are trying to* pretend it hasn't happened.

The top ranking Soviet official at the United Nations Arkady Shevchenko a 47 yr. old protégé of Foreign Minister Gromyko * has defected and refused to return to Russia. Shevchenko is privy to the Kremlins foreign policy secrets and it's espionage efforts aimed at us & our allies.

Our experts in this field say this could be the biggest & most important breakthrough for us since W.W.II. In their opinion Shevchenko has to be fully informed of Russias strategy & it's worldwide goals. He is in addition fully informed as to what the Soviets hope to achieve in the strategic arms limitation talks—Salt II.

From what he has revealed so far we can demolish Russias claim that the Backfire bomber is only a medium range, not a strategic bomber. He has ~~the~~ knowledge of Russias use of Cuban troops and it's plans for Africa. How much is it worth to us to have laid out the Soviet plans for using Cuba as a base?

The concern of our intelligence forces is that policy makers in the State Dept. may try to hush up Shevchenkos revelations possibly because they'll expose the weakness of our own policies.—~~e~~*E*xpose them not to the Russians who already know about them but to us—the American people. There is also the possibility that we cant continue trying to buddy up to the Russians if we learn too much about what they have planned for us. There have already been off the record statements that this neatly tied gift of great value couldn't have come at a worse time. It's almost as if someone was complaining that he'd al-

* Soviet Foreign Minister Andrei Gromyko.

most made friends with a fellow ~~until & then someone~~ *and was sorry to* learn the fellow was stealing his wallet.

I suppose we must always be on guard against a Soviet plant who will feed us mis-information but I believe we have personnel who can check against our own ~~information concerning~~ *knowledge of* KGB agents & operations. As a matter of fact since his defection we have arrested two Soviet U.N. employees as Russian spies.

Who knows Shevchenko might have information of possible ties between the Weatherman Underground, ~~the radical group~~ & the Soviet U. which could prove the FBI agents the justice dept. is prosecuting were right in doing what they did a few years ago. Those agents have based their ~~case~~ *defense* on proving the Weathermen were working closely with Soviet agents.

With defense budgets being debated, arguments *going on* about the B-1 *Bomber* & the neutron warhead why shouldn't the American people hear Shevchenko's story & know once & for all whether we do or do not need ~~to~~ an arms buildup against a Soviet threat?

This is RR Thanks for listening. ❖

*After being kidnapped by the Symbionese Liberation Army in Berkeley, California, on February 4, 1974, Patty Hearst, an heir of the William Randolph Hearst publishing family, participated in a bank robbery and shoot-outs in California. Arrested by FBI agents on September 18, 1975, Hearst was freed on $1 million bail in November 1976. One month before the taping of this broadcast, Hearst returned to prison, as her appeals had been denied.**

Hearst
June 5, 1978

I have an urge to do a postmortem on a story that was front page for a long time but ~~that~~ now is old & therefore dead news. I'll be right back.

Patty Hearst is back in prison to serve a term for participating in a bank robbery and ~~firing a gun in another holdup of sorts in which a companion (if I remember correctly) had stolen a pair of socks.~~ *other crimes.*

There is no question about her participation in these events. She freely admitted it and apparently identified her fellow participants. Her only defense was that she had been kidnaped by a terrorist band calling itself the Symbionese Liberation Party and frightened into doing the things she did. That kidnaping occurred 4 years ago. She was in the hands of her kidnapers or with

* In September 1978, Hearst's lawyers sought executive clemency for their client in an appeal to the Justice Department. On February 1, 1979, President Jimmy Carter granted executive clemency. On January 20, 2001, President William J. Clinton pardoned Hearst.

them, however you want to put it for almost 2 years. In those last 2 years she has of course been involved in the trials ~~& appeals~~ which resulted in her conviction.

During this latter period we were treated to *frequent* newsreel shots of Patty & her family ~~especially on those occasions when she was~~ *& those high priced lawyers. We saw her* being pushed through crowds of press & photographers on her way into court appearances. There were countless columns, editorials & articles ~~about the ≠ stature & cost of her attorneys and always~~ *and always* the drumbeat that as a rich little girl she was getting favored treatment.

Is this really true? Would a ~~gil~~ girl from a *FAMILY OF* modest means [have] been thrown into prison willy nilly without a fair trial? ~~Or is Patty Hearst in prison because she her family is rich?~~

Let's recast the scenario & see how it looks if ~~Patty "Not So Rich" in fact~~ *Patty Hearst is PLAYED BY* Patty "Almost Poor" who is brutally dragged from her home and spirited away by terrorists. We see news photos of her grief stricken family in their modest home but as the months go by the press turns to other stories. The police, F.B.I., all the agencies of our justice system are helpless to find her.

Then her suffering, bewildered family receives a message that she has renounced them & joined her kidnapers in their revolution. A photo months later shows her ~~en~~ apparently engaged with them in a bank robbery. She is subsequently arrested & charged with this & other crimes.

Her family ~~mortgages~~ hires the best lawyer they can afford possibly after mortgaging their home & the case comes to trial. Patty "Almost Poor" takes the stand and admits to her participation in the crimes. Then she goes back to the kidnaping (which a lot of people seem to have forgotten)

Her lawyer asks her to tell in her own words what happened to her in those almost 2 years prior to her arrest. A jury listens intently as this lone girl tells how she was bound, blindfolder and crammed for an interminable time in a closet so small she sat for hours on end with her knees tucked beneath her chin. She told of being moved from one hideout to another, sexually abused, beaten, threatened over & over again with death because her parents were somehow enemies of society.

Yes she finally did as they ordered—because she was afraid; too afraid even to try and escape because she thought they'd find her & kill her. After all they were able to escape capture by all ~~of law enforcement.~~ *the power of the law.*

~~Our law says~~ ~~*In our society* the ≠ accused must be proven guilty beyond a reasonable doubt. Isn't there some doubt here; a possibility that Patty was telling the truth? Our courts regularly free rapists, muggers & even killers on what appear to be technicalities. Would Patty "Almost Poor" go free? Is Patty Hearst in prison because her family is rich?~~

In our socicty the accused must be proven guilty beyond a reasonable doubt. Every day rapists, muggers & even killers are freed because of technicalities or some ~~question about~~ *questionable* evidence. ~~Would there be no do~~

~~reasonable doubt~~ Isn't there a possibility that Patty "Almost Poor" was telling the truth? Is Patty Hearst in prison because her family has money?

This is RR Thanks for listening. ❖

Spending
June 5, 1978

The Budget is blossoming in Wash. & ~~it is~~ *in* full bloom it's going to be quite a bouquet. I'd like to tell you about a few of it's petals. I'll be right back.

It's impossible anymore to itemize the Fed. budget ~~in an effort~~ to see how it managed to grow to it's present size but you might be interested in a few scattered bits of extravagance. For example the cost of running 41 Fed. regulatory agencies has gone up 115% in 5 yrs. ~~That expense alone pro rates out to $470 for every man, woman, & child in America.~~

~~And of c~~ I suppose it's foolish to mention anything in less than mil's. & bils. when you are talking about a half trillion dollar budget. But then maybe that's why the Sec. of the Energy agency doesn't feel extravagant when he decides to spend $32,000 for private restrooms in the new agencies quarters. The Federal Home Loan Bank tops him ~~with almost twi~~ *by spending* almost twice that much to tear out it's new washrooms and replace them with private rooms & showers for it's executives.

Then over in Congress the House Admin. Comm. will double that amount spending $126,000 for 450 ~~17~~ *17* inch color TV sets *for it's members*. The committee chairman says they are ~~buyin~~ doing it to help correct the deficit in our balance of trade with Japan. They are buying American made sets.

This one I'm sure will touch your heart. The health planners in Wash. are determined to cut public health care costs by reducing, quote "unnecessary surgery" unquote. According to them that terms fits *such* things as cataract operations & hysterectomies. However if a man agrees to dress in womens clothes for a year the Pub. Health Service says medicare should pay for *his* quote, "gender reassignment surgery," unquote.

On the subject of health the House Appropriations Committee has discovered that Labor Dept. employees in the Office of Worker Compensation, filed 10 times as many injury claims for themselves as did employees in other govt. offices. Maybe it's all in knowing how. Anyway their take came to half a mil. dollars tax free.

Some time ago on one of these broadcasts I mentioned some of the shortcomings of the C.E.T.A. program. Those initials stand for Comprehensive Employment & Training Act. It has $11 bil. to spend and where the money is that big a little scandal is not an unusual thing.

In Dade County Fla. a grand jury has found waste, false record keeping & criminal violations in the Federally funded programs. One C.E.T.A. employer turned out to be a pool hall operator who hired his nephew~~.~~ *with the Fed. money.*

In another Fla. county I dont know whether it's dishonest or not but the Fed. money will be used to pay $2.65 an hour (the minimum wage) to illiterate students for going to school.

Is it any wonder that Sen. Jesse Helms * suggested that the Senate recess for 1 min. on May 6th in honor of the taxpayers. May 6th was the day the average worker started working for himself. From Jan. 1 until that ~~dayte~~ ~~*day*~~ date he's been working ~~for govt.~~ *to pay* his share of the cost of govt.

This is RR Thanks for listening. ❖

Energy

June 5, 1978

The ability of Burocracy in the field of self preservation should be an inspiration to all those who teach survival courses. I'll be right back.

I've been waiting to see if Wash. would be rocked by another "scandal of the tapes" but so far all is quiet. Of course the tapes I'm talking about are computer tapes but even so there has ~~been~~ unquestionably been monkey business in the marble halls.

A state representative from Louisiana, spokesman for 5 major energy producing states according to an A.P. news dispatch several weeks ago charged the new Fed. energy agency in Wash. with computer rigging. The idea was to produce false data proving the Admin's energy plan would work.

Billy Tauzin ** chairman of the Southwest Regional Energy Council says; "The plan dosen't & cant work. It will fall far short of it's projections in all forms of energy production—oil, natural gas, coal & nuclear."

Now if this were just an expression of opinion representing one side of a debate we could wait to hear the other side. It's far more than that and it follows on 2 or 3 other coverups regarding our energy situation. The Council had to invoke the Freedom of Information Act to get the computer tapes from the Dept. of Energy. According to Tauzin, ~~"~~the computer model was tampered with or, "manipulated 21 different ways between Dec. of 1976 & last April so it would coincide with what the planners wanted this country to believe about the plan." The 5 member states congressional delegations & the White House have been advised of this. So far no comment that I've heard or read from the Dept. of Energy on the charge that in addition to the manipulating, 3 ~~blank~~ *unusable* tapes & one that was blank were delivered to the council before the

* R–North Carolina, 1973–2002.

** Wilbert Joseph (Billy) Tauzin was elected to the U.S. House of Representatives in 1980. He remains a Democratic representative from Louisiana.

Dept.—eventually yielded the information. Apparently the idea had been to hide ~~the correct~~ *basic* information about the energy plan until Congress had acted on it. Acted of course on the basis of false information & figures.

~~The plan was called for the production of energy by 1985 equal~~

Projections of energy production between now & 1985 were falsified. The plan before Congress would result in a big shortfall & major ec. & pol. problems in the country. A federal audit advisory team said that changes in the computer model were made by persons in the Dept. of Energy—the policy planners who wanted the plan to be approved. The audit team said no outside agencies or experts were consulted about the changes. In other words it was a nice cozy little in house operation.

I'm no expert in the field of producing natural gas & oil but for those who are, 2 *MAJOR* changes contributed to the false conclusion. Data was projected that no additional natural gas would be produced if the price was allowed to rise to $1.75 per 1000 cubic feet & that the equivalent of 30 barrels of oil is produced for each ft. ~~of~~ a well is drilled. That last one sounds fishy to even an amateur like myself.

But of even greater importance than the monkey business with our need for oil & gas is ~~that~~ the arrogance of burocratic officials who would distort the facts if the facts didn't support their theories.

This is RR Thanks for listening. ❖

Oil

June 5, 1978

If the rate of inflation we've had for the last 5 years continues for the next 5 that 20 gal. tank of gas that now costs $13.28 will cost $24.16.

I'll be right back.

In 1976 during the primary campaign in Calif. I had been talking about the failure of Congress to do anything constructive about the, "energy crisis." Oh Congress had done something but it couldn't be called constructive. The energy bill they came up with didn't encourage the increase*d* ~~of~~ production of oil by a single barrel. In fact *SCORES OF* ~~*NEW*~~ drilling rigs exploring for new oil *HAD* closed down all over the country.

~~Probably because of what I'd~~

One day I was invited to visit an oil field in the Los Angeles harbor area. The reason for the invitation?—~~e~~*E*very well was closed down. Thousands of barrels of oil not being ~~brought to the~~ pump*ed* because ~~the~~ our govt. had set a well ~~or~~ head ~~oil~~ price on those wells of $4.50 a barrel & ~~they~~ it costs more than $4.50 to bring that oil to the surface.

But standing there in the midst of those silent pumps we could look across ~~the the channel~~ *a harbor slip* and see a Japanese tanker unloading Arab oil at

$13.50 a barrel. Well a few days ago I ran into the gentleman who had invited me to that oil field 2 yrs. ago. He told me those hundreds of pumps are still closed down because the govt. price ceiling is still $4.50 & the cost of pumping is 6. So each & every day 37,000 barrels of oil have to be replaced by that high priced Arab oil. Since that first visit 2 yrs. ago that totals more than 27 mil barrels of oil we could have had for the pumping.

In 1973 at the time of the embargo we had only been importing 23% of our oil—now it's 47%. The admin. has told us we must learn to conserve & thus reduce the amount of oil we have to import. Well economists have it figured out that for every 5% increase in price we allow we'll increase domestic supplies by 1%. They also tell us that because we are maintaining our domestic price at 30% less than the import price we are consuming about 3 mil. barrels per day more than we otherwise would. Now add 3 mil. barrels we'd save if the price were allowed to go higher & 2 mil. barrels ~~more~~ *more* per day ~~*more*~~ we'd pump domestically if the price were higher & you have a 5 mil. barrel a day reduction in our imports. ~~That~~ At $13.50 a barrel that just about wipes out the deficit in our balance of trade.

I know that's a lot of arithmatic to absorb by radio especially if you are driving. ~~b~~*B*ut when you stop to think that ~~oil~~ *gasoline* at our present rate of inflation will rise by 82% over the next 5 yrs. if that inflation rate continues and food will only go up 54% it makes you wonder why govt. has such a blind spot with regard to oil & natural gas.

This is RR Thanks for listening. ❖

Russia
June 5, 1978

Clichés ~~are~~ *become* clichés because they are nothing but simple truth repeated so often that we begin saying, "I've heard that before." I'll be right back.

No one can make a headline or a news flash by proclaiming that "travel is broadening." But in the sense of adding to ones knowledge & understanding it really is.

Congressman John Wydler of N.Y. ~~has *POSSIBLY* discovered~~, just possibly, has re-discovered the truth of the old adage. He has recently returned from a trip to the Soviet U. and has told his constituents ~~that~~ the trip was an eye opening experience.

When Congressman & Mrs. Wydler* arrived in Moscow American officials there gave ~~him~~ *them* a kind of checklist. It was a security briefing that told them a great deal about life in the workers paradise.

There were 5 specific points. "No. 1. All telephone calls," they were told,

* Congressman John W. Wydler (R–New York, 1963–1981) and Brenda Wydler.

"were monitored by the Soviets. No. 2—They were to assume that all rooms have electronic eavesdropping equipment, and that all conversations will be monitored. No. 3—Assume that all drivers understand English & are required to report all conversations. No. 4 Assume that any luggage or briefcases in your rooms will be searched while you are absent. No. 5—Assume all trash thrown in wastebaskets will be examined.

The Wydlers had an experience that made them believe*rs* in the checklist. They returned to their hotel room one day to find all the window drapes had been removed. Mrs. Wydler pointed out to her husband that there was no way to cover the windows and have any kind of privacy.

The Congressman turned toward the chandelier and yelled "Bring back those drapes—right now." And they did. Now you know that ~~has to~~ *would* be a funny scene in a movie; the Congressman shouting at a lamp and the door bursting open with a half dozen people rushing to the windows ~~to~~ hanging curtains as fast as they can.

That part of the checklist having to do with drivers who all understand English reminded me of an experience in Sac. a few years ago. A delegation of Soviet journalists was touring America and our state dept. called to say they wanted to interview me. We had a kind of press conference with an interpreter translating their questions to me & my answers to them. I got a little curious so at one point I told a joke. About ⅔ of them laughed before the interpreter opened his mouth

Another Congressman returned from Russia with a little "travel *is* broadening" experience he related to the Am. Security Council. John Breckenridge told of a meeting with Soviet deputy, defense minister N.V. Ogarkov.* The Marshal told him; "Today the Soviet U. has military superiority over the U.S. and henceforth the U.S. will be threatened. You had better get used to it."

~~Well~~ Congressman Breckinridge** told the Council; "The U.S.—not it's people—in spite of an economy unmatched in the world has either accepted or bungled into a position of inferiority predicated on budgetary insufficiency."

This is RR Thanks for listening. ❖

Responding to the U.S. Air Force's call for short takeoff and landing aircraft (STOL), Boeing began constructing the YC-14 in the early 1970s. The Carter administration contended in 1977, however, that budget constraints made it necessary to halt government funding of the new aircraft.

* Nikolai V. Ogarkov.

** John Breckinridge (D–Kentucky, 1973–1979).

Planes
June 5, 1978

From Congressman Bill Dickenson of Alabama* a member of the House Armed Services Comm. comes a bit of information you might not have heard. I'll be right back.

Many of us have had our say about the B-1 bomber, the neutron ~~bomb~~ warhead, the cruise missile etc. Now there is the case of another type aircraft and I doubt if many of us know about it or of it's military importance. Congressman Bill Dickenson of Alabama knows about it ~~pro~~ probably because he's a member of the House Armed Services Comm. And thanks to him you're going to hear about it if you'll stay with me for the next few minutes.

By way of setting the stage, one of our ~~key~~ major defense areas is the western front in Europe; the Nato line. Russia has a vast offensive force with tens of thousands of tanks arrayed against the combined Am. & European contingents. Part of our strategy is based on our ability to move forces swiftly across the Atlantic in the event of a Soviet attack. This means aerial transport of men & equipment. ~~a~~And equipment means armored vehicles & tanks to counter the overwhelming advantage in numbers of tanks the Soviets already have combat ready & in place.

Our initial force would be the mechanized brigade which has 21 different vehicles including tanks. All in all the brigade consists of 4295 troops & 1130 vehicles. The C-130 transport is our present aircraft for moving this force. It can only carry 7 of the 21 vehicles & cannot transport tanks. I'm sure the Soviets are well aware of this.

An amazing new type aircraft is under development. It bears a great many initials in the description of it's ~~ab≠~~ characteristics but they all boil down to "Advanced Medium Short Take Off & Landing Transport." It will carry heavy outsized cargo—tanks & armored vehicles. And it can travel long distances & land on ~~short runways~~ as well as take off from short runways. I'm talking about the Boeing YC-14. Two wings of these aircraft could transport an entire brigade & equipment to Germany in 12 hours. It would take a combination of C-130's & ground or sea transportation a lot longer. The C-130 can only land on 93 of Germany's airfields—the YC 14 can land on 306.

All of this sounds reassuring dosen't it. ≠ But there is a kicker in the story.—Last Dec. the admin. cancelled the YC-14 program in one of it's nat. security—or perhaps I should say—insecurity decisions.

Meanwhile by some strange coincidence the Soviet U. just happens to be ploughing full speed ahead on an airplane ~~bil~~ building program. ~~a~~And the plane they are building looks ~~like~~ for all the world like a mirror image of the

* William L. Dickinson (R–Alabama, 1965–1993).

YC-14. Well why not? The YC-14 is the most advanced idea ~~for this type of~~ in cargo transport of combat forces & equipment in the world today.

This is RR Thanks for listening. ❖

Drugs
June 5, 1978

This is going to be a little discussion of drugs—the kind you take to get healthy not the ones you take to get high. I'll be right back.

Back in 1962 the late Estes Kefauver* tacked an amendment onto the Food, Drug & Cosmetics act. It was the time of near hysteria over the Thalidomide tragedies** in Europe. No one paid much attention to the fact that Thalidomide had been banned in the U.S. ~~for~~ since 1938. The seemingly innocuous amendment was passed and we're still suffering from the unexpected repercussion.

The Fed. Drug Admin. exists to protect us from drugs or medicines such as Thalidomide that could prove harmful to our health. Sen. Kefauvers amendment simply stated that in addition the F.D.A. had to establish that the drug was effective.*** This is a near impossible task. What is effective for one patient may do nothing at all for another. So long as the medicine is not a menace to health the Dr. discovers which of his patients respond to various medications.

The immediate result was a toboggan ~~ride~~ *slide* for the U.S. pharmaceutical industry which until then had led the world in the discovering & production of health giving medicines. The *average* time for developing a new drug went from about 2 yrs. to 8 or 10 ~~& some~~ *or more*. The cost jumped from an average of about $1 mil. to $20 mil. & sometimes twice that. *THE TIME BETWEEN APPLICATION FOR A LICENSE & APPROVAL JUMPED FROM 7 MO. TO MORE THAN 2 YRS.* We dropped from about 56 new medicines a year to 17 in the 1st yr. the amendment was in effect.

Smaller firms were forced out of the market and only a few major corp's. could carry on. The F.D.A. protests that we haven't been denied any "important" drugs because of the '62 amendment. Is that true? Hardly.

All but 1 of the 11 drugs introduced for epilepsy in the U.S. since '62 were 1st introduced in England ~~so~~ by margins of up to a dozen years. Half of the drugs for epilepsy in use in the Eng. are still not available here.

* Carey Estes Kefauver served as congressman (D–Tennessee, 1939–1949) and as senator (D–Tennessee, 1949–1963).

** In Europe in the late 1950s, thalidomide was an approved medication to help pregnant women control nausea and restlessness, but it was soon discovered that it caused severe birth defects.

*** The amendment was passed in August 1962 as Public Law 87–781, "The Drug Amendments of 1962," and signed into law October 10, 1962.

I chose this particular illustration because the F.D.A. has just gotten around to ~~allowing~~ *approving* Sodium valproate, the most effective drug known to medical science in the treatment of epilepsy. It's been in use in Europe for 10 yrs. The Commission for the ~~c~~Control of ~~e~~*E*pilepsy says it can prevent a million epileptic seizures a year.

F.D.A.'s claim that Americans have not been denied access to important drugs is just not true. ~~&~~ In addition to ~~the~~ Sodium valproate there are medications for high blood pressure, hypertension & Asthma which were proven successes in Europe for years before they were made available in the U.S. And many are still banned here.

A Congressman from Idaho, Steve Symms * has introduced a bill to simply repeal the Kefauver ~~amendment~~ *amendment*. He has 113 co-signers—he needs more & we need the result ~~his~~ that repeal of the amendment would bring.

This is RR Thanks for listening. ❖

Money
June 5, 1978

We're hearing a lot of reasons for the declining value of our money but about all we can really be sure of is that it is declining. I'll be right back

It is easy to dismiss our dollars attack of anemia as due to the high price of Arab oil but dont look too closely at that excuse if it gives you comfort to believe it. W. Germany & Japan import <u>all</u> of their oil not half and their currencies are still very robust.

It wont make you feel better to know that an editor of Nat. Review magasine more than 10 yrs. ago—long before there was an oil crisis wrote a book called "Death of The Dollar." ** In it he prophesyed exactly what was going to happen to the dollar & it has happened.

Among the causes he listed for the dollars coming death were inflation, govt. hobbles on enterprise, payment for not working and ~~tax~~ punitive taxes on saving, ~~&~~ investment and honest labor. All of these & more have been standard during these past 10 yrs.

Incidentally for whatever part the high priced Arab oil has played in our spiralling inflation here is one *ex*~~s~~ample of how we've deallt with that problem. A Fed. judge in Mass. issued an injunction prohibiting the sale of oil exploration leases for the Georges Bank off Cape Cod on the grounds that "irreparable" ~~enviro~~ *ecological* harm would follow such exploration. What

* R–Idaho, 1973–1981. Symms also served in the U.S. Senate (R–Idaho, 1981–1993).

** William Frost Rickenbacker, *Death of the Dollar: Personal Investment Survival in Monetary Disaster* (New Rochelle: Arlington House, 1968).

are the facts? In ~~the~~ 25 years ~~since~~ *from* 1950 to 75 the total annual catch of fish in Mass. dropped from almost 600 mil. pounds to less than 300 mil. without any oil or gas drilling activity. In Louisiana where there was great offshore drilling & production the fish catch increased 400%.

But look at the evidence of some of those other factors and their inflationary effects; govt. regulation for example. A new car this year will cost almost $700 more than it should because of Fed. regulations. This was listed in a report ~~of~~ by the Joint Ec. Comm. of Congress along with a finding that govt. red tape, Fed. St. & local was adding about $2500 to the cost of a new house.

The study set the total cost to business & therefore the public ~~at~~ for complying with Fed. regulations alone at 20 times the cost of operating the multitude of agencies. It will come to about $100 Bil. this year.

Some time ago on one of these broadcasts I told of how the Renogiation ~~b~~*B*oard slated to go out of business in 1976 had made itself virtually permanent by way of it's backlog and by taking upon itself tasks it ~~had~~ was never set up to perform. It is, by the way, a temporary board set up during the Korean war to renogiate contracts where it is believed there have been overcharges to the govt.

Sen Lugar of Ind.* has reported to a Sen. appropriations sub-committee that the board in the last 2 yrs. has cost the govt. from 3 to $10 for every $1 in excess profits it recovers.

This is a small agency. If ~~govt.~~ *Congress* cant kill it why should we believe it can save us from the entrenched ~~behem~~ leviathons of burocracy? It will only do so when we the people tell our Congressmen the agencies go or they go.

This is RR Thanks for listening. ❖

Salaries

June 5, 1978

You may not be aware that you've been taking on a lot more dependents lately than you see around the breakfast table every morning.

I'll be right back

According to the census bureau there are 218M men, women, child~~&~~*ren* & babies in America—218 mil. of which more than half—124 mil. are dependent on tax dollars for all or a great part of their income. Let me hasten to say we shouldn't rise up in wrath ~~au~~ automatically assuming these are all parasites. Many are legitimate pensioners, social security recipients & of course govt. employees.

But with less than half the population supporting more than half—in addition to themselves and their own dependents it ~~makes~~ *behooves* us to makes

* Senator Richard Green Lugar (R–Indiana, 1977–present).

sure there are safe guards against extravagance, waste and/or cheating. What it comes down to is a workforce of roughly ~~71 mil~~ 70 mil. or so in the private sector ~~putting~~ paying the whole bill out of their earnings. Remember that. The private sector is govt's. only source of revenue. True, govt. employees pay taxes but even those dollars first had to be taken from the 70 odd mil.

~~Now~~ What I'm ~~saying~~ *going to say* now should not be taken as an attack on public employees. There are about 15¼ mil. of those with some 32 mil. dependents of their own and I'm sure all of us feel they too are entitled as we are to a fair days pay for a fair days work. Indeed we have insured that this will be so by passing statutes that govt. workers will be paid at a rate comparable to ~~the~~ pay in the private sector for similar work.

The Pres. has proposed a 5% TO 5½% pay raise for all Fed. workers but the increasingly powerful federal unions say THIS isn't enough. It's possible those union leaders are trying to justify their own existence by making loud & bellicose statements.

The fact is federal salaries ~~up~~ through the upper, middle levels are well above private-sector salaries. The Commerce dept. says the average federal ~~salary~~ SALARY in 1976 was $16,201 about $4,700 higher than the $11,483 private sector ~~salary level~~ *average*. And the Fed. employees received a 7%+ increase in '77. It is apparent that comparability has been replaced by political considerations with regard to fed. salaries.

~~We can not afford to~~

We can no longer afford unrestrained growth in the size of govt. or retention of personnel not absolutely essential to our needs. Govt. is the biggest growth industry in America. A $38 bil. payroll in 1973 is $68 Bil. in 1978. ~~The~~

The old days of government employees talking about getting out of govt. to make money are long gone. In 1973 there were 5,000,000 inquiries about ~~govt~~ Fed. jobs—last year there were 12,000,000. Govt. workers get twice as many holidays, have the best retirement program in the nation, pay raises are automatic and there is no question about job security.

It is not well known but I can assure you that as Fed. salaries go up the pressure at local & state govt. levels for comparable increases becomes almost impossible to resist.

This is RR Thanks for listening. ❖

Education
June 5, 1978

I'd like to spend a few minutes talking about a different kind of school—different that is from our own. I'll be right back.

This wont be another instalment in the recent travelogue I did about our trip to Asia but it is about one of the nations we visited. It just happens to be about someone elses trip.

Last fall a group of west coast editors visited the Repub. of China on Taiwan. One of them Joe Gendron of Pomona did an article on the tour they were given of an elementary school on their final day in Taiwan.

For almost 10 yrs. now free public education has been compulsory for all Chinese children through the 9th grade. Japan is the only other Asian nation where such educational opportunities are offered. Beyond 9th grade, high school & college ed. is provided on the basis of competitive exams. This does have a tendency to make the children a bit serious about their schoolwork.

The school day starts at 8 A.M. & ends at 4 P.M. The students also go half a day on Saturdays. There is of course a summer vacation such as we have here in our schools but with a slight difference. Once each week during the summer the children return to school to hand in their homework and keep the teachers posted on what they are doing during the summer.

The teachers get about $200 a month and are paid year round even though their summer work is only part time. But hear this—there is very little support personnel unlike our own schools where non-teaching employees have been increasing twice as fast as the number of teachers. There are no custodians in the Taiwan schools. Mr. Gendron says all the housekeeping chores are done by the students & teachers during the noon lunch break. Incidentally they all bring their lunches. There is no cafeteria in the school.

Great emphasis is placed on physical ~~educ~~ education. The school has a large outdoor swimming pool and the students go swimming every day during the school year. The pool by the way has no heating system—just sunshine.

Mr. Gendron says their group arrived at the school just in time for the ~~daily~~ routine which ~~begins~~ *starts* each day. On a voice command 5000 boys & girls poured out of classrooms & lined up in the outside corridors facing on the schoolyard. Another command and they started marching to the music of "It's a Small World." Gendron said it was a moving experience to see this number of children take their positions in ranks in the schoolyard. Students all wear a distinctive uniform which keeps down the clothing expense for parents.

Standing at attention they doffed their hats and sang their national anthem as the flag of the Republic of China was raised to the top of the flagpole. Then an instructor led teachers & children in calisthenics.

I know the picture of uniformed students marching & obeying commands will be ~~prob~~ denounced by some as regimentation and authoritarianism. It really isn't when you recall the news photos of ~~mainland~~ Chinese children on the mainland, also in uniform but learning how to throw hand grenades & use a bayonet.

This is R.R. Thanks for listening. ❖

In 1978, both chambers of the U.S. Congress passed the DC Voting Rights Amendment. The amendment would grant the District of Columbia federal voting representation already granted to states by the U.S. Constitution; allow the District to vote on amendments to the Constitution; and repeal the

Twenty-third Amendment. An affirmative vote by three-fourths of the states is needed for an amendment to be added to the Constitution. The 1978 DC Voting Rights Amendment never met this requirement.

District of Columbia
June 27, 1978

†Wash. D. C. How often we say it but how much thought do we give to those letters ~~& what~~ —*D.C. & what* they stand for? I'll be right back.

Thirteen colonies have become 50 sovereign states each with it's own capital, it's own govt. with powers firmly fixed by the constitution. And these states are joined together in a Federation.

Which colony or which of the 50 states should be the locale of the national capital? The Founding Fathers solved that problem with great, good, commonsense. Wanting to make sure we preserved the system of Sovereign states, an idea unique in all the world they created a district separate & apart from the states to serve as the site for the nations capital. That very simply is the "D.C."—District of Columbia.

By doing so the issue of conflict of interest was neatly solved, the national govt. cannot in any way be charged with favoring one state over *THE* others. Fed. employees living in the nat. capital cannot have an undue influence on the ~~govt. becau~~ *Congress with* regard to their own interests because they dont vote for representatives in Congress. It is all spelled out in Article 1 Sec. 8 of the Const. that the seat of govt. would be exempt from the pol. process so that Fed. govt. would remain the servant of the people & not become their master.

Over the years as the nat. govt. has taken on more & more tasks and thus assumed greater & greater power Wash. has become the fastest growing city in America probably because it created the fastest growing industry—govt. The citizens of the ~~city~~ *district* elect officials of city govt. & also vote for Pres. & V. Pres. The district ~~also~~ receives an annual grant from the Fed. govt.—no strings attached—~~+~~ *which* makes up 38% of ~~the~~ *it's* budget. Fed. aid amounts to more than $1000 per capita per year. No state receives that level of handout from Wash. Incidentally Wash. is the richest metropolitan area in the U.S. Problems in the rest of the country mean more prosperity for Wash. where the govt. will happily try to solve anything. Per ~~Emp.~~ *HOUSEHOLD* Inc. averages $10,000 higher than in N.Y. City, possibly because 38% of those working in the district are employed by the Fed. govt. & another 25% work in related service industries.

But now comes Sen. Edward Kennedy of Mass.* who says the citizens of the District of Columbia are victems of taxation without representation and that possibly they ~~are~~ *also* suffer racial discrimination. His answer is to make

* Senator Edward M. Kennedy (D–Massachusetts, 1962–present).

the District our 51st state. Properly lobbied his bill soared through the House 289 to 127 and moved to the Senate for hearings.

Once implemented the District of Columbia would have 2 U.S. Senators & one or two representatives in the House. Their constituency would be for the most part govt. employees who already enjoy a Fed. subsidy for much of their municipal services.

There is no way that the 51st states representatives could free themselves from a built in conflict of interest. ~~First & foremost would be a requirement that~~ They would undoubtedly vote for higher taxes, & expansion of the govt. payroll claiming that was in the best interest of their constituency. How about making the District of ~~This~~ Columbia the 51st state—if it promises to secede?

This is RR Thanks for listening.

† This should go in the 1st 3. RR ❖

Cities
June 27, 1978

With people finally aroused about the high cost of govt. have we done all we could to provide essential services at a more reasonable price? I'll be right back.

Whenever anyone brings up ~~govt~~ cutting govt. costs the inevitable ~~answer~~ *question* is ~~in the form of a question—~~"what programs do you want to eliminate?" Well without getting into ~~the~~ a discussion of whether or not there are programs that should be eliminated may I suggest there may be ways to reduce the cost of govt. without ~~eliminating~~ eliminating services.

I've spoken *before** about Scottsdale Arizona's fire protection costs running ~~at~~ at ⅔ less than for other ~~si~~ cities of the same size. Scottsdale has no city fire dept. It contracts out to a private, profit making fire fighting company for protection.

Now through a Santa Barbara-based research group on means of lowering spending we learn that many cities have found free enterprise solutions to ~~some~~ *a number of* costly problems. Pres. of the research group Robt. W. Poole writing in the paper Human Events tells of Camden N.J's. ~~switch~~ experience with garbage collection.** Four years ago Camden had a city dept. with 90 garbage collectors operating 16 trucks. Today a private firm does it with 35 employees & 9 trucks.

That same firm has branched out. Last January it took over the trash collection job in Collingswood N.J. & replaced a dozen pub. employees with one

* See "Government Can Cost Less I pp. 193–94."

** Robert W. Poole, Jr., "Cities Discovering Merits of Private Contracting for Services," *Human Events*, June 17, 1978, 15.

man and a side loading truck. In another *nearby* community 3 men & 1 truck replaced 14 ~~#~~ city employees & 5 trucks.

Other cities have found they can maximize their investment in highly trained police officers by using guards from a qualified protection agency for building security (including even the police station). This frees higher priced police for crime fighting duty.

Several weeks ago ~~in~~ *when* the debate over Prop. 13 was at fever pitch in Calif. a TV newscaster reported the results of a little private sleuthing in one of our Calif. cities. He had witnessed the planting of a tree ~~on~~ *along* one of the cities streets. The tree was sapling size in a 15 gal. can. It arrived at the planting site in a truck along with 6 city employees. The newscaster who like all of us has done a little home gardening checked with the city & found the charge for labor on that tree planting ~~(at taxpayers expense)~~ *by pub. employees* came to more than $150. He then called several nurseries & inquired ~~what~~ what they would charge for planting such a tree & how the job would be handled. All of them said they'd have a fellow bring it over in a pickup truck & plant it. The charge? Well the lowest estimate was $7.50 & the highest $15.

Private contracting eliminates cities having inventories of expensive equipment often sitting idle for long periods and even more expensive personnel for whom *at times* work must be found.

A year ago Mr. Poole says an economist at the University in Santa Barbara carried out a statistical analysis of contract ~~vers~~ *versus* non-contract cities in Los Angeles County. On the average he learned, that street maintenance in cities that contracted out cost 43% less than in those maintaining their own dept's.

There were many more examples than I have time for but maybe your home town ~~ought~~ *might want* to get some information from the "Local Govt Center" in Santa Barbara Calif.

This is RR Thanks for listening. ❖

In the spring of 1978, the Postal Rate Commission raised the price of U.S. first-class stamps for the third time in a decade. The price increased from 13 to 15 cents. The price increase went into effect on May 29, a month before this broadcast.

Stamps
June 27, 1978

Even if you aren't a stamp collector you might find it interesting to take a look at the new stamps. I'll be right back.

Ben Stein, An author, former *columnist for the* Wall St. Journal ~~columnist~~ & currently writer for the Los Angeles Herald Examiner ~~did~~ *offered* a most interesting bit of information in that paper about a month ago.

~~Ben Stein~~ Two years ago he wrote a book in which he described a hypothetical economic disaster befalling America in the early '80's.* In writing the book he had done extensive research ~~of~~ *on* the economic collapse of the Weimar Republic in Germany—1918 to 1923. That was a time when people literally ~~wheeled~~ *hauled* money around in wheelbarrows *when they shopped* & very often the wheelbarrow was worth more than the money.

Germany went through in those 5 years an inflation of one trillion percent.—Yes I said one trillion. Employers ~~gave~~ *paid* workers every hour so they could rush out and buy things before the prices went up. I remember as a boy being given a 50 million mark note by a ~~returning visitor to~~ *visitor returning from* Germany. *It was worth about one American penny.*

In his research Ben Stein learned that the denominations on postage stamps ~~changed~~ *increased* so ~~quickly~~ *rapidly* that to avoid the expense of constantly changing them ~~and~~ the German govt. decided to ~~simply~~ issue stamps bearing *SIMPLE* letters of the alphabet. This not only avoided the psychological upset of putting out ~~one billion~~ stamps bearing ~~the~~ *a* price *of* one billion marks ~~but~~ *or so* but they could sell the A ~~sta~~ or the B stamp for whatever the new price might be each day & save printing new stamps.

It seems impossible I know that any great nation could go through & survive such a wild & unbelievable inflation but it happened. And possibly because of the post war bitterness we felt toward Germany, Americans joked about what was happening over there.

Right now I dont particularly feel like joking~~—Ben Stein~~ certainly not about postage stamps without prices—just letters of the alphabet on them. Take a look at ~~the~~ *our* new 15 cent stamps. ~~They dont say 15 cents.~~ ~~*There is nothing on the stamp that* that says 15¢~~ *It dosen't say 15 cents.* There is just the letter "A."

Ben Stein reached two members of the White House press bureau by phone. That isn't hard to do because ~~the press~~ the White House press aides outnumber the Nat. Security council. When he asked why the stamps bore only the letter A the answer was—"Well it's so that if we have to raise the price we wont have to print a lot of new stamps."

Now I'm sure Ben Stein wasn't trying to frighten the readers of the Herald Examiner with images of billion dollar stamps but he was in a sense uttering a ~~wa~~ legitimate warning. Indeed he quoted an old family friend, an Austrian economist who had lived through that German inflation who said of us "You are going down that path too."

This is RR Thanks for listening. ❖

Although Governor Jimmy Carter pledged to reduce the number of U.S. military personnel in the Republic of Korea during the 1976 presidential campaign, U.S. troop strength in the country remained stable throughout Carter's

* Benjamin Stein with Herbert Stein, *On the Brink* (New York: Simon & Schuster, 1977).

presidency. When this essay was written, the United States had approximately 42,000 military personnel in South Korea.

On December 15, 1978, the United States and the People's Republic of China issued a joint communiqué stating that bilateral relations would be established on January 1, 1979. The communiqué also said: "The United States recognizes the Government of the People's Republic of China as the sole legal Government of China. Within this context the people of the United States will maintain cultural, commercial, and other unofficial relations with the people of Taiwan." *

Asia
June 27, 1978

A very well qualified observer of world affairs has returned from a swing through Asia with some comments you might find interesting. I'll be right back.

An executive with what must be the worlds biggest news agency recently made a trip to Asia where because of his position he met with govt. officials, industrial leaders, publishers and others able to contribute sound views on the countries he visited. He has returned with information that ~~present~~ *does not* always jibe with the doctrinaire views we get from diplomats & some commentators who often see things only in the light of their own bias. He was protected against ~~a~~ indoctrination by the variety of his contacts; he could check the things he gathered from one source against the views of others.

He told me that he too had found an almost universal anxiety over our foreign policy. Everyone in S. Korea was convinced that N. Korea would attack if the U.S. presence was reduced. He was astounded to learn from qualified sources in detailed breifings that N. Korea is capable of producing it's own ~~armored forces~~ ~~*vehicles*~~ *armor.* Also that most of it's artillery is concentrated in hardened positions along the demilitarized zone capable of shelling Seoul & the surrounding area in which is located almost all of S. Koreas industry.

In all of his contacts in Korea he found no hostility toward the U.S. He also found a resolve on the part of the people to counter communism at any cost. That's a little ~~contrary~~ *contrary* to the view we're so often given of S. Korean unhappiness with their own leaders. The 2 questions he was asked most often were: "What must we do to show you that we are your true friends?" And "Dosen't your Pres. know that a communist attack on S. Korea will eventually engulf all of Asia?"

His next step was Taiwan where he met with many of the same officials I had met with plus numerous others in business & the press. He came away with a feeling that Taiwan might not find a 2 China's policy impossible to live

* President Jimmy Carter signed the Taiwan Relations Act on April 10, 1979. The legislation reaffirmed U.S. commitment to the peace and security of Taiwan.

with; that we could pursue establishing diplomatic relations with Communist China without renouncing our treaties & our recognition of the Free Repub. of China. Our Sec. of State should discover that.

He found as we did on our visit that the Chinese on Taiwan are hardworking and very proud of their economic achievements & their constant progress toward a more democratic govt. Being there on an election day he visited polling places and watched not only the voting but the counting of ballots. He suggests we might have a few precincts in some of our *own* cities where that ~~might not~~ *wouldn't* be possible.

On Taiwan he ran into one oft-repeated question; "Why must you slap your friends in the face while kowtowing to those who have never shown their friendship toward you." Do any of us have an answer to that?

The windup on Taiwan was his briefing on "intelligence operations." ~~Very~~ Mainland Chinese manage to get hundreds of reports a week over to Taiwan on conditions in Red China. Some are written by *members of the* military. ~~personnell~~ All present a picture quite different from the canned tour Americans are given when they visit Peking.

This is RR Thanks for listening. ❖

On September 21, 1972, President Ferdinand Marcos imposed martial law in the Philippines. The ostensible reason was an attempted assassination of Juan Ponce Enrile, the secretary of defense, yet government corruption, poverty, and political unrest had been rising for years. Marcos lifted martial law on January 17, 1981, but his firm rule continued.

Asia II

June 27, 1978

On the last broadcast I quoted reports by a friend, an executive with the worlds greatest news agency who has just returned from Asia. Today is the wrap up.

I'll be right back.

Today I'd like to tell you ~~about~~ what the Philippines look like to a qualified observer who had an opportunity to meet with leaders in every field as well as journeyman members of the press ~~and~~ *TOPPED OFF BY* several hours with Pres. & Mrs. Marcos.*

The Pres. is very sensitive to the wave of criticism he & his admin. are receiving in the American press following his declaration of martial law. We here in America have been given a ~~picture~~ story of repression, arrest of pol. prisoners and torture. The gentleman ~~I'm~~ I quoted with regard to S. Korea & Taiwan

* Imelda Marcos.

~~yesterday~~ *on the last broadcast* & who I am quoting today regarding the Philippines said: "Maybe there have been human rights violations & torture. I dont know. I can tell you, however, that a close friend who has been in the Philippines as a representative of the Drug Enforcement Admin. for 5 yrs. told me that he has never seen or even suspected mis-treatment of prisoners by the police. I questioned him closely & he told me that he had been to numerous prisons, including those for pol. prisoners. He said that some of the prisons housing pol. prisoners are country clubs compared to U.S. prisons." Then he added; "I trust my friend implicitly."

He found both the Pres. & Mrs. Marcos still staunch friends of America & as anti-communist as ever. They know that their insistence that our *mil.* bases there be ~~made~~ *leaseholds* under Philippine sovereignty has been interpreted as anti-Americanism but ~~the~~ Pres. Marcos said; "the people of the Philippines must be given some nat. pride & shown that their country is running it's own affairs."

That shouldn't be so hard for our govt. ~~which bled so freely~~ *TO UNDERSTAND AFTER THE WAY it bled* over Panamas desire to feel nat. pride by obtaining sovereignty over the Canal. The Pres. went on to say that the payments he was asking for the bases would be applied toward the purchase of an early warning radar system.

Brace yourself for a slight surprise. My friend expressed the opinion that this was hardly necessary since ~~of course~~ *obviously* the U.S. already had such a system in operation there. Pres. Marcos laughed and said that was the response of both Pres. Carter & Sec. Vance.* Neither of them were ~~aware~~ ≠ *aware* that we had no such long range warning system in the Philippines.

Other surprise revelations; the average man in the street said living conditions had improved more in the 5 yrs. of martial law than in the previous 50 yrs,

There are stories about Mrs. Marcos "putting the arm" on industry for money with which to build some of her pet projects such as the Philippines Cultural Center. She stated very frankly that she did exactly that. She added, there isn't public money for such construction so she asks industry to contribute & smilingly agreed that maybe, ~~she leaned more~~ "*there was more* leaning than asking" but what usually isn't reported is that all such contributions are tax deductible just as they are here in America.

This news agency executive summed up that on the Philippines as elsewhere in Asia he found only friendship for the U.S. but worry as to what our foreign policy really was. *Well that's something we have in common.*

This is RR Thanks for listening. ❖

* Secretary of State Cyrus Vance.

Tass, the Soviet news agency, called Johnny Harris, a death-row inmate in Alabama, a civil rights martyr, yet Harris was not a civil rights activist, and was placed on death row following a charge of murdering a prison guard. Harris won a retrial in 1981, and in 1983 was convicted of first-degree murder for a second time.

Free Press
June 27, 1978

It's amazing what you can do if you control the media—the means of communication. Russia does that & has created an instant hero you might like to know about.

I'll be right back.

The Soviet U's. two great newspapers—~~are~~ *both* govt. operated, are Pravda & Isvestia. Now ~~Pra~~ the word Pravda means truth & Isvestia means news. There is a joke the Russian people tell but not out loud. They say "There is no Isvestia in Pravda & no Pravda in Isvestia."

But one thing is certain, when they put on a propaganda effort it succeeds. There is no one to blow the whistle on them & cry foul.

They have created ~~virtually~~ a national hero in Russia using an American prison inmate you probably never heard of. Russians are flooding Pravda & Isvestia with mail as well as the office of the Gov. of Alabama. Alabama is where the man is in prison awaiting execution.

Execution the Russians say because he is, "an eloquent pointer to the violation of human rights, the lawlessness & arbitrary rule that has become part of America today." A member of the Presidium of the Soviet Womens committee see's in the impending execution an indication that; "U.S. racists want to electrocute the young worker for adhering to progressive views. The rector of a Soviet University says American talk about human rights is worthless if a person can be sentenced to death for daring to protest against oppression & lawlessness.

The Soviet media on orders of course has produced an instant celebrity. From the Ukraine to Siberia the Russian man ~~&~~ *or* woman in the street knows that a "young worker" is about to be slaughtered for his beliefs, after trial in a rigged court on prefabricated charges.

A team of Soviet reporters came all the way to the U.S. & to Alabama to interview the man to whom they had given nationwide celebrity status in their own land. The interview never took place ~~because~~ Alabama like Calif. & a number of other states has a policy forbidding interviews with death row inmates.

One of the Russian reporters was given a tour of the prison and a look at the electric chair which hasn't been used in 13 years. Then all the Soviet news delegation interviewed "civil rights" activists in the state.

Interestingly enough the man who has been the object of so much attention in Russia has had his execution postponed pending an appeal. That probably wouldn't be of interest to the Russian journalists. They'd have to explain to their readers about the right of appeal which ~~dosen't~~ isn't much of a commonplace in the Soviet system of justice.

And you can be sure they wont tell their readers at home why their celebrity is really on death row. ~~He~~ *It isn't because he's a fighter for human rights nor is he a martyr for his beliefs. He* murdered a guard ~~for~~ *while* serving a life sentence for robbery & rape.

This is RR Thanks for listening. ❖

As Reagan discusses in the next two broadcasts, Soviet dissident Aleksandr I. Solzhenitsyn was the commencement speaker at Harvard University on June 8, 1978. In 1974, following the publication of Gulag Archipelago, *a book critical of the Soviet Union's labor camps and incarceration methods, Solzhenitsyn went into exile.*

Alex. Solzhenitsyn
June 27, 1978

A month or so ago Alexander Solzhenitsyn delivered a graduation address here in our land. Some of his eloquent remarks deserve quoting. I'll be rite back.

Remembering the anti-Vietnam war sentiment of the late '60's & early '70's some might find a bit of irony in the fact that ~~early~~ last month Alexander Solzhenitsyn was Harvard U's. graduation speaker. It is always good to see ourselves as others see us so I'd like to quote just a few paragraphs from his address which dealt uncompromisingly with, "the ~~d~~ *decline* of courage in the West."

He saw that decline in all of the Western world; in each country, each govt., each pol. party & in the United Nations. He said; "It is particularly noticeable among the ruling groups & the intellectual elite causing an impression of loss of courage by the entire society." He made plain however that possibly there was courage to be found among our people but they were not making their influence felt in govt.

"Pol. & intellectual bureaucrats show depression, passivity & perplexity," he said, "in their actions and in their statements to explain how reasonable & even morally warranted it is to base state policies on weakness & cowardice." He went on to say they can be inflexible & even angry when dealing with weak ~~govt's.~~ *countries.* But—quote, "they get tongue tied & paralyzed when they deal with powerful govt's., aggressors & international terrorists."

He reminded his Harvard audience of our own Dec. of Independence; that "when the modern ~~w~~*W*estern states were created they proclaimed that govt's. are meant to serve man & man lives to be free & to pursue happiness."

Saying there are "meaningful warnings which history gives ~~to~~ a threatened or perishing society," ~~such as~~ Solzhenitsyn described the fight for our planet earth, physical & spiritual, as of cosmic proportions. And he said, "it was not a vague matter of the future; it has already started. The forces of evil have begun their decisive offensive, you can feel their pressure, & yet your screens & publications are full of prescribed smiles & raised glasses." ~~What~~ And he asked: "What is the joy about?"

For those who think hopefully that Angola might become the Soviet Unions Vietnam or that Cubas adventuring in Africa can be stopped by being polite to Castro he has an answer. He describes their failure to understand the Vietnam war as, "the ~~"~~most cruel mistake.~~"~~ Members of the U.S. anti-war movement wound up being involved in the betrayal of Far Eastern nations in a genocide & in the suffering today imposed on 30 mil. people" ~~a~~*A*nd he asked: "Do those convinced pacifists hear the moans coming from there? Do they understand their responsibility today? Or do they prefer not to hear?"

On the next broadcast I'd like to ~~tell~~ *give* you a few more of Alexander Solzhenitsyns thoughts.

This is RR Thanks for listening. ❖

Alex. Solzhenitsyn II
June 27, 1978

This is more from Alexander Solzhenitsyns speech last month at Harvard U's. graduation ceremony. I'll be right back.

On the last broadcast I quoted from ~~the~~ last months Harvard graduation address by Alexander Solzhenitsyn. It was a very frank description of how our society appears to this man who lived through the horror of the Soviet Gulag and still had the courage to defy ~~his~~ the slave masters of his homeland. I've quoted him because he does not see in us that same courage.

Speaking of the Vietnam conflict he said: "The American intelligentsia lost its nerve and as a consequence there~~f~~*of* danger has come much closer to the United States. But there is no awareness of this. Your shortsighted politicians who signed the hasty Vietnam capitulation seemingly gave America a carefree breathing pause; however, a hundredfold Vietnam now looms over you." He continued: "That small Vietnam had been a warning & an occasion to mobilize the nations courage. But if a full fledged America suffered a real defeat from a small Communist half country, how can the West hope to stand firm in the future?"

If the West dosen't have the will to stand firm Solzhenitsyn says ~~"~~nothing is left then but concessions & betrayal to gain time. He criticized our diplomats

~~at~~ *at the* Belgrade conference who backed away from any confrontation over ~~the~~ Soviet violations of the Human Rights provision in the Helsinki pact. This is the provision for which men like Orlov * have gone to Siberia & others have died. It ~~makes~~ *reminds* us of the ~~now~~ *arrogant* statement by the *chief* Soviet delegate at Belgrade who said “If you take out everything we dont like, it's ~~g~~ quite a good document.”

Then he said that while the next war would probably not be an Atomic one still it might very well bury Western civilization forever. He said he wasn't, “examining the case of a world war disaster & the changes it would produce in society. There is a disaster, however, which has already been under way for quite some time. ~~now~~ I am referring,” he said, “to the calamity of a despiritualized & irreligious humanistic consciousness.” We have lost the concept of a Supreme Complete Entity which used to restrain our passions & our responsibility. We have placed too much hope in pol. & soc. reforms only to find that we were being deprived of our most precious possession; our spiritual life.

Solzhenitsyn told the Harvard graduates that since ~~we ou~~ *our bodies* are all doomed to die our task while on earth must be of a more spiritual nature. And he left them with this charge, “that one's life journey may become an experience of moral growth, in that one may leave life a better human being than one started it.”

Isn't it too bad that young men & women graduating from the U. of Moscow cant have a speaker like Alexander Solzhenitsyn~~?~~.

This is RR Thanks for listening. ❖

Inflation
June 27, 1978

Looking ahead to the next 5 years can be a dismal thing to do unless we deal suddenly & solidly with inflation. I'll be right back.

Not too long ago I gave a figure ~~in~~ *on* one of these broadcasts about what a tank full of gasoline ~~for the car would~~ *would* cost 5 yrs. from now if we ~~c~~ continue the rate of inflation we've had for the last 5 yrs. Right now a tank of regular runs about $13.28—5 yrs. from now it could be $24.16.

That ~~item~~ *line* from a broadcast I did on energy started me thinking about what other items in our daily living might cost if we dont get some common sense & end ~~this~~ inflation ~~like day before yesterday.~~ *before it ends us.* A $50 shopping cart of food for example will cost $77. I should point out that while we have a cost of living index not all items making up that index increase at the same rate. Gasoline went up 82% in the last 5 yrs. food went up 54%.

A new house at $55,000 today will be $89,600 in 5 years. In Los Angeles or

* Yuri Orlov was a Soviet dissident. He and Irina Valitova, his wife, were allowed to leave the Soviet Union in 1986.

Wash. D.C. you'd have to multiply those figures quite a bit. A $5000 car will be $6,875. A year in college will go from $5200 to $7,740.

But the most telling figures have to do with ~~what~~ *how* our earnings must increase ~~to~~ just to maintain the same level of living we had 5 yrs. ago & today. I've done some broadcasts on how much our ~~Fed.~~ taxes go up every time we get a cost of living increase so the salary figures I'm going to give you are for maintaining your buying power after you've paid your Fed. taxes. There is no way of course to project local & state taxes because they vary from town to town & state to state.

If you were making $5000 a year 5 yrs. ago you have to be earning $7,011 today to have the same buying power ~~(~~after you've paid your Fed. taxes.~~) that you had then.~~ If we continue inflation at the same rate for another 5 yrs. you'll have to make $11,108.

Now if *the* Fed. ~~taxes~~ *inc. tax* were indexed to allow for inflation we could simply multiply ~~by #~~ to get the figures for other levels of earning. But the tax isn't indexed so that wont work. *You're going to move up into* higher *surtax brackets*. If your income was $10,000 in 1973 it has to be $14,601 today to keep even & 5 yrs. from now it must go to $22,530 that's $422 more than double the figure for the $5000 inc. At $15,000 in 1973, you must be earning $22,452 today & if inflation continues 35,280 in 1983.

Were you in the $20,000 a year range in 1973? Well if you aren't earning $30,195 today you are worse off than you were then & you'll have to earn $48,056 ~~in 1983~~ *5 yrs. from now*. Twenty five thousand in '73 calls for $38,211 ~~in '78~~ *TODAY* & $61,744 in 1983. Let's jump up to that standard of affluence the $50,000 inc. *If you were making that* in 1973, it has to be $79,463 now and brace yourself—$124,038—5 yrs. from now. As an example of the part the Fed. inc. tax plays, inflation over the 10 yrs. ~~was~~ amounts to 65% but you have to increase your earnings 150% to stay even at a ~~6 &~~ 6½% annual inflation rate.

Those are some of the prices we pay ~~for Fed. defi~~ *because the Fed.* govt. *continues to* spends more than it takes in.

This is RR Thanks for listening. ❖

Government
June 27, 1978

Every now & then as you well know I'm moved to write about the curious doings of officialdom in the marble halls of govt. I'll be write back.

Not too long ago a friend sent me a clipping from the Pasadena Star News. That is the Rose Parade Pasadena in Calif. It seems that Pasadena couldn't qualify ~~for~~ as a distressed area eligible for the Presidents urban program to help distressed areas.

Now that hardly qualifies as a headline bit of news that would make one lift an eyebrow and say "how come?" To be eligible a*n* ~~city~~ area must meet 3 of 4 criteria; have an unemployment rate above the nat. average; a 5 yr. growth rate of employment below the nat. average, a 5 yr. growth rate of population below th~~ate same~~ *nat.* average & it's 5 yr. absolute change in per capita income is below the nat. average.

Pasadena is a stable area and what is usually termed a wealthy community so it isn't surprising that it didn't meet the "need" requirements for an Uncle Sam handout. No—that isn't what made the news clipping interesting. ~~The~~ It was the cities that did qualify that raised a few eyebrows in Calif.

San Marino, La Canada, Flintridge & Bradbury are all *on the* eligible list. It's true these cities aren't filled with industries and they probably have quite a few people who aren't working at regular jobs. But that's because they are the kind of communities where a lot of people dont need jobs. As a matter of fact a pretty good percentage of the people in those communities are better off than the Fed. govt. ~~There debts (if they have any) dont aren't greater~~ if you compare their credit ratings. I doubt they'll be rushing to Wash. for a handout.

Meanwhile business in the Nations Capital goes on as usual. Sec. of H.E.W. Joseph Califano ~~described~~ *summed up* his agency this way: "If you combined the budgets of all 50 states the total would be $50 Bil. shy of matching HEW's budget." ~~HEW has the 3rd largest~~ This one agency of our govt. has the 3rd largest budget in the world, topped only by the budgets of the U.S. *it's self* & the Soviet U.

Now that we're all past the inc. tax date you might be interested to know that the worlds most confusing document is the Internal Revenue Services official manual. It has 38,000 pages in 12 volumes. That's bad enough but they continue to make changes every month to such an extent that the Agencies librarian cant keep pace with the indexing.

One *I.R.S.* special agent who needs the manual in his work (which involves criminal *tax* investigations) became so fed up he went out & bought a commercial copy. When tax time came & he took the cost of his purchase as a tax deduction—(the manual being an essential tool in his work as an I.R.S. agent) ~~the I.R.S.~~ *HIS BOSS, the I.R.S.* refused to allow it.

In closing—the Treasury Dept. proposed making tax regulations more simple. They said: "A regulation which would otherwise be eligible for consideration as a significant regulation, may, nontheless, with secretarial approval, be determined not to be a significant regulation." Doesn't that make you feel better?

This is RR Thanks for listening. ❖

Mirages
June 27, 1978

Someone has come up with a scientific explanation for some of the miracles recorded in both the old & new Testaments. I'll be right back

I suppose it's only natural for any of us regardless of our faith to speculate at times ~~about some of the miracles contained in the Bible and~~ *as to whether or not* there might be a natural explanation for some of the biblical miracles. I'll confess to doing it in idle thought on occasion but always winding up unable to explain away the happening ~~as told in both old & new~~ *described in either the old or new* Testaments as natural phenomena.

But today just as there are revisionists trying to re-write history so are there scholars—yes & theologians trying to de-spiritualize the Judeo-Christian tradition. Some time ago I commented on this with regard to the Christmas story.*

Now a scholar has come up with a scientific explanation of two of the better known miracles. He says they were simply mirages. The first is the parting of the Red Sea which allowed ~~the Is~~ Moses & the Israelites to escape the pursuing Egyptians and the second is Jesus walking on the waters of the sea of ~~Gallile Galillee *GALLILEE*~~ Gallilee.

Most of us know something about mirages, particularly those of us who live in the West. And I dare say most of us have been driving on a hot day & seen the highway ahead take on the appearance of water shining in the sunlight. We dont put on the brakes because we know it is simply heat waves rising from the pavement ~~and~~ giving the illusion of water. Of course there is much more scientific knowledge about the often elaborate mirages & reflected images ~~in~~ *seen* in desert areas and I'll admit I'm not blessed with that knowledge.

But this scholar who is has suggested that the Israelites were simply led across desert sands at a time when a mirage gave them the appearance of walking through water. ~~He says much the same explanation is given has probably *situation could probably explain* the belief that Jesus walked upon the water.~~

As I say I'm not an informed scholar on the ~~science of the phenomena we refer to as mirages.~~ *subject of mirages.* ~~b~~*B*ut even giving the writer that edge I'm still left with some questions. The mirage might (and let me emphasize *THE WORD* might) explain the Israelites crossing ~~of~~ the Red Sea but that leaves the story very much unfinished. The Armies of the Pharaoh tried to follow & the waters closed on them crushing chariots & drowning men and horses. ~~That I'm convinced can not be done by a mirage.~~ *A mirage can do that?*

The~~ren~~ *there* is an unanswered question or two about Jesus walking on *the* water if we assume he was on dry land & part of a mirage. First of all it was

* "Christmas," January 9, 1978, pp. 247–48.

night and the Disciples were in a wave tossed boat. Jesus walked from the shore ~~toward them~~ *to join them in the boat.* If that was a mirage & he was really on dry land—what was the boat doing there?

I'm afraid our scholar has asked too much of heat waves & reflections on cloud & desert sand. It will take more than a mirage to do a successful re-write of the all time worlds best seller—the Bible.

This is R.R. Thanks for listening. ❖

Lumber

June 27, 1978

It's very easy to hear the word lumber & then let your mind picture rapacious exploiters leveling the forest in their lust for profit. True or false?

I'll be right back.

I'm sure I wont be surprising anyone ~~if I~~ *by* saying that lumber prices which are about 15% of all construction are a major factor in the high cost of building. Some contractors find it almost impossible to give a ~~sub~~ reasonable estimate on a project because of the uncertainty of lumber prices. Can all of this be laid at the door of the lumber industry—or is there something to be done that is beyond the power of the industry?

Columnist John Chamberlain* recently gathered *together* some ~~statistics~~ *information* having to do with lumber & forests ~~and~~ which points to an attainable solution and once again it is a simple matter of using common sense.

The problem is of course ≠ the unconscionable high cost of new homes. Our private forest industry at present plants more trees than it cuts. No longer does the industry de-nude the forest land & then move on. But that industry only owns 16% of the nations standing softwood. States own about 12% ~~&~~ *BUT* the Fed. govt. owns 52%. So as Chamberlain points out ~~it is~~ the U.S. dept. of Agriculture could be the key to lower housing costs.

Right now the Forest service (operated by the Agri. dept.) sells about 12½ billion board ft. of lumber annually to the saw mills, the forest industry from it's much smaller holdings sells almost 16½ billion & another 14½ comes from non-industrial sources. That does indicate that Uncle Sams 52% offers the best chance of increased supply.

Now I'm sure all of us want conservation of ~~forest land~~ *trees* in our national forests. No one of us would suggest wholesale cutting ~~back~~ to meet commercial demand. But what John Chamberlain has discovered is that the Fed. govt.

* In 1930, John Chamberlain became the first daily literary critic for *The New York Times*. He wrote a syndicated column on political, economic, and social issues for King Features from 1960 to 1985 and authored eight books.

is allowing ~~enough~~ lumber to go to waste each year which could increase the supply by 6 bil. board feet.

Trees aren't like minerals which stay where they are until some one removes them from the earth. Trees grow up, sometimes get sick, grow old, & ~~they die~~ DIE. This apparently is not recognized by some of our environmental extremists who confuse conservation with preservation. *Dead trees are pure waste & harmful to the Forest.*

Take the example of ~~one~~ *Lassen* national forest in Calif. This preserve allows a cut of 150 mil. board feet a year. It could raise that to 268 mil. board feet if the timber cutters were allowed to harvest only the overmature & dying trees. ~~And~~ Lassen would be a better national forest & one much safer from the threat of forest fire if the additional cutting were done. As it is, it's choked with rotting wood.

Chamberlain points out that this additional cutting in Lassen Nat. Forest alone would *also* provide a*n* ~~job~~ increase of 1200 jobs in Calif. And it would ~~make~~ lower the price of lumber.

This is RR Thanks for listening. ❖

Reagan opposed President Gerald Ford signing the Helsinki Pact on August 1, 1975, on the grounds that it codified Soviet control of Eastern Europe. He labeled the Helsinki Pact immoral during the Republican primaries of 1976, and inserted language to this effect in the 1976 Republican platform.

Freedom of Speech in Russia
June 27, 1978

Young students from the countries of Western Europe are risking imprisonment in the Soviet Gulag for the cause of Human Rights. I'll be right back.

A while back National Review magasine presented an article by Lennart Frantzell that revealed how much idealism there is in the world and exposed how much hypocracy there is behind the Iron curtain.*

The author gives an accounting of young students *& others* from France, Belgium, Norway, Finland & other countries ~~outside~~ of Western Europe who journey to Russia as tourists. These particular tourists however aren't interested in sightseeing. They smuggle *in* books & leaflets which they then openly hand to Russians on the streets. These are books the Russians are forbidden to read such as the writings of Solzhenitsyn. Invariably the ~~students~~ book distributing tourists are arrested. One young Belgian girl ~~t~~ handing out ~~lis~~ lists of pol. prisoners names was ~~rushed~~ *seized by KGB agents* so quickly she could only throw the leaflets in the air before she was arrested.

* Lennart Frantzell, "The Book Smugglers," *National Review,* June 23, 1978, pp. 776 and 795.

Now the Soviet Const. guarantys freedom of speech but like the Helsinki pact the Russian govt. dosen't feel obliged to observe it. Nevertheless ~~the~~ Soviet officialdom is taking it's lumps and is very uncomfortable ~~about~~ in the face of these tourists who argue back with full knowledge of the*ir* ~~leg~~ legal rights & the terms of the Helsinki pact.

Listen to this exchange between a 22 yr. old French girl & the 2 KGB officers who arrested her.

~~"Who is your friend?"~~ "Are you a member of a political party?" "Yes."

"What does your father do?" "He is a politician."

"Does he have a high position?" "High enough."

"Does your father know of your trip to the USSR?"

"Yes of course."

"Well both you & he know that it is forbidden to bring books into the USSR!" "Really? But why? To our country for example, one can bring *IN* any books. In our country people have the right to read anything."

"Well this isn't Belgium but the USSR." "How does the USSR differ from Belgium?" "We want our nation to think according to our ideology." "You are really naive people! Do you really believe that 250 mil. people will think the way you want them to think?" The K.G.B. agents didn't have an answer to that one. All they could say was; "It is forbidden to bring in books! You may get 10 yrs. for it." To which she replied "I know we already packed some things in case we would have to go to camp."

The smugglers have the help of the Russian émigré organization and ≠ contacts in the Soviet U. who help pass the literature along. Leaflets have appeared in cities & towns far distant from Moscow and books are regularly circulated among dissident intellectuals in Moscow.

Sokolov a member of the section in charge of the confiscated books was arrested a couple of years ago for selling those books to black market dealers. He hasn't been heard from since. But the smuggling goes on and significantly the Russian people show a great eagerness to get their hands on the forbidden literature.

This is RR Thanks for listening. ❖

Stanley Yankus
June 27, 1978

Reading a Chi. paper on a recent airplane flight I ~~learned~~ *discovered* the ~~finish of~~ *end to* a story I first heard & repeated almost 20 yrs. ago. I'll be right back.

~~Being~~ *As* a veteran of the mashed potato circuit~~—(the~~ (*my name for the* after dinner speaker ~~route~~ ~~*routine*~~ routine) I'm always on the lookout for interesting anecdotes & examples. The other day on a flight to the midwest I was reading the Chi. Tribune when a familiar name caught my eye. It wasn't the name of ~~some~~ *a* well known public figure but it had been a part of a speech I'd made almost 20 years ago.

Stanley Yankus was a chicken farmer in Mich. back in the late '50's when our govt. was deeply involved in the control & regulation of American agriculture. Some of you will remember those days of acreage allotments, & subsidies for not growing things. It was not the best of times for farmers and coincidentally there are signs that Wash. is anxious to return to those days.

But back to Stanley Yankus. His chicken farm was the culmination of a dream. He had worked for years in Chi. as a hog butcher, saving for the day when he could have his own farm. With his dream realized he worked from dawn until long after dark when he & his wife ~~candled~~ *would candle* eggs on the back porch. Maybe I'd better explain to a younger generation that candeling meant holding each egg up to a light to make sure it wasn't a fertile egg containing an embryo chicken.

Stanley was a good family man & citizen serving on the local school board and educating his children. He raised wheat on his little farm which he harvested & fed to his chickens. Then in the late 50's the govt. told him he couldn't do that. The govt. had a wheat control program in which farmers were given allotments of how much wheat they could raise.

Yankus protested that he wasn't in the Wheat business, he was just raising enough to feed to his own chickens. He refused to plow his wheat under as the govt. ordered him to do. The govt. attached his small bank account. When he still didn't give in they fined him $5000 and threatened him with worse penalties.

I remember citing his experience & ~~the~~ a judges ruling that said in effect, "the govt. had usurped the right to tell a citizen what he could raise on his own land for his own use." Stanley Yankus said: "This is the action of a police state—the sort of life we were brought up to detest."

He sold his farm to pay the fine and became the first American I know of to leave the U.S. in search of freedom. He & his family moved to Australia. There unfortunately he learned ~~govt.~~ *life* was also pretty much regulated by govt. Becoming a salesman he started in to reclaim his dream of once again having a farm.

A few weeks ago, 19 years after he had left America his dream was near realization. He ~~closed a deal~~ *bought a 10 acre* almond farm *in ~~Aus~~ his new homeland* and was awaiting plans for the ~~home~~ *house* he would build on his own land. ~~Sta~~

Stanley Yankus was then 59 yrs. old. He died of a heart attack before the house plans arrived.

This is RR. Thanks for listening. ❖

Charity
July 1978

† I'd like to tell you about a wonderful undertaking by a group of your fellow citizens who saw a problem & decided to do something about it.
†† I'll be right back.

You've heard me criticize govt. many times for taking on tasks that properly ~~belon~~ should be left to the people. To tell you the truth a very real fear of mine is that govt. with it's many social ~~welfare~~ reforms may rob ~~o~~ us of that great sense of ~~generosity which is characteristically American~~ *GENEROSITY & charity which is our American heritage.*

Not too long ago I received a letter from a longtime friend, Robert Young. To younger listeners I'm speaking of the Robert Young you probably know as Dr. Welby.* In his letter he told me some facts about child abuse; that it is the number one killer of children under 5 yrs. of age; ~~&~~ *that* 60% of abuse victems are ~~under~~ *not yet* 2 yrs. old; ~~More than~~ *that* 325,000 cases are on record but experts say the real total including the unreported is probably over a million.

Those of course are just statistics. ~~He told me of a~~ *They dont tell about a* father plunging a squirming 14 month old son into a tub of scalding water because he cried~~. Then there was the case of~~ *or* a 9 yr. old retarded boy beaten while he knelt on carpet tacks. They dont tell of little Mary Beth.

~~But Bob really brought it home to me when he told me the story of a *one particular* little girl. Neighbors had reported to the police that~~ *sounds of repeated* ~~terrified screams.~~ Investigating officers went to a typical suburban residence~~. They~~ *where they* were greeted by a neatly dressed young mother. There were 2 boys ages 6 & 8 ~~who~~ in the room who seemed to be uncommonly quiet. When the officers mentioned that neighbors ~~complaint~~ *had reported hearing screams* the young mother said she had ~~had~~ disciplined one of ~~ch~~ her children for misbehaving. As she was talking the officers heard a soft whimper, like the sound of a hurt animal come from a room down the hall.

While the 2 boys cowered in fear & the mother protested, the officers threw open a bedroom door. ~~Bob said t~~*T*here was an overpowering stench of urine, vomit & defecation. Then they saw the little girl ~~hudded~~ huddled naked in a corner of the bed—one wrist tied to the bedpost with an electric cord. Her body was a mass of bruises & welts. An ugly blue, black swelling had closed one eye, her lip was split & her mouth was swollen.

As her mother followed the officers into the room, ~~the little girl~~ *little Mary Beth* through her bruised & swollen lips said, "Mommy if I die—then will you love me?"

* Robert Young played the title role in the long running television series *Marcus Welby, M.D.* The show ran from 1969 to 1976.

Neighbors said this little battered animal was in reality a bright, beautiful & charming child. ~~The~~ *Her* punishment had been for wetting the bed.

~~Then *in*~~ *In* his letter Robt. Young told ~~me he~~ *me* about "Childrens village;" a modern residential facility near Los Angeles on 119 acres where abused children can be cared for; where they will hear possibly for the first time a kind voice as they are tucked in bed with a Teddy bear or a doll.

Childrens Village U.S.A. is a non-profit organization, it's entire program supported by voluntary contributions ~~of~~ $5–$10–$100 or whatever.—It's on Ventura Blvd. in Woodland Hills Calif. 91364.

Childrens Village U.S.A.—because some of your fellow citizens wanted to make a battered, hurting child whole again.

This is RR Thanks for listening.

† Send a copy of this to Robert Young. If we dont have his address I'm sure Sue Taurog can get it.

†† For files in case of inquiry the address is Childrens Village U.S.A. 22554 Ventura Blvd. Woodland Hills Calif. 91364 ❖

Wedding

July 1978

† I'm going to talk about a wedding and maybe you'll feel better about life in general ~~+ after~~ *when* you've heard about this one. I'll be right back.

On Sunday July 15th in Chicago Linda Fraschalla ~~& Pete Saraceno~~ walked down the aisle and ~~were~~ *was* married *to* Pete Saraceno.* As they led the wedding party from the church the pace was a little slow because Pete had to ~~+~~ use a walker.

Actually the marriage itself was about 2 yrs. late. Linda & Pete had planned to wed in 1976 right after he was released from the Marines. Then Pete and a buddy crashed an automobile. Pete was critically injured~~. When he arrived at Westlake hospital he was pronounced dead. Then the~~ *and pronounced dead on arrival at Westlake hospital. But a* Dr. felt for a pulse one last time & found a very faint one. Pete was alive, but ~~barely so and he was in a coma.~~ *in a coma.*

After 12 days ~~the Drs. told~~ *in a respirator* & with 5 other life ~~machine~~ support machines attached to him the Dr's. told his mother to pull the plug. She replied that if God had wanted him, he would have taken him in the accident. ~~Pete remained~~ *He would remain* in the coma for 3½ months. At 3 months he ~~developed~~ *contracted* double ~~pneumnia~~ *PNEUMONIA* and was given only a few hours to live.

Linda works in the admitting office at Presbyterian—St. Lukes hospital.

* Anne Keegan, "She Held on to Dream during a 2-yr. Nightmare," *Chicago Tribune,* July 11, 1978, p. 1. The wedding date was actually July 16.

Every night after work she visit[ed] Pete ~~For 3½ months he~~ *who* never so much as moved an eyelash. ~~but~~ *Nevertheless* Linda was there decorating his room with a lighted tree for Christmas, spending New Years eve with him. Sympathetic Drs. told her to go out, ~~&~~ have fun & try to forget ~~Pete~~ *him*. She refused.

Then ~~after 3½ months~~ *one day* Pete ~~eyes~~ opened his eyes & his eyes began following Linda as she moved around the room. Later a finger moved, then an arm and finally he tried to speak. Linda was the only one *who* could understand him. Even when he made no sound she could read his lips. ~~and later when he could only blurt out sounds she said she knew what he meant.~~

He spent 7 months at Westlake, then to the Chicago rehabilitation Inst. & finally home. Linda quit her job ~~and moved in with Pete & his widowed mother. She~~ *&* used her savings to buy a 28 ft. backyard swimming pool to help him exercise his legs.

One day his mother took him back to Westlake to meet the nurses who had cared for him during the long months of Coma. He stepped off the 3rd floor elevator using a walker and Mrs. Saraceno says there wasn't a dry eye on the floor.

When Pete asked Lindas father for permission to marry her Mr. Fraschalla said, "When you can walk down that aisle, she's all yours."

Linda has returned to her job but has spent her evenings decorating a garden type apartment in Melrose Park where they are now at home. Pete had wanted to become a Chi. policeman but still has trouble with his left arm. Linda says he can do some kind of desk work.

Pete says, "The Dr's. call me the miracle boy & I guess they are right. I'm lucky to be alive & I'm lucky to have Linda." Yes he is. When the Drs. told Linda that he would never make it, she ~~said: "But~~ *told them* I love~~d~~ him, ~~I~~ *and she* refused to believe them SHE SAID "I wanted to help him so I stayed at his side as much as I could." Pete says; "She sure taught me about love." ~~Congratulations Pete &~~ *I think she taught all of us something Pete. Congratulations.* And to you Linda a lifetime of love & happiness.

This is RR Thanks for listening.

† PUT THIS IN 1st 15 RR ❖

The Soviet Union and Cuba coordinated much of their military involvement in Africa throughout the final decades of the cold war. For instance, a few months before Reagan taped this commentary, the Soviet Union airlifted thousands of Cuban troops to help Ethiopia prevail in the Ogaden war. Primarily populated by Somalis, the Ogaden was a desert territory in Ethiopia that the Somalis had invaded in an attempt to unite the Somali people.

Cuba
July 1978

I'm going to talk again about Cuba and what some of our leaders in Wash. on both sides of the aisle have suggested we do about it. I'll be right back.

Unless you've boycotted the daily press or refused to listen to the evening news you are aware that the admin. in Wash. has had some harsh things to say about Cuba. Castro has been told to remove his mercenary troops from Africa or we'll,—or we'll,—or we'll what? Come to think of it the admin. has never mentioned what the—"what" might be. And you can bet that Mr. Castro is well aware of that.

There are now 50,000 Cubans in Africa propping up a whole cluster of 3rd. world nations and training an assorted pack of guerillas in the gentle art of butchery. And not so incidentally threatening ~~the~~ *to* cut off ~~t~~ minerals vital to the industrialized western world.

Some of the senior members of Congress on both sides of the aisle have ~~be-coming~~ become very much aware of that unanswered "what" in the Presidents rhetoric. Like prompters coming to the aid of an actor who has forgotten his lines they are trying to give him the next sentence.

House minority leader John Rhodes of Ariz. urged the Pres. to stop wringing his hands and take some specific action which he then outlined.* I bring this up because if you weren't in the House gallery on the day Congressman Rhodes spoke you probably have never heard or read of his proposal. For some reason this subject ~~has~~ seems to be of no interest to the news media.

Then a short time later Democratic Senator Talmadge of Georgia** took the Senate floor to charge Cuba with aggression & subversion in Central America & support of Puerto Rican terrorists who have been responsible for numerous bombings in our own country.

The Senator said that outside of a few feeble protests our only response has been to exchange diplomats with Cuba, lift the ban on travel to Cuba, send athletes, performers, businessmen & Congressional delegations down there. He added: "We seem to be bent ~~on~~ upon treating our enemies as friends & our friends as enemies."

Senator Talmadge didn't have any trouble suggesting some practical steps;—close the Cuban mission in Wash., ban travel to Cuba, prohibit sending dollars to Cuba & restore the ban on diplomatic & economic relations. But for all the press he received he might as well have marked his speech "top secret."

Shortly thereafter the Democratic, majority leader of the Sen. Robert Byrd

* Congressman John Rhodes (R–Arizona, 1953–1983). His statement is found in *Congressional Record* (House), May 16, 1978, p. 13883.

** Senator Herman Talmadge (D–Georgia, 1957–1981).

of West Va. echoed his colleagues words & added that we should cut back sales of advanced technology to the Soviet's who, "have not swerved from their commitment to foment chaos wherever ~~it~~ *they* believe it can benefit." He made P.-14 of the N. Y. Times and was mentioned in ~~a~~*the* Wash. Post in a story hailing the split between "McGovern & Byrd."* McGovern got 10½ paragraphs, Byrd 3½ but his proposals about the action we should take were not mentioned.

The visit of the Cuban ballet to the U.S. was given more than one full page.

This is RR Thanks for listening. ❖

Trains

July 1978

I'm an old train buff and therefore am more than a little unhappy about what the govt. is doing to the railroads. I'll be right back.

A good case can be made that the ills of railroading were brought on by excessive govt. interference in the running of the railroads. Now of course that same govt. has ridden to the rescue ~~of the~~ with Amtrack & in the East a combine called Conrail. Both are losing horrendous sums of taxpayers money every day.

I just have to read you a letter ~~from~~ to the Dept. of Transportation from the "Texas South Eastern R.R." responding to the Dept's. order that strobe lights be mounted on locomotives to reduce railroad crossing accidents. This letter was inserted in the Congressional record.** There are several references to Conrail in the letter, possibly because Conrail has recently been trying to explain to Congress why it is losing millions & millions of dollars at the same time it wants to give a hefty pay raise to those who are managing Conrail.

The letter reads: Gentlemen: The best solution would be to require all motor vehicles to STOP, LOOK, AND LISTEN at all railroad grade crossings. . . . This of course will never be considered because it would probably eliminate 95 per cent of all crossing accidents. . . . It would also place a heavy drain on the legal profession and that alone will keep such action from ever being taken.

Therefore, we have on our own and without any government grant of any kind made an independent survey. . . . We have determined that one strobe light on each locomotive will probably eliminate 1 per cent of all grade crossing accidents. Based on this assumption, if one hundred strobe lights were

* Senator George S. McGovern (D–South Dakota, 1963–1981) and Senator Robert Byrd (D–West Virginia, 1959 to present).

** *Congressional Record*, 95th Congress, 2nd session, 1978. Vol. 124, pt. 11. p. 14504. This letter was entered into the *Congressional Record* on May 18, 1978, by Congressman Charles Wilson (D–Texas, 1973–1997).

placed on each locomotive we could eliminate 100 per cent of all grade crossing accidents. We would also suggest that no trains be operated during daylight hours as daylight will reduce the effectiveness of the strobe lights.

Probably the next best method would be to require that all trains stop at all grade crossings. This, of course, would greatly increase the railroads' operating expenses. We have estimated this figure to be $697,492,654,552.27 annually. . . . Our figures were arrived at with the help of a cost expert on loan from Conrail.

This same gentleman advises us that this amount is insignificant, and that we could, of course, expect a government grant for this expense. One method would be to add this to Conrail's request for the next six months' Operating Expenses, where it would probably go unnoticed.

One other suggestion would be to require all vehicles to approach all grade crossings at 90 mph. This would allow many motorists to beat the trains at a legal speed. Those that did not could be almost certain of not being crippled in the resulting collision.

Respectfully submitted,

George T. Honea
Vice President, General Manager

This is RR—Thanks for listening. ❖

As governor of California, Reagan spearheaded support for Proposition 1, a spending and tax limitation measure. Although voters rejected the proposed amendment to the state's constitution in a special election on November 6, 1973, Californians later approved Proposition 13, a property tax reduction measure, a month before this commentary was taped.

Proposition 13
July 1978

Proposition 13 in Calif. may be giving us one of those terms that become part of the language. "Prop 13" is becoming a symbol for citizen rebellion.

I'll be right back.

Following the passage of Proposition 13 in Calif. and the wave of comment, criticism and just plain cheering that swept the nation, Gallup took a very interesting poll. His first question aimed right at those who pooh! pooh! cuts in govt. spending because, (they claim), the people still demand services & handouts from govt.

Mr. Gallup asked: "Would you favor or oppose a proposal in your state to cut or limit property taxes—even if it means a reduction in certain local services, or an increase in other forms of tax?" Nationwide the response was 57% would favor such a proposal 30% said no. I wont bother giving the "dont knows."

Then Mr. Gallup asked how much the respondents believed *PROPERTY TAXES* could be cut ~~from~~ without a serious reduction in local services or an increase in other kinds of taxes. All in all 71% felt there could be a cut ranging from 10% to 50% or more. It broke down to 29% believing a 10% cut was possible, 23% thought a 20% cut, 11% a 30% cut & 4% each for a 40 & a 50% *TAX* cut.

People of a more liberal bent continue to insist that the sales tax is unfair & that ~~the~~ average citizens believe in the present graduated inc. tax. Gallup found this too was part of the ec. mythology of our times. Only 10% thought the property tax was the fairest, 36% the inc. tax ~~and~~ *but* 43% approved the sales tax as most fair.

Continuing on that theme the 5th question asked respondents to name the tax they most objected to. Income tax (Fed. St. & local) tied with real estate tax at 31% each. Sales tax was ~~most~~ objectionable to only 16%.

Then came a question as to the amount of increase the respondants had in their taxes in the last few years. Ranging from a fair amount of increase to a great deal, 63% said Fed. inc. taxes. More than half, 52% said Local or state inc. tax and a whopping 76% named the real-estate tax. Only 35% listed sales tax.

The poll indicated the correctness of the Founding Fathers in wanting to keep govt. as much as possible at the local level. When asked which level of govt. gave the most value for the tax dollar, 22% said Fed. 23% ~~said said~~ State & 35% local.

When the poll asked why local taxes have increased in the past few years 34% gave as a "very important" reason that people expect too many services from local govt. But 57% said money is spent on programs & services that are not really needed and 70% said too much money is spent on overhead & administration.

~~In o~~One final question e*i*nquired as to whether the respondants ~~local~~ community spent too much, too little or just the right amount on each of a list of local services. The replies revealed general satisfaction with those basic govt. services that burocrats all too often treat as luxurys. Fire & Police protection, public libraries & sanitation were rated ~~as~~ *highest* with regard to costing about the right amount. They averaged 57% only 8% thought they cost too much.

This is RR Thanks for listening. ❖

By mid-1978 the percentage of the adult population in the labor force—that is, either holding a job or looking for one—had increased steadily since its post–World War II low of 55.8 percent in 1946 to 63.0 percent in April 1978 *(and 63.6 percent in December 1978), primarily because more women joined the labor force.* As Reagan points out, the unemployed include people seeking a job for the first time and those who have quit to look for other work as well as those who have lost jobs or are reentering the labor force. The unemployment rate declined from 7.9 percent in January 1976 to 5.9 percent by the end of 1978, held steady in 1979, and began to increase in 1980.*

Employment
July 1978

Has talk of unemployment become a hard to break habit? And is it a habit we should break because there is no reason for it? I'll be rite back.

In past broadcasts I've talked of the probability that we aren't getting an honest count & haven't for some time with regard to unemployment. For months past metropolitan papers in their Sunday editions have carried scores & scores of pages of help wanted ads.

Why then should we continue to be given information that indicates large scale unemployment with all it's heartbreak for those vainly seeking jobs? One answer could be that so many govt. programs in the social reform field exist only if there is chronic & persistent unemployment.

Curiously enough "we the people" with that an almost instinctive wisdom have given indications that we no longer consider unemployment a top priority. When polled as to what are our most important *national* problems, inflation is number one by an overwhelming majority. Unemployment is down with the also rans. And as is so often the case—the people are ~~cor~~ right.

~~First of all there is no truly accepted definition of what *the percentage of unemployed which* is a proper percentage level on full employment.~~

Last April the number of unemployed fell below 6 mil. for the 1st time since 1974. Now jobless people numbering 6 mil. ~~seems~~ would indicate *that* we do have a problem but that is not necessarily so. There are many of those who are 1st time job seekers, ~~and~~ even more who are voluntarily unemployed~~.~~, *And it is estimated that possibly 2 MIL ACTUALLY HAVE JOBS BUT ARE WORKING FOR CASH TO AVOID TAXES.* Really significant figures have to do with *among other things* how long the unemployed remain out of a job. The average for all labor is *LESS THAN* 13 weeks but for skilled workers it is less than a month. Add to this the fact that a greater number are moonlighting—holding down 2 jobs ~~and. m*Many*~~ *and it's easy to understand why many* industries are hoarding manpower ~~because of the~~ fearing a shortage.

* It is possible for employment and unemployment to increase at the same time if more people enter the labor force—perhaps because they finish school—than find new jobs. The Bureau of Labor Statistics of the U.S. Department of Labor collects a wide range of information about employment and the labor force.

More than 100 mil. Americans are working—the greatest number in our history. The most astounding figure however, at a time when ~~the govt's. attitude is~~ *govt. is still claiming* that unemployment is a problem, ~~is~~ *has* to do with the percentage of ~~popul~~ adults who are employed; ~~For this statistic adulthood is considered as starting at age 16. and~~ 63% of ~~all adults~~ *all those over age 16* in America are employed. That too is an all time high figure and establishes the fact that more women must be in the work force than at any time in our history.

It's time to re-order our priorities. The jobs those 100 mil. Americans hold are ~~threatened if~~ vulnerable to an energy shortage. An even greater threat is declining productivity due to aging & obsolescene of our industrial plant~~.~~ ~~That has been~~ brought on by unnecessary govt. regulation and short sighted tax policies.

Meanwhile back at the ranch—we have double digit inflation & that is the biggest threat of all.

This is RR Thanks for listening. ❖

Religious Freedom
July 1978

How much do we really know about religious freedom in the land of Karl Marx? Some of the more "Detente" minded would have us believe it's alive & well.

I'll be right back

I think sometimes there is a built in optimism in Americans that makes us want to believe that things are alright ~~not only here but~~ in other lands & other places. Perhaps it is this happy outlook that makes us accept the stories of returning travellers from behind the iron *or the bamboo* curtains.

There is plenty of evidence *indicating* that visitors to the various "workers paradises" are treated to showcase tours ~~and~~ *but* carefully kept from seeing things as they really are. Of late we've had the make believe exposed by visitors to Cuba, China & elsewhere who, with courage & persistence risked possible imprisonment to look behind the false front.

One of the more prevalent myths has to do with religious freedom & whether it does or does not exist in those lands where Karl Marx is hailed as the Messiah. The World Council of Churches seems unable to believe that religion might be forbidden fruit in the Communist world. The fact that a few churches in Russia remain open & are attended by an ever shrinking group of senior citizens makes the Council ignore the uncompromising *MARXIAN* denial of God.

~~Karl Marx preaches that we are accidents of nature, here for a brief time & then dust.~~ He swore that his paradise could only be realized by destroying the church. ~~and h~~*H*e had a special hatred for the Hebrews, possibly because the God of Moses is also the God of Christianity.

Not too long ago ~~the~~ Austrian journalists got hold of a*n* ~~test~~ *examination* being given school children in Czechoslovakia. They made their findings public & it does seem to answer those who have denied that communism & religious persecution go hand in hand.

There are 15 questions in the examination but I think 3 are enough to settle any argument. In giving the test the students are instructed that they are to answer "correctly, truthfully & honestly." ~~Our first sample is this question:~~ *Question one:* "If you are religious, are you aware that your relgious rating will form a serious obstruction with a view to your future career?" If that one isn't discouraging enough try this one: ~~on~~ "Our school is educating you as a skilled worker of the future. Since you will participate in the leadership of the production process, your attitude toward religion must be clear. For this reason the school has the right to influence your religious attitude and your feelings in respect to your future job. Does the school—the teaching staff—do this with conviction? Answer Yes or No."

Now if that one isn't enough to put little Ivans teacher on ~~guar~~ notice here is sample *NUMBER 3*. "During your ~~time~~*erm* of study at the school, was enough insight & help given in the battle against religion & its pressures, and in the formation of a scientific view of the world?"

SO MUCH FOR RELIGIOUS FREEDOM IN THE WORLD OF COMMUNISM. I doubt that many children ~~there in Marxist Schools~~ *behind the curtains* treasure gold stars for Sunday school attendance.

This is RR Thanks for listening. ❖

In 1947, the United Nations formed the Trust Territory of the Pacific Islands (TTPI) and the United States was designated the Trustee. On July 12, 1978, a referendum was held in several districts of the TTPI to move toward self-determination and sovereignty as supported by the Constitution of the Federated States of Micronesia (FSM). The process began the following year, and on October 1, 1982, a compact was signed with the United States that allowed the FSM to have autonomy over domestic affairs. The United States continued to maintain control over military affairs for the territory until November 3, 1986, when President Reagan officially ended all U.S. administration of the territory, and the FSM became a fully independent state.

South Seas
July 1978

Do you ever dream of a blue lagoon surrounded by Palm trees; a South Pacific Island where the trade winds blow and life is sun, sea & sand? I'll be right back.

Most of us at some time or other have gone Polynesian in our daydreams. The very words, "South Sea Island" bring up pictures of white coral sand, blue sky & water, balmy breezes and just possibly a ukelele ~~back~~ providing background music.

I'm sure there still must be such islands. If there aren't I dont want to ~~find~~ *know* that. ~~out.~~ But I'm having trouble clinging to my daydream. A married couple from New Mexico set out on a cruise to the S. Pacific and I've been reading an account of their trip.

Several days beyond Hawaii they came to one of the Micronesian islands awarded to the U.S. after W.W.II. Some of the indestructible charm of the S. Pacific is there—after all blue sea is blue sea & sand is sand but it wasn't helped by beer cans & rusting automobile bodies. That dreamy island music is now a jukebox.

It seems that back in the early '60's we decided to improve life for our Micronesian wards. Thousands of civil servants journeyed to the islands to supervise ~~education,~~ *education,* hygiene and various sociological programs. Financial aid followed of course—about $1000 per native. It is estimated that an average of $162 of each 1000 is regularly invested in bottle goods. This has led to further advantages of civilization such as alcoholism & crime. One does not go for an evening stroll neath the coconut palms unless one wants to get bopped on the noggin & <u>not</u> by a falling coconut.

The natives do not go forth at daybreak in their canoes to spear fish for a luau. Japanese fishing boats have caught the fish which ~~is~~ *are* canned and sent back to the island for sale. Somehow it's hard to get romantic ~~ab~~ over a can opener.

Our touring couple asked an elderly man what it was like under the Japanese occupation during the war. He said, "very bad—much work, no money. Then they asked how it was under good old Uncle Sugar and he answered; "No work, plenty money."

A plebiscite was held offering the people a choice between economic development & welfare—welfare won by a country mile. The growth in population is increasing and like feeding deer we have made the natives on this island so totally dependent on our help there would be great suffering if we put them back on their own. The rice fields are gone and the mills are idle & deteriorating.

But hold on to your dream. Our touring couple sailed on to another island and while it showed some signs of modern day culture it was still So. Pacific as it should be—largely due to the efforts of missionaries who feel their duty is to import religion & the ~~dignit~~ dignity of honest toil.

There's a lesson in ~~there~~ *here* someplace. Both govt. & the missionaries have the same motive—they want to help the Islanders. ~~One does it with handouts and the others with One takes them Gold the other brings them God. But one brings them Gold and destroys One gives a handout—the others give a hand up.~~

~~The~~

Maybe the govt. should try bringing God instead of Gold

This is RR Thanks for listening ❖

Prisoner Exchange
August 7, 1978

† There is talk of prisoner exchanges with the Soviet U. It sounds easy but there are a few complications. I'll be right back.

Anatoly Shcharansky* has been sentenced. ~~in and~~ *He* will now disappear into the Soviet Unions Gulag Archipelago for 13 long years of inhuman labor on a starvation diet, plus whatever additional tortures come to his jailers minds

Free people all over the world are outraged at this further example of Russias cruel hypocrisy. From Moscow has come the accusation that ~~Sch~~ *SHCHARANSKY* is an American spy. ~~The~~*Our* President ~~of the U.S.~~ has of course denied this. and ~~branded it for the baseless charge that it is.~~ There have been hints that the Soviets might be willing to free Shcharansky in exchange for a couple of ~~proven~~ *known* Soviet spys ~~now in jail in our country.~~ *we have in jail.*

At first hearing most of us would probably say, "why not?" We caught the spies, they cant do any more damage, send them back. ~~to their Kremlin bosses.~~ In return a man who had the courage to stand up to Russias slave masters would be free to tell the world what life is like behind the iron curtain just as Alexander ~~Sohl~~ Solzhen~~y~~*i*tsyn & others have done. Unfortunately things aren't that simple in the world of international diplomacy.

If we made such an exchange the Soviets would have a great propaganda victory. They would challenge the Presidents credibility. ~~declaring this was proof he had lied. about~~ Hadn't he been willing to exchange their spies for ours?

Now however Alexander Yanov, exiled from Russia 4 years ago, a distinguished professor of slavic languages, has suggested a way to get Shcharansky out of Russia and the slave labor camp.

Some weeks ago on one of these commentaries I told of the great Soviet propaganda campaign concerning a prisoner on death row in Alabama. Soviet press & television has made this man John Harris a national hero to the Russians. ~~They say he is~~ *They have told their people he is* being executed for simply ~~stating his principles~~ ~~criticizing our govt.~~ *expressing his views.* ~~Their propaganda was helped by Ambassador Youngs recent foolishness about political prisoners in America.~~ The truth is, Harris is a convicted robber, rapist & murderer. He is not a political prisoner, in fact he committed murder while serving a life sentence for the other crimes.

Yanov has made a brilliant suggestion. We say ~~Sharanksy~~ *SHCHARANSKY* is a pol. prisoner. The Russians say he is a common criminal. They say Harris is

* On July 14, 1978, Anatoly B. Shcharansky was sentenced to 13 years in prison by a Soviet court. After years of intense negotiations with Soviet leaders, the Reagan administration secured Shcharansky's release in an exchange of prisoners from the United States, the Federal Republic of Germany, and the German Democratic Republic in February 1986.

a pol. prisoner & we say he is a common criminal. Why not trade them—Harris for SHCHARANSKY? After all their build up & propaganda about Harris in their own land they'~~ll~~*d* look pretty silly if they refused to save him from the electric chair when they could bring ~~their Har~~ *him* to Russia for a ticker tape parade. Come to think of it we'd have to send them the ticker tape too.

Yanov has suggested that Ambassador Andrew Young, in view of his charge that our prisons house hundreds if not thousands of pol. prisoners, is the logical one to propose the Harris, Shcharansky trade.* He could follow up & ~~save~~ *free* scores more of those Harris type pol. prisoners ~~by exchanging~~ *he says we have by exchanging* them for Piatkus, Ginsberg, Yuri Orlov, Kovalev, Slepak** and ~~many others of Russias other~~ *other* inhabitants of Gulag.

~~I like Yanovs final suggestion~~ *YANOV HAS ANOTHER SUGGESTION;* if any of our prisoners refuse to leave their jail cells in America for freedom in Russia—let Brezhnev explain such a puzzling phenomenon to the world.

This is RR Thanks for listening.

† Make this number 1 in the next session.

RR ❖

Income Tax
August 7, 1978

A battle may be brewing ~~over~~ between the increasing number of Congressmen who want to lower the inc. tax and the entrenched burocrats who dont.

I'll be right back.

With the fever for tax reduction running high throughout the land, Congress is debating changes in the income tax law. Much of that debate is over how much to reduce the tax which in itself is something of a monumental breakthrough. Very few voices are raised in opposition to a cut and none suggest an increase.

~~But~~ Of course I'm talking about elected representatives who will submit themselves to the voters in November. Over in the offices & corridors of the Internal Revenue Service no such foolishness as reducing the citizens *TAX* burden is tolerated. Jerome Kurtz, Internal Rev. Commissioner has suggested that if a taxpayer wants to pay less income tax he should, "take a lower paying job."

If Congress wont give him new laws increasing the tax, Commissioner Kurtz just might use his authority to pass a few regulations on his own. U.S.

* Ambassador Andrew Young caused a stir during the trial of Shcharansky when he said that the United States has "hundreds, maybe thousands, of people I would categorize as political prisoners."

** Viktoras Petkus, Alexander Ginsburg, Yuri Orlov, Sergei Kovalev, and Leonid Slepak.

News & World Report recently listed some 40 so called fringe benefits the I.R.S. is assessing as ~~possibilities for including as~~ *POSSIBLE* income subject to tax.*

Time wont permit listing all 40 but let me read you some to show how phoney is ~~the Wash.~~ *the constant* talk of loopholes with it's inference that tax deductions benefit only the well heeled. ~~The I.R.S. assessors have in mind one thing & one thing~~ only~~—more money for govt. And~~ ~~since the agency cant change rates~~ ~~it can by regulation declare fringe benefits should be given a cash value and included as part of your *taxable* income.~~

For example, "Free parking on employers premises." "In kind benefits such as free or cut-rate telephone & power service for retired employees of phone companies & other utilities." That of course aims directly at senior citizens on fixed incomes as does the idea of taxing ~~as income,~~ *residents of* "Old age homes provided by companies for their retired employees."

And listen to these ~~tax evasions~~ ~~*deductions*~~ *FRINGE BENEFITS* the I.R.S. would ~~eliminate~~ *tax:* "Christmas gifts worth more than $25 ~~to~~ *from* employers; Vacation facilities maintained by companies for free use by employees; Employee cafeterias & executive dining rooms offering subsidized prices; Lunch & dinner money provided for employees in all sorts of situations; Company picnics, Christmas lunches, parties; Taxi fares for employees coming or going after dark & free transportation to plants or offices in distant locations or unsafe neighborhoods."

All of these are the things we've always thought of as the mark of a good, responsible employer. And speaking of employers there are of course ~~all the~~ fringe benefits the I.R.S. would tax; "Free receptions & entertainment for wives at trade conventions." That smacks a little of using taxation to separate husband & wife. ~~An executive~~ *Another so called* fringe benefit is the provision of bodyguards for corporate executives. With the number of businessmen who have been kidnape & murder victems of terrorists that hardly seems to be a luxury. *There are of course*

~~This is RR Thanks for listening~~

all the perquisites of country club memberships, company jets etc. But all in all the I.R.S. is putting itself in the management role by using taxation as more than a means of raising revenue.

This is RR Thanks for listening ❖

British Health Care
August 7, 1978

Great Britains socialized medical system marked it's 30th anniversary recently but there was gloom & doom in place of a celebration. I'll be right back.

* "40 Fringe Benefits IRS Wants to Tax," *U.S. News & World Report*, May 8, 1978, p. 76.

Back in 1948 when *Englands* Prime Minister Bevon * saw his dream of socialized medicine come true, he believed it heralded the beginning of an England so healthy, Dr's. would go out of style. Maybe that is extreme, but he was sure that the new system would ~~make England~~ *bring* ~~*England*~~ such improvements in the health of the people that medical costs would become less & less.

In it's first year however the costs were double what had been anticipated and now after 30 yrs. the program is the target of bitter criticism by Dr's., patients & politicians. For a year now a royal commission has been studying to find a way out of what is openly called a health care crisis.

With nationalized health service being pushed by our own politicians we'd better hear some of the things the *royal* Commission has learned. First is that hospitals are worn out & antiquated, lacking modern equipment. Half of them were built in the last century.

There is an enormous waiting list for what are called non-urgent operations such as hernia, arthritic joints or varicose veins. They may be called non-urgent but more than 600,000 people are waiting ~~for operations~~ & will wait years for operations to correct proplems that are painful & disabling.

A top heavy administrative burocracy has created an unworkable mass of red tape. There is great anger & frustration among Drs. & patients over this elaborate decision making machinery which does everything it seems but make decisions.

Top quality Drs. ~~in~~ are leaving England or at least the National Health plan out of sheer frustration. Their places are taken by foreign Drs. & nurses many of whom ~~have not had~~ *are not up to the level of* training ~~of the level~~ *of the personnelle* they are replacing.

There is such a breakdown in morale on the part of hospital staff that strikes, slowdowns and outright rebellion are becoming commonplace among professionals once hailed for their dedication.

Rising medical costs have created a technology gap between available treatment and the kind of treatment that is possible in view of recent advances in medical science. Any figures the British system can point to as evidence of success such as reducing infant mortality are either matched or topped by other countries including our own.

One orthopedic surgeon called the 127 patients he has on a waiting list to tell some of them they may have to wait more than 30 yrs. ~~at~~ *for* their operations at the present rate of scheduling. This dosen't mean he's that busy—it's the unavailability of operating room time and/or recovery beds in the ancient hospitals.

Some of the patients he called ~~are~~ were elderly people in wheelchairs waiting for replacement of arthritic hip joints so they can walk again. The surgeon

* Aneurin Bevan was actually the minister of health and Clement Attlee was the prime minister.

was only able to do ~~su~~ 2 such operations in all of 1977 because so little time in the operating room was available to him.

The royal commission is supposed to come up with some answers in 1977. In the meantime I would think we have all the answers we ~~have~~ need for Wash.

This is RR Thanks for listening. ❖

Brainwashing I
August 7, 1978

At a news conference on July 12, 1977, President Jimmy Carter stated that he had not decided whether to deploy the neutron bomb, a thermonuclear weapon the effects of which are confined to a limited area surrounding the blast. On April 7, 1978, he announced his decision to defer production of the neutron bomb. He added that future decisions about enhanced radiation weapons, another name for the neutron bomb, would "be influenced by the degree to which the Soviet Union shows restraint in its conventional and nuclear arms programs and force deployments affecting the security of the United States and Western Europe."

Brainwashing is not a word Americans like to hear ~~used~~ applied to themselves but the Soviet U. is pretty good at it. I'll be right back.

The Soviet U. must really be uptight about the neutron warhead; seldom have we seen such a campaign to kill off a weapon before it even goes into production.* In our own country well intentioned people have joined in the campaign but without (and let me emphasize that without) any realization that their own concern might possibly be the result of subtle, Soviet brainwashing.

Recent polling has revealed a strange dichotomy in peoples view of this weapon which could be the greatest ~~threat~~ defense ~~of~~ against the Russian tanks massed on the Western front ~~aga~~ opposite our Nato forces. A year ago our people favored going ahead with production of the weapon 44 to 38. Now the poll reads 47 to 35 against.

Strangely enough those same Americans while opposing production & deployment of the weapon believe 46 to 25 that it is the most effective defense we COULD have against the threat of an attack on the Nato line. By a lesser margin 36 to 34 they still see it as an effective deterrent that would reduce the chance of war. But, (and here is where the possibility of brainwashing comes in) a large majority 74 to 12 fears that use of the bomb *neutron weapon* might

* See Christopher S. Wren, "Moscow Assails Carter for Funding Neutron Bomb," *The New York Times,* August 10, 1977, p. 5.

lead to the use of other nuclear weapons, meaning the exchange of the ultimate in destructive weapons the arsenals of intercontinental ballistic missiles.*

The President has indicated from the first his opposition to the weapon but under pressure from our Nato allies and our own mil. leaders he has held off a final no. His position is that he might cancel production of the warhead if the Soviets agree to a new Salt treaty.

Now, while the Soviets normally oppose the idea of any weapon for us, as they proceed with their own buildup of the greatest offensive mil. machine the world has ever seen, they have been ~~+~~ *unusually* excited about the ~~net~~ *neutron* weapon.

We and our Nato allies have responded to the Soviet tank forces massed on the German border with some pretty potent anti-tank weapons. There are small ~~but~~ but effective guided missiles that can be carried & fired by one or two men and heavy caliber infantry missiles such as the American T.O.W. All have the ability to penetrate the Russian armor & knock out or disable ~~thei~~ their tanks.

Now we learn the Soviets have developed and field tested a new tank, the T-80 and according to all available information it is immune to our anti-tank missiles. They have invented a new type of composite armor. It is a kind of honeycomb of steel, ceramics & aluminum *WITH* 3 times ~~as~~ the protective quality of conventional steel plate, yet it weighs practically the same.

We know how good it is because by coincidence our English allies have come up with virtually the same thing for our own tanks. It is impervious to present day anti-tank weapons. But, and this explains Russias anxiety about the neutron warhead, the new armor is no better against the neutron weapon than the present steel plate

With an order to go ahead on our weapon we can nullify ~~their~~ their new T-80 tank.

This is RR Thanks for listening. ❖

Brainwashing II

August 7, 1978

Nicolai Ogarkov** of the Soviet U. has recently made an *arrogant* statement that reflects the growing superiority of Soviet military power. I'll be right back.

The Soviet Unions Nicolai ~~Ogarkop~~ *OGARKOV* has delivered a message to the American people. He says: "You once had mil. superiority & felt secure.

* The poll figures are found in "Poll Shows More in U.S. Opposed to Neutron Bomb," *The New York Times*, May 26, 1978, p. 19.

** Nikolai Ogarkov.

You no longer have that superiority and you will never have it again. And now you will know what it means to feel threatened."

On the last broadcast I called attention to a new invention of the Soviets which could make their tanks invulnerable to present day anti-tank weapons. It would not protect them against our neutron warhead—that is if we had our ~~neu~~ neutron warhead.

The June issue of "The Officer," the official reserve officers journal carried a story based on data & material authenticated by the American Security Council and presented by Major Gen. J. Milnor Roberts.

The article opened with what the Gen. called a worst case scenario. Let me read portions of that scenario to you. "Suddenly and without warning, hundreds of Soviet-bloc divisions spearheaded by 15,000 assault tanks and amphibious armor, spin from Warsaw pact maneuvers and lunge westward. Their target the English Channel.

Swarms of Soviet warplanes, armed with missiles, bombs & cannisters of death dealing chemicals, strike Nato bases & stockpiles of U.S. tactical nuclear weapons.

Outnumbered & outgunned allied forces retreat before the massive Communist blitzkrieg. At sea Soviet submarines pre-positioned hours before, intercept and attack U.S. convoys attempting rush reinforcements. Behind the lines, Communist saboteurs emerge in Western Europes cities & industrial centers creating widespread havoc.

With Western Europe about to be overrun, the Pres. of the U.S. is faced with a life or death decision: To accept the Soviet conquest of all Europe or to unleash Americas nuclear counterforce, thereby risking a worldwide holocaust."

The Gen. admits this, "worst case" scenario may never happen. But he does say, "the possibility that it might is the constant nightmare of allied leaders. Then he quotes Gen. Haig* our Supreme Allied Commander in Europe, "the greatest single threat to stability and peace continues to reside—as it has for 29 years—in the immediate presence of massive Soviet mil. power . . . the greatest peacetime aggregation of mil. power the world has ever seen."

The article then goes on to catalog the statistics of Russias power and the continued retreat by the U.S. over the last couple of decades.

In 1962, the time of the Cuban missile crisis our superiority was so great that Krushchev had no choice but to back down. Eleven years later in the 1973 Arab-Israeli war Russias power was such that a threat ~~of intervention by Russia~~ *by them to intervene* in that war forced the Israelis to halt their drive against Egypt. Our Chief of Naval Operations said, "had their been a confrontation ~~in the~~ between the U.S. & Russia in the Eastern Mediterranean "we would have lost."

Production of the neutron warhead could very probably eliminate the

* Alexander M. Haig, Jr., served as supreme allied commander in Europe from 1974 to 1979, and served as the U.S. secretary of state from 1981 to July 1982.

nightmare of that "worst case" scenario at best & at least buy us some much needed time.

This is RR Thanks for listening. ❖

Following the approval of Proposition 13 by California voters in June 1978, a tax revolt swept across the country with voters in many other states approving property-tax limitation measures.

Tax Revolt
August 7, 1978

It dosen't look like Proposition 13 will go away as a converstaion piece. ~~o~~Or should I say *the subject of* taxes wont go away? I'll be right back.

Recently a Calif. newspaper did a survey, *undoubtedly* inspired by Prop. 13 but aimed at learning peoples attitude toward govt. services & govt. spending. As it turned out 73.6% of the respondents had voted for Prop. 13. The poll ~~was~~ sought answers as to the areas where govt. could be reduced, how much fat, those polled, thought there was in govt. etc.

When they were asked how much fat they thought there was in local govt., the biggest percentage, (just over half) estimated 25% or more. But almost 94% put it at ~~10~~ above 10%. A somewhat smaller number but still 77% said ~~fro~~ *10% or more of* local govt. employees ~~ranging from 10% & up~~ should be cut from the payroll. Here again the biggest percentage. 22.2% would ~~cut~~ *eliminate* 25% or more. Personally I've always felt the better & yes the humane way to reduce *the* govt. payroll is by attrition. ~~Freeze the~~ *Put a freeze on* hiring ~~of~~ replacements for those who retire or leave govt. service. We made this work in Calif. ~~without any~~ *and there were no* layoffs.

Most interesting in the poll however was where people thought the cuts should be made. They were given a pretty complete list of city functions and asked, yes or no on whether cuts should be made in each of these services. More than 85% said no to reducing police or fire protection. Next highest support—a fraction over 65%—was for street maintenance.

But in the yes vote—where *they felt* cuts should be made—more than 95% said, "in admin. ~~More~~ Around 85% would cut aid to non-profit groups & size of the city workforce. From ~~almost~~ *about* 78% to 80% those polled would cut downtown redevelopment & planning.

Switching to County functions almost 82% would <u>not</u> make cuts in the Sheriff's dept. But almost 88% would reduce welfare & public assistance, 80% would cut planning & more than 82% would reduce the size of the workforce. But here again the biggest cut ~~f~~ by far would be in admin. overhead—95.7%.

Finally the poll took up school spending. In basic Ed. activities 84.2% said no to any cuts and more than 63% would not reduce the number of teachers or increase class size. However almost 94% would cut admin. And 86.3% would cut special ed. programs such as bi-lingual ed. Around 65% would close neighborhood schools with low enrollment, child care centers and 58% *would* trim spending on extra curricular activities such as band, art classes & driver ed. Almost 80% would reduce the size of the workforce.

The final 2 questions in the poll should be of special interest to elected pub. servants. More than ¾ (76.7%) said they would favor a state const. amendment that would limit how much money state & local govt's. could spend. And 77.6% said they did <u>not</u>—repeat—<u>not</u> want other taxes increased to help pay for services that may be cut as a result of Prop. 13.

Just maybe, someone in govt. had better be listening.

This is R.R. Thanks ~~for~~ YOU FOR listening. ❖

The Average Man
August 7, 1978

With all the gloom & doom, the pessimism it's so easy to accept today, there is still good reason to be optimistic. I'll be right back.

I know that I do ~~as much~~ *a lot of* criticising ~~as anyone~~ *on these* commentaries, pointing to things that need correcting, but please believe me I'm an optimist. I truly believe the people of this country will justify the faith the Founding Fathers had when they said, the people themselves were the best custodian of freedom and their own security.

An old friend from college days regularly sends me the magazine he publishes. It is called "Sunshine." * The ultra-sophisticates might think it corny. I find it is just what it's name implies and it's good for the soul.

There was a short article in the Aug. issue which refurbished my optimism. I thought you might like to hear it—it's about the Average Man. ~~You know that fellow some refer to as the common man—he's really pretty uncommon. Then some lump him in with the something called the "masses". And most demeaning of all is that dogooder phrase—"the little people."~~ Sunshine magazine says; "The progress and prosperity of the free world is based ~~upon~~ upon the basic decency of the average man." ~~It~~

It goes on to say: "This average man is a fellow who respects himself. If he buys something he will pay for it. He expects to work for the money he needs. He wants a home & he is willing to accept the responsibility for the care of his children. He is a temperate person in every sense of the word. He wants to <u>use</u> the <u>good</u> things in life. He doesn't want the headaches that come from abuse. He is a law observer with common sense enough to know that you have to

* *Sunshine* was published by Garth Henrichs of Litchfield, Illinois. Reagan corresponded with Henrichs from 1949 to 1981 (see *Reagan: A Life in Letters,* pp. 98–100).

have law enforcement for a few. He knows that freedom is rooted in self discipline, that rights & responsibilities go hand in hand.

The free world has it's problems, for freedom is not Utopia. It has individuals who are misfits, who do not measure up to the average man. It has the individual who scoffs at law observance, who has to be held in check by law enforcement. It has those who confuse anarchy with freedom, and privileges with rights, who think law & order is oppression. And these people get more than their share of the news media's attention.

But all the time the good, decent, law abiding average man is going about his job of earning a living, ~~supporting~~ *supporting* his country, contributing to worthy programs to help the less fortunate, and participating in the religious life of his community. He is the backbone of the free world. He is the one who is doing the plain, everyday, seldom spectacular things that are slowly making this a better world for everyone.

Sometimes he wonders if those in public office have any interest in his right to use the streets in peace & safety. He wonders if they are concerned with his right to be secure from violence in his own home. He wonders if working for what you need, saving for what you want, & living for what you believe is right is out of date.

But even as he wonders, he keeps on doing his job & keeping faith in what he knows in his heart is best."

~~Well~~ That's the average man. Some do gooders demean him by lumping him into something called the "masses," or even worse "the little people." And sometimes he's called "the common man." Well he's very uncommon and he'll probably wind up saving those do-gooders in spite of themselves.

This is RR Thanks for listening. ❖

Government Cost
August 7, 1978

† The other day I commented on the spreading tax revolt signalled by ~~Prop~~ passage of Prop. 13 in Calif. But what added up to revolution? I'll be right back.

It is possible ~~the~~ *a* tax revolt was already on the way and that Calif's. Prop. 13 just set the date for it's happening? What city in America has the highest level of per-capita earning? What city has the highest percentage of household income over $25,000, the highest average household income, the highest percentage of white collar employment, the most banks & Mercedes-Benz automobiles per capita? Well one city ~~has~~ *is 1st in* all of these things; our nations capitol Wash. D.C.

Of course Wash. was smart enough, as someone once pointed out, to latch onto the fastest growing industry—govt. Wash. has the highest average income and the majority of it's earners work for govt. or in related ~~fields~~ *FIELDS*.

Maybe it's only coincidence but Sacramento ~~Calif.~~ capitol of the most populous state—Calif. is in the top 5 cities in those same categories.

I remember back about 15 or 16 years ago reading an item about a young man—age 19—in Ark. who was charged by the govt. with overplanting his 5 acre cotton allotment by a fraction of 1 acre. In those days the govt. would survey *LAND* to make sure farmers hadn't exceeded their acreage allotments. The govt. sued the young man to collect penalties of $52.38. They spent $61.10 on travel expenses for deputies to serve the papers. In the meantime bad weather and boll weevils had ruined the crop. No cotton was picked & the young man had joined the navy.

I thought at the time it was quite a comedy of errors and much ado about nothing. I certainly didn't realize *THEN* it was just standard operating procedure. Today it's ~~just~~, "ho-hum," when you discover that CETA the Comprehensive Employment & Training Act is putting up $31,000 to build a 30 ft. high concrete monolith in Salem Oregon. It's for rock & mountain climbers to practise on.

In Fall River Mass. the state dept. of Public Welfare spent $450 a day ~~to~~ on room & board for a 15 yr. old boy. No, the young man hadn't been charged with any crime. He was classified as a child needing services. So while officialdom was trying to decide what to do with him, he was put up in a motel with 2, $8 an hour guards. For more than a week he swam in the motel pool, fished in a nearby cove and lived high on the hog. At one breakfast he made away with a dozen pancakes & half a dozen eggs.

Then there is San Francisco's ~~rapid~~ bay area rapid transit system known as Bart. So far it has cost double the planned amount $1.6 Bil. It has only attracted half the passengers it expected and serves only 2% of the trips in the district. It was supposed to reduce auto traffic but ~~only~~ *less* than ⅓ of it's riders came from automobiles. About half switched over from buses. Now the Bart ride costs twice as much as the bus & half again as much as the private car. The transit system could buy a fleet of *NEW* buses capable of handling all of Barts passengers until 1980 for less than half of what Bart is losing each year.

I know you can match me with hundreds of equally silly examples & that's why there is a tax revolt.

This is RR Thanks for listening.

† Make sure this doesnt go on before "Tax Revolt." RR ❖

Land

September 19, 1978

† I wonder how many Americans are aware of their govt's. insatiable hunger for land. Probably not as many as should be. I'll be right back.

Back when terratories were ~~still~~ *first* becoming states the rule was that federal lands became the property of each new state to be disposed of as the state saw fit. Some place along the ~~way~~ *line* that policy just went the way of the Buffalo. As the ~~country~~ *nation* moved west and the younger states were admitted Uncle Sam held on to the land. In the case of one of the latest *Alaska* the Fed. govt. holds about 96%. In states like Ariz., Nevada, New Mexico etc. Fed. lands range *anywhere* from ~~the~~ 43% of Calif. ~~the govt. owns~~ to 70% of Idaho ~~to~~ *& on up to* 80 & 90% of *the* others. Uncle Sam is the biggest landlord in the country.

Some dozen years ago Wash. pushed the panic button claiming it was necessary to acquire land for outdoor recreation. We were told of the population explosion and how if we didn't provide for future recreational areas our children would grow up in a paved over totally ~~urban~~ *URBAN* America. Well the population explosion fizzled, we have more schoolrooms than we need and you have to wonder about those mining claims in the mountains the govt. cancelled on top of all the other land grabs in the name of outdoor recreation.

It was during that period that one of the Wash. officials involved made a statement ~~abou~~ we should all keep in mind. He said: "In an earlier time the govt. encouraged private ownership of land in order to get it developed. Now it is necessary for the govt. to regain control of the land."

When the recreation story ran out of steam the environmental issue was just getting underway. We've had Fed. land planning bills presented ~~& now unable to get them passed they are back with pretty much the same thing only now it's~~ *& voted down in Congress but our land hungry burocracy never gives up. It is back with another bill this time* called the "Land ~~Diversity~~ *DIVERSITY* Bill.

Up in Colorado the Bureau of Reclamation ~~is building~~ *intends to build* a dam & reservoir for an irrigation project. It will harness the La Plata & Animas rivers. There is no quarrel with the project which will be of great benefit to agriculture. But the land that will be taken for a reservoir ~~is~~ belongs to the Colorado Division of Wildlife and is used ~~for~~ as winter range for anywhere from 50 to 200 Elk ~~depend~~ depending on who is talking. *The Division of Wildlife insists on an acre for acre replacement &* ~~The Division of Wildlife~~ has set it's sights on a group of ranches. ~~and~~ *It* has declared if the ranchers wont sell voluntarily ~~they will~~ *their property will* be taken by condemnation. The ranchers dont want to sell. One of the largest has been in the same family for 78 yrs. and is a haven for Elk, Wild Turkey & other game because no hunting is allowed. In fact the Elk use the ranch as a migration route.

There are ranches of good size ~~in~~ *FOR SALE IN* the area ~~but the for sale~~ but the Division of Wildlife refuses to consider them. The 7 or 8 the Division has zeroed in on have been owned by the same families for from 30 to 78 years. It would seem this is another example of the "arrogance of officialdom" ~~first spoken of by Cicero in ancient Rome~~.

This type of acquisition is ~~being~~ going on in a dozen western states all in the name of a need for more wilderness areas. In such areas there are no roads or structures or vehicles of any kind allowed—only a few backpackers will ever see them. Yes there are natural beauty spots which should be so protected but how many covering how much of our land? I hope the Colorado ranchers win this one.

This is RR Thanks for listening.

† When typed send a copy to Violet Steward Gwaltney Writer of attached letter. RR ❖

Pot

September 19, 1978

The arguments go on about Pot—(Marijuana) and whether it is or is not harmful but for some reason one side of the argument dosen't get much play in the news.

I'll be right back.

~~About the time Dr. Peter Bourne *BOURNE* was leaving the White House and taking his final shot at the White House staff~~

In discussions with young people about the possible health hazards from smoking Marijuana I never cease to be amazed at how familiar they are with reports downplaying the danger. They have no comparable knowledge of the scientific studies which ~~give~~ *tell* a different story. I dont believe they are deliberately closing their eyes to these contrary studies, there just isn't wide circulation of such reports in the media.

Let me for a few minutes try to even up the coverage. Not too long ago 41 scientists representing 13 countries met in France* to present new research findings. Now first of all let me point out that scientists dont have a grudge for or against "pot." They seek the truth, they have no prejudice which makes them want to find it harmful or harmless for that matter. It so happens that these scientists have found pot, grass, weed—whatever you want to call it definitely bad news.

They linked it's use with harmful effects on human reproduction, the brain and other organs including the lungs. Past studies have been criticized on the grounds that dosages of marijuana were used which were far greater than a pot smoker indulges in. Not so this time. Rhesus monkeys were used in the experiments because their systems metabolize marijuana similar to the way humans do. They are also similar in their reproductive systems & hormonal control. The dosages used were comparable to those humans are subjected to in light, moderate & heavy smoking.

The scientists reported significant tissue breakdown in the lungs after expo-

* Symposium on Marijuana, Rheims, France, July 22–23, 1978. Proceedings of the conference were published as *Marihuana, Biological Effects,* edited by G. G. Nahas and William D. M. Paton (Oxford: Pergamon Press, 1979).

sure from 8 months to a year; and structural brain changes adversely affecting emotions & behavior.

What is the extent of the problem in our own country? Well a recent study by the Nat. Inst. on Drug Abuse reveals that 1 out of 11 high school Seniors smoke marijuana on a daily basis. Three years ago it was only 1 out of 17. In the month preceding the survey 29% of 16 & 17 yr. olds had smoked pot. So had 15% of the 14–15 yr. olds & 4% of the 12 & 13 yr. olds. It is estimated that about 11 mil. Americans now use it at least weekly.

At the meeting in France Dr. Carol Grace Smith of the Uniformed Services Medical School, Bethesda Maryland expressed particular concern about the steady use of pot by teenagers. She said the effect on the developing reproductive system of teenagers is particularly vulnerable to disruption by drugs. One or two "joints" a day will inhibit sex hormone development.

To sum it up the International Narcotics Control Board—(this is the board elected by the United Nations Ec. & Social Council)—reported to the meeting in France that: "*MARIJUANA IS* far from being a harmless substance, either for the individual or for society."

I've only touched on the full findings of the scientists but is anyone listening? Why aren't our young people made to read this ~~body of~~ scientific evidence before they wreck the ~~only~~ bodies & minds they are going to have to live with the rest of their lives?

This is RR Thanks for listening. ❖

Utilities
September 19, 1978

~~On the last broadcast I~~
Some professions, ~~and~~ some trades & some businesses seem to acquire a questionable image which somehow they can never seem to change. I'll be right back.

Among the arts & professions actors down through the years have lived ~~under~~ with a false image that they are somehow lacking in what might be called normal attributes. Plumbers have put up with the stock jokes that they always forget their tools & the customer has to pay by the hour while they make the round trip to pick up the missing items. In the industrial world Utility Companies rank high on the villains list. Always the myth prevails that they produce a necessary item in a monopolistic manner, cheaply & easily & ~~force~~ *extract* an horrendous profit from the helpless customer.

I'll leave defense of actors & plumbers til another time and plead the case of the utilities today. How many of us have stopped to think that in this long era of inflation ~~our telephone~~ electricity is one of the only major commodities that has gone down in price? Now before you scream & say look at my last months bill ~~let m~~ hear me out. We actually pay less per kilowatt hour of electricity than we did 20, 30 or 50 years ago. Our bills are up because we ~~do~~ use electricity for many more things.

When I was a boy we cooked with a wood burning stove & kept warm with a coal furnace. There was no air conditioning, we had an ice box not a refrigerator and electricity was used only for lighting. Now we shave, brush our teeth, watch TV, have all manner of electrical tools—we even carve the Christmas turkey with an electric carving knife. If it still cost as much per kilowatt hour we couldn't afford the electrical gadgets *THAT TODAY* we cant live without.

And we aren't being ripped off by the producers of that electricity. Just let me read you some figures from the report to the stockholders of the Middle South Utilities Inc.* Last year the company reported *TOTAL* operating revenues of $1,251,600,000. That was a 25.7% increase over the previous year. More than a bil. & a quarter dollars sounds like a good business~~.~~ *and a 25% increase is something to cheer about.*

The report, however also shows operating costs of ~~$1,073,293,647~~ *more than a bil. dollars* leaving a net profit of ~~$106,566,954 which~~ *SLIGHTLY OVER 100* ~~$~~ *MIL.* ~~*that*~~ *which* figures out to $1.72 a share for the stockholders—6 cents less per share than they received last year. Nevertheless it is a normal & respectable return. ~~but~~ *It is* hardly a windfall or as some pundits love to declare, "an obscene profit."

Fuel to generate the electricity cost more than twice as much as the *TOTAL* profit which makes another part of the report very interesting. The stockpile of uranium which opponents of nuclear energy say is the great threat to life on earth would be the fuel used to generate electricity once we finished developing the breeder reactor. The admin. in Wash. as you know does not want to continue *it*'s development. But that present stockpile which lies there for the taking, no one would have to find it, or go into a mine to dig it out, would meet our energy needs literally for centuries. It represents a fuel value of between 10 & $20 trillion.

I respect the right of the opponents of nuclear power to dissent but with that right goes a responsibility to know what they are talking about.

This is RR Thanks for listening. ❖

Free Enterprise
September 19, 1978

I guess one of the great things about free enterprise is that someone can always find an opportunity to provide a new & different service.

I'll be right back.

* Middle South Utilities served customers in Arkansas, Louisiana, and Mississippi.

I'm usually near the head of the line in pointing out the miracle of the marketplace. I never cease to be amazed *at* how new products come into being or what new ~~f~~ service is provided for our convenience by someone just getting an idea & having a go at it.

Right now however I have a direct mail advertisement ~~on my desk~~ offering a new service and I'm filled with mixed emotions—admiration for the fellow who thought of it but anger that the opportunity he seized exists at all.

The ad opens with a colorful, ~~blazing~~ picture of a hand ~~full of~~ *holding* ~~*m*~~ money and a blazing caption which reads: "Are you getting your share of the $5,276 per family—<u>tax free</u>—that the govt. will give out this year alone?" In smaller print underneath the picture it goes on to say: "If the answer is 'no' and you'd like to start getting, right now, your fair share of the $5,276 per year—tax free—perhaps for life—then simply read the startling information inside! Well of course I looked inside where a letter started out, "For example—Dear Friend," which puts things on a cozy basis right away.

But then you learn that our govt. has set aside a "mind boggling" (their words not mine) "$286.bil. to ~~p~~ be paid out to people just like you & families just like yours." That's $1,319 per person. ~~The letter goes~~

The letter goes on to explain that while the money is put aside ~~to but~~ *it is* not necessarily being paid out, because we're not asking for it. Then follow about 5 pages of black alternating with red print describing the funds available; giving examples of individuals who are receiving checks and explaining that we who aren't don't realize ~~the~~ *that the way to get the* money, is buried in over 100 different govt. documents~~, pe~~ where the ordinary person cant find it.

In a box under a red headline you are urged to think about "these startling facts": In one program 31 mil. of your fellow Americans are getting a U.S. govt. check every month. Then it tells you *there are* 19 mil. more in another program, 11 mil. in another & 5 mil. in ~~another~~ *a 4th* & these are only 4 of 137 programs.

~~Now~~ The ad is leading up to a service for a fee. ~~A~~ Send in $8.98 for a confidential report which will come in a plain paper wrapper. Read it from cover to cover, the ad says & see how much money is waiting for you without gambling a penny. If you dont think any of that money is for you ~~send back~~ *return* the report & get your ~~money~~ *$8.98* back. Then there is an ongoing newsletter called "New Govt. Cash For You." You subscribe to that but somehow except for the 1st 3 issues on a dollar trial basis they dont tell you the price.

Now I'm not going to name this advertiser or give an address because the whole thing points ~~out~~ up the extent to which our govt. has departed from reality. Obviously if <u>every</u> family could collect $5,276 then <u>every</u> family would have to pay the govt. $5,276. The only money govt. has is the money it takes from us.

Right now it is true 124 mil. Americans—more than half our population are receiving all or most of their income from tax dollars. Right now the total unfunded obligations of our govt. pro-rate out to more than $30,000 for every man, woman, child & baby in the nation. *We all get splattered when the bubble bursts.*

—This is RR Thanks for listening. ❖

In 1978, the U.S. Congress voted to amend the U.S. Constitution so that the District of Columbia could have representation equivalent to a state in the U.S. Congress. The legislatures of 38 states would have to approve the measure in order for the Constitution to be amended.

District of Columbia
October 10, 1978

We have another constitutional amendment to worry about and it's one we might be better off without. I'll be right back.

In the process prescribed for amending our Constitution the Congress has passed and sent to the legislatures of the 50 states for ratification an amendment to ~~make~~ *give* the District of Columbia ~~our 51st state.~~ *representation equal to a state in the U.S. Congress.* A potent lobby pushed this through the Congress using high flown phrases such as taxation without representation, end the 2nd class citizenship of those who dwell in the district & so on ad nauseum.

We have a nation unique in all the world. It is a Fed. of Sovereign States and that is probably our greatest guaranty against tyranny by a centralized nat. govt. Those Founding Fathers whose like the world hasn't seen since thought of just about everything. They said, "if Federalism is to work how can any of the Sovereign States be the locale of the Nat. capital without opening the door to possible conflicts of interest?" So the District of Columbia was established on land ceded by Maryland & Virginia.

To say that residents of the Dist. who vote for city ~~govt. *officials*~~ officials & for Pres. & V. Pres. are without representation is ridiculous. The District is represented by the entire Congress of the U.S. Wash. is a one industry city & that industry is the Fed. govt. It is a company town—look at the pop. figures for 1976. Some 223,900 employees in the Dist. worked for the Fed. govt—149,200 for industries servicing govt. and only 16,100 were employed in manufacturing.

The Congress has been most generous to the district in the handing out of Fed. grants. It is the most affluent city in America. And the district is a city—~~smaller~~ a 70 sq. mile enclave with a population smaller than 11 other cities.

But if 38 state legislatures ratify this latest congressional foolishness Wash. will be the only city to have 2 United States Senators and at least one ~~Congress~~ representative in the house. They'll have no stake in agricultural problems. Their constituents demands will be for more govt. growth & the perquisites that go with govt. employment. And those 2 new Senators are the reason for the lobbying effort.

If they aren't & if the promoters of this idea sincerely mean ~~ju~~ they just want representation for the citizens of the district there is a very simple answer & an established precedent: cede back to Maryland the residential portion of the city just as Alexandria was returned to Va. in the last century. Then they'll be represented by Marylands 2 Senators & they can vote ~~to~~ in Marylands Senatorial elections.

One thing certain, the American people should be contacting their state legislators & telling them to vote <u>no</u> on ratification.

This is RR Thanks for listening. ❖

Amtrak

October 10, 1978

Should the U.S. Govt. continue in the railroad business & what are Americans getting out of it?

I'll be right back.

In 1971 with most of our railroads pleading that passenger rail service had become so costly that freight traffic could no longer subsidize it, the U.S. govt. stepped in and created Amtrak. This of course was the nationwide network of passenger lines which would service the most popular routes with a govt. run railroad.

In that 1st year Amtrak required a $40 mil. subsidy to keep the wheels turning. By last year that subsidy had grown to $500 mil. a year and it is estimated that will be a Bil. $ if Amtrak is still around in 1984.

Now I'm a train buff. For many years into the jet age I traveled exclusively by train out of personal choice. Becoming Gov. changed that and ~~planes~~ *jet travel* became a necessity. Nevertheless I'll admit to a great nostalgia for the conductors, "All aboard" & for seeing the country through a pullman window. But the numbers dont add up anymore & maybe we should settle for nostalgia.

The average Amtrak passenger takes a 226 mile trip. This costs Amtrak $44 but the passenger pays $16 leaving $28 to be ante'd up by the taxpayers. Amtrak could save $2 by buying the passenger an airplane ticket or could save ~~$~~ $27 by putting him or her on the bus. The fare *there* is only $17. As a matter of fact Amtrak could pick up the whole fare, buy ~~hi~~ *the* passenger ~~a~~ lunch and still save money.

Of course some may bring up the matter of energy and point out that rail travel must save a lot of scarce oil. I'm afraid that argument is worth about as much as my nostalgia. On the average Amtrak is only about one-half as energy efficient as those busses we see out on the highway. Worse yet—with the exception of what is called the "Northeast corridor" where commuter type traffic is heavy Amtrak uses more energy per passenger mile than does the automobile. And before you bring up the environmental argument about air pollution—trains pollute more than busses.

It is true that trains have a safety record with regard to fatalities that is better than the automobile—but so do planes and busses. No there are only 2 reasons for Amtrak—one I've already mentioned, nostalgia and I'm afraid the other is politics. Too many of us even though we dont take train rides anymore just like to think they are there. ~~to And~~ As for the other reason, they run through too many congressional districts to ever expect Congress to say, "enough already." If it wasn't for this the money losing ~~lines~~ routes could be eliminated and possibly the crowded North East corridor retained where the losses aren't so great.

It will take something of a miracle to keep us from buying a lot of railroad tickets for other people to use—so sit back ~~& charge it of~~ *& enjoy nostalgia.*

This is RR Thanks for listening. ❖

Twelve years before this commentary, Reagan complained about hyphenated names and policies that seemed to divide Americans in a handwritten letter to President Dwight D. Eisenhower: "I am in complete agreement about dropping the hyphens that presently divide us into minority groups. I'm convinced this 'hyphenating' was done by our opponents to create voting blocks for political expediency." *

Bi-Lingual
October 10, 1978

How far do we go in our effort to change ~~T~~*t*his land from a melting pot into ~~a nati~~ *an all nations* smorgasbord? I'll be right back.

From the very first this nation has been made up of a collection of minorities forming a majority we called Americans. We hyphenated ourselves, yes, to explain the origin of ~~our~~ family; calling ourselves German-American, Irish-American, Italian-American ~~and so forth~~ *etc.* And as 1st generation Americans began to be replaced by 2nd & 3rd generation Americans the success of the melting pot became evident as more & more of us described our heretage as French & Dutch or Irish, Scotch & English, Austrian & Italian—you name the mix we had them all.

Our ancestry traces to every corner of the world but with one common characteristic which ~~made~~ *makes* us Americans. Those forefathers of ours &

* Reagan's July 22, 1966, letter to President Eisenhower is reprinted in Kiron K. Skinner, Annelise Anderson, and Martin Anderson, eds., *Reagan, A Life in Letters*, pp. 700–701.

yes todays modern immigrants had & have an extra love of ~~freedom~~ *liberty* and *an extra* ounce of courage which made it possible for them to tear up roots & journey to a faraway land in search of *more personal* freedom & *better* opportunity for themselves & their children. Yes we keep our pride of origin, perpetuate the memory of *ancestral* song & custom, dress up in ethnic costume for certain ceremonial days. ~~but~~ *We also* carry the Stars & Stripes and sing the Star Spangled Banner on those occasions.

Of late however and possibly for pol. purposes we seem bent on doing away with the melting pot, ~~and maintaining~~ *recreating* strict ethnic divisions. A few weeks back I commented on ~~the failure of bi lingual ed. in our schools~~ *bilingual ed. and it's failure* to do anything toward improving the ability of students speaking a foreign tongue, to master English.

The other day a ~~successful~~ *TYPICAL* American drove me to the airport in a town where I'd been speaking. He decried our ~~Calif.~~ law which requires the printing of our ballots in 2 languages. Then he told me how he had come to this country *FROM ITALY* when he was 10 yrs. old. Like millions before & since he learned English with*out* ~~no~~ *the help of* special programs and he said at ~~night~~ *home in the evenings* he & his brothers & sisters would help ~~teach English to their parents~~ *their parents learn English*. He's *STILL* a fairly young man & as American as baseball.

A Calif. news item the other day reported on the cost of printing ballots ~~+~~ in 2 languages and the waste because hundreds of thousands of them were thrown away, uncalled for at the polling places in our ethnic neighborhoods.

Now from the Nat. Review Bulletin I glean the following item. The Fed. govt. has ordered 3 counties of No. Carolina to print ballots in the language of the Lumbee Indians. There is a problem—there is no Lumbee language. There was once but the Indians abandoned it long ago in favor of English when white settlers moved into the area.

County officials are considering asking for a Fed. grant to invent a Lumbee language & teach to the Lumbees so they can carry out the law requiring dual language ballots.

Wash. isn't doing too well in English these days. Here is an H.E.W. working paper: "In terms of heads who worked, as one would expect, the proportion of heads who worked is greater for total poor heads compared to poor heads eligible for welfare, greater still for non-poor heads eligible for welfare."

Try that in Lumbee.

This is RR Thanks for listening. ❖

Environment
October 10, 1978

I dont want you to lose sleep over this but it is reported the Whydah bird* found only on Digue Island may become extinct in 15 years. I'll be right back.

If you've ever heard of the Whydah bird—that's spelled W-H-Y-D-A-H—you're ahead of me. As a matter of fact I'll have to look at an Atlas or Encyclopedia to find out where Digue Island** is, ~~located. Digue is~~ the only place where the Whydah bird is found. But apparently we are supposed to be upset because an ornithologist says the Whydah bird may be extinct in 15 years.

Maybe CETA the "Comprehensive Employment & Training Act," could help a little. In Wisconsin CETA workers are *being* paid to record the sounds of Quail calls, why not the Whydah birds?

But in Calif. We have an environmental problem which could pit environmentalists against environmentalist. The Pacific Legal Foundation a non-profit organization ~~usually~~ *consistently* found on the side of common sense & fairness has filed suit against the Environmental Protection Agency. It seeks an injunction to stop E.P.A. activities which violate the Endangered Species Act. To make this action even more unusual the U.S. Fish & Wildlife Service is also named in the suit.

All this started with an E.P.A. order banning waste disposal in the Ocean by ~~the~~ Los Angeles & other nearby cities. E.P.A. would have them switch to a land disposal system at a cost of hundreds of mil's of dollars. Now you must understand we're not talking of raw sewage or sludge but treated effluent which is piped out to sea. Scientists have found this not to be polluting so much as it is fertilizing. They say that the Santa Monica bay area is rich in Plankton because of the nutrients brought into the sea by this waste disposal.

Plankton it so happens is an important food supply for the great Gray Whales & for anchovies. ~~And the~~ Brown Pelicans feed on anchovies. Now the Whales & the Pelicans are both on the endangered species list. The Pacific Legal Action committee is asking whether the E.P.A. order ~~by~~ which would reduce the food supply of the Plankton would not subsequently endanger the Whales, the Anchovies & the Pelicans.

Curiously the Fish & Wildlife people who rushed to stop ~~a~~ dams that threatened the Snail Darter, the Furbish Lousewort and the Daddy Longlegs Spider aren't anxious to buck the E.P.A. The Legal group actually has a serious and worthwhile purpose. They are trying to establish the absurdity of the present endangered species law which gives priority to tiny fish, weeds & spiders regardless of the merits of any proposed project.

* The Whydah is a finchlike bird of the genus *Vidua*. Various Whydahs are native to Asia and Africa.

** La Digue is an island in the Seychelles chain in the Indian Ocean northeast of Madagascar.

Through a confrontation they hope to achieve a balance between environmental concerns & economic ~~concerns~~ *values* important to the American people. They advocate ~~environmental impact statements requiring~~ that no new species be put on the endangered list until environmental impact statements have shown what the loss to society would be in comparison to the loss of projects such as dams and reservoirs etc.. I told you they were on the side of common sense.

This is RR thanks for listening. ❖

Welfare
October 31, 1978

In Wash. the word, welfare is usually followed the word, mess. That mess can be eliminated but not by Wash. I'll be right back.

The Sec. of H.E.W. admitted with apparently no great discomfort that last year $7 bil. ~~in~~ was lost in welfare fraud. A number of big city mayors routinely ask Wash. to take over Welfare as do some Governors and the admin. when it talks welfare at all advocates federalizing it.

From our experience in reforming welfare in Calf. I am convinced the welfare mess is a Wash. mess. It can be straightened out if Wash. will close down it's welfare shop and turn welfare over completely to the states & local govt. This of course must include turning the necessary tax sources over the states at the same time.

Right now welfare is administered at the local level but under ~~the~~ thousands of all encompassing, ever changing Fed. regulations. In spite of this there is evidence that locals can eliminate a lot of the mess even with the Fed. handicaps. Los Angeles County is a classic example, one which makes you wonder what could be accomplished if Wash. would get out of the way.

In comparing local management it is interesting that Wash. D.C. has a 35% rate of fraud & error, ~~Los Angeles has only 2.67%.~~ N.Y. *City* won't even reveal it's fraud/error figures but the overall state average is 12.1%. The nat. average is 8.5, ~~and~~ all of Calif. is ~~only~~ 3.6 and Los Angeles County is only 2.67%.

Th~~is~~*ese* figures indicate the extent of Calif's. accomplishment in the welfare reforms which went into effect in 1971. Additional savings ~~of~~ estimated *at* $100 mil. *could be made* if Wash. would make the welfare forms readable by recipients. Simplifying the eligibility rules could lead to at least $150 mil. in savings and it's anyones guess what could be saved by computerizing the welfare management system at the local level.

Calif's. 1971 reforms reduced the caseload by 350,000 persons in 3½ yrs. reversing what had been a 40,000 a month increase. Key elements were tougher enforcement of child support ~~laws~~ *LAWS*., enforcing work requirements & cracking down on fraud & error. Now L. A. County is an excellent case study of what computers & good management can do. ~~Their~~ *It's* error/fraud rate was 12%. By 1976 it was down to 4.4 & now as I said is down to 2.67.

Keith Comrie the L.A Co. Dept. head has streamlined operations to the point of reducing welfare employees from 13,000 to 11,000 in JUST the last 2 years. A computer cross check can reveal in 3 seconds whether a recipient is getting welfare in any of the other 26 district offices. The system automatically cross checks the state disability files, unemployment offices & Fed. St & local govt. employees. When that program started it turned up 2000 co. & city employees on the welfare roles.

I submit Mr. Comrie makes the case for state & local management of welfare without Fed. interference.

This is RR Thanks for listening. ❖

Crime

October 31, 1978

Once again we have a tragic example of what can happen when we go too far in our effort to be fair or charitable to law breakers.

I'll be right back

~~If they haven't caught him already Los Angeles police are trying to find & arrest a man accused of~~

An off duty police officer working as a security guard at a Los Angeles bus depot recently placed a man under citizens arrest for loitering in the early morning hours. When Los Angeles police checked the man's identity he turned out to be a suspect they had been seeking since Sept. 28th.

They had already arrested two members of his family as accomplices in the Sept. 28th crime but he had escaped. The crime was the kidnaping, rape & murder of a University librarian. He was also wanted in connection with 3 other kidnapings & rapes including an 18 yr. old co-ed.

It is alleged that the suspect kidnaped the young librarian from a bus stop at gunpoint. She was taken to his family home where she was (as the press reported it) sexually molested and then shot at close range. Her body was then dumped in an alley a few blocks away.

The suspect, according to the police, was also wanted along with others for kidnapping 2 women, taking them to the same house where at gun point they were forced to perform unnatural acts ~~on~~ *with* each other~~)~~ & raped by 5 men~~,~~. *One was* pistol whipped, suffering a broken jaw.

On the following night the young coed was kidnaped from in front of a cafe by 2 men, taken to the same home where she too was raped and held for 11 hours. She was released in the morning and subsequently led the police to the house where she had been held & where it is assumed the other crimes had taken place. Now the suspect & his sister have been charged with murder. In all, he is charged with 15 felonies including the murder, in addition to kidnaping, rape, robbery and others.

One cant help but have an overwhelming feeling of compassion for the victems who were forced to endure such nightmares of horror & degredation. And in the case of one—death.

But let me make it clear, I did not subject you to this account of brutal crimes just ~~to~~ for the shock of telling a horror story. The shock is (& this is my reason for telling the story) the man charged with these crimes was sent to state prison for bludgeoning a man to death in 1976. On Sept. 13th 1978—just 2 years later ~~we~~ *he* was paroled and put back on the street where in a matter of days he allegedly committed the crimes I have described.

Our system of justice calls for punishment only if guilt is proven beyond a reasonable doubt. Is it too much to ask of a parole board that they have confidence in a mans rehabilitation beyond reasonable doubt before they free him?

This is RR Thanks for listening. ❖

On August 17, 1978, President Carter vetoed a defense bill because it included $2 billion for a Nimitz-class *aircraft carrier. On September 7, the House of Representatives sustained the veto. On October 13, President Carter finally signed the bill.*

Nuclear Carrier
October 31, 1978

It is hard to understand the veto of the recent defense budget bill if, as was stated, it was because of the inclusion in that bill of a nuclear carrier.

I'll be right back.

When the defense bill was vetoed the reason given for the veto was the provision in that bill for construction of a Nimitz-class *aircraft* carrier. The veto message stressed the greater cost of a nuclear carrier as compared to the conventional kind. That was a little less than accurate for a number of reasons, one being that the stated cost of the nuclear carrier included fuel for 13 yrs. Adding fuel cost to the price of the conventional carrier for ~~that~~ those 13 yrs. brings ~~the cost~~ it into the Nimitz class price range—*but not it's battle effectiveness.*

What makes the veto hard to understand though is a report to Congress ordered by the Carter admin. making an unanswerable case in support of the giant carriers.

In fact there were 2 studies submitted early last spring both of which were thorough analysis of naval force planning. One was the, "Sea-based Air Platform" study comparing the cost-effectiveness & "survivability" of small, medium & large aircraft carriers. The 2nd was the "Sea Plan 2000" study which analyzed the mission & the needs of the U.S. Navy from now til the end of the century.

The admin. delivered these studies without deleting or repudiating a single recommendation or finding. Then ignoring the studies completely, submitted a 1979 Navy budget providing for no carriers at all and ~~redu~~ a shipbuilding program reduced by half.

To say the members of Congress were surprised is an understatement. The first study had informed them that the Nimitz class carrier is individually the most effective & survivable ship. It's massive armor *plate* protecting ~~it's~~ magazine & power plant, structural strength & compartmentalization make it capable of absorbing a great many enemy hits and STILL keep on fighting. This is not true of the smaller ships.

The "Sea Plan 2000" study found that our surface ships & carrier battle groups will become less vulnerable over the next 10 or more years. This is laid to the expectation that 3 U.S. developments will more than match Russias advances in cruise missiles, attack bombers & ~~the~~ submarine threat. They are the F-14/Phoenix fleet air defense system, the introduction of ~~an air~~ *a close in* defense against missiles that get through the fighter barrier and improvements in our anti submarine warfare.

Over ~~all~~ & above all, the studies demonstrated that a 13 carrier, 600 ship navy could take on the vastly improved & increased Soviet navy in it's own waters and win. We are far short of those numbers right now.

Admiral Holloway * who has just retired as Chief of Naval Operations had recommended the giant carrier. Sec. of the Navy Claytor ** said if Congress would authorize a big carrier he would build it with enthusiasm.

It is hard to understand the complete reversal of the admin. when it's own studies and arguments were aimed at convincing Congress ~~that~~ the nuclear carrier was needed. Congress was convinced but the Pres. said "April Fool," and the Soviets smile happily.

This is RR Thanks for listening. ❖

Pensions

October 31, 1978

Not too long ago ~~Sec. of H. E~~ a proposal—or at least a suggestion came out of Wash. which causes one to wonder about our govt's. approach to problem solving.

I'll be right back.

* Admiral James L. Holloway.

** W. Graham Claytor, Jr.

There are several ways by which an American can provide for his non-earning years. First of course he can earn an income which permits him to accumulate enough wealth to see him through those years. Second he can invest his earnings in a retirement insurance plan or annuity. But this in turn *also* requires a pretty high level of earnings. Third he or she can be a participant in a Union or industry type pension plan in which the employer ends up ~~making~~ retiring the worker on a fixed percentage of earned salary. This would also cover public employees who long ago opted not to participate in Soc. Security. And of course the latter—(Soc. Security) is the retirement plan for a great many.

Unlike the other plans the ~~retire~~ *Soc. Security* retirement income is not based on the payroll tax paid over the individuals working years by employer & employee. That was the original idea but the plan has actually become a pay as you go ~~basis~~ arrangement whereby todays workers pay a tax to support the workers of yesteryear. Today workers in turn expect to be supported by a payroll tax on tomorrows workers.

Social Security was predicated on a projection that the number of workers would increase faster than the number of retirees so the payroll tax would as time went on become less of a burden. Unfortunately that was a false projection, fewer & fewer workers are supporting more & more recipients and the program is trillions of dollars out of actuarial balance. ~~as we look down the next 75 years.~~

Public employees pension funds are to a large extent unfunded liabilities even though pub. employees contribute a percent of their income to such funds. The employer—in this case govt's. Fed. St. & Local simply count on future tax funds to pay their part of the obligation. Federal unfunded *PENSION* liability is estimated at around $450 bil. & growing. States & municipalities are unfunded by about $300 bil.

Now curiously enough the Fed. govt. which does not regulate the solvency of it's own plans subjects private pension plans to a tough scrutiny by something called "Erisa."* The contributions by employees & employers are invested in Americas industry. Indeed they are an important source of capital—the very life blood of our economy.

A survey of the 1600 largest companies reveals they can meet their *PENSION* obligation with only 3 months of *PRE* tax ~~free~~ earnings. Employee pension funds own ⅓ the equity capital of American industry.

Now Sec. Califano has suggested that maybe the answer to Soc. Securities' problem is for it to take over the private funds. That's like the Capt. of the Titanic telling the passengers to scuttle the lifeboats & stay on the ship. He even suggests it is unfair ~~of~~ *for* workers who pay both for their pensions & the Soc. Security tax to have retirement incomes better than those offered by Soc. Security.

* The Employee Retirement Income Security Act of 1974 sets minimum standards for most voluntarily established pension and health plans in private industry.

In other words scuttle the fully funded programs in an effort to bail out Soc. Security. With nearly ⅔ of the nations work force covered by private pension wouldn't it make sense for Soc. Security to join them? ~~Why not?~~ Why wont they do that? Well a pretty sizeable burocracy might find itself with nothing to do.

This is RR Thanks for listening. ❖

Toys
November 1978

†Govt. has taken aim at another Am. institution. A childs letter to Santa may soon be a thing of the past. I'll be right back

For a great many years,—certainly all that I have lived, parents have waited for their childrens letters to Santa Klaus to get some idea of what to put beneath the Christmas tree. As growing up changed that a more direct form of communication took place. After all raising a family presents enough problems without having to guess about what *WILL BRING JOY TO* your children on Christmas morning.

Now where do ~~the~~ children get the ideas they incorporate in those letters to Santa or in later years that they carefully ~~in~~ hint to ~~their~~ *us* parents in elaborately casual conversation? In my childhood it was very often a Sears Roebuck catalog that fired up desire for an electric train or an erector set. Then & now it ~~is~~ *can be* the walk through the toy dept. to see Santa in person. But whatever, a childs imagination isn't up to inventing the toys he or she wants to find under the tree on Christmas morn.

In short they see something some childhood friend has, they see store window displays, catalogs & now in living color TV commercials and from any or all of these ~~decide on~~ *choose* those toys they'd like to have. ~~Bu~~t There is of course the element of parental judgement which often modifies the expressed desire, sometimes for ~~reas~~ *economical* reasons, sometime because of unsuitability. I remember wanting a mechanical boat (I'd seen in a catalog) at a time when there wasn't a body of water of any size within miles of where we lived. A couple of years later we moved to a river town and there ~~one~~ *on* the 1st Christmas was my boat.

~~Now the~~ This system of communication between parent & child has ~~work~~ worked very well & for a long time. Now govt. wants to get ~~in on~~ *in the act.* The Fed. Trade commission is considering a ban on *TV* advertising of toys to children. I'm not sure whether they intend ~~the~~ applying the ban to other forms of advertising. But with regard to TV they say children must be protected since they are too young to see the distinction between program & commercial. I think they underestimate our children.

Isn't this really an interference in the parent, child relationship? The F.T.C.'s concern should extend no farther than insuring that the advertising is not deceptive or misleading and that the toy ~~is~~ meets legal requirements as to safety etc. From then on it is the parents responsibility to decide whether a toy is or is not suitable for their child.

Right now the industry itself regulates all toy advertising. Every commercial is submitted for approval by the Nat. Assn. of Broadcasters, the networks & the Council of Better Bus. Bureaus.

~~The responsibility for w~~What children watch on TV & for that matter how much they watch is a parent responsibility. The fact that some parents dont exercise that responsibility as they should is hardly the province of the Fed. Trade Commission.

As for me I'm still trying to find out what Nancy wants for Christmas. Our children have long since given us the word.

This is RR Thanks for listening.

† Send copy when typed to writer of attached letter. RR ❖

Horse and Rider I

November 1978

Every once in a while a news story reminds us of the indomitable spirit of man and for a while we can forget the cynics. I'll be right back.

Anne Keegan writing in the Chicago Tribune on Nov. 3rd* is the source of todays commentary. She wrote of a husky young man (age 27) who worked on an Illinois river barge until one day a two inch metal cable broke. As it snapped back it whipped ~~around Jim Hendricks~~ *around his body* like a boa constrictor, crushing his lower spine. Jim Hendricks became a paraplegic. That was 4 yrs. ago.

After a period of feeling sorry for himself (which I'm sure we can all understand) he made up his mind that he wouldn't settle for growing old in a wheel chair doing nothing.

Jim had been raised around horses all his life & his first love had been riding. He decided he was going to ride again. You know there is an old cavalry saying that nothing is so good for the inside of a man as the outside of a horse. I dont know whether Jim was familiar with that saying but he knew riding would make him, as he put it, feel human again.

First of course he needed a horse—a big boned, stocky, quiet horse with common sense & intelligence. He found his mount, standing in *a* pasture, unbroken as yet. But that was alright because he would have to be trained in a special way.

* Anne Keegan, "This Team is More than a Man and His Horse," *Chicago Tribune,* November 3, 1978.

Borrowing money from the bank to buy the horse, a truck to haul him and some ≠ left over to pay for training, he put up his mobile home as collateral. Then he went hunting for a trainer. A special kind of trainer who could teach a horse to lie down so Jim could get aboard & then get up carrying his rider.

He found his man—an old trick rider—now blind. Bud Jones was more than a little doubtful about the project but when he saw how determined Jim was he gave it a try. It was a good try and Calvin ~~(the horse)~~ *that's what Jim named his horse* learned in 3 mo's. what they had thought would take a year.

Jim & Calvin became close friends & Calvin seemed to sense the need to take care of his friend. He learned a number of tricks. Jim made himself a leg brace & with crutches could *STAND &* move around just a little. But he rode with out any straps or safety devices.

Then one day Bud suggested that Jim & Calvin should do the horse show circuit & perhaps some country fairs. Jim said no at first but when Bud pointed out it might ~~be~~ *be* helpful to & inspiring to other's with handicaps he went on the road billed as "Hopalong the Worlds only Paraplegic Trick Rider & His Horse Calvin." They did rodeos, fairs and just about anything that would take them. When people would marvel at Jims ability to ride, he'd give the credit to ~~his horse~~ Calvin.

It would be nice if the story of Jim Hendricks, paraplegic, Blind Bud Jones and Calvin ended right here but unfortunately there is more. I'll tell you about it in the next broadcast.

This is RR Thanks for listening. ❖

Horse and Rider II
November 1978

This is more about Jim Hendricks—paraplegic and ~~his~~ *the* horse Calvin, he rides at fairs & rodeos.

I'll be right back.

On the last broadcast I told of how Jim Hendricks a paraplegic as the result of an accident decided to take up horseback riding. He mortgaged his mobile home to buy ~~a truck~~ *an unbroken horse & truck* to haul his horse. He found an ex-trick rider now blind who taught his unbroken horse to lie down so he could be mounted and to do a number of tricks.

Then Jim & his horse Calvin went out on the ~~show tour~~ *circuit*, playing rodeos, horse shows & ~~fairs.~~ *FAIRS*. They received a fee but actually only broke even what with feed bills & hire of an assistant at each stop. In fact Jim never took a motel or hotel room but slept in the stable with Calvin. But they were having fun and life had a purpose. His support was from Social Security disability out of which he paid the instalments on his mortgage.

Then last August Jim & Calvin came in off the road and found his disability had been cut off because he had missed a medical re-examination. He was told he'd have to appeal the decision and that would take 3 or 4 months. But then they added that even if he won the appeal & was declared medically eligible he still wouldn't get any checks because he'd become a performer. They turned a ~~def~~ deaf ear when he explained he didn't actually make any money—that he was doing it to encourage other handicapped people.

Finally the bank notified him that unless he could resume payments on his loan they'd have to take his mobile home, his truck & Calvin. Trainer Bud Jones says that would probably mean the slaughter house for Calvin because he wont let anyone but Jim ride him. Others have tried & been thrown. Calvin seems to be more understanding than the people at Soc. Security. He has a 6th sense about his ~~*handicapped* owner and~~ handicapped owner and takes care of him.

Jim has begged the bank to take his trailer & his truck~~s~~ but not Calvin. He says; "I'd lay down my life for that horse. He's everything to me. He's my pleasure & my protector. He's given me a purpose in life since my accident." Jim feels his back is to the wall. If his disability isn't restored there is no way that he & Calvin can go on. ~~H~~ As he puts it: "I'm the type I dont worry if it's just a can of beans on the table for supper. So they can come & take everything to my name. But I dont know how I'll get along if they come & take my best friend away."

Anyone who rides knows how Jim Hendricks of Pleasantview Ill. feels. Social Security Computers cant know ~~&~~ *nor* apparently can any of those desk jockeys who live by the book. I wonder how many discouraged & depressed people with handicaps have been encouraged to find a purpose in life after seeing Jim Hendricks as "Hopalong the Worlds only Paraplegic Cowboy & His Horse Calvin"?

This is R.R. Thanks for listening. ❖

Lt. General Victor H. Krulak, USMC (Ret.) and Ronald Reagan exchanged many letters during Reagan's presidency. Krulak typically enclosed his nationally syndicated column in his letters to Reagan. As president, Reagan would share the columns with White House staff. Here he shares Krulak's reporting on the People's Republic of China and Taiwan with millions of listeners.

China
November 1978

Here is a little human interest story with a happy ending—I thought you might like to hear.

I'll be right back.

A long time friend, former Gen. in the U.S. Marine Corps V.H. ~~Krulak~~ *KRULAK* recently made the acquaintance of a young man named Chou Shui-liang.

Gen. Krulak was so impressed with his story that he made it the subject of ~~hi~~ a syndicated column he writes.

~~As the Gen.~~ Chou Shui-liang ~~a citiz~~ is *an entertainer,* a juggler by profession. He was a member of a troupe sent to the Sudan by the Communist rulers of mainland China. I suppose it was in the nature of a cultural exchange.

One night after a performance in Khartoum Chou decided to leave the troupe. What he really had in mind was parting company with his homeland, the Peoples Republic of China. He reached the American Embassy in Khartoum late that night where he announced he wanted out.

I'm sorry to say our embassy decided he was diplomatically a little *TO* hot to handle what with Wash. getting ready to cozy up to the rulers in Peking. So Chou was passed on to the Sudanese govt. ~~Gen.~~ *where according to Gen.* Krulak ~~*where*~~ ~~reports that~~ no one could speak Chinese. This was no problem for Chou. He walked over to a map, ballpoint pen in hand, drew a big X across Peking and pointing to himself made a circle around Taiwan.

The Sudanese got the idea immediately & did what I wish our embassy had done; they bought Chou a ticket to Taiwan—right to the capital city Taipei.

Gen. Krulak had ~~an~~ *a* personal meeting & interview with the now free Chou Shui-liang. He asked, "weren't you scared? Here you were brought up under the communists, no real experience anywhere else. You didn't have the slightest inkle of what you were getting into." Chou had an answer ~~for~~ *to* that. He said: "Thats right. I didn't know what I was getting into, but I sure knew what I was getting out of." Then he added, "and there are millions more just like me."

He went on to say that he was ~~only~~ a child ~~when~~ *before* the communists came into power in 1949. "I remember," he said, "we didn't have much, but we were never hungry. We could go to church or travel or criticise the govt. & nobody ~~sa~~*cared.* But now there is a ration coupon for everything, you cant move across the road without permission and there's always some commissar around trying to tell you what to think."

Chou sounds like a very forthright young man & one who has his values pretty straight. He makes us wonder whether we can go forward, as the admin. apparently intends to, with ~~plans to~~ a program ~~intended~~ calling for a relationship with Red China based on betrayal of the Free Chinese on Taiwan.

One thing is certain, we cant do that & pretend we are concerned about human rights

This is RR Thanks for listening. ❖

Wood I

November 1978

† Are you ready to learn that we really haven't been able to see the forest for the trees?

I'll be right back

When we ~~get a chance~~ *have an opportunity* to go to the ranch, which is not as often as we'd like, we're off & running. And once there we never have to ask, "what will we do"? There is an ongoing perpetual chore we can always turn to after a horseback ride or before for that matter.

Our house is heated only by fire places so the chainsaws are always gassed up & waiting. But they are used for more than ~~firewood~~ *building* up the woodpile. Much of the ranch is covered by *a* beautiful forest of Calif. Live Oaks & Madrone trees. It's beautiful to look at but not easy to walk or ride through. ~~and I guess that's true of most woodland in America.~~ You really cant see the forest for the trees.

Nancy & I and our friend Barney have taken to clearing pathways & even entire groves with ~~ha~~ *2* chainsaws, *a* pruning saw, ~~&~~ jeep & trailer. Our beautiful forest is a jungle of underbrush, windfalls, dead trees & dead limbs on live trees. The sun cant get through to the forest floor so new young trees die aborning.

We've concentrated on one grove near the house. It is *an* arduous, backbreaking and slow job but the reward is great. The dead limbs & the prunings are piled high in the trailer and then hauled out to a clearing and ~~piled~~ *stacked* for burning when ~~the~~ *our Calif.* rainy season comes. ~~(to Calif.).~~ The heavier limbs & fallen trees are cut to ~~firewood~~ *fireplace* length & used to heat the house. Gradually this one grove has become parklike. The good trees can be seen, and the sun dapples the earth beneath as we walk *OR RIDE HORSEBACK* through that particular grove. ~~or ride the horses beneath the trees.~~ Already we've seen an increase in wildlife as deer ~~come for~~ *browse on* the new growth. Unfortunately there is no way we can ever complete the job on the entire forest and ~~doing it~~ *having it* done would cost ~~a few~~ hundreds of dollars an acre.

Now what I've described is true of just about all the ~~woo~~ forest land in America. Whether we're talking commercial lumber land, privately owned timber or national forest, if there isn't a trail you cant go very far into the woods. But what if I told you <u>that</u> forest land, which covers half the country—not counting groves of noncommercial lumber like ours, cannot only become beautiful & parklike with increased wildlife but it can do a lot to solve our energy problem?

No—I'm not suggesting we cut down our forests. Quite to the contrary. Even the most ardent environmentalists approve the idea of clearing ~~those~~ forests of dead wood & fallen limbs which make forest fires more ~~possible~~ probable ~~but~~ *and* also more uncontrollable.

For some time now a gentleman named Norval Morey has been pleading the cause of harvesting junk wood as an energy source. He is Pres. of Morbark Industries Inc. in Winn Mich. He explains that junk wood consists of trees in our forests that are dead, dying, diseased, overcrowded & overmature. He not only pleads the cause, he's doing something practical about it. Dont miss our exciting next instalment with it's amazing figures on a perpetual energy source and ~~it~~ easily it can be ours.

This is RR Thanks for listening.

† When typed up send copies of these 2 scripts to Mr. Norval Morey—Morbark Industries Inc. P.O. Box 1000 Winn Mich. 48896. ❖

Wood II

November 1978

~~Yester~~ On the ~~last~~ *preceding* broadcast I said there was an energy source close at hand~~;~~ *&* inexhaustible. It's also more economical than oil, gas or coal. I'll be right back.

On the last commentary I referred to the Pres. of Morbark Industries Inc. ~~of~~ *in* Winn. Mich. Norvel Morey who has been trying to ~~get~~ make Wash. aware of a self perpetuating energy source ~~here~~ *close* at hand *&* ~~which is~~ greater than our entire import of oil from the OPEC nations.

In the U.S. (not including Alaska) we harvest about 1% of our wood *PER YEAR* for lumber and paper. Our forest lands produce each year 6 to 7 bil. tons of new fibre. This means about 5 bil. tons of fibre is wasted each year as trees die or become old & cease to increase in size. ~~l~~*L*imbs fall, disease & rot set in. Young trees are stunted, ~~and~~ unable to grow because they are smothered by windfalls or are unable to get needed sunlight. This 5 bil. tons of ~~woo~~ waste wood is the equivalent of 8½ bil. barrels of oil. We *ONLY* import 3½ bil. barrels a year.

What Mr. Morey is pointing out is that ~~40% of junk~~ *less than half of* the ~~wood~~ waste or junk wood in our forests (which makes for a giant forest fire danger) ~~if~~ *can be* used *INSTEAD* to produce steam or electricity equal to what we produce with all the oil ~~(3½ bil. barrels)~~ we import. ~~each year.~~ And the forests will be healthier & more attractive.

Anticipating a question as to how we harvest this ~~jungle~~ tangle of underbrush, dead trees, stunted trees & old trees ~~that is what~~ *THE ANSWER IS* Morbark Industries is ~~"~~doing *THIS* every day. We all have some idea of regular ~~lumbering lumbering~~ *harvesting* practises, the chain saws, bulldozers, ~~etc. &~~ *cable skidders &* the ~~d~~ debris left behind; tops, limbs etc. This *conventional* method produces some 3 to 10 tons *OF WOOD* per man/day. Morbark produces 50 tons per man/day of uniform size *WOOD* chips ready for the pulp mill.

An hydraulic shear reaches out and cuts the diseased or overage tree like you snip a cutting from a rose bush with a pair of clippers. A grapple pulls the tree ~~limbs, top & all to a machine into which it is fed~~ and feeds it, limbs, top & all into a chiparvestor. The chiparvestor is a machine that chews up the tree and spits it into a waiting truck in the form of wood chips and the truck heads for the power plant, factory or papermill. Morbark is already delivering to paper mills 2 grades of chips: One, the top grade is used to make the paper and the lower grade fuels the boilers.

There has been a recent addition to this mechanical chain—a gasifier which turns the waste wood into a natural gas increasing it's heat energy. One fellow put it this way—"it even burns up the smoke." ~~W~~ Incidentally whether burned as chips or gas, wood fibre is free of the pollutants found in other fuels. And when the machines pull out they leave a parklike forest behind with new shoots sprouting from the ~~stump~~ root systems~~.~~ *providing ~~feed~~ FOOD & SHELTER FOR WILDLIFE.*

The term used to describe the process is environmental thinning and we have in the U.S. 736 mil. acres designated as commercial grade forest~~,~~. We dont know how many mil's. of acres of ~~just~~ groves & ~~for~~ timber in addition. ~~b~~*B*ut in that commercial forest land there is an estimated 100 bil. tons of trees of which 40% is junk or waste wood and the supply renews itself on a permanent basis. ~~Several states~~

This is RR Thanks for listening. ❖

By the time Reagan taped this commentary, President Carter and General Torrijos had signed the Panama Canal treaties and the U.S. Senate had ratified them.

Panama Canal
December 12, 1978

I'll bet you thought you'd heard the last of the Panama Canal. Well brace yourself—It will be back with us right after New Years Bowl games.

I'll be right back.

I've just recently been shown a *copy of* [a] letter from a special assistant to the Commissioner of U.S. Customs addressed to the head of our Panama Canal Company. The letter reads: "Due to the cost items incorporated in the Panama Canal Treaties, tolls at the Canal will be increased approximately 40 to 100%. Shipping industry officials based in New Orleans are highly concerned that large toll increases at the Panama Canal will drive cargo away from the Port of New Orleans, the Gulf & East Coast to West Coast ports; approximately 20% of the cargo passing through the port of New Orleans transits the canal." I wonder if some Senators who voted for the treaties knew what they ~~were~~ *might be* doing to the economy of their states? ~~"~~The letter concludes: "I would appreciate your comments & forecasts as to the impact this will have on the shipment of goods bound for the gulf & East Coast Ports & the effect it will have on the Canal usage. This information would assist us in future allocations of Customs resources at the ports of entry along the U.S. coastline."

And we were just getting used to not hearing about the Panama Canal anymore. Well we'll be hearing when Congress returns in Jan. For obvious reasons the admin. did not send the Congress proposals for legislation to carry out the provisions of the treaty before the election. But in Jan. they'll all have to face up to a deadline. The treaty requires us to hand over to Panama certain bldgs. & facilities no later than *next* Oct. 1.

Panama will take over the headquarters of the 193rd Infantry Brigade, the 210th Aviation Battalion, mil. intelligence for the entire Southern Command and the Mount Hope Cemetery on the Atlantic side. Some 1200 mil. & civilian graves will have to be moved to the Pacific side.

All of this involves some $38 mil. in new construction by us. The new treaty prohibits the new canal commission from operating such things as bowling alleys & theatres so these will have to be taken over by the military.

Very simply the problem is this; the date for turnover is Oct. 1st, the rainey season starts in April. Construction is virtually impossible. Once the rains start— The place becomes one big puddle & Congress wont be back til Jan.

The Senate ratified the treaties but all the legislation implementing this construction, the transfers and the appropriations must be passed by both the House & the Senate. The treaties themselves can stand or die in this coming legislative session.

One thing sure—we'll be reminded that all these mil's. of dollars ~~in~~ *worth of* new construction to house our men~~,~~ (because we're giving Panama the present facilities)~~,~~ will also be given to Panama in the year 2000.

Yes we'll be hearing about the Canal—at least until the rains start in April.

This is RR Thanks for listening. ❖

Taxes

December 12, 1978

"Soak the rich," has been a standard part of tax policy for a long time now—but who has it really helped? I'll be right back.

Our progressive income tax structure is founded on the idea that those who earn more should pay more and there can be no arguing with the fairness of that. Indeed it is part of our Judeo-Christian tradition—the idea of tithing. The Lords share is considered to be a tenth. And we are told that if the Lord prospers us ten times as much we will give to him 10 times as much. In other words *if* you earn $10,000 you devote 1/10, ~~or~~ $1000 to good & charitable ~~causes.~~ *works.* If you prosper 10x as much and earn $100,000 you give ⅒—$10,000 to those good & charitable causes; in other words to the Lord.

It is when we "render unto Caesar" that we find ~~that~~ *the* proportionate tax which satisfies the Lord is totaly unacceptable to govt. Under what is called a progressive tax if you are prospered 10x as much, ~~your~~ *you are* taxed 50x as much—sometimes even more. This is the philosophy of "soak the rich," which theoretically lightens the burden for the less affluent—those with lower earnings.

To suggest exchanging ~~a~~ *the* progressive tax for a proportionate system would be political suicide for any office holder. Even the Kemp-Roth bill which ~~would~~ called for an across the board tax cut (and which I supported) would have retained the progressive feature.* Who today would dare say as a Scottish economist said a century ago; "to tax a man ~~on anything~~ *in any way* other than ~~on proportion to of his ta~~ *PROPORTIONATE TO his* earnings is to put to sea without rudder or compass. There is no end to the mischief you can do."

Alright having said that—brace yourself. I would like to see the rich pay more tax. I do not however believe that can be accomplished by increasing their tax rates. To the contrary I believe lowering the steeply progressive rates on the upper income brackets would not only increase their taxes it would mean more prosperity for all of us.

People in the upper income levels have a certain flexibility in arranging their affairs. When for example tax rates become too punitive they refrain from ~~risking~~ *putting* their money in *RISKY* investments because they would get so little benefit from any return ~~on the investment. There are~~ *because of the high tax. They can buy* school ~~bonds to buy; The return is low but it's tax free.~~ *& municipal bonds which are safe and while the return is low it is nontaxable.* Or they can buy works of art, land or ~~a govt.~~ *treasury* notes.

The truth is, real tax revenue from those who should be ~~investing in American industry, making it possible for us to increase productivity has been shrinking. Let me~~ *making business & commercial investments has been shrinking. Let me* give you some figures to prove that govt. gets more revenue when the punitive tax rates are lowered. In the 3 years 1961, 62 & 63 the top surtax rate was 91%. ~~Govt. averaged getting from those with incomes $100,000 a year & up $2.681 Bil. In 1964 John F. Kennedy backed a measure to lower the 91% rate to 77%—the govt.~~ ~~*tax*~~ ~~receipts jumped to $2.953 bil. In the 2 following years the 77% rate was dropped to 70% and the govt. share went up to just under $4 bil.~~

In each of those 3 yrs. Govt's. actual tax revenue from people earning $100,000 & up was a little over $2½ bil. ~~a year~~ In 1964 Pres. Kennedy backed a measure to reduce the 91% rate to 77% and tax receipts went up to almost $3 bil. In the 2 following years the 77% rate was dropped to 70% and govt. received about $4 bil. each year. They were better off & so were we.

This is RR Thanks for listening. ❖

* The bill, introduced on July 14, 1977, by Congressman Jack Kemp (R–New York, 1971–1989) and Senator William Roth (R–Delaware, 1971–2001), called for cutting income tax rates 30 percent across the board over a three-year period. Reagan eventually signed the Economic Recovery Tax Act of 1981, which incorporated such tax cuts, on August 13, 1981.

Keep Off the Grass
December 12, 1978

† Keep off the grass may be the newest edict to come down from the keepers of our public lands.

I'll be right back.

I've commented once or twice about what appears to be a move by the Fed. govt. to tie up more & more of the land area of the United States. Right now something called "Rare II" is going on. Rare stands for Roadless Area Review & Evaluation. It is a program by the Bureau of Land Management & the Forest Service to take about 62 mil. acres of Nat. forest & nat. grasslands in 37 states & Puerto Rico and designate them as wilderness areas. This would mean of course the closing of all roads. ~~in those areas.~~ In other words only those robust enough to go backpacking would have ~~the use of~~ *access to* those mil's. of acres of scenic land.

To show what this means to many Americans let me read you a portion of a letter I received. It reads: I happen to be what is popularly called a "rockhound," as is my husband. Many areas have been open~~ed~~ to us for many, many years, for hunting gem & rock materials (from which we make jewelry we sell to make a little extra money) if these plans (Rare II) go through some 500 rockhound areas in the Southwest alone will be closed to us."

Mrs. Corey then explained how rockhounds have certain areas posted for ~~them~~ their use; how it is traditional with rockhounds that they leave no litter behind & even engage in cleanups of areas where campers have carelessly left rubbish etc. She goes on to say, "our hobby happens to be one in which senior citizens participate to a great extent. Many of us are disabled so that we can not backpack, but we can go on the club trips if we can use the 4 wheel drives or the recreation vehicles. The ~~Bl~~ BLM & NFS plans would deny us all this. It is a healthy hobby which gets us outdoors & helps keep us active—good for both the morale & the body. If my husband & I did not have this type of recreation, I'm afraid we might become very inactive & do only sedentary type things, which you know is the worst possible thing for older people." Mr. Corey will be retiring in 2 years & they both look forward to continuing their hobby.

In a P.S. she added "We want to be entirely self supporting by our own hands. I believe you will find most of us feel this way—that is in our particular generation." Amen! She closed by pleading not for just rockhounds but for all who enjoy the great outdoors.

Mrs. Corey is right to be concerned and I think we all should be ~~concerned~~ lest a handfull of extremists plus ~~some~~ *these* govt. agencies lock up in a preserve the great scenic areas of our land for the benefit of a privileged few.

The Philips Co. News in Montana reports that 2 special agents of the Dept. of Interior appeared at the home of a retired rancher with a search warrant and confiscated the collection of arrow heads he had hanging on his living room wall.

Mr. Oshio had been collecting such artifacts for years as a hobby—not to sell. The Fed. agents said he had broken the law by taking them from public land. I find it inconceivable that a hiker coming upon an arrow head in the desert or nat. forest is breaking the law if he picks it up. As the song says—"This land is our land." It is not a burocratic private preserve.~~)~~

This is RR Thanks for listening.

† Send copy of this to Mrs. Corey (see letter attached) RR ❖

During the five years that Reagan recorded radio commentaries, he visited London twice, in 1975 and 1978.

Bread
December 12, 1978

In England there is an expression, "use your loaf." In America we say, "use your head." They mean the same thing. I'll be right back

A few weeks ago we took off for Europe to ask questions about some of the problems confronting the United States and our allies in the Free World. Meetings were scheduled with business & govt. leaders ~~including~~ in England, France & West Germany with London the first stop.

There are several ways to Fly to London. You can go to N.Y., overnight there and take the Concorde for a fast 3 hours or so the next day or the trip can be made in one day. Of ~~course~~ course the one ~~f~~ day trip upsets your life routine a bit. Leaving Calif. during the noon hour you take the big circle route up toward the pole, over Iceland, Scotland and South to Heathrow airport in London. The upsetting thing is that in those 9½ hours you fly into night, crossing 8 time zones and arriving at what is bedtime in Calif. but ALREADY morning in London. This we did and spent the next few days trying to adjust ~~to~~ *our* sleeping, waking & eating ~~on~~ *to* English time.

But enough about ~~je~~ jet lag. I mentioned eating and that has something to do with what I wanted to tell you. England had been undergoing a bakers strike for about 3 weeks before we got there. The press reported it as "industrial action." Naturally we figured on doing without bread, buns & pastries and had already counted the calories we'd ~~saved.~~ *save.*

To our surprise we never sat down to a meal that didn't include a variety of breadstuffs & pastries. We assumed this resulted from pre-strike hoarding or possibly imports until we read a news item under the headline: "Use your loaf Sam." That translates in American "use your head," and the Sam was Sam Maddox, General Sec. of the striking Bakers Union.

It seems that in spite of the, "industrial action"—(the strike called by

Sam's union)—more than 80% of the normal supply was reaching the market *every day.*

At first Sam claimed it ~~was~~ *was* coming from private sources. Later when that was proven to be untrue, he accused the large bakeries with dumping frozen stock they'd had in storage. *That also was untrue*

~~That also was untrue.~~ What the press had to report was something of a miracle of the loaves. About 2000 bakers in all of England had defied their leaders and returned to work; More than 20,000 remained on strike. Mr. Maddox is faced with trying to explain how ~~fewer~~ fewer than 10% of the normal workforce is providing 80% of Englands bread supply—seemingly with little strain or upset.

The paper ~~+~~ suggested there was evidently "an alarming degree of overmanning," in the bakeries and said, "It is time the leaders of the bread strike faced up to reality." Ironically the newspaper workers who voiced those thoughts were planning to go on strike ~~when we left~~ themselves~~.~~, before we left.

This is RR Thanks for listening. ❖

Business Tax
December 12, 1978

At last voices are being raised challenging the demagogery so widespread about business, profits & taxes.

I'll be right back.

Louis Rukeyser * recently did a column about a corporations annual report to the stockholders. The particular corp. was Winn-Dixie Stores Inc. a major food chain.

It must have been a pleasant report for the shareholders to receive because it announced a 20% increase in profits over the previous year and the shareholders dividend was $3.94 per share.

But that wasn't the reason Mr. Rukeyser did his column on Winn-Dixies *ANNUAL* report. There was another figure in that report that is not usually included in such a document. Profits were up 20%, *YES,* but taxes were up 22% and the shareholders could read for the first time that *while* their ~~share~~ *dividend* was $3.94 ~~but~~ govt's. ~~share~~ take for each share of stock was $5.93.

The chairman of the board admitted that some of the stockholders were quite shocked by their first time look at the tax bite. Actually that $5.93 was not the total amt. of taxes paid by Winn-Dixie. It included Fed. inc. tax, Soc. Security taxes, franchise & occupational licenses, state income taxes & personal property taxes. It did not include indirect taxes such as the portion of the

* Louis Rukeyser wrote a syndicated newspaper column and also does radio and television commentary on economic and financial matters.

considerable rent the corp. pays which of course includes property tax on the rented facilities.

Let us hope this is only a beginning & that other businesses will fall in line & publish this figure in their reports. They will help to expose much of the economic mythology prevalent in our land. In the first place we ~~see~~ can see more clearly the inequity of the double tax. Each shareholder has paid in effect $5.93 in tax on the $3.94 he is allowed as his return. But now he must *ALSO* pay an income tax on that $3.94 which the Internal revenue service calls unearned income & therefore subject to a tax rate of as much as 70%.

Ah! but you say that's for a ~~pret~~ pretty well heeled person. Alright are you in an employee pension plan? Such plans own ⅓ of the stock in American business & industry. Dividends from those stocks will determine how much will be in the fund when you retire. Do you have an insurance policy? Premiums you & others pay for 380 mil. insurance policies are invested in shares of stock in Americas industry. *Your policy dividends come FROM THE DIVIDENDS EARNED BY THOSE INVESTMENTS.*

The fair answer of course would be a single tax. If there were no corporate tax, nontaxable funds such as Union pensions, endowments for schools & hospitals etc. would get twice as much money for their investments & would pay no tax on it. On the other hand individuals would receive ~~their~~ *INCREASED* dividends and pay income tax at whatever rate was called for by their income tax bracket. The retired couple with only a few dollars investment would pay no tax. As it is now they've been taxed ~~mo~~ at more than a 50% rate before they get their money. The high salaried individual in a 40 or 50% bracket would pay that rate of tax on his dividends.

By the way, Winn-Dixie did not make that healthy profit by gouging the customers. Their gross profit on each dollar of sales was less than 2 cents.

This is RR Thanks for listening. ❖

E.R.A.

December 12, 1978

Can Fed. employees be forced to actively work for a pol. cause even if they are personally opposed to that cause? Apparently the answer is yes. I'll be right back.

For a long time we have confidently assumed that govt. employees cannot be forced to participate in pol. activities. Apparently we have been wrong. ~~and u~~*U*nder certain circumstances their personal views notwithstanding they can be ordered to support a cause if not a candidate.

Thanks to a state legislator in Arizona, Rep. Donna J. Carlson* we learn of

* R–Arizona, 1974–1982. She was the Arizona coordinator for "STOP ERA."

a memo within a Fed. agency which not only orders support for the ratification of E.R.A. but requires interference by Fed. employees in the state ratification process.

Now let me hasten to say ~~this is~~ *I am* not bringing up the Equal Rights Amendment* for a pro or con discussion. The Congress has approved an extension of time for the state legislatures to vote for or against ratification of this constitutional amendment. What I am bringing up is what Rep. Donna Carlson calls, "blatant interference into the ratification process by the executive branch."

It seems that Rep. Carlson came into possession of a memo from the Lower Colorado Regional office—Bureau of Reclamation, U.S. Dept. of the Interior. It reads as follows: "Subject: Elimination of Sexual Discrimination." The body of the message then follows: "In a memorandum to the heads of dept's. & Agencies, the Pres. emphasizes that every resource of the Fed. govt. is to be applied in eliminating discrimination & inequality based on sex."

If the memo ended there I'd be in complete agreement & I'm sure Ms. Carlson would be also. But it continues: "He states that ratification of the Equal Rights Amendment will remain a priority ~~of~~ *with* the present admin. and further directs the Head of each dept. & agency to (1) make the most of public appearance opportunities to demonstrate the administrations commitment to the Equal Rights Amendment and (2) include in public speeches, where appropriate, language emphasizing the importance of ERA and assure that similar language is included in the speeches made by officials of their agency or dept."

Perhaps that paragraph can be defended by some as within the administrations right. But there can be no justification for the final paragraph of this memo to employees of the Dept. of Interior.

"Accordingly, I am asking each supervisor & manager in this Region to comply with the above ~~directives~~ directives regardless of personal preferences or political opinions. This is not to be considered a partisan issue, but one which Fed. employees are now obliged to support."

It was signed by the regional director and sent out on Oct. 23rd. It was made public in the Phoenix Gazette in Nov.

This is RR Thanks for listening. ❖

* The proposed equal rights amendment to the U.S. Constitution, never ratified, read: "Section 1. Equality of rights under the law shall not be denied or abridged by the United States or by any state on account of sex. Section 2. The Congress shall have the power to enforce, by appropriate legislation, the provisions of this article. Section 3. This amendment shall take effect two years after the date of ratification."

Textbooks
December 12, 1978

I know you've heard it before but evidently we need to hear it again—"We should take the time & trouble to read our childrens schoolbooks."

I'll be right back.

Columnist Patrick Buchanan (Bless his soul) has written a column reminding us that people write schoolbooks and therefore some schoolbooks will reflect the bias of their authors and students will accept that bias as truth.

If you are troubled now & then by a dinner table discussion in which your ~~children~~ *teenagers* attack your views with pronouncements they deliver as ~~unalterable~~ unassailable fact—check their source. You'll probably find ~~it's~~ it isn't TV or the newly befriended classmate. It's that ~~history~~ *text* book you're going to send them to their rooms to read. After all you're a parent and parents are supposed to see that homework is attended to. But let's add for the umpteenth time—parents ~~are also supposed to~~ *should* know what is in those text books.

Pat Buchanan reports that the Georgetown U. Ethics & Public Policy Center requested a veteran diplomat Martin F. Herz to examine 6 best selling high school history texts on how they treated 16 cold war topics.

He delivered a sobering 76 page report* on everything from the Yalta agreement, to the Berlin blockade, the Cuban missile crisis, the Korean war & the tragedy of Vietnam. "With the exception of a <u>single</u> paragraph in a <u>single</u> history book," Pat says ~~that "~~Herz reported, ~~"~~that, "none of the textbooks can be said to present an overly ~~friendly~~ *favorable* view of U.S. foreign policy. On the contrary there is a tendency of several to give the Soviet U. greater benefit of the doubt than is given to the U.S."

Only 2 of the 6 texts dealt with Soviet aims at all & one of those 2 was flattering & sympathetic to Lenin, Stalin & Soviet communism. It described the Truman doctrine** as committing the U.S. to intervene in "Democratic revolutions" whereever in the world they occurred.

While the books made no mention of communist subversion in America they painted ~~quiet~~ quite a picture of the excesses of the McCarthy era. And 2 of them found Fidel Castro an admirable fellow who saved Cuba from Batista.*** One falsified completely when ~~he~~ it said that Castro took the land away from a few ~~wealthy~~ immensely rich families & gave it to the poor farm

* Martin Florian Herz, *How the Cold War Is Taught: Six American History Books Examined* (Washington, DC: Ethics and Public Policy Center, Georgetown University, 1978).

** On March 12, 1947, President Truman requested that Congress appropriate $400 million and civilian and military personnel to help Greece and Turkey fight communist influence in the region. Congress agreed to do so. Supporting countries in danger of falling under Communist influence became a basic U.S. policy.

*** Fidel Castro led a seven-year revolution against Fulgencio Batista Zaldívar, leader of the Cuban government. He succeeded in taking control of Cuba in February 1959.

workers. What he did was confiscate all the land from rich & poor alike and set it up like the state owned collective farms of Russia.

Vietnam of course was described as an oppressive, dictatorial regime. That is S. Vietnam was described that way. No mention was made of the rampant totalitarianism in N. Vietnam nor was it mentioned that Ho Chi Minh was a communist.

Pat Buchanan drew a sobering & yes frightening conclusion. What if an American Pres. is faced some day with rallying his countrymen to the defense of this nation in an East-West Clash. And what if he is faced with an indifferent or even hostile young America made that way by our nations schools?

This is RR Thanks for listening. ❖

The following seven undated essays were drafted by Reagan and typed, but we have found no evidence that they were ever recorded. One was published as a newspaper column. We have estimated the time when they were written from their content.

Reagan wrote "Young People" as a radio essay, but it was distributed January 13, 1978, through King Features Syndicate as a newspaper column.

Young People
January 1978

Those of us who were on the over age 30 side during the riotous days of the 60's can be happy about what seems to be a reversal in the swing of the pendulum. I'll be right back.

Something called the "Who's Who Among High School Students" has been tracking our young people for about 10 yrs. now by way of a nationwide poll. Almost 24,000 High school Juniors & Seniors are chosen each year as leaders. Their principals, counselors and national youth groups make the selection on the basis of scholarly achievement, extra curricular activities, ~~&~~ athletics, and community service.

This years poll is the eighth and it would seem that certain trends of 10 yrs. ago have been reversed. Both morally & politically they are more conservative than their counterparts of a few years ~~ago~~ *back*.

Here for example is the score on one turnaround; a majority (54%) listed Nat. Defense as the top priority ~~sp~~ for Fed. spending. This is the first time in any of the 8 polls that defense has ~~been~~ received ~~a~~ majority support. Seventy seven percent would either increase or maintain the present level of spending. Just 4 yrs. ago only 8% suggested *an* increased ~~n~~ defense budget.

In 1971 only 30% of the student leaders favored capital punishment. This year 66% favor reinstituting the death sentence. Almost as many 64% would approve of censoring certain movies, TV programs, books & magazines. That is a complete reversal. The same percentage opposed such a thing in 1971.

I share their view that something needs to be done but I cant support the idea of govt. censorship. It is too ~~good~~ powerful a weapon to be put in govt. hands. Someone has said that anyone with enough character to be a censor would have too much character to be one. Still I hope Hollywood and Madison Ave. are listening. ~~It is they~~ That is where the problem can be solved with voluntary code of ethics such as the motion pic. industry once had. In the meantime I could suggest something these young people might do; stop buying tickets and what they dont like will go away.

Here are some other figures to gladden a parents heart, 49% have never hoisted a stein of beer, 46% have never sipped wine & 61% ha~~d~~*ve* never tried hard liquor. Contrast that with the poll of 5 yrs. ago when 85% said "yes" they had tried alcohol. About 88% ha~~ve~~*d* never used drugs, only 9% said they had tried marijuana and 85% had never even smoked a cigarette. ~~which adds to~~ *There were* 8% who had quit *smoking* for a 93% Total.

What is most heartwarming in this day when the media seems so obsessed with sex is to learn that 70% ~~were~~ *are* virgins & 56% said this was not because of parental pressure or lack of opportunity. It simply reflected their own moral standards.

~~Only 2 out of 7 would approved an intimate relationship without marriage.~~

Nearly 80% are members of an organized ~~reli~~ religion & 60% attend church on a weekly basis. Almost half said religion has become more a part of their lives in the last few years.

I hope this has brightened your day a little—it has mine. This is RR Thanks for listening. ❖

The following two essays, "Vietnam I" and "Vietnam II," address the findings of Guenter Lewy of the University of Massachusetts on the validity of charges made about the conduct of the military in Vietnam. Lewy's 21-page article, "Vietnam: New Light on the Question of American Guilt," was the cover story of the February 1978 issue of Commentary *magazine. The article was adapted from Lewy's book,* America in Vietnam *(New York: Oxford University Press, 1978) published later in the year.*

Vietnam I
February 1978

I'm sure you remember Vietnam—there was a war there once. Finally history is catching up with what has to be our most lied about war.

I'll be right back.

Why should anyone want to do a commentary about the ugly, cruel and apparently useless war in Vietnam? Well maybe because *too* many of our young people consider our defeat there a justified humiliation and that our presence in Vietnam was the epitome of evil. Of course they only know what they've heard & read. Now Prof. Lewy of U. of Mass. who spent 5 yrs. researching classified documents, ~~of the military,~~ command directives, field reports & staff studies, intelligence reports, investigations of war crimes etc. states that charges of officially condoned crimes & immoral conduct have no basis in fact.

The Prof. says that whereas we bombed civilian targets in W.W.II. with no criticism, somehow Vietnam was different. Every mistake or misdeed was reported by journalists who were generally critical of the American effort. Then the Communists put their worldwide propaganda machine into high gear and found many Western intellectuals ready to accept at face value every *false* charge.

Richard Falk of Princeton U. charged us with using cruel tactics against the civilian population. Prof. Lewy responds that the enemy practised, "clutching people to their breast," converting villages into fortified strongholds. ~~&~~ It was this that brought combat into populated areas.

Probably no attrocity (so called) was more widely heralded ~~an~~ than our use of napalm. We used it in W.W.II. air raids & everyone cheered. But in Vietnam we were led to believe we were burning innocent children by our indiscriminate use of this firey weapon.

~~But~~ a*A*s far back as 1967 and continuing through the war a team of noted American Doctors formed a committee & visited Vietnamese hospitals. This committee we now learn reported it found no justification for the charges of civilian napalm burns. We also learn now that in Dec. 1967, 600 Vietcong armed with Russian napalm flame throwers attacked a Montagnard village and burned 252 people (most of them refugees) to death.

In 1973 an antiwar group in America managed to get the words of the Rev. Chan Tin a So. Vietnamese anti-war activist ~~who was~~ before a U.S. Congressional Committee. He was free to criticize his own govt. ~~and~~ yet he charged ~~that~~ *his* govt. held more than 200,000 pol. prisoners. Two years later it was discovered the ~~humanitari~~ humanitarian priest was a member of the Viet Cong underground. We also learn now there were only 35,000 prisoners of all kinds *including common criminals* in all the jails of S. Vietnam at any time.

Then there were the tiger cages described by Sylvan Fox of the N.Y. Times as small concrete trenches with bars on top and several prisoners crammed into a space only 5 ft. wide, 6 ft. long & 6 ft. high. The so called cages actually numbered 48, they were built by the French in 1941, they were above ground and they were 6 ft. 3 inches wide, 10 ft. 6 inches long & 10 ft. high.

Next broadcast I'd like to reveal a few more facts about Vietnam as discovered by Prof. Lewy.

This is RR Thanks for listening. ❖

Vietnam II
February 1978

This is a continuation of the last broadcast with a few more honest facts about the war in Vietnam.

I'll be right back.

On the last broadcast I talked about Prof. Lewy *(LEWY)* of the U. of Mass. who has spent 5 years studying all the classified documents having to do with the war in Vietnam. Prof. Lewy is the 1st to do this and he turns a spotlight of truth on the unconscionable flood of propaganda that was loosed on us by our own media & the communist apparatus. ~~duing during the war.~~

I've already told you of how the records expose one of the foremost heros of the peace groups, a South Vietnamese clergyman who posed as just an outraged opponent of the war. When the enemy finally won, he turned out to be a secret agent of that enemy.

The Prof. comes up with another one—Huynh Tan Mam. He led demonstrations in Saigon against Pres. Thieu & the war. He was befriended by American reporters. On May 1st 1975, a day after the fall of Saigon he was honored & rewarded for his service to the Communist cause. ~~and made a speech as part of the celebration of the Communist victory.~~

Then the Prof. takes up the matter of whether ~~our forces violated the rules of international warfare as was charged; that~~ our men committed atrocities in response to orders by our high command. The truth is our men fought under restraints that amounted to ~~ty~~ tying one hand behind their backs. When Sen. Barry Goldwater was shown in 1975 some of the restrictions which had been placed on our men, he said: "It is absolutely unbelievable that any Sec. of Defense would ever place such restrictions on our forces. I am ashamed of my country for such restrictions to have been placed *up*on men who were trained to fight."

One of the most successful propaganda groups was the "Vietnam Veterans Against the War." They engineered a hearing in Detroit ~~with~~ *PRESENTING* witnesses ~~testifying~~ *WHO TESTIFIED* about war crimes. Now we ~~know~~ *discover* some of the witnesses had never been in Vietnam and others had never been in the combat zones where the alleged crimes were supposed to have occurred.

It's hard for most of us to realize how correct Hitler was when he said, "the bigger the lie, the more apt we are to believe it. One of the most widely heralded war crimes was ~~supposed to be~~ one in which American G.I's. threw a living Vietnamese out of a helicopter. That ~~one~~ *story* appeared in papers with photos of the falling body. The Army's Criminal Investigation Division (and this you didn't read in the papers) came up with the 2 anti-war soldiers who faked the incident by throwing a dead body out of the chopper, photographing ~~the incident~~ *it* & sending the photos to the girlfriend of one of the men.

~~Another~~ *A* televised story ~~of torture~~ was arranged by a reporter for one of the networks who ~~had~~ persuaded a soldier to cut the ear off a dead VC soldier for the TV cameras. The soldier was court martialed ~~but~~ *by the army but* the network never corrected the story or reprimanded the reporter who staged it.

And finally the N.Y. Times printed as byline dispatches *from a top correspondent* stories from a North Vietnamese propaganda pamphlet, "Report on U.S. War Crimes in Nam Dinh City."

Do you have the feeling we should apologize to those young men of ours who fought so bravely ~~with~~ *under* so many handicaps & with so little appreciation?

This is RR Thanks for listening. ❖

The Department of Health, Education and Welfare came into existence April 11, 1953. A separate Department of Education was signed into law in 1979, and the Department of Health, Education and Welfare became the Department of Health and Human Services on May 4, 1980.

Birthday Party
April 1978

†Some weeks back there was a birthday party in Wash. D.C. It was quite a whingding & you should know about it because you paid for it.

I'll be right back.

You might have seen some mention of the party held in Wash. several weeks ago, celebrating the 25th Anniversary of the Dept. of Health, Ed. & Welfare. It lasted 2 days and cost $15,000 which came from the "Office of Pub. Affairs budget & contingency funds"—those are tax dollars of course. But then we shouldn't begrudge H.E.W. it's moment of joy, even if the moment lasted 2 working days. And what is $15,000 to an agency that spends an average of $500 mil. a day?

The party was held in front of & within the lobby of the "Humphrey Bldg" (that's the name of the H.E.W. Headquarters). There was, according to the Wash. Post, "wall to wall music." * The Post also noted that in the lobby was ~~a 12~~ *what* amounted to a 12 ring circus.

At noon they sang "Happy Birthday Dear H.E.W." and there were numerous speeches. You might be interested in some of the facts revealed in those speeches. The Sec. of H.E.W. Mr. Califano ** in recognizing that this was the 25th anniversary, proudly announced that the ~~depts.~~ *agencies* budget is 26

* Joseph McClellan and William Gildea, "HEW Throws a Party for Itself," *Washington Post,* May 24, 1978, pp. C1, C3. A follow-up story (*Washington Post,* April 10, 1979, p. A8) put the cost at more than $100,000.

** Joseph Califano was secretary of the Department of Health, Education, and Welfare from 1977 to 1979.

times bigger than it was when it started. That's a lot of size to put on in 25 yrs. A 20 inch baby at birth would be more than 43 ft. tall at age 25 if it could achieve such a growth rate.

A number of legislators were invited to the party and apparently to qualify for an invite each one had to have a satisfactory voting record in welfare spending. Naturally they were introduced for a few words & each received warm applause. The last one to be recognized (he was saved for last) was Sen. Magnusen* of Wash., chairman of the Appropriations Committee; ~~thus a~~*A*nd since he was on hand at the birth of H.E.W. he had a hand in that fantastic growth rate.

He called attention to that when he said: "We started out very small." Then he spoke of the tremendous responsibility that had been placed on the dept. by congress & the courts. He said: "I asked the Sec. one day how many people are employed in H.E.W. How many are paid out of the pub. till. Well he said it was a little difficult to get that figure. Finally he came up with it 1,124,000 people." The Sen. added that was more than the army or the navy but he said Congress was proud ~~not~~ of that—not critical.

Now that figure takes some explaining and it was explained in Mr. Califano's speech. He explained that the 35,000 H.E.W. employees in 1954 had increased to 145,000 today but that HEW pays the salaries of 980,000 state, local & private employees. The Sec. says this growth was, "thrust upon," the dept. by the American people and it has, "created a more just & caring society."

How many of you remember doing any of that "thrusting," he speaks of?

This is RR Thanks for listening.

† ~~Maybe this should replace one of the others in this taping session. If there is one that ≠ isn't important time wise. RR~~ ❖

Doing Something About Government
Undated

Every day there is increasing evidence that Americans are stirring themselves and doing something on their own about the problems which plague us.

I'll be right back.

I once suggested that if the American people were given a single bill once each year telling them how much they owed as their share of the cost of govt. there would be a revolution. ~~Polls indicate that r~~*R*eal govt. ~~cost are~~ *cost* is hidden behind ~~the~~ *a* multitude of hidden & indirect as well as direct taxes. Thus when polled as to how much the individual thinks he or she pays for govt. the great majority only come within about ⅓ of the real cost.

* Senator Warren G. Magnuson (D–Washington, 1944–1981). Magnuson had previously served as congressman (D–Washington, 1937–1944).

For a long time it has been my belief that ~~only~~ business could do more to show the ~~people~~ *consumer* how much of the price for various products is made up of hidden taxes. Now I'm happy to say that various trade associations, ~~&~~ individuals and volunteer groups are springing up and doing their best to expose the economic mythology so widespread in our land.

Just recently I received a small easy to read pamphlet that is being circulated by a nonprofit educational foundation manned entirely by unpaid volunteers. They call themselves "Truth About Taxation Inc." Their mailing address is Box 923 Davenport Iowa.

The pamphlet using govt. figures, tax foundation research and estimates based on previous years statistics tells us where we are with regard to govt. spending. ~~a~~*A*nd you dont have to have a degree in economics to get the message. For example *PRESENT* total govt. liabilities pro rate out to about $40,000 for every man, woman, child & baby in America. Hidden consumer costs, meaning taxes, ~~business must pass on in the price,~~ govt. required regulatory costs etc. *which business must pass on in the price* amount to $1,818 per man, woman, child & baby.

But the pamphlet isn't the only effort being made by "Truth About Taxation Inc." This obviously grass roots operation makes available a display card for retailers, manufacturers & marketers of consumer products. The card is suitable for counter display or hanging on the wall. With it comes a folder outlining hidden cost estimates for use in answering customer questions. Very briefly the card, called a tax disclosure statement reads: "The estimated average amount of taxes and govt.-mandated ~~taxes~~ costs included in the price of this product is"—and there is a blank space for putting in the amount.

Now obviously the figures will be reasonable estimates and averaged because of the thousands of different tax jurisdictions in the U.S. Nevertheless some of our larger corporations have proven the feasibility of such accounting. General Motors for one discovered that compliance with govt. regulations over a 2 yr. period had added some $3 bil. to the cost of operation.

Tax Disclosure is not suggesting a General Motors type operation. It uses *SIMPLE* economical materials distributed at cost so that individual customers can know how much of the price of consumer items is really govt. costs. There before you is the price tag broken down into actual price plus accumulated tax.

Well you can read the pamphlet for yourself. It's available at "Truth About Taxation Inc." P.O. Box 923 Davenport Iowa.

This is RR Thanks for listening. ❖

Nonsense

After June 6, 1978

Today a few words from a public servant who didn't vote for Prop. 13 but who is trying to make it work. I'll be right back.

Not too long ago I read a letter to the editor ~~tha in~~ *of* our local paper that I thought you'd like to hear. Hugh Cameron, business manager of one of our So. Calif. school districts has a legitimate beef. In his letter he said he had not voted for 13* but he could & would listen to the voice of the voters.

Then he described himself as frustrated & blankety blank mad. But not at the voters for passing 13. He explained that he, along with the school board, teachers, administrators, ~~&~~ students & their parents were agonizing over what cuts could be made to live within the amount of money available & still make things work. And he said they'd get the job done.

So who is he mad at? Well he's pretty definite about that. "The real culprit," he says, "the real enemy of taxpayers, schools, teachers, students etc. reared it's ugly head again–Fed. bureacratic nonsense." Now you know he touched a nerve in me with those words.

He then went on and cited a case of counter-productive, costly & ridiculous application of rules that would be laughable if it weren't for the dollars involved.

It seems there is a tremendous amount of paper communication between the school districts & the County Supt. of Schools. The school districts also have to communicate with ~~oth~~ each other. Several years ago some of the business managers in the area ~~decided~~ hired a private courier to carry budgets, payrolls, directives etc. They found this was cheaper than using administrative personnel and faster than the U.S. mails. In fact the idea was so practical that the County Supt. ordered it implemented countywide.

Letters to school districts, notices to Supt's., directives etc. were sent quicker & cheaper by what came to be called the "Blue Bag" system.

Then as Mr. Cameron says; "some ever alert, watchful, Fed. agent caught us. The County School Office was investigated. We were all guilty of saving some of your tax dollars (and incidentally saving the Post Office some work)." Of course that says Mr. Cameron was not the way the Post Office saw it. The County School Office was illegally transporting letters to avoid payment of postage.

Now the Post Office doesn't say the "Blue Bag" system has to be abandoned—not at all. They can continue to transport the directives, letters, bulletins etc. in the Blue bags so long as they affix proper U.S. postage to each message & a county employee hand cancels each letter. In other words you & I will pay more tax dollars to transfer tax dollars from one public agency to another.

I can understand Mr. Camerons anger. I'm a little teed off myself.

This is RR. Thanks for listening ❖

* Proposition 13 was passed June 6, 1978; it limited property taxes.

Part Five

1979

Nineteen seventy-nine was a tumultuous year. Economic conditions at home and abroad imperiled incumbents with high inflation and little real economic growth. OPEC raised oil prices 9 percent to $14.55 a barrel in March and even higher in June. On March 28 the Three Mile Island nuclear power plant near Harrisburg, Pennsylvania came close to a meltdown, putting an effective end to the possibility of expanding nuclear power, the only energy alternative that could ultimately make a real dent in oil imports. Californians sat in long gasoline lines for hours in May and June; in the summer the East Coast experienced shortages, apparently the consequence of regional allocations by the U.S. Department of Energy.

In this final year as he prepared for his run for the presidency, Reagan continued to devote about 70 percent of his radio commentaries to domestic matters. His primary focus was on major issues of national domestic policy—the economy, energy policy, and major federal programs. Reagan argued for tax cuts, for a constitutional amendment to limit taxes and spending, for line-item veto authority for the president, for budget control, for more reasoned regulation, for deregulation of energy prices, and for more sensible consideration of nuclear power. He opposed national health insurance and supported welfare reform. He compared the benefits of capitalism to the devastations of socialism and explained his views on the role of government in a free society. His domestic commentaries were rounded out with his views on crime, drugs, education, the family. And he told stories about Americans, famous and unknown, whom he admired. They were a vehicle for his expression of confidence in the American people and the economic and political institutions of the United States.

Although domestic policy issues were Reagan's major emphasis, historic shifts were taking place in the international scene, and Reagan did not neglect them. On January 1, diplomatic ties between the United States and the People's Republic of China (PRC) became official and the U.S. broke relations with Taiwan. Two weeks later, the political unrest that had been taking place in Iran since 1978 was punctuated when Shah Mohammad Reza Pahlavi and his family fled the country, thereby ending the shah's long reign. On February 1, Ayatollah Khomeini returned to Iran after many years in exile. A conservative Islamic government was soon installed in Iran under Khomeini's guidance, and the United States lost an ally that shared a long border with the Soviet Union. In the wake of Vietnamese aggression in Cambodia as the

Khmer Rouge seized power from Pol Pot, the PRC invaded Vietnam and the two countries engaged in fighting in February and March.

Crises and historic events were also occurring in other parts of Southwest Asia and the Middle East. In February and March, North Yemen and South Yemen became involved in a brief border war. Reeling from the "loss" of Iran, the Carter administration provided assistance to North Yemen. The Soviets assisted South Yemen. On March 26, Egypt and Israel ended three decades of hostility when President Anwar Sadat and Prime Minister Menachem Begin signed a peace treaty brokered by President Carter at Camp David. Arab nations promptly severed diplomatic ties with Egypt and imposed an economic boycott against the country.

In May of 1979, conservatives came to power in some of the countries most closely allied with the United States. On the third, Margaret Thatcher was elected prime minister of Great Britain. On May 22, Joseph Clark, of the Progressive Conservatives, was elected prime minister of Canada.

President Jimmy Carter and Soviet General Secretary Leonid Brezhnev signed the second strategic arms limitation agreement, a national security issue on which Carter staked much of his presidency, in Vienna on June 18. In the months that followed, the Carter administration undertook a major campaign in support of U.S. Senate ratification of the treaty. Opponents of the treaty lobbied against ratification, arguing that it favored the Soviets and would sacrifice U.S. and allied interests to appease Soviet expansionism.

Members of the influential Committee on the Present Danger (CPD)—a bipartisan national defense group of Democrats and Republicans—campaigned against SALT II, as the arms control treaty was known. Prominent in the CPD were Paul Nitze, a national strategy expert, and Yale professor Eugene W. Rostow; Reagan had met Nitze and Rostow in January of 1979. Ambassador Edward Rowny, an army general who represented the military in the SALT II negotiations, had resigned after the negotiations were complete; he testified against the treaty. Reagan called him in December 1979 and they met the following month. Rowny, like Nitze and Rostow, would later be appointed to key negotiating posts in the Reagan administration.[1]

In the second half of 1979, military actions of the Soviet Union undermined the ratification of the SALT II nuclear treaty.

In the summer, U.S. intelligence reported the existence of a Soviet military brigade, around 2,000 officers and men, in Cuba. Treaty opponents charged that the "discovery" was evidence that the Soviet Union could not be trusted to comply with international agreements and that the United States lacked effective monitoring capabilities to enforce Soviet compliance. These arguments persisted even though what was identified in 1979 was a remnant of a much larger Soviet brigade that had been in Cuba since the 1960s. The brigade was not covered under the Kennedy-Khrushchev understanding that ended the Cuban missile crisis in 1962. President Carter defused the issue of Soviet forces in Cuba on October 1 by stating that the brigade was not a combat unit. A major blow to SALT II, however, had already been dealt.

The most substantial blow to prospects of Senate ratification of the treaty occurred on December 25–26, when the Soviet Union began a massive invasion of Afghanistan to prop up a puppet regime in the country. As part of the package of sanctions against the Soviet Union, President Carter asked the Senate in January 1980 to temporarily table SALT II even though the United States would abide by its terms.

Also in December, the Carter administration was faced with another dimension of the nuclear equation. A majority of the members of the North Atlantic Treaty Organization decided to deploy 572 intermediate-range nuclear weapons in Western Europe by 1983 to counter Soviet nuclear weapons pointed westward. The deployment in fact would occur in 1983 with the firm support of President Reagan.

Nineteen seventy-nine was an important year in Reagan's growing involvement with national security issues. On July 12, he had an extensive briefing, which included a presentation by General George M. Seignious, director of the Arms Control and Disarmament Agency, on SALT II. On July 31, Reagan visited NORAD, the North American Aerospace Defense Command. He commented afterward to Martin Anderson that "the only option we would have would be to press the button or do nothing. They're both bad. We should have some way of defending ourselves against nuclear missiles."[2] It was an issue he took up in his January 1980 meeting with Ambassador Edward Rowny.

On September 15, Reagan gave a comprehensive speech on SALT II in San Diego. The speech built upon his study of the issues and radio commentaries on the treaty. Reagan now categorically opposed the treaty. He had concluded that the U.S. Senate should not ratify SALT II because it was an agreement for an arms buildup instead of arms limitation. In making this speech, which was reprinted in the *Washington Star* and introduced into the *Congressional Record* by Senator Barry Goldwater, Reagan had squarely entered the debate on the U.S.-Soviet nuclear arms race.[3]

As the 1970s came to a close, the pains of political transition were being felt around the world. In July, the long rule of the Somoza dynasty came to an end as President Anastasio Somoza Debayle fled Nicaragua and the Sandinista National Liberation Front (FSLN) came to power. A resistance movement quickly formed, and for the next decade Nicaragua would be immersed in a civil war. On November 4, Iranian extremists took 66 Americans hostage and seized the U.S. embassy in Tehran. The hostage takers demanded that the Shah, in the United States for medical treatment, be returned to Iran to face charges of torture in exchange for freeing the Americans. Although some hostages were released in November, most were held captive until the day of Ronald Reagan's inauguration on January 20, 1981, prolonging the worst crisis of Jimmy Carter's presidency. On December 21, Rhodesia moved closer to becoming black-ruled Zimbabwe when the warring factions, including the Patriotic Front led by Robert Mugabe and Joshua Nkomo, signed a cease-fire in London. In 1980, Mugabe became president of Zimbabwe. Reagan addressed these regional crises in his newspaper column, radio addresses, and speeches in 1979.

Reagan also thought seriously about the Western Hemisphere. Five days after his briefing on SALT II, he traveled to Mexico to meet with President José López Portillo to discuss his idea of concluding a North American Accord between the U.S., Canada, and Mexico that would mainly address security and trade issues. López Portillo seemed responsive to the idea. Due to scheduling difficulties Reagan was unable to travel to Canada to make his case.[4]

Meanwhile, the Reagan for President Committee was announced March 7 by its chairman, Senator Paul Laxalt of Nevada. It was an exploratory committee. Unlike the much smaller 1976 exploratory committee, this one had 365 names.

President Jimmy Carter faced a primary challenge from Senator Edward M. Kennedy. Reagan too had competition. Representative Phil Crane of Illinois, an articulate conservative, had announced his candidacy in 1978. By the time of Reagan's formal announcement, other candidates in the race included John B. Connally, George H. W. Bush, Howard Baker, Robert Dole, and John Anderson; Charles Percy had already withdrawn. Reagan was, however, well in the lead; Connally came in second and Baker third in a poll published in *Time* magazine November 26.

Reagan spoke to many groups between 1975 and 1979. At any given time he had two basic "stump" speeches—one for political groups and one for business groups. Each speech was slightly different, but the basic topics—economic problems and national defense—were recurrent themes. It was through his radio commentaries that he developed the details of his positions on many issues.

Reagan's final pre-presidential radio commentary, called "Miscellaneous & Goodbye," was broadcast on November 13, 1979, the day he formally announced for the presidency. He concluded it by saying:

> Believe me, my friends, I speak to you today with mixed emotions . . . This has been my final commentary.
>
> I'm going to miss these visits with all of you. I've enjoyed every one. Even writing them has been a lot of fun. I've scratched them out on a yellow tablet in airplanes, riding in cars, and at the ranch when the sun went down.
>
> Whenever I've told you about some misfortune befalling one of our fellow citizens you've opened your hearts and your pocketbooks and gone to the rescue. I know you have because the individuals you helped have written to let me know. You've done a great deal to strengthen my faith in this land of ours and its people. You are the greatest.
>
> Sometime later today if you happen to catch me on television you'll understand why I can no longer bring you these commentaries.
>
> This is Ronald Reagan, and from the bottom of my heart—thanks for listening.

On January 1, 1979, relations were officially normalized between the United States and the People's Republic of China.

Taiwan III
January 1979

Once more I'd like to talk about the change in our relations with the Repub. of China on Taiwan & the Communist rulers in Peking. Ill be right back.

In the first days following the Dec. 15th announcement that we were abrogating our treaty with Taiwan, spokesmen for the admin. and some pundits of the press declared we were simply recognizing a reality. After all there are something like a bil. Chinese on the mainland and only 17 mil. on Taiwan. It was foolish to pretend the govt. on Taiwan was the govt. of China. But isn't *it* just as foolish to pretend that the govt. ~~on~~ in Peking is the rightful ruler of Taiwan?

If we're going to put this on the basis of looking at reality there are a few things we shouldn't overlook. The Peking govt. once allied with Russia as part of the world communist ~~govt.~~ movement now see's Russia as not being true to the ~~ten~~ principles of Karl Marx. Soldiers of the 2 great communist powers face each other across a long border and China proclaims Russia is ~~the~~ an enemy & a threat to peace.

But China also says we are an *imperialist* enemy ~~that~~ *which* must eventually be destroyed. To their own people the Communist leaders explain that we aren't an immediate threat as is the Soviet U. so first things first. ~~If & when they turn on us they can do so with a clear conscience. They'll only~~

And if they should ever decide we're enemy number 1 not number 2, they can do so with a clear conscience. They'll only be doing to us what we've done to Taiwan.

With Congress back in session there are things we can do to lessen the damage that ~~Presidents~~ has been done. We dont have just one treaty or agreement with Taiwan. We have about 50. We do around $7 bil. worth of business with Taiwan.

The President can say all these things will continue on a non-governmental basis but that's impossible. Granted he has the power to close the embassy and re-open it in Peking but govt. representation by us in Taiwan & by the Repub. of China ~~is~~ here is essential. The same *daily* functions performed now by embassies & consulates must *STILL* be performed if we are to maintain trade & cultural relations.—So we call them liason offices but they are official govt. institutions.

Congress can make sure that most of those 50 treaties & agreements remain in force & that we *REALLY DO* provide the ~~R~~ people of Taiwan with the weapons they need to defend themselves. Your congressman needs to hear from you right now with regard to this.

This is RR Thanks for listening. ❖

Jim Hendricks
January 1979

†I told a story about a man & his horse and found out once again how truly wonderful people are.

I'll be right back.

Some time ago on one of these broadcasts* I told the story of a young man in Bridgetown Ill: Jim Hendricks & his horse Calvin (*CALVIN*). Since then I've had a number of letters from neighborly people who want to ~~lift~~ *give* a hand to Jim & Calvin. Before this commentary ends I'll give Jims address in case you want to be ready to take it down.

Jim Hendricks, a young man in his middle or late 20's was working on a river barge when a 2 inch cable snapped and crushed his spine. He is a paraplegic living in a trailer home and was ~~receiving~~ *living on* disability payments from Soc. Security. Those payments were suspended a while back as the result of a burocratic "snafu." It's curious how quickly the payments could be cancelled ~~but~~ *yet* now that the "snafu" is cleared away, Soc. Security tells him it will still be several months before ~~he can~~ *his* payments can be reinstated.

Meanwhile Jim is being pressed by a bank because he mortgaged his trailer & everything he owns including his horse Calvin. Of course with no income

* See "Horse and Rider I" and "Horse and Rider II," pp. 374–76.

he is unable to keep up the mortgage payments & could very possibly lose his home & Calvin.

Now Calvin is the thing that makes this story pretty special. Jim Hendricks ~~determined~~ *resolved* that he would not spend his life sitting in a wheelchair watching the world go by. He had grown up on a farm riding horses as a boy. He decided that he wanted to ride again even though he was paralyzed from the waist down.

He set out to find the right horse. Having done this he looked for & found a trainer; a blind man who had trained trick horses for the circus. In 3 months they had a horse that would lie down so Jim could get aboard~~. Jim rides him~~ *& could be ridden by him* with no braces or straps. Strangely enough Calvin seems to understand & is protective of his rider but wont allow anyone else to ride him.

If the mortgage is foreclosed Jim will lose ~~this~~ Calvin. Well this is the story I told a while back. I've received letters ~~with checks enclosed for~~ *from disabled people telling me* what Jim & Calvin have done to inspire them. Others have written wanting his address so they can help. So here it is—Jim Hendricks P.O. Box 229, Bridgetown Ill. 62618. I'll repeat—Box 229, Bridgetown Ill. 62618. And thank you all—sincerely.

This is R.R. Thanks for listening.

† Make this 1st after the Taiwan 5 scripts. RR ❖

Patent Medicine I
January 1979

Step right up folks and for one dollar get a bottle of cure all made from a secret recipe. Was a time when that was the bottom line in the traveling medicine show. I'll be right back.

Not too many people are around who remember the flamboyant, painted wagon that used to ~~pull~~ *roll* into town~~; the~~ *with an* entertainer (dancer, banjo player or Indian tom tom thumper)~~; then the~~ *and a* huckster peddling a medicine guaranteed to cure any & all ailments.

The routine was always the same, the side of the wagon would open providing a small stage, the entertainer would attract a crowd & then the *medicine* salesman would make his pitch.

I was reminded of this old time medicine show a few weeks ago when a subcommittee of the U.S. Sen. came to the Los Angeles area supposedly to hold hearings on Nat. Health Insurance. Now a hearing by a legislative committee is supposed to gather fact & opinion to help the committee determine policy on a given matter. The sub-committee that came to Calif. after appearing in ~~Chi. (and several other cities I'm told)~~ *Wash., West Va., Detroit, Chi. & Denver,* wasn't gathering information: It was beating publicity drums in support of legislation. The chairman of the sub-committee, Sen. Ted Kennedy* ~~had~~ *is* already ~~decided~~ for the legislation, his own Nationalized Health Insurance bill.**

I think it is ~~*alright*~~ *proper* to question whether taxpayers money should be used in this manner to ~~lobby~~ *drum up support* for a legislative proposal. ~~In Chi. the Sen. had~~ The Sen. came to Calif. & as he did in those other cities had a road show troupe of several Canadians & several of our citizens all of whom had suffered catastrophic illnesses. ~~The~~ In Calif. there was an audience of over a thousand to hear first the Canadians tell how the great cost of their illnesses was paid by the govt. Then the Americans would tell their story of wiped out savings, lost homes etc. as they tried to pay for their catastrophic ills. Now let me say I'm not belittling these witnesses who have suffered long & costly illnesses. Catastrophic injury or disease can strike any of us & the tremendous costs can go on for years. But this is a particular problem to be solved and it should not be used to justify compulsory govt. medical care for everyone.

At *each stop* Sen. Kennedys road show attracts opposing witnesses who have difficulty getting on the agenda. In Chi. the Pres. of the Ill. medical society surprised the Senator by turning his time over to a Dr. from Canada. Senator Kennedy was not pleased. He curtly addressed this Canadian saying—"Well get on with it. Where are you from?"

Dr. Robillard, a neurosurgeon, trained at Harvard now Pres. of the Fed. of Medical Specialists of Quebec. said; "I have no axe to grind but let me say one thing loud & clear. America has the best medical care in the world. In your haste to copy our (Canadian) system do not bring Am. medicine down to the Canadian level. For now we look up to you." The Sen. tried to rebut the Dr. in an emotional outburst and the hearing ended. No *SUCH* surprises were allowed in the Calif. show.

This is RR Thanks for listening. ❖

Patent Medicine II

January 1979

This is the 2nd instalment on Nat. Health Insurance and the all out effort to propagandize the Am. People and sell the idea of Govt. medicine.

I'll be right back.

On the last broadcast I told of the Senate subcommittee that is roadshowing the country under the pretense of holding hearings when in truth it is ~~a~~

* Edward M. Kennedy (D–Massachusetts, 1962–present).

** The Kennedy bill, "Health Care for All Americans Act," was announced in May 1979. It proposed a government subsidized program funded by additional payroll taxes. President Carter proposed less sweeping legislation in June. Both bills failed; Kennedy's did not get out of committee.

campaign*ing* to sell the people on Socialized medicine. And the taxpayers are footing the bill for this sales trip.

Part of the sales pitch is based on how much medical costs are increasing and how much they'll be *in a few years* if we dont adopt a program of compulsory govt. medical care. Nothing is said however about the cost now & in the future ~~of~~ if we do adopt such a system.

Health care now costs us about $150 bil. a year. The Dept. of H.E.W. even though it wants govt. medicine has estimated that the Kennedy proposal would add $80 bil. to that the 1st yr. Supporting this is the evidence in all & let me emphasize all—the nations in the world who have already instituted nationalized, that is socialized health care. This includes *among others* Canada, Britain & Sweden. In these latter two some kinds of care are being denied to people because of cost. This denial takes the form of setting an age limit above which things like transplants wont be given. Patients are denied care if a disease is too far advanced reducing the odds of saving the patient. Several thousand kidney patients in one of those countries die each year because ~~of~~ the cost of keeping them alive is too great.

But we have evidence close at hand of the part govt. intervention in health care can play in raising the cost of such care. The Hospital Assn. of New York State reveals that almost ¼—24% of the costs of hospital care in that state result from govt. regulations aimed at cost & quality control. This report was based on a study of 148 hospitals.

It was found that admin. ~~procedures spent~~ *personnel* SPEND from 50 to 70% of their time complying with regulation. Even nurses spend more than ¼ of their time on such matters instead of in the care of patients.

In that one state alone, N.Y., this is the equivalent of employees engaged full time in paperwork on a year round basis equalling in number what it would take to fully staff 75 hospitals with 250 beds each. Or put another way they could provide full hospital services to 600,000 ~~patients~~ people.

Possibly N.Y. is above the average in this regulatory extravagance but it indicates a problem that must be serious in all of the country. In N.Y. regulatory costs add almost $40 a day to each patients bill.

Can any of us believe that total takeover by govt. would not vastly increase the paperwork, the regulations and the cost of healthcare? ~~which~~ We have provision now for the elderly & the destitute and more than 130 mil. Americans hold some kind of health insurance. If the govt. really wants to help, let it give citizens *income* tax deductions or credits for ~~money~~ *health* insurance premiums.

This is RR Thanks for listening. ❖

Federal Trade Commission
January 19, 1979

Probably nothing is so politically rewarding as denouncing monopoly and professing to save consumers from price gouging. But sometimes it can be downright dishonest. I'll be right back.

Yale Brozen Prof. of Business Ec's.—the Graduate School of Bus. at the U. of Chi. has called attention in Nat. Review magazine to a "strange notion brewing in the Anti-trust Division of the Fed. Trade Commission." * It is a notion Prof. Brozen says would be suicidal for our nation to adopt.
In simple language the Trade Commission & the Justice Dept. are going to attack as monopolists, firms that by operating efficiently and making consumer goods available at a fair price have won a large share of the mkt.

Now we all understand the purpose of the Anti-trust laws. They are to prevent a single firm or a group of firms from getting together, holding back on production so as to create a shortage & then jacking up the price to the consumer. But now the F.T.C. is apparently going to punish a firm or firms who increase production, lower prices and as a result win a large share of customers. As Brozen says, Henry Ford who captured about 60% of the automobile mkt. because he made a car the average man could afford ≠ when up til then they had been affordable only by the rich, today would have the F.T.C. assailing him as a monopolistic fiend.

A present day perversion of the anti-trust laws is being carried out against DuPont. That company developed a low cost method for producing titanium, Dioxide pigments. They passed these savings through to the customer in a lowerd price thereby capturing about 40% of the mkt. Business is so good they are building a new plant to make more available to the consumers. Now the anti-trust laws are supposed to prevent "restraint of trade," the fixing & raising of prices, not the increase in production to make more product available for purchase. But an anti-trust complaint has been filed against DuPont.

The F.T.C. is prosecuting Kellogg, General Foods & General Mills. They are charged with "brand proliferation." In other words because these companies offer us a variety of breakfast cereals they are guilty of, "a shared monopoly." Apparently they are guilty of trying to give us what we want, bran cereals, vitamin enriched cereals, grapenuts etc. They'd be alright in the eyes of the govt. if they had just stuck to corn flakes.

When the Sherman anti-trust bill was passed in 1890 Sen. Sherman ** said it was intended to outlaw arrangements which tended to raise the cost to the consumer. Indeed when the Sen. Judiciary Committee explained the bill to

* Yale Brozen, "Antitrust Witch Hunt," *National Review,* November 24, 1978, pp. 1470–1471, 1476–1477.

** Senator John Sherman (R–Ohio, 1861–1877 and 1881–1897).

the Sen. they declared that a man ~~“~~who, “got the whole business because nobody could do it as well as he could” ~~wont~~ would not be in violation of the Sherman act.

From 1921 to 1925 Ford supplied more automobiles than all the other companies put together. Then in 1927 it shut down for a year to retool for production of the model A. The price of cars didn’t go up because of the shortage. They went down.

The Fed. trade commission is embarked on a witch hunt which could very conceivably result in increased prices for all of us. This is RR Thanks for listening. ❖

Counterintelligence

January 19, 1979

The Justice Dept. continues to press the case against several F.B.I. agents who are charged with violating the privacy of citizens by use of wiretaps & other means. I’ll be right back.

I have commented before about what I think is the Justice Dept’s. foolishness in rendering ~~and~~ our F.B.I. & the C.I.A. impotent, all in the name of protecting our privacy. Now I dont want “big brother” to have a key to my front door or to listen in on my phone calls. On the other hand when there is credible evidence that someone is plotting crimes & violence I want agencies such as the F.B.I. to be able to do all the snooping necessary to apprehend the plotters.

The Copley News Service recently carried a story by James Cary.* So far I’ve seen no word of the story in any of the rest of the media. I hope you wont mind my passing it on.

The “Black September” Palestinian terrorist group—this is the outfit that murdered 2 of our diplomats in Khartoum in 1973** and 11 Israeli athletes at the 1972 Olympics—this “Black September” band sent agents to the U.S. in 1972 to kill ~~the~~ *FORMER* Pres. ~~of~~ Nixon, Henry Kissinger *AND ISRAELI PRIME MINISTER* Golda Meir, & Jordans King Hussein ~~These latter two~~ were visiting ~~in~~ America at the time.

The plan was broken up by the F.B.I. thanks to tips received from Israeli intelligence. The plotters were quietly deported. So called illegal entry & wiretaps were used by the F.B.I. to prevent the planned asassinations. Should the agents involved be arrested for violating the terrorists privacy?

* James Donald Cary was a senior correspondent with Copley News Service when Reagan wrote this commentary.

** In early 1973, the outgoing American chargé d’affaires, George C. Moore, and Ambassador Cleo A. Noel were killed in the attack on the Saudi Embassy in Khartoum by Palestinian guerrillas known as Black September.

In January of 1973 a citizen of Iraq entered our country by way of Montreal. Again there were tips by Israeli intelligence—which by the way is one of the most effective intelligence forces in the world. The suspect changed residences frequently while gathering explosive materials. Were our F.B.I. agents committing a crime by trying to keep him under surveillance?

Actually he managed to almost carry out his mission and would have if the hand of the Lord had not intervened. He placed his explosive devices plus 5 gal. cans of gasoline in ~~cars~~ *automobiles* which were then parked outside the Israeli airline at Kennedy Airport, and at 2 other locations in downtown N.Y. Fortunately one of the cars was in a no parking zone and the N.Y. police towed it away. The detonating devices failed to work in the other two even while F.B.I. and police were desperately trying to locate them.

The police later exploded one of the devices in a remote area. They reported the fireball would have killed anyone within 100 yards of the blast.

The terrorist fled the country & is still at large although he has been traced through 4 different countries. If we continue our policy of handcuffing our own law enforcement officers he may decide this is the safest country in which he can operate even though he has been indicted by 2 Fed. grand juries in N.Y.

"Black September" agents, Mr. Cary reports are still in this country in considerable numbers & pose a serious threat in Wash. D.C. & Northern Va.—Pleasant Dreams. This is RR Thanks for listening ❖

Australia I

January 19, 1979

Having visited Australia several years ago* when ~~the labor govt.~~ *socialism* was ~~in charge~~ *in vogue* I was greatly interested to learn recently of the near miracle that has taken place there.

I'll be right back.

With inflation plaguing these United States and our mkt. place coming more & more under govt. domination I thought you might like to hear of what has happened almost overnight ~~in~~ *to* the land down under—our ally Australia.

Less than 6 yrs. ago runaway inflation there was at an annual 20% rate. Taxes were punitive if not confiscatory, *and* govt. costs had gone up 50% in 2 yrs. Unemployment was high, the strike record was 3rd worst in the world and labor costs were rising 70 times faster than productivity. Foreign capital, lifeblood of Australian ec. progress had dried up and key industries were threatened with nationalization.

* During his tenure as governor of California, Reagan made four trips abroad on behalf of President Richard M. Nixon. During one trip, in November and December 1973, Reagan visited Australia, Indonesia, and Singapore.

Then came a change. Taxes were cut $1 bil. Annual budget increases were cut to ⅔ of what they'd been, interest rates went down, strikes fell to ¼ of what they'd been and the inflation rate fell from 20% to *far* less than what we have ~~by far~~—5.2%. Now foreign investment is back with hundreds of millions of dollars being invested in mines & other ~~industries~~ *ventures*.

The turnaround began when a coalition of parties opposed to the socialist policies of the labour party elected Malcolm Fraser, Prime Minister.* The Prime Minister would be the 1st to say however that a most important element in the turnaround was a new management organization which advocates better cooperation & understanding in labor, management relations. It is called "Enterprise Australia." It's cheif executive says they are trying a new approach emphasizing consensus & cooperation between management & labor instead of conflict & confrontation.

The election of Fraser was the catalyst which brought former adversarys together. In short they stopped talking about each other & began talking to each other. Employers & employees found they had more they agreed on than they disagreed on. Labor turned away from nationalizing industries after they were shown that employees took home more than 10 times as much as there was profit.

"*Enterprise* Australia" imported John Q. Jennings from N.Y. one time Fed mediator & now a ~~la~~ management-labor consultant. A breakthrough was made with R. J. Hawke Pres. of the Trade Union Congress, Australia's counterpart to George Meany of our AFL-CIO.

Jennings persuaded management to send their employees company statements—annual reports telling clearly how the companies income is shared between employees & stockholders. Prime Minister Fraser told management: "How can I explain to the people that free enterprise is the best system for them if you cant be bothered to explain it to your own employees." One labour spokesman said: "The old enemy capitalists—no longer exist. Today in our society corporate management has reached the stage where real ownership of capital is all of us ~~sitting~~. There are no capitalists of a form you can identify." And all this came about by talking to each other. TRW corp. for example sent it's employees a highly graphic report showing among other things that after other expenses are paid, out of every dollar available for payroll & profit 91.3¢ goes to the employees, 4.1 cents to the stockholders & 4.6¢ is re-invested in the business. Nationalization of a steel co. was rejected by the workers when they recv'd. a report showing they were getting 95¢ out of the dollar.

Would this work in America? I think so—listen to the next broadcast.

This is RR Thanks for listening. ❖

* Malcolm Fraser was prime minister of Australia from 1975 to 1983.

Australia II
January 19, 1979

On the last broadcast I asked if the system that has brought labor, management peace to Australia could work here. I'll be right back.

On the last broadcast I told of how the new Prime Minister of Australia—Malcolm Fraser and a labor, management group called "Enterprise Australia" turned Australia's ec. around. They knocked an inflation rate down to 5% from 20, cut govt. costs & taxes, increased productivity~~,~~ *&* cut man days lost in strikes to ¼ of what it had been.

One of the key tools was an idea brought to them by an American troubleshooter John Q. Jennings of N.Y. It was the institution of annual reports by management to the workers with color graphics & illustrations. Workers learned that they took home better than 90% of the companies earnings only 4 & a fraction % wento stockholders and 4.6% was re-invested in the companies.

On that last commentary I asked if it would work here. I'm convinced it would and I'm happy to say Dart industries working with the graduate school of business at Uni. of So. Calif. is doing something of the kind.

With all of our knowledge & all of the 'gillion' words of information pumped at us each day we still believe in a number of ec. & pol. fairy tales. When opinion research asked a cross section of Americans how they thought corporate income was divided between employee payroll & profits the answer was 25% to employees—75% for profit. Students at Kings college near N.Y. City thought the split was 60–40 in favor of profits. The facts were 90.6% went for employee compensation and the rest went for profits—which had to be divided between stockholders & re-investment in plant & machinery.

It's no wonder the kids made this kind of mistake, 52% of their teachers said they believed the largest ≠ *PORTION* of nat. inc. went to owners. The fact is after taxes only 3½% went to owners.

Another poll found Americans in general believed that 10% net on sales after taxes would be a "fair" profit. They believed however that manufacturers were getting 20% Profit.

So far "Enterprise Australia" hasn't aroused a lot of interest in either management or labor circles in Am. That's too bad. The founder of the A.F.L. that great labor statesman Samuel Gompers* would have understood "Enterprise Australia." He said management & labor were partners and the worst sin management could commit against the worker was to fail to make a profit.

* Samuel Gompers was the first president of the American Federation of Labor (AFL), from 1886 to 1924.

I would add another—it is a sin against the worker, it is a sin against the citizen at large and truly a sin against our sons & daughters to not do everything we can to dispel the ec. mythology so prevalent in our land. I hope enlightened employers will create an "Enterprise America."

This is RR Thanks for listening ❖

Founded in 1961, the Peace Corps was a Kennedy administration initiative to carry American models of political and economic progress to developing countries. President John F. Kennedy, appointed his sister Eunice's husband, Sargent Shriver, the first director of the Peace Corps. In 1971, President Richard M. Nixon placed the Peace Corps under ACTION, a government entity that managed several volunteer programs. In 1977, President Jimmy Carter appointed Sam Brown, an organizer of the Vietnam Moratorium during the 1960s, director of ACTION. In November 1978, Brown forced Carolyn Payton, a black psychologist at Howard University, to resign as director of the Peace Corps due to ideological differences. This action added to the growing criticism of Brown's management style and policy objectives, which many saw as too radical and politically oriented for a government agency. A few months after this commentary was taped, President Jimmy Carter signed an executive order making the Peace Corps an autonomous agency within ACTION.

Peace Corps
January 19, 1979

Back in session Cong. faces some interesting situations, not the least of which involves a change in directors over the Peace Corps. I'll be right back.

For some years now we've had a "peace corps" operating throughout the world. Starting out as an idealistic effort to benefit people in the underdeveloped countries particularly, it has pretty generally been accepted as something akin to theo*se* unselfish ~~contributions made by~~ *good* ~~*Samitans*~~ SAMARITANS *our American* missionarys.

Young people were recruited mainly from our colleges. They were trained in a variety of ways. Then they journeyed to faraway places where they lived in native villages, teaching the people about sanitation, better ways to farm, health care and helping in any ways they could~~:~~.

But what Congress will face is the possibility that the one time idealism of the peace corps volunteer has given way to ~~some~~ *pure* pol. activism somewhat out of line with the corps original purpose.

The Peace corps is a branch of an agency called "Action." Action under this admin. is headed up by a young man named Sam Brown. A number of Congressmen of both parties have been concerned for more than a year that Director Brown has packed his agency with "New Left" activists, veterans of the Anti-Vietnam war radicals & others and that Action dollars are being used to finance the programs of the new left.

Sam Brown was an organizer in 1969 of the so called moratorium demonstration. Well after his appointment to "Action" he attended the rally in N.Y. to welcome the North Vietnamese conquerors to the U.N. He listened to the denunciations of our country as "imperialists" who had fought a bloody colonial war and openly expressed his joy at seeing a 15 yr. dream come true—namely a communist victory over the U.S.

Brown has surrounded himself with veterans of the riotous '60's—Marge Tabankin to run the Vista program, Associate Dir. John Lewis formerly of the Student Non-Violent Coordinating committee, some of whose spokesmen were Rap Brown ~~Sto~~ Stokely Carmichael * and a former ~~Berkeley~~ *BERKELEY* city councilwoman who gained attention by refusing to stand for the pledge to the flag.

What Congress will be looking at is the recent ~~resignation~~ *ousting* of the Peace Corps Director Carolyn Payton. Dr. Payton a 53 yr. old black ~~woman~~ *psychologist* had confronted her superior Sam Brown protesting that ~~politic~~ the Peace Corps had been enmeshed in politics. She said it was, "pursuing objectives which have nothing to do with promoting world peace & friendship."

Dr. Payton made it clear that Peace Corps volunteers were being used to export a particular ideology and encouraged to engage in pol. activism. Their ~~over see~~ *superiors* would be pleased to see them demonstrate *overseas* against corporations which engage in practises with which they disagree.

I believe Sam Brown has a budget of about $200,000,000. You can stir up a lot of trouble with that kind of money. I hope Congress listens to Dr. Carolyn Payton—we all should listen. This is RR Thanks for listening. ❖

A Policeman
January 19, 1979

†Today I'd like to talk about a man,—one of those rare men who leave the world a little better than it was before they ~~came here.~~ *walked among us*. I'll be right back.

Every once in awhile I take the 20 min. flight from Los Angeles to San Diego—usually to address a convention of one kind or another. I always enjoy the visit; San Diego is a beautiful part of our Calif. southland.

I made such a trip recently and while the beauty was unchanged one thing

* Margery Tabankin was a prominent civil rights and anti-Vietnam War activist in the 1960s. John Lewis, H. Rap Brown, and Stokely Carmichael were members of the Student Nonviolent Coordinating Committee (SNCC), a 1960s civil rights organization.

was sadly different. A familiar face was missing at planeside when I ~~debarked~~ came down the ramp. Officer Gene Spurlock * of the San Diego police was not on hand. He had been laid to rest the day before my visit.

Gene became a policeman in 1966 at age 29. ~~When I knew him and over the years became a delea~~ *In all the years I was Gov. he would be one of those* on hand whenever I visited San Diego. For a long time I didn't know he always asked for the assignment. I was very proud when I found that out.

A former highschool athlete in San Diego—(he still holds the Lincoln High school broad jump record) Gene insisted on serving in the *RUNDOWN* Southeast part of the city. ~~He~~ *where he was born. He* became the most decorated officer ~~in~~ *on* the force but he was much more than that. Probably no man on the force has even been more loved & respected by his fellow officers. He was also loved, respected & totally trusted by the people in the district he served.

At his memorial services the police chaplain said: "His ability to bridge the chasm between races & between all people was uncanny. He had what could be called a 'natural knowing' in handling delicate matters involving tensions between the races. He had the ability to create a trust whether arresting them or giving them the last 5 bucks he had in his pocket." Another tribute came from Mama Williams, a black woman of great dignity who'd had her share of troubles. She said: "He was my friend. How many people can say they had one." Her 7 yr. old grand son said: "He gave me my nick name, "Tiger"—just say he was my friend."

He believed in justice, he would tear the town apart to clear someone he believed was wrongly accused. Sometimes he paid the bail for the very individuals he had arrested.

About 5 years ago he was attacked by a painful disease, Reiters syndrome, still he refused to take a less demanding assignment. He stayed with his people, in his neighborhood.

Gene met his wife Betty Lou when they were in 6th grade, he married her when they were in 12th grade. Betty tells how their ~~house~~ *home* was open house on weekends. Black, Brown & White "his people" would gather just to talk or to have him fix their cars—he was good at that. It was only ~~with~~ *when* his illness grew serious that anyone knew he'd been caring for several needy families for years.

He & Betty knew a great love for 24 years. They have a fine son & 2 lovely ~~daughetrs~~ *daughters*. Gene Spurlock was a legend in the force he was proud to serve. He was 42 years old. This is RR Thanks for listening.

† Send copy to Mrs. Spurlock. Dave will get address for you.

* Spurlock was born November 4, 1936; he died in January 1979.

Regulations
January 19, 1979

Now I'm sure you'll think it strange that I'm going to talk a few minutes about govt. regulations—but that's the way it is. I'll be right back.

~~I know that~~ I've used this commentary many times to call attention to the ever increasing burden of govt. regulations covering every facet of our lives. And here I go again.

Alexander Hamilton said: "It will be of little avail to the people that laws are made by men of their own choice if the laws be so voluminous that they cannot be read, or so incoherent that they cannot be understood; if they be repealed or revised before they are promulgated, or undergo such incessant changes that no man who knows what the law is today can guess what it will be tomorrow." *

Hamilton was speaking of laws written by our elected representatives. He had no way of ~~knowing~~ *foreseeing* that multitudinous regulations having the power of law would be written by permanent employees of govt. who were not elected by ~~us~~ the people. Today more & more Americans are discovering that by obeying the mandate of one agency they violate the rules of another. For example the eEnvironmental Protection Agency wants hoods over coke ovens in the steelplants to reduce air pollution. The Occupational Safety & Health Admin. wants them removed because they increase the noxious ~~fu~~ gases breathed by coke oven workers. The steel industry is blanketed by 5600 regulations ~~admini~~ *enforced* by 26 separate agencies.

Officials of the Mass. Inst. of Technology obtained approval from the Smithsonian Inst., Nat. Park Service & the Nat. Endowment for the Arts, to stage a laser-light show on the mall in Wash. D.C. The Bureau of Radiological Health let the show open & then closed it for failing to comply with Fed. Safety standards.

OSHA requires vehicles at some construction sites to have alarm bells which sound as warnings to workers when the vehicles back up. OSHA also requires those workers to wear ear plugs as protection against excessive noise—which it turns out includes those *WARNING* bells.

OSHA is involved in another conflict *THIS TIME* with H.E.W. It seems H.E.W. claims jurisdiction over a hospital because Fed. money was involved in it's construction. When an HEW inspector found the hospital putting plastic bags in wastebaskets it ordered them removed, charging that a careless tossing of a cigarette butt into a wastebasket ~~would~~ *could* start a blaze & the fumes of the burning ~~basket~~ *plastic* would be injurious to the patients. The hospital has a problem,—OSHA ordered the bags in the baskets to protect employees from contamination when they empty the wastebaskets.

* Federalist Paper Number 62.

A study ~~by~~ published in the Yale Law Journal describes this bureaucratic chaos as, "a patchwork of specialized & fiercely independent agencies with different perspectives whose concerns necessarily overlap & whose actions may contradict one another." The report might have added they create problems instead of solving them because the problems are their only reason for existing. We are up to our necks in alligators & it's time to drain the swamp. This is RR Thanks for listening. ❖

On December 10, 1978, NBC-TV aired an hour-long report on the negative effects of marijuana.

Pot
February 13, 1979

Todays commentary is about one of televisions finer hours—a program on NBC some weeks ago. I'll be right back.

If this were a true–false test and I should ask, "Smoking pot (marijuana) is no more harmful than smoking regular cigarettes~~—true or false~~ *or drinking alcohol*—true or false?" And you answered, "true," I'd be sure of one thing, you didn't see NBC's. special on marijuana several weeks ago, called "Reading, Writing & Reefers." I'd also have to give you a failing grade on the test.

Edwin ~~Newman~~ *NEWMAN* hosted the TV special which featured a variety of medical experts, ~~and~~ among them Dr. Robert Dupont* the former director of the Nat. Institute for Drug Abuse. He was one of those who formerly believed marijuana was ~~≠~~ no more harmful than regular cigarettes or alcohol. On the program he stated that he now knows he was wrong. He said: "We know a lot more about the health hazards of marijuana now and how dangerous it really is." He went on to say that the earlier comparison to tobacco & alcohol was a disaster and that he felt badly about having contributed to that.

Dr. Carlton Turner** who works for the govt. analyzing the chemical content of "pot" told of finding ~~that~~ more cancer causing agents in ~~Pot~~ a marijuana cigarette than in tobacco.

Dr. Sidney Cohen*** director of marijuana studies at UCLA's school of medicine told the N.B.C. audience: "It is entirely possible that youngsters who smoke lots of good pot over long periods of time sustain some mental impairment which is not completely reversible." He said that some, "may be so im-

* Dr. Robert L. DuPont was director of the National Institute on Drug Abuse from 1973 to 1978.

** Dr. Carlton Edgar Turner was director of the Marijuana Research Project at the University of Mississippi at Oxford when Reagan wrote this commentary. During the Reagan administration, Turner held numerous positions in the White House related to drug abuse policy.

*** Dr. Sidney Cohen of UCLA and the Narcotics and Drug Abuse Center at the National Institutes of Mental Health.

paired that they will never function at their best level of effectiveness." He cited a UCLA study which ~~deliv~~ proved that smoking just 5 marijuana joints had the same effect as smoking 112 tobacco cigarettes.

NORML—the Nat. Organization for the Reform of Marijuana Laws has campaigned for ~~easing~~ easing if not actually eliminating restrictions on sale & use of Pot. But now Keith Stroup director of "Norml" expresses worry that young people underestimate the danger in psychoactive drugs and he cautioned against making marijuana a habit.

I've talked to many young people who defeneded "pot" and were able to quote *ALL THE* statements ~~by~~ ever made about the harmlessness of ~~pot~~ the weed. Somehow they seem never to have heard the other side. Never heard for example that marijuana contains 300 or more chemicals & 60 of those are found in no other plant. The most potent is THC. Unlike alcohol it accumulates in the body and remains there for a long time mainly in the brain & ~~the~~ reproductive system. The more pot smoked the greater the accumulation. Chronic users have to smoke more & more to get the high feeling they are after. They dont realize they are already partly intoxicated. ~~already.~~

N.B.C. did a real service. Youngsters have been propagandized by celebritys who admit publicly to marijuana use but who of course have no real knowledge of it's ~~effects~~ long range effect. The medical authorities we saw on TV have no axe to grind for or against the weed. They simply state the facts they have learned through research. NBC 30 Rockefeller Plaza N.Y. will send transcripts of the show if you write.

This is RR Thanks for listening. ❖

Lawrence Welk
February 13, 1979

† The son of immigrants who has truly lived the American dream offers a lesson in Americanism in his book "My America, Your America." * I'll be right back.

As our country was approaching it's bi-centennial a man wrote a book called "My America, Your America." In the foreword he says: "I know that this wonderful life of mine could never have happened anywhere but here. My parents knew this long before me. Searching for freedom they came to this country as immigrants, from a land where they and their parents before them, had been bitterly oppressed—trapped in a life where there was little or no chance to better themselves."

You can see & hear this man any week on T.V. Just treat yourself to an hour's entertainment that will (if you're old enough) bring *back* nostalgic

* Lawrence Welk, with Bernice McGeehan, *My America, Your America* (Englewood Cliffs, NJ: Prentice-Hall, 1976).

memories of the big band era. There he is, one time farm boy, son of immigrants, ~~Lawrence Welk~~ telling us, "Its Wunnerful, Wunnerful."

And Lawrence Welk * has done something to make life wonderful for those around him. Take a look at his company of more than 50 people and see if you cant feel the genuine warmth & camaraderie of his musicians & artists. You can because it's there.

In this cynical world where too often a broken promise dosen't count unless it was in writing the Lawrence Welk company operates with no written contracts. This is part of the "Welk Training & Sharing Plan." A great many business executives & industrialists could do themselves a favor by having Lawrence explain his plan to them.

Very simply the plan consists of 3 parts. Number one is the training program. Young talent is discovered, is trained by the employer & senior employees. The trainees are paid during a training period which does not exceed one year. At the years end employee & employer review progress & decide whether to continue the relationship. If the decision is, yes, the trainee becomes a full employee & begins from that day to share in the profits & other benefits of the business.

~~The~~ Part 2 of the plan is a corporation which sets aside an amount equal to 15% of the gross payroll. This money is deposited & invested for the sole benefit of the employees. If & when they retire or leave the company they get their share. There are in addition, special benefits for & bonuses for meritorious effort. The corp. also assumes all or part of the payment for medical coverage, life insurance, union assessments etc.

And Part 3 is the no contract basis. As Lawrence explains it: ~~"We all realize the only way to maintain our~~ "The prime goal of our job training and sharing program is to develop the individual person to the highest possible degree of his inborn talents and potential in every way—personally, professionally, morally & spiritually. This goal is the basic, underlying motivation for our entire system."

Does the system work? In the backstage life TV viewers never see there is an unmistakable family spirit. They babysit for each other, take trips together & help each other in time of trouble. Sounds real American dosen't it? Maybe Lawrence Welks bicentennial book "My America, Your America" should be required reading for all of us. It's wunnerful, wunnerful.

This is RR Thanks for listening.

† Send typed copy to Mr. Lawrence Welk 100 Wilshire Blvd. Suite 700 Santa Monica Calif. 90401 ❖

* Lawrence Welk (1903–1992) was a musician and entertainer specializing in "champagne music" who led a touring big band throughout the 1930 and 1940s, and in 1955 started *The Lawrence Welk Show,* a variety show specializing in soft dance music. It ran on the ABC network and later in syndication until 1981.

Hamburgers
February 13, 1979

When is a hamburger not a thing of beauty? When it's in Martha's Vineyard—that's when.

I'll be right back.

There is a famous resort community—a part of the Massachusetts coastline, Martha's Vineyard, rich in history, beauty and the nostalgic charm of yesterday. Now thanks to my friend M. Stanton Evans that lovely place is here in a commentary I'd intended to do about the "junk food" fuss.

In a recent Nat. Review bulletin Stan reported on a battle that has brought rancor & bitterness to the normally peaceful vacation climate of Martha's Vineyard. It seems that McDonalds the franchise ~~food~~ purveyor of hamburgers wants to open a place in that village.

Standing in the way is a hastily mobilized group called the "No-Mac committee." Stan quotes a spokesman for the group as saying: "The consensus of the community is to reject many of the 20th century values which have homogenized American culture."

Now lest you think this is a problem ~~a~~ of scenery & esthetic values let me hasten to say that "Big Mac" has made it plain there will be no neon signs or golden arches. The plan is for a building in keeping with the local architecture. It is described as "like a captains house"—sea captain that is.

One cant escape the idea that opposition to a "Big Mac" in Martha's Vineyard springs from a touch of snobbery.~~—that e~~Elitists who'd have no objection to a new tearoom are ~~opposed to a~~ *horrified by the* low cost, mass merchandising of food. Well there is no argument that MacDonalds & all the other so called "fast food" merchandizers are aiming at supplying food of guaranteed quality in clean (if not atmospheric) surroundings at low cost. They do not pretend to be gourmet cafés with exotic menus. ~~And~~ *But* just in passing let me point out *that in addition to selling good food at low cost* they provide employment for thousands of young people who have no particular job skill or trade.

Well as I said, I was going to do a commentary on all the fuss now being raised about junk foods. Stans article sidetracked me only because the "fast food" chains are often lumped in with the sugar coated tooth~~,~~ destroyers, soft drinks etc. which are supposedly ~~destroying~~ threatening the health of the young. To do this is unfair and a false accusation.

A research group in Wis. for example, focused on ~~Mac~~ McDonalds and found that a meal consisting of a Big Mac, french fries & a chocolate milkshake provides 70% of daily protein needs, 60% of niacin, 50% of calcium, 50% of phosphorus, 45% of vitamin B-12, 30% of iron & substantial percentages of other dietary requirements.

The director of ~~the~~ Food & nutrition of the Am. Medical Assn. agrees ~~wit~~

there is adequate nutritional value in such a meal and adds, "most of the products used are just about as good or maybe even better than the products that are prepared at home." They make it plain of course that such a meal as a steady, daily diet would ~~lack in~~ not meet all *our* nutritional needs.

Stan Evans in his article called attention to ~~another fact~~ *a coincidence* which of course has nothing to do with the good people of Martha's Vineyard. "New Times," a Soviet weekly paper has accused McDonalds of exploiting youth, financing secret armies & a host of other sins and a Swedish communist charges that "the hamburger culture is a danger to the working people."

You know it's funny—but all of a sudden I want a hamburger. This is RR Thanks for listening. ❖

Long Walk
February 13, 1979

†I hope you are in the mood to feel good about things because with all that's wrong in our land, one young man has found a lot that's right.

I'll be right back.

I'm *i*ndebted to a columnist in a ~~Hollywood~~ *movie* trade paper, "The Hollywood Reporter" for todays commentary. George Christy wrote of an amazing ~~saga~~ *book*—"A walk ~~a~~*A*cross America,"* and the young man who did the walking & writing of the book.

In Oct. 1973, 22 year old Peter Jenkins left his home in Conn. and started a back packing trip across America. This was no hike to get from one ocean to the other, or to see how quickly it could be done. The hike ended 5 years later *in Oregon* when he waded out waist deep into the Pacific Ocean.

When Peter left Conn. he didn't think he'd discover America—he thought he knew America & he didn't like it. He was ashamed of the American flag & he didn't believe in God. ~~He~~ *Peter Jenkins* was one of the youthful rebels from the Woodstock era, convinced that ~~the South was racist.~~ Whites ~~he knew~~ *in the South* hated ~~b~~*B*lacks and ~~b~~*B*lacks were all barefoot. He was sure he'd confirm this as he headed South.

He arrived in Murphy N. Car. flat broke on a Friday night. There was no point in looking for work on a Fri. night so he joined a group of black youths who were playing basketball. When the game broke up some of them invited him to their home for dinner. He was afraid but he went. He shared corn bread & fried chicken and spread his bedroll in their yard.

Continuing on he decided Mobile Alabama was the most beautiful city he'd ever seen. He fell in love with the way of life on the gulf coast & wanted to live there. He discovered the pleasure of a Louisiana "shrimp boil," where he

* Peter Jenkins, *A Walk Across America* (New York: William Morrow, 1979).

waded with his hosts into the bayou for shrimp and helped with the cooking pots. In Texas he saw the children of oil millionaires and of workers happily going to school together & no way to tell them apart.

Zigzaging across country, moving north as spring came he herded, wrestled, & dehorned cattle. Somewhere in the 5 years of hiking this young rebel who had vowed marriage was not for him; that he would find & leave girls as it suited him, met & married Barbara. It's all in the book.

Marriage wasn't the only thing he changed his mind about. He describes his walk as a pilgrimage in search of himself. But he found America & he found God. He writes: "Finally I've come around to enjoying being an American. I appreciate ~~what it means~~ *being able to go to* the grocery store to buy what I want, fish & hunt. I want to become involved with the operation of our schools & govt. We often overlook the fact that everyone has an opportunity to have his own home, to create his own world here."

Last Christmas he & Barbara sent out Christmas cards inviting everyone they'd met on the trek to join them for the last mile in Oregon. Over 150 came, ranchers from Idaho, oilmen from Texas, the black family from Murphy ~~Alabama~~ *N. Car.*, his & Barbaras families. They waded out waist deep in the ocean, laughing, crying & embracing.

In his book "A Walk Across America," he sums it up, "there <u>is</u> great love and wonder & hope here, and you're free to pursue your dreams."

This is RR Thanks for listening.

† Send copy when typed to George Christy—"The Hollywood Reporter" and the attached note. RR* ❖

Four years after Vietnam was unified under Communist rule, the country was at war with a neighboring Communist state, the People's Republic of China. In January 1979, Vietnam overthrew the Khmer Rouge in Cambodia. The following month the PRC, which supported the Khmer Rouge, retaliated by attacking Vietnam. In April, Sino-Vietnamese peace talks began.

P.O.W.
March 6, 1979

Vietnam is back in the news and it's only natural that some memories have been reawakened.

I'll be right back.

~~Several~~ A *few* weeks ago the U.N. was asked to deal with the matter of Chinas' attack on Vietnam and Vietnam's attack on Cambodia. Specifically a

* The note reads: "Dear George, Just a line to confess I plagiarized your column. Thanks very much for writing a most heartwarming story and one that should make a cynical world look a little brighter. Best regards, Ron"

resolution called for each side to withdraw it's forces to within it's own borders. Chinas Teng Tsiao Ping* immediately proclaimed his support of such a plan.

If ~~I~~ memory serves me correctly Pres. Lyndon Johnson asked the U.N. on more than one occasion to involve itself in the Vietnam situation when we were ~~involved~~ *fighting* there. ~~The Tower of Babel on the Hudson~~ *The U.N.* remained obstinately aloof & silent.

~~Now with regard to~~ *Regarding* the present ~~solution~~ resolution I think an amendment would be appropriate. Yes the Chinese should return to their own border & yes the Vietnamese should return to theirs; ~~But we are talking about~~ the <u>North Vietnamese</u> who broke their pledged word given in the Paris Peace Accords and conquered an independent neighbor <u>South</u> Vietnam. ~~These two countries~~ *The Vietnam war was not a civil war. They* have been separate nations for centuries. ~~even though for~~ a time ~~both were part of Frances colonial empire.~~ Let the resolution be amended to read that N. Vietnam will not only leave Cambodia, but WILL LEAVE S. Vietnam as well. And while they are at it they could also withdraw from Laos which turned out to be one of the dominoes we were told would fall if N. Vietnam had it's way. You'll remember how some apologists ridiculed the "domino theory."

We've been treated to news photos of prisoners taken by the N. Vietnamese in the present fighting. Someone had better be sure provision is made for their release in view of the Vietnamese record. Those photos bring back some unhappy memories.

A U.S. Navy fighter pilot, Jim Stockdale** parachuted from his crippled plane over N. Vietnam on Sept 9th 1965. He was released almost 8 years later on Feb. 12 1973. ~~He had endured~~ *after* 2,714 days in prison including 3 years in solitary confinement and over a year in total isolation.

He was tortured for days on end throughout those years and reduced as he put it to total submission on 15 occasions by his own count. In 1969 when ~~th~~ his captors wanted to use him in a propaganda film he beat his own face to a pulp with a wooden stool & inflicted wounds on his head & face with a razor. He was not used in the film.

Months later, fearing that he might be so weakened he would eventually reveal secrets to the enemy he stabbed both his wrists with broken glass to end an interrogation. He said he felt the only way he could stop the questioning was to make them believe he was willing to die rather than yield. For this he has received the Congressional medal of honor.

Today Vice Admiral James Stockdale is an instructor in the Naval War College. ~~He is~~ teaching mid-career officers philosophy. It is a ~~military type of~~ philosophy designed to help the military, quote "regain our bearings" enquote.

Admiral Stockdale says, "a lot of training in the military tells you how ~~to~~

* Deng Xiaping.

** Vice Admiral James Bond Stockdale.

YOU SHOULD act but dosen't give you the why." And he adds: "No philosophical survival kits are issued~~"~~ when man goes to war."

What about us? ~~Do we~~ *DONT WE* have a moral obligation to continue reminding the world that *the* S. Vietnam*ese are* a conquered people?

This RR Thanks for listening. ❖

The 100 Club
March 6, 1979

† I'm never happier than when I come across a story that reaffirms my belief in the capacity of our people for great & noble deeds.

I'll be right back.

About 20 yrs. ago 4 men in Boston Mass. ~~had an idea. That wasn't strange because they were~~ all successful in their fields of endeavor~~. Their idea was~~ ~~*HAD AN IDEA*~~ *decided* to create an organization simply because they cared. *THEY WERE* Catholic, Jewish & Protestant.—They said, "we care for those who care for us." That is today the slogan of the unique organization they created ~~and which is called~~, "The 100 Club of Mass. Inc.

Only one of those founders is alive today, Norman Knight, Pres. of the 100 club. The Club which started with 4 men now has a membership of *MORE THAN* 2000 ~~and~~ business, professional & civic leaders *from* all over Mass. and a long waiting list of people who want to join *THEM* in providing a magnificent service.

You'll understand that slogan, "we care for those who care for us," if I read a line or two from one of the clubs pamphlets. "A piercing bullet, a raging fire, a terrifying explosion or a sudden heart failure can quickly flick out the life of our heroic protectors against crime & holocausts. There's lonely grief, mounting bills, the world becomes bleak."

These words of course are about the men who serve in law enforcement & those who protect us from fire. ~~a~~*A*nd the families they leave when the hazards of their work cost them their lives.

~~In the~~ The 4 founders of the 100 club wanted to do something for these men who care for us. Twenty years ago they started helping the families who had met with tragedy. ~~Then~~ At first it was a $1000 check to a widow. Now it's $2500, plus paying $10,000 worth of bills, summer camp for children, college assistance and a host of other benefits. But even more it is a warm & continuing relationship not just the impersonal mailing of a check. More than 15 functions a year for widows & children are arranged ~~covering~~ *ranging* from baseball games to the famous Boston "Pop" concerts.

Right now the club is caring for some 200 families across the state. There are no fixed regulations nor is the help limited to families of men killed in the line of duty. It is an effort by private citizens who want to help their neighbors. And in these 20 yrs. they have helped—some $2 mil. worth.

Here are a few lines from the letters that arrive almost daily at *100* club headquarters. "We shall never forget how our lives were touched by many kind, loving & caring people."

"I was at the hospital this evening when the lovely basket of fruit arrived for my son. He broke down & cried."

"We're enjoying ourselves at camp. We learned how to field, hit, steal bases & a lot more things."

"I would like to sincerely thank everyone for once again making it financially possible for me to return to college this Fall."

And from a bereaved widow: "God bless you for caring & understanding."

What if we had 50 statewide 100 clubs?

This is RR Thanks for listening.

† Send copy of this to Mr. Norman Knight 100 CLUB OF MASS. INC.—17 GLOUCESTER ST. BOSTON MASS. 02115 cc: Wm. Loeb ❖

*In 1978 consumer prices rose 9 percent; the rate for 1979 was 13.3 percent.**

Inflation
March 6, 1979

There is a risk in talking about inflation. We must all wonder if there is anything left to say that hasn't already been said. I'll be right back.

In spite of the umpteen million words that have been written, *&* spoken about inflation I'm going to add a few more. ~~In spite of~~ *With* all the rosy predictions about the fight against inflation & the possibility of victory we now know that *the* inflation rate in 1978 was 9% and there are hints it might actually have been 10.

Have you ever wondered what things would be like if that rate continued for the next 20 yrs.? I'll use the 10% ~~figure~~ *rate* not just to look on the dark side but because it's easier to figure.

In 1998–20 yrs. down the road with a 10% inflation rate when your grandchild asks for a candy bar you'll give him $1.35. Maybe you'll make it an even $1.50 & tell him to keep the change~~. Maybe it~~ *and maybe that* will buy him a stick of gum. Todays $50,000 home will cost $336,000 and if you can still afford to eat, the food you can buy now for $100 will set you back $673. That modest $4000 car sitting in the driveway will have a $26,910 price tag. College tuition which averages $5000 a year now will be a hefty $33,638. Heaven only knows what kind of money ~~j~~*J*unior will be writing home for.

Well that's 10% inflation 20 yrs. down the road. We're being encouraged to think the ~~relatio~~ inflation rate might be brought under control at say a reasonable 6%. And sometimes it sounds as if those in govt. plus their ec. advisors

* *Economic Report of the President, 1980,* Table B54.

are willing to settle for that as a kind of status quo. That's a little like rolling over & going ~~to~~ back to sleep because the fire in the house is only on the 1st floor.

Would you like to hear that same set of figures I just gave, readjusted down to a 6% inflation rate? That $50,000 house will be a bargain at $160,357. The candy bar for little Johnny or Alice will only cost 64¢ & that $100 basket of food will run you $321. Your modest compact car will only cost ~~$16,036~~ $12,830 & college tuition will be $16,036 a year.

All we have to do to prevent these ridiculous figures from becoming a fact of life is *to* end deficit spending by govt. How did we get into this situation anyway? Well back in the '60's it was a decision to fund a great many social reforms we called the "great society" and the war in Vietnam without raising taxes.

It takes political courage to raise a tax. Inflation is a tax but not easily recognizable as such and no one in office has to cast a vote for it. As a matter of fact inflation is kind of fun for awhile. The govt. without saying anything to anyone turns on the printing presses and ~~grinds out~~ runs off several billions of dollars, all green & crisp. Business seems to pick up, money is easy to come by and everyone feels good. You get a raise and find yourself in a higher surtax bracket. At first you're inclined to be proud of that. It seems like you're getting ahead in the world.

But then the warm glow turns out to be a fever. You discover you're earning twice as much but suddenly you dont seem able to afford the same things you could back when you earned less. Maybe we cant go back but we can head off that $1.35¢ candy bar right now at 20¢ by simply telling Govt. the party's over.

This is RR Thanks for listening. ❖

Human Rights
March 6, 1979

We've been told that "Human Rights" is the very heart of our foreign policy. If that is true it explains the inconsistency of that policy. ~~This is RR. Thanks for lis~~ I'll be right back.

By coincidence three situations dealing with our policy on Human Rights became news items almost simultaneously in recent weeks and they pointed up our own inconsistency with regard to this subject. In fact it is an inconsistency that perhaps should be called hypocrisy.

The first news item was that our state dept. has decided violation of human rights is ~~not~~ no longer a barrier to normalizing relations with Castros Cuba. We still have two other unresolved matters standing in the way, Cubas forces in Africa and lack of compensation for private property seized by Castro during the revolution. But the slate is clean on human rights because a few hundred of ~~the~~ *Castros* thousands of pol. prisoners have been freed and allowed to join their families in the U.S.

The 2nd item had to do with a cutback in economic aid to Nicaragua and the withdrawal of American personnel. This we are doing because according to the State Dept. President Somoza* is in violation of our standards of human rights. He may be—I dont know. I do know, because it's a matter of public record, that the revolutionary forces ~~he is dealing with~~ *who are fighting against his regime* are marxists for the most part & many were trained & armed by Castro's Cuba. So it's one off & one on our human rights black list.

~~B~~ Item number 3 is the release of a report that has been in the making for about a year and a half. It was in Sept. of 1977 that Panama invited the Organization of American States to send it's Inter American Commission on Human Rights to visit Panama and investigate what were called, "unfounded, unjust & irresponsible charges of violations of human rights." These charges had been made in the discussion & debate over the Panama Canal treaties.

The results of that investigation have just been made public and they confirm the charges the govt. of Panama declared were unfounded & unjust.** The Commission concludes that between 1968 & 1972 ~~that~~ Pol. activity was practically suppressed by the military regime. From 1972 to '77 Panamanian citizens were deported in violation of the const. Restrictions were imposed on freedom of assembly, expression & association and there was interference in the judicial process.

All of that is only for openers. The commission reported on torture tactics engaged in by the Panama national guard; Electric shocks to the vital & most sensitive parts of the body, physical beatings of male & female prisoners usually with a hose, the insulting fondling of female prisoners ~~with~~ *and* threat of rape and long interrogation of prisoners while denying them food, water or sleep.

The commission also reported a written statement from Leopoldo Aragon who was a pol. prisoner for 2 years and then exiled to Sweden where he burned himself to death in a protest against our turning over the canal to Panama.

Here is some of what he wrote; "prisoners were running like cattle under the whippings & savage cries of the guards who were hitting them with clubs." In addition to this he told of prisoners being hung from tree limbs by their wrists, chaining them to thorn trees & tying them on top of ant tunnels.

* Besieged by pressure from the Sandinista National Liberation Front (FSLN), the Somoza dynasty was faltering in 1979. In February, the month before Reagan recorded this broadcast, the Carter administration announced that it was ending the United States' military relationship with Nicaragua and reducing economic aid. In July, President Anastasio Somoza Debayle fled the country as the FSLN took power.

** See "Report on the Situation of Human Rights in Panama," Organization of American States, June 22, 1978.

We will ~~turn over~~ begin the turnover of the canal to Panama on Oct. 1st. This is RR Thanks for listening. ❖

On March 28, 1979, less than a month after Reagan wrote this address, the Number Two reactor at the Three Mile Island nuclear power plant on the Susquehanna River near Harrisburg, Pennsylvania suffered a partial meltdown, causing panic and a renewed national debate about the safety of nuclear power. Three Mile Island became a rallying point for anti-nuclear activists, and it was this incident (in combination with a low national demand for electricity and more restrictive regulation of the industry) that was responsible for the U.S. slowdown in private nuclear power plants in the late 1970s. No new nuclear power plants have been started since 1977. Prompted by a Carter-appointed commission to review the Three Mile Island incident, in October 1979 the industry created the Institute of Nuclear Power Operations (INPO).

Nuclear Power II
March 6, 1979

† This is going to be a little more on nuclear power which hopefully will expose the ignorance of those who demonstrate against such power. I'll be right back.

On the last broadcast I commented on the misconception many of us have had regarding the dangers inherent in generating electricity by the use of nuclear reactors. Today I'd like to give you some of the economic advantages of nuclear power.

We presently generate about 12% of our power ~~by~~ in nuclear plants. That saves us 450 mil. barrels of oil each year. If we had to import that oil it would add $6 bil. to our trade deficit. It also means consumers have saved between 2 & 3 bil. dollars on their electric utility bills. Incidentally we are increasing our need for electricity at a steady rate. It amounts to almost 40% of all energy consumed at present & will be more than half in 20 years.

Let's take one example of what nuclear power means in Americas north east. I'm sure we've all seen *or heard* the news stories the last couple of years about the Seabrook plant in New Hampshire. A very active anti-nuclear power group calling itself the "clamshell alliance" has successfully delayed construction of the Seabrook ~~allia~~ plant. The groups name comes from the fact that it based it's opposition on the ~~charge~~ *claim* that discharge of heated water from the plant into the ocean would destroy a few acres of seabottom as a breeding area for clams. Seabrook answered by changing it's design & creating a ~~colli~~ *cooling* tower so that no hot water would bother the romancing clams. That didn't however cool down the demonstrators.

Construction resumed thanks to the herculean efforts of New Hampshires then Gov., Mel Thompson. ~~His~~ but he paid a considerable price for carrying out what was clearly his duty. ~~H After~~ In spite of having kept his state economically sound with the lowest tax burden in the nation he was narrowly defeated in the '78 election because of a small TEMPORARY charge added to utility bills to cover the ongoing Seabrook construction costs. The charge will be ~~lift~~ removed when the plant is completed.

Unfortunately the good people of New Hampshire (undoubtedly influenced to a certain extent by the loud mouthed "clamshellers") weren't aware that the Public Service Co. of N.H. is providing them with electric*ity* ~~power~~ at a savings of more than 19% right now because of nuclear power. Nor did they know that every year that Seabrook is delayed they pay almost $60 mil. extra. That's a pretty high price for letting the antinuclear demonstrators have their fun.

~~A~~ *The* ~~h~~*H*ouse ~~c~~Committee on Govt. Operations his issued a report that nuclear fuel is about ⅙ the price of coal & 1/18 the price of oil in generating electricity. A recent report also set the cost for 3 yrs. delay in construction of *a* nuclear plants at $350 mil. All of which must, of course, be paid ULTIMATELY by the consumers.

The history of mans progress is directly tied to mans access to power or if you will—energy. It started with his discovery of the use of fire, the wheel and then fossil fuels to produce steampower & finally electricity. Our standard of living is directly proportionate to our ability to reduce the cost of energy. We have brought development of nuclear power almost to a ~~halt~~ complete halt here in the U.S. ~~This is RR Thanks for listening.~~ ~~*Why?*~~ *at* ~~*what*~~ *a cost to us of what must be trillions of dollars. Why?*

This is RR Thanks for listening. ❖

† Send copy to Gov. Mel Thompson (we must have his home address) He's no longer Gov. RR

Small Business I
March 27, 1979

† How many of us are aware when we use the word capitalism that it exists in it's purest form in what we call small business? I'll be right back.

Corporate America may get the headlines but nearly 90% of the business ventures in our nation are classified as small business. And small business is responsible for half our Gross national product, affecting directly or indirectly the lives & the livelihood of more than 100 mil. Americans. It gives jobs to more than half the workers in our land.

All of us see them, know them & associate with them every day. The average small business man is the tool & diemaker who takes his savings & a bank loan and goes into business for himself. ~~The~~ He is the fellow *on the corner* we buy our gasoline from, the druggist, the lunch counter proprietor or the man or woman who has parlayed a lunch counter into the towns top cafe.

Small business is the backbone of the free market and the starting point for corporate or big business. Much of corporate America was once an individual with an idea for a service or product he thought people might want. And today we all take for granted massproduced conveniences and products which were once just an idea in someones head. Henry Ford fits that description, so does a tailor who once made sail cloth ~~p~~ work pants for the miners in Virginia City. His name was Levi.

You'd think our govt. would handle with care this unique heretage which has so much to do with our way of life. Unfortunately that is not the case. For every 10 small businesses that start up today 5 will be gone inside of 2 yrs. A repressive tax code which makes it difficult to get start up capital or ongoing capital to expand or even operate is part of the reason that small business is undernourished. Then there are Fed. regulations which overburden the proprietor with paperwork and limit his or her ability to be innovative.

Just recently an item appeared calling attention to the decline in patents issued to Americans ~~on~~ *for* inventions. In fact 35% of the patents granted by our U.S. Patent office today go to foreigners.

In 1969 one hundred new, "high risk" small business firms in such fields as electronics, energy research & development & environmental management were incorporated. But that was 10 yrs. ago. By 1976 there was not a single new small business formation in these fields.

One former small business man is now a U.S. Congressman from the 5th district of Pennsylvania, Richard T. Schulze.* Based on his experience in business he has come up with some solutions to the problems of the small business man & woman. They are not the usual Wash. approach of govt. loans and help funneled through a burocracy. He wants to free this important segment of our ec. structure from the harassment of govt. which caused the problems in the 1st place.

His colleagues on the Ways & Means committee are in full support. He's getting up to 100 co-signers of his program which calls for 7 simple steps and he needs our help. Last year his bill passed & was vetoed. He is back with a "Small Business Tax Relief Act of 1979." On the next broadcast I'll give you a rundown on his 7 points.

This is RR Thanks for listening.

† Send copies of this & script no. 2 to Congressman Schulze (letter attached) along with my note to him. RR ❖

* R–Pennsylvania, 1975–1993.

Rhodesia
March 27, 1979

If anyone can justify OR EXPLAIN the attitude of the U.S. govt. with regard to Rhodesia I'd be more than happy to listen. I'll be right back.

Writing in the Wash. weekly "Human Events" Allan C. Brownfeld* reminds us of the truth of a line spoken by Adolph Hitler: "If you kill one man it is murder, while if you kill millions it simply becomes a statistic." And then Mr. Brownfeld goes on to illustrate that to our govt. the dead both black & white in Rhodesia, killed by the terrorists of Nkomo & Mugabe have become just a statistic.

Allan Brownfeld had attended a press conference in Wash. where he listened to a survivor of the Rhodesia passenger plane ~~brought~~ *shot* down by terrorists last Sept. You'll recall the incident, the guerillas using Soviet ground to air missiles blasted the airliner out of the sky. I believe 54 died in the crash and 10 of the survivors were gunned down by the terrorists after escaping ~~death in the crash.~~ *from the downed plane.*

The man Brownfeld heard in the press conference was Hans ~~+~~ HANSEN one of 8 who escaped death in the crash & the later massacre. He told how the survivors crawled from the plane and were met by the terrorists who ordered them to stand & move away from the plane. Hansen & his wife** were apart from the rest having returned to the plane for clothing for those who were seriously hurt.

When they heard the order to stand he asked his ~~Rhodesian~~ wife if they should obey and she being a Rhodesian (he is Danish) said, "No way." They saw the terrorists rob the passengers of all valuables then ~~they~~ *sho~~t~~ot* them all ~~and bayonetted~~ *after which they bayonetted* them—men, women & children.

The Hansens were invited to America by the American Security Council to tell their story. Our State dept. refused to give Mrs. Hansen a visa because she is Rhodesian. Hans Hensen travelling on a Danish passport couldn't be kept out. Our State dept. if you aren't aware, gave visas to both Nkomo & Mugabe for visits to this country & *they were granted* audiences with our Sec. of State.

Mrs. Hansen insisted that her husband come without her so that we the American people could hear the truth about the murderers our govt. insists on calling "The Patriotic Front."

I'm afraid HOWEVER not too many Americans heard the story. According to Alan Brownfeld none of the 3 major networks sent cameras or crews TO THE PRESS CONF., and not one word was carried in The N.Y. Times, the Wash. Post or any other major paper.

* Allan C. Brownfeld, "U.S. Indifferent to Rhodesian Terrorism," *Human Events,* March 17, 1979, p. 14.
** Hans and Diana Hansen.

Hansen has expressed surprise that so many of us seem to have completely different views than those of our State dept. This has made him optimistic. He says, "I believe there is a great future in Rhodesia under majority rule. Blacks & Whites will be able to work together if only the terrorists are prevented from destroying what we have built."

Meanwhile ~~our govt.~~ *terrorists* are being trained in Angola by Cuban & Soviet military advisors. We have that from one of the trainees who gave himself up after he & a companion killed 17 civilians in the Zwimba Tribal Trust Land.

I wonder if Mrs. Hansen will accept an apology from at least one American who thinks our State Dept. is shaming our country.

This is RR Thanks for listening. ❖

District of Columbia
March 27, 1979

Are the govt. workers living in the District of Columbia suffering taxation without representation?

I'll be right back.

Some time ago I discussed on one of these commentaries* the matter of whether the District of Columbia should be given voting representation in the House of Representatives & 2 United States Senators. In other words the District which in effect is our national capital, the city of Wash. would be treated as a state. As you know ~~this has been~~ *a const. amendment to do this has been* presented to the states for ratification. ~~by state legislators. If the required number vote yes, the citizens of Wash. D.C. will elect a congressman & 2 Senators.~~

On that previous broadcast I expressed my opposition to such a plan & gave some reasons for that opposition. Now a young Congressman from Maryland, Rep. Robert Bauman** has delivered an eloquent argument against changing the present status of the District.

He points out that our Founding Fathers made two very important decisions: One that our nation would be a Federation of sovereign states & two that the new nations capital would be a city created for that purpose in a Fed. district. If we give up those 2 principles we wont be creating a new state. We will be establishing ~~an entity~~ *a non state* with all the benefits of statehood.

There would be no state const., no Governor, no legislature and no responsibility for it's own financing. It would still be under the control of Congress. Voices raised in support of this mutation cry, "No taxation without representation!" Yet they have proposed ~~taxing~~ *charging* citizens of Maryland & Virginia who work in Wash. a commuters tax.

* See Reagan's commentary titled "District of Columbia," taped on June 27, 1978.
** Congressman Robert Bauman (R–Maryland, 1973–1981).

The~~se~~ owners of these voices say nothing about the fact that citizens of the 50 states presently are taxed to support the district. Residents of Wash. pay Federal taxes as do we all. But for every 29¢ they pay they get $1 in return. In neighboring Maryland the citizens pay $1.16 for each dollar they get back.

Wash. D.C. receives a direct $300 mil. grant ~~to~~ from the Fed. govt. to offset the revenue loss from untaxable federal land. No other state gets such a grant & yet some states have as much as 80 to 90% of their land in federal ownership. In Calif. it's about half.

A point has been raised that the district is larger than seven of our states. One could reply that we all know the Fed. govt. is bigger than it should be. But even more to the point so is Baltimore bigger than 7 of our states, or N.Y.. Should we start giving our large cities 2 Senators?

Congressman Bauman points out that Puerto Rico inhabited by 3 mil. people who are legally citizens of the U.S. and who have debated the question whether to apply for statehood or continue as a territory might have another alternative. If this amendment passes they could just follow precedent and say, "never mind statehood, just treat us like a state & give us 2 Senators."

I hope a great many of us will let our state legislators know we like things the way they are.

There's an old saying, "if it aint broke dont fix it." Well the district isn't broke—we are.

This is RR Thanks for listening. ❖

Washington Weather
March 27, 1979

It is a known fact that anything more than an inch of snow in Wash. D.C. brings that city to a crashing halt. I'll be right back.

With the freakish weather we've been having in these last 2 yrs. particularly in the East & Midwest, it's easy to think maybe the govt. has stopped predicting it and started regulating it.

Anyone having business in our nations capital has learned at one time or another that a light snow fall is a major disaster. ~~& n~~Normal living isn't even attempted until nature rights itself & melts the snow.

But we're indebted to a *Wash.* writer ~~for the~~ *with* ~~*magazine,*~~ Nat. Review* ~~Bulletin~~ for a new slant on how the Capital deals with this assault by nature.

In the most recent snow flurry this writer was listening to an all news radio station when the *regular* news was interrupted for a special report directed to all govt. workers. Remember Wash. is a one industry town and we all know what that industry is, dont we?

Anyway the special bulletin was; "Because of the winter storm the Office of

* "Letter from Washington" (weekly column), *National Review,* March 16, 1979, p. 338.

Personnel Management has declared a Condition 3 effective immediately. We repeat for all Fed. employees Condition 3 is in effect today." That almost has the dramatic sound of those wartime bulletins calling all mil. personnel to report to their posts immediately. You used to wonder if the enemy had landed on Long Island.

Well our alert Wash. correspondent for Nat. Review got on the phone and made a few calls. He learned that, "Condition 3 is a rare civil service bird, a day in which only those workers identified as 'essential'—identified by themselves—need report to work. In other words all workers receive full pay regardless of whether they show up & those who do show receive no overtime pay." Well there you have it, and all this time millions of trusting Americans thought all govt. employees were essential.

Our source for this story continued his phoning, starting with the 12 cabinet officers. There were 3 no shows but then at cabinet level they could have been out somewhere in other parts of the nation.

At the State dept. a suspicious young lady guessed at about 120 employees on hand. In answer~~ed~~ to a follow up question she admitted ~~a~~ *the* normal force was about 7000. I'll confess I've always suspected that only about 1 out of 600 at *the* State Dept. could be called essential. ~~That~~ *With 6900 absentees that* must have been one of our better days in foreign relations.

We weren't so lucky at H.E.W. They said about half of their 37,000 employees living in the metropolitan area were on hand. But we can put a question mark on that one. Our writer offered ~~a~~ *to* pay a dollar for everyone who filed a time card if the fellow on the other end of the phone ~~who~~ would put up a dollar for every one who didn't. It was no deal.

Maybe we could really streamline govt. if we moved the capital to Northern Maine.

This is RR Thanks for listening ❖

James Warren (Jim) Jones formed the People's Temple, an independent church, in the 1950s in Indianapolis, Indiana. Jones moved his church to Northern California in 1965 and in 1977 he and hundreds of followers established a compound in Guyana. In 1978, Congressman Leo J. Ryan (D–California) traveled to Guyana to investigate the activities of People's Temple. Ryan and those traveling with him were shot and killed at the airport as they sought to return to the United States. Soon thereafter, on November 18, Jones and approximately 900 of his followers participated in a mass suicide. Most took poison, but some were shot.

Jonestown
April 16, 1979

Todays subject is not a pleasant one but before we put it completely behind us there are a few facts we should know. I'll be right back.

The terrible tragedy of Jones~~borough~~*town* is fading into the past and well it should. It isn't a pleasant topic and I dont relish bringing it up. ~~b~~*B*ut there is a little known facet to the horrifying series of events which should have received more attention than it did.

There has been talk of investigating cults for the purpose of learning how we might possibly be able to anticipate & ~~therefby~~ *THEREBY* prevent another such happening. Some who knew the Rev. Jim Jones in the beginning of his ministry remember him as a sincere clergyman who somehow went wrong. But little attention has been given to what you might think would be the cap to the entire story—Jim Jones own personal account of his career as a minister or cult leader.

Yes there is such a document—a transcript of a tape that he recorded in which he told literally his life story & his philosophy. It was found at Jonestown after the mass suicides & murders. The full text was printed last Dec. 6th in the Georetown Guyana Chronicle, a time when Georgetown was teeming with American reporters.

The only Am. paper that ~~I know~~ *carried* the ~~paper~~ *story* so far as I know was the N.Y. Times on page 20 under a heading that read, "Paper Calls Jones Communist In 1950's." *

Now that headline on the story was a bit mis-leading. It was Jones who called Jones a communist. In his own rambling account he made it clear that he was a communist from the beginning & occupied the pulpit only for the purpose of furthering his *COMMUNIST* philosophy. His entire account is filled with profanity & vulgarities as he tells how a legitimate clergyman offered him a church even though he was cursing religion & the church. Jones expresses the belief that the ~~minister~~ clergyman who put him in the pulpit did so deliberately because he too was a communist.

I know it is hard to believe such a thing but ~~I remember~~ years ago when the American Communist Party moved to get control of the Motion Pic. Industry it had the help of a clergyman in one of our established religions. ~~as an ally~~ At first many of us thought he had been duped by the party and wasn't aware of what was really going on. Then when it became clear that he was ~~knowlin~~ knowingly doing their work we found ourselves asking—"how does a man of ~~God~~ *the* cloth become a communist?" The answer came from a man in law enforcement who was a specialist in communist tactics. He said—"Men of the cloth dont become communists—communists become men of the cloth."

So it was with Jones. In his taped account ~~account~~ ~~autobiograph~~ ~~*autobiograph*~~ *autobiographical* account he said, "Life is a gamble and I'd rather gamble on the side of communism." He expressed great admiration for Stalin & turned to Mao Tse Tung when Stalin was put down by the Soviets. He also admired Castro and wished he could have led a revolution as Castro did.

Obviously I haven't been able to recite in full the amazing story of Jim Jones

* Nicholas M. Horrock, "Paper Calls Jones Communist in 1950's," *The New York Times*, December 20, 1978, p. A19.

but it should be more widely known. Jonestown ~~did~~ *WAS* not the result of religious fanaticism—quite to the contrary.

This is RR Thanks for listening. ❖

Bilingual Education I
April 16, 1979

Maybe it's time we asked ourselves what we really mean by the term "bilingual ed." & what we want it to accomplish. I'll be right back.

Not very many Americans would hold still for scratching out ~~that~~ *the* inscription on the base of the Statue of Liberty in N.Y. Harbor. "Give me your tired, your poor, your huddled masses yearning to breathe free, the wretched refuse of your teeming shore. Send these, the homeless, tempest-tost to me. I lift my lamp beside the golden door."

There are some who call her Miss Liberty & others equally appropriately call her "The Mother of Exiles." But ~~whi~~ by whichever title she symbolizes the fact that for 200 yrs. this nation has been the melting pot of the world.

From the earliest pioneer to the most recent immigrant we are a collection of people from every spot on earth. We have in common a love for freedom that made us or our ancesters willing to tear up roots come to a strange land, learn it's ways & it's language and create a new ethnic breed called "American."

Learning our language never seemed to be an insurmountable problem in the melting pot process. A man of Italian origin told me one day he & his brothers & sisters learned *English* in our public schools & at night taught their parents. We provided free night time classes for newcomers to our shores. They all learned & no one thought we were asking to[o] much. Each was aware that if someone had come to ~~their~~ *his or her* motherland—a Frenchman to Germany, a German to Italy or vice versa they would be expected to learn that country's language.

As a new Gov. I first learned of bilingual ed. ~~in our schools~~—or rather the lack of it in our schools. In Calif. the problem had to do with our large *Spanish speaking* community. ~~of~~ Children coming from homes where Spanish was spoken had difficulty learning other subjects in the classroom because of their inability to speak English.

This was 1st brought to my attention by a group of mothers of such children. ~~and~~ They told tragic stories of children being put in classes for *the* backward or handicapped when their only problem was language. I asked why mothers of ~~S~~ Mexican heretage couldn't serve as volunteers to aid English speaking teachers. If a child was having a problem such a volunteer could talk to him or her in Spanish & see if the difficulty was misunderstanding due to unfamiliarity with ~~our language.~~ *English*. I was informed that the law required that anyone helping in the classroom have a teachers certificate.

Frankly I think that's silly. If a good purpose can be served by granting a waiver with regard to our legalities then that waiver should be granted. But, getting to the point: bilingual ed. was presented to me as a case of training a cadre of teachers in two languages so they could be assigned to particular schools where a sizeable percentage of students were of an ethnic background—~~Ca~~ in Calif's. case, Mexican. My thought was that such teachers would be entitled to premium pay for the extra training they had received.

Next broadcast.* I'll tell you what bilingual ed. has come to mean in our schools.

This is RR Thanks for listening. ❖

The Salcido Family
April 16, 1979

Once again tragedy duly reported in the press reveals how warm & kind Americans *can* be when they are given the chance. I'll be right back.

A few weeks ago the Los Angeles Times carried a story of tragedy striking a Calif. family. The victems were not public figures and possibly the accidental death of a family head would not normally result in press attention beyond the obituary column. There were however facets to this story that made it well worth reporting.

Jose Salcido a kindly, conscientious 50 yr. old father of 13 children, liked by his neighbors and fellow workers for his uncomplaining acceptance of life was killed in a senseless, unexplainable accident. Unloading his pickup truck he walked around the front of the parked vehicle~~. which It suddenly~~ which suddenly lurched forward crushing him against a brick wall.

For Jose it was the last of a chain of personal tragedies. His wife had died after suffering the agony of cancer ~~for~~ *over* a long period of time. A son had been killed by gun fire from a roving gang in a passing car and another son had accidentally drowned.

The Times told this story and printed a picture of the heartbroken children of Jose Salcido. A few days later the Times wrote another story about the Salcidos. I thought you might like to know about that story too.

On March 23rd the day after Jose's death a man from Beverly Hills drove to La Puente. He handed the eldest daughter $300 & left without giving his name. A short time later a woman in the neighborhood, suffering from arthri-

* "Bilingual Education II," in *Reagan, In His Own Hand,* p. 346. Reagan states that bilingual education has shifted from helping non-native English speaking students transition to English to helping them maintain their native languages.

tis and barely able to walk made her way to the Salcido home with the $100 she had collected ~~door~~ in a door to door solicitation from neighbors. Two tourists visiting Calif. from Pennsylvania sent a donation. The Times was receiving calls & letters from all over So. Calif.

One woman gave a check for $500. She said she wanted to provide, "immediate help." That immediate help was deeply appreciated by the 13 children of Jose Salcido because it took care of a large part of the funeral costs.

Their parish church started a drive and by this time the L.A. Times had received several hundred dollars from people who asked that it be forwarded to the family. This money was deposited in a special checking acct. in the name of the eldest son, Frank Salcido.

The children of Jose Salcido have been amazed by the help that has come to them from strangers. They have also ~~been~~ discovered how kind the people of this land can be. One letter accompanying a check ~~says~~ *said* it all. "This is for the children of Jose Salcido. It is for them to know that there are always others who care; that despite personal tragedy, the world is not always the dark place it seems to be; that their father would have wanted for them to go on with courage & strength, and still open hearts."

Because I know that some of you will ask; that bank acct. is in the name of Frank Salcido—Crocker Nat. Bank, E. Valley Blvd. La Puente Calif.

This is RR. Thanks for listening. ❖

Following a series of chance factors and human mistakes, Unit Two of the nuclear power station, Three Mile Island, malfunctioned on March 28, 1979. Although the amount of radioactive gas released into the environment was considered minimal, there was a strong public outcry against the use of nuclear power in the United States. Public concern about nuclear power found expression in The China Syndrome, *starring Jack Lemmon, Jane Fonda, and Michael Douglas. A dramatic depiction of an accident at a major American nuclear power plant, the movie was released two weeks before the accident at Three Mile Island.*

Three Mile Island I

May 8, 1979

I probably should apologize for doing a commentary on a news story that's already been overdone—but I wont.

I'll be right back

† I'm sure all of us feel we've had all the news about Three Mile Island and the nuclear accident there, that we want to hear. My only excuse for doing this commentary on that subject is because I'll be using news that somehow & for some unknown reason didn't get widely reported.

My decision to talk about this was triggered by a N.Y. Times CBS poll that found 36% of the people think a nuclear power plant can blow up like an atom bomb & another 40 odd percent dont know whether it can or not. The simple unarguable truth is—no it cannot. The fuel *used in nuclear power plants* has been reduced to where it can only continue getting hotter, it cannot explode.

I think the media has been largely irresponsible in its sensationalism about Three Mile Island and it's near boycott of the less sensational facts. Now since I'm part of the media by way of these commentaries I'll contribute my bit to ~~clearing~~ ~~the~~ *balancing the* news.

The accident is still *being* called the "worst ~~nuclear~~ *catastrophe* in the history of nuclear power. Some catastrophe! No one was killed, no one was injured and there will not be a single additional death from cancer among the 2 mil. people living within a 50 mile radius of the plant.

Dont take my word for it. Sen. Edward Kennedy* chaired a Sen. subcommittee on April 4th which summoned Wash's. top authorities in the field of ~~health~~ *HEALTH* & environment, to report on the accident. Sec. of H.E.W. *JOSEPH* Califano provided the information on the 2 mil. people. He further stated that the 25,000 people living within 5 miles of the plant had received at most, radiation equivalent to 2 chest x rays. This will not produce a single case of cancer. The maximum safe exposure is more than 6x as much as any ~~of the 25,000~~ received by the 25,000 people.

The Surgeon General told the committee there was no significant risk to the public even in the close vicinity of the plant. The head of the ~~e~~*E*nvironmental ~~p~~*P*rotection ~~a~~*A*gency & the head of the Fed. Food & Drug Admin. ~~who~~ *an agency that* often errs on the side of being too cautious said there was no increased health risk from the drinking water or the food. The gases that escaped from the plant are a type that disperses rapidly and loses its radioactivity in only a few days. Insignificant traces of iodine were found in the milk in the area amounting to ~~between 1/10 & 3/10 of 1%~~ ~~*one of the permitted level*~~ *at most* one 300th of the safe permissible level.

One of the networks interviewed a man on TV who owns a few goats. He said he didn't think the goats milk was safe to drink even though govt. inspectors had assured him it was. The network didn't say that his wife was a member of an anti-nuclear protest group. She showed up on another program with what she said was a sick sheep & she was sure it's illness was due to the accident.

Incidentally the total radioactivity the people & the animals were exposed to in the immediate vicinity of the plant was less than the difference between living in Dallas or living in the higher altitude of Denver Col.

There were (as I said earlier) no injuries, no deaths, ~~there~~ *there is* no residual radioactivity & that is the worst catastrophe in the hist. of nuclear power. Oh yes—one more thing, the supposedly radioactive cooling water released

* Senator Edward M. Kennedy (D–Massachusetts).

into the Susquehanna river turns out to be the water from the plant lavatories which has always been released in the river—after an automatic checking process.

This is RR Thanks for listening.

† Maybe this should be among the 1st we tape.

RR ❖

Three Mile Island II
May 8, 1979

Just a little more about the Three Mile Island Nuclear accident & the movie that benefited by the fallout. I'll be right back.

† On the previous commentary I reported the testimony of govt. officials such as Sec. of H.E.W. Califano, the Surgeon General, Head of Food & Drug & others that the event at *the* Three Mile Island power plant was more an incident than a catastrophe. Sec. Califano & the others said there would be no additional deaths from cancer among the 2 mil. people living within a 50 mile radius of the power plant.

Now Califano has changed his testimony. He says there was more fallout than he had previously stated and as a result there might be 1 additional case of cancer ~~ease~~ in the ~~decades~~ lifetime of those 2 mil. people. No one can take this lightly but the question arises—will we ever know? Can we be so accurate in ~~the~~ predicting how many ~~of 2 mil~~. *among* 2 mil. people will develop cancer in the next 30, 40 or even 60 or 70 years ~~?~~ that we'll know if there is one extra?

There was fallout of a beneficial kind to one small group of Americans—the cast, crew & investors in the movie "The China Syndrome." The story line of this picture ~~was one of a nuclea~~ *involved a threatened* nuclear disaster and the attempted cover up by the utility bigwigs who being businessman were of course more concerned with finances than human lives. I say, "of course," because businessmen are portrayed as villains more often than not in todays movies.

Anyway the box office receipts for "China Syndrome" boomed with every scare headline about "3 mile island." The screenwriter admitted to an interviewer that ~~his~~ his script reflected his personal views about nuclear power. He obtained his technical help from engineers aligned with the anti-nuclear forces. He also stated that his first target was going to be the oil industry but then he switched to nuclear.

Recently the Knight Ridder newspapers carried a story by Mike Lavelle* that revealed something of the fanaticism indulged in by the anti-nuclear group and how opposed they are to giving the other side a fair hearing.

* Mike Lavelle was a columnist with the *Chicago Tribune*.

David Rossin was invited to a preview of "The China Syndrome." Rossin is an engineer with Chicago's ~~Common~~ Commonwealth Edison Co. Jane Fonda, Jack ~~Lemmon~~ *LEMMON* & Michael Douglas had invited about 50 editors of college newspapers to the preview, which Lavelle says was to be followed by a question & answer period.

A young girl led off asking a question critical of the movie. According to the news story Michael Douglas "asked her sneeringly if she worked for Commonwealth Edison." She said that she had once worked part time for the company. With that he asked if anyone else in the audience worked for Commonwealth Edison. David Rossin raised his hand. He was asked to leave & ~~no~~ not wanting to make a scene—he did.*

One wonders if any of the college editors wrote about the one sidedness of the Q. & A. session or did they accept the anti nuclear brainwashing? One wonders also if the makers of "China Syndrome" were pleased that the ~~power plant didn't~~ *accident at Three Mile* ~~burned out~~ *caused no* deaths from radioactive fallout. I'd like to think so.

This is RR Thanks for listening

† I sent in a script about the 3 Mile nuclear plant. Make it no. 1 & this one no. 2 RR ❖

I'm only 17
May 8, 1979

Todays commentary is somewhat different. It just seemed to be something we all should hear. I hope you'll agree. I'll be right back.

Maybe you'll think "Dear Abby" an unusual source for a commentary. I hope though you'll agree she was well worth quoting.

A 17 yr old high school student wrote Dear Abby asking for permission to re-print *in her high school paper* a column *Abby had* written 2 yrs. ago. The young lady said it had made her do a lot of thinking. Abby graciously gave permission and here is that 2 yr. old column—because it made me do some thinking.**

The day I died was an ordinary school day. How I wish I had taken the bus! But I was too cool for the bus. I remember how I wheedled the car out of Mom. "Special favor," I pleaded, "all the kids drive." When the 2:50 bell rang, I threw all my books in the locker. I was free until 8:40 tomorrow morn-

* This story is recounted in David Burnham, "Nuclear Experts Debate "The China Syndrome," *The New York Times*, March 18, 1979, p. D1.

** The "I'm Only 17" column was also reprinted following the request of a reader in 1985. See the "Dear Abby Column" in the *Chicago Tribune*, August 26, 1985, section 5, p. 8. The column is titled "Please, God, I'm Only 17."

ing! I ran to the parking lot, excited at the thought of driving a car and being my own boss. Free!

It doesn't matter how the accident happened. I was goofing off—going too fast. Taking crazy chances. But I was enjoying my freedom and having fun. The last thing I remember was passing an old lady who seemed to be going awfully slow. I heard the deafening crash and felt a terrific jolt. Glass and steel flew everywhere. My whole body seemed to be turning inside out. I heard myself scream.

Suddenly I awakened; it was very quiet. A police officer was standing over me. Then I saw a doctor. My body was mangled. I was saturated with blood. Pieces of jagged glass were sticking out all over. Strange that I couldn't feel anything.

Hey, don't pull that sheet over my head. I can't be dead. I'm only 17. I've got a date tonight. I am supposed to grow up and have a wonderful life. I haven't lived yet. I can't be dead.

Later I was placed in a drawer. My folks had to identify me. Why did they have to see me like this? Why did I have to look at Mom's eyes when she faced the most terrible ordeal of her life? Dad suddenly looked like an old man. He told the man in charge, "Yes, he is my son."

The funeral was a weird experience. I saw all my relatives and friends walk toward the casket. They passed by, one by one, and looked at me with the saddest eyes I've ever seen. Some of my buddies were crying. A few of the girls touched my hand and sobbed as they walked away.

Please . . . somebody . . . wake me up! Get me out of here. I can't bear to see my Mom and Dad so broken up. My grandparents are so racked with grief they can barely walk. My brother and sisters are like zombies. They move like robots. In a daze, everybody! No one can believe this. And I can't believe it, either.

Please don't bury me! I'm not dead! I have a lot of living to do! I want to laugh and run again. I want to sing and dance. Please don't put me in the ground. I promise if you give me just one more chance, God, I'll be the most careful driver in the whole world. All I want is one more chance.

Please, God, I'm only 17!

This is RR Thanks for listening. ❖

Oil

May 8, 1979

When is a monopoly not a monopoly? And more to the point, is the oil industry in America a monopoly? I'll be right back.

A few weeks ago I was flipping the TV dial during the early morning news programs looking for a weather forecast when I came upon a discussion—discussion! It was an argument.

Forgetting the weather I watched and listened to a top oil co. executive and Sen. Metzenbaum of Ohio.* They were evidently guests on a talk show and the subject under discussion must have been the Presidents ill conceived energy program.

The Sen. was pounding away on the oil co. profits, their increase, the increase they'd have with decontrol of oil prices and that the only answer to these obscene profits was a windfall tax. Oh yes, he also cited the upsurge of oil co. stocks on Wall st.

When the oilman responded with a list of major corps. all of whom had a higher percentage of profits and an even greater increase in the market price of their stocks, Metzenbaum said "Yes but that's different. The oil industry is a monopoly." The oilman broke out laughing.

I didn't get to see the rest of the show, the clock ran out on me but I think I know why the gentleman from the oil industry was laughing. How do we determine whether an industry is competitive or monopolistic? Well there is no mystery about that. How concentrated is it? Is there freedom for newcomers to enter the field? And what is the record or history of profits?

On the 1st point—concentration of the industry for example the top 4 automakers account for 91% of that bus.*INESS*. The top 4 aluminum co's. make & sell 96% of the total output of aluminum. By comparison the top 4 oil co's. share only 33% of all the oil products sold in America.

As for freedom of entry there has been a 65% increase in the number of new oil co's. since 1951. Independent oil co's. have increased their share of the business about 30% over just the last 10 yrs.

We are so used to thinking of the entire industry in terms of the several most familiar trademarks it comes as something of a surprise when we take a census of the industry as a whole. There are 8000 different oil & gas producers, 130 refiners, 16,000 wholesalers & 186,000 service stations mostly run by independent businessmen.

The 3rd point in determining whether a monopoly situation *exists* has to do with the history of profits. I'm well aware as we all are that oil is a profitable business. ~~b~~*B*ut it's only about ½ as profitable as television or the major newspaper publishers and comes about in the middle range of all American industry.

There is an oil monopoly. It is made up of the OPEC nations. We can break that monopoly only by finding & producing more oil in these United States thereby lessening our dependence on OPEC oil. And if our govt. will trust in the incentives of the mkt. place we'll find & produce that additional oil. Then we'll all be laughing—maybe even Sen. Metzenbaum.

This is RR. Thanks for listening. ❖

* Senator Howard M. Metzenbaum (D–Ohio).

Disaster Area
May 8, 1979

It's hard to believe that people can suffer a disaster and not be aware of it but our govt. says it <u>can</u> happen. I'll be right back.

When we read in the daily press that some part of our country has been declared a disaster area ~~it~~ we assume that fire, flood, earthquake or some other natural calamity has struck. The declaration is official notice that victems of the calamity qualify for various kinds of federal ~~assis~~ *aid*. Such a calamity is usually a pretty obvious thing as we'll [we've] all seen numerous times on the TV news. And of course the victems are well aware that a disaster has taken place.

Just recently Cloud Lake Fla. received an official notice from the Fed. govt. that it had been declared a "major disaster area." The Treasury Dept. notification came to Town ~~cle~~ *CLERK* Dorothy Gravelin. Under a bold type heading "Disaster Notice," she read that her town—pop. 128 had been declared a major disaster area by the Pres. of the U.S.

Now Town Clerk Gravelin hadn't heard of any trouble. She looked out the window and everything appeared to be normal. ~~Sh~~ Picking up the phone she called Tallahassee and several other near by towns to ask if they were disaster areas too. Evidently they had been spared, only Cloud Lake had suffered.

In the meantime word had spread through the community but no one could recall any disaster and none of them could figure out how they'd missed it.

Clerk Gravelin's next call was to Wash. She finally reached the Florida coordinator in the U.S. Office of Rev. Sharing who didn't know what the disaster might be but would check it out.

Finally the answer came. Cloud Lake had suffered a crop freeze in Jan. of 1977. That of course should have solved the mystery and ended the suspense—But it didn't. Cloud Lake hadn't suffered any crop damage in 1977 or any other year because the nearest crops are about 20 miles west of Cloud Lake.

But Wash. had an answer for that. There probably had been some indirect effect like farmers who wouldn't be spending as much money in town. There are seven business establishments in Cloud Lake, all lined up on Southern Blvd. The busiest happens to be the Cloud Lake Adult Book Store. A check of that establishment found there had been no let up in business—in fact the proprietor just laughed at the idea.

But Wash. dosen't take such things lightly. Cloud Lake has been declared a disaster area and Wash. wants Cloud Lake to forget it's pride, get off the dime and admit it's had a disaster. The Town Council is supposed to ~~approve signing~~ *fill out* the govt. form and ~~and~~ *saying,* "Yes the disaster had an effect on us," sign it and mail it in. Then Wash. can do it's thing ~~and~~ *by* sending Cloud Lake—pop. 128 the federal funds it is entitled to because of a freeze that took place somewhere in Fla. back in Jan. of 1977.

I'm sorry I dont have word as to whether the Town Council ~~took~~ *has taken* the action or whether the Fed. check is still lying there in Wash. The check is for $22.61.

This is RR Thanks for listening. ❖

*The political turmoil in Iran followed by the fall of Mohammad Reza Shah Pahlavi in January 1979 led Carter administration officials to make a number of public pronouncements about the energy crisis. In February, Secretary of Energy James R. Schlesinger said, "The elimination of Iranian oil production has reduced world oil production by 5 million barrels a day." On March 19, President Carter held a widely discussed daylong meeting with some of his top advisers to discuss inflation and the energy crisis. On April 5, in a televised address on energy, President Carter warned that the United States was "dangerously exposed" to the disruption caused by Iran unexpectedly ceasing oil exports in the late fall of 1978.**

Oil
May 29, 1979

The gasoline shortage is like the weather these days. Everyone is talking about it but no one does anything about it.

I'll be right back.

During the Arab oil boycott in 1973–74 the lines at the oil stations were long and tempers were short. We've had a re-run of that situation HERE in Calif. and maybe before the summer is over it will happen in other states as well.

Summer is a time of heavy driving but it's also a time when refinerys are building up a reservoir of ~~fuel~~ *heating* oil for the winter that follows. At the moment they are behind schedule in that dept. If rumors were crude oil we'd have no problems.

Everyone seems to be looking for someone to blame. But where to begin. Well there is the Fed. allocation system. The Arabs & Iran have all reduced the amount of oil they are pumping so ~~the~~ *our* govt. has reduced each states allotment ~~by~~ to a percentage of what they were getting last year.

In doing that they overlooked something. Some states have fewer people & hence fewer cars than they had last year. And some states like Calif. for instance have ~~thou~~ hundreds of thousands of new citizens & 10's of 1000's of

* See "Iran General Vows to Reinstate Order," *The New York Times*, November 19, 1978, p. 21; Terence Smith, "Carter Discusses Oil and Inflation with Top Aides," *The New York Times*, March 20, 1979, p. A1; and Richard Halloran, "Carter Figures on Big Oil Shortfall at Issue," *The New York Times*, April 9, 1979, p. D4.

additional automobiles. That's why business seems normal in other states while motorists spend 4 hours in line out here waiting to buy 10 gals. of gas.

Then there is a refinery shortage due to environmental regulations. There is the case reported by UPI a short time back; Jack Evans applied for permission to build a refinery in Portsmouth Va. in 1969. It is now 1979—10 yrs. & $7 mil. later. The money went for environmental impact statements & legal fees. He still dosen't have permission to build the refinery.

Then there is the ~~dema~~ increasing demand for unleaded gas as more & more cars are equipped with smog control devices—federally ~~authorized.~~ *mandated.* It takes more oil to produce unleaded gas, and the unleaded gas dosen't give as ~~much mileage~~ *many miles* per gal. And incidentally unleaded refinery capacity has not been allowed to grow to meet demand. Ask Jack Evans.

It's easy to look at the big oil companies and blame them but can we be sure we'd have the right target? I know their profit picture has been improving still when you buy a gal. of gas the Fed. govt. get's 10 times as much from your dollar as does the oil co. and *the* OPEC *countries* gets 17x as much.

Now the Environmental Protection Agency has dreamed up some new regulations. ~~that~~ *They* will take a lot of oil industry money that might better be spent exploring for new oil. Drilling mud, oil production brines & crude oil residue are to be classified *BY E.P.A.* as "hazardous waste." Total cost of that decision would come to about $6 Bil. more than our entire bill for imported oil—somewhere around $45 bil. a year.

One thing does seem very clear—if we could produce more domestic oil and thus reduce our dependency on Arab oil we might find that Arab oil ~~was~~ suddenly had a lower price. We'd also find the lines *of cars* had disappeared from around our gas stations.

This is RR Thanks for listening. ❖

Chapter 14 of the New Jersey Code of Criminal Justice states: "An actor is guilty of sexual assault if he commits an act of sexual contact with a victim who is less than 13 years old and the actor is at least four years older than the victim." Some people, like Ronald Reagan, were appalled by this law.

Sex Education
May 29, 1979

This commentary will be ~~something of~~ a correction of something I said recently but it may also be a shocker for you as it was for me.

I'll be right back.

Not too long ago in talking about Sex ed. in our schools I mentioned (if I remember correctly) that someone had recommended lowering the age of consent to 13 yrs. Let me correct that statement. ~~No one ha *Some*~~ Someone didn't

JUST suggest it. It's a part of the 212 page criminal code signed into law last Aug. in the state of New Jersey. It has just been discovered by a N.J. ~~peace~~ *POLICE* officer who sounded the alarm.

The new law reads that age of consent for sexual intercourse is lowered to 13 and even lower if there is less than 4 yrs. difference *in age* between children having sex.

The purpose of the change was to exempt consenting youngsters from statutory rape charges while strengthening ~~prof~~ protections for actual rape victems according to the 2 feminist groups who drafted the legislation. Spokespersons for the groups said, "A rape prosecution is too high a price to pay for adolescent sexuality." They also said this brought the law up to date with the sexual habits of teenagers; "that" quote, "many parents dont *KNOW OR* want to admit it, but the number of sexually active teenagers is increasing rapidly."

In fairness let me say these spokespersons evidently were not representative of many in the feminist groups who were not aware they were sponsoring such a law. Remember it was in a 212 page bill—Chapter 14 section 2 C:14-2.

In fact it had slipped by many of the legislators who had voted yes and who now have introduced a bill to repeal the provision.

But it was the parents, the clergy, the NAACP and other groups who manned the ramparts. One father said, "I look at my 13 yr. old & other youngsters and I just cant see that they can handle sex emotionally."

Ironically this slipped through a legislature that is considering raising the legal drinking age from 18 to 19 or 20.

But in all of the furor and understandable distress of parents one thing should warm the hearts of all of us. God bless the wisdom that often goes with youth.

An 8th grader said; "I'm against the law. A lot of kids who didn't do it before are going to try it now—it's like giving them permission. And if they get pregnant who's going to marry a 13 yr. old?"

A teacher held a discussion of the law in her class when the publicity about ~~the law~~ it had made it a subject of general conversation. ~~She reported that~~, "The kids said they weren't ready for that kind of responsibility," she reported and then added this wonderful line. "And they were surprised there were adults who thought they were."

Well as someone once said, "some people grow up and some people just grow older."

This is RR Thanks for listening. ❖

Student unrest at U.C. Berkeley hit its zenith in early 1969 when protests mounted as the university sought to wrest control of the university-owned People's Park from students and squatters. On May 15, the rioting became bloody and local law enforcement officials were unable to control the situation. Reagan was governor of California at the time, and upon the advice of local law enforcement and university officials, he called upon the National Guard. For more than two weeks, the National Guard helped quell the crisis.

People's Park I
May 29, 1979

On May 15th ~~a few weeks ago~~ an anniversary was observed in Berkeley Calif. It was marked by a subtle re-writing of history. I'll be right back.

~~On May 15th 1969 violence erupted on & near the campus of the U. of Calif. at Berkeley.~~

A few weeks ago the press reported that about 150 people gathered on the campus of the U. of Calif. at Berkeley to observe what was called the 10th. anniversary of the "Peoples Park." Nothing was reported as to the makeup of the group or what was said at the occasion.

At least one of Calif's. largest newspapers however printed a piece by the former owner of a Berkeley bookstore ~~Mr.~~ Fred Cody. Mr. Cody's article was a nostalgic memorial to that day, May 15th 1969 when the ~~long~~ several years of campus ~~rioting~~ *rioting* in Berkeley acheived a new peak of violence resulting in ~~one~~ death for one person * & blindness for another.

Cody mentions that. ~~b~~*B*ut from there on his memory ~~must~~ *seems to* have been pretty vague because his account of that tragic day ~~does~~ *is* not supported by historical fact.

Describing the property owned by the U. as a "kind of no mans land—a muddy, junk strewn parking lot," he said hundreds of students and others tried to beautify it by planting flowers, trees, etc. *In* ~~Q~~*q*uoting a Prof. as saying this was, "a beautiful example of spontaneous community effort to improve it's ecology," he may have been accurate. There were faculty members at the time who looked kindly on any effort to disrupt campus & community life.

But then Mr. Cody tells of the University fencing off the property, the ensuing struggle that resulted in the tragedys I've mentioned, ~~&~~ the arrest of thousands & injury to additional hundreds. I dont dispute these figures but there is a subtle switch of good guys & bad guys in the way the events are described. "Police discharged "shot guns loaded with buckshot" into the crowd of protestors." Demonstrators on the campus were sprayed with tear gas from a low flying helicopter." And then he adds that, "the precedent had been set for the fatal shootings soon to come at Ohio's Kent State and at Jackson State in Miss."

I come in for some personal attention in Mr. Cody's article. "To many, in-

* James Rector of San Jose was shot by one of the sheriff's deputies and died from his wounds. See Lou Cannon, *Reagan* (New York: G. P. Putnam's Sons, 1982), p. 152.

cluding an angry Gov. Ronald Reagan, Peoples Park seemed an act of revolutionary insurrection aimed at subverting property rights. As such it was to be put down savagely, lest the youthful rebels capture Berkeley and make it a "liberated zone," a citadel of a nat. youth revolution." He goes on to say "the nat. guard occupied Berkeley for several weeks. *(They weren't there that long.)*

There is no question ~~th~~ but that the riot over the so called "Peoples Park" was an event ~~report~~ of national interest. But when Cody refers to it as an almost "romantic memory" and says it "remains—quietly & stubbornly—still a symbol of the city's legacy of unorthodoxy & dissent," he is asking for a rebuttal. And since ~~we~~ I'm out of time today—the rebuttal will be given on the next commentary. ~~Liste~~ *Tune in, same station, sametime.* This is RR Thanks for listening. ❖

People's Park II
May 29, 1979

Instalment 2 coming up on the "Peoples Park" episode of 10 yrs. ago in Berkeley Calif. and the attempt now to re-write hist. I'll be right back.

On the last commentary I discussed an article which appeared on the 10th anniversary of the tragic & ugly "Peoples Park" riot at the U. of Calif. Berkeley. One person died & ~~ano~~ *another* was blinded on that terrible May 15th. Hundreds were injured.

Here is the truth about that riot. The U. had acquired a piece of property ~~across the street from~~ *a few blocks from ~~the~~* the campus. The intention was to develop it as an outdoor recreational field for the students.

Berkeley had attracted a colony of squatters known as the "Street People." They aligned themselves with the radical dissenters on the campus. Their current cause was that no one had the right to own land just because they'd bought it. The land ~~was~~ *according* to them belonged to everyone.

They homesteaded the U. property & defied ~~the U.~~ *~~it~~ the U.* to proceed with it's plans for development. The Chancellor met with & tried to reason with them and of course got nowhere. At the same time he was receiving countless complaints from the homeowners neighboring on the Park. Their nights were made miserable by raucous all night parties complete with bonfires & bongo drum serenades. Their lawns were used for romance ~~&~~ as well as substitutes for the parks non-existent toilet facilities.

Housewives were afraid to use the sidewalks even in daylight hours and evidence was overwhelming that drug use among the squatters was commonplace.

May 15th was set as the day work would start on the recreational field. A fence was erected in the early morning hours. A noon time rally on the campus ended with the ~~emotio~~ cry, "on to the park!" ~~Several~~ *A mob of* 2000 ~~street~~

~~people & apparently~~ armed with broken chunks of concrete & foot long pieces of steel reinforcing rod, which were thrown end over end, with horrifying results swept down on the Berkeley police.

The officers never drew their guns and in a matter of seconds *75 of them* were on the pavement overrun by the mob. Sheriffs deputies had been held in reserve. Armed with shotguns they fired the lightest of birdshot into the mob as they came to the rescue of the downed police ~~&~~ more than 40 of whom had to be hospitalized.

The mob grew and spread out into the shopping areas near the campus. A reserve policemans car was overturned & ~~burn~~ *set* on fire. He was knocked down by the rock throwing mob & might have lost his life if he hadn't been rescued by citizens who dragged him into a bldg. *under a shower of rocks.*

It was late afternoon when I received a call from the Pres. of the U. who told me he was with the Mayor, the Sheriff & the Police Chief & they were unanimous in their belief they could no longer ~~protect~~ *guarantee the safety of* the citizens of Berkeley. They asked ~~for~~ *that* the Nat. Guard be sent in.

The "Peoples Park" is not, as the author of the news article said it was, "a romantic memory."

This is RR Thanks for listening. ❖

Marijuana
May 29, 1979

We all know about the drunken driver & hope we dont meet one on the highway. Now it seems we must also watch out for the pot smoking driver.

I'll be right back

Marijuana *SMOKING* has been decriminalized in 11 states and enforcement of anti-marijuana laws in the other 39 is lax or non-existent. This has probably contributed to the widespread belief among young people that pot, grass or weed as marijuana is called by it's users is really a harmless, mild intoxicant.

Surveys indicate that 1 out of 9 high school seniors are daily pot smokers. When those seniors entered high school 4 yrs. ago the rate among seniors was only 1 out of 20 or so. Of course the percentage of high school students who smoke marijuana less frequently than every day is far greater.

Now the Nat. Inst. of Drug Abuse has sounded a warning which has received far too little attention from the press. The Pot smoker who drives a car is a threat to himself or herself and to everyone else on the road. And the Inst. says 60 to 80% of the marijuana smokers they've questioned admit to driving while high on pot. I myself have had young people tell me they are actually better drivers when they've been smoking marijuana.

They are living in a dream world and that's not just a figure of speech. They think they are driving better but actual research has discovered their vision, memory span, attention, skill & tracking ability are all impaired. They imagine they are holding a steady course in the proper lane when in truth they are weaving from one lane to another.

A Prof. of psychiatry at the U. of British Columbia conducted actual driving tests with 64 individuals all of whom had had experience in smoking marijuana. A third were asked to smoke 1 joint, a third smoked 2 joints and the rest smoked a harmless fake. They were all put in cars with dual controls and an observer in each car *and asked* to drive a closed course. Those who had smoked a single joint showed a ⅓ decline in driving skills. Those who had smoked twice as much had a 55% decline.

Then they drove a 16 mile route through the heavy traffic downtown area—again with someone ready on the dual controls. They were ~~judged as~~ *rated on* the basis of taking ~~a~~ *the* ~~drivers for~~ *examination* for a drivers license. Here the low dose group had a 42% decline in skill, the higher dosage group a 63% decline. *The* Observers noted ~~their~~ *a* failure to ~~observe~~ *see* signals, stoplights etc. *& an* unawareness of pedestrians and stationery vehicles.

Significant also was the fact that several hours after smoking pot when the subjects ~~had no se~~ *no longer had a* feeling of being high their driving skills were *STILL* impaired~~.~~ *&* There was a lingering effect as much as 24 hours later.

Readers Digest in the May issue* did an article on these tests and others and concluded with the warning that states should enact laws to deal with marijuana intoxicated drivers. At present only 2 states, Alaska & Minn. have any such laws. The article also recommended an educational campaign including brochures to be distributed at gas stations, spot ads on radio etc. *pointing out that it's "dangerous to drive stoned."*

The author of the article Peggy Mann tells of a driving instructor who gave a marijuana joint to a student driver "to relax." The Calif. Dept. of Justice has made a study of Highway Patrol arrests and found a vast increase in the number of traffic violators who are intoxicated by marijuana.

This is RR Thanks for listening. ❖

Crime
May 29, 1979

We've had a lot of theorizing about crime & punishment and we still have a lot of crime. Maybe we should take a longer look at punishment.

I'll be right back.

I know that I've given reports on these commentaries of studies linking crime *directly* to the lack of punishment. The studies have been sound. ~~and~~

* Peggy Mann, "Marijuana and Driving: The Sobering Truth," *Reader's Digest,* Vol. 114. No 685, May 1979, p. 106.

~~*r*Reverse studies indicating that crime rates fall when punishment is swift &~~ severe confirm the other studies.

Why then cant we act on this research? Columnist Pat Buchanan has collected several recent incidents that make one wonder if anyone weeps for the victems of crime. Plea bargaining which reduces the sentence in order to avoid a costly trial, judges granting probation, mental hospitals releasing the criminally insane—possibly to free up a bed, all of these ~~of~~ things add up to more victems.

Picture this scene as if it were on TV. A man holds a knife to a womans throat while he robs her. Then he throws her off the subway *platform* on to the tracks below, breaking both her legs. Still she manages to pull herself back on to the platform. He kicks her in the face sending her reeling back on the tracks where she is almost crushed by an onrushing train.

He is arrested and allowed to plead guilty ~~of~~ to robbery instead of attempted murder. He can be out on another subway platform in 4 yrs. *He had done the same thing to a 90 yr. old man but was released because of inadequate identification.*

In Calif. a man was sentenced in 1975—15 yrs. to life for a 2 hour horror scene in which he raped a young lady twice, pressed a carving knife to her throat & sexually abused her in a depraved & brutal manner.

Last year the State Sup. Ct. decided he had not inflicted great bodily harm on her—he'll be back on the streets next year. Incidentally a year before the crime I just described he had plead guilty to a sexual assault on an 8 yr. old girl. He was given probation—that's why he was free to commit the crime in 1975.

Another Californian was convicted in 1974 of 2 separate ~~sexual~~ assaults on children for which he spent 16 months in a mental hospital. Six months after they let him out he committed a sexual assault & this time went to prison—for 22 months. He was paroled and now stands accused of 20 counts of kidnapping, rape and assault in connection with 2 child molestation incidents *just* last winter.

In Wash. D.C. a man is charged with stabbing & strangling an 18 yr. old girl. At the time of his arrest for this crime he was on parole from a Fed. prison in Fla. and *also* free on his "personal recognizance" from the District of Columbia jail, having been arrested for larceny.

I have just reported the crimes of 4 individuals. The total number of victems is 12. Had these 4 law breakers been in prison for their first convictions 8 of their 12 victems would not have been harmed.

It's almost as if we're opening the cages at the zoo and turning the wild animals loose. That isn't fair though—the animals would probably leave us alone if we didn't bother them.

This is RR Thanks for listening. ❖

Vietnam War
May 29, 1979

Not everyone is applauding the ~~ac Motion Pic.~~ Academy Award recognition given to the movie "The Deerhunter." I'll be right back.

The Oscar was given on Academy Award Night to the motion picture "The Deer Hunter." I'm sure you all know the movie deals with the Vietnam war. If you haven't seen it then possibly you dont know that it is ~~the~~ *a* story of friendship among young men; that it certainly does not glorify war bu~~t it~~ *although it* is unashamedly patriotic and it dosent ~~preach a sermon about calling~~ *call* down punishment on the U.S. for being in that war.

It is this last point that has caused some ~~among us~~ to withhold congratulations for it's award of the Oscar. Those who in the 1960's & early '70's saw no virtue in anything America did and only nobility of purpose on the part of North Vietnam cannot of course accept any story about that war which doesn't follow that theme.

Indeed they cant accept the truth let alone a fictional version. I wish some one in the world of TV or the movies would do a film about the men who endured captivity for 6, 8 & 10 years in the Hanoi Hilton as it was called or any of the other Communist torture camps.

Capt. John McCain U.S. Navy spent 6 yrs. in the hands of the North Vietnamese. One day he was told he was to meet an "American Actress" who was for peace. Recognizing a propaganda trick he refused. He was beaten, ~~&~~ starved, ~~and~~ finally put in an unventilated box 5 ft. long & 2 ft. wide and kept there for 4 steaming summer months.

If the producing gentry in Hollywood want to follow up on the Deer Hunters success there is plenty of material at hand. Scott Blakey has written a book called "Prisoner At War—The Survival of Commander Richard A. Stratton." It's published by Anchor Press/Doubleday.*

Dick Stratton was a prisoner more than 6 yrs. His story is one of love as well as war; Of a wife who never lost hope. And it's the story of dozens if not hundreds of the men who were his fellow prisoners. There are amazing tales revealed for the first time. One such concerns Admiral Jeremiah Denton.

If you remember that long night** when we all watched TV waiting for the ~~rel~~ landing at Clark field in the Phillipines of that 1st plane bringing our

* Scott Blakey, *Prisoner at War: The Survival of Commander Richard A. Stratton* (Garden City, NY: Anchor Press/Doubleday, 1978).

** The first group of American POWs released from Vietnam as part of the January 27, 1973, Paris agreement touched down at the Clark Air Base in the Philippines during the early morning hours of February 12, 1973. Naval Captain Jeremiah A. Denton, Jr. was the senior ranking officer among the men and was the first one off the plane. Denton was mentioned again in President Reagan's January 26, 1982, State of the Union address as a "hero," and served in the U.S. Senate (R–Alabama, 1981–1987).

P.O.W.'s home, Jeremiah Denton was the 1st man we saw. He made his way down the ramp, saluted the flag & thanked us for bringing them home.

You might not remember that you had seen him a few years before on TV when his captors forced him through torture to be filmed telling us how well they were all being treated. He stood there before the microphone his eyes blinking in the ~~TV~~ harsh TV lights. But now ~~we~~ *thanks to Scott Blakeys book we* know it wasn't the lights that made him blink.

~~His blinking spelled~~ *He was spelling* out in Morse Code the word "tortured" over & over again.

When the film was played on network TV in America a Naval Intelligence officer recognized & read the message. Naturally this had to be kept secret while our men were still prisoners.

You'll learn a lot from the book and you'll get a little impatient with those who dont like pictures that dont hate America.

This is RR Thanks for listening. ❖

Nuclear Power
June 29, 1979

D-C 10's have replaced Three Mile Island as the source of panic in our daily ration of news but the anti-nuclear forces are still beating their drums.

I'll be right back.

Several weeks ago our modern day Luddites were out in full force. For those who dont know, the Luddites were people who wanted to stop the industrial revolution back in the last century. They took to the streets and tried to smash factory machinery then.

Todays Luddites are against generating electricity by the use of Nuclear ~~energy~~ *generators*. I'm quite sure many of them are sincerely motivated and truly believe there is great danger to mankind in the developement of nuclear energy for peaceful purposes.

I'm also sure many of them aren't aware that the whole anti-nuclear movement is infiltrated by ~~the~~ *SOME OF THE* same disruptive elements who sent so many young people into the streets to riot during the Vietnam war. We are naive indeed if we think that day of worldwide anti-nuclear demonstrations several weeks ago just happened by accident. There were disturbances and violence in West Germany, France, Spain and I dont know how many other countries besides the dozen or so demonstrations here in the U.S.

I said the movement was worldwide but I have to qualify that. There were no such demonstrations behind the Iron Curtain. "Nuclear Power not only gives mankind the key to a practically limitless source of energy, but also means the creation of one of the most modern branches of industry which significantly contributes to the development of science & technology."

Now who do you suppose said that? Well it was Soviet Prime Minister Alexei Kosygin who was in Prague to ~~+~~ *see* the 1st Czechoslovakian nuclear power station go into full operation. That was in May. Earlier & by coincidence on the same day as the Three Mile Island accident the Soviet U. Czechoslovakia, Poland & Hungary signed an agreement to start a huge new plant in the Ukraine.

Industrial output is directly proportionate to the energy supply a nation has available. Both Czechoslovakia & East Germany hope to be getting 40% of their electrical power from Nuclear generators by 1990. That's only 10 years & a few months down the road. Restrictions in our country are such that if we started a new plant tomorrow it couldn't be operating by 1990. Incidentally there w~~as~~*ere* no news stories about Three Mile Island in the Soviet controlled press.

I dont have the figures on how many nuclear generators are operating in the Soviet U. itself but there are 4 in E. Germany & 4 more planned, Romania has ordered ~~5~~ *4* from Canada, Bulgaria has 2, Hungary is building it's 1st and Czechoslovakia is to build 4 more.

If the U.S. were producing 40% of it's electricity from nuclear generators we would be almost ~~totally~~ independent of ~~outside of~~ the OPEC oil cartel if not totally so. What a hole that would make in our imbalance of trade and inflation.

As I said before I'm sure many of our anti-nuclear protestors are sincere. I just cant help but wonder why they dont stage some demonstrations in E. Germany, or Czechoslovakia or Russia for that matter.

This is RR Thanks for listening. ❖

Molecules
June 29, 1979

Very frankly ~~bet~~ todays commentary has been cribbed from another radio broadcast.

I'll be right back.

On May 1st the news broadcast on WIBC Indianapolis carried a story that more Americans should hear. If you are a listener to that station and by chance missed it stay tuned. I think you'll be interested.

In all my commenting about the foibles & follies of burocracy I dont think I've ever compared burocrats to children. I like children. But we all know that idle hands can tempt youngsters into mischief. Could that be the excuse for the govt. shenanigans reported on that May 1st broadcast?

The Indiana Farm Bureau struck oil in Gibson County about 2 years back. And as so often happens got natural gas along with the oil. "Citizens Gas" of Indianapolis contracted to buy the gas. Since there was no pipeline, Texas Gas

Transmission Co. agreed to use it's pipes providing connecting ~~fedder~~ feeder lines were built.

Enter the govt. The gas well is in Ind., the gas was to be shipped in Ind., sold in Ind. and used in Ind. But Texas Gas Transmission is an ~~intra~~ interstate carrier. The Fed. govt. stopped the ~~sale~~ sale claiming it had the right to regulate it.

The Farm bureau in Gibson Co. established that it would put X number of cubic ~~ftt~~ ft. of gas into the pipe line each day and take the same number of cubic ft. out each day in Indianapolis. Therefore there would be no shipping of this gas across statelines even though the pipeline ~~was~~ is used for interstate shipments.

The Fed. govt. said it was true that you *could* accurately measure the *amount of* input and outtake of ~~the~~ gas but ~~that~~ there was no way to be sure that the actual molecules of gas taken out were the same molecules that were put in. And horrors of horrors some of the molecules put into the pipe in Gibson Co. might stray past Indianapolis and thus cross a state line.

Silly as it sounds the govt. was demanding that it had regulatory power because there was no way to be sure that the exact same gas would be removed from the pipe in Indianapolis.

The Farm Bureau had no other way to move the gas & no storage facility so for almost 2 years it burned off $10,300 worth of gas a day.

Comes now the end of story. The govt. finally gave in. The Farm Bureau prepared to lay a feeder pipe across the bottom of the White river. The Army Corps of Engineers has said no because a Prof. claims there might be an endangered species of mussel in the 12 ft. wide ~~strip~~ section of river the pipe is supposed to go in. The Prof. has searched the section 7 times without finding one of the endangered mussels but he's going to keep on trying.

So ends this tale of Molecules & Mussels.

This is RR Thanks for listening. ❖

A month before the next two broadcasts were taped, an "Open Letter to the Socialist Revolution of Vietnam" by Joan Baez, the famed folk singer and civil rights activist, appeared in major American newspapers, including the The New York Times. Later in 1979, Baez traveled to Southeast Asia to investigate reports about the treatment of people under Communist rule. On October 30, she met with President Jimmy Carter at the White House to discuss relief aid for Southeast Asian refugees.

Joan Baez I
June 29, 1979

Memories of the tragic & Violent '60s are being revived by one individual whose forthrightness may correct some misunderstandings of that era.

I'll be right back.

Back in the '60s when our campuses were in turmoil & a quarter of a mil. demonstrators disrupted the business of govt. in the nation's capital, singer Joan Baez was a prominent figure in the Anti Vietnam war movement.

Today Miss Baez may be making a major contribution to better understanding of that *TRAGIC* decade. Some of us at the time insisted that while many in the so called peace movement were sincere there were others who were using it to further ~~other~~ *different* and longer range goals.

By her recent actions Miss Baez has proven that she was sincere in her anti-war activism. ~~She has been disturbed~~ *DISTURBED* by the stories coming out of Communist Vietnam—stories of persecution by the North Vietnamese conquerors she once thought of as liberators, Joan Baez is ~~speaking up for~~ ~~*calling for*~~ condemning the Hanoi govt. for it's inhumanity. She serves as Pres. of the Humanitas/International Human Rights Committee and in that capacity ~~she~~ took out full page ads in 5 major newspapers on May 30th demanding an end to the imprisonment & torture of innocent men, women & children in Vietnam.

Joan did more. She mailed out to reporters & columnists packets of material documenting her charges against the communist regime, including in it a map pinpointing the location of the prisons & torture camps. She has appeared on ~~#~~ nat. television and has been joined by ~~some but definitely not all of~~ *a few—but only a few* of her former associates in the anti war movement.

Miss Baez is probably still a socialist in her political leanings and possibly hasn't changed her mind about our participation in the war but she *NO LONGER* has any illusions about the communist conquerors of S. Vietnam.

By her own admission it took some time for her to accept the reality of what was going on. The first horror stories out of South East Asia found her trying not to believe them but she didn't close her mind. She sought the truth.

Probably the final proof came from Dr. Tran Xuan Ninh who later appeared with her on a national press conference. The Dr. had spent 27 months in one of the re-education camps where he witnessed the torture and beatings of his fellow prisoners. He bribed his way out of the camp and with his family escaped Vietnam by boat. While only a few hours from safety in the Philippines his youngest child and only son died in his arms.

Joan Baez took her facts to Vietnams ambassador to the U.N. and asked him to let a team of neutral observers go to S. Vietnam. He refused on the grounds that this would be an interference in Vietnams internal affairs.

On the next commentary I'd like to tell of some of those in the antiwar movement who apparently had other causes they served and who have refused to help Miss Baez.

This is RR Thanks for listening. ❖

Joan Baez II
June 29, 1979

This is instalment 2 about the efforts of former anti-war protestor Joan Baez to get help for the victems of communist cruelty. I'll be right back.

On the last commentary I spoke of singer, and one time anti-war activist Joan Baez and how she has come to realize that communist N. Vietnam is guilty of the utmost in inhumane treatment of the S. Vietnamese people.

She published an open letter ~~accusing~~ *in which she* said the facts, "form a grim mosaic" of torture & terror. "People disappear & never return; people are shipped to re-education centers, fed a starvation diet of stale rice, forced to squat ~~hours~~ bound wrist to ankle, suffocated in boxes; People are used as human mine detectors, clearing live mine fields with their hands & feet. For many life is hell & death is prayed for."

Joan has asked help in her present mission of mercy from those who were once allied with her in the anti-war movement. Her 2 letters to Jane Fonda have gone unanswered.

Nothing has made it more clear that some of the one time anti-war leaders were less sincere than Miss Baez; that indeed they perhaps had a cause that went beyond peace, than the response to her open letter by Wm. Kunstler, well known lawyer & activist in New Left causes.*

Kunstler calls her open letter, "a cruel & wanton act." Tens of thousands of Vietnamese, men women & children put to sea in boats to escape the cruelty of their communist tormentors even though they know the odds are ~~50 / 50~~ 50/50 they'll die. Mr. Kunstler excuses this by saying, "the sudden release of long pent-up emotions can easily result in regrettable instances of the denial or subversion of fundamental rights & liberties." And then he says these "violations of human rights are not relevant to this discussion."

What discussion does Mr. Kunstler refer to? Well he says that excoriating Vietnam for this slaughter of the innocents serves "to divide the left over an absolutist mythology at precisely the moment when the near tragedy at Three Mile Island seems to be pulling it together." In other words the new left party line is now "anti-nuclear power" and like the Vietnam war it can be used to decieve sincere people into helping the new left influence American policy once again.

Let me remind you there is no anti-nuclear movement behind the iron curtain where any number of nuclear power plants are being constructed.

When Joan Baez called Daniel Ellsburg** and asked him to sign her human

* William Kunstler.

** Daniel Ellsberg, an analyst at the Defense Department, leaked to the press the classified *Pentagon Papers* about U.S. decision making related to the Vietnam War.

rights letter, he gave her a pitch about her "future in the anti-nuclear movement."

These people who reveal that the anti-war movement was only a means to an end now have another means to an end—anti-nuclear power. Is it to much to ask what the end really is? Or is that pretty evident without asking?

This is RR Thanks for listening. ❖

Corruption

June 29, 1979

Our faith in govt. has been tried, tested & undoubtedly eroded by changes of corruption among elected officials. We'd better widen our view.

I'll be right back.

These last few years have made it difficult to urge morality on our sons & daughters. Never has there been less respect for our basic institutions. No little share of the blame for this goes to the numerous cases of & charges of corruption in high places in govt. particularly among elected officials.

But now comes word of a more direct form of corruption—outright theft and not at the exec. level. Is it perhaps indicative of a general decline in moral standards ≠ that millions of dollars worth of property & office equipment is being stolen from govt. offices on a daily basis?

The General Services Admin. says theft from govt. offices is general throughout the country but most severe in Wash. Last year in the Wash. area theft of both Fed. property & personal possessions of Govt. employees totaled some 3000 items valued at more than ½ a mil. dollars.

Those who pilfer are expected to do better this year based on first quarter figures. From Jan. through March in our Nations Capital alone more than 1250 items valued at $277,000 were stolen from govt. offices.

If you are curious about just what is being taken they aren't items you can slip in your lunch box or pocket. The loot includes electric typewriters, calculators—not just the pocket ~~size~~ kind but the expensive desk size ones; *and* automobiles. The personal possessions of employees range from fur coats & radios to handbags.

No dept. or agency is exempt not even our top law enforcement agency ~~in the land~~ the U.S. Justice dept. One can wonder about our national security TOO and protection against theft of defense secrets when the Pentagon has to admit to theft of 79 typewriters, 68 calculators and 44 personal items—most of them in the month of Jan. alone.

Even the C.I.A. is included but H.E.W. and the Dept. of Agriculture top the list. Maybe AT H.E.W. they are so used to giving things away it just comes naturally.

Blame for the crime wave ~~is~~ *has* been laid BY SOME on Congress which

~~have~~ *has* stressed an open building policy to make public bldgs. more accessible. Other officials say the need is for more security personnel. That dosen't hold up very well because the best guarded bldgs. have the highest rate of theft.

No one pretends this theivery is the result of breaking & entering which leaves us with the ugly thought that Fed. employees who average about $4000 a year more in income than the ~~rest~~ average worker are to blame. But let us be careful not to blanket indict. I'm sure the overwhelming majority of public emp's. are honest—indeed are victems of some of the crime themselves.

Surely someone can come up with a system for aprehending a thief walking out of a building with an electric typewriter under his arm.

This is RR Thanks for listening. ❖

Assembly Line Medicine I

July 9, 1979

Can medical care be delivered like groceries or luggage at an airport on a conveyor belt and still be good medical care? I'll be right back.

From time to time on these commentaries I've taken issue with the advocates of nationalized health insurance which is the title used for compulsory socialized medicine. Some time ago* I called attention to Sen. Kennedy's attempt to use ~~Canidas~~ Canadas national health plan as proof that such plans are better than our own pluralistic system.

Now with 2 plans for govt.health care, the Senators and the Presidents, up for consideration by the Congress, some further information about the Canadian plan might be in order.

In 1953 the province of Manitoba suffered the worst epidemic of polio to ever hit any part of the North American continent. Polio of course is a catastrophic illness and an epidemic such as struck Manitoba left families totally destitute. There was no denying the need for some kind of community help for catastrophic cases.

Manitoba until 1969 had a fairly successful medical insurance plan run entirely by the medical profession. It offered unlimited medical & surgical care, laboratory tests, xrays, drugs, ambulance ~~etc.~~ *service,* nursing care and physical checkups. And of course free choice of Dr. It covered 65% of the population.

In 1969 this plan was ordered disbanded by the govt. of Canada which had introduced a program of compulsory, universal care. F.S. Manor writing in the

* See "Patent Medicine I," p. 405.

American Spectator* describes in detail what happened then. He calls the govt. program a conveyor-belt system administered through community clinics. These clinics consist of "all powerful administrators, social workers, paramedics and a small number of salaried doctors doing shift work & restricted in the number of X-rays or laboratory tests they can order per day." And believe it or not the doctors are low men on the medical totem pole.

You arrive at the clinic as a patient. You are assigned to a social worker who determines whether you really need medical care or if it is all in your head. If the decision is that you probably do have some ailment you are turned over to a paramedic. This individual decides whether it's something he or she can treat or whether you should see a doctor. If you do see a doctor he or she diagnoses your case and makes an appointment for treatment. But treatment may be by a doctor you've never seen before because your appointment happens to fall on his or her shift.

Now obviously this whole procedure is backward. Your first interview should be with a trained doctor who decides whether you need a doctors care, whether a paramedic can handle your case or whether you just need to be talked to by a social worker. The system is backward because it's cheaper that way. The top men on the totem pole—the administrators have ruled that the conveyor belt will run backwards.

This is RR Thanks for listening ❖

Free Speech for Business?
July 9, 1979

Not long ago the Supreme Ct. ruled that corp's. are entitled to the right of free speech. Can a corp. speak it's mind in public? I'll be right back.

Recently one of our major corp's. produced 3 ~~commercials~~ *messages* for television drawing attention to 3 issues they felt were of major concern to the people of America.

I'd like to read you the scripts for these ~~commercials.~~ *messages*. The 1st dealt with free enterprise and the voice over the picture said; "Is free enterprise an endangered species? How much govt. regulation is enough? Is business bad just because it's big? Or does a country like ours require a diversity of business—both big & small? Will excessive control over big business lead to control over all our business? The answers are up to you. Whatever your views let your elected representatives know. People, one by one, need to speak up now. You can help keep free enterprise free." Then followed the corp's. signoff with a tag line added, "One person can make a difference.

* F.S. Manor, "Wheelchairs and Bedpans: Canada on the Move," *American Spectator* Vol. 12 No. 7, July 1979, p. 26.

The second commercial had to do with the energy crisis. The announcers voice over delivered this msg. "Some people are calling the energy crisis a hoax. Others say that at the rate we're using up our oil reserves we'll be down to our last drop in our childrens lifetime. Whoevers right, one thing is clear. America needs an energy plan for the future now. One that uses all ~~our~~ resources available from coal & nuclear power to solar. But we're only going to get it if people, one by one, demand it. Whatever your views, let your elected representatives know now. There's not much we can do when the light goes out."

Again there was the corp's. signoff & the tag line, "One person can make a difference."

Now if you are wondering why I'm reading these T.V. messages I'll explain right after this third and last one. It has to do with govt. red tape and opens with several voices overlapping, speaking the following lines: "Applications should be filled out in triplicate. Forms should be returned by the 19th or penalty charges. The Bureau requires all permits to. The Dept. must be notified. Send one copy to."

Then the [announcers] voice is heard saying; "Its red tape. In 1977, America spent $100 bil. on Fed. paperwork alone. And in the end we all pay for it. But if people ~~speak out,~~ one by one, start speaking out, we can begin untangling Americas knottiest problem. A message from Kaiser Aluminum. One person can make a difference."

Yes the corp. offering these messages was Kaiser Aluminum & Chemical corp. They submitted these to the 3 TV networks as commercials for which the corp. was, of course, willing to pay. The networks refused to put them on the air. There was nothing false, inaccurate or misleading about them. The networks said they were controversial or not acceptable material. One network cited the fairness doctrine, the F.C.C.'s requirement that a fair balance of opinion be presented on television. We're all agreed on that but for the life of me I find no threat to such a balance in the messages I've just read and which Kaiser was going to present as paid commercials.

Well to quote from the 2nd message if you think someones right of free speech was denied by the networks "let your elected representatives know now."

This is R.R. Thanks for listening. ❖

America
July 27, 1979

T'was Bobby Burns who said "if only we had the gift to see ourselves as others see us."

I'll be right back.

This commentary is going to be a condensed version of a love letter to America by a British Journalist, John Rosen who fell in love with this country at first sight. I'm sorry time wont permit all of his article but you'll get the idea.

Mr. Rosen writes; "You Americans are spoiled rotten. You dont know how good you've got it. ~~h~~*H*ere you are living in Paradise—all of you—in the Utopian States of America and all you ever do is gripe. ~~About everything~~.

Compare this magical ~~land~~ *country* of yours to any other place on planet earth. And in every case and from any angle this country comes out on top. Way on top.

Very few of you ever realize how incredibly lucky you are to live in this marvelous, magnificent country. The freedom is simply intoxicating. Theres precious little of it around the world and most of it is right here at your feet. But you Yanks take it all so much for granted.

Your cops are the friendliest, toughest, fastest, and most politely deferential defenders of your freedom of any cops in this galaxy. Yet all you do is bad mouth them. Go break the law anywhere else—and see what happens.

As I travel the suburbs, slums, cities, towns and farmlands of this most beautiful country in the world—people ask me what I think of the place. When I say it's the best place in the world I'm rewarded with suspicious looks. My crime? I dare to love America.

My qualifications for making such glowing statements about your country are the 85 other countries Ive been to.

The people here are the worlds friendliest, most hospitable, most outgoing individuals anywhere.

People in other countries have so much ≠ less to live with and to live for. They live out lives of quiet desperation and deprivation, no hopes, no dreams. Just their stomachs to worry about.

Only in America and no place else do you sometimes get a free refill for your coffee.

Only in America can you walk across the road. In every other country you run for your life.

Only in America can you get a drivers license the same day you decide you want it. In every other country "they" keep you waiting (sometimes years) and automatically flunk you unless you grease the mans palm with cold cash.

Only in America do the phones work, all the time. Only here do you get a bill telling you who you called, when you called & how much you pay for each call.

The minimum ~~wage~~ hourly wage is higher than the average daily wage in most countries and the average weekly wage in others.

So my American friends a word of loving advice.

Love what you've got here because there is nothing better anywhere. And remember—97% of the worlds people would like to trade places with you."

He's right you know.

This is RR Thanks for listening. ❖

Free Speech
July 27, 1979

One of the most common & often used truisms is that free speech does not ~~mean~~ give one the right to yell, "fire" in a crowded theatre. I'll be right back.

Let me start this commentary by stating a personal position I take on freedom of speech & press. I believe a free press is essential to liberty. I believe we all have the right to express our opinions and beliefs so long as we dont incite to riot, advocate violent overthrow of the govt. or impose ~~ourselves~~ *on the* rights of others. By that latter phrase I mean that freedom of speech shouldn't be taken ~~to as~~ *to mean we have* the right to shout our opinions under someones bedroom window at 3AM. or shout down a speaker who is expressing his.

But there is another qualifier on freespeech—call it a restriction if you will. Does freedom of speech mean we must guaranty an audience to anyone who wants to express an opinion? Personally I dont think so and I'm sure most of you dont.

Now all of this brings me to the point of expressing our opinion to elected officials. We can & do write to our state legislators, our Congressmen & Senators and yes Governors & the Pres. of the U.S. But should a very busy Congressional committee inviting testimony to aid it in recommending legislation have to listen to everyone who wants to express an opinion even if they ~~lack~~ *have no* expertise in the topic before the committee?

For that matter should the committee feel bound to invite testimony from special interest groups who could do as the rest of us do and write the committee a letter? I bring this up because a while back Ralph Nader appeared before a sub-committee of the House Interior Committee. If a John Doe citizen had written a letter to the committee advocating the same action Nader recommended I have a hunch his letter would have ended up in the wastebasket and a Sec. would have sent him routine form letter number 11.

Nader's pitch to the Congressmen was that Congress should scrap the 92 nuclear power plants presently under construction and the 70 plants already in operation producing the electricity we need. He waved off the billions of dollars this would cost as "a cheap price to pay compared to alternative risks," and added that the whole process should only take 2 or 3 years.

A man who is far better qualified to speak on this subject than Ralph Nader, Arthur Spitzer for whom the Chair of Energy & Management at Pepperdine U. is named ~~&~~ evaluated Ralphs testimony. He said: "It is easy for Ralph Nader to preach that he would rather live by candlelight instead of nuclear ~~ener~~ energy. Since he makes a living with this kind of preaching and he knows it will never happen, he can easily preach this kind of nonsense."

All of us are aware that there are risks and dangers inherent in nuclear power and we want the utmost in protective measures. We also look both ways before we cross a street. In short common sense is called for.

To put things in focus, Dr. Alvin Weinberg of Oak Ridge brought a Geiger counter to a committee room of the U.S. Senate. It registered higher radioactivity than escaped at Three Mile Island. The radioactivity comes from the granite building stones—just as we get radioactivity from sunshine or burning coal.

This is RR Thanks for listening. ❖

In 1977, Edward Schwartz and George St. Johns started Showcase U.S.A., *a news magazine. The first issue was published in January 1978.*

Showcase U.S.A.
July 27, 1979

This will be about a new kind of catalogue—another example of the virility of the free mkt. place.

I'll be right back.

There is something about a catalogue that grabs everyone. When we were kids we called them wish books. I've wondered now & then if we didn't have a secret weapon we've never used. What if we dropped umpteen million Sears catalogs on Russia? When the people there saw the kind of consumer goods available to those who worked & earned in a free society there would be another revolution.

Well this commentary is about a magazine not a catalogue but there is something of a relationship. There is also further evidence of the magic of the free mkt., this way of life that allows an individual to dream & turn that dream into a saleable commodity.

"Showcase U.S.A." is the magazine I'm talking about—the dream that became reality. It isn't on the news stands. It has a controlled circulation aimed at a particular reader list for whom it performs a most useful purpose.

A young man named George St. Johns is the publisher. ~~whose~~ His dream became a 6 issue a year magazine aimed at importers throughout the world who are interested in American exports. "Showcase U.S.A." brings *them* useful information on every facet of Americas export business.

A look at the index of the current issue indicates why this magazine fills an heretofore unmet need. There are articles on Trade Shows & Conventions, transportation featuring information on American Ports & shipping facilities. Others are titled "Small Business The Available Resource" & " "Expanding Trade for Small Business." There is another, "The Futures Mkt.; an Essential Trade Tool." ~~Those are just a few of the informative features~~

A couple of those titles reveal what could well be a new chapter in International trade, the entry of small & independent American businesses in the export ~~trade~~ mkt. Then there are sections—(permanent features of the publication) listing companies in export and an Industry roundup. In this latter are breif summaries of products available, separated into types such as commodities, foodstuffs, manufactured goods, consumer goods etc.

From the beginning publisher George St. John encouraged correspondence from his readers with regard to inquiries directed to American companies. He sees that the correspondence reaches the proper business or provides the answer such as sending a foreign executive a complete roster of companies making automotive air conditioners. ~~Th~~

This correspondence has led to a new feature in the magazine, "Trade Inquiries & New Products" which is published in cooperation with the Dept. of Agriculture & the U.S. Dept. of Commerce. Adding to the flavor of the magazine is the colorful & great variety of advertising ~~which~~ by American companies involved in export trade—another evidence of the free mkt. in action.

Showcase U.S.A. published in Woodland Hills Calif. a handsome and interesting magazine, filled with illustrations is performing a real service for buyer & seller ~~alike~~ alike. And isn't that what free enterprise is all about?

This is RR Thanks for listening. ❖

Reagan often did commentaries on a series of short subjects. This one mentions Proposition 13, which limited property taxes, and the all volunteer armed force.

Miscellaneous III
July 27, 1979

A few items today ranging from Prop. 13 to education & environment.

I'll be right back.

Getting out of Calif. into the other ~~50~~ 49 states I ~~frequently~~ FREQUENTLY am asked how Calif. has fared under our famous or notorious (depending on how you look at it) proposition 13.

You'll remember loud voices warned that every disaster short of Calif. sliding into the Pacific Ocean would follow passage of 13. Now Fortune magazine has turned it's considerable reporting ability to that question and provides the answer.

The several bil. dollar reduction in property taxes has resulted in a 14% increase in personal income. Consumer spending & retail sales rose by that same percent and while 17,000 govt. workers were laid off & 100,000 quit or retired 532,000 new jobs were created in the private sector. Govt. received an additional bil. dollars in business & sales taxes alone & the state ~~will~~ ended the fiscal year with a $3 bil. surplus. So much for the great Calif. disaster.

This next item is not so happy, but it does have to do with Calif. Yosemite

Nat. Park ~~is~~ has been described as one of the few spots in the world that completely lives up to it's advance billing for sheer beauty.

I recently received a letter from an old friend who backpacks into our high Sierras and therefore is a true environmentalist with real love for the beauty of this earth. He had just completed a 4 day hike in the high area of Yosemite, from Tuolomne meadows to Glen Aulin.

He wrote that he was appalled at the condition of the lodgepole pines. The needles are turning brown not only in the high country but on the valley floor as well. These trees have been attacked by an insect known as the Lodge Pole Pine Miner. If an effort isn't made to save those forests, the trees will die and much of the beauty of Yosemite will be gone.

There is a spray that will control those insects but so far the Forestry people are dragging their feet while the needles turn brown & fall from the trees. The environmentalists and the Earth people, vocal & well organized are opposed to the spraying of the trees. ~~and t T~~he Foresters apparently are intimidated.

One last item has to do with national defense and our all volunteer army. It seems the army is having trouble recruiting young men who can read. This is an expensive problem because the inability to read requires longer training. It is ~~mor~~ *a* serious problem for another reason. The army is about to introduce an entire generation of new, sophisticated mil. hardware that will require study by these men who cant read.

Now before you jump to the conclusion that dropouts & illiterates are being recruited—listen to this. The all volunteer army has the highest percentage of high school graduates of any army in ~~U.S.~~ *the* history of our nation. ~~This is~~ *Our* problem isn't the army—it's our schools.

This is RR Thanks for listening. ❖

On July 16, 1979, President Jimmy Carter addressed the nation on the energy crisis. He stated that he wanted to reform the nation's energy policy "even if it costs me another term," and emphasized the need for more domestic energy production. The president struck a pessimistic tone: "The true problems of our Nation are much deeper—deeper than gasoline lines or energy shortages, deeper even than inflation or recession." The problem facing the United States was, he said, "a crisis of confidence." The Washington Post *declared that President Carter had made "malaise a household word."* *

The Magic Money Machine
August 1979

With all the hassle over the Presidents energy speech of several weeks ago we may have overlooked it's possible impact on our wallets. I'll be right back.

* "Changing the Way Things Are," *The Washington Post*, July 15, 1979, p. E6.

The long delayed, Presidential energy address has come & gone, some weeks ago. ~~b~~*B*ut there may be costly echoes. He called for a windfall profits tax on the oil industry and made it sound as if no one but those quote, unquote greedy oil barons would have to pay.

A closer look at what he was proposing reveals that he would, if the Congress went along, have himself a magic money machine. The total take could amount to $146 bil. over a 10 yr. period. And no matter how many times they say it would be paid by the oil companies we should be asking, "where will the oil companies get ~~it?~~ $146 bil? The answer of course is from their customers & guess who they are. In other words, no matter how much we pretend ~~he~~ the Pres. has come up with a magic money machine the $146 bil. will be an added 146 bil. the govt. is removing from the private sector.

Now when our public servants see a windfall like that they just naturally prove the truth of a century old statement by the French statesman Bastiat;* "Public Funds seemingly belong to no one and the temptation to bestow them on someone is irresistable."

† The White House wants to use the money for an energy trust fund. But liberal do gooders in Congress want to use it for welfare. Other members (& we should be grateful for them) want it to substitute for an income tax cut. In other words our tax burden wouldn't be increased we'd just collect it in a different way.

Then someone realized the windfall tax would be an excise tax & therefore deductible in figuring the corporate income tax thus it wouldn't ~~gain~~ add a net 140 odd bil. $ to govt's. haul. Suddenly the Pres. countered with wanting to earmark part of the regular corporate tax for his pet program the energy trust fund.

Then some in the Congress decided to exempt some oils from taxes to restore incentive for exploring & finding the new oil we need. And who can quarrel with that?

I*f* ~~cant begin to follow the figures as~~ *we follow the figures closely enough* the 140 bil. becomes with one idea only 28 bil. and with another 2 or 3 times that much. Then there is a new proposal to use the tax to roll back Social Security taxes but that inspired someone to suggest a new conservation plan financed by the, by now not so magic money machine.

The battle will rage but hasn't everyone forgotten that we started out to find a way to ~~enco~~ encourage the discovery of more oil so as to reduce our dependence on ~~Arab oil?~~ the imported stuff? I have a feeling that if our govt. was as good at getting oil out of the ground as it is at getting money out of us we'd all be driving gas guzzlers with nothing to worry about except how to pay for them.

This is RR Thanks for listening

† *SORRY WE'RE FLYING THRU BUMPY WEATHER*** ❖

* Claude Frédéric Bastiat.

** Reagan drafted this commentary on a bumpy flight and was apologizing to his typist.

Power
August 1979

The dream that one day we can harness the sun & get rid of all our nuclear, coal & oil ~~*electric* generating~~ *fueled electric generating* plants is just that—a dream. I'll be right back.

The emotional campaign against nuclear power not only exaggerates the hazards of ~~gener~~ using such power to generate elecricity but is equally irrational in it's advocacy of Solar power as a substitute. This is the theme of a book authored by ~~a~~ Prof. Beckmann of the U. of Colorado entitled, "Why Soft Technology Will Not Be Americas Energy Salvation." *

Perhaps I should explain that "soft technology" is the term applied not only to the sun as an energy source but to others as well, geothermal, hydropower etc.

Now before you get a chip on your shoulder ~~regarding his~~ thinking the Prof. is writing off solar power entirely let me assure you that his book ~~ma~~ starts out by declaring that, "Solar energy is a good thing." And he advocates using it wherever it's practical. I think it's safe to say we all agree.

Quoting him, he says of solar power; "It can supplement more concentrated & more versatile sources of energy when only small amounts of energy are needed. It is well suited for residential space heating & cooling, & for domestic water-heating—certainly in Fla. & the SouthWest."

Here are some of the examples he uses to point up the reality of solar energy and it's limits. ~~It~~ Visualize the sun shining unobstructed and perpendicular on a collecting panel of about 11 sq. ft. That is what it takes to produce 1 kilowatt. Compare that to coal. It only takes *a little under* 1 pound of coal to ~~equal~~ *make* 1 kilowatt of electricity. That lump of coal held in the sun would cast a shadow of about 15 square inches. The sun would have to shine on that 15 inch square for almost 3 months out in the Ariz. desert where it shines 12 hours a day to produce 1 k.w. hour of energy.

Dr. Beckmann says the energy source which, per unit of energy produced, costs less in human lives & health than any other concentrated source is nuclear. ~~But beyond that~~ Then he draws another ~~paralell~~ comparison illustrating that solar energy would have a considerable environmental impact.

To construct a 1000 megawatt solar plant you'd assemble 35,000 tons of aluminum, 2 mil. tons of concrete, 600,000 tons of steel, 7,500 tons of copper, 75,000 tons of glass, 1,500 tons of chromium, titanium & other materials. All of that totals an amount of materials 1000 times greater ~~that~~ than the amount needed to build a coal-fired or nuclear plant that would produce the same power.

* Petr Beckmann, *Why "Soft" Technology Will Not Be America's Energy Salvation* (Boulder, CO: The Golem Press, 1979).

Prof. Beckmann suggests that proponents of "soft power" aren't just against nuclear power, they are against ~~any kind of~~ *an* increase in power *period.* They oppose dams for hydro-elec. power, off shore drilling for oil, pipelines and even geo-thermal development. One environmental group *actually* opposes geothermal operations within 1 mile of thermal pools, hot springs, mud pots etc. In other words they are for geothermal development anywhere except where there is ~~a~~ geothermal energy to be had. In ~~short~~ *other words* they are against growth. Dr. Petr Beckmann should be required reading. The title again; "Why Soft Technology Will Not Be America's Energy Salvation."

This is RR Thanks for listening. ❖

Food Stamps
August 1979

Some years ago a cabinet member told some irate citizens, "watch what we do not what we say." That's good advice. I'll be right back.

Energy & Salt II seem to be all that is concerning Wash. these days but that isn't true. Any number of special interest axes are being ground and *the* sieve through which our tax dollars are leaked away is being passed from hand to hand in the marble halls of govt.

Those halls, it is true, are resounding with the usual ~~rhetoric re~~ ~~*ret*~~ rhetoric about cutting budgets, fighting inflation and all the other things that became fashionable after Calif's. proposition 13 passed. But lets pay heed to "what they do not what they say."

For instance we should be more than a little concerned about what is being done to the food stamp program. Now food stamps are supposed to be an additional help to those who might not be able to afford a nutritional diet for themselves. And no one of us wants anyone in the land to go hungry. Food stamps exchangeable for groceries in the marketplace came into being in the 60's. They were free to some and purchasable by others depending on income but the cost could not exceed 30% of their value. And of course there were strict rules ~~that they~~ *that food stamps* could be used <u>only</u> to purchase staple foods. Remember that point please because in a moment I'll refer back to it.

In 1965 there were ~~400,000~~ less than half a mil. people receiving or buying food stamps and the budget for them was $35 mil. By 1977 there were 15 mil. recipients and a budget of $5.6 bil. There were also charges of extensive fraud. Official figures suggested at least ~~3 of~~ 3 mil. recipients were ineligible.

Congress declared the need for reform of the runaway program was imperative. So they reformed it. And what do you know—they made it easier to get food stamps & made them entirely free, ~~and~~ *there would* no longer *be* any charge for them.

Opponents of this kind of reform were thrown a fish to quiet their protests—a ceiling of ~~$6 + 6 Bil.~~ *a little over $6 bil.* was put on the budget for fiscal 1979. And, oh yes! there would be tighter certification of eligibility to crack down on fraud.

The burocrats over at the Dept. of Agriculture put the cancellation of any charge for the stamps into effect immediately. It took them several months to get around to any of the ~~other~~ provisions about tighter eligibility. Now the 15 mil. recipients have become 19 mil. The estimate for this year is that another 3½ mil. will be added. And that ~~6 and a fraction~~ $6 bil. dollar ceiling is now over $7 bil. There is also a projection that the program is $650 mil. in the red—so the White House is telling Congress they'll have to lift the ceiling or there will be a cutback which will result in hardship for the truly needy. This is an old welfare trick;—~~threate~~ a form of blackmail in which the elderly & infirm are held as hostages to extort more money from Congress.

All of this came from a supposed reform. I told you I'd refer back to the rule that food stamps can only be used to purchase food. In Mo. there is a theatre which runs mainly X rated, pornographic films. ~~It's marquet~~ It's lighted marquis reads "We accept food stamps."

This is R.R. Thanks for listening. ❖

Talking Back
September 11, 1979

Radio is a 2 way communications system as you find out if you do a commentary on current events. I'll be right back

Since Current Events are very often subject to debate, if not downright ~~controversial~~ *controversy* it's understandable that now and then I hear from some of you with regard to something I've reported.

For example someone recently called to my attention a ~~Wash.~~ Wash. Post headline *which* proclaim~~inged~~ ~~that~~; "Vaunted Taxpayer Revolt Only a Skirmish So Far." * Now possibly the paper was mistaking the summer doldrums for a let up in the fever that followed passage of Prop. 13 in Calif. I dont know. I do know I've done some commentaries on what has seemed to me ~~an~~ *to be* a new awareness on the part of people about govt. costs & high taxes.

Anyway I decided to do a tally sheet on what had happened around the country in the aftermath of Prop. 13. Thank Heaven Nat. Review magazine ** saved me from a research chore before I'd gotten too deeply involved. If the

*Art Pine, "Vaunted Taxpayer Revolt Only a Skirmish So Far," *Washington Post,* June 3, 1979, p. A8.
**"Sons of Proposition 13," *National Review,* July 20, 1979, p. 903.

Wash. Post can call ~~the~~ what has happened "~~a~~ *only* a skirmish"—the Chi. fire was a backyard cookout.

Here is the aftermath of Prop. 13; Idaho & Nevada *have* limited prop. taxes to 1% of mkt. value. Six states Kansas, Maryland, Ind., Ark., Miss. & Vermont lowered their inc. tax. Another 5, Ala., Mass., Mo., N. & S. Dak. passed various tax reductions. Minn. reduced it's taxs by $712 mil., Va., Kentucky & N. Mex. froze the amount that can be collected through Prop. taxes. We refunded a bil. $ ~~tax~~ *Bud.* surplus, gave a 2 month moratorium on inc. taxes & lowered the surtax brackets. Ariz., Hawaii, Mich., Texas and Utah fixed spending limits. Ill. voters approved, 4 to 1, an advisory referendum calling for a spending ceiling. And just to round things off a sizeable group is pushing for a ~~nat~~ const. amendment ~~in Wash~~ at the nat. level to set a spending ceiling on the Fed. govt.

Maybe someone at the Wash. Post should put Nat. Review on their ~~redding~~ *reading* list.

On an entirely different subject, I've had some inquiries about Nat. Health Insurance and why I seem to be so adamantly opposed. I wont repeat my arguments here but will answer some questions that came up about health insurance of the private kind and whether it could possibly be an answer to our health care problems.

Today in America, not counting the mil's. of needy & elderly who have medicaid or medicare or those eligible for treatment in Veterans hospitals, private hospital insurance including group plans covers 179 mil. Am's. Of these 179 mil. 9 out of 10 have insurance covering surgery, physicians services other than surgery & 8 out of 10 *ALSO* have major medical insurance.

I'm sure we can improve on this but it dosen't seem to me we have a health care crisis requiring national, compulsory, govt. health care for everyone in the U.S.

This is RR Thanks for listening. ❖

Ships
September 11, 1979

Flanked as we are by 2 great ~~nations~~ *oceans* do we have a maritime policy that recognizes our dependence on a merchant marine & keeping the sea lanes open?

I'll be right back.

This is one of those good news bad news situations and I'll give you the bad news first. The law with regard to maritime policy states that a merchant marine is necessary for defense and commerce. Our nation is committed to maintaining a merchant fleet under our flag and efficient facilities for building & repairing ships.

† The law further provides that at least half of the gross tonnage of commodities purchased by the public treasury must be transported in U.S. flag ships. Right now about 90% of such cargos are carried by ships flying foreign flags. We are utterly dependent on foreign ~~vessells~~ ships for 68 of the 71 raw materials considered critical to our economy & our defense.

We've fallen from 923 ships 20 yrs. ago to a few more than 500 today. The Soviet U. has 2400. Of the 26 major shipbuilding yards in our country it is estimated only 8 or 9 will still be in business by 1984. Estimates ~~the~~ are that 50,000 shipbuilders will lose their jobs in the next 2 yrs. Right now we have less than 10% of the ships we'd need to support a conflict in Western Europe involving Nato.

Ironically we could reverse this by simply complying with our own law.

Well that's the bad news—that & the fact that the Soviet U. has a blue water navy capable of operating anywhere in the world. Their ships outnumber ours in everything but aircraft carriers and they are building those.

But now for the good news. We've heard a lot about navy shipbuilding, ~~and~~ cost overruns *and late delivery* as well as ships failing to meet navy specifications & requirements.

Well here's a different story. Up in Bath Maine on the banks of the Kennebec river the Bath Iron Works which started building ships for our navy in 1890 is turning out a new kind of destroyer, on time and believe it or not—under the agreed upon price.

The new kind of destroyer is classed as a guided missile frigate, it's prime function to keep the sea lanes open if there should be a war.

The first such ship was delivered to the navy last Dec. Christened the "Oliver Hazard Perry" she went through her sea trials and a very pleased Rear Admiral J. D. Buckeley called her, "the best ship in 20 yrs.

The "Oliver Hazard Perry" is a victory for those naval strategists who've been calling for smaller, cheaper ships. She is smaller than the conventional destroyer and comes in at well under half the price including research costs.

Bath Iron Works is a bright spot in what has been a dark picture because of a management team that didn't try to grab more than it can handle and some solid Maine citizens who like to build ships. They have promised 11 more, 7 weeks under schedule.

This is RR Thanks for listening.

† Send copy of this & attached letter to Mr. Frank Kerr—Bath Iron Works Corp. Bath Maine 04530 ❖

Department of Education
October 2, 1979

If you believe in local control of education it's letter writing time again. Time for letters to our Senators & Representatives. I'll be right back.

When the two houses of Congress each vote out a bill to create, say a new agency, but the bills differ in some details, they are sent to a conference committee. This committee of Sens. & Rep's. attempts to reconcile the differences in the bills and send a compromise version back to each house for another vote.

Some time ago both house & senate approved ~~&~~ the creation of a new *cabinet level* Dept. of Ed. This was in response to the Presidents pledge to the Nat. Ed. Assn. that he would try for such a new dept. It means of course Fed. regulation of our schools under the domination of the Nat. Ed. Assn. which is in truth a great & powerful union. Another union, the Am. Fed. of tchrs. is opposed to such a dept.—as all of us should be. ~~Should~~ *Is* the govt. that administers the postal service & Amtrak—to say nothing of energy—qualified to educate our children?

If the conference committee hasn't acted before you hear this we should be letting our elected representatives know we dont want it. The House ~~only~~ passed it by *only* 4 votes after it had been amended in umpteen different ways—mainly, one has to suspect, to make it unacceptable to the Sen.

For example this bill to create a nat. ed. agency now carries an amendment forbidding Fed. funding of abortions. Another amendment would require voluntary prayers be permitted in public schools. ~~I could support that one~~ I've never thought they should have been stopped. An amendment forbids racial or sexual quotas in inst's. of higher learning that accept Fed. subsidies. One also forbids the new dept. from directing school bussing for racial integration. And another removes nurses, ~~&~~ medical trainees ~~from~~ and Indians from the new Dept's. jurisdiction.

Our best hope is that this measure with all it's attached baggage will linger with the conference committee until the end of this session of Cong. Letters to Representatives & Senators can help bring this about.

I've said before on these broadcasts, the Nat. Ed. Assn. has a long standing dream of a Fed. school system with everything from curriculum to textbooks dictated by Wash. Of course the Assn. has in mind that Wash. will look to it for guidance on setting policy. The N.E.A. has contributed ~~&~~ a half mil. dollars *over the last 5 years* to members of Cong. who have brought this dream to it's present near reality.

A Nat. Dept. of Ed. would extend it's power ~~ov~~ to cover independent & parochial schools. Indeed part of it's dream is incorporation of such schools in the pub. system. It would enlist thousands of employees and have a budget some congressmen have said would top $10 bil.

This ugly blossom on the academic tree should be left to die of committee neglect.

This is RR Thanks for listening. ❖

Hollywood East
October 2, 1979

Wash. D.C. has been called many things but "Hollywood on the Potomac," is a new one.

I'll be right back.

Sen. Bill Roth* of Deleware has done some digging into one area of Fed. spending and learned that a new "tinsel town" called "Hollywood on the Potomac" may be abuilding.

It's hard to picture eager young performers with stars in their eyes turning their backs on Calif. and rushing to Wash. for that big break. Or what our nations capital might be like if the ~~lobbyests~~ lobbiests, burocrats and "pols" were found themselves elbowing ~~each other and~~ theatrical agents for office space.

Cant you see some new starlet writing home and saying; "it's finally happened! After my bit part in 'Sanitary Design for Drinking Fountains,' I have the lead in a biggie called 'Rhesus Monkeys of Santiago Island.'

Believe it or not those are titles of movies being made by our govt. in Wash. Here are a few others, "Identification of Some Common Sucking Lice," "Days of a Tree" and "How to Succeed with Brunettes." Now that last one does sound as if it might be worth seeing.

Sen. Roth has caught our attention. The nearest estimate of govt. spending on film making is $600,000,000 a year. But that is only a guess. The truth is there is no central accounting system to control expenditures and help eliminate useless spending.

"There is no accurate record," the Sen. says, "of how many govt. films are in circulation, or are in production, no single catalogue or guide listing existing films and tapes, and no centralized process for contracting Fed. movies & TV advertisements. We simply have no way of knowing who is doing what, for how much & for what reason."

We learn that a half hour bicentennial film was made at a cost of $460,000 & seen by fewer than 500,000 people. By contrast a ½ hr. TV show ~~made~~ produced commercially for $180,000 in 1977 had an audience estimated at 30 mil.

~~By~~ In true Wash. ~~styp~~ style many of ~~W~~ the audio-visual productions are made toward the end of the fiscal year to use up an agencies budgeted funds so they can ask for more money in the next budget. And like as not many of those films are never seen by anyone. The Sen. learned that agency personnel stockpile projects so their bosses can ask "What do you have that ~~will~~ might cost X number of dollars before we have to turn back our money"?

And many agencies spend money on films that simply glorify the agenc~~y~~*ie*'s

* Senator William Roth, Jr. (R–Delaware, 1971–2001).

image thus enhancing the agencies potential for continued existence. One last point must be made; very often the numerous agencies engaged in filming duplicate each others product. No cross check is made to see if someone else has made or is making the picture an agency has listed for production.

I'm sure there is a legitimate reason for some govt. films. ~~b~~*B*ut wouldn't it ~~be~~ make ~~f~~ more sense to farm that picture work out to Hollywood where there is the greatest pool of technical & artistic talent to be found anywhere in the world? And where there is also a considerable amount of unemployment.

This is RR Thanks for listening. ❖

Defectors
October 2, 1979

The Cultural Exchange between the U.S. & the Soviet U. was intended to promote better understanding & friendship between our people. It did a little more than that.

I'll be right back.

When the Cultural Exchange began between the U.S. & the Soviet U. ~~with artists of both *each* country performing in the~~ there was concern on the part of many Americans that the Soviets might try to use the program for espionage purposes. Whether they did or not I have no way of knowing. But as it turned out the Soviets did get more than they bargained for. Or perhaps I should say they lost more than they bargained for.

Artists & entertainers in the Soviet U. are a special class in the classless society of the "Workers Paradise." They live at a higher standard than the average Russian and have priveleges matched or exceeded by only the party heirarchy. Even so there must be something lacking. Could it be something so simple as individual freedom?

Late August & early Sept. found the cultural exchange a losing deal for the men in the Kremlin. On August 22nd the superstar of the touring Bolshoi Ballet, Alexander Godunuv walked off the stage in N.Y. City and asked for sanctuary in this country. On Sept. 22nd the Bolshoi was in Los Angeles, Godunuv's replacement Leonid Kozlov did the same thing taking his *ballerina* wife Vallentina with him.*

The very next day in Switzerland where a Soviet ice show was appearing the top two Russian skating stars, both Olympic champions, defected.**

Of course there have been other defections in years past but spaced out at greater intervals. We have in our country the former conductor of the Soviet national symphony, the virtuoso cellist Kondrashin, and the world renowned

* Aleksandr Godunov, Leonid Kozlov, and Valentina Kozlov.
** Oleg Protopopov and Lyudmila Belousova.

ballet stars Nureyev, Natalia Makarova & the inimitable Baryshnikov.* The Kremlin theme song these days could very well be that old W.W.I. ~~s~~ditty, "How You Going To Keep Them Down On the Farm After They've Seen Paris."

~~Now~~ On Sept. 27th the shaken leaders in the Kremlin came up with ~~a~~ something of an answer to that musical question. They cancelled the 24 city *U.S.* tour of the Moscow symphony scheduled to open in N.Y. Oct. 2nd. at Carnegie Hall. The symphony was also scheduled to officially open the season at the Kennedy Center in Wash. Some 3500 tickets had already been sold.

This would have been the 5th U.S. tour for the Orchestra. There has only been one defection from that group and that one in 1969.** Apparently the Soviet leaders had reason to believe things might be different this time for they asked our govt. to refuse sanctuary to any of the musicians if they tried to defect. This of course we could not do ~~—so the tour was cancelled~~.

† You see there are those words engraved on the Statue of Liberty which the men in the Kremlin can never understand. "Give me your poor—get correct quote—"Yearning to breathe free. I lift my light beside the Golden Door."

This is RR Thanks for Listening.

† Get correct quote ❖

Coal

October 2, 1979

We have more coal than anyone. The Pres. says we should burn more coal than we are burning. Why dont we? I'll be right back

Some time ago when the Pres. addressed us on energy he advocated converting more of our utilities & industrial plants ~~to~~ from oil & natural gas to coal. He even set a figure for utilities—substitute coal for 50% of the oil they are presently using.

Well you cant argue with the fact that we have enough coal to last 900 yrs. We have an estimated ⅓ of all the known coal reserves in the world. But you can ask, why aren't we burning more? You can even ask why ~~we~~ aren't WE mining more? We are producing about 150 mil. tons a year—below our capacity to produce.

The answer to these questions was given a few years ago by a spokesman for the energy industry. He said very simply; "Under Fed. policies and regulations, we cant mine it, and we cant burn it." "It" of course ~~was~~ *being* coal.

* Kirill Kondrashin, Rudolf Nureyev, Natalya Makarova, and Mikhail Baryshnikov.

** Vsevolod Lezhnev.

A massive network of regulations has led to our present situation. Wash. is aware of this problem because Carl E. Bogge Pres. of the Nat. Coal Assn. sent a lengthy memo to the White House listing the Federal practices that made the President's request for conversion impossible to fulfill.

I'm indebted to a fine journalist & friend M. Stanton Evans for collecting & making public these govt. roadblocks to more use of coal.* They are: A moratorium on ~~Fed.~~ leasing ~~of~~ Fed lands for coal mining since 1971: The unworkability of the Dept. of Interiors coal leasing program: That same dept's. regulations under the Surface Mining ~~&~~, Control & Reclamation Act which may even put some operators out of business; Some policies under that same act which will declare some coal bearing lands "unsuitable" for mining: Public lands withdrawal: And emission standards under the Environmental Protection Agency which could make unusable large shares of the most economically recoverable U.S. coal reserves.

Stan went on to cite more of Mr. Bogges memorandum such as taxes on the industry, price controls on other fuels which held them so low, coal cant compete ~~with them.~~ and increased royalty payments to the govt. There is also a refusal to allow ~~a~~ coal slurry pipelines for transporting coal which would compete with existing means of transportation.

By far however the biggest roadblock are the so called "ambient air standards." Every air quality control ~~district~~ region in the U.S. is in violation of those standards, mainly because of what are called "suspended particulants." Now these aren't necessarily man caused pollution. These particulants can be dust, swamp gas and other of natures wonders. But because they are present we cant add whatever particulants might be produced by mining or burning coal.

It would seem that a study is called for weighing the regulations & their benefits against the benefits of utilizing our biggest natural fuel supply.

This is RR Thanks for listening. ❖

California
October 2, 1979

Calif. the golden state, home of Hollywood, land of oranges & sunshine has had a tough time buffing away ~~the~~ a little tarnish on it's image lately.

I'll be right back.

Those of us who love Calif. have had a hard time lately fighting an unattractive image that has come upon our state in the closing weeks of summer. First there were the long lines at the gas stations dutifully shown on nation-

* M. Stanton Evans, "The United States Has Plenty of Energy." *Human Events,* September 22, 1977, p. 15.

wide TV. Some commentators had a field day with that one. Californians were portrayed as gas greedy road hogs in a panic at the prospect of not being able to drive in their usual profligate way.

It was pretty hard to get the truth across that on a per ~~#~~ driver basis Californians averaged less mileage *per month* than ~~the~~ our fellow Americans in Maryland, Virginia & even in the limited area of the District of Columbia. It was even harder to convince the Dept. of Energy that basing Californias gasoline allocation on the 1972 census was an error of sizeable proportions. Calif. has 4 mil. more automobiles than it had in 1972.

But it was nature that gave us our latest pasting. In a spell of weather not experienced in more than half a century a heat wave settled on the state. The cooling ocean breezes off the Pacific stayed well out in the Pacific. Our nights which ~~even~~ even in summer are usually 20 to 30 degrees cooler than daytime temperatures stayed *at* the same level as the baking days.

Born of the heat an inversion layer settled in at 400 ft. And since the mountains surrounding Los Angeles ~~are~~ are higher than 400 ft. the smog just piled up under that inversion layer until the air was thick enough to stir with a spoon. Then, and also born of the heat the brush fires started, adding billowing smoke & ashes to the smog.

Well the heat wave broke, the inversion layer lifted, the fires were doused as they always are and apparently the crisis was over. ~~U.S.C.~~ The Trojans of Southern Calif. were rated the number 1 ~~team~~ football team in the nation and things seemed to be pretty normal.

Then came the unkindest blow of all. One of the summer sports most Californians are denied is swatting mosquitos. Oh—we have a few places where the little monsters can be found—in the High Sierras, the Delta & so on but certainly not in So. Calif.—That is until this very unusual year.

Now ~~in~~ the San Diego area—particularly the community of Imperial Beach has been invaded by swarms of large, economy size "skeeters." Like the plot of one of our horror films the source of the plague has been located. It is several hundred acres of swamp in the Tia Juana river estuary. So you say—like in those same movies—"happy ending." But no—the Fed. govt. is in the cast of this story and the U.S. Fish & Wildlife service refuses to allow (on environmental grounds) spraying of the swamp. Meanwhile the humans in the area are being eaten alive.

But never sell Calif. short. The Mayor of Imperial Beach has declared the swamp will be sprayed even if it means going to jail. And he has declared he'll be at the nozzle of the 1st sprayer jail or no jail. I'm on his side.

This is RR Thanks for listening. ❖

Red Tape
October 2, 1979

I've talked before about red tape & burocratic nonsense but this time it's with a worldwide view.

I'll be right back

There are now 151 nations in the United Nations Organization. There are several who aren't there—good ~~+~~ ones too. Their govt's. range from totalitarian to ~~Republics~~ *authoritarian; from monarchies to* representative; from dictators to more dictators and until recently even an Emperor—*(Bokassa the first)* now deposed. But all of them have one characteristic in common, varying only in degree; the stultifying hand of burocracy.

I've talked about our own burocratic problems, criticized ~~them~~ *burocratic* excesses & deplored ~~their~~ *burocratic* arrogance. Today I'd like to show what citizens of other countries have to put up with. You'll probably find yourself saying we're not so bad off after all. But I hope you'll also say lets get our own act together before we are that bad off.

In one country ~~+~~ in S. America the post office was charged with burning 3 mil. pieces of mail rather than delivering it. The postal officials vehemently denied burning 3 mil. pieces of mail—they ~~only~~ *said they had only* burned 300,000.

An American businessman in a European country had to "nationalize" his car which he had brought into the country. It took 12 different procedures in offices as much as 15 miles apart with hours of waiting in each office. He now hires a private company to expedite such problems. The expediters are all former ~~g~~ burocrats.

A Swiss woman living in Paris France wanted to marry a Lebanese. Every time she applied to the Prefecture of Police she learned of another govt. form she'd have to fill out. Always there was another bit of information she hadn't supplied—such as her grandmothers maiden name.

One day in desperation she tucked a pillow under her dress, went to another office, shed buckets of tears and told them she was pregnant~~. She~~ *and* received instant approval of her marriage.

There was the case of a woman who was billed for 11 years for her mothers TV set license *RENEWALS*. He[r] mother had been dead for 11 years. She was threatened with fines for not accepting a registered letter addressed to her mother. She had gone to the post office & tried to get the letter by showing them her mothers death certificate. They refused to give it to her because she didn't have written authorization from her mother.

We usually seem to follow *in* our English cousins footsteps by 10 or 12 years. Prime Minister Margaret Thatcher may have some tips for us a few years down the road. ~~Right now 4 out of 10 workers in England is a~~ *are* ~~public employees.~~

A Senior Civil Servant fired half of his staff, closed down a bunch of govt. run ventures & cut his *$23 mil.* ~~#~~ budget by a full one third. When he tried to show his superiors in London how his methods could be used throughout the country they yawned in his face.

There ~~are~~ *is* 1 govt. employee to every 2½ other workers in Eng. We have a little way to go yet—here it's 4 to 1.

This is RR Thanks for listening ❖

Radioactivity
October 2, 1979

I've been hearing from some of you with regard to my commentaries on nuclear generating plants.

I'll be right back.

There have been some questions in the mail recently about my stand on nuclear power. Some have challenged that the problem of nuclear waste has not been solved. Others have taken the position that the very existence of nuclear plants threatens us with the dread, invisible spread of radioactivity. The things we have now learned about the ~~low~~ harmful effects of low level radiation from the WWII bomb tests is offered as proof that nuclear elec. generating plants will be an ongoing source of silent death.

Well it is true that mistakes were made in those early days of atomic testing; that there was a lack of information even among nuclear scientists. It is equally true that we now do have *an enormous* fund of knowledge ~~on~~ which makes it possible to accurately appraise potential risk.

When Madame Curie's* discovereys led to the developement of the X-ray we know there was little thought given to possible side effects. Undoubtedly there were casualties associated with xray use. But would anyone suggest that the X-ray has not been a boon to mankind with benefits far outweighing the unanticipated side effects?

Samuel A. Wenk, research & development manager for the South West Research Inst. has tried to put risk & benefit in proper perspective. He says: "We live in a world of natural radiation. Everyone panics at the terms 'nuclear' & 'radiation' when it comes to power plants; in truth however we are getting daily doses of radiation from the sun, the ground and the buildings we live in that is 10 to 20 times greater than what is put out by nuclear power plants."

Wenk is peculiarly well qualified to speak of this—not alone by his scientific training: He had a skin cancer removed that was caused by too much exposure to the sun.

But here is his assessment of the annual natural radiation we're all exposed

* Marie Sklodowska Curie.

to. Ground level radiation from cosmic rays is about 45 millirems. If you fly an average of 10 hrs. ~~of~~ a month add another 62½ millirems. The average in ~~/~~ the U.S. of radiation from the ground we walk on is 60 ~~mir~~ *millirems*. The building materials in our homes gives off 40 and in driving 10,000 miles we get an additional 4 from the ~~aggrgate~~ aggregate used in street & highway paving. That totals about 211.5 millirems per year.

That is the equivalent of 10 chest X rays and we ~~*haven't*~~ counted what we eat & drink. The intake from that is 25 millirems. Then Wenk says there is localized exposure. A wearer of dentures gets Alpha radiation which fortunately has limited penetration. Wearing glasses adds rems of Alpha radiation to the corneas. Cooking with natural gas exposes us to ~~/~~ Radon, which is also found in our drinking water—there are no average figures on this. You get more radon from taking a shower than you do if you take a bath.

An efficient 1000 megawatt coal generating plant exposes the nearby population to 380 millirems a year. A nuclear power plant is restricted to less than 10 at it's own fence.

Anyone interested can get all this information & more from the Environmental Protection Admin. report~~—"Radiol~~ "Radiological Quality of the Environment In the U.S. 1977." *

This is RR Thanks for listening. ❖

The Golden Fleece

October 2, 1979

The Golden Fleece of legend & mythology has in recent years become a recognition of govt. extravagance.

I'll be right back.

Wisconsins Senator Wm. Proxmire ** has faithfully for 5 years now called attention to examples of govt. extravagance & foolish spending. The Sen. makes public his award of the "Golden Fleece" to individual, dept., agency or branch of govt. ~~which~~ guilty of unnecessary, unwise or ~~carle carless~~ careless expenditures of taxpayers money. There have been 55 such awards in these 5 years.

If you are curious about why his award bears the title, "golden fleece," just look at it this way; we the taxpaying citizens are the wooly creatures being shorn everytime some one in govt. gets extravagant.

Sen. Proxmire really hit home with his most recent award. He presented it to those who you might say govern the govt.—his colleagues in the U.S. Con-

* *Radiological Quality of the Environment in the United States, 1977* (Washington, DC: Environmental Protection Agency, Office of Radiation Programs, 1977).

** D–Wisconsin, 1957–1989.

gress. Said the Sen. "I am giving my fleece of the month to Congress for the eruption in it's staff and spending over the past decade. In that period the staff of the House & Senate has grown by about 70% and the cost of that staff by 270%."

The growth is remarkable when you look at the figures. The House has increased staff from 7,300 ten years ago to 11,600 today. The Sen. ~~did~~ did better by doubling it's staffing—from 3400 to 6800 (that figures out to 68 staff members per Senator).

Total staff cost this year is $550,000,000 up from $150,000,000 ten years ago. A pay raise has been proposed which will increase this even more.

In reality however this is only the tip of the iceberg. The real cost to us is the increased spending generated by congressional staff. There is no way to estimate what that total may be but there is no ~~way~~ denying that staff makes a sizeable contribution.

The next time you read somewhere that the coming $552 bil. budget is in response to demands *BY THE PEOPLE* for more govt. services ~~by the~~ take that with a large grain of salt. Far more legislation is generated by govt. agencies than by popular demand.

It works like this; those entrusted with operating a govt. program, very often with the best of intentions, decide they can do even more for the people if only they can get more money ~~and yes~~—more personnel and of course a little more power. They put their proposal into legislative form and then look around for a Rep. or Sen. to introduce the bill.

Enter the congressional staffers. They have to justify their existence so they are on the lookout for things they can present to the boss as worthwhile things to do. The dept. promoters contact staffers they are acquainted with. The staffers take the proposal to their boss as a politically sexy bill he can ~~aut~~ author. ~~a~~And presto up goes the budget~~., g~~Govt. grows larger and the 1st thing you know the congressional staff has grown 70% in 10 yrs.

This is R. R Thanks for listening ❖

In September 1979, the Western Conference of the Council of State Governors and the Western Region of the National Association of Counties voted in favor of a resolution that supported a bill put forth by Senator Orrin G. Hatch (R–Utah) that would give states control over some federal land.

Land
October 2, 1979

There may be a new Mason-Dixon line in our Nation but this one is running North & South.

I'll be right back.

On Sept. 9th a meeting took place in Reno Nevada. Those gathering there were representatives of the Attorneys General of the ~~4~~ *13* western states. They met in response to ~~Nevadas~~ a law passed by the Nevada legislature in July in which that state laid claim to 49 mil. acres of land owned by the U.S. govt. and administered by the Bureau of Land Management.

Nevada has started what is being called the "Sagebrush Rebellion." From the Rockies, across the deserts and all the way to the Pacific the western states are voicing their angry resentment of a powerful absentee landlord—the Fed. govt. which has overlaid the West with controls & regulations ~~which~~ as irksome as barb wire was in an earlier day. ~~when the open range was fenced.~~

The West has a legitimate beef (and I dont intend that to be a pun). Early in our history as territories became states the Fed. lands within their borders were turned over to the states for development or sale to private owners. Naturally the Fed. govt. retained title to lands it had actually developed for use. These included mil. reservations, Fed. instalations, national parks etc.

As the nation expanded westward however and the newer, western states were added a change occurred. The 100th meridian marked the change. To the East of the meridian Fed. ownership of land ~~averages~~ ranges from ~~6.~~ 6/10 of 1% in Iowa to a high of 12% in N.H. In the District of Columbia, our nations capital it only amounts to 26%.

But west of the meridian it is a different story. It [is] almost as if the govt. said, "we're being foolishly generous giving all this land away." Fed. ownership at the 100th meridian goes from *the* 6 states ~~north to south~~ *east* of the meridian averaging about 3% to the 4 states west of them averaging 37% Federally owned. And as you continue to move West through the most recent additions to the Union the percentage goes up in all but Wash. which ~~is~~ has 29% of it's land in Fed. ownership. Ariz. is 43%, Utah 66%, Idaho 64%, Nevada 87%, Ore. 53% & Calif. 45%. But then comes our largest ~~st~~ & newest state Alaska & the Fed. govt. stubbornly holds onto 96%.

This Fed. land has been made available for multiple use—lumbering, mining, cattle grazing & recreational. But now the B.L.M. is writing all manner of new regulations and in effect changing the rules in the middle of the game. Out in Idaho a rancher whose *cattle* operation is based on the lease of 15,000 acres of grazing land—(a lease his family has held for 92 yrs.) is told the govt. is taking back the land as a winter range for deer. The E.P.A. tells him he cant poison coyotes and the F.D.A. has ordered that only a Veterinarian can administer anti-biotics to cattle. The nearest Vet is 60 miles away & dosen't make house calls. The B.L.M. is suspending the 10 yr. leases and changing to a year to year basis and imposing 212 separate environmental impact statements on the ranchers.

Is the Fed. govt. a better custodian of 700 mil. acres than the states would be? In a recent fire the B.L.M. managers refused to let a rancher help put out the fire.

This is RR Thanks for listening.

Ronald Reagan's Radio Addresses

1975–1979

Of 1,027 unique radio addresses taped by Ronald Reagan and distributed by O'Connor Creative Services between 1975 and 1979, handwritten drafts by Reagan have been found of 673 of them. This book includes more than 337 of them; 237 were previously published in *Reagan, In His Own Hand*.[1] All of these, and the unpublished addresses, are available at the Ronald Reagan Presidential Library. In the following listing the Page in Book column indicates the page in this book or in *Reagan, In His Own Hand* in which the radio address appears.

In addition to the recorded radio commentaries, we found Reagan drafts of another nine that were not recorded. Most of these are included in this book; two of them were used as newspaper columns. In addition to the 1,027 unique radio addresses Reagan delivered, there were 17 repeat broadcasts and 14 that were written and recorded by guests.

O'Connor used batch numbers (such as 75-01 and 75-02) to identify sets of radio addresses; each batch was sent out on a vinyl long-play record or on tape to the radio stations subscribing to the program. The 1976 series begins in September 1976, when Reagan returned to broadcasting after the 1976 presidential primary campaign, and continues for a year. Reagan did a taping session once every three weeks or so. The batches as O'Connor sent them out sometimes included radio addresses taped in the previous session or earlier. Batch 76-08 includes radio addresses taped in late 1976 and early 1977, and is included in this book in the 1976 chapter. The year 1977 includes batches 76-09 through 76-19 and 77-20 through 77-24. For 1978 and 1979, the O'Connor batch numbers match the calendar years.

The radio addresses for which we have handwritten drafts by Reagan are indicated in bold type in the Title column and a document description in the Handwritten Draft column. For example, 14-2 is legal-size paper, two pages; 11-3 is letter-size paper, three pages. Sometimes the color of the ink is noted; p indicates pencil. The "ldt" designation means that a line was drawn through the document by a secretary indicating it had been typed. Few documents are marred in this way. Where someone else is known to have written the initial draft, the author's name is shown in the Handwritten Draft column. Reagan himself edited all the typed drafts before delivering them at the microphone. The radio addresses written by Reagan but not used on the radio are at the end of each year and identified with xx instead of a batch number for the year. Thus, 78-xx-1 through 78-xx-7 are the seven unrecorded essays written, we believe, in 1978. The other two are 76-xx-1 and 77-xx-1, written in 1976 and 1977 respectively.

Almost all the documents were found in the Pre-Presidential Papers collection in the Reagan Presidential Library, a collection not open to the public. A few are held in private collections, and three were found in boxes 923 and 924 of the 1980 Reagan-Bush Campaign files, another collection at the Reagan Presidental Library not open to the public. The Pre-Presidential Papers storage boxes in which handwritten documents were found were originally numbered 12, 14, 15, and 21, but archivists have reorganized the collection and have the radio addresses available for research.

Various collections in the Hoover Institution Archives have copies of the typed radio addresses that Reagan used when recording them (double-spaced, and sometimes including handwritten changes) and single-spaced copies of the addresses as recorded, which were prepared by O'Connor Creative Services and distributed to the radio stations with the vinyl records or tapes so that each station could respond to requests for copies of the programs. The O'Connor distributions do not include Reagan's introduction to each broadcast or his sign-off line, "This is Ronald Reagan. Thanks for listening."

Some taping dates are estimated, especially those that indicate only a month and year. The sides of the vinyl records are indicated by A and B; where there are only numbers, the addresses were distributed on tape. The radio addresses included on the audio CD in this book are indicated with an asterisk following the book page.[2]

O'Connor Number	Title	Side/ Number	Taping Date	Handwritten Draft	Book Page
75-01	Food Stamps	A1	1/8/1975		
	Consumer Protection	A2	1/8/1975		
	Inflation	A3	1/8/1975	9-4	RIHOH 255
	Boondoggle	A4	1/8/1975		
	Cuba	A5	1/8/1975		
	Unemployment (1)	B1	1/8/1975		
	Unemployment (2)	B2	1/8/1975		
	Unemployment (3)	B3	1/8/1975		
	Bureaucrats	B4	1/8/1975		
	Civil Service	B5	1/8/1975		
	3 R's	B6	1/8/1975		
	Postal Service	B7	1/8/1975		
	Fair Trade	B8	1/8/1975		
75-02	Inflation Fighting	A1	2/1/1975		
	Supply and Demand	A2	2/1/1975		
	Surprise Tax Bills	A3	2/1/1975		
	Energy Problems	A4	2/1/1975		
	Rocky's Story	A5	2/1/1975		
	Public Employees	B1	2/1/1975		
	Viet Nam Policy	B2	2/1/1975		
	Capitalism-Socialism	B3	2/1/1975		
	Volunteerism	B4	2/1/1975		
	Incredible Bread Machine	B5	2/1/1975		
	Red China	B6	2/1/1975		
75-03	Federal Budget	A1	2/14/1975		
	Detente	A2	2/14/1975		
	Peru Revolution	A3	2/14/1975		
	Mozart vs Sibelius	A4	2/14/1975	Peter Hannaford	
	The Delta Queen	A5	2/14/1975		
	A Cuba Documentary	A6	2/14/1975	14-2	5
	Farm Facts	B1	2/14/1975	14-2	6
	Tax Plan #1	B2	2/14/1975	14-3	8
	Tax Plan #2	B3	2/14/1975	14-3	10
	Tax Plan #3	B4	2/14/1975	14-3	11
	Arms Limitations	B5	2/14/1975		
	Crisis of Democracy	B6	2/14/1975		
75-04	**Unemployment #1**	A1	2/27/1975	14-2	13
	Unemployment #2	A2	2/27/1975	14-2	14
	W. Germany/Inflation	A3	2/27/1975		
	National Debt #1	A4	2/27/1975		
	National Debt #2	A5	2/27/1975		
	Congress & Security	A6	2/27/1975		
	The Work Ethic	B1	2/27/1975		
	Land Planning	B2	2/27/1975	14-2	RIHOH 338
	Price of Beef	B3	2/27/1975	14-2	15
	Private Government	B4	2/27/1975		
	N.H. Senate Contest	B5	2/27/1975		
	Recession vs Inflation	B6	2/27/1975	14-2	RIHOH 264
75-05	Southeast Asia	A1	3/12/1975		
	Energy Sources	A2	3/12/1975		
	Capital Punishment	A3	3/12/1975		
	Vacation Exchange Program	A4	3/12/1975		
	The Superintendent's Dilemma	A5	3/12/1975		
	Oil Talk	A6	3/12/1975	14-2	17

O'Connor Number	Title	Side/ Number	Taping Date	Handwritten Draft	Book Page
	Tiffany & Company	B1	3/12/1975	14-2	18
	Cold Beer	B2	3/12/1975		
	Regulations	B3	3/12/1975	14-2	RIHOH 294
	Federal Retirement Pensions	B4	3/12/1975		
	Easy Voting	B5	3/12/1975	14-2	19
	The Money Supply	B6	3/12/1975		
75-06	Portugal #1	1	March-75		
	Portugal #2	2	March-75		
	Energy #1	3	March-75		
	Energy #2	4	March-75		
	Campaign Law	5	March-75		
75-07	**Indochina #1**	A1	April-75	14-2	21
	Indochina #2	A2	April-75	14-2	RIHOH 48
	Satellites	A3	April-75		
	Utility Subsidies	A4	April-75		
	Postal Feedback	A5	April-75		
	Patent Proposals	B1	April-75		
	The New Congress	B2	April-75		
	Abortion Laws	B3	April-75	14-2	RIHOH 360
	Welfare Program #1	B4	April-75	14-2	22
	Welfare Program #2	B5	April-75	14-2	RIHOH 389
	Welfare Program #3	B6	April-75	14-2	24
75-08	London #1	A1	April-75		
	London #2	A2	April-75		
	London #3	A3	April-75		
	Regulations-New Wave #1	A4	April-75		
	Regulations-New Wave #2	A5	April-75		
	Farm Workers Union	A6	April-75	14-2	
	No Time To Confuse	B1	April-75		
	Vietnam	B2	April-75	14-3	25
	Land Use	B3	April-75		
	Peace	B4	April-75	11-3	RIHOH 4
	Government: Big vs Small #1	B5	April-75		
	Government: Big vs Small #2	B6	April-75		
75-09	The Amazing DeBolts	A1	May-75		
	The Washington Media	A2	May-75		
	Italian Bureaucracy and the U.S. Treasury	A3	May-75		
	United Nations	A4	May-75	14-3	RIHOH 159
	Red Sea	A5	May-75		
	Nuclear Power	B1	May-75	14-2	RIHOH 323
	Recession's Cause	B2	May-75		
	Portugal	B3	May-75		
	Government Computers	B4	May-75	11-2	27
	Adoption	B5	May-75	11-2	28
75-10	Agency for Consumer Advocacy	A1	May-75		
	George Meany and Economics	A2	May-75	14-3	29
	Communism, The Disease	A3	May-75	14-2	RIHOH 10
	Soviet Superiority	A4	May-75		
	The EPA Strikes Again	A5	May-75		
	Panama Canal	A6	May-75		

O'Connor Number	Title	Side/ Number	Taping Date	Handwritten Draft	Book Page
	Boondoggles' Foe	B1	May-75		
	Radical Chic Revisited	B2	May-75		
	Falling Dominoes	B3	May-75		
	Truth in Spending	B4	May-75		
	Congress vs. Local Government	B5	May-75	14-2	30
	Tax Loopholes	B6	May-75	14-2	RIHOH 268
75-11	Is This the Land of Our Fathers?	A1	Jun-75	Maureen Reagan (recorded by MR)	
	Is Government Our Big Brother?	A2	Jun-75	Maureen Reagan (recorded by MR)	
	Seen Your Doctor Lately?	A3	Jun-75	Maureen Reagan (recorded by MR)	
	Big Mo	A4	Jun-75	14-3	
	Inflation As Tax	A5	Jun-75	14-3	32
	Cost Overruns	A6	Jun-75	11-2	34
	Gun Control #1	B1	Jun-75		
	Gun Control #2	B2	Jun-75		
	Gun Control #3	B3	Jun-75		
	Button Button	B4	Jun-75		
	Letters to the Editor	B5	Jun-75	14-2	RIHOH 15
	Business Profits, Myths & Realities	B6	Jun-75	14-2	35
75-12	Free Enterprise	A1	Jun-75		
	Law and Order	A2	Jun-75	14-2	37
	Job Hunting	A3	Jun-75		
	Budget "Uncontrollables"	A4	Jun-75		
	Aquaculture	A5	Jun-75		
	Stopping Vandalism	A6	Jun-75		
	Mariana Islands	B1	Jun-75		
	Congressional "Perks"	B2	Jun-75		
	Samizdat	B3	Jun-75		
	M.I.A.	B4	Jun-75		
	Pacific Legal Foundation	B5	Jun-75		
	Polls on Government	B6	Jun-75		
75-13	**Chile**	A1	Jul-75	14-2	
	UNICEF	A2	Jul-75	14-2	38
	Socialized Medicine I	A3	Jul-75	14-2	RIHOH 364
	Socialized Medicine II	A4	Jul-75	14-2	39
	Community Work Experience Program	A5	Jul-75	14-3	41
	Phu Quoc	A6	Jul-75	14-2	42
	Welfare Reform Corporations I	B1	Jul-75		
	Welfare Reform Corporations II	B2	Jul-75		
	Welfare Reform Corporations III	B3	Jul-75		
	Do Away with IRS?	B4	Jul-75		
	Turtles and Aquaculture	B5	Jul-75		
	Somalia	B6	Jul-75		
75-14	Equal Rights Amendment-Pro [Maureen Reagan]	1	Aug-75	Maureen Reagan (recorded by MR)	
	Equal Rights Amendment-Con	2	Aug-75		

O'Connor Number	Title	Side/ Number	Taping Date	Handwritten Draft	Book Page
	Soviet Life	3	Aug-75		
	World Affairs Report	4	Aug-75		
	"Why don't they ____?"	5	Aug-75		
75-15	Oil and the Shah of Iran	1	Aug-75		
	Cuba, O.A.S. and Us	2	Aug-75		
	The Helsinki Document	3	Aug-75		
75-16	**CIA Commission**	A1	Aug-75	11-2	RIHOH 121
	Letter to Congress	A2	Aug-75		
	Permits to Plow	A3	Aug-75		
	Ruritania	A4	Aug-75	11-3	RIHOH 130
	Gun Control	A5	Aug-75	Patrick J. Buchanan	
	Mr. Nader's Great Treasury Raid	A6	Aug-75	Patrick J. Buchanan	
	Images	B1	Aug-75	14-2	RIHOH 252
	Indians' Plight	B2	Aug-75	14-2	RIHOH 386
	Crime—Care and Prevention	B3	Aug-75	14-2	
	Pollution #1	B4	Aug-75	14-2	44*
	Pollution #2	B5	Aug-75	14-2	46
	Pollution #3	B6	Aug-75	14-2	47
75-17	Washington Ironies (HOT LINE)	1	Sep-75		
	Tax Limitation (HOT LINE)	2	Sep-75		
	Update—School Vandalism, UNICEF	3	Sep-75		
	Saving Energy and Lives on the Freeway	4	Sep-75		
	Reducing the Federal Burden	5	Sep-75		
	Academic Freedom	6	Sep-75	11-2	RIHOH 362
	Strengthening Social Security I	7	Sep-75		
	Strengthening Social Security II	8	Sep-75		
	Strengthening Social Security III	9	Sep-75		
	Regional Government	10	Sep-75		
75-18	A Few Ironies (HOT LINE)	1	Sep-75		
	National Economic Planning (HOT LINE)	2	Sep-75		
	Public Employee Strikes	3	Sep-75		
	Hudson Institute on Education	4	Sep-75	11-3	49
	Federal Registry I	5	Sep-75	11-2	RIHOH 293
	More on Regulations II	6	Sep-75		
	New York	7	Sep-75	11-2	RIHOH 404
	The Federal Rathole	8	Sep-75		
	Nuclear Power	9	Sep-75		
75-19	Cedu Foundation	A1	Oct-75		
	"Double-Dipping"	A2	Oct-75		
	Castro, Cleaver & Puerto Rico	A3	Oct-75		
	"Peoples' Bicentennial Commission" Survey	A4	Oct-75		
	Can You Persuade a Leftist?	A5	Oct-75		

O'Connor Number	Title	Side/ Number	Taping Date	Handwritten Draft	Book Page
	Producers in the Minority	A6	Oct-75		
	Uncle Sam the Advertiser	B1	Oct-75		
	U.S.P.S.'s Kokomo Plan	B2	Oct-75		
	Gun Laws, Drug Laws	B3	Oct-75	14-2	50
	Communist Conspiracy? #1	B4	Oct-75		
	Communist Conspiracy? #2	B5	Oct-75	14-3	RIHOH 232
	Communist Conspiracy? #3	B6	Oct-75		
75-20	Economic Planning	A1	Oct-75		
	The Russian Wheat Deal	A2	Oct-75	14-3	RIHOH 26
	Secret Service	A3	Oct-75	14-3	51*
	Detente	A4	Oct-75		
	Some Thoughts on Unemployment	A5	Oct-75		
	Samizdat	A6	Oct-75		
	Common Situs Picketing	B1	Oct-75		
	New Gasoline Lines?	B2	Oct-75		
	The Superintendent's Dilemma	B3	Oct-75	repeat	
	The Incredible Bread Machine	B4	Oct-75	repeat	
	A Break for the Handicapped	B5	Oct-75	Julie Nixon Eisenhower (recorded by JNE)	
	Welfare Abuses	B6	Oct-75	Julie Nixon Eisenhower (recorded by JNE)	
75-21	Clearingcutting	1	Nov-75		
	Government Pay	2	Nov-75		
	Letter To Employees	3	Nov-75		
	Panama Canal	4	Nov-75		
	Welfare Letter	5	Nov-75		
	National Land Use Policy #1	6	Nov-75		
	National Land Use Policy #2	7	Nov-75		
	National Land Use Policy #3	8	Nov-75		
	The Trouble With New York City	9	Nov-75		
75-22	Crime	1	Nov-75		
	What Would You Do If You Woke to Find a Burglar In Your Home?	2	Nov-75	William F. Buckley Jr. (recorded by WFB)	
	Is Gerald Ford Ganging Up On New York City?	3	Nov-75	William F. Buckley Jr. (recorded by WFB)	
	Should Ex-CIA Employees Be Treated as Second-Class Citizens?	4	Nov-75	William F. Buckley Jr. (recorded by WFB)	
	How Do You Talk Back to Eric Sevareid?	5	Nov-75	William F. Buckley Jr. (recorded by WFB)	
	Should We Really Give Away The Panama Canal?	6	Nov-75	William F. Buckley Jr. (recorded by WFB)	
	Women In Government and Politics #1	7	Nov-75	Julie Nixon Eisenhower (recorded by JNE)	
	Women In Government and Politics #2	8	Nov-75	Julie Nixon Eisenhower (recorded by JNE)	
	Women In Government and Politics #3	9	Nov-75	Julie Nixon Eisenhower (recorded by JNE)	
76-01	**Convention #1**	A1	9/1/1976	14-2	RIHOH 235
	Platforms A	A2	9/1/1976		

O'Connor Number	Title	Side/ Number	Taping Date	Handwritten Draft	Book Page
	Platforms B	A3	9/1/1976	14-2	61
	Platforms C	A4	9/1/1976	14-2	62
	Panama Canal	A5	9/1/1976		
	Getting Back at the Bureaucrats A	A6	9/1/1976	14-2	64
	Bureaucrats B	B1	9/1/1976	14-2	65
	Congress' Automatic Pay Raise	B2	9/1/1976		
	Women's March	B3	9/1/1976	14-2	67*
	China	B4	9/1/1976		
	Shaping the World for 100 Years to Come	B5	9/1/1976	14-2	RIHOH 9
	Tax Reform	B6	9/1/1976	14-2	68
76-02	The Median Is the Message	A1	9/21/1976		
	Panama's Press	A2	9/21/1976		
	Mao's China	A3	9/21/1976		
	About the Press	A4	9/21/1976	14-2	RIHOH 247
	Education (A)	A5	9/21/1976	14-2	70
	Education (B)	A6	9/21/1976	14-2	RIHOH 344
	Herman Kahn, Futurist	A7	9/21/1976		
	Paperwork & Bureaucrats	B1	9/21/1976	14-2	RIHOH 295
	Institute for Contemporary Studies	B2	9/21/1976		
	Humphrey-Hawkins Bill (Jobs A)	B3	9/21/1976	14-2	71
	Humphrey-Hawkins Bill (Jobs B)	B4	9/21/1976	14-3	RIHOH 265
	FORBES on "Full" Employment	B5	9/21/1976		
	President Coolidge	B6	9/21/1976	14-2	72
	Nuclear Wastes	B7	9/21/1976		
	The Hope of Mankind	B8	9/21/1976	14-2	RIHOH 224
76-03	The Ford Strike	A1	10/18/1976		
	Election Day, November 2, 1976	A2	10/18/1976		
	Vietnam	A3	10/18/1976	11-3	74
	Reporters, Sources & Laws	A4	10/18/1976		
	The Fate of 14 (b)	A5	10/18/1976		
	The Speedy Trial Act	A6	10/18/1976		
	Welfare	A7	10/18/1976	11-2	75
	Running Fence	B1	10/18/1976		
	"Bread Machine" and Janeway	B2	10/18/1976		
	Soviet TV and America	B3	10/18/1976	Peter Hannaford	
	Government Forms	B4	10/18/1976	11-2	77
	Milton Friedman - #1	B5	10/18/1976		
	Milton Friedman - #2	B6	10/18/1976		
	Sweden 1	B7	10/18/1976	11-3	78
	Sweden 2	B8	10/18/1976	11-2	79
76-04	Diamond Lanes	A1	11/2/1976		
	Tax Reform I	A2	11/2/1976	11-2	80
	Tax Reform II	A3	11/2/1976	11-2	82
	Hoover's America Plan	A4	11/2/1976		
	Africa	A5	11/2/1976	14-2	83
	Freedom Train	A6	11/2/1976	11-3	RIHOH 230

O'Connor Number	Title	Side/ Number	Taping Date	Handwritten Draft	Book Page
	Glomar Explorer	A7	11/2/1976		
	Katyn Forest	B1	11/2/1976	14-2	RIHOH 31
	Big Government and the Cities	B2	11/2/1976		
	San Francisco	B3	11/2/1976	14-2	RIHOH 406
	Berkeley's Street Tax	B4	11/2/1976		
	The Politics of the Federal Government	B5	11/2/1976		
	The Alaska Gas Pipeline	B6	11/2/1976		
	The Communes	B7	11/2/1976	11-3	84*
	New Directions	B8	11/2/1976		
76-05	Centralized Planning	A1	11/2/1976		
	Bureaucrats Revisited	A2	11/2/1976	14-2	86
	Inflation and the Property Tax—I	A3	11/2/1976		
	Inflation and the Property Tax—II	A4	11/2/1976		
	Land Use Planning	A5	11/2/1976		
	Education I	A6	11/16/1976	14-2	RIHOH 342
	Education II	A7	11/16/1976	14-2	87
	Campaign Reminiscence	B1	11/16/1976	14-2	88
	Citizen's Choice	B2	11/16/1976		
	Liberals	B3	11/16/1976	14-2	90
	Red Hen	B4	11/16/1976	1/8p. intro	RIHOH 262
	Government Cost I	B5	11/16/1976	14-2	91
	Government Cost II	B6	11/16/1976	14-2	RIHOH 270
	Solar Energy	B7	11/16/1976		
	Britain	B8	11/16/1976	14-2	93
76-06	Unemployment & Inflation I	A1	11/16/1976		
	Unemployment & Inflation II	A2	11/16/1976		
	Unemployment & Inflation III	A3	11/16/1976		
	Unemployment & Inflation IV	A4	11/30/1976		
	Unemployment & Inflation V	A5	11/30/1976		
	Cuba	A6	11/16/1976	14-2	RIHOH 195
	Terrorism	A7	11/16/1976	14-2	94*
	United Nations	B1	11/30/1976	14-2	RIHOH 164
	Vietnam I	B2	11/30/1976	14-2	RIHOH 50
	Vietnam II	B3	11/30/1976	14-2	RIHOH 134
	Pardons	B4	11/30/1976	14-2	95
	Child Services Act	B5	11/30/1976	14-2	
	Socialism	B6	11/30/1976	14-2	
	Soviet Visas	B7	11/30/1976	11-3	RIHOH 144
	Human Rights Double Standard	B8	11/30/1976		
76-07	Postal Profits	A1	11/30/1976		
	Special Parents; Special Kids	A2	11/30/1976		
	Update on Social Security	A3	11/30/1976		
	Crime I	A4	11/30/1976	14-2	RIHOH 401
	Crime II	A5	11/30/1976	11-3	
	America's Strength	A6	12/22/1976	11-3	RIHOH 12

O'Connor Number	Title	Side/ Number	Taping Date	Handwritten Draft	Book Page
	Crime	A7	12/22/1976	11-3	RIHOH 400
	Public Broadcasting	B1	12/22/1976	11-3	RIHOH 250
	Welfare	B2	12/22/1976	11-3	RIHOH 390
	Tricentennial	B3	12/22/1976		
	The Family . . . and Other Living Things	B4	12/22/1976		
	Milton Friedman and Chile	B5	12/22/1976	11-3	97
	South Vietnamese Boat People	B6	12/22/1976		
	New Hampshire & Vermont	B7	12/22/1976		
	Memo to a Liberal	B8	12/22/1976		
76-08	Strategic Stockpiles	A1	1/19/1977		
	Farewell Speeches	A2	1/19/1977	14-2	RIHOH 64
	Campaign Law Violated?	A3	1/19/1977		
	Panama	A4	1/19/1977	11-1	
	Television	A5	1/19/1977	11-2	
	Korea	A6	1/19/1977	11-3	107
	People Power	A7	1/19/1977	John McClaughry	
	Tax Limit	B1	12/22/1976	14-2	98
	Television & Profits	B2	12/22/1976	14-2	
	Health Care	B3	12/22/1976	14-2	
	Rapid Transit	B4	12/22/1976	14-2	RIHOH 307
	Junk Food	B5	12/22/1976	11-3	
	Building Codes	B6	1/19/1977	John McClaughry	
	OSHA	B7	1/19/1977	14-2	109
	More About OSHA	B8	1/19/1977	14-2	110
76-xx	**Planned Economy**	1	12/22/1976	14-2	100
76-09	**The Real China?**	A1	1/19/1977	14-2	111
	Capital Gains	A2	1/19/1977	14-2	113
	More About Taxes	A3	1/19/1977	14-2	RIHOH 271
	Postcard Registration	A4	1/19/1977	14-2	RIHOH 244
	Poverty	A5	1/19/1977	14-2	RIHOH 391
	Amnesty	A6	2/2/1977	14-2	114
	Foundations	A7	2/2/1977	14-2	116
	Conservation	B1	2/2/1977		
	China	B2	2/2/1977	14-2	
	Tom Wolfe's New Book	B3	2/2/1977		
	Torrijos, Human Rights and Money Lenders	B4	2/2/1977		
	IBM	B5	2/2/1977	14-2	118
	Congress	B6	2/2/1977	14-2	119
	Civil Service	B7	2/2/1977	14-2	RIHOH 237
	Rhodesia	B8	2/2/1977	14-2	RIHOH 179
76-10	**Minimum Wage**	A1	2/2/1977	14-2	121
	Taxes I	A2	2/2/1977	14-2	122
	Taxes II	A3	2/2/1977	14-2	123
	Taxes III	A4	2/2/1977	14-2	RIHOH 281
	Agriculture Day	A5	3/2/1977	11-2	
	Update on Cuba	A6	3/2/1977	John McClaughry	
	Cuba II	A7	3/2/1977	14-2	125
	England	B1	3/2/1977	14-2	
	Seabrook	B2	3/2/1977	14-2	127
	Germany	B3	3/2/1977	14-2	
	Added Inflation	B4	3/2/1977	14-2	128
	Census	B5	3/2/1977	14-2	RIHOH 239

O'Connor Number	Title	Side/ Number	Taping Date	Handwritten Draft	Book Page
	Sports and Religion	B6	3/2/1977	14-2	130
	Amtrak	B7	3/2/1977		
	Free Press and Property Rights	B8	3/2/1977		
76-11	**Economic Plan**	A1	3/23/1977	14-2	131
	Equal Rights Amendment	A2	3/23/1977		
	Taxes	A3	3/23/1977	14-2	133
	Intelligence	A4	3/23/1977	14-2	RIHOH 117
	Saccharin	A5	3/23/1977		
	National Review	A6	3/23/1977	14-2	134
	Chile I	A7	3/23/1977	14-2	135
	Chile II	B1	3/23/1977	14-2	136
	Chile III	B2	3/23/1977	14-2	137
	Labor	B3	3/23/1977	14-2	RIHOH 245
	Murphy's Law	B4	3/23/1977	14-2	139
	Day Care Centers	B5	3/23/1977	14-2	RIHOH 377
	Charity	B6	3/23/1977	14-2	
	Argo Merchant	B7	3/23/1977	14-2	
	Government by the People	B8	3/23/1977	14-2	
76-12	**Redwoods**	A1	4/13/1977	14-2	140
	Capital Punishment	A2	4/13/1977	14-2	142
	Electoral College	A3	4/13/1977	14-2	RIHOH 242
	Panama	A4	4/13/1977	14-2	143
	Brezhnev	A5	4/13/1977	14-2	RIHOH 212
	Gasohol	A6	4/13/1977	14-2	
	Coal Tar	A7	4/13/1977		
	Human Rights	B1	4/13/1977	14-2	RIHOH 165
	Jamaica	B2	4/13/1977	14-2	145
	Recycled Theater	B3	4/13/1977		
	Environment	B4	4/13/1977	14-2	RIHOH 326
	Education & Religion	B5	4/13/1977	14-2	RIHOH 359
	Miranda	B6	4/13/1977	14-2	146
	Student Letter	B7	4/13/1977	14-2	148
	Arson	B8	4/13/1977	14-2	149
76-13	F.B.I.	A1	5/4/1977		
	A Renewable Source	A2	5/4/1977	14-2	150
	Rhodesia	A3	5/4/1977	14-2	152
	Lawnmowers	A4	5/4/1977	14-2	153
	Cuba & Africa	A5	5/4/1977	14-2	RIHOH 183
	Kidco	A6	5/4/1977	14-2	155
	Keng Piao	A7	5/4/1977	14-2	RIHOH 35
	Punishment	B1	5/4/1977	14-2	RIHOH 399
	Drugs & the F.D.A.	B2	5/4/1977	14-2	RIHOH 297
	Lord Chalfont	B3	5/4/1977	14-2	156
	Recycled Streamliner	B4	5/4/1977		
	Strategy I	B5	5/4/1977	14-2	RIHOH 110
	Strategy II	B6	5/4/1977	14-2	RIHOH 111
	Bill Niehouse	B7	5/4/1977	14-2	157
	Postcard Registration	B8	5/4/1977		
76-14	**Korea**	A1	5/25/1977	14-2	RIHOH 66
	F.B.I.	A2	5/25/1977	14-2	159
	Voting	A3	5/25/1977	14-2	RIHOH 241
	Public Servants	A4	5/25/1977	14-2	RIHOH 298
	Cuba—Trouble in Paradise	A5	5/25/1977		
	National Review	A6	5/25/1977	14-2	

O'Connor Number	Title	Side/ Number	Taping Date	Handwritten Draft	Book Page
	Cambodia #1	A7	5/25/1977	14-2	RIHOH 36
	Cambodia #2	B1	5/25/1977	14-2	RIHOH 38
	Cambodia #3	B2	5/25/1977	14-2	RIHOH 40
	Soviet Workers	B3	5/25/1977	14-2	RIHOH 146
	Why Government Costs Money	B4	5/25/1977	14-2	160
	Marijuana	B5	5/25/1977	14-2	162
	Government Spending	B6	5/25/1977	14-2	RIHOH 256
	Inflation	B7	5/25/1977	14-2	163
	Russians	B8	5/25/1977	14-3	RIHOH 33
76-15	Privacy Bureau	A1	6/15/1977	Peter Hannaford	
	Vietnam	A2	6/15/1977	14-2	165
	Oil I	A3	6/15/1977	14-3	RIHOH 318
	Oil II	A4	6/15/1977	14-2	166
	Cuba	A5	6/15/1977	14-2	RIHOH 156
	Episcopal Controversy	A6	6/15/1977	Peter Hannaford	
	Intelligence	A7	6/15/1977	14-2	RIHOH 124
	OSHA	B1	6/15/1977	14-2	RIHOH 288
	DNA Research	B2	6/15/1977	Peter Hannaford	
	Indexing	B3	6/15/1977	14-2	RIHOH 272
	Force Account Work	B4	6/15/1977	Peter Hannaford	
	Common Sense Bureaucrats	B5	6/15/1977	Peter Hannaford	
	Economic Fairy Tales	B6	6/15/1977	14-2	168
	Health Costs	B7	6/15/1977	14-3	169
	Names	B8	6/15/1977	14-2	171
76-16	**Private Property**	A1	7/6/1977	14-2	172
	The Hatch Act	A2	7/6/1977	14-2	**173**
	South Africa	A3	7/6/1977	14-2	RIHOH 185
	Food Stamps	A4	7/6/1977	14-2	RIHOH 393
	Man's Castle	A5	7/6/1977	14-2	RIHOH 291
	Jamaica	A6	7/6/1977	14-2	RIHOH 196
	Endangered Species	A7	7/6/1977	14-2	RIHOH 329
	Socialized Medicine	B1	7/6/1977	14-2	RIHOH 366
	The Principal's Principles	B2	7/6/1977		
	Property Rights	B3	7/6/1977	14-2	RIHOH 167
	Cambodia	B4	7/6/1977	14-2	175
	Bulletins	B5	7/6/1977	14-2	
	Spending	B6	7/6/1977	14-2	176
	Government Cost	B7	7/6/1977	14-3	178
	Quiz	B8	7/6/1977	14-2	179
76-17	Food Stamps	A1	July-77		
	Neutron Bomb I	A2	July-77		
	Neutron Bomb II	A3	July-77		
	Ukraine	A4	July-77		
	Tax Shift	A5	July-77		
	Drunk Driving	A6	July-77		
	Korea I	A7	July-77		
	Korea II	A8	July-77		
	Korea III	B1	July-77		
	Laxalt	B2	July-77		
	Human Rights	B3	July-77		
	Snail Darter	B4	July-77		
	Busing	B5	July-77		
	NEA	B6	July-77		

O'Connor Number	Title	Side/ Number	Taping Date	Handwritten Draft	Book Page
	Porpoises And Tuna	B7	July-77		
	Small Business	B8	July-77		
76-18	**Panama**	A1	8/15/1977	14-2	RIHOH 198
	Cover Up	A2	8/15/1977	14-2 ldt	
	Justice Department	A3	8/15/1977	14-2 ldt	
	Unemployment	A4	8/15/1977	14-2 ldt	RIHOH 266
	Medical Care	A5	8/15/1977	14-2 ldt	181
	World Research	A6	8/15/1977	14-2	
	TRIS	A7	8/15/1977	14-2 ldt	
	Montage	B1	8/15/1977	14-2 ldt	
	Dream World	B2	8/15/1977	14-2 ldt	182
	Tom Hayden	B3	8/15/1977	14-3 ldt—gr	183
	Business	B4	8/15/1977	14-2 ldt—gr bl	185
	Inflation	B5	8/15/1977	14-2 ldt—gr	186
	Korea	B6	8/15/1977	14-2 bl.	RIHOH 41
	Rhodesia	B7	8/15/1977	14-2 gr.	188
	Foreign Aid	B8	8/15/1977	14-2 ldt bl	RIHOH 168
76-19	***L.A. Times***	A1	9/6/1977	14-2	RIHOH 199
	Panama Canal I	A2	9/6/1977	14-2	RIHOH 201
	Panama Canal II	A3	9/6/1977	14-3	RIHOH 202
	The Bible	A4	9/6/1977	14-2	RIHOH 409
	Kettering	A5	9/6/1977	14-2	RIHOH 309
	Government Costs	A6	9/6/1977	14-2	189
	Cuba I	A7	9/6/1977	14-2	191
	Cuba II	B1	9/6/1977	14-2	192
	Youth Employment	B2	9/6/1977	14-2	RIHOH 303
	The Olympics	B3	9/6/1977	14-2	RIHOH 214
	Government Can Cost Less I	B4	9/6/1977	14-2	193
	Government Can Cost Less II	B5	9/6/1977	14-2	195
	Pensions	B6	9/6/1977	14-2	RIHOH 373
	Blackout	B7	9/6/1977	14-2	196
	Furbish Lousewart	B8	9/6/1977	14-2	197
77-20	**Pot**	A1	9/27/1977	14-2 ldt	199
	Rhodesia	A2	9/27/1977	14-2 ldt	
	Carter Welfare Reform #1	A3	9/27/1977		
	Carter Welfare Reform #2	A4	9/27/1977		
	The Stalinoids	A5	9/27/1977	John McClaughry	
	Hospital Costs	A6	9/27/1977	14-2	200
	Mozambique	A7	9/27/1977	14-2	RIHOH 186
	Olympics	B1	9/27/1977	14-2 ldt	201
	Tax Limitation	B2	9/27/1977	14-2 ldt	202*
	Air Bags	B3	9/27/1977	14-2 ldt	204
	Camps	B4	9/27/1977	14-2 ldt	205
	The Military	B5	9/27/1977	14-2 ldt	RIHOH 69
	Property Rights	B6	9/27/1977	14-2	RIHOH 340
	Congressional Committees	B7	9/27/1977	14-2 ldt	RIHOH 126
	The Myth of the Medicare Millionaires	B8	9/27/1977		
77-21	**Energy**	A1	10/18/1977	14-2	206
	Carter Welfare Reform	A2	10/18/1977		
	Treaties	A3	10/18/1977	14-2	RIHOH 51
	Panama I	A4	10/18/1977	14-2	RIHOH 204
	Panama II	A5	10/18/1977	14-2	RIHOH 205

O'Connor Number	Title	Side/ Number	Taping Date	Handwritten Draft	Book Page
	Panama III	A6	10/18/1977	14-3	208
	Steel	A7	10/18/1977	14-2 dark	209
	Land	B1	10/18/1977	14-3 dark	
	Taxes	B2	10/18/1977	14-2 dark	RIHOH 274
	Energy I	B3	10/18/1977	14-2 dark	212
	Energy II	B4	10/18/1977	14-2 dark	213
	Equal Time	B5	10/18/1977	14-2	214
	Items	B6	10/18/1977	14-2	
	Investigative Agencies	B7	10/18/1977	14-2	216*
	Drugs	B8	10/18/1977	14-2	
77-22	**SALT**	A1	11/8/1977	14-2 gr	RIHOH 75
	Pushers	A2	11/8/1977	14-2	217
	Kearney	A3	11/8/1977	14-2	
	Alaska	A4	11/8/1977	14-2	RIHOH 336
	Good News	A5	11/8/1977	14-2	
	Youth and Crime	A6	11/8/1977	14-2	218
	Free Enterprise	A7	11/8/1977	14-2	220
	Aid to Vietnam	B1	11/8/1977	14-2	221
	The Individual	B2	11/8/1977	14-2	222
	Taxation	B3	11/8/1977	14-2 dark	223
	Energy	B4	11/8/1977	14-2	225
	Restitution	B5	11/8/1977	14-2	226
	Freedom	B6	11/8/1977	14-2	227*
	An Angry Man I	B7	11/8/1977	14-2	229
	An Angry Man II	B8	11/8/1977	14-2	230
77-23	Superintendent's Dilemma	A1	11/21/1977	repeat	
	Capitalism/Socialism	A2	11/21/1977	repeat	
	Socialism	A3	11/21/1977	repeat	
	Inflation and the Property Tax I	A4	11/21/1977	repeat	
	Inflation and the Property Tax II	A5	11/21/1977	repeat	
	Public Employees	A6	11/21/1977	repeat	
	Red Hen	A7	11/21/1977	repeat	
	President Coolidge	B1	11/21/1977	repeat	
	Education	B2	11/21/1977	repeat	
	Christmas 1977	B3	11/21/1977		
	Bread Machine and Janeway	B4	11/21/1977	repeat	
	The Incredible Bread Machine	B5	11/21/1977	repeat	
	People Power	B6	11/21/1977	repeat	
	Button, Button	B7	11/21/1977	repeat	
	America's Strength	B8	11/21/1977	repeat	
77-24	**Snail Darters**	A1	11/29/1977	14-2 gr dark	231*
	Nicaragua I	A2	11/29/1977	Peter Hannaford	
	Nicaragua II	A3	11/29/1977	Peter Hannaford	
	Visas	A4	11/29/1977	14-2	232
	National Security	A5	11/29/1977	14-2	233*
	National Health Insurance I	A6	11/29/1977	14-2	235
	National Health Insurance II	A7	11/29/1977	14-2	236
	Social Security	B1	11/29/1977	14-2	RIHOH 370
	Martin Luther King	B2	11/29/1977	14-2	RIHOH 385
	Coffee	B3	11/29/1977	14-2 gr dark	
	Automobiles	B4	11/29/1977	14-2 gr dark	237
	NEA	B5	11/29/1977	14-2	RIHOH 351

O'Connor Number	Title	Side/ Number	Taping Date	Handwritten Draft	Book Page
	Kidco	B6	11/29/1977	14-2	
	Apples	B7	11/29/1977	14-2 gr bl	RIHOH 301
	Herman Kahn, Futurist	B8	11/29/1977	repeat	
77-xx	**The Execution**	1	Jan–77	14-3	239
78-01	SALT II	A1	1/9/1978		
	Christmas	A2	1/9/1978	14-2	247
	American Farm School I	A3	1/9/1978	14-2	248
	American Farm School II	A4	1/9/1978	14-2	250
	Human Rights I	A5	1/9/1978	14-2	RIHOH 53
	Human Rights II	A6	1/9/1978	14-2	RIHOH 150
	Human Rights III	A7	1/9/1978	14-2	RIHOH 152
	Taxes	B1	1/9/1978	14-2	251
	Our Country	B2	1/9/1978	14-2	252
	Crime	B3	1/9/1978	14-2	254
	Miscellaneous	B4	1/9/1978	14-2	
	Welfare	B5	1/9/1978	14-2	RIHOH 394
	Healthy Competition	B6	1/9/1978	John McClaughry	
	Pot	B7	1/9/1978	14-2	255
	Social Security	B8	1/9/1978	14-2	RIHOH 372
78-02	**Big Mo**	A1	1/27/1978	14-2	
	Panama	A2	1/27/1978	14-1 red	256*
	St. Stephan's Crown	A3	1/27/1978	14-1	
	Korea	A4	1/27/1978	14-2	RIHOH 68
	Oil	A5	1/27/1978	14-2	257
	"Independents" vs. IRS	A6	1/27/1978	John McClaughry	
	Regulation	A7	1/27/1978	14-2	259
	Welfare Reform	B1	1/27/1978	14-2	260
	Miscellaneous	B2	1/27/1978	14-2	
	Looking Out a Window	B3	1/27/1978	14-2	RIHOH 18
	Jobs	B4	1/27/1978	14-2	261
	Miscellaneous	B5	1/27/1978	14-2	
	Pity the Middle Class	B6	1/27/1978		
	Miscellaneous	B7	1/27/1978		
	Father & Son	B8	1/27/1978	14-1	262
78-03	**Panama Canal Debate**	A1	2/20/1978	14-2	264
	Spaceships	A2	2/20/1978	14-2	265*
	Redwoods	A3	2/20/1978	14-2	266
	Swordfish	A4	2/20/1978		
	Farm Day	A5	2/20/1978	14-2 blue	268
	Tax Limitation 1978 Style	A6	2/20/1978		
	Steel	A7	2/20/1978	14-2	269
	Labor	B1	2/20/1978	14-2	270
	Economy	B2	2/20/1978	14-2	272
	Neighborhoods	B3	2/20/1978	John McClaughry	
	Cuba	B4	2/20/1978	14-2	
	Treaties	B5	2/20/1978	14-2	273
	Neutron Bomb	B6	2/20/1978		
	Bakke	B7	2/20/1978	14-2	274
	Blind on the Left	B8	2/20/1978	14-2	RIHOH 136
78-04	**Canal**	A1	3/13/1978	14-2	
	Treaties	A2	3/13/1978	14-2	RIHOH 54
	SALT Talks I	A3	3/13/1978	14-2	RIHOH 76
	SALT Talks II	A4	3/13/1978	14-2	275*
	Cubans & Russians	A5	3/13/1978	14-2	RIHOH 207
	SALT II	A6	3/13/1978	14-2	RIHOH 77

O'Connor Number	Title	Side/ Number	Taping Date	Handwritten Draft	Book Page
	Two Worlds	A7	3/13/1978	14-2	
	War	B1	3/13/1978	14-2	RIHOH 99
	Suicide Lobby	B2	3/13/1978	14-2	RIHOH 139
	Budget	B3	3/13/1978	14-2	276
	Mineral King	B4	3/13/1978	14-2 green	278
	Local Control I	B5	3/13/1978	14-2	279
	Local Control II	B6	3/13/1978	14-2	280
	A Gift	B7	3/13/1978	14-2	RIHOH 388
	Items	B8	3/13/1978	14-2	
78-05	**Canal**	A1	4/3/1978	14-2	RIHOH 208
	Tax Time	A2	4/3/1978	14-2	
	Crime	A3	4/3/1978	14-2	281
	China	A4	4/3/1978	14-2	RIHOH 58
	Bill Simon	A5	4/3/1978	14-2	
	Missing Person	A6	4/3/1978	14-2	RIHOH 411
	Three Martini Lunch	A7	4/3/1978	14-2	283
	Government	A8	4/3/1978	14-2	
	Spies	B1	4/3/1978	14-2	284
	No Pay, No Vote	B2	4/3/1978	14-2	RIHOH 171
	B-1 Bomber	B3	4/3/1978	14-2	RIHOH 103
	Farm	B4	4/3/1978	14-2	
	Regulators	B5	4/3/1978	14-2	285
	Miscellaneous	B6	4/3/1978	14-2	
	General James	B7	4/3/1978	14-2 dark	287
	Desk-Cleaning	B8	4/3/1978	14-2 dark	RIHOH 141
78-06	**Guinea**	A1	2/20/1978	14-2	RIHOH 170
	Christmas	A2	2/20/1978	14-2	RIHOH 415
	Do Right	A3	2/20/1978	1/2	288
	Life & Death	A4	2/20/1978	14-2	290*
	School Days	A5	2/20/1978	14-2	RIHOH 345
	Government Security	A6	3/13/1978	14-2	291
	Sports	A7	3/13/1978	14-2 dark	292
	Fighting Cal Graham	B1	3/13/1978	John McClaughry	
	Greensville County Elections	B2	3/13/1978	John McClaughry	
	Snails & Signboards	B3	3/13/1978		
	Nit Picking	B4	4/3/1978	14-2	
	Communications I	B5	4/3/1978	14-2 dark	RIHOH 300
	Communications II	B6	4/3/1978	14-2	
	Soviet Consumers	B7	4/3/1978	John McClaughry	
	Air Cargo De-Regulation	B8	4/3/1978		
78-07	**Japan I**	A1	5/15/1978	14-2p	293
	Japan II	A2	5/15/1978	14-2p	RIHOH 287
	Japan III	A3	5/15/1978	14-2p	RIHOH 114
	Taiwan I	A4	5/15/1978	14-2p	RIHOH 43
	Hong Kong	A5	5/15/1978	14-2p	RIHOH 113
	Women	A6	5/15/1978	14-2p	295*
	Education	A7	5/15/1978	14-2	296
	Alger Hiss	B1	5/15/1978	14-2	297
	Rhodesia	B2	5/15/1978	14-2	299
	The Pacific	B3	5/15/1978	14-2	RIHOH 116
	Seal Hunt	B4	5/15/1978	14-2	RIHOH 334
	Dulles Airport	B5	5/15/1978	14-2	300
	Castro's Prisons	B6	5/15/1978	14-2	301
	Miscellaneous	B7	5/15/1978	14-2	
	Health Care	B8	5/15/1978	14-2	302

O'Connor Number	Title	Side/ Number	Taping Date	Handwritten Draft	Book Page
78-08	**Taxes Again**	A1	6/5/1978	14-2	RIHOH 277
	National Security	A2	6/5/1978	14-2	304
	Hearst	A3	6/5/1978	14-3	305
	Spending	A4	6/5/1978	14-2	307
	Energy	A5	6/5/1978	14-2	308
	Oil	A6	6/5/1978	14-2	309
	Russia	A7	6/5/1978	14-2	310
	Planes	B1	6/5/1978	14-2	312
	Drugs	B2	6/5/1978	14-2	313
	Foolishness	B3	6/5/1978	14-2	
	Money	B4	6/5/1978	14-2	314
	New Talk from a Labor Leader	B5	6/5/1978	John McClaughry	
	Salaries	B6	6/5/1978	14-2	315
	Davis-Bacon Act	B7	6/5/1978		
	Education	B8	6/5/1978	14-2	316
78-09	Normalization	A2	6/27/1978		
	U.S.–China Relations	A1	6/27/1978		
	District of Columbia	A3	6/27/1978	14-2	318
	Fraud	A4	6/27/1978	14-2	
	SALT Talks	A5	6/27/1978	14-2	RIHOH 79
	Cities	A6	6/27/1978	14-2	319
	Stamps	A7	6/27/1978	14-2	320
	Asia	B1	6/27/1978	14-2	322
	Asia II	B2	6/27/1978	14-2	323
	Free Press	B3	6/27/1978	14-2	325
	Alex. Solzhenitsyn	B4	6/27/1978	14-2	326
	Alex. Solzhenitsyn II	B5	6/27/1978	14-2	327
	Inflation	B6	6/27/1978	14-2	328
	Malibu	B7	6/27/1978	14-2	RIHOH 331
	Miscellaneous	B8	6/27/1978	14-2	
78-10	**Government**	A1	6/27/1978	14-2	329
	Mirages	A2	6/27/1978	14-2	331
	Lumber	A3	6/27/1978	14-2	332
	Freedom of Speech in Russia	A4	6/27/1978	14-2	333*
	Stanley Yankus	A5	6/27/1978	14-2	334
	Charity	A6	Jul-78	14-2	336
	School Busing	A7	Jul-78		
	Wedding	B1	Jul-78	14-2	337*
	South Africa	B2	Jul-78	14-2	RIHOH 188
	Cuba	B3	Jul-78	14-2	339
	Castro	B4	Jul-78	14-2	RIHOH 59
	Walter Knott	B5	Jul-78		
	Trains	B6	Jul-78	14-1	340
	Chiefs of Staff	B7	Jul-78	14-2	RIHOH 70
	Proposition 13	B8	Jul-78	14-2	341
78-11	**SALT Talks I**	A1	Jul-78	14-2	RIHOH 82
	SALT Talks II	A2	Jul-78	14-2	RIHOH 84
	Employment	A3	Jul-78	14-2	343
	Economics I	A4	Jul-78	14-2	RIHOH 258
	Economics II	A5	Jul-78	14-2	RIHOH 259
	Paperwork	A6	Jul-78	14-2	
	Religious Freedom	A7	Jul-78	14-2	344
	Miscellaneous	B1	Jul-78	14-2	
	Rome	B2	Jul-78	14-2	RIHOH 238

O'Connor Number	Title	Side/ Number	Taping Date	Handwritten Draft	Book Page
	South Seas	B3	Jul-78	14-2	345
	Prisoner Exchange	B4	8/7/1978	14-2	347
	Local Government Center	B5	8/7/1978	John McClaughry	
	Alternative Energy and Uncle Sam	B6	8/7/1978	John McClaughry	
	A Refugee Success Story	B7	8/7/1978	John McClaughry	
	Accidents	B8	8/7/1978	14-2	
78-12	**Income Tax**	A1	8/7/1978	14-2	348
	British Health Care	A2	8/7/1978	14-2	349
	History	A3	8/7/1978	14-2	
	Brainwashing I	A4	8/7/1978	14-2	351
	Brainwashing II	A5	8/7/1978	14-2	352
	Tax Revolt	A6	8/7/1978	14-2	354
	Left & Right	A7	8/7/1978	John McClaughry	
	The Average Man	B1	8/7/1978	14-2	355
	Polls and Guns	B2	8/7/1978	14-2	RIHOH 403
	Guantanamo	B3	8/7/1978	14-2	RIHOH 209
	Government Cost	B4	8/7/1978	14-2	356
	Pay Raise	B5	8/7/1978	14-2	
	Miscellaneous	B6	8/7/1978	14-2	
	Two Worlds	B7	8/7/1978	14-2	RIHOH 13
	Technology	B8	8/7/1978	14-2	RIHOH 313
78-13	Mexico's Oil	A1	9/19/1978		
	Olympics	A2	9/19/1978	14-2	RIHOH 147
	Prop. 13 Fallout	A3	9/19/1978	14-2	
	Terrorism	A4	9/19/1978		
	Land	A5	9/19/1978	14-2	357
	Pot	A6	9/19/1978	14-2	359
	Nuclear Power	A7	9/19/1978	14-2	RIHOH 324
	Needed—Better Use of National Forests	B1	9/19/1978		
	Mail	B2	9/19/1978	14-2	RIHOH 407
	Africa	B3	9/19/1978	14-2	RIHOH 193
	Utilities	B4	9/19/1978	14-2	360
	Bugs	B5	9/19/1978	14-2	RIHOH 333
	Government Payroll	B6	9/19/1978	14-2	
	Free Enterprise	B7	9/19/1978	14-2	361
	Miscellaneous	B8	9/19/1978	14-2	
78-14	**District of Columbia**	A1	10/10/1978	14-2	363
	Amtrak	A2	10/10/1978	14-2	364
	Bi-Lingual	A3	10/10/1978	14-2 dark	365*
	Federal Lands	A4	10/10/1978	14-2	RIHOH 337
	Ocean Mining	A5	10/10/1978	14-2	RIHOH 173
	Rostow I	A6	10/10/1978	14-2	RIHOH 92
	Rostow II	A7	10/10/1978	14-2	RIHOH 93
	Rostow III	B1	10/10/1978	14-2	RIHOH 94
	Rostow IV	B2	10/10/1978	14-2	RIHOH 95
	Rostow V	B3	10/10/1978	14-2	RIHOH 97
	Rostow VI	B4	10/10/1978	14-2	RIHOH 98
	End of An Emergency	B5	10/10/1978		
	Argentina	B6	10/10/1978		
	Environment	B7	10/10/1978	14-2	367
	Soviet Nuclear Power	B8	10/10/1978		
78-15	Letelier I	A1	10/31/1978		
	Letelier II	A2	10/31/1978		

O'Connor Number	Title	Side/ Number	Taping Date	Handwritten Draft	Book Page
	Intelligence and the Media	A3	10/31/1978	14-2	RIHOH 127
	Welfare	A4	10/31/1978	14-2	368
	The Escalator	A5	10/31/1978	14-2	
	Nuclear Power I	A6	10/31/1978	14-2	
	Nuclear Power II	A7	10/31/1978	14-2	
	Crime	B1	10/31/1978	14-2	369
	Waste	B2	10/31/1978	14-2	
	Nuclear Carrier	B3	10/31/1978	14-2	370
	Pensions	B4	10/31/1978	14-2	371
	Self-help in the Neighborhoods	B5	10/31/1978	John McClaughry	
	Chinese Libertarians	B6	10/31/1978	John McClaughry	
	Davis-Bacon Act	B7	10/31/1978		
	Miscellaneous	B8	10/31/1978	14-2	
78-16	**Private schools**	A1	Nov-78	14-2	RIHOH 354
	Toys	A2	Nov-78	14-2	373
	Hope for the Cities	A3	Nov-78	Peter Hannaford	
	Basketball	A4	Nov-78	14-2	RIHOH 378
	Horse & Rider I	A5	Nov-78	14-2	374
	Horse & Rider II	A6	Nov-78	14-2	375
	China	A7	Nov-78	14-2	376
	SALT II	B1	Nov-78	14-2	RIHOH 85
	Jokes	B2	Nov-78	Peter Hannaford	
	An Accurate Thermometer	B3	Nov-78	Peter Hannaford	
	Miscellaneous	B4	Nov-78	14-2	
	Wood I	B5	Nov-78	14-2	377
	Wood II	B6	Nov-78	14-2	379
	Bilingualism	B7	Nov-78	Peter Hannaford	
	Taxation	B8	Nov-78	14-2	RIHOH 279
78-17	Christmas Day	A1	12/12/1978		
	SALT II	A2	12/12/1978	14-2	RIHOH 86
	Panama Canal	A3	12/12/1978	14-2	380
	Gambling on the Dollar	A4	12/12/1978	John McClaughry	
	The Checkoff Ripoff	A5	12/12/1978	John McClaughry	
	Gas	A6	12/12/1978	14-2	
	Taxes	A7	12/12/1978	14-2	381
	Keep Off the Grass	B1	12/12/1978	14-2	383
	Helsinki Pact	B2	12/12/1978	14-2	RIHOH 154
	Bread	B3	12/12/1978	14-2	384
	Business Tax	B4	12/12/1978	14-2	385
	E.R.A.	B5	12/12/1978	14-2	386
	Miscellaneous I	B6	12/12/1978	14-2	
	Miscellaneous II	B7	12/12/1978	14-2	
	Textbooks	B8	12/12/1978	14-2	388
78-xx	**Young People**	1	Jan-78	14-2	389
	Vietnam I	2	Feb-78	14-2	390
	Vietnam II	3	Feb-78	14-2	392
	Birthday Party	4	April 78	14-2	393
	Doing Something About Government	5	Undated	14-2	394
	Miscellaneous	6	After April 78	14-2	
	Nonsense	7	After 6/6/78	14-2	395
79-01	Taiwan	A1	Jan-79		
	Taiwan I	A2	Jan-79	11-2	RIHOH 61
	Taiwan II	A3	Jan-79	11-2	RIHOH 45

O'Connor Number	Title	Side/ Number	Taping Date	Handwritten Draft	Book Page
	Taiwan III	A4	Jan-79	11-2	403
	Jim Hendricks	A5	Jan-79	11-2	404
	Patent Medicine I	A6	Jan-79	14-2	405*
	Patent Medicine II	A7	Jan-79	14-2	406
	Human Rights	B1	Jan-79	11-2	RIHOH 155
	Health Insurance	B2	Jan-79	11-3	
	Telescope I	B3	Jan-79	11-2	RIHOH 310
	Telescope II	B4	Jan-79	11-2	RIHOH 311
	Miscellaneous I	B5	Jan-79	14-2	
	Miscellaneous II	B6	Jan-79	14-2	
	Miscellaneous III	B7	Jan-79	11-2	
	South Africa	B8	Jan-79	11-2	RIHOH 189
79-02	**Phone**	A1	1/19/1979	11-3	RIHOH 316
	OPEC	A2	1/19/1979	11-2	RIHOH 321
	Federal Trade Commission	A3	1/19/1979	11-2	408
	The Official Rules	A4	1/19/1979	John McClaughry	
	Anti-Poverty Abuses I	A5	1/19/1979		
	Anti-Poverty Abuses II	A6	1/19/1979		
	Wind Energy in Denmark	A7	1/19/1979	John McClaughry	
	Counterintelligence	B1	1/19/1979	11-3	409
	Australia I	B1	1/19/1979	11-3	410
	Australia II	B3	1/19/1979	11-2	412
	Peace Corps	B4	1/19/1979	11-2	413
	A Policeman	B5	1/19/1979	11-2	414
	Miscellaneous 1	B6	1/19/1979	John McClaughry	
	Miscellaneous 2	B7	1/19/1979	11-2	
	Regulations	B8	1/19/1979	11-2	416
79-03	Proposition 13 and the Post Commission—I	A1	2/13/1979		
	Proposition 13 and the Post Commission—II	A2	2/13/1979		
	Deregulation	A3	2/13/1979		
	Dishonest Environmentalists	A4	2/13/1979	John McClaughry	
	Fish	A5	2/13/1979	14-2	RIHOH 290
	Constitutional Amendment	A6	2/13/1979	14-2	RIHOH 284
	Pot	A7	2/13/1979	14-2	417
	Saying "No"-Part I	B1	2/13/1979	14-2	
	Saying "No"-Part II	B2	2/13/1979	14-2	
	Conspiracy	B3	2/13/1979	14-2	RIHOH 234
	Lawrence Welk	B4	2/13/1979	14-2	418
	Income Tax	B5	2/13/1979	14-2	RIHOH 280
	Hamburgers	B6	2/13/1979	14-2	420
	Long Walk	B7	2/13/1979	14-2	421
	Miscellaneous	B8	2/13/1979	14-2	
79-04	**Nancy**	A1	3/6/1979	14-2	RIHOH 355
	Lettuce Strike	A2	3/6/1979		
	Taiwan's Future	A3	3/6/1979	14-2	RIHOH 72
	P.O.W.	A4	3/6/1979	14-2	422
	Cuba	A5	3/6/1979	14-2	RIHOH 158
	The 100 Club	A6	3/6/1979	14-2	424
	C.I.A.	A7	3/6/1979	14-2	
	Miscellaneous	B1	3/6/1979	14-2	
	Inflation	B2	3/6/1979	14-2	425
	Human Rights	B3	3/6/1979	14-2	426*
	Comparisons	B4	3/6/1979	14-2	RIHOH 229

O'Connor Number	Title	Side/ Number	Taping Date	Handwritten Draft	Book Page
	Nuclear Power I	B5	3/6/1979	14-2	
	Nuclear Power II	B6	3/6/1979	14-2 gr bl	428
	Higher Standard of Living	B7	3/6/1979	14-2 gr dark	
	Student Economists	B8	3/6/1979		
79-05	**Panama**	A1	3/27/1979	14-2	RIHOH 211
	Small Business I	A2	3/27/1979	14-2	429
	Small Business II	A3	3/27/1979	14-2	
	Scared Straight	A4	3/27/1979		
	Palestine	A5	3/27/1979	14-2	RIHOH 215
	Miscellaneous	A6	3/27/1979	14-2	
	Agriculture	A7	3/27/1979	14-2	RIHOH 304
	Rhodesia	B1	3/27/1979	14-2	431
	District of Columbia	B2	3/27/1979	14-2	432
	Miscellaneous II	B3	3/27/1979	14-2	
	Rural Renaissance	B4	3/27/1979	John McClaughry	
	Washington Weather	B5	3/27/1979	14-2	433
	SALT II - Part I	B6	3/27/1979	14-2	RIHOH 88
	SALT II - Part II	B7	3/27/1979	14-2	RIHOH 89
	Miscellaneous III	B8	3/27/1979	14-2	
79-06	New England Energy Barriers	A1	4/16/1979	John McClaughry	
	Land Use: The California Precedent	A2	4/16/1979		
	The Real Impact of Inflation	A3	4/16/1979		
	Real Estate Signs	A4	4/16/1979	1979	
	Jonestown	A5	4/16/1979	14-2	434
	David & Goliath	A6	4/16/1979	14-3	
	Schools	A7	4/16/1979	14-2	RIHOH 352
	Budget	B1	4/16/1979	14-2 p	RIHOH 285
	Food Stamps	B2	4/16/1979	14-2	
	Bilingual Education I	B3	4/16/1979	14-2	436
	Bilingual Education II	B4	4/16/1979	14-2	RIHOH 346
	Regulations Go to College	B5	4/16/1979	14-2	RIHOH 360
	The Salcido Family	B6	4/16/1979	14-2	437
	Miscellaneous	B7	4/16/1979	14-2	
	Free Enterprise	B8	4/16/1979	14-2	RIHOH 228
79-07	**T.K.E.**	A1	5/8/1979	14-2	RIHOH 209
	Three Mile Island - I	A2	5/8/1979	14-2	438
	Three Mile Island - II	A3	5/8/1979	14-2	440
	Whistle Blowers; Poverty's Causes	A4	5/8/1979		
	Parable of the Talents—Updated	A5	5/8/1979	William Gavin	
	McCarthy	A6	5/8/1979	14-2	
	Miscellaneous	A7	5/8/1979	14-2	
	Grove City College	B1	5/8/1979	14-2 p	
	I'm Only 17	B2	5/8/1979	14-1 p	441
	Oil	B3	5/8/1979	14-2 p	442
	Fluid Flame Burner	B4	5/8/1979	14-2 p	
	Disaster Area	B5	5/8/1979	14-2	444
	Sex Education	B6	5/8/1979	14-2	RIHOH 347
	Graffiti	B7	5/8/1979		
	Banned Words	B8	5/8/1979		
79-08	**California Gas Shortage**	A1	5/29/1979	14-2	RIHOH 322
	Oil	A2	5/29/1979	14-2	445
	Sex Education	A3	5/29/1979	14-2	446

O'Connor Number	Title	Side/ Number	Taping Date	Handwritten Draft	Book Page
	People's Park I	A4	5/29/1979	14-2	448
	People's Park II	A5	5/29/1979	14-2	449
	Free Trade vs. Protectionism	A6	5/29/1979		
	Political Bestiary	A7	5/29/1979		
	Marijuana	B1	5/29/1979	14-2	450
	The Delaney Amendment	B2	5/29/1979		
	Miscellaneous I	B3	5/29/1979	14-2	RIHOH 104
	Miscellaneous II	B4	5/29/1979	14-2	RIHOH 46
	Investment Lag	B5	5/29/1979		
	Crime	B6	5/29/1979	14-2	451
	Vietnam War	B7	5/29/1979	14-2	453
	Operation Get Smart	B8	5/29/1979		
79-09	**John Wayne**	A1	6/29/1979	14-2 dark	RIHOH 412
	Double Standard	A2	6/29/1979		
	The Pope in Poland	A3	6/29/1979	14-2	RIHOH 174
	Nuclear Power	A4	6/29/1979	14-2	454
	Oil Profits	A5	6/29/1979	14-2 dark	
	Miscellaneous	A6	6/29/1979	14-2	
	Money	A7	6/29/1979	14-2	RIHOH 261
	A Green Lawn	B1	6/29/1979	1/3	
	Bukovsky	B2	6/29/1979	14-2	RIHOH 149
	Molecules	B3	6/29/1979	14-2 dark	455
	A Tale of Two Countries	B4	6/29/1979	14-2	RIHOH 176
	Joan Baez I	B5	6/29/1979	14-2	456
	Joan Baez II	B6	6/29/1979	14-2	458
	The Family	B7	6/29/1979	14-2	RIHOH 375
	Corruption	B8	6/29/1979	14-2	457
79-10	Busing Amendment	A1	7/9/1979		
	Sen. Jackson on SALT II	A2	7/9/1979		
	Soviet Trade	A3	7/9/1979	14-2	RIHOH 73
	Trains	A4	7/9/1979	14-2	RIHOH 306
	Nigeria	A5	7/9/1979	14-2	RIHOH 16
	Assembly Line Medicine I	A6	7/9/1979	14-2	466
	Assembly Line Medicine II	A7	7/9/1979	14-2	RIHOH 368
	Namibia I	B1	7/9/1979	14-2	RIHOH 190
	Namibia II	B2	7/9/1979	14-2	RIHOH 192
	The MSHA Test	B3	7/9/1979		
	Free Speech for Business?	B4	7/9/1979	14-2 dark	461
	Energy-Saving Computer	B5	7/9/1979		
	Project Match	B6	7/9/1979		
	Miscellaneous	B7	7/9/1979	14-2 dark	
	Elementary Energy Lessons	B8	7/9/1979		
79-11	Congressional Promises and Performance	A1	7/27/1979		
	Income Tax Indexation	A2	7/27/1979		
	Chile	A3	7/27/1979	14-2	RIHOH 142
	International Year of the Child	A4	7/27/1979		
	Tax Expenditures	A5	7/27/1979	14-2	RIHOH 283
	Another Side of the U.N.	A6	7/27/1979		
	A Different Watergate Story	A7	7/27/1979		
	Miscellaneous I	B1	7/27/1979	14-2	
	Neoconservatives	B2	7/27/1979		
	Common Sense from a Neighbor	B3	7/27/1979		

O'Connor Number	Title	Side/ Number	Taping Date	Handwritten Draft	Book Page
	America	B4	7/27/1979	14-2	462
	Miscellaneous II	B5	7/27/1979	14-2	
	Free Speech	B6	7/27/1979	14-2	464
	Showcase U.S.A.	B7	7/27/1979	14-2	465
	Miscellaneous III	B8	7/27/1979	14-2	466
79-12	What to Expect from the Soviet Succession	A1	Aug-79		
	Thank You, Chairman Brezhnev	A2	Aug-79		
	Better Representation for Skilled Tradesmen	A3	Aug-79		
	Government Housing Programs	A4	Aug-79		
	Alaskan Anger	A5	Aug-79		
	Waiting in Line	A6	Aug-79		
	Citizen vs. Chicago Transit Authority	A7	Aug-79		
	Tax Revolt Going Strong	B1	Aug-79		
	The Magic Money Machine	B2	Aug-79	14-2	467
	Administration Report Clears Oil Companies	B3	Aug-79		
	Marijuana	B4	Aug-79	14-2	RIHOH 396
	Voting Records	B5	Aug-79	14-2	
	Power	B6	Aug-79	14-2	469
	Food Stamps	B7	Aug-79	14-2	470
	Living Dangerously . . . Sometimes	B8	Aug-79		
79-13	**Defense I**	A1	9/11/1979	14-2	RIHOH 105
	Defense II	A2	9/11/1979	14-2	RIHOH 107
	Defense III	A3	9/11/1979	14-2	RIHOH 108
	Defense IV	A4	9/11/1979	14-2	RIHOH 119
	Talking Back	A5	9/11/1979	14-2	471
	Miscellaneous I	A6	9/11/1979	14-2	
	Ships	A7	9/11/1979	14-2	472
	SALT II	B1	9/11/1979	14-2	RIHOH 62
	Miscellaneous II	B2	9/11/1979	14-2	
	Miscellaneous III	B3	9/11/1979	14-2	
	Miscellaneous IV	B4	9/11/1979	14-2	
	In Business	B5	9/11/1979	John McClaughry	
	How to Handle Dissident Bureaucrats	B6	9/11/1979		
	Local Energy Solutions	B7	9/11/1979		
	Temperature Restrictions	B8	9/11/1979		
79-14	**Vlasenko**	A1	10/2/1979	14-2	RIHOH 177
	Six Lies on Energy	A2	10/2/1979		
	Department of Education	A3	10/2/1979	14-2	473
	SALT II	A4	10/2/1979	14-2	RIHOH 90
	Hollywood East	A5	10/2/1979	14-2	475
	Defectors	A6	10/2/1979	14-2	476
	In Defense of Success	A7	10/2/1979		
	Coal	B1	10/2/1979	14-2	477
	California	B2	10/2/1979	14-2	478
	The Draft	B3	10/2/1979	Martin Anderson	
	Red Tape	B4	10/2/1979	14-2	480
	Radioactivity	B5	10/2/1979	14-2	481

O'Connor Number	Title	Side/ Number	Taping Date	Handwritten Draft	Book Page
	The Golden Fleece	B6	10/2/1979	14-2	482
	Gadgets	B7	10/2/1979		
	Land	B8	10/2/1979	14-2	483
79-15	Cuba Overseas	1	10/25/1979		
	Cuban Conditions	2	10/25/1979		
	Israel I	3	10/25/1979		
	Israel II	4	10/25/1979		
	SALT	5	10/25/1979		
	Health Care	6	10/25/1979	14-2	RIHOH 369
	Miscellaneous and Goodbye	7	10/25/1979	14-2	RIHOH 416*

Notes

Introduction

1. Peter Hannaford, *The Reagans: A Political Portrait* (New York: Coward-McCann, 1983), pp. 55–56, and Lou Cannon, *Governor Reagan: His Rise to Power* (New York: Public Affairs, 2003), p. 399.
2. Cannon, *Governor Reagan,* p. 394. The national poll was conducted by a well-known pollster, Robert Teeter.
3. Nancy Reagan with William Morrow, *My Turn: The Memoirs of Nancy Reagan* (New York: Random House, 1989), p. 179.
4. Cannon, *Governor Reagan,* p. 397.
5. Gerald R. Ford, *A Time to Heal* (New York: Harper & Row, 1979), pp. 142–43.
6. Cannon, *Governor Reagan,* p. 400.
7. Ibid.
8. Dictated letter to Dwight Myers, 1980 Reagan-Bush Campaign Files, Box 923, Ronald Reagan Presidential Library.
9. "Reagan's Radio Producer," *Television/Radio Age* (September 8, 1980): 16, and Kiron K. Skinner's telephone interview with Harry O'Connor on March 2, 2004.
10. These documents are found in Deaver and Hannaford Collection Box 1, Hoover Institution Archives. See also a September 19, 1974, memo from Peter Hannaford to Ed Meese and copied to Mike Deaver. DH 1.
11. Doug Willis, "Reagan's Radio Show Instant Hit," undated AP wire newspaper clipping, Deaver and Hannaford Collection, Hoover Institution Archives.
12. According to a document titled "Viewpoint with Ronald Reagan" and dated March 14, 1975, 162 radio stations carried Reagan's radio program. Another document with the same title but dated May 15, 1975, lists 270 stations carrying the radio program. See the following sources in the Pre-Presidential Papers at the Ronald Reagan Library: PPP Box 12 Folder 'Viewpoint'—Business Info., and PPP Box 19 Folder 'Viewpoint' Julie Eisenhower. In a May 23, 1975, memo to Governor Reagan, Peter Hannaford wrote: "As of this date you are on 286 radio stations and 226 newspapers, via O'Connor and Copley, respectively. O'Connor expects to break the 300 mark within the next two weeks." See PPP Box 12 Folder 'Viewpoint' Correspondence. In a July 2, 1975, memo to Michael Deaver, Peter Hannaford wrote that about 320 stations carried the program. PPP Box 12

Folder " 'Viewpoint'—Business Info." An October 13, 1975, press release from O'Connor Creative Services noted that 300 stations carried "Viewpoint," and that Mutual radio network would be taking over the marketing of Reagan's program, and Mutual had more than 1,300 affiliated stations. Deaver and Hannaford Collection, Box 61, Hoover Institution Archives.

13. Letter in Harry O'Connor's personal collection.
14. Reports on the size of Reagan's listening audience vary. In a February 17, 1977, memo to Bill Stetson of Citizens for Republic, Peter Hannaford reports that Reagan is now on 234 radio stations with an approximate audience of 5-7 million per week, according to Harry O'Connor, of O'Connor Creative Productions, Hollywood, which produces and syndicates the program nationally. It is heard in 42 states and DC." Citizens for Reagan Collection, Box 106 Folder 106-3-3 Radio Stations with RR Broadcasts and Newspaper with RR Column. Peter Hannaford drafted a letter to Admiral Elmo R. Zumwalt, Jr., for Reagan that addressed the size of the listening audience. The typed version of the letter, signed by Reagan, is dated October 30, 1978, and states: "My every-weekday radio broadcasts and my twice-a-week newspaper column reach an estimated 20 million Americans every week." PPP Box 6 Folder XYZ RR Correspondence 1978. In an article for which Harry O'Connor, the producer of Reagan's radio commentary, was interviewed, the size of Reagan's audience was placed at 30 million per week. "Reagan's Radio Producer," *Television/Radio Age* (September 8, 1980): 16. Besides allowing him to speak to America, the speeches, newspaper columns, and radio commentaries also earned Reagan an estimated $800,000 in 1975. Cannon, *Governor Reagan,* p. 399.
15. Peter Hannaford mentions objections to Reagan's broadcast in a July 2, 1975, memo to Michael Deaver. See " 'Viewpoint'—Business Info.," PPP Box 12.
16. For example, in a letter dated July 18, 1975, to John Moon of Copley News cancelling Reagan's column, Thomas Keevil, editor of *Daily Pilot,* wrote: "As Reagan's candidacy becomes more and more obvious, I am more and more nervous about running his column. Please count us out until it is absolutely clear he will not be a candidate. . . . We can't give editorial page prestige to a candidate for office." For this and other such letters see Folder Copley News Service. PPP 12.
17. See an Associated Press article found in DH Box 61.
18. For instance, on September 8, 1977, Reagan testified before a committee of the U.S. Senate on the Panama Canal treaties. His testimony is closely reflective of the many handwritten drafts of his radio commentaries on the Panama Canal.
19. *Reagan, In His Own Hand,* edited by Kiron K. Skinner, Annelise Anderson, and Martin Anderson (New York: Free Press, 2001) includes 237 of Reagan's handwritten commentaries; 337 others are in this book, including eight of the nine not broadcast. The handwritten drafts of the radio commentaries that constitute the initial discovery were found mainly in boxes 12, 14, 15, and 21 (since reorganized) of a collection of President Reagan's private papers at the Ronald Reagan Library titled the Pre-Presidential Papers, 1921–1980 (PPP). Three other commentaries were found in the 1980 Reagan-Bush Campaign Files, a collection of private papers at the Reagan Library.
20. This is part of a letter (dictated) that Reagan wrote to Tommy Thorson. See Kiron K. Skinner, Annelise Anderson, and Martin Anderson, eds, *Reagan: A Life in Letters,* p. 335.
21. "Reagan's Radio Producer," *Television/Radio Age* (Septemter 8, 1980): 16.

A Note on Editorial Methods

1. Kiron K. Skinner, Annelise Anderson, and Martin Anderson, eds., *Reagan, In His Own Hand: The Writings of Ronald Reagan That Reveal His Revolutionary Vision for America* (New York: Free Press, 2001).

1975

1. Kiron K. Skinner, Annelise Anderson, and Martin Anderson, eds., *Reagan, In His Own Hand: The Writings of Ronald Reagan that Reveal his Revolutionary Vision for America* (New York: Free Press, 2001), p. 9.
2. Hannaford, *The Reagans,* p. 68, and Christopher Lyndon, "Six Form a 1976 Group for Reagan," *The New York Times,* July 16, 1975, p. 19.
3. These commentaries are in Kiron K. Skinner, Annelise Anderson, and Martin Anderson, eds., *Reagan, In His Own Hand,* pp. 4–9, 10–12, and 26–31.
4. In his radio essay titled "The Russian Wheat Deal," Reagan asked, "But isn't there also a moral issue?" He was referring to selling wheat to the Soviet Union, which he described as "a Godless tyranny." He continued: "The moral question then is can America alone force the change to peaceful pursuits on Russia by refusing to sell or would we have to persuade the other free Nations to do the same. Following such a course what would we do then about our farmers and the surplus they'd have on their hands? . . . Maybe there is an answer. We simply do what's morally right. Stop doing business with them. Let their system collapse but in the meantime buy our farmers wheat ourselves and have it on hand to feed the Russian people when they finally become free." In "Nigeria," a radio broadcast taped on July 9, 1979, Reagan said that the distinguishing characteristic of "a representative government such as ours is virtue. If virtue goes the government falls." He then questioned whether the United States supported Nigeria's stance on Rhodesia/Zimbabwe because the U.S. buys oil from the country: "Are we choosing paths that are politically expedient and morally questionable? Are we in truth losing our virtue? . . . Are we as Americans so thirsty for oil that we'll forget the traditions upon which our country is founded and let our foreign policy be dictated by anyone who has oil for sale? If so we may be nearer the dustbin of history than we realize." Kiron K. Skinner, Annelise Anderson, and Martin Anderson, eds., *Reagan, In His Own Hand,* pp. 30 and 31, and 16–17. For a classic study of the centrality of the tension between power and principle in the history of American foreign policy, see Samuel P. Huntington, "American Ideals versus American Institutions," *Political Science Quarterly,* (Spring 1982): vol. 97, no. 1, pp. 1–37.
5. See Reagan's speech before the Southern Republican Conference banquet in Houston, Texas, on December 13, 1975. The speech is found in Citizens for Reagan, Box 103, and Ronald Reagan Subject Collection Box 1 Folder RR Speeches 1975–76.

1976

1. Although U.S.-Soviet relations and defense policy were central issues for Reagan, he wrote and spoke about international relations more broadly in 1976. For instance, in radio commentaries and speeches he discussed issues such as U.S.-

Republic of China relations, political developments in Latin America, and international organizations.

2. See *Public Papers of the President, Gerald Ford,* 1976–1977, vol. 1, p. 6, and "Ford Abandons 'Détente' (The Word, Not the Policy)," *Manchester Union Leader,* March 4, 1976, p. 21.
3. Reagan's speech was excerpted as an article in *The Wall Street Journal.* See Ronald Reagan, "Tactics of Détente," February 13, 1976, p. 8. The full text is in Citizens for Reagan Box 40 Folder Presidential Campaign January 15, 1976–April 22, 1976, Hoover Institution Archives.
4. Quoted in James M. Naughton, "Ford Says 'In Time' He Expects To Talk With Nixon on China," *The New York Times,* March 2, 1976, p. 12.
5. See for example *Denver Post,* March 5, 1976, p. 20: "Mr. Ford's political opponent, former California Gov. Ronald Reagan, undoubtedly has affected the President's stand [on détente]."
6. Quoted in Martin Anderson, *Revolution* (New York: Harcourt Brace Jovanovich, 1988), p. 71.
7. September 14, 1976, memorandum from Peter D. Hannaford, Ronald Reagan Subject Collection Box 9 Folder Newspapers 1976, Hoover Institution Archives.
8. Kiron K. Skinner, Annelise Anderson, and Martin Anderson, *Reagan: A Life in Letters* (New York: Free Press, 2003), pp. 223, 224.

1977

1. Peter Hannaford, *The Reagans: A Political Portrait* (New York: Coward-McCann, 1983), pp. 142–43.
2. The Gallup Poll #982, August 16, 1977. All Gallup Poll data are from the Gallup Organization's online database at http://brain.gallup.com (Documents: Decade Breakout 1970–79).
3. The final legislation provided business tax credits, immediate rebates to some individual taxpayers, and increased taxes on incomes over $13,750 for taxpayers using the standard deduction.
4. David Binder, "Conservative Lobby Bids U.S. Keep Panama Canal," *The New York Times,* November 5, 1975, p. 89, and Hannaford, *The Reagans,* pp. 144–45.
5. Reagan discussed foreign policy issues, including the Panama Canal negotiations, in a speech before the Conservative Political Action Conference in Washington, D.C. on February 6, 1977. See Citizens for Reagan Collection Box 104 Folder 1–5 and Ronald Reagan Subject Collection Box 3 Folder RR Speeches—1977, Hoover Institution Archives. On February 8, President Carter appointed Sol Linowitz and Ellsworth Bunker as co-negotiators for the Panama Canal discussions.
6. Hannaford, *The Reagans,* pp. 144–45.
7. See Citizens for Reagan Box 104, Hoover Institution Archives.
8. Reagan often discussed the importance of principles and values in American foreign policy on their own terms, but sometimes he weighed these issues against international realities, as he does here.
9. See Joseph B. Treaster, "Reagan Is Critical of Carter on Rights: He Accuses the Administration of Practicing 'Double Standard,' " *The New York Times,* June 10, 1977. For Reagan's speech see Citizens for Reagan Box 104 Folder 1–4, and Ronald Reagan Subject Collection Box 3 Folder RR Speeches—1977.

10. Campaign 1980, Box 9, Reagan Presidential Library.
11. "Reagan on the Canal," *Newsweek,* September 19, 1977, p. 50.
12. See the Gallup Polls of February 25, 1975; December 30, 1975; October 5, 1976; October 22–25, 1976; October 18, 1977; March 15, 1977; July 19, 1977; April 11, 1978; July 5, 1978; September 5, 1978; October 24, 1978; February 20, 1979; May 1, 1979; August 7, 1979; and October 12–15, 1979.

1978

1. For a copy of the September 5, 1978, stump speech Reagan gave in Palm Springs, California, see Citizens for Reagan Box 104 Folder 1–5 and Ronald Reagan Subject Collection Box 3 Folder RR Speeches 1978, Hoover Institution Archives.
2. Quoted in Peter Hannaford, *The Reagans: A Political Portrait,* p. 159.
3. Reagan's March 17 address before the Conservative Political Action Committee is found in *Vital Speeches,* May 1, 1979. A copy of it is also in RR Speeches 1978, RRSC Box 3 Folder RR Speeches 1978.
4. RRSC Box 3 Folder RR Speeches 1978.
5. Peter Hannaford, who accompanied Reagan on the Asian tour, believes that Reagan's "decision was rooted in the first meeting [with Mansfield] at the Hotel Okura in April, 1978." *The Reagans: A Political Portrait,* p. 162.
6. Reagan's speech in Taipei on April 21, 1978, is found in *Vital Speeches of the Day,* July 1, 1978, and Ronald Reagan Subject Collection Box 3 Folder RR Speeches 1978.
7. The essays are "Japan I" (78-07-A1, p. 293) and five published in *Reagan, In His Own Hand,* "Japan II" (78-07-A2), "Japan III" (78-07-A3), Taiwan I (78-07-A4), "Hong Kong" (78-07-A5), and "The Pacific" (78-07-B3).
8. A copy of the interview is found in RRSC Box 3 Folder RR Speeches 1978.
9. Peter Hannaford, *The Reagans: A Political Portrait,* p. 190.
10. Ibid., p. 171.
11. For accounts of the dinner see Martin Anderson, *Revolution* (New York: Harcourt Brace Jovanovich, 1988), pp. 169–70, and Peter Hannaford, *The Reagans,* pp. 176. Other guests included Peter Hannaford, Michael Deaver, Glenn Campbell, and Rita Ricardo-Campbell. Several of the people would serve in the Reagan administration—Shultz as secretary of state, Weinberger as secretary of defense, and Greenspan as chairman of the Federal Reserve Board of Governors.
12. Hannaford, *The Reagans,* p. 172.

1979

1. Edward L. Rowny, *It Takes One to Tango* (New York: Brassey's, 1992), pp. 125–31, 135–36.
2. Martin Anderson, *Revolution* (New York: Harcourt Brace Jovanovich, 1988), pp. 80, 83.
3. Reagan's handwritten draft of the speech is found in Campaign 1980 Box 924. The typescript of the speech is found in RRSC Box 3 Folder RR Speeches 1979.
4. Peter Hannaford, *The Reagans: A Political Portrait,* pp. 209–210. Reagan presented his idea about a North American Accord in his November 13 announcement that he would seek the Republican Party's nomination for the presidency.

Ronald Reagan's Radio Addresses

1. Kiron K. Skinner, Annelise Anderson, and Martin Anderson, *Reagan, In His Own Hand: The Writings of Ronald Reagan That Reveal His Revolutionary Vision for America* (New York: Free Press, 2001). *Stories In His Own Hand: The Everyday Wisdom of Ronald Reagan,* edited by Kiron K. Skinner, Annelise Anderson, and Martin Anderson (New York: Free Press, 2001) includes five commentaries not published in our other books.
2. *Reagan, In His Own Voice* includes 87 radio addresses, including some of those on the CD with this book.

Acknowledgments

This book is the fifth in a series based on the writings of Ronald Reagan. Over the years, especially the years since he first ran for governor of California, Reagan spent thousands of hours sitting on airplanes, in the backseats of automobiles, on trains, in hotel rooms, at a desk in his bedroom at home, and at his ranch in the mountains of Santa Barbara—writing. This book holds 337 policy essays he wrote for his syndicated radio broadcasts in the late 1970s; carried by over 300 stations his broadcasts covered virtually the entire United States and reportedly reached between 20 and 30 million listeners a week.* The handwritten drafts that survived were stored in cardboard boxes. And many people were links in the chain of events that transformed those unsorted, undated stacks of yellow, legal-size paper into this book, which shows the major role these essays played in the five-year odyssey (1975–1979) that led to Reagan's successful run for president in 1980. We will try to acknowledge all the men and women who helped make that happen.

Most important was Nancy Reagan, who recognized the historic importance of these papers and gave us permission to study and publish them. Married to Reagan for more than fifty years, she and she alone knew the extent of how much Reagan read, studied and wrote as he moved up the American political ladder, and she wanted others "to know Ronnie" as she did.

George Shultz, who was at Reagan's side for six and a half years as his secretary of State when the Cold War was won, gave us significant counsel and support as we worked on the five books based on Reagan's papers. And he wrote the introductory Foreword for each of them.

A special note of thanks goes to Joanne Drake, chief of staff to Ronald Reagan, to Mark Burson, former director of the Ronald Reagan Presidential Foundation, and Duke Blackwood, who is both director of the Ronald Rea-

* Interview with Harry O'Connor, head of O'Connor Creative Services, the producer of Reagan's radio commentaries, April 5, 2004, and "Reagan's Radio Producer," *Television/Radio Age* (September 8, 1980): 16.

gan Presidential Library and director of the Ronald Reagan Presidential Foundation. As we worked on these five books they were all instrumental in facilitating access to the private papers kept in the Ronald Reagan Presidential Library in Simi Valley, California, and in giving us valuable guidance and advice.

Throughout this process the scholarly resources of the Hoover Institution were invaluable—from staff support, computers, fax machines, scanners, copiers, and funds to travel to the Reagan Library and other places that held Reagan's writings. But most important was the backing of the director, John Raisian, who not only supported us at key times over the past four years, but who encouraged us enthusiastically. Carnegie Mellon University, where Kiron Skinner is an assistant professor, similarly provided strong support for the books, as did the John M. Olin Foundation.

We want to express special gratitude and thanks for the funding provided to the Hoover Institution in support of the project on the Reagan papers. A major grant for the Reagan project and the efforts of the Hoover Institution to make it possible came from the late Barton A. Stebbins of Laguna Beach, California, and his trustee, Donald W. Crowell of San Marino, California. Mr. Stebbins, who died in 1999, held Ronald Reagan in the highest regard, both as a person and as an inspirational leader. He "would have been deeply honored by the opportunity to help underwrite the communication of the powerful message about the man who changed our world for the better, in public ways and, as this book shows, in so many private and personal ways," said his trustee, Mr. Crowell.

Tad Taube of Woodside, California, a longtime overseer of the Hoover Institution, was one of the first to recognize the importance of understanding Reagan's character and leadership style, and he provided generous support in the early stages of the project. Taube was joined by the Honorable L. W. "Bill" Lane, Jr., of Portola Valley, California, an old personal friend of Reagan's, who also provided support and counsel.

Kiron Skinner would also like to thank Bruce Bueno de Mesquita, Charlie Hill, Condoleezza Rice, Ellana Schwartz, Thomas Schwartz, George P. Shultz, Byron Skinner, Gloria Skinner, and Ruby Skinner for support and counsel throughout the writing of this book. She would also like to thank several staff members and producers at CNN-TV for providing unusual assistance during a crucial time of her research and writing for this project: Emily Atkinson, Joy DiBenedetto, Jessie Malter, and Stephanie Siegel. Skinner would like to similarly acknowledge Kai M. Schellhorn and Kerstin Meerwaldt of BMW Stiftung Herbert Quandt in Munich, Germany.

The archivists at the Hoover Institution were especially helpful in providing access to the many Reagan documents in their collections—the director of Library and Archives, Elena Danielson; deputy archivist, Linda Bernard; manuscript cataloger Dale Reed; assistant archivist Carol Leadenham; and Grace Hawes, archivist to George P. Shultz.

The administrative staff of the Hoover Institution was vital to the effective functioning of the Reagan project, especially deputy director David Brady, senior associate director Richard Sousa, Bill Bonnett, Helen Corrales, Craig Snaar, Kelly Doran, Frank Coronado, Claudia Hubbard, Karen Kenlay, Celeste Szeto, Deborah Ventura, and Dan Wilhelmi.

Anne Hawkins, our agent, was suggested to us by one of our colleagues at the Hoover Institution, Bruce Bueno de Mesquita. Throughout she has played an important role in the complex negotiations that were necessary for this project to proceed, and has often been a source of keen advice and inspiration.

Our publisher, the Free Press of Simon & Schuster, has been superb throughout. One of their former editors, Paul Golub, was the first to see the importance of Reagan's handwritten papers and offer us a contract. Paul left shortly thereafter and was replaced by Bruce Nichols, who filled Paul's shoes and then some. For all our books Bruce has been our main editor, and he has been terrific. His organizational suggestions and editing have greatly improved our original manuscripts. At every step in the drafting of these books—from the initial reading, to proofing the manuscript to writing and editing the jacket copy—his advice and counsel have been invaluable. In addition, his assistant, Hui Xie, was especially helpful in working with us pulling together the manuscript as we worked on it from both coasts. But perhaps most important has been the quiet, consistent encouragement Bruce Nichols gave to sometimes difficult authors, as the books were driven to completion. We thank him.

We would also like to thank Cassie Dendurent, publicity director at the Free Press, and her staff for graciously promoting our books.

At the Reagan Presidential Library the archivists were uniformly helpful and professional, and all did much to make our many days of research in the papers both productive and enjoyable. Sometimes it was fun. We want to express our appreciation and thanks to archivists Diane Barrie, Kelly Barton, Steve Branch (audio-visual), Greg Cumming (who is now the head archivist at the Richard Nixon Library and Birthplace), Mike Duggan, Sherrie Fletcher, Lisa Jones, Cate Sewell, and Jenny Sternaman for their enthusiastic support.

While we were studying the hundreds of policy essays that Reagan wrote on his way to the presidency we conducted many interviews. Of special significance were the small number of people who were physically with Reagan during the times he read, studied, and wrote his radio commentaries, and who worked with him directly after he had finished writing them and when he taped his broadcasts. They include Peter Hannaford, his top assistant on the radio commentaries, William P. Clark, Michael Deaver, Edwin Meese, Thomas C. Reed, Harry O'Connor, who was in charge of broadcast production and donated those papers and tapes to the Hoover Institution, Dennis LeBlanc, and David Fischer, who traveled with him during this time, and Elaine Crispen Sawyer and Helene von Damm, who were his secretaries—the people who saved the rough drafts and made this part of history possible.

The heart of this book are Reagan's handwritten drafts of his radio commentaries. The difficult, painstaking work of reading the original drafts and translating them into clear English, showing all of the editing that was done, was primarily done by the following research assistants at the Hoover Institution and Carnegie Mellon University—Nancy Cloud, who did most of the first typed copies, Allison Asher, Reagan project research assistant, Heather Campbell, assistant to Annelise Anderson, Lillie Robinson, assistant to Martin Anderson, Lydia Anderson and Rosa Stipanovic, assistants to Kiron Skinner, and Susan Schendel, assistant to George Shultz. The handwriting of Ronald Reagan is unusually clear and easy to read, but not his editing. Often, while editing, he did such a thorough job of crossing out words that it is difficult, and sometimes impossible, to discern his first thoughts. Reagan also used many abbreviations in the handwritten drafts, depending on his secretaries to flesh out the words in the typed script he used to record from in the studio. They all did an excellent job of untangling those edits and abbreviations so that, in almost all cases, we can easily follow the flow of his words.

Researching issues raised in Reagan's commentaries was also central to this book. Kiron Skinner would like to thank a highly skilled team of researchers at Carnegie Mellon University, New York University, and Stanford University: Kaiting Chen, Suneal Chandran, Lela Gibson, Leslie Johns, Mojan Movassate, Julia Myers, Lara Panis, and Alex Porfirenko.

In addition, our assistants provided comments and suggestions that often found their way into the book and, in the final stages of the work, identified and located many obscure items that Reagan mentioned in his commentaries and that are now footnoted.

Index

About the Editors

Kiron K. Skinner is an assistant professor of history and political science at Carnegie Mellon University and a research fellow at the Hoover Institution. In 2004, President George W. Bush appointed her to the National Security Education Board, and Secretary of Defense Donald Rumsfeld appointed her to the Chief of Naval Operations Executive Panel. Her articles have appeared in *Orbis, National Interest, The New York Times,* and *The Wall Street Journal.*

Annelise Anderson is an economist who has been fellow at the Hoover Institution since 1983. From 1981 to 1983 she worked in the Reagan administration as associate director of the Office of Management and Budget and was a senior policy adviser to Ronald Reagan's 1976 and 1980 presidential campaigns.

Martin Anderson is the Keith and Jan Hurlbut Senior Fellow at the Hoover Institution. He served two tours of duty in the White House, first as a special assistant under Richard Nixon and then as chief domestic and economic policy adviser to Ronald Reagan. He was also a top adviser in the Nixon and Reagan presidential campaigns and is the author of seven books, including *Revolution,* the first comprehensive history of the Reagan administration.